History of Berkeley County West Virginia

Willis F. Evans

"A people who have not the pride to record their history will not long have the virtues to make history worth recording; and no people who are indifferent to their past need hope to make their future great."

HERITAGE BOOKS
2007

HERITAGE BOOKS
AN IMPRINT OF HERITAGE BOOKS, INC.

Books, CDs, and more—Worldwide

For our listing of thousands of titles see our website
at
www.HeritageBooks.com

A Facsimile Reprint
Published 2007 by
HERITAGE BOOKS, INC.
Publishing Division
65 East Main Street
Westminster, Maryland 21157-5026

Copyright © 1928 Willis F. Evans

Copyright © 2001 Heritage Books, Inc.

— Publisher's Notice —
In reprints such as this, it is often not possible to remove blemishes from the original. We feel the contents of this book warrant its reissue despite these blemishes and hope you will agree and read it with pleasure.

International Standard Book Number: 978-0-7884-1945-4

PREFACE.

A century and a half ago Berkeley County was formed. Over two hundred years ago the first cabin home was erected within its present confines and also the first in what is now West Virginia. Two hundred and fifty years ago the first white man set foot upon her soil. Before the coming of these and for a hundred years later, another race of people inhabited this fair valley, and their passing furnishes history of immense value.

No other county in the State is so rich in historical substance, in deeds of valor and heroic actions and trials attendant upon the settlement of a new country. The history of Berkeley County is a history of the Nation. She sent more soldiers to the wars of the country per capita than any other county of the State. Not all did her people accomplish by wars alone. The pioneer cleared the lands, established homes along the streams and on the surrounding hills. They planted orchards, established schools and churches, made roads and adopted a code of morals as strict and righteous as any. In later years some served in legislative halls and pulpit; some wielded the axe and the hoe while others wielded the pen.

The history of Berkeley County reads like a romance. We read of tales of adventure of olden times; we have them. We read of heroes doing mighty deeds; we have them. We hear of statesmen, guiding the destinies of nations; we have them. We read of warriors, successfully fighting great battles; we have them. We observe men heading mighty industries; we have them, and we observe men, experts in every industrial activity under the sun, but none can surpass ours, skilled or unskilled.

It is regretable that the deeds of thousands of men and women, of patience, toil, sorrow, anxiety; deeds of which we will never know and whose names will never adorn history's pages cannot be recorded because such deeds were not done in the glare of public inspection, but in the silent watches of the night, within the solitary confines of the home and in the incessant toil of the work-shop or the farm.

The home builder is the nation builder and no more fitting tribute could be paid to these than that to them this work be respectfully dedicated.

WILLIS F. EVANS.

(Arden) Martinsburg, West Virginia.
November 8, 1927.

CHAPTER I.

VIRGINIA.

In the year 1492, Christopher Columbus, a Genoese navigator, crossed the Atlantic, (the Sea of Darkness), and returned to Spain. He had supposedly reached Cathay or India and had supposedly discovered a short, all-water route to Asia. He had, unknown to himself and the world, reached the shores of America. Columbus was hailed by the court of Spain as a great navigator.

King Henry VII, of England, hearing of Columbus' successful venture and wishing to share in the glory of discovering new land in the west, in 1497 commissioned John Cabot and his son Sebastian, famous sea captains then residing in Bristol, England, to make explorations for him. They struck out boldly across the Atlantic and in due course of time reached a land which they took possession of for the English king. They landed on what is now Newfoundland, and thus named it New Found Land, a name it has retained to the present day. They sailed along the coast from Labrador to probably what is now the vicinity of North Carolina, and returned to England. John Cabot was at once proclaimed a mighty navigator and was received with delight by the English people, and was proclaimed the "Great Admiral" by them.

On account of this voyage England laid claim to the continent of America; a claim which wielded a mighty influence upon the future history of this continent, this state, and this county. In asserting her claim to any future portion of North America, English statesmen always based their rights of possession upon this voyage, and this basis was the predominating factor in the early settlement of our own particular region. When the French, by discovery and by exploration, attempted to obtain the Ohio valley, the English, acting upon the old argument that "Possession is nine points in law", offered every inducement possible to settlers to occupy the land west of Blue Ridge.

But it was not by John Cabot nor through his discoveries that our state received its name. That was left to another man, Sir Walter Raleigh. England did not immediately take advantage of the discoveries of the Cabots, as Spain did of that of Columbus. In fact, England did not want America. It wished to trade with the rich countries of India and China, where it had been obtaining its gold, its spices, its silks and precious stones from remote times. It wanted a short, all-water route to these lands. But there lay America, stretching across its path from North to South, presenting a formidable barrier to its plans. In fact, the greatest minds of that day heartily wished no such country as America existed. So, with this attitude in view, nothing was done towards exploiting this vast empire to the west for upwards of a hundred years.

While Spain was taking advantage of the new lands to the south, which, as it were, thrust upon her, and France, of the lands to the north, England sat idly by. And it was not until one after another of Spain's energetic adventurers returned with shipload after shipload of treasure and had advanced Spain to a first rate world power, and France, in the north, had added another empire to its domains, that England began to take notice.

In 1558 came to the throne of England, a young woman who was destined to make her country take first rank in the affairs of nations; none other than the illustrious Queen Elizabeth. This energetic queen at once surrounded herself in the affairs of state with the best talent England could produce. She encouraged navigation. She promoted art and literature, and engaged in statescraft, the best counsellors. In so doing, she commissioned Walter Raleigh with a patent to explore the coast of America. Raleigh, who never did things by halves, sent out in the summer of 1584, Sir Richard Greenville and William Sanderson, who explored the entire coast of America and brought back such a glowing description of the country that the queen was delighted. She gave Raleigh a title of nobility and to the whole of the country he had explored, the name of Virginia, in honor of her own maiden name, signifying "Virgin Queen". By this act, the State of Virginia received its name.

Virginia has been called the "Mother of Presidents", from the fact that she has given so many of her illustrious sons as Presidents of the United States. From the fact that so many magnificent states have been carved from her domains, she might rightly be called the "Mother of States", for the domain that Walter Raleigh bestowed upon England stretched from the St. Lawrence on the north to Florida on the south and from the Atlantic to the Pacific.

Sir Walter Raleigh advised the Queen that this country was well worth possessing, and, in order to hold it against the encroachments of the French and Spaniards, settlements should be made at once. Accordingly, he sent out a shipload of emigrants who landed on Roanoak Island, off the coast of what is now North Carolina, and began a settlement. The vessel then departed for England. Nothing was ever again heard of these colonists. When the place was again visited, no trace of them could be found. This has been styled the "Lost Colony of America". Raleigh made a second attempt to plant a colony in Virginia, but this also ended in failure, but these attempts at colonization were not without results for they encouraged others to make the attempt and in the year 1607, the first permanent English settlement was made in Virginia.

On April 10, 1607, James I, King of England, granted a charter to each of two companies, the "London" and the "Plymouth", for the purpose of making settlements in Virginia. The former, composed of London merchants, who agreed to finance the undertaking, was the first to make an attempt to plant a colony. This patent included all the territory extending from the mouth of the Potomac river on the north, to Florida on the south, and from the Atlantic to the Pacific. In fact, all early grants of land in America extended from ocean to ocean as no one, at that time, knew of the extent of the territory such a term implied. On all early maps, America was represented as being a narrow peninsula probably not over a hundred miles in width.

This Company immediately set to work to procure men and equipment to plant a colony within the confines of this grant. One hundred and five persons were collected and under the leadership of Captain Christopher Newport, set sail for Virginia on December 20, 1606. The colonists were induced, for the most part, to come to Virginia by alluring prospects of obtaining speedy fortunes. Stories were rife in London at this time, of the fabulous riches to be obtained there for the mere gathering. In fact, one of the conditions imposed upon the colonists by the Company was that the one-fifth of all the gold obtained was to be paid to them.

These colonists were not the type of men to make a permanent settlement. Some were spendthrifts, broken in fortune. Some were "gentlemen", with all the term implied. Some were soldiers, just returned from the late European wars, and some "just joined for the fun of the thing".

In the spring of 1607, the colonists reached Chesapeake Bay. They found the mouth of a broad river up which they sailed, and which they named James, in honor of their sovereign who had granted them their charter. They sailed up this river until they found a place suitable for a settlement and landed. This place they named Jamestown, also in honor of their king. They had intended to settle at the old spot of Sir Walter Raleigh's on Roanoak Island, but adverse winds drove them from their course, to Chesapeake Bay.

At first, the colonists did not build substantial houses, but lived under the trees or under old sail-cloth tents hastily constructed for the weather was delightful and they had no intention of remaining any definite time. All fell to searching for gold. Troubles began. Soon the food gave out. The Indians were troublesome. Many sickened and died. Instead of planting corn, they found a yellowish clay, known as "fool's gold", and proceeded to fill a ship with it and dispatch it to England.

But there was one man among them made of firmer stuff. That was Captain John Smith, and if it had not been for him, the colonists would have given up and gone back to England. He contrived to be chosen Governor of the colony. He set the well men to work building houses. He nursed the sick and buried those that died. He coerced the Indians into selling the settlers corn. When the colonists seized a ship and attempted to leave for England, he turned the cannon of the fort on it and threatened to knock it to pieces. After a winter of untold hardships, more emigrants arrived, bringing plenty of provisions, and the colony took on a brighter outlook. Each settler was given a piece of land for his very own. The cultivation of tobacco was begun and the colony took firm root.

Thus was established the first English speaking colony in Virginia and in all America. From this settlement others have sprung, and in this way the State of Virginia was made.

Subsequent charters were granted to the company by the King, James I, for the better governing of the colony. One of these (1619), granted a legislative council, called the General Assembly. It was "to assist the Governor in the administration of justice, advance Christianity among the Indians, direct the colony in obedience to His Majesty, maintain the people in Christian conversation, and strengthen them against their enemies."

To fully portray to the reader what was embodied in this charter the following instructions are given in full (dated, July 24, 1621):

INSTRUCTIONS TO GOVERNOR WYATT.

"To keep up religion of the Church of England as near as may be:—to be obedient to the king and do justice after the form of the laws of England, and not to injure the natives and forget old quarrels now buried.

"To be industrious and to suppress drunkenness, gaming, and excess in clothes; not to permit any but the council and heads of hundreds, to wear gold in their clothes, or to wear silk till they make it themselves.

"Not to offend any foreign princes; to punish piracies; to build fortresses and blockhouses at the mouths of the rivers.

"To use means to convert the heathen, viz: to converse with some; each town to teach some children fit for the college intended to be built.

"After Sir George Yeardly has gathered the present year's crop, he is to deliver to Sir Francis Wyatt, the hundred tenants belonging to the governor's place: Yeardley's government to expire the 18th November next, and then Wyatt to be published governor: To swear the council.

"George Sandis appointed treasurer, and he is to put into execution, all orders of court about staple commodities to whom is allotted fifteen hundred acres and fifty tenants. To the marshal, Sir William Newce, the same. To company's deputy, the same. To the physician, five hundred acres and twenty tenants, and the same to the secretary.

"To review the commissioners to Sir George Yeardly, governor, and the council dated 18th November, 1618, for dividing the colony into cities, burroughs, &c., and to observe all former instructions (a copy whereof was sent) if they did not contradict the present: and all orders of the court (made in England):

"To make a catalogue of the people in their plantations and their conditions; and of deaths, marriages, and christenings:

"To take care of dead persons, for the right owners, and keep a list of all cattle, and cause the secretary to return all copies of the premises once a year.

"To take care of every plantation upon the death of their chief, not to plant above one hundred pounds of tobacco per head: to sow great quantities of corn for their own use, and to support the multitudes to be sent yearly; to enclose lands: to keep cows, swine, poultry, &c., and particularly, which are not to be killed yet:

"Next to corn, plant mulberry trees, and make silk, and to take care of the French-men and others sent about that work, to try silk grass, to plant abundance of vines, and to take care of the vignors sent.

"To put prentices to trades, and not let them forsake their trades, for planting tobacco or any other useless commodity:

"To take care of the Dutch sent to build saw-mills and to seat them at the falls that they may bring their timber by the current of the river:

"To build water-mills and blockhouses in every plantation:

"That all contracts in England or Virginia, be performed and the breaches punished according to justice:

"Truants not to be enticed away: to take care of those sent about an iron work, and especially Mr. John Berkeley, that they don't miscarry again, this being the greatest hope and expectation of the colonies:

"To make salt, pitch, tar, soap, ashes, &c, so often recommended and for which materials had been sent: to make oyle of walnuts, and employ apothecaries in distilling of beer and searching after minerals, dyes, gums and druggs &c. and send small quantities home.

"To make small quantity of tobacco, and that very good: that the houses appointed for the reception of the new comers and public storehouses built, kept clean &c. to send the state affairs quarterly and a duplicate next shipping:

"To take care of Captain William Norton, and certain Italians sent to set up a glass house:

"A copy of a treatise of the plantation business and excellent observances made by a gentleman of capacity is sent to lie among the records and recommended to the councellors to study:

"Mr. William Claybourne, a surveyer, sent to survey the planters lands and make a map of the country:

"To make discoveries along the coast and find a fishery between James River and Cape Cod:

"As to raising commodities, the chief officers ought to set examples and to aim at the establishment of the colony:

"Chief officers who have tenants reprimanded for taking fees; but require that the clerks have fees set for passes, warrants, copies of orders, &c.

"Governor and council to appoint proper times for administration of justice, and provide for the entertainment of the council, during their session; to be together about one whole month about state affairs, and law suits; to record plaints of consequence, to keep a register of the acts of quarter sessions, and send home copies:

"If the governor dies, the major part of council to choose one of themselves within fourteen days: but if voices be divided, the lieutenant governor shall have the place and next the marshall: next the treasurer; and one of the two deputies next:

"Governor and chief officers not to let out their tenants as usual.:

"The governor only to summon the council, and sign warrants, or give authority to execute council orders, except in cases that do belong to the marshall, treasurer, deputy, &c:

"The governor to have absolute authority to determine and punish all neglects, and contempts of authority, except the council who are to be tried at the quarter and censured. Governor to have but the casting voice in council or court, but in the assembly a negative voice:

"That care be taken that there be no engrossing commodity, or forestalling the market:

"All servants to fare alike in the colony, and their punishment for any offense, is to serve the colony in publick works:

"To see that the Earl of Pembroke's thirty thousand acres be very good:

"And lastly not to let ships stay long, and to freight them with walnut and any less commodity.*

---

*Henning's Statutes at Large.

From the above extract of the laws for the governing of the colony of Jamestown it will be seen that they exerted a great influence upon the government of our county when it was formed some one hundred and fifty years later. For if these laws are not printed word for word upon the statutes of West Virginia, as they appear here, the main principles are embodied and we are governed by some of these same statutes, laid down for the government of that first colony upon the soil of Virginia.

Many of these instructions could not be carried out as they were impractical but in the main were very good laws.

In 1619 the General Assembly met at Jamestown. It was the first legislative council to convene in America.

The English evidently wished to keep at peace with the natives, but on the 22nd of March the next year, the Indians suddenly fell upon the whites and a bloody massacre ensued and it was so horrible that the assembly, in March 1623, directed "that the 22nd of March be yearly solemnized as a holiday", to commemorate the escape of the colony from total extinction. This bloody event is known in history as "Opecancannough's Plot", this Indian chief attaining to the leadership of the Indians in Tidewater, Virginia, upon the death of his brother, Powhatan.

From this massacre began a hatred upon the part of the white settlers which continued for a hundred years, until the Indians were driven beyond the Blue Ridge mountains.

Several laws were enacted by the Assembly in 1623, a few of which are here given, relating to the dealings of the whites with the Indians:

"That every dwelling house shall be palisaded in for defense against the Indians."

"That no man go or send abroad without a sufficient party well armed."

"That people go not to work in the ground without their arms, (and a sentinel upon them)."

"That the inhabitants go not aboard ships or upon any other occasions, in such numbers as to weaken and endanger the plantations."

"That the commander of every plantation take care that there be sufficient of powder and ammunition within the plantation under his command, and their pieces fixed and their arms complete."

"That there be due watch kept by night."

"That no commander of any plantation do either himself or suffer others to spend powder unnecessarily, in drinking or entertainment, &c."

"That at the beginning of July next the inhabitants of every corporation shall go upon their adjoining salvages, as we did last year."*

In 1629, the Assembly enacted again: "ordered that every commander of the several plantations appointed by commissioners from the governor shall have power and authority to levy a party of men out of the inhabitants of that place so many as may well be spared without too much weakening of the plantations, and to employ these men against the Indians."

---

*Hen. Stat. at Large: vol. I, p. 127, 128.

"It was the opinion of the whole body of the Assembly that we should go three several marches upon the Indians, at three several times of the year, Viz: first in November, second in March, thirdly in July."

In 1631-2, "It was ordered that no person or persons shall dare to speak or parly with any Indians, either in the woods or in any plantation, if he can possibly avoid it by any means."*

In giving the above extracts from the laws passed by the General Assembly, relative to the Indians, it is intended to show to the reader the feeling of the settlers towards them. And it is not thought expedient at this time, to enter into a discussion as to which were the aggressor. Suffice it to say that here was begun a system of warfare which lasted until the Indians were finally conquered and driven upon reservations where he is compelled to keep the peace.

Another important event having much bearing upon the history of our county occurred at Jamestown in the year 1619. In that year a Dutch ship arrived at Jamestown, bringing twenty African negroes which were sold as slaves to the planters. This was the beginning of African slavery upon this continent and this institution was not eradicated until in 1866, when the Thirteenth Amendment to the Constitution abolished it from the country.

Henning's Statutes at Large.

CHAPTER II.

THE INDIAN.

The American Indian was a strong factor in the history of this country and much of the early history of the county is connected with him.

The Indian was a savage. He kept no written record and hardly any other, or if he kept any, it was handed down from generation to generation by word of mouth, not unlike the custom among the Arabs of today. As he had no written record, he had no books and no written history. True, he had built up a sort of legendary account of himself but it was vague in the extreme. One of these legends was to the effect that he had fallen from the moon; that he had crawled up out of a great hole in the ground by the aid of grape-vines and many other legends as equally absurd. Nothing in his legendary history points to his having migrated from any other country.

In recording the history of his tribe, five young men were selected from it to learn its history. These young men were each compelled to learn its history, word for word. A year and a half was allotted them in which to learn it. At the end of that time each in turn repeated it to each other in the presence of the Sachem and each was compelled to repeat it to the Sachem. In this manner, the history or traditions, were kept pure—not a word being added or removed from the original. At the death of all but two of these, other five were chosen to learn the history and in this way, a tolerable accurate account was kept of the events and traditions of the tribe. The reason for selecting five men instead of one can readily be seen that in case only one knew the history and he died, the history would be lost.

The Indian's religion consisted in the worship of a Great Spirit and evil spirits. The evil spirits were worshiped more than the Great Spirit, for the Indian reasoned that the Great Spirit, being good, would do him no harm, while if the evil spirits were appeased and not angered, they would let him alone also. The Indian believed that a "brave" after death entered the "Happy Hunting Grounds", but a coward was forever flogged by relentless demons. This made the Indian a fighter and war was his favorite pastime. He fought for personal glory and for the admiration of his tribe and his women. He fought for the sake of fighting to appease his savage spirit. His connection with the history of the early period of our country deals almost in every instance with war on the settlers, with massacre and rapine and murder.

Whether the Indian was the original inhabitant of this country is a mooted question. Few historians consider them as such. In several places, notably in the Ohio valley, at Moundsville, W. Va., in Yucatan, in Mexico, and Peru, are remains of a race of people who must have occupied this land at a remote period. In the Ohio valley are found mounds of earth resembling serpents. In Mexico and Peru were found a people who had acquired a high degree of civilization. They had built cities and temples of solid masonry, built roads and bridges, and viaducts for conveying water from distant sources, terraced mountains and cultivated fields. In Yucatan, the traveller still beholds ruins of mighty temples.

All these facts point to this continent having been peopled long before the Indians came.

It is probable that these people came to America from Asia. To substantiate this claim, Mr. Snowdon, in his history of America, advances the theory that the Kamschatka peninsula in Asia, and the Aleutian peninsula in North America might have been united in a solid land area; that an earthquake might have submerged this neck of land, leaving only the tops of the highest mountains above the water. Many islands are found extending from Alaska in a direct chain to the peninsula of Kamschatka in Asia; that in the narrowest point between these two continents the distance is only thirty-nine miles with two islands intervening. In the middle of this narrow strait could lead one to believe if this channel always existed it would not be impossible to pass this current in open boats as that is the common practice of the Esquimeaux at the present day. And as this strait is covered with ice the major part of the year, it would not be improbable that whole nations could pass by this way from one continent to another. Mr. Snowdon further argues:

"As mankind increased in numbers, they naturally protruded one another forward. Wars might be another cause of migrations. No reason appears why the Asiatic north might not be an 'officina vivorum' as well as the European. The overteeming country to the east of the Riphean mountains, must have found it necessary to discharge its inhabitants; the first great increase of people were forced forward by the next to it; at length reaching the limits of the Old World; found a new one with ample space to occupy for ages unmolested; 'til Columbus in an evil hour for them, discovered their country; which brought again new sins and new deaths for both worlds. It is impossible, with the lights which we have so recently received to admit that America could receive its inhabitants (that is, the bulk of them) from any other place than Eastern Asia."

In speaking of the customs or dress common to both worlds, Mr. Snowdon further relates:

"The custom of scalping was a barbarism in use with the Scythians, who carried about them at all times this savage mark of triumph. A little image found among the Kalmucs of a Tartarian deity, mounted on a horse and sitting on a human skin with scalps pendant from the breast, fully illustrates the custom of the ancient Scythians as described by the Greek. This image, we well know by horrid experiences, is continued to this day in America. The ferocity of the Scythians to their prisoners extended to the remotest part of Asia. The Kamschatkans, even at the time of their discovery by the Russians, put their prisoners to death by the most lingering and excruciating torments, a practice now in full force among the aboriginal Americans. A race of the Scythians were named Authropophagi, from their feeding on human flesh; the people of Nootka Sound still make a repast on the flesh of their fellow creatures."

"The savages of North America have been known to throw the mangled limbs of their prisoners into the horrible cauldron and devour them with the same relish as those of a quadruped. The Kamschatkans in their marches never went abreast, but followed one another in the same track. The same custom is still observed by the uncultivated natives of North America. The Tungusi, the most numerous resident nation in Siberia prick their skins with small punctures in various shapes with a needle; then rub them with charcoal so that the marks become indelible. This custom is still observed in some parts of South America. The Tungusi use canoes made of birch-bark distended over ribs of wood and nicely put together; the Canadian and many other primitive American nations use no other sort of boats. In fine, the conjectures of the learned respecting the vicinity of the old and new world, are now by discoveries of late navigators lost in conviction, and in the place of an imaginary hypothesis, the place of migration is almost incontrovertably pointed out."*

Berkeley County was the home of a tribe of Indians known as the Tuscarowas, from which Tuscarora Creek derived its name. Their principal town was located at the present site of Martinsburg. Evidence of their handiwork is occasionally picked up even at this late date, such as arrow-heads, stone hatchets, stone bowls for grinding corn, pipes, tomahawks and axes.

Several Indian graves or mounds existed as late as the year 1880, but none of these remain. All have been plowed down and destroyed.

The town of the Tuscarowas Indians occupied the hills surrounding the springs of the old water-works on East John street, namely: The King's Daughters Hospital, the County Courthouse, the Martinsburg High School, the old Fair Grounds, and Green Hill Cemetery. That they should choose for their villages the surrounding hills of these magnificent springs is due to the fact that the Indian, though possessing no technical knowledge of sanitation, knew that surrounding hills were healthier places to live and the hills afforded a better place of defense against the enemy; and their lodges, being built near the springs, afforded them abundance of pure water at all times. According to tradition, the Great Sachem, or Chief of the Tuscarowas, "Crane," lived in a wigwam much larger than the others, occupying the site of the King's Daughters Hospital, and that the great council fires of the nation occupied the site west of this wigwam near where the Court House now stands. If this be true, where we to-day decide questions of law and equity, another tribunal of kings meted out justice and decided cases of their government.

The Tuscarowas must have had a large population for when they suddenly left the county (supposedly at the instigation of the French), in 1753, and moved westward across the Alleghenies, they were strong enough to be embraced by the Five Nations, and when after this Indian confederation was formed, it became known as the Six Nations.

This portion of the country now occupied by Berkeley County was a favorite hunting-ground for the Indian, as well as a favorite dwelling-place. The portion of country lying between the Potomac and the Shenandoah rivers,

---
*Kerchival's Hist. of the Valley.

with its deep forests and fertile, broad *savannahs*, was a favorite spot where plenty of wild game existed. Such wild animals as the buffalo, deer, elk, bear, fox, with other smaller animals, were found here in abundance. Wild birds were plentiful, as duck, geese, quail, pheasants, while the streams teemed with freshwater fish. No wonder the Indian considered this a "happy hunting grounds".

At the time this valley was first known to the white people, the Delaware and Catawba tribes were engaged in bloody wars and each tribe continued its onslaught upon the other after our section became pretty thickly settled by the whites. The Tuscarowas took no part in these bloody encounters, but remained neutral.

The Delawares inhabited the region now occupied by the States of Maryland and Pennsylvania, while the Catawbas resided principally in what is now southern Virginia and the Carolinas. In Gerrardstown district, two miles west of Arden, is a hollow, or small valley, known to-day as "Indian Hollow", from the numerous number of flint arrowheads which have been picked up, some of them found to the present day. In a battle here, about 1650, over a thousand warriors were engaged on both sides. This valley is now owned by the North Valley Orchard Corporation, and was formerly owned by the late James S. Pitzer. On the site of the old Evans homestead, near this place, is evidence of another battle-grounds, from the presence of numerous flint arrowheads and hatchets having been found. At the former battle the Delawares were successful. Other engagements took place at the mouth of the Opequon and in Back Creek valley, south of the present site of Jones' Spring.

On the Maryland side of the Potomac, at the mouth of the Antietam Creek, another fierce battle was fought between these two tribes. The Delawares had advanced to the south, committing depredations upon the Catawbas, and on their retreat were overtaken at the above mentioned place and every Delaware put to death but one; and every Catawaba but one procured a scalp. This was a disgrace not to be borne, and he gave chase and overtook the Delaware at the Susquehannah River, (a distance of one hundred miles), killed and scalped him, and returned in triumph to his friends.

Another conflict ensued between these two tribes at the mouth of Conocacheague Creek and just one Delaware escaped by hiding in a white settler's cabin, and the owner would not give him up. There is a tradition of a great Indian battle being fought at what is now called Hanging Rock, in Hampshire County. A large party of Delawares had invaded the Catawba country, taking several prisoners. When they reached this spot where the South Branch of the Potomac breaks through the mountains the party halted and began fishing. The Catawbas, in close pursuit, discovered them and, throwing a part of their warriors across the river, another in front and another in the rear, began the assault which ended in the massacre of almost all of the Delawares.

The Indian has left many beautiful names to the streams adjacent to and within our county. The Potomac, from its source to its junction with the Shenandoah river at Harper's Ferry, was known as the Cohongoruton. Later it was changed to Po-to-meck, and later to its present name. The Shenandoah River, on the south of Jefferson County, is an Indian name denoting "Daughter of the stars". Opequon creek, or as it was known in the early history of the county, "Opequon river," is a name of Indian origin. Tuscorora Creek, upon which Martinsburg is situated, was named from a tribe of Indians which lived upon its banks when the white man first visited this section.

In the surrounding sections the Indian also gave names to rivers and streams, some of which they still retain. Others have been changed to suit the white conquerors. Antietam Creek, which empties into the Potomac on the Maryland side, opposite Jefferson County, is an Indian name. The Conococheague Creek, which empties into the Potomac opposite Berkeley County, is another. The South Branch of the Potomac wasanciently called the Wappatomaka, an Indian name; the Allegheny mountains, of which North Mountain is the first range, is an Indian name, and signifies "the place of the foot-print", or "the impression of feet", on account of the winter snows which fell at an early period of the winter and lasted to well on into the spring months.

Had the Indian continued in unmolested power to this day, the condition of America doubtless would have remained the same, only a trackless forest or barren waste; whereas millions of human beings find happiness and a peaceful existence. No doubt the Divine Creator created this world for the benefit of the greatest numbers of his people and not for a favored few. Traditional history has handed down to us places where once these people dwelt but no marks of any kind are left to show at least where their long resting-places are. Interesting would it have been for posterity if some of these places or their burying grounds had been marked in some way or the location of them been preserved, so that future generations could have had a conception of where these people lived, moved, and had their being. There are those who claim that the Indian has been unjustly treated at the hands of the white man; that instead of him having been driven off and his lands taken from him, he should have been assimilated. But this could not be. His tastes, temperament, and thoughts were different. He occupied the land but it cannot be truly said that he possessed it. This was a land for him to roam over, hunt over, and fight for. It has been estimated that it took the production of two hundred acres to keep an Indian. The white man can live upon considerable less. It is the law in a state of nature that the strong shall dominate the weak, and it must naturally follow that he should fall before the onslaught of a superior race. He did not give up without a struggle and many a settler was killed and many a home broken up before he was finally exterminated.

CHAPTER III.

EARLY EXPLORATIONS AND SETTLEMENTS.

As Jefferson County was a part of Berkeley until the year 1801, when by an act of the Virginia Assembly it was made a separate county, and Morgan County was taken from Berkeley in 1820 and made a separate county by the same process, the history of Berkeley County must needs include the events transpiring within these two counties up to the time of their formaation. The original Berkeley County included all the territory in what is now the "Eastern Panhandle", and extended from the Potomac to the Shenandoah rivers on the north and east, to the confines of Hampshire County.

This section first became known to the white man in about the year 1660 when John Lederer, an explorer employed by Sir William Berkeley, colonial governor of Virginia, visited it. On several occasions, prior to this time, he had made journeys to the Shenandoah valley to the southern part, but in this year he had decided to see what country lay in the northern section of the valley. On this expedition he crossed the Blue Ridge in the vicinity of what is now Harper's Ferry, explored the valley there and penetrated to the west as far as the valley of the Cheat River. He was probably the first white man to set foot upon the soil of Berkeley County.

A few years later came John Howard and his son, who, on a journey to this section, discovered the valley of the South Branch of the Potomac; continued across the Allegheny mountains, and when they reached the Ohio River, killed a large buffalo, or bison, removed its hide, and with the help of ribs of wood, made a rude boat in which they set sail on that river and floated with the current to New Orleans.

Previous to this time Robert Cavalier La Salle had discovered the Ohio and Mississippi and planted a fort at the mouth of the latter and called it Fort New Orleans. These two, father and son, were arrested as suspicious characters. They were sent to France, tried, but as nothing criminal was found against them they were released and then returned to England. Lord Fairfax, then residing in England, chanced to hear of Howard's discoveries in the Shenandoah and South Branch valleys and in an interview with him learned of the fertility of the soil and the beauty of the country and determined to gain possession of it for himself. How he succeeded is set forth in another chapter.

In those days this section was covered by almost impenetrable forests and people were slow to take advantage of its natural resources, and over sixty years had passed away before another white man traversed this trackless wilderness. In 1725, John Van Matre (as the name was written at that time), a member of a prominent family of New York and Holland, traversed this county. He crossed the Cohongoruton (Potomac) River at what is now Shepherdstown, and penetrated to the Wapatomacka (South Branch) River where John Howard had been many years before. He was an Indian trader; when in this section resided with the Delawares on the Susquehanna River in Pennsylvania. He wished to trade with the Catawbas also, and on his journey happened to traverse this valley. He was so charmed with it that when he returned home he advised his sons that if they ever migrated to Virginia, to obtain land on the South Branch as the "Trough" contained the finest land he had ever seen. On one occasion he led an expedition of Delawares against the Catawbas. They met at where the Pendleton County court house now stands, and a fierce battle was fought which went against the Delawares. John Van Matre was the ancestor of the Van Metres which later settled in Berkeley County on the Opequon and in Hardy County on the South Branch.

In 1716 Governor Spottswood, colonial governor of Virginia, organized a party of thirty men; provisioned and equipped them at Williamsburg—which was then the capital of Virginia—and proceeded at the head of this party to make explorations in the Shenandoah valley. The party crossed the Blue Ridge and the Shenandoah valley and reached the summit of the Alleghenies. The party returned to Williamsburg and the Governor organized what he termed the Trans-Mountain Order, or "Knights of the Golden Horseshoe". He gave to each one who had accompanied him a miniature horseshoe which bore the inscription "Sic jurat transcudere montes", or "Thus he swears to cross the mountains". All others who would comply with the terms of the inscription were given one.

Although this expedition did not reach this section, such acts as these led to the settling of the valley at an early date.

To Morgan Morgan belongs the honor of building the first cabin-home in Berkeley County and, in fact, in all of what is now West Virginia. In 1726, he settled on Mill Creek at what is now the town of Bunker Hill. He was a native of Wales, having migrated to Pennsylvania at an early period and from thence to the valley of Virginia. He was an Episcopal minister and established the Episcopal Church at Bunker Hill. He was afterward appointed one of the King's Gentleman Justices for Berkeley County.

The first emigrants to come to Berkeley County in a body was in 1727, when a number of persons from Pennsylvania crossed the Cohongoruton (Potomac) at the "Old Pack-horse Ford", two miles below Shepherdstown. This section, with its gray limestone cliffs bordering the river at this place, reminded them so much of their old home in Germany that they decided to stop here and begin a settlement. They named their settlement New Mecklenburg for the old town in Germany. This is the oldest town in West Virginia. Thirty-four years later (1761), the Virginia Assembly by legislative enactment established a town there and named it Shepherdstown in honor of Thomas Shepherd, who laid it out.

John Van Matre, the Indian trader, who had advised his sons that if they "ever came to Virginia, to secure lands on the Wapatomaka" (South

EARLY EXPLORATIONS AND SETTLEMENTS

Branch), was rewarded by seeing his two sons, John and Isaac, securing a patent from Governor Gooch, then Colonial Governor of Virginia, for forty thousand acres of land. This was in the year 1730. John settled in what is now Berkeley County and Isaac proceeded west to the South Branch in Hardy County and each became the progenitor of large families in either section. A large portion of this grant included land in what is now Berkeley, Jefferson, Morgan, Hampshire and Hardy Counties, West Virginia, and Frederick County, Virginia. From this settlement it will be seen that John Van Matre was one of the original emigrants to Berkeley County.

The next large body of emigrants to come to this section was that of Joist Hite, with his family, in 1732. In that year he purchased from John Van Matre a portion of the 40,000-acre tract granted to him by Governor Gooch. This portion was located in Frederick County. Those accompanying Hite were his sons-in-law, George Bowman, Jacob Chrisman and Paul Foreman with their families; Robert MacKay, Peter Stephens, Robert Green, William Duff and others. The party, comprising sixteen families in all, removed from the vicinity of what is now York, Pennsylvania, crossed the Cohongoruton about two miles above Harper's Ferry, and proceeded to about five miles south of Winchester. There they founded a settlement, or colony, on what is now the Valley Pike. They cut their way through the forest as they went and a part of this is now the Winchester Pike through Berkeley County which was formerly known as the Great Winchester Road. None of these settled in what is now Berkeley County but this is mentioned here as an enterprise of this nature induced others to make their homes in this section.

In 1734 Richard Morgan obtained a grant for a tract of land in the neighborhood of what is now Shepherdstown and from him the famous Morgan Springs in Jefferson County are named. It is now owned by the Morgan's Grove Fair Association, at which place a great annual agricultural fair is held, and this spring furnishes water for thousands of visitors at this place.

Among the first settlers at New Mecklenburg (Shepherdstown) and in the vicinity were: William Stroop, James Foreman, John Lemon, Richard Mercer, Thomas Forester, Thomas Shepherd, William Forester, John Wright, Samuel Taylor, Robert Stockton, Robert Buckles, Van Swearingen, Richard Morgan, Jacob Van Metre, William Foster, Israel Friend, Thomas Swearingen, Edward Lucas, Jacob Hite, Edward Mercer, and John Taylor.

Robert Harper settled nearer where Harper's Ferry now stands and the ferry established across the Potomac at that place some years later was named for him. These settlements were made about the year 1734-5.

Another patent for 13,000 acres of land was granted by the Colonial Governor of Virginia. The owner of this land by gambling and sporting had become deeply involved in debt. To satisfy his creditors, it was sold under the hammer at Williamsburg, then the capital of Virginia. General Washington happening to be present and, who knew of it, persuaded Ralph Wormley to buy it, which he did. He had been imbibing too freely of spirits and, after reflection, was disgusted with his purchase and wished to get rid of it. Washington still advised him to retain it as he thought it would develop into a valuable piece of land, and if he was still dissatisfied with his purchase he (Washington) would take it off his hands. This led Mr. Wormley to still retain it and it did develop into a valuable piece of property, as Washington had predicted, had his children known how to take care of it, but it passed into other hands. Much of this tract was in Berkeley County in that portion which is now Jefferson County.

John Van Metre settled on the Opequon in the vicinity of Vanclevesville. John Evans settled on the Opequon near where the State Road crosses it from Martinsburg to Charles Town.

John Boyd settled at the east base of North Mountain in the vicinity of Tuscarora Creek. All these settlements were made prior to the year 1740. The record of other settlements are meager but they must have been numerous for at the outbreak of the French and Indian War, in 1754, Colonel George Washington raised three hundred men to fight the Indians and many of these were collected from Berkeley County.

It is evident that the Quakers were among the first inhabitants. These, the Indians never molested, and they were invited to make settlements in the section of what is now our county, and, from the following letter, it will be seen that they were inclined to deal with the Indians in a wise and just manner.

"Virginia, at John Cheagles, 21st., 5th month, 1738"
"To Friends of the Monthly meeting at Opequon.

"Dear friends who inhabit Shenandoah and Opequon—Having a concern for your welfare and prosperity both here and hereafter and also the prosperity of your children, I had a desire to see you; but being in years and heavy, and much spent and fatigued by my long journeys in Virginia and Carolina, makes it seem too hard for me to pay a visit to you in person, wherefore I take this way to discharge my mind of what weighs weighty thereon: and:

"First;—I desire that you be very careful (being far and back inhabitants), to keep a friendly correspondence with the native Indians, giving them no occasion for offense; they being a cruel and merciless enemy where they think they are wronged or defrauded of their rights as woful experience has taught in Carolina, Virginia and Maryland, especially in New England, etc., and—

"Secondly;—As nature hath given them and their forefathers the possession of this continent of America (or this wilderness), they had a natural right thereto in justice and equity; and no people, according to the law of nature, and justice, and our own principle, which is according to the glorious gospel of our dear and Holy Jesus Christ; ought to take away and settle on other men's lands or rights without consent or by purchasing the same by agreement of parties concerned; which, I suppose, in your case is not done.

"Thirdly:—Therefore my counsel and Christian advice is, my dear friends, that the most reputable among you do with speed endeavor to agree with and purchase your lands from the natives or inhabitants. Take example of our worthy and late proprietor William Penn, who by his wise and religious care, in that relation has settled a lasting peace with the natives, and through his prudent management, hath been instrumental to plant in peace one of the most flourishing provinces in the world.

"Fourthly; Who would run the risk of the lives of their wives and their children for the sparing a little cost and pains? I am concerned to lay these things before you under an uncommon exercise of mind that your new and flourishing settlement may not be laid waste, and (if the providence of the Almighty doth not intervene) some of the blood of yourselves, wives or children be shed or spilt on the ground.

Fifthly, Consider that you are in the province of Virginia holding what rights you have under the government; and the Virginians have made an agreement with the natives to go as far as the mountains and no farther; and you are over and beyond the mountains, therefore out of that agreement; by which you lie open to the insults and incursions of the Southern Indians who have destroyed many of the inhabitants of Carolina and Virginia and even now have destroyed more on the like occasion the English going beyond the bounds of their agreement, eleven were killed by the Indians while we were traveling in Virginia.

"Sixthly, If you believe yourselves to be within the bounds of William Penn's patent from King Charles the second, which will be hard for you to prove, you being southward of his line, yet if done, that will be consideration with the Indians without a purchase from them, except you will go about to convince them by fire and sword, contrary to our principles; and if that were done, they would ever be implacable enemies, and the land would never be enjoyed in peace.

"Seventhly, please to note that in Pennsylvania that no new settlements are made without agreement with the natives; as witness Lancaster County, lately settled, though that is far within the grant of William Penn's patent from King Charles the second; wherefore you lie open to the insurrections of the Northern as well as the Southern Indians; and

"Lastly, Thus having shown my good will to you and to your new little settlement, that you might sit, everyone, under your own shady tree, where none might make you afraid,· and that you might prosper naturally and spiritually, you and your children; and, having a little eased my mind of that weight and concern (in some measure) lay upon me, I at present desist, and subscribe myself, in the love of our Holy Jesus Christ, your real friend, T. C."*

Probably in the year 1742 or 1743, fifteen families, members of the Baptist faith, left their homes in New Jersey and settled in the vicinity of Vanclevesville. They shortly afterward began the erection of a log church on a hill to the left of the State Road leading from Martinsburg to Charles Town. The remains of this church can be seen just beyond where the new bridge crosses Opequon Creek on that road. This church was founded by Rev. John Gerard and was the first Baptist church founded west of the Blue Ridge mountains.

The Indians did not object to the Quakers settling the country, on account of William Penn's just dealings with them, but they hated the Virginians whom they designated as "Long Knives", and opposed their occupying the land with all their power. At first, the Indians regarded the English as neighbors and as joint occupyers of the land but not so the English. They

---

*Letter from Kercheval's History, 1833.

regarded the Indians as savages and treated them as such and determined upon a course of extermination.

The Virginians did not like the Quakers on account of their refusal to contribute in any way to the support of the wars against the Indians both by refusing to bear arms and to pay taxes for the support of the war. In retaliation, the Legislature of Virginia in March, 1660, enacted the following law:

"An Act for Suppressing The Quakers.

"Whereas there is an vnreasonable and turbulent sort of people, commonly called Quakers, who contrary to the lawe do dayly gather together vnto them vnlaw"ll assemblies and congregations of people, teaching and publishing lies, miracles, false visions, prophecies and false doctrines, which have influence vpon the communities of men, both ecclesiasticall and civill, endeavoring and attempting thereby to destroy religion and lawes, communities, and all bonds of civil societie, leaving it arbitrarie to everie vaine and vitious person, whether men shall be safe, lawes established, offenders punished, and governors rule, hereby disturbing the publique peace and just interest; to prevent and restraine which mischiefe, *It is enacted,* That no master or commander of any shipp or other vessell do bring into this colonie any person or persons called Quakers, vnder the penalty of one hundred pounds sterling to be levied vpon him and his estate by order from the governor and council, or the commissioners in the severall counties where such ships shall arrive: That all such Quakers as have been questioned, or shall hereafter arrive shall be apprehended, wherever they shall be found, and they shall be imprisoned without baile or mainprize till they do adjure this country, or putt in security with all speed to depart from the colonie and not to return again: And if any should dare to presume to return hither after such departure to be proceeded against as contemners of the lawes and magistracy, and punished accordingly, and caused again to depart the country, and if they should the third time be so audacious and impudent as to return hither, to be proceeded against as felons: That no person shall entertain any of the Quakers that have been heretofore been questioned, by the governor and council, or which shall hereafter be questioned, nor permit in or near his house any assemblies of Quakers, in the like penalty of one hundred pounds sterling: That commissioners and officers are hereby required and authorized as they will answer the contrary at their perill, to take notice of this act, to see if fully effected and executed: And that no person do presume on their perill to dispose and publish their books, pamphlets or libells, bearing the title of their tenets and opinions." *

These cruel and unjust laws were passed at a time when people were biased and prejudiced in their opinions. They could not understand why all the people would not bear their just share of the burden of government, both civil and military. Furthermore, the Church of England was the established church in this colony and if any people or sect did not wish to worship as they did, they could depart and the authorities decided that they did depart. To-day, there is not a more inoffensive, orderly and strictly moral people than the Friends or Quakers, and their presence is welcomed in any community.

Notwithstanding this unreasonable legislation, many Quakers at an early period, migrated to this section, and later hundreds of this faith settled on

---

*Henning's Statutes at Large. Vol. I, pp. 532-33.

the Opequon and in the vicinity of Apple Pie Ridge. At the breaking out of the Revolution, quite a number of them had settled in the vicinity of Arden and in the southern section of the county.

At this time it might be appropriate to relate the legend of how Apple Pie Ridge got its name. At the monthly meetings of the Quakers on the Opequon it was the custom for Friends, coming from a long distance, to bring provisions with them for their two days' meeting. The good Quaker wives always included apple pies in their list and were profuse in passing samples of their culinary art to their friends. On one occasion, a visiting minister inquired who had brought such delicious pies. When told they had come from "the ridge", to the west near North Mountain, he suggested that that ridge afterwards be designated as "Apple Pie Ridge". The name clung and is still known as the best apple producing region in the two Virginias.

Thus it will be seen that the early migration to this section was from New York, Pennsylvania, New Jersey and Maryland; colonies to the north of it rather than from Tidewater Virginia. As this region belonged to Virginia it would naturally have been supposed that the emigrants to this region would have been from that colony. The authorities did offer every inducement to get settlers to come to this section, but the Blue Ridge mountains formed a barrier to them. Lord Fairfax, who at one time owned all the land comprising the County of Berkeley, sold smaller tracts to settlers at a very low figure, and Governor Gooch also practically gave away large tracts to the Van Matres, who in turn sold it to the settlers for practically nothing (ten dollars per hundred acres).

The settlement of this section was slow; the Indians were hostile except to the Quakers; the roads—if any—were mere trails through the forest and transportation was by pack-horse. The land had to first be cleared of trees and was unfit for extensive farming for several years or until the stumps had decayed. "New ground" farming was accomplished with the severest toil, and, even after the crop was gathered in the fall,, it was not an uncommon ocurrence for the Indians to make a raid upon the settler and destroy the results of his whole summer's work.

CHAPTER IV.

LORD FAIRFAX.

One of the most picturesque figures in the later colonial history of Virginia, and one who had more to do with the settling of our county than any other man, was Lord Fairfax. And because many of the early deeds of conveyance for lands in this county bear the signature "Fairfax", it is appropriate that mention be made here of the one who was so intimately connected with the history of this region. Many families exhibit with pride old deeds for their lands which were at one time conveyed to their ancestors by Lord Fairfax. Let us pause and reflect what manner of man this was and how he had the power to deed so much land to others.

Born in 1692, of Catherine, only child of Alexander, Lord Culpepper, Baron of Thorsway, who was appointed Governor of Virginia by King Charles II, July 8, 1675, and the fifth Lord Fairfax whom she married in 1690, and who was a descendant of the commander-in-chief of the parliamentary army in the English civil war. He was a descendant of the English nobility. His grandfather, Lord Culpepper, has been described as an able but artful and covetous man. At the age of eighteen he inherited from his mother the estate of Lord Culpepper and the Fairfax estate in England, and an immense tract of land in America, and the title of nobility—sixth Lord Fairfax—from his father. At this time he was a student at the University of Oxford. The Culpepper estate was heavily involved in debt and in order to save it his mother and maternal grandmother prevailed upon him to cut off the entail of the Fairfax estates in England. This he did, not being very well able to do otherwise. For doing so he was given the Culpepper estate in America.

Prior to this, King Charles II of England had, in 1644, granted to Lord Hopton, Lord Culpepper, Lord Berkeley, the Earl of Saint Albans, Sir William Morton and Sir Dudley Wyatt an immense tract of land in America.

This tract extended between the Potomac and Rappahannock rivers in Virginia and to the Blue Ridge (these rivers supposedly rising in these mountains) and was known as the Northern Neck of Virginia, a territory now embracing the Counties of Lancaster, Northumberland, Richmond, Westmoreland, Stafford, King George, Prince William, Fairfax, Loudon, Faukuier, Culpepper, Madison, Page and Shenandoah in Virginia.

This grant was in the same nature as those given to William Penn and Lord Baltimore, with the exception that it did not form a colony as the others had. Perhaps Lord Culpepper, the proprietor, was shrewd enough to save the expense of founding a colony while he could sell his lands to settlers from other colonies already founded, and still retain the proprietary title. Until the American Revolution changed the old order of things, this immense tract of land was regarded as distinct from the Virginia colony.

In 1681 Lord Culpepper bought the other grantees' shares and became the sole owner of the Northern Neck. Hence at his death this estate descended to his daughter Catherine.

As has been stated in a preceding chapter, John Howard and his son, by exploration, discovered that the Potomac and Rappahannock rivers had their first fountains in the Alleghenies and not in the Blue Ridge as was first understood. Lord Fairfax, learning of Howard's discoveries, sought an interview with him, and found that by the grant of 1664, he was entitled to an additional large territory beyond the Blue Ridge—a territory almost as large as his one east of it, and comprising the present Counties of Jefferson, Berkeley, Morgan, Hampshire, Hardy, Grant, Mineral, and a part of Tucker in West Virginia, and Frederick County in Virginia. By the terms of the grant of lands by King Charles II. to Lord Culpepper and others, it included all the lands between Potomac and the Rappahannock, which meant to their sources, and Lord Fairfax hastened to acquire this additional territory.

In the meantime the colonial governors of Virginia, notably Governor Gooch, had granted immense tracts of land in the lower Shenandoah valley to several parties, among them John and Isaac VanMatre, who in turn had sold a part of it to Joist Hite. Several other grants of smaller denominations were sold to others. This land really belonged to Lord Fairfax. His lordship visited Virginia in 1736 and, when he found that immense tracts of this territory was granted to others by the governor, he returned to England and instituted his petition in the court of king's bench for the possession of this territory. Fairfax and the crown compromised the matter. In the compromise it was expressly stipulated that those persons holding under the King's grant were to be quited in their right of possession. Fairfax now sold large tracts of this same land to other individuals. Joist Hite and his partners instituted a law suit in the year 1736 against Fairfax which was not settled until the year 1786. During these fifty years purchasing of these farms went on apace. Lord Fairfax returned to Virginia in the year 1742. He lived with William Fairfax, a cousin, at "Belvair" on a plantation twelve miles below Mount Vernon. Then he decided to remove to a 10,000-acre tract which he called a "manor" and which he reserved for himself from his thousands of acres. This was in Frederick County, Virginia, eleven miles southeast of Winchester. There he built himself a house and called it "Greenway Court." He removed here to be in close proximity to his lands to the westward and opened an office for the transacting of any business which might come under his hand, such as surveying, rents and the selling of lands to settlers.

In 1746 a line was surveyed from the headwaters of the North Branch of the Potomac to the source of the Rapid Ann (Rapidan) to determine the western boundary of his estate. Previous to this time, in 1733, he had petitioned the King for commissioners to determine the bounds of his patent. The petition was heard, commissioners appointed and assembled at Fredericksburg, Va., in 1734, and began the exploration of the Potomac. They proceeded to explore that river from its mouth to the mouth of the South

Branch. It was determined to continue to the headwaters of the North Branch as that was the real Potomac. This contention over whether the North Branch or the South was the true Potomac brought forth a contention between Maryland and Virginia over the land between these two branches which will be discussed in another chapter.

Lord Fairfax employed George Washington, then a young man of seventeen, to survey his lands in Frederick, Berkeley, and Hampshire Counties, or as we might say, in territory now included in them, and lay off the land into lots to suit the purchasers. Lord Fairfax had met the young man when he, Fairfax, had resided at "Belvair." He attained an affection for him which lasted through life, although Fairfax never forgave Washington for taking sides with the colonies in their struggle against the King. George had, among other things, studied surveying and in this art had become efficient notwithstanding his extreme youth. Christopher Gist, the eminent surveyor for the colony of North Carolina, was also employed by Fairfax and accompanied Washington on several surveying expeditions into the wilds of this section. Washington in this capacity gained his first experience of life in the wilderness. By thus being employed he also acquired a knowledge and foresight of the vast opportunities the acquiring of western Virginia afforded. Being employed in this capacity made Washington a "western man".

Joist Hite had advertised his land acquired from the Van Matre brothers for sale at three pounds ($10.00) for one hundred acres. This advertising brought many settlers from older neighborhoods, mainly from the colonies to the north, Pennsylvania, Maryland, and New York, to this region. All went well until Lord Fairfax came to reside in Virginia, when he demanded a tax called a quit rent from them to himself as a sort of proprietary rental, and he demanded that these quit rents extend back to 1745, the year which he acquired possession of the additional territory west of the Blue Ridge. These quit rents amounted to practically nothing (two shillings—50c—per fifty acres yearly), yet the people resented them on the grounds that they cast a shade of doubt upon the title to their homes.

Lord Fairfax called his 10,000-acre tract a "manor". When he built his country home, "Greenway Court," he had thought of building a castle but the demand by the granting of lands and surveying, the collecting of quit rents and the suits of Joist Hite and others so engaged his time that he gave up the idea and contented himself with "Greenway Court". And it has been stated also that his love for hoarding English gold made him reluctant to part with it in erecting a great house.

This house was erected in 1748. It consisted of a long story and half building with a veranda the entire length facing the Blue Ridge. Three dormer windows adorned the roof on either side. On top of the roof were two wooden belfries, one at either end, in which hung two bells used in giving alarms and in summoning the numerous slaves to and from work. The center of the roof was ornamented by a large bird house or nesting place for swallows and martins. A sundial stood near to the entrance to the veranda. The cabins for the slaves were arranged all about the great house.

Around all was woods and the proprietor made no attempt to clear or cultivate but lived off the money from quit rents and sale to settlers whom he termed "retainers". He was fond of the chase and retained these 10,000 acres as a hunting reserve for himself and his few friends.

Greenway Court stood for more than a hundred years, being torn down in 1859. Interesting it would have been if this old mansion had been preserved as were Mount Vernon and Monticello, homes of Washington and Jefferson.

Fairfax was fond of books and had literary ability, although he did not use it. At home he was hospitable to the male friends only. He had an aversion for the fair sex, supposedly for two reasons: his mother and maternal grandmother causing him to give up his estates in England, and being jilted by the woman to whom he was engaged. He remained a bachelor throughout his life.

He had a velvet suit of each of the following colors: brown, blue, drab, scarlet and green; silk coats, scarlet laced, green damask laced, gold tissue vests, and scarlet plush and black velvet breeches. He always appeared in silk stockings and slippers adorned with immense silver buckles.

He lived at Greenway Court for the remainder of his life, never returning to England. When warned of the approach of the Indians he refused to leave and barricaded himself and his slaves within the great house and by threats and persuasions, fought the Indians. He lived to the ripe old age of ninety-one. Shortly after the surrender of Cornwallis at Yorktown, upon hearing of this event he remarked to his old servant: "Come, Joe, and put me to bed for it is now high time for me to die." He expired shortly afterward and was buried in the old Episcopal Church at Winchester. When the building was no longer in use his remains were removed to the chancel of the church, at the corner of Water and Washington streets, where a tablet was erected to his memory. Notwithstanding his faults, he was honorable and public spirited. He advanced money to the settlers for the betterment of their lands, although this advancement netted him additional income. He helped to defend the frontier against the French and Indian war by giving money to help pay the soldiers. He was quite popular, being a member of the county court, a county lieutenant, and an overseer of the poor.

For hundreds of years the system of granting special privileges to certain of the King's favorites had been in vogue and the last of these to pass was Lord Fairfax. He lived at the time when this system was responsible and not the man. He attempted to live a baronial life in democratic America and he was a misfit. Thoroughly in sympathy with all things English, he had no patience with things American, especially to the westward. He did not leave England until well advanced in years and had been nurtured under a government which believed in kings and nobles, while the great mass of common people were considered underlings.

Therefore, we should think kindly of this man who has done much for the development of our country, especially this part of it.

CHAPTER V.

"NORTHERN NECK OF VIRGINIA."

In the year 1681, King Charles II. of England granted to Lord Hopton and several others, whose names appear in a preceding chapter, a tract of land in the northern section of Virginia including all the territory between the Potomac on the north and the Rappahannock on the south and extending to the Blue Ridge Mountains, or in that vicinity, as the western boundaries of grants in those days were vague in the extreme. This immense tract of land was known as the "Fairfax Land Grant", and was called the Northern Neck of Virginia. It was the fashion for those two Charles' (Charles I. and Charles II.) to give grants for immense tracts of land in America to their favorites as in the case of William Penn, Lord Baltimore, and Lord Clarenden. The difference between these and Lord Fairfax was, each of the former wished to found a settlement for people persecuted for religious beliefs, while the latter wished to enrich himself at the expense of others. The former *gave* their land to the settlers while the latter *sold* his to them.

To fully understand what one of these grants meant to the grantee, it must be remembered that the country was a trackless forest filled with savage beasts and more savage men. There were no white settlements except a narrow fringe of sparsely settled communities along the coast, and if any of us today were handed a tract of land like this we would hesitate to accept it. It would be like being granted a tract of land of a hundred thousand acres in the heart of Africa. It would be of no use unless we could develop it.

The Northern Neck was considered an independent government separate from the colony of Virginia, although it was a part of the same. It was a domain within a domain. Lord Fairfax considered it such and the King of England backed him up in his claims. Fairfax sold his lands to settlers as leaseholds running ninety-nine years, demanding what he called "composition money" when he made the transfer. The settlers were to pay for each fifty acres, ten shillings in "composition money", and an annual quit rent of ten shillings yearly. This caused so much contention on the part of the people that the Virginia Legislature passed an act in 1785 absolving the landholders from any further payment of these quit rents, of which a section reads as follows: "And be it further enacted, that the landholders within said district of the Northern Neck shall be forever hereafter exonerated and discharged from composition and quit rents, any law, custom of usage to the contrary notwithstanding."*

After his lordship's death, in 1781, Denny Martin, a nephew, living in England, became sole proprietor of what interests Lord Fairfax had possessed within America, he having left them to him by will with the condition that

---

**See Revised Code of the Laws of Virginia, page 351, Vol. I.*

he would ask the British Parliament by act to make him a Lord. This was done and Denny Martin became the seventh Lord Fairfax. He, like his uncle, never marrying, left no issue, and devised his estate to his two maiden sisters who sold it to Marshall, Colston and Lee. But the law relative to the stoppage of the payment of quit rents having been passed by the Legislature having made these estates not quite so valuable, Martin did not receive so much rental as his uncle had done. At his death he left his property to General Philip Martin. He speedily sold these interests in America to John and James Marshall, Raleigh Colston and General Henry Lee. John Marshall afterwards became Chief Justice of the Supreme Court of the United States, Raleigh Colston's name again appears in this work as one of the founders of this county and General Henry Lee became a great general in the Revolution.

This purchase was called the Manor of Leeds, and included South Branch Manor, Patterson's Creek Manor and various other tracts of land.

Denny Fairfax left part of his estate to Col. Thomas Bryan Martin, another nephew who had resided with him at "Greenway Court Manor," as he had styled Greenway Court. Col. Martin never married. He is the one for whom Martinsburg was named and the last owner of a very small portion of the Fairfax estate, an estate which comprised nearly the one-fourth of the whole State of Virginia.

CHAPTER VI.

OF THE EARLY SETTLERS.

FOUNDING A HOME.

The pioneer who wished to found a home in the wilderness would first make a journey to the section where he desired to locate, select a site, go to the proprietor for his deed and return for his friends. A few males would cross the mountains by packhorse in the spring, leaving their families behind, to raise a crop of corn, pumpkins and potatoes, etc., to build their cabins and bring their families out in the fall.

All went well if sufficient corn was raised to feed the family till the next summer vegetables grew, but if the corn ran out the family had to subsist on lean venison and breast of wild turkey which was roasted and served as bread. Bear flesh was denominated meat. After living in this way for some time they became sickly and the stomach seemed to be always empty. In addition to this, was the constant fear of the savage tomahawk and scalping knife. In time of great danger while working in the fields to keep their families from starvation the coming winter one of their number was compelled to stand watch while the rest labored. Often after the crops were gathered into the garner, a prowling band of Indians would appear and set fire to it all and drive the settlers off. If the family reached civilization intact, it was in the most wretched condition.

Generally, several families would migrate together. When the company arrived at its destination the men cast lots to determine whose house should be built first. Then all set to work; some felling trees, others cutting the logs into proper lengths, others rolling them into place. One man was placed at each corner of the building and each would put them into position. The "sleepers" upon which the lower floor rested were usually placed upon the first or foundation log. When the building was of proper height the joists for the upper floor were placed. The roof was formed by making the end logs shorter until the single log called the "ridge pole" formed the comb of the roof. Over these logs clapboards were laid which overlapped each other and were held in their proper places by logs being placed upon them. Openings were afterwards made for the door, windows and chimney.

Puncheons for the floors were split out by an instrument called a frow, and were smoothed by a drawknife. The crevices between the logs were "chinked" (that is, filled) with short pieces of wood and sometimes stone, and daubed inside and out with stiff clay.

The window panes were made of paper soaked in bear's oil. These let in some light and kept out the cold in winter. During the summer season they were removed entirely. The door was barricaded inside with a stout wooden crosspiece fitted into a mortice at each side of the door. When thus secured a "man's house was his castle" indeed, and he felt quite secure against the attack of savage or wild beast.

At one end of the room a huge fireplace was built of stone. For a chimney, short logs were used in like manner as the house, and were daubed inside and out with stiff clay. This was called a "cat and clay" chimney. None of these houses are left standing. The last one in Berkeley County was torn down in 1902, and stood on the farm owned by the late Colonel Stuart W. Walker on the Dry Run Creek, in Hedgesville District. Houses of a later date were built in like manner with the exception that the logs were hewn flat on two sides. These kind of houses presented a much better appearance both inside and outside.

At a later period it was found that in numerous places in the county large deposits of shale and clay existed for the making of brick. Then began the construction of houses of brick. Some of these are of large dimensions.

Utensils. The furniture was simple; a table was made of boards or puncheons, sometimes made of a single board hewn from a tree down to the proper thickness with four stout legs; three-legged stools for chairs; and the bed usually a framework of boards fastened to the walls by pins of wood to one side of the room. The mattress or "tick" was stuffed with straw, leaves, moss or occasionally with feathers, and the spinning-wheel and loom for making the family clothing constituted about the only household articles.

For a lamp "grease lamps" or tallow dips were used. The grease lamp consisted of an iron bowl in which bear's oil or lard was poured in, from which a short rag or wick extended. A tallow dip was made by taking a wick about a foot in length and dipping it into melted tallow until it acquired the correct thickness.

Afterward molds of tin were used, sometimes six, sometimes ten candles constituting a mold, for molding tallow candles. A wick was inserted through the center of this, the melted tallow poured into the mold and allowed to harden. It was the custom to make several dozen of these and lay them by for future use. A pair of "snuffers" were used to remove the charred end of the wick, as the candle burned down, to make the flame brighter. The candle was placed in a brass candlestick, some of them beautifully carved. These curios are now eagerly sought after by collectors of "antiques".

The early settlers had not much use for lights for they usually arose with the break of day and retired at nightfall.

For time the early settlers used the sun. Clocks and watches were not yet invented and, as there was no hurrying to catch trains and no worrying about meeting engagements, this mode of determining the time of day was sufficient.

The cooking was simple and was done on the open fire. Boiling was the universal method employed; occasionally roasting and frying. Each fireplace was equipped with the crane which consisted of a long bar of iron suspended across the top of the fireplace. If roasting was resorted to or corn pone was to be baked, the "Dutch oven" was used. This "oven" was a round, flat-bottomed pot, which was heated before the open fire by placing live coals under and around it.

The family washing was done at the bank of the stream. The clothes were thrown into the stream and beaten with a short stick until clean, and then hung on the bushes to dry.

Food. The food was plain but nourishing. Johnny-cake and corn pone were the only forms of bread used. For breakfast or dinner hominy cooked in bear's oil or eaten with a gravy made from fried meat was used. For supper mush and milk (when it could be had) were eaten. If food became scarce "sawdust pudding" was eaten. This was made of pounded corn stirred in a bowl of water. The larder was generally supplied with venison, fish, bear's meat, and wild turkey, and the yield of the truck patch. This manner of living and diet tended to produce a hardy race of people, a people perfectly able to cope with its savage adversary and who, when the time came, were able to throw off the yoke of British oppression and form a new government according to its own ideas.

If a settler wished to kindle a fire he used a piece of steel to strike sparks into a piece of tow. Tow was the lint gathered from a piece of goods while weaving it. This spark was then blown into a blaze. Or he could use the Indian method of rubbing two sticks together until they took fire by friction. Usually the coals were "banked" upon the hearth by burying them with ashes to "keep" the fire till morning. If none of these methods were at hand he would be compelled to borrow fire from his more fortunate neighbor.

Occasionally a dance would be held in the neighborhood, if the weddings were too far apart. And occasionally someone would hold a "log-rolling" or a "raisin'". The former consisted of chopping the trees and rolling the logs into huge heaps to be burned and thus clear the land; the latter was given when one wished to build a house. Often at these frolics wrestling was indulged in which usually wound up in a fist fight, the whole company forming a ring and watching the two combatants "fight it out". The one that "hollered 'Nuff'" first was declared whipped and that was the end of the matter.

These were strenuous times but with this simple fare and labor in the open, added to the constant menace of the Indian, produced a hardy race of people. Many of the descendants of these people are still living, filling positions of trust and responsibility in our nation and in the various walks of life, and we owe them a great respect, that such men and women laid the foundation on which our present citizenship stands.

Dress. The dress of the pioneer was admirably suited to the needs of the strenuous life in the wilderness. The women wore clothes made of coarse woolen cloth or "linsey", and sometimes of coarse linen, the wool dyed and spun by hand. Often the wool was grown and woven by them. Cotton was expensive; silk was not to be obtained. The men adopted, with few modifications, the dress of the Indian. It consisted of a loose coat reaching nearly to the knees and caught at the waist by a belt; knee-breeches, leggings and moccasins. The material was woolen linsey, or deerskin, or "buckskin" sometimes dressed with the hair on. He wore a cap made of 'coon skin and adorned with two raccoon tails fastened at the front, and extending around the head on either side, and terminating in two tips at the back.

This was the dress worn by Washington and his "Virginians" when they accompanied General Braddock on his ill-fated expedition against the French on the Ohio in 1755. This manner of dress of Washington's brought forth the sarcastic remark from that egotistical general, when Washington advised him to proceed with more caution, that "it was high time that a young buckskin should teach a British general how to fight."

Barter. Money was scarce. Almost the only mode of exchange was by barter or trade.

Of course the English pound sterling was one medium of exchange. If money could have been had it would have been a hindrance rather than a help. Each colony had its own money, and, if a person should have traveled in those days from Maine to Georgia, he would have had thirteen kinds of money to handle.

This system of trade was almost universal and its use extended well into the present century that the merchants of Martinsburg gave a few cents more "in trade" for farm commodities than for cash.

It is a tradition that in those days, when a settler wished to purchase a drink of rum or purchase some article of small value, he would walk up to the counter, throw down a fox hide, get his purchase, and receive in "change" a raccoon and opossum hide.

At one time in the early Virginia colony, the colonial governors were paid in tobacco. Also at that time the clergyman's salary was set at so many pounds of tobacco per year. The first wives of Virginia were bought at one hundred and fifty pounds of tobacco.

The settlers were extremely pious and always included a church in their building program in the thickly settled communities. There were no resident ministers and the only sermons delivered were by the "circuit rider" who made occasional visits to the settlement and preached for the people. Services were regularly held each Sabbath by the deacons of the church. These deacons were stern men who fought as hard as they prayed, many of them were like Captain Myles Standish of Puritan fame who, when he died, left three good swords and three well worn Bibles.

Weapons. The trusty rifle, as was the powder horn and the bullet pouch, were as indispensible to the settler as was the axe or grubbing hoe. The rifle was of the flint-lock pattern. A steel hammer swept the spark into a pan which held the powder. The spark ignited the powder in the barrel and discharged the rifle. These rifles were loaded from the muzzle with powder and bullets and rammed home with a ramrod. This was a clumsy weapon compared with the modern breech-loading repeating rifle but was far superior to the bow and arrow of the savage and was much more accurate. Many a backwoodsman, and woman, too, became expert in the use of it and one man with it was equal to ten Indians in a fight with bows and arrows.

Sports. Throwing the tomahawk was a sport in which many became proficient. The tomahawk of the Indian consisted of a stone blade, sharp on one end and blunt on the other. The middle of it was inserted in a cleft handle, the cleft being bound around by strings of deerskin. The white man's was made of hardened iron with a cleft in the tomahawk into which the handle was inserted not unlike our hatchets of the present day. The blade was made sharp by grinding while the other end was elongated into a sharp point. All frontier soldiers were required to carry a tomahawk, as it was a part of their equipment.

The tomahawk with its handle of a certain length will make a given number of turns in a given distance. Say, at five steps, it will strike with the edge, the handle downward; at a distance of seven and half it will strike with the edge of the handle upwards, etc. A little experience enabled the boy to measure the distance with his eye, when walking through the woods, and strike a tree with his tomahawk in any way he chose. In fights with the Indians the tomahawk was retained in the hand and not thrown at the enemy only when necessity required it, as in that case his most proficient weapon in a hand encounter would be lost to him. But in numbers of cases the accuracy with which this weapon was thrown decided whether he should carry his scalp a little longer or not.

Dancing was the principal amusement indulged in by the young of both sexes. These dances were of the simplest forms—three or four-handed reels and jigs. The music was furnished by the neighborhood fiddler, who upon all occasions was called upon to flourish his bow.

Shooting mark was a pastime which was indulged in by old as well as young men, when the supply of ammunition warranted it. Off-hand shooting was not then in use but shooting from a rest was the custom and at a great distance. Rifles of that period were for a long range and carried bullets at forty-five bullets to the pound. Bullets of smaller size were not considered large enough for hunting and warfare.

When a boy arrived at the age of fourteen he was furnished with a small rifle and shot-pouch* and powder-horn. He then became a fort soldier and had his port hole assigned to him. This was indeed a proud day for him.

The Wedding. In the days of which we write the inhabitants generally married young. And as the social circle in which the young people moved was small compared to the present day, the first impression of love usually resulted in a speedy marriage. No worry on the part of the groom as to whether his salary was sufficient to support a wife and a home ever entered

---

*These pouches were really bullet-pouches. Why they were called shot-pouches is not known.

his head, for a home then was easy to establish and with little labor and no cost.

A wedding usually engaged the attention of the entire neighborhood, and was looked forward to with eager anticipation, for this was the only diversion that the people had that was not attended with labor, such as harvesting, log-rollings, house-raisings, scouting, or hunting. On the morning of the wedding day the groom and his attendants assembled at the home of his father, the object being to reach the home of the bride before noon, at which time the nuptials were celebrated. Imagine a large concourse of people without a store, dressmaker or tailor within a hundred miles, and an assemblage of horses without blacksmith or saddler within an equal distance; the gentlemen dressed in moccasins, leather breeches, leggings, and linsey hunting shirts, the ladies attired in linsey petticoats, linsey or linen bedgowns, coarse shoes, stockings, and handkerchiefs, all homemade. If there were any buckles, rings, buttons, or ruffles, they were heirlooms brought from the old home and treasured for the occasion, or were gifts handed down from parents or grandparents. The horses were caparisoned with old saddles and bridles, or halters, and pack-saddles with an old blanket thrown over them, a rope or string often serving as a girth.

The march of the party of the groom, double file, was often interrupted by the narrowness of the road, and often by the ill-will of the neighbors by felling logs or tying grapevines across the way. Often the party would be ambushed by a party of friends at which time guns were fired to envelop the party in smoke. The horses would rear and plunge, the girls would shriek, and occasionally someone would be thrown which resulted in a sprained ankle or wrist, but a handkerchief was tied about it and nothing more was said or thought of it.

When in sight of the bride's home, two of the young men were delegated to race for the bottle, "Black Betty," as it was called. The father of the bride stood at the door with a bottle of whiskey in his hand, and the one who first reached it and conveyed it back to the groom was declared the winner and he was decorated with a wreath of leaves as a token of his championship. After each had taken a liberal swig from the bottle (the groom first, of course,) the party would take up the line of march for the bride's home.

The wedding preceded the dinner, which consisted of beef, pork, fowls and sometimes venison and bear meat, roasted or boiled with a plenty of potatoes, cabbage and other vegetables. After the dinner, the dancing commenced and lasted until the next morning. The figures of the dances were three or four-handed reels or square sets and jigs. About nine or ten o'clock a deputation of young ladies would steal away the bride and put her to bed. In doing this a ladder would have to be ascended to the loft above. This done, a deputation of young men stole off the groom and placed him snugly by the side of his bride. Meanwhile the dance went on. If one wished to get away from the crowd and snatch a few minutes of sleep he was hunted up and paraded upon the center of the floor, and the fiddler was made to play "Hang out 'til morning".

In the midst of all this hilarity the bride and groom were not forgotten. Someone would suggest that they might stand in need of refreshments. Black Betty was procured and sent up the ladder accompanied by enough bread, pork, beef, and cabbage to feed half a dozen hungry men. The young couple were compelled to eat and drink more or less of what was sent up to them.

If anyone wished to help himself to a dram and the young couple to a toast, he would call: "Where is Black Betty? I want to kiss her sweet lips." The bottle was handed to him and, holding it up in his right hand, he would say: "Here's health to the groom, not forgetting myself; here's to the bride, thumping luck and big children." This, so far from being taken amiss, was considered a very proper and friendly wish; for big children, especially boys, were of great importance as the settlers were few in number and were continually engaged in warfare, with the Indians, and every big son was therefore considered as a young soldier. Often times some of the neighbors who had not been invited to the wedding would be revenged by cutting off the manes, foretops, or tails of the horses.

The feasting and dancing often lasted for several days, at the end of which the whole company was so exhausted with loss of sleep that it was several days before they were fit for their usual work.

Tomahawk Rights. One way of establishing rights to land in those days was an inferior kind of land title known as "tomahawk right", which was made by deadening a few trees at the head of a spring and marking the bark. The clumps of dead trees could be seen from an eminence for a long distance and sometimes were used to mark the boundaries or corners of various grants. The initials and sometimes the entire name of the owner would be cut into the bark of these trees. These rights designated the ownership of the land and resembled somewhat the marking or staking of claims in the western gold-fields. But if it conferred any right of ownership on the settlers it was asserted among themselves and not by the governor of the colony. These rights were often bought and sold; the settlers preferring to buy the tomahawk rights than to quarrel with the ones who made them.

At one time the western or mountain section of the country belonged to the government of Virginia and that body being desirous of getting rid of waste land would send its agents to negotiate on sale of this land. One instance of this sale is amusing: It was the custom to mark cattle (the earmark being preferred, each owner having a certain earmark), and turn them out in the spring and gather then in in the fall to sell them to drovers. A young man (of the vicinity of Glengary, a Mr. Parson by name), out hunting up some cattle he had turned out in the spring, came upon two government men. They asked him if he had any money. Upon answering in the negative, they asked him if he had any tobacco. Upon answering negatively, they asked: "Well, what have you got?" Upon examination it was found that he had four grains of barley in his pockets. He had been threshing some barley a few days before and these four grains had become lodged in his pocket by chance. The agents took the four grains of barley and immediately filled him out a deed for four hundred acres of this government land, each party being perfectly well satisfied with the bargain. The instructions to these agents were to get rid of this land at whatever price could be obtained.

An enterprising German by the name of Jacob Stover, who had accumulated considerable fortune, conceived the idea of obtaining a large grant in this county and vicinity. He applied to the Governor of Virginia but was informed that he must settle this tract with heads of families within a certain length of time. Knowing that he could not meet the requirements, he went to England and petitioned the King to direct his grant to issue. He again appeared before the Governor with the King's request and a long list of "families" which he had secured. In the meantime he had given a human name to every cat, dog, pig, horse, cow, and chicken that he owned representing them as "heads of families". He immediately sold out his land in small divisions to the settlers for three pounds (equal to ten dollars per hundred acres), cleaned up handsomely and left with the money. This was in 1733. This deal would not have stood inspection before the King and Council, perhaps, but he had gone; and in a way he had done a great service to Virginia by inducing actual settlers to obtain land to the westward and to build homes in the far wilderness.

Morals. At the time of the settlement of our county nothing was known of courts, magistrates, sheriffs, lawyers, or constables. There was neither "law nor gospel", for in a sparsely settled community, where everyone knew everyone else, each was a law unto himself. It must not be construed that a state of lawlessnes and anarchy existed among these inhabitants. Far from it! The liars, thieves, worthless and cowards were speedily punished, while industry, bravery, candor, honesty, and steadiness of deportment received its reward at the hands of one's neighbors. The imperial court of public opinion ruled; idleness, dishonesty, lying and ill-fame were punished by "hating the offender out", as they expressed it, and when this general expression or indignation was meted out he speedily reformed or left for other parts.

At the frolics commonly indulged in, such as house-raisings, log-rollings and harvest-parties, everyone was expected to do his full share. In war every able-bodied man was expected to do his full duty in the defense of his home. If he shirked, "he was branded as a coward," or "hated out as lazy," and when he was branded thus his peace of mind was forever at an end as far as that community was concerned. Each man was supposed to keep himself supplied at all times with war equipment, such as rifle, ammunition, a sharp flint or priming wire, scalping knife and tomahawk. If a man for any unexplained cause failed to take his part in any community enterprise, he was branded as a coward and a loafer and epithets of dishonor were heaped upon him without mercy. He might live them down but it took a long time. Debts were unknown and after the depreciation of the continental paper no money of any kind was used. A good cow and calf was often the price of a bushel of alum salt.

Theft was punished by condemning the culprit to Moses' law: forty stripes save one. Some able-bodied man was selected to lay on the stripes on the bare back with the injunction that they be "well laid on".

Even as late as 1800 the whipping-post, the pillory, and the stocks occupied a prominent place in front of the court house in the public square. For petty thefts the accused had his choice of going to jail or taking a whipping. The latter punishment was usually chosen and was immediately inflicted, after which the culprit was ordered to "clear out".

If a woman was given to tattling and slandering her neighbors, she was given a patent right to say whatever she pleased without being believed,—her tongue was then considered harmless or to be no scandal.

The people were given to hospitality and would share anything they had with a stranger or neighbor, and it was considered an offense to be offered pay in return. They toiled, feasted, suffered and fought together. They were in constant friendship. On the other hand, they were revengeful in resentment, and woe unto one if he gave offense to another without due cause. If one man called another a liar, it was considered a challenge to his honor and he must resent it then and there or be deemed a coward. Personal quarrels were usually settled with fists, teeth, and feet. The combatants would fight until one of them "hollered 'nough," as they expressed it; then they shook hands and remained good friends. Often these quarrels extended to duels; if fought with swords the one who first drew blood of his adversary was considered the victor. The more deadly duelling pistol was often resorted to. In this case the combatants were placed back to back and ordered to walk ten steps, turn, and fire. If one combatant took advantage of the other in any way other than the rules of duelling laid down, he was immediately dispatched on the spot by the seconds who had arranged the duel.

Seduction or bastardy did not often happen, and when it did the guilty one was in great danger of losing his life at the hands of the girl's brothers or father; family honor being held in high esteem.

The Sabbath was considered a day of rest for the aged and a play-day for the young, as there were no churches or resident ministers as there are now. The wedding nuptials were performed either by the "circuit rider" or a magistrate from an adjoining town would be sent for and conveyed by horseback to the bride's home. Or, better yet, the groom on horseback, with his bride-to-be seated on a "pillion" behind her father, also on horseback, would journey to the nearest magistrate's office and there be married; the new bride accompany the groom on his horse to the new home.

OMENS, SIGNS, TOKENS, INCANTATIONS, ETC.

The sturdy pioneer relied greatly upon the signs of the Zodiac, which were published monthly in a little pamphlet of some eight or ten pages, and which was called the "Almanack". This "Almanack" gave the phases of the moon, the rising and setting of the sun, eclipses of the sun and moon, the rising and setting of the most conspicuous of the planets, and fixed stars, a conjecture or forecast of the weather. This little pamphlet was interspersed with useful information of various subjects. These were read by thousands, and it is stated that Benjamin Franklin made a fortune publishing his "Poor Richard's Almanack". A pamphlet similar to these is still published at Hagerstown, Md., and it is widely read, even to this day.

The early settler would no more think of starting a certain piece of work without first consulting his almanac to see if the sign was right than he would think of going without eating. There were twelve costellations said to govern man's body: Ram (aries), head and face; Bull, (Taurus), neck; Twins, (Gemini), arms; Crab, (Cancer), breast; Lion, (Leo), heart; Scales, (Libra), veins; Virgin, (Virgo), bowels; Scorpion, (Scorpio), secrets; Archer, (Sagittarius), thighs; Goat, (Capricorn), knees; Water-boy, (Aquarius), legs; and Fishes, (Pisces), feet.

A few of these signs might be mentioned: If a rail fence was begun when the sign pointed down, the fence would settle surfficient to require repairing its entire height in a few years; otherwise if it was begun when the sign pointed up, it would remain on top of the ground and would retain its original height for a number of years. As high fences were required to keep the stock in the fields, the rail fences were always built when the sign pointed up.

Manure was always hauled to the field when the sign was down, for then it would sink into the earth where it was needed.

All climbing plants were planted when the sign pointed up so that they would run up the poles and trellis and a goodly crop might be assured.

Potatoes and all root crops were planted in the dark of the moon, and all stock plants, like corn, wheat, and other grains, in the light of the moon to insure an abundant crop.

All grasses and plants of a spreading nature and all vines were planted in the sign of the Crab (Cancer). Flower seeds, to insure abundant bloom, was always planted in the sign of the flower girl (Virgo). Grain, to insure good weight, was sown in the sign of the Scales (Libra). Fruit trees were planted in the sign of the Lion (Leo), to insure a strong, sturdy tree. Plants of the pod variety, as beans and peas, were planted in the sign of the Twins (Gemini), to promise a multiplicity of pods.

Rain was sure to fall when two signs of the Water-boy (Aquarius), followed by the two signs of the Fishes (Pisces). The old Indian signs were prevalent among the early settlers: namely, if he could hang his powderhorn on the edge of the new moon, he could go hunting, for it would be dry weather for two weeks.

The death-bell or ringing in the ears, the death-tick or noises of the larva of insects in the walls of the house, the nightly barking of a dog and the croaking of a raven were sure signs of a coming death in the family and were dreaded signs. At this late day we understand these things by the use of ,enlightened minds, but our rude forefathers were ignorant of the cause of these phenomena, and attributed them to the supernatural, tokens, and warnings.

If a person was on a journey and a black cat happened to cross his path it was considered bad luck and he must turn back and make the journey another day or time.

When a family moved into a new habitation a broom and a bag of salt were carried into the first room by a person walking backwards to insure against the intrusion of witches while the house was inhabited by them.

More Sports. The early inhabitants had not much time for indulgence in sports, but occasionally a day was given over to the them. Young men were instructed in woodcraft, and were taught to imitate the various calls of the wild life of the woods. The white man never became very proficient in the use of the bow and arrow, but he did excell in the use of the long rifle. All the games indulged by the youth of that time tended to fit him for proficiency in warfare with his savage foe, and in almost every instance where the woodcraft of the white man was pitted against that of the Indian, the white man came out best. This is proved in the instances of our pioneer scouts. Lewis Wetzel learned to load his rifle while running, a feat hard to accomplish as, in order to load the ancient flint-lock rifle, it was necessary to measure a charge of powder, pour it into the barrel, place a wad upon this and then ram it down with a wad. The next and most difficult act was to place a little powder in the pan. It would be an easy matter to put a bullet in a modern rifle while running.

Mechanic Arts. As there were no mills of any kind among the first settlers, no shoemakers, no weavers, each family had to provide its own mill for grinding the corn, and do all other work by hand.

The hominy block and handmills were made by them and were a part of every household's utensils. The hominy block was made of a large block of wood about three feet long, set on end with an excavation burned in it. This was wider at the top than at the bottom so that the pestil working within the excavation continually threw the corn up to the slides towards the top of it, from whence it continually fell down into the center. This instrument did very good work while the corn was soft in the fall but was rather slow when the corn became hard. Another method of grinding or pounding was to suspend a block of wood the same size as the depression in the hominy block to a bent sapling, which, by raising this block up and sending it down, pounded the corn into a coarse quality of meal. The best method of making meal was with a handmill. This was made by placing two stones one on top of the other, the lower stationary and the other fixed to turn round upon the lower. A wide hoop was placed round these to retain the meal. These stones were scored or "picked" in such a manner as to compel the meal to run out at a spout fixed in the side of the hoop; two handles were put in the upper stone to turn it by. This was slow work but necessity compelled its use. Each family tanned its own leather. Ashes were used to remove the hair in place of lime. The clothing was made by hand; the goods being woven from wool or flax raised by the settler himself, and the goods dyed by using walnut bark and other native plants for dye peculiar to the region.

Medicine. In a backwoods settlement on the outskirts of civilization physicians were unknown and the people had to rely on "home remedies" when they were sick. Our forefathers were a hardy race of people, made so by their simple mode of living. Civilization is not conducive to well-developed physical bodies. Privations, long hours of severest toil often lasting fifteen or sixteen hours at a time, plain fare, and life in the open, was calculated to produce a hardy race of people, which were well able to subdue the forest and till the soil. Consequently when a person of that day became ill or met with an accident he usually got well quickly. Diseases of children were mostly ascribed to worms, and there were several remedies used, as: half a tablespoonful of common salt, scrapings of pewter spoons, sulphate of iron, or green copperas, were given.

The elder portion of the population were afflicted with rheumatism caused by hard labor and exposure. To relieve them hunters usually slept with their feet to the fire. The Indian seldom had this disease as, when his feet became wet by wading in water or tramping after a rain (and the moccasin usually became quickly soaked owing to the porous nature of deerskin), he would dig a large pit in the ground, heap logs upon it and set it afire. After the logs had burned to a bed of coals in the bottom of the pit, the Indian would sleep with his feet hanging over the sides of the pit. In this way his feet became dry in a short time. The whites used the oil of rattlesnakes, bear's grease, ground-hogs, pole-cats or raccoons to rub over the afflicted parts, bathed in before the fire.

Croup was another common disease of children. The best remedy for this was the juice of roasted onions or garlic, or skunk grease applied externally. For fevers sweating was the general remedy. Strong decoctions of Virginia snakeroot were also given in large doses. If a purge was needed, half a pint of strong decoction of walnut bark was given. In very early times bleeding or blood-letting was resorted to, the object being to get rid of the "bad blood" of the sick person.

For burns or scalds poultices of scraped potato, Indian meal, roasted turnip, or slippery-elm bark were used.

Snake bite was a common occurrence. In case of rattlesnake bite, the snake was killed and a piece was cut from the body and applied to the wound, the piece of snake having the property to absorb the poison from the wound (as they thought). The remainder of the snake was burned in the front yard. After this process was over, a large quantity of chestnut leaves were boiled and the decoction was poured on the leg and allowed to run down into a pot. Then the boiled leaves were bound to the leg. They all usually recovered, they having implicit faith in the remedy; but we in this day of modern science know that it was owing to the rugged constitutions that they were able to withstand the attack of the poison left by the sting of the snake.

Other remedies were cupping, sucking, and making a deep incision and filling the wound with salt and gunpowder.

Gunshot and other wounds were treated with slippery-elm bark, flaxseed and other poultices. Coughs and colds were treated with a great variety of syrups. Here I might insert a recipe for a "Cough Medicine" which was used even as late as the 1870's:

        Spikenard root   Brown sugar or molasses
        Elecampane root   Wild cherry bark
                  Hoarhound root

This decoction was boiled or brewed, strained, and placed in bottles ready to be taken in case of a cough or a cold. This mixture was not unpleasant to take and a certain aged lady was noted for her "cough medicine" and the neighbors never failed to cough and complain of a cold when on a visit to her house in order to get a "dose" of her medicine.

In later years there was a remedy for colds and especially a "run-down condition", and a "cure-all" sold at stores throughout the country under the name of "Iron Tonic Bitters". It was said to contain the extract of a few harmless barks such as wild-cherry bark and sweet anis. But the greatest "healing" property was attributed to the sixty or more per cent alcohol which it contained, and it was a favorite remedy for many years whether it cured anyone or not.

Witchcraft. To more fully set forth the superstitious beliefs of our early forefathers, a paragraph on this subject might not be amiss. The most outstanding of these delusions was a belief in witchcraft, or a belief in witches, ghost stories, ghosts and signs. Witchcraft is a delusion which is prevalent among many uneducated people, in that part of the country farthest from any seat of learning. I do not wish to be understood as saying that there were no learned men or women among our early settlers. There were many. But in building homes, clearing lands or fighting the Indian, the settlers had little time for the study of refinement or for the education of their children. Hence the majority of the inhabitants were not educated in schools of science or natural philosophy, and attributed the mysterious to some supernatural agency. To the witch was ascribed the tremendous power of inflicting spells, mysterious diseases, curses, "hoo-doos", etc., on persons or things. The witch power was supposed to be possessed by some woman of the settlement, who was said to have the power to mount a broom and sail through the air whenever and wherever she wished to go; to enter rooms through keyholes or cracks in the walls or down the chimney and torment little children by sticking them with pins, in case of diseases of children, rickets, dropsy or intestinal diseases. Diseases which could neither be cured nor accounted for were attributed to witchcraft. On the ignorance of these settlers the "witch-doctor" flourished. He was usually someone in the community who claimed to have power to counteract the witches' actions, to remove or break a spell, or curse placed upon the victim by witches. For instance, any farmer's wife knows that it is easier to churn butter in the summer season than in the winter; that cream must be heated to a certain temperature before it will produce butter. I have heard of one instance where the good housewife on a cold winter morning started churning her cream. She churned and churned but no butter. So she dispatched one of the children for the witch-doctor. The first thing that he did when he arrived was to move the churn close to the fire, make a few passes over it with his hands, mutter a few mysterious words, and call for some boiling water which he immediately poured into the cream. Then he told the housewife to go on and churn. She did so and in a few minutes the cream had turned into butter. He charged a handsome fee for his services and departed. I have heard of cases where a sickly child was said to be bewitched by being "liver grown", that was the liver had grown fast to some other organ. The remedy was to take the little one by the heels and give it a sharp jerk to loosen it of its adherence. If the child recovered the witch doctor's reputation was made. If not, the incantation was worked in the wrong sign. The fees were collected just the same, for the mother stood in constant fear that the witch-doctor would put some greater spell on her already suffering offspring. Sometimes to cure a disease inflicted by witchcraft, the picture of the supposed witch was drawn upon a piece of board and a bullet moulded with a small amount of silver in it. This was then fired at and the part of the figure struck was supposed to be afflicted with the disease of the sufferer. If a cow became weak and thin in the spring from lack of proper care through a hard winter, she was supposed to be bewitched. The witch-doctor would come, make an incision in the skin of the tail about two inches long, fill it with salt and pepper and bind it up. This was called "Wolf in the Tail", and this treatment drove the disease away. Another witchcraft disease of cattle was "Hollow Horn" and the remedy was to bore a small hole in the horn, with an awl or gimlet, to let the witch out of the hollow of the horn. When a small boy I have seen "witch stirrups" plaited in the manes of the horses said to have been ridden by witches at night to some of their nightly rendezvous. When the cows decreased in their flow of milk they were said to have been milked by witches. This was done by fixing a new pin in a new towel for each cow intended to be milked. The towel was hung over the witch's door and by incantations the milk was extracted from the fringes in the same manner that a cow is milked. The witch-doctor was sent for. He made a few mysterious passes with his hands over the cow's back and then ordered the feed to be increased, and Presto! more milk was found in the bucket at each milking.

Ghost stories used to be told and retold; the most popular one was the "headless horseman" or the ball of fire seen hovering over swamps and graveyards on damp and dark nights. As a boy I have sat and listened to the recital of these stories until my flesh would creep and my hair would raise on end. These stories of ghosts and spooks made such a lasting impression on my mind that to this day there comes to me when out alone on a dark night the presentiment or sign of the proximity of some ghost or spook ready to touch me or glide past me.

The early settlers, even to the time of the latter part of the nineteenth century, believed in signs. The old almanack always hung in a conspicuous place, and our forbears consulted this little book with rigor. When contemplating planting seeds, building a fence, going on a journey, or cutting out a dress, they would consult this little pamphlet to see whether the sign was right, whether the sign was up, or down, whether it was the "light" or the "dark" of the moon. The signs have been carefully studied and drawn out by our Experiment Stations and, after exhaustive researches, it has been proved beyond a doubt that there is nothing to them. Fortunately, we now have more time to devote to education than formerly and as we become more highly educated the less will be the beliefs in these old superstitions. Superstition is always associated with ignorance.

Testing the Fertility of the Soil. If our forefathers wished to test the fertility of the soil the test was this: "Dig a hole of any reasonable dimension or depth, and if the soil taken from it when thrown lightly back into it does not fill up the hole, the soil is fruitful; if it more than fills the hole, the soil is barren."

Hunting. Hunting, by the early settlers, was a necessity rather than a sport as it is now considered. It was not uncommon for families to live for months without corn bread. Wheat bread was unknown or could not be had. If the corn crop was short on account of drouth or destruction by the marauding Indians, that article of diet was sure to be lacking. The family had to subsist on wild meats. There was no way of keeping these meats by refrigeration, hence the hunting was generally done in the late fall or early winter. At this time of year, the hides of animals were in better condition, the fur being thicker and "prime", as they expressed it. Also the hibernating animals had to be taken before they went into winter quarters, which was before the first snows. Therefore the settlers wished to lay in a goodly supply of salted meats for use during the long winter.

The hunt furnished the meat used by the settlers before cattle, sheep, hogs and poultry were introduced into the settlements. After a time, these furnished the meat for them and hunting became less popular. The hunting season began as soon as the first skift of snow fell, or after a heavy frost or two, for it was a saying among the inhabitants that all game was good and all hides were prime during every month in which the letter "'R" occurred. Several hunters usually camped together. choosing a site for a camp, the place chosen had to be sheltered, by the surrounding hills from every wind, especially that from the north and the west. A half-faced camp was hastily constructed. This was built in the following manner: two stakes were driven in the ground about four inches apart, eight or ten feet from each other at the corners. These stakes received the logs comprising the back, and the sides of the camp. The cracks between the logs were stuffed with leaves or moss, the front was always open. The roof was made of slabs, skins or bark, and sloped from the front to the rear. In front of this opening a fire was built, and after the day's hunt was over the party would gather around the fire and tell tales of the chase or boast of the prowess of the hunter.

These camps were located in secluded spots, and nothing of the presence of the white hunter's camp or his hunting, other than the crack of his rifle, or by some prowling Indian, happening to stumble on his camp, was ever known. Oftentimes this would happen and then the hunters would be killed and scalped and the camp destroyed. But this danger did not deter the white hunter. The call of the hunt got into his blood and nothing would satisfy him but to hunt it out. When game, a deer, a bear, or a wolf was killed, the carcass was hung up on the limb of a tree, out of the reach of wolves or other animals. These were afterwards gathered, skinned, and the meat packed upon the backs of the packhorses, brought along for that purpose, and conveyed to the settlement to be either packed in huge home-made "hogs-heads" in brine, or hung up and dried and smoked for the future supply of meat for the family. Occasionally the male inhabitants of a village would be selected for the final end of a hunt of this character, the whole party would form a wide circumference and, by whooping and beating the brush, would gradually lessen the ring until all the wild game would be driven to a central point where it would be shot down in heaps. Any deer or bear attempting to escape could be shot down, but none of those remaining within the circle could be shot until the final central point was reached. This was the rule strictly adhered to in a hunt of this kind.

As the country became more thickly settled and game became scarcer, the inhabitants began to import cattle and hogs to be raised on the farms, which took the place of wild animals for meat. Lord Fairfax derived a snug income from rental from this branch of husbandry from his numerous tracts of land which he owned throughout this section.

As the years rolled on and all settlements grew numerous and timber was cut off, the large game, as elk, deer, bear, were either killed or driven to the remoter parts of the State among the Allegheny mountains, and came near being extinct until the Legislature of West Virginia passed stringent laws against the killing of game. This action has resulted in the deer again becoming pretty numerous in our western counties, but all large game has forever been driven from Berkeley County, and the hunter of today must necessarily confine himself to procuring such small game as the rabbit, quail, pheasants, squirrel, and to trapping the mink, skunk, and muskrat. Occasionally fox hunts are staged in the mountains in the western part of our county, but this is confined to the red fox alone. The silver fox is no more.

The indulgencies of our foreparents were simple and inexpensive. As little was spent on luxuries and less on clothing and fine carriages, so, little was spent on tobacco, liquor, and such things. The money spent of a single Saturday night in Martinsburg now-a-days for soft drinks, ice-cream, pool, motion pictures, automobile riding, dance halls, etc., etc., would have staggered the imagination of a resident one hundred and fifty years ago. Yet the people seem to get along now as well as they did at that time, and seem to have as much money to spend. The only solution to this problem seems to be in the keeping of the inevitable dollar in circulation and not letting it stop in the hands of one hoarder. Benjamin Franklin, in his day, showed the people how to become thrifty by starting a pound sterling into circulation, and keeping it circulating. I have read somewhere of a statement in which a person declared that he could pay off the entire World War debt with a five dollar banknote if everybody kept it in circulation and nobody stopped it and I believe it could be done.

The early settlers of the country were inveterate users of tobacco, women as well as men. The Indian always carried a leaf of it with him on his long journey for, as he said, "It cured being tired." The first settlers raised a little tobacco in their "truck patches", along with their vegetables. This was usually cut before frost, hung in the corner of the cabin home, and, when dried, crumbled in the hand and smoked in a "chalk" pipe. Many of our grandmothers smoked a pipe made of a clay substance moulded in a single piece; a hole through the stem from the bowl to the lip piece. Probably the art of making these pipes is lost as none are ever seen or used, whereas fifty years ago they could be purchased at any store for a nickel apiece.

Occasionally the men used this kind of pipe, but their favorite was one made from a corn cob with a hollow reed stuck in it for a stem. The early Dutch and German settlers of the country preferred the long reed stem; some of these stems were a foot long, they claiming that the long stem made a cooler and more soothing smoke than the short stems.

As this county is not adapted to the raising of tobacco (on account of the short summers), it was not long before the settlers began to depend on the section east of the Blue Ridge for their tobacco, and when the annual or semi-annual caravan was made up by them to visit the eastern settlements or trading posts, preferably at Baltimore or Richmond, to exchange furs, corn, and venison for salt, lead, powder, iron, tobacco was usually included in the list brought home by packhorse. For convenience the leaves were pressed together by heavy weights into "plugs", hence we have to this day the plug tobacco, used for chewing. If the packhorse trips above mentioned were of long intervals, or there was danger of the supply running short, the settler was known to lay up his "chews" for drying and at a later date these chews were used for smoking. Snuff taking became a habit among the European people shortly after the colonization of this country. At first snuff was taken by the nose. As snuff is tobacco stems dried and ground to powder, it derived its name from the habit of taking a pinch of this material between the thumb and forefinger and snuffing it into the nostrils. Hence the name "snuff", a name it still retains, although snuff now used is taken into the mouth and chewed as any other form of tobacco.

Some of the snuff-boxes were costly affairs, made of silver or even of gold, and occasionally inlaid with gems. Eventually the custom of taking snuff died out until today a few women and fewer men use it.

The cirgarette is of recent origin, probably thirty years, the cigar being much older. The West Virginia law forbids the selling of cigarettes to children under eighteen years of age, on account of the serious injury to the health and growth of the child. Chewing tobacco seems to be more prevalent among the rural people, while smoking is indulged in more by suburban and city residents.

In the early colonial period of Virginia, tobacco formed a medium of exchange but was not used as such in the early times of our county, partly because the inhabitants did not produce it and partly because of the late date of the settlement of our county. Hides of furbearing animals peculiar to this region were used for exchange instead.

The settlers brought with them the art of distilling whiskey and "New England Rum". At first corn was scarce but plenty of wild fruits, as grapes and berries, were at hand, and the housewives became adept at making sour wines. Later a still was brought in and one person engaged in making "co'n licker" for the entire neighborhood. These developed later into "still houses" where a farmer could take his corn and have it made into whiskey for twenty-five cents a gallon. About the same time "grist-mills"—mills for grinding corn meal—were set up and run by water power, and as the numerous swift-running streams produced abundant water power, almost every community had its grist-mill.

Drinking was prevalent; nothing important was begun or carried out without ardent spirits. The building of houses, log-rollings, harvestings, dances, weddings, huntings, frolics, and even the building of new churches, all came in for their share of drinking by the male attendants. Fights and altercations resulted occasionally, but these were taken as a matter of course and none thought anything of it.

CHAPTER VII.

FRENCH AND INDIAN WAR.

The history of Berkeley County proper does not begin as a county until 1772, when it was organized by an act of the Virginia Legislature, but prior to that time many settlements were made in that territory embraced by what is now that county. These settlements were fostered and encouraged by the colonial government of Virginia, by the large landholders of this region, such as Fairfax, Hite, and VanMetre, and by the restlessness and a desire to acquire new territory by the people themselves, which seems to be a natural trait of the human race—that unsatisfied desire to explore the unknown, that longing to seek new lands to conquer. The settlers were not molested by the Indians for a period of about twenty years, after the first settlement in the confines of Berekeley County, because there was land enough for all, and the English were very particular to obtain land from the Indians by treaty, as the treaties of Lancaster and Fort Stanwix will show; also by purchase, as many of our settlers were of the Quaker faith which, by the wise and just treatment of William Penn of the Indians, insured a lasting friendship on their part and modified to a great extent their conduct towards the whites.

At the end of the twenty years above mentioned the French made friends with the Indians, a policy which would have been better for the Virginians, had they adopted it, but the latter entered upon a policy of extermination, while the former sent missionaries among them; namely, Joliet, Marquette, and Father Hennipen, who visited them and preached to them, and, though they did not, perhaps, make many converts, they had shown that they came as friends and not as enemies. The French, by making them presents and supplying them with the white man's arms, and promises of more presents and many scalps, had so turned the heads of the Indians that they were ready to fight on the side of the French at any time.

Therefore, when emissaries from the western Indians came among the Indians of the Shenandoah Valley, especially the Tuscororas, they suddenly moved across the Allegheny mountains and joined the Five Nation confederation, which after this event became the Six Nations. This was in the spring of 1753.

In 1754, began the war known in American history as the French and Indian War. It lasted for nine years, or from 1754 to 1763, and during that period, death and desolation reigned supreme throughout the region west of the Blue Ridge. That portion of territory embracing what is now Berkeley County received its full share of savage barbarity and French intrigue. All but a few of the settlements of this region were broken up, and the inhabitants driven east of the Blue Ridge mountains.

All the lands in western Virginia were claimed by three nations. The Six Nations by right of possession, the English by grant of King James II., May 23, 1609, by the sixth section of the second charter granted to the Virginia Company of London, settling the boundary as follows: "All those lands lying and being in that part of America called Virginia, from the point of land called Cape or Point Comfort, all along the sea coast to the northward two hundred miles, and all that space and circuit of land from the seacoast of the precinct aforesaid up into the land throughout from sea to sea and northward."* From sea to sea meant from the Atlantic to the Pacific oceans; and the French by the discovery of the Ohio River by Robert Cavalier La Salle in 1669.

It will be seen from the above that each nation laid claim to this region with excellent authority for asserting its claims.

The French made the first move for asserting their claim to this valley in 1749, by sending out an expedition from Canada under the leadership of Captain Bienville de Celoron, with about 275 men to plant leaden plates at the mouths of the tributaries to the Ohio River. On these plates were inscriptions asserting France's right to the region.

Governor Robert Dinwiddie, Colonial Governor of Virginia, resolved at first to use diplomacy, thinking that perhaps he might divert hostilities.

The French had erected a fort on the Allegheny River, a few miles above the present site of Pittsburg, named Fort Le Boeuf. Thither Governor Dinwiddie sent Major George Washington in the fall of 1753, to deliver a message to the commander there, stating that the fort was erected on the territory belonging to Virginia. The French commander politely sent back a refusal stating that he had orders to hold the territory of the Ohio Valley in that vicinity.

Virginia retaliated by organizing and equipping a party of men from Berkeley and Hampshire counties and appointing Capt. William Trent, who proceeded to the forks of the Ohio and began the erection of a fort there. In a short time this uncompleted fort was attacked by a large force of French and Indians from Canada who captured the fort from the Virginians. The French finished the erection of the fort and named it Fort Duquesne in honor of Marquis du Quesne, Governor General of Canada.

Virginia raised a force of men and placed them under the command of Lieutenant-Colonel George Washington, who proceeded to Will's Creek (Fort Cumberland). Not waiting for reinforcements, he pushed westward through the forest toward Fort Duquesne. When he arrived at Great Meadows, upon hearing of the approach of a force of the enemy, he halted his little army and hastily built a fort which he named Fort Necessity. Here he was attacked by a superior force of French and Indians and was compelled to surrender the fort but marched out with all the honors of war and began the tedious march back to Fort Cumberland, and, after his men rested, marched back to

---

*Henning's "Statutes at Large."

Philadelphia. The end of the year 1754 closed with the French in full possession of the Ohio Valley.

The English were as anxious to get possession of this valley as were the Virginians, and in 1755 sent an expedition to America composed of the 44th and 48th Royal Infantry Regiments under command of General Edward Braddock. The 44th Regiment was commanded by Sir Peter Halket and the 48th by Colonel Thomas Dunbar.

The force landed at Alexandria, Va. Braddock met many of the Colonial Governors at a conference at Annapolis, where it was decided to begin operations by attacking Fort Duquense at the forks of the Ohio.

General Braddock proceeded with his army to Frederick, Md., thence up the Maryland side of the Potomac to Fort Frederick near what is now called Williamsport, Md. We are indebted to Lieutenant Robert Orme, who was the chief aide to the General, for a narrative of the expedition through this section of the country.

ROBERT ORME'S REPORT.*

"As no road had been made to Will's Creek on the Maryland side of the Potomack, the 48th Regiment was obliged to cross the river at Congogee (Conococheague Creek, Washington County, Maryland) and to fall into the Virginian Road near Winchester. The General ordered a bridge to be built over the Antietam (creek) which being finished and provisions laid on the road, Colonel Dunbar marched with his Regiment the 48th, from Fredericktown, Maryland, on the 28th of April, and about this time the bridge over the Opequon, in Virginia (now Berkeley County, West Virginia) was finished for the artillery, and flats were built on all the rivers and creeks."

The following extract from the same report is noted, and was quoted by Lewis from "Seamans Journal", doubtless written by Lieutenant Spendelow, of the detachment of Marines sent by Commodore Kippel of the British fleet with Braddock on his expedition to the Ohio:

"Apr. 29th, 1755. We began our march (from Fredericktown) at 6 but found much difficulty in loading our baggage, so that we left several things behind us, particularly the men's hammocks. We arrived at 3 o'clock at one Walkers, 18 miles from Frederick, and camped there on good ground; this day we passed the South Ridge (South Mountain) or Shannandoah (Shenandoah) Mountains very easy in the ascent. We saw plenty of Hares, Deer and Partridges: This place is wanting of all refreshments.

On the 30th:—At 6 we marched in our way to Connechieg, where we arrived at 2 o'clock, 16 miles from Walkers'; this is a fine situation close to the Potomack. We found the Artillery Stores going by water to Will's Creek and left two of our men here.

May 1st:—At 5 we went with our people, and began ferrying the Army, &c., into Virginia, which we completed by 10 o'clock, and marched in our way to one John Evans, where we arrived at 3 o'clock—17 miles from Connechieg and 20 miles from Winchester. We got some provisions and forage here. The roads now begin to be very indifferent.

On the 2nd:—As it is customary in the Army to halt a day after 3 days' march, we halted today to rest the Army.

---

*From Lewis' Third Biennial Report, pages 24, 25, 26. Dept. Arch. & Hist. W. Va.

On the 3rd:—Marched at 5 in our way to one Widow Barringer's, 18 miles from Evans: this day was so extremely hot that several officers and many men could not go on till the evening, but the body got to their ground at 3 o'clock. This is 5 miles from Winchester, a fine station if properly cleared.

On the 4th:—Marched at 5 in our way to one Potts; 9 miles from the Widow's—where we arrived at 10 o'clock. The road this day was bad: we got some wild turkeys here: in the night it came to blow hard at N. W.

On the 5th:—Marched at 5 in our way to Henry Enoch's being 16 miles from Potts' where we arrived at 2 o'clock; the road this day over prodigious mountains and between the same we crossed over a run of water called Kahapetin (Cacapon) where our men ferried the Army over and got to our ground, where we found a Company of Peter Halket's encamped.

On the 6th:—We halted this day to refresh the army.

On the 7th:—We marched at 5 in our way to one Cox's, 12 miles from Enoch's. This morning was very cold but by 10 o'clock, it was prodigiously hot. We crossed another run of water 19 times in 2 miles and got our ground at 2 o'clock and encamped close to the Potomack.

On the 8th:—We began to ferry the Army over the river into Maryland, which was completed by 10 o'clock and then we marched in our way to one Jackson's, 8 miles from Cox's. At noon it rained very hard and continued so till 2 o'clock, when we got to our ground and encamped on the banks of the Potomack. A fine situation with a good deal of cleared ground about it."

In reading the narrative of General Braddock's expedition from Alexandria to Fort Duquesne, the reader will doubtless wonder why that general made such a wide *detour* through the section of what is now West Virginia, thus exposing his army to such long delays when he could have marched straight to Fort Cumberland on the north side of the Potomac. And we, who pass over the Old National Road today in our highpowered automobiles at fifty miles per hour, no doubt think it was a lack of judgment that he exhibited in taking this circuitous route. Yet we must remember that was one hundred and seventy years ago; that there was no road from Williamsport to Cumberland; that the whole region between these points was one unbroken wilderness. A road from where Williamsport is now located to Winchester was known as the old "Indian Road"; and crossed the Potomac at Evan Watkin's ferry, which had been established Oct. 9th, 1744, by act of the Virginia Assembly. John Evans Fort, southeast of what is now Martinsburg, was a fort of considerable importance, and capable of accommodating Braddock's army during his brief stay there. The route taken to Widow Barringer's, Potts', Henry Enoch's, Friend Cox's and back across the Potomac at the mouth of Little Cacapon River were on an established road. This route was well known to Colonel George Washington and many of his Virginians who accompanied Braddock, and it was he that advised him to make the *detour*.

Lieutenant-Colonel George Washington accompanied this expedition with 1209 Virginian troops. Many of these were recruited from the region now occupied by Berkeley County. Among the men who accompanied Braddock on that expedition and fought under Washington, from Berkeley County, and who afterward became famous were: Colonel William Crawford, General Adam Stephen, General Daniel Morgan, General William Darke, and General Horatio Gates.

How different was the movement of General Braddock through Berkeley County in 1755 as compared to the movements of General Stonewall Jackson or General J. E. B. Stewart's troops through the same section in 1862. General Braddock had to contend with bad roads but his movements were unnecessarily slow. He wasted valuable time, as Lieutenant Orme states in his Journal. "Floats were built on all rivers and creeks." Washington remonstrated with him for this delay and proposed to him that they pass on with the light infantry and leave the heavy military stores to come later, but Braddock haughtily gave him to understand that *he* was the General in command and not Washington.

Braddock left Fredericktown with his staff and a body guard of light horse. At Alexandria he had purchased from Governor Horatio Sharpe of Maryland, a sort of two-wheeled chariot, one of the cumbersome vehicles of that day. In this chariot he made his way through this section. The John Evans mentioned in Lieutenant Orme's Journal was the builder and defender of John Evans Fort, a stockade fort, which was begun in 1755 and completed the next year. It had hardly been completed before it was attacked by the Indians, and the people of the neighborhood who had sought refuge within its walls so gallantly defended it that the Indians were driven off and the inmates saved from massacre.

A description of a stockade fort might be of interest to my readers. The fort was built in the form of a square or a rectangle and contained from one-fourth to one-half acre enclosure. Trees of about eighteen inches in diameter were felled and logs cut from them ten feet in length and hewn flat on opposite sides. These were firmly plantd in the ground, the flat sides adjoining, which formed the sides and ends of the fort. At the four corners, bastions were placed and built of logs placed on end in like manner as the walls. These bastions protruded six feet beyond the walls of the fort to prevent the enemy from getting close to the walls. Port holes were bored at regular intervals of sufficient diameter to enable the garrison to thrust the long rifle through in firing at the enemy. The portal or gate was made of the same material as the walls and swung on enormous hinges. The inside was fastened with a huge crossbar which fitted into slots in the gate and into mortices at either side jamb. Within the stockade was another fort built of logs square and roofed, this building erected similar to the houses of the settlers. These forts were built over a spring or creek to insure plenty of water in case of a seige. The inner fort was well supplied with grain and ammunition, especially at times of Indian troubles. The stockade fort was much safer from destruction than the other types as was shown in the instance of the John Evans Fort, which, though attacked several times, was never destroyed.

After the defeat and death of General Braddock in Western Pennsylvania,

Colonel Dunbar conducted the retreat of that General's army to Philadelphia, and the defense of the frontier of Virginia fell upon the Virginians. Not much help was afterwards received from England. Virginia and her neighboring colonies, Maryland, Pennsylvania and the Carolinas, carried on the struggle and placed Colonel George Washington in command. In Pennsylvania the Quakers predominated the Legislature, and, as members of that faith were adverse to war or munitions of war, they, nevertheless, came to the defense of their country by voting appropriations in that body "for internal improvements and OTHER GRAINS". The grains referred to here meant "grains" of powder. In this way Pennsylvania helped in the defense of the western frontier stretching from the Great Lakes to Georgia against the horrible massacres and destruction of homes and settlements which began immediately following that disastrous defeat. Washington retreated to Winchester and erected Fort Loudon in the fall of 1755. The people immediately erected stockade forts in every part of the valley, to which places the people of their vicinity flocked for safety.

Notwithstanding the erection of these forts, many people were driven east of the Blue Ridge. It looked as if our valley was to be conquered by the wiley savage. Washington, with what colonial troops he could collect, marched against the Indians in western Virginia. In the meantime, several forts were erected at considerable expense to the colonies at various places to be used as a chain of defense against the attacks of the French and Indians. Fort Cumberland had been erected. This has become the busy city of Cumberland, Maryland. Another fort of importance to the inhabitants of Berkeley County and surrounding sections was Fort Frederick. This fort was begun in 1755 under the direction of Governor Sharpe of Maryland, and finished in 1756. It was to serve as a place of safety for the inhabitants of the surrounding country and is still standing. It is located between Hancock and Clear Spring, Md., about three and a half miles south of the Old National Road overlooking the Potomac. When visited by the author, July 4, 1927, it was still in a fine state of preservation excepting a few feet of the southern wall which had been torn down and used for a stone foundation and a bridge wall of a large barn which had been erected near it by a former owner. The farm of 180 acres, upon which the fort now stands, was recently purchased by the State of Maryland and placed under the supervision of the Maryland State Forestry Commission. It is now kept up by the State.

The bronze tablet standing in the center of the fort bears the following inscription:

"This fort was erected after Braddock's defeat as one of a chain of frontier defenses and posts of refuge upon 150 acres of land bought by Governor Horatio Sharpe, and named Fort Frederick the seventh and last Lord Baltimore. The Maryland Assembly voted 20,000 pounds for defense, of which some 2000 pounds were spent to build the fort. The site was 100 feet above the Potomac. It contained stone barracks and was first garrisoned by 200 men under Captain John Dogworthy in August, 1756. The fort was square with corner bastions each defended by a cannon. Its sandstone walls reach the height of 17 feet and at the top were 2 feet thick, 4 feet at the base and contained one acre and a half. The portal was 12 feet wide: the gate hinges weighed 42 pounds apiece. Seven hundred people have been sheltered at the same time within the fort. Hessian prisoners were kept here in the Revolution. In 1790, Maryland sold land and fort. Colonel Kenley's First Maryland Regiment, U. S. A., used it in 1861."

As Fort Frederick was the most important of all the chain erected extending from Fort Loudon (Winchester) to Fort Duquesne (Pittsburg), and it being in close proximity to Berkeley County (just across the Potomac in Maryland, near the northwestern portion of the county), a description in detail is given above.

At each of the four corners, bastions, or protruding walls, were built. These extended twelve feet beyond the sides of the walls and were built to prevent any lurking enemy or any body of the enemy from getting too close to the sides of the fort. A cannon was placed on each bastion and was mounted on a pivot so as to be fired in any direction. Within the fort at the exact spot where the British flag was planted, the Maryland State flag now floats to the breeze. To the east of this, a large United States flag is raised. Within the fort was a barracks for the use of the garrison, one story high, 120 feet long by 15 feet wide. At another side was a two-room building, 15 by 30 feet, used as headquarters for the officers. Near the barracks was an oven for baking bread for the occupants. All these buildings were built of sandstones but have been removed and used for other purposes.

A circular hole was made three feet in diameter, through which a heavy cannon was thrust for the defense of the Chesapeake and Ohio Canal and the Baltimore and Ohio Railroad against Colonel Thomas J. Jackson, the Confederate leader, who was bent upon destroying each to cripple the transportation of men and material from the west to Washington during the Civil War. This defense was made by Colonel Kenley in 1861.

East to the fort, and adjacent to it, is a burying ground in which over 300 graves were made. In them lie buried those who happened to die of disease during its occupancy.

This fort was never attacked by the French or the Indians. In 1756, Captain Jeremiah Smith, of Hampshire County, Virginia, with a small force of settlers, attacked and defeated a body of 50 Indians led by a French officer at the head of Cacapon River. The French officer was killed and when his clothing was searched, his commission and written instructions were found upon him to meet another party of 50 Indians at Fort Frederick, attack the fort, destroy it and blow up the magazine. This heroic defense by Captain Smith no doubt saved the fort from attack at this time.

Another fort of the chain of defense was John Evans Fort. This fort was situated upon the east side of Opequon Creek, a few hundred feet above the bridge that crosses that stream on the right side of the State Highway leading from Martinsburg to Charles Town. This was one of the forts hastily erected for defense against the Indians and French. Its chief defender was not a man, but a woman—Polly Evans. This estimable woman was the daughter of Abraham Van Metre, who had married John Evans II., after whom the fort was named.*

In the spring of 1756, this fort had scarcely been completed, when it was attacked by a party of Indians. None were in the fort at the time but the women and children of the neighborhood. Polly Evans made the women load rifles and she did the firing from one port hole after another and kept up such a raking fire on the Indians, that they abandoned the attack, supposing from the incessant firing from the fort that it was heavily garrisoned. When all the other forts in this section were destroyed, this one alone withstood the attacks of the savages.

Fort Neely stood farther up the Opequon about two miles. On one occasion it was attacked by a party of fifty Indians. The fort was destroyed and the inmates murdered or carried away to the Indian towns to the west.

Painter's Fort stood up on Mill Creek in the vicinity of Woodstock. This fort had been erected in 1757 by George Painter and the inhabitants of the nieghborhood took refuge in it, when in the summer of 1758, it was attacked by a body of forty Indians and four Frenchmen. George Painter was killed. The fort surrendered and the Indians dragged the body of Painter to the house, threw the body into it and set fire to it. They took four infant children from their mothers' arms hung them up in trees, and while the distracted mothers were compelled to look on, shot the four little one in savage sport. They then set fire to the stable near by containing a number of sheep and calves, and while the helpless dumb brutes writhed in agony, the savages danced around the burning building. They then beat a hasty retreat, taking about forty persons with them. After six days of constant travel they reached their settlement west of the Allegheny Mountains. A council was held and they decided to sacrifice one, Jacob Fisher, a boy of about twelve years of age. He was compelled to gather a large quantity of dry wood. When he had done this, they cleared a space around a sapling, tied him by one hand to it with a thong five or six feet long, then formed a ring of dry sticks around him and set fire to it. The poor boy was compelled to run around the tree until the thong drew him to it, then back again until he came in contract with the fire. This inhuman torture was kept up for several hours while his parents and friends were compelled to sit helplessly by and hear his agonized cries for succor. His savage tormentors became beastly drunk so that they fell prostrate to the ground. The squaws with long poles would pierce the flesh with the burning ends of them until the poor helpless sufferer fell and expired with the most excruciating agonies. And yet there are people who exclaim, "The poor Indian! How he has been mistreated!" A Christian people are supposed to apply the Golden Rule to all cases, yet as we read this narrative our hearts are filled with indignation and we turn away with a shudder with the belief that the Indian deserved just what he got from the hands of the white man.

---

*See account of Lieutenant Spendelow's "Seaman's Journal" of General Braddock's march through Virginia for a further account of Johns Evans Fort.

The present generation can thank their lucky stars that these forefathers of ours rid this country of this savage hoard and made it a pleasant and safe place in which to live.

Hedges Fort stood on the road leading from Martinsburg to Bath (Berkeley Springs), just east of the North Mountain. This was in the vicinity of what is now Hedgesville. This fort was built for the protection of the settlers of that section, which at that time were quite numerous.

These were probably all the forts erected within the present limits of Berkeley County for protection against the Indians and their French instigators. There are traditions of other forts having been located at other places but a diligent research has failed to reveal any others than those already mentioned. The Indians continued to be a menace to the people of this lower Shenandoah region until after the close of the Revolution, when, under such men as Darke, Clarke, and Wayne, the savage power was broken forever.

The leader of the Indians in this struggle was Killbuck, a famous chieftain who had visited this region when, a young man and had become familiar with the settlements. He was, by this knowledge, a valuable leader to them. He lived to be over one hundred years of age, and on account of his great age had become totally blind. If all the exploits of this noted chief should be written they would fill a good sized volume. One instance portraying his activities might be included here as it will doubtless be of interest to readers of this work: As Kill-buck often visited this and adjoining regions, he was offered a reward for capturing a runaway servant belonging to one Peter Casey. His reward was to be a pistol (a gold piece worth three dollars and seventy-five cents). Kill-buck captured the absconding servant and delivered him to Casey, but he (Casey) refused to pay the reward. They quarreled and Casey knocked Kill-buck down with his cane. During the French and Indian war Kill-buck on several occasions tried to kill Casey but could not succeed. During the Lord Dunmore war a son of Peter Casey was appointed to a lieutenantcy and sent to Wheeling. Kill-buck was living there with his tribe. Young Casey, hearing of him and knowing of his fame as a warrior, requested to meet him. Kill-buck was old and blind, but when he heard the name Casey, he asked if he knew Peter Casey. The lieutenant replied: "Yes, he is my father." Kill-buck exclaimed: "Bad man, bad man, he once knocked me down with his cane." He then related to young Casey the circumstances pertaining to the assault. Casey proposed to settle the difficulty. "Will you pay me the pistol?" Casey not having it, proposed to give the old man a quart of rum. The old warrior assented, saying: "Peter Casey old man, Kill-buck old man." He then stated that he had watched for an opportunity to kill him but concluded with: "Him too lazy—would not come out of the fort. Kill-buck now friends and bury the tomahawk."

CHAPTER VIII.

FROM THE CLOSE OF THE FRENCH AND INDIAN WAR TO THE BREAKING OUT OF THE REVOLUTION.

The victory of the English forces in America over the French in 1763 and the treaty with the Indians (Six Nations) at Fort Stanwix (now Rome, New York) brought a cessation of hostilities in this section. In fact, the Indians never molested the inhabitants in what is now Berkeley County again. By this treaty the whole of what is now West Virginia was ceded to England for money and goods amounting to ten thousand four hundred and sixty pounds, seven shillings and three pence. The settlers who had been driven from their homes by the Indian and French atrocities now returned and new settlers began to pour into this section from Virginia, beyond the Blue Ridge, Maryland, Pennsylvania, New Jersey and as far north as New York State.

The records of the settlements of the county from 1763 to 1772 are meager, but by searching what were available a few of them were found. The Quakers seem to have continued to make settlements during all these years of conflict, as they had never been molested by the Indians. They were pretty numerous on Middle Creek, and on Apple Pie Ridge, in the vicinity of Arden and Darkesville, for in 1791 adherents to that faith built a stone church at Arden. This edifice was used by them until shortly after the Civil War; the Quakers having moved westward, and the congregations becoming small, they sold it to the M. E. Church South. In 1904 the old Quaker Church was torn down and the commodious building erected almost upon the same spot. Nearby is a burying ground in which many of Quaker persuasion lie buried. As was their custom, no tombstones or markers were placed at their graves. Only small limestone stones mark the place where the Jobs, Throckmortons, Lees, and Moons lie buried.

On the road leading from Pikeside to Shepherd's Flying Field is a stone house, now owned by Richard and Roland Gano (brothers, which was the home of Tillotson Fryatt; also at Shepherd Flying Field is another, now owned by Alex. Shepherd, built about the same time by Alexander Shepherd.

Another pioneer of this period was John Boyd, who purchased a large tract of land from Lord Fairfax at the east base of North Mountain at the headwaters of Tuscorora Creek. He was the father of General Elisha Boyd of War of 1812 fame and the founder and builder of "Boydville", the present home of Hon. Charles J. Faulkner.

On the same creek is the Seibert house, erected by George Seybert (Seibert), and another erected by Wendall Mong, who became one of the King's Justices of the Court of Berkeley County.

Another settler on this creek of that period was John Miller, who afterwards became an officer in the Second War with Great Britain, and a representative in Congress from Missouri, also Governor of that State.

In the vicinity of Bunker Hill, on Mill Creek, stands a house erected by Levi Henshew, for many years a member of the County Court of Berkeley County, and four times a member of the Virginia Legislature.

The "Old Stone House", built in 1727, and now owned by I. D. Van Metre, Esq., (a descendant of John Van Matre, one of the original settlers), was erected by Abram Van Matre, and was the residence of General Adam Stephen, a distinguished soldier of the Revolution, and the founder of Martinsburg.

John Hite and Jacob Barney settled in the upper region of Back Creek Valley, while Jacob Stuckey settled at Tomahawk Springs, and Michael Rooney settled at Cherry Run, both in the lower region of that valley. Michael Rooney was, at one time, Sheriff of Berkeley County.

Hezekiah Hedges settled in the vicinity of what is now Hedgesville, and in his honor that town was named. He also built Hedges Fort, near that place, which served as a defence against the Indians.

John Myers (Hunter John Myers) located in Meadow Branch, a valley in the western section of the county.

This era of peace was the time for clearing land and enlarging farms, and the people took advantage of it. Many erected substantial residences of hewn logs or stone. Martinsburg assumed the aspect of a thriving village. All this peace and prosperity could have continued had not the Indians, in 1773, killed and robbed two white men (Indian traders), John Martin and Guy Meeks, on the Hockhocking River in what is now the State of Ohio. The next year they committed murder and robbery upon two men on the Ohio River. Colonel Angus McDonald and a body of other bounty men* went to the Ohio and Kanawha Rivers to survey lands, allotted to the soldiers by the King of England for their services in the French and Indian War. These were driven off by the Indians. Colonel McDonald appealed to John Murray, Earl of Dunmore, who was Colonial Governor of Virginia, for protection. Colonel McDonald also reported that the Indians were otherwise hostile and had violated their treaty (Fort Stanwix Treaty). The Governor authorized him to raise a regiment of four hundred men and proceed to punish the Indians. He speedily raised the required army and proceeded to the Indian country, destroyed several villages and cornfields, and returned. This act caused all the Indians of the Ohio Valley and westward to unite under the leadership of Cornstalk, a famous chieftain, and the

---

*"Bounty Men" were men who had been soldiers who had served in the Indian wars in the military service of Virginia and were given tracts of lands in the Ohio Valley as a bounty for such services. These lands were situated on the Ohio River on the eastern bank, and included the rich alluvial soil of that valley. In time they became valuable and include those fertile sections of West Virginia now so valuable as farming regions.

whole western frontier of Virginia was again thrown into a condition of savage warfare.

Lord Dunmore ordered Colonel Andrew Lewis to collect a body of one thousand men and to proceed to the Indian country. This was done, and Colonel Lewis immediately moved to the mouth of the Great Kanawha River. His men were collected from southern and western Virginia. In the meantime Lord Dunmore raised an army of an equal number of men, principally from the counties of Berkeley, Hampshire, Frederick, and Shenandoah, and assuming the command in person, proceeded to Fort Cumberland and Wheeling by the route of General Braddock. Cornstalk attacked Colonel Lewis' army at Point Pleasant and after a fierce battle, which lasted the entire day, the Indians were defeated. Colonel Lewis (now General) crossed the Ohio with the intention of invading the Indian country, but received orders from Lord Dunmore to return. This he did, marching back home by the Kanawha and Greenbrier Rivers. Lord Dunmore returned with his army to Williamsburg and thus ended what is known in history as Lord Dunmore's War.

This war affected Berkeley County in so much as many of the men engaged in it were from its confines. It is unfortunate that a roster of the men serving in that war from our county was not preserved, but no record is available other than "five hundred men were collected from Berkeley County under Colonel Adam Stephen."

CHAPTER IX.

FORMATION OF BERKELEY COUNTY.

The closing of the French and Indian War and the subsequent treaties with the Indians whereby they gave up all claims to the Shenandoah Valley caused a great influx of people from older settlements into this region and it became apparent that steps should be taken for the formation of a new county. Therefore, on the 19th day of May, 1772, the first court of the county was held and Berkeley County began her existence.

Spottsylvania County, Virginia, formed in 1720, was the first county to claim jurisdiction to any portion of the valley west of Blue Ridge. Orange County was taken from Spottsylvania in 1734. Its western confines were vague but were supposed to include the territory to the westward as far as Virginia laid claims—notably: to the Ohio River. Frederick County was laid off and defined by the Virginia Assembly in the year 1738. Thirty-four years elapsed before Berkeley County was taken from Frederick (1772). It included all the territory lying between the Potomac on the north, and the Shenandoah on the east, and all the region of western Virginia, and constituted all the territory included in the "Eastern Panhandle" of West Virginia, a territory which includes the present counties of Jefferson, Berkeley, and Morgan. Hampshire County was formed in 1753 from Frederick.

Let us pause and take a survey of the conditions existing which led to the formation of a new county.

Hampshire County had been laid off by the Virginia Legislature, and Winchester was the county seat of Frederick County, which county included the territory of the present counties of Jefferson, Berkeley, and Morgan. One of the main reasons for establishing a new civil unit to the northward was that the county seat was too far away. At the present the town of Winchester is not quite an hour's drive from any section of Berkeley County, yet in those days this distance meant a trip of two days at least, which was too far for the convenience of the inhabitants over the miserable roads of that period. If a settler wished to procure a legal deed for his farm, it necessitated a long trip to the far-away town of Winchester, the county seat, to get his deed filed among the proper records. In 1765, the county seat was as far away as Washington or Pittsburg is today.

There were few roads and travel was by horseback. The only road to Winchester was a road crossing the Potomac at Williams' Ferry, now Williamsport, Md., and extending as far as Harrisonburg, Va., and following almost identically the Williamsport Pike, the Winchester Pike, and the Valley Turnpike, was known as the "Indian Road", of which mention has already been made. This road was used for centuries by the red-man in passing from the north and south. This road with little improvement was broad enough for a wagon. Hence the settlers never thought of making another when there was already one in existence. Another was the famous "Old Packhorse Road", from the Potomac at Shepherdstown westward across the mountains to Bloomery Furnace, in Hampshire County. Another was the "Warm Springs Road" from Shepherdstown by Hainesville and Hedgesville to Bath or Warm Springs. After the establishment of Martinsburg this road extended from Harper's Ferry by Martinsburg, and followed almost identically the route of the new State Road from Harper's Ferry to Berkeley Springs.

In the spring of the year 1745, the County Court of Frederick County accepted the "Indian Road" as a public highway and designated it such under the title of the "Great Winchester Road".

Another factor which instigated the desire for a new county was the fact that the majority of the inhabitants had established their homes in a trackless wilderness by the severest toil and by enduring untold hardships. They had rid the country of a savage foe and had reached the point where they felt perfectly capable of managing the affairs of their section. The Colonial Government of Virginia was ever ready to lend a hand in the establishment of local government in the western section, and by this act strengthening its claims to the Ohio Valley and beyond. Hence when application was made for the formation of a new county it readily consented.

Berkeley County was named from Norborne Berkeley, Baron of Boutetort, Colonial Governor of Virginia under King George III. and not from that other Berkeley (Sir William), the "Tyrannical Governor of Virginia," who hanged Nathaniel Bacon's followers for daring to resist his authority, and of whom King Charles II. said, when he heard of it, "That old fool has hanged more people in that naked country than I for the murder of my father."

Commissions were issued and dispatched by Lord Dunmore, Colonial Governor of Virginia, and on the 19th day of May, 1772, at the "Red House" in the northern limits of Martinsburg, the first officers of the county were sworn in and Berkeley County began her career. This house is still standing, just off the Williamsport Pike to the west on land now owned by George Tremble.

The following is a record of Berkeley County's first "birthday" and is on file in the office of the Clerk of the County Court at the Court House:

BERKELEY COUNTY, S.S.

Be it remembered that at the House of Edward Beeson, the Nineteenth Day of May, Ano Domini, 1772, A Commission of the Peace and a Commissioner of Oyer and Terminer from his Excellency Lord Dunmore, dated the 17th day of April in the year aforesaid directed to Ralph Wormley, Isaac Hite, Van Sweringan, Thomas Rutherford, Adam Stephen, John Neaville, Thomas Sweringan, Samuel Washington, James Nourse, Wm. Little, Robert Stephen, John Briscoe, Hugh Lyle, James Strode, William Morgan, Robert Stogdon, James Seaton, Robert Carter Willis, and Thomas Robinson, Gent, and also Dedimus's for Administering Oaths directed to the same persons (or any two of them) were produced and read whereupon the said Van Sweringan having first taken the usual oath to his Majesty's Person and Government Reported and Suscribed the Test taken the Oaths of a Justice of the Peace of the Justice of the County Court in Chancery and of a Justice of Oyer and Terminer which was administered to him by the said James Nourse, William Little, be the same Van Sweringan administered the oaths unto Thomas Swerengan, Samuel Washington, James Nourse, William Morgan, Wm. Little, James Strode, Robert Stephen, Robert Stogdon, Robert Carter Willis and James Seaton who severally took the same and repeated and suscribed the Test

At a Court held for Berkeley County the 19th Day of May, 1772:

Present:

VAN SWERENGAN
THOMAS SWERENGAN
SAMUEL WASHINGTON
JAMES STRODE
ROBERT STOGDON
JAMES SEATON
JAMES NOURSE
WILLIAM MORGAN
WILLIAM LITTLE
ROBERT STEPHENS
ROBERT CARTER WILLIS
Gent. Justices.

The first clerk of this court was William Drew. The first sheriff was Adam Stephen appointed by Lord Dunmore, Colonial Governor of Virginia. His bondsmen were Samuel Oldham, George Cunningham, Archibald Shearer, George Stogdon, William Handshew, Henry Newkirk, Daniel Morgan and George Briscoe.

The first attorneys admitted to practice law in this court were James Thieth, John MacGill, George Brent, George Johnston, Philip Pendleton, and Aexander White, all sworn in by Adam Stephen, Sheriff.

The first Commonwealth Attorney was Alexander White and was appointed by the Attorney General of Virginia.

As there was no town of Martinsburg at the time of the formation of Berkeley County, the little village of perhaps 200 people, which was the nucleus of the present city, was called "Berkeley Court House". It was understood that the seat of justice for the county should be as near the center of the county as possible. Prompt arrangements were made for a court house and jail. The authorities rented the dwelling house of Edward Beeson at the north end of the town. Here the first court was held—May 19th, 1772. This building is still standing and is known as the "Red House". Court was held here until a new court house could be erected. This new building was of stone, one story high and located on the south side of the Public Square opposite to where the present one now stands. The jail was erected in the Public Square, where the Band Stand now stands. It was built of logs with a market house attached to the rear end. The whipping post occupied a prominent place in front of the Court House door on King Street. The stocks and pillory above it stood east on East King Street in front of the building now owned by Downey & Henson, lawyers, in which house was the Clerk's Office.

FORMATION OF BERKELEY COUNTY

The county was not laid off into districts until the year 1863. Then they were designated as "townships". In assessing the property of the county several assessors were appointed for the various sections. From these appointments it appears that the people had settled for the most part along the creeks.

The following is a record of the first assessment and the assessors of Berkeley County:

Thomas Swerengan, Assessor. "From the Mouth of Opequon, up the same to the Warm Spring Road, thence down said road to Robert Lemmon's, thence to Potomack at Mecklenburg."
"William Morgan—Eastern Section Near Mecklenburg.
James Nourse—Southern Section.
William Little—Southwest Section.
James Seaton—South.
James Strode—Center.
Robert C. Willis—Back Creek.
Robert Stephens—Sleepy Creek.
Robert Stogdon—Northwest."

The first constables were: James Quigley, William Ward, Stephen Boyles, and Thomas Batt.

The first coroners were: Robert Worthington and David Shepherd.

The assessors, coroners, and constables were appointed by the court. The other officers for the county were appointed by or through the Governor.

There were one hundred and twenty-six dedes recorded the first year of the existence of Berkeley County. These were all written with a quill pen, no other kind being in use, and are in a perfect state of preservation in regards to the quality of the ink and the paper, but the location of the portions of lands first recorded are vague, merely stating that they are "of the County of Berkeley and the Colony of Virginia." The first deed recorded was for 77 acres of land and reads as follows:

"Twentieth day of September in the Year of our Lord one thousand seven hundred and seventy one between John Lemmon, of Frederick County, Colony of Virginia, to Jacob Vandever, of the County and Colony aforesaid, for Fifty Seven Pounds, Eleven Shillings, Current money of Pennsylvania, containing 77 acres."

Other deeds recorded the same year were:

Dougal Campbell to James Campbell.
Ephraim G. Albertis to William Albertis.
Andrew Bowman to William Porterfield, jr.
John Borden to John Copenhaver.
John Burry to Robert Rutherford.
Isaac Evans to Joseph Evans.
Jacob VanMetre to William Haucher, Etc., Etc.

Several old records are preserved in the County Clerk's office at Martinsburg. Among them is a trust bond dated 1769. This bond was written upon sheepskin and is in a perfect state of preservation. The seal is attached to the face as in the case of our bonds at the present, but is appended to the bottom and contains the seal in use by the British Government at the time. It reads as follows:

"This Indenture made this sixth day of February in the nineth year of the Reign of our Sovereign Lord George the Third by the Grace of God of Great Britain France and Ireland, King, Defender of the Faith and soforth, and in the Year of our Lord One Thousand seven hundred and sixty nine Between Catharine Burton of Exmouth in the County of Devon, Widow and Relict of Joseph Burton late of Exmouth aforesaid Esquire, deceased of the one part and Joseph Palmer of Lincoln Inn, in the County of Middlesex, Gentleman, and William Hughes of the Parish of Saint Paul Convent Garden in the same county. Linnen Draper of the other part.

Whereas the said Catharine Burton, with her own proper money purchased the sum of five hundred pounds in the Capitol or Joint Stock of Consolidated Four Per Cent Annuities (Created by Two Acts of Parliament Of the second year of the reign of his present Majesty, One entitled An Act for raising Annuities in manner therein mentioned the sum of Twelve Millions &c. The other entitled an Act for charging certain Annuities granted in the year One Thousand seven hundred and sixty on the Sinking Fund &c.) transferrable at the Bank of England which said sum of Five Hundred Pounds. Four Per Cent Annuities, by the direction of the said Catharine Burton, John Palmer and William Hughes."

The trust bond was executed by the three above mentioned for Catherine Burton Nourse, "the God Daughter of the said Catherine Burton," and one of the daughters of James Nourse, one of the founders of Berkeley County and a member of the first Court.

On file in the office of the County Clerk are records of commissions appointing sheriffs, justices and overseers of the poor. Many of these were issued by the Governors of Virginia who afterwards became noted men in the affairs of the nation. Several were issued and signed "Dunmore" who was John, Earl of Dunmore, a Colonial Governor of Virginia. Some of these are instructions to the Justices relating to the trial of slaves and Indians for crimes and insurrections, others in regard to the administering oaths by the Justices. One of these has a seal of wax in the form of a crown attached to a narrow silken ribbon and attached to a Commission (the only one known to be in existence), others have a seal in wax stamped on them. Dunmore's commissions were issued from Williamsburg, Virginia. Several were signed by Patrick Henry when he was Colonial Governor of Virginia. One of these Commissions appointed Horatio Gates to fill the position of Gentlemen Justice, who looked after the affairs of the county in its early history. One signed by Thomas Jefferson on May 20, 1780, appointing Justices for Berkeley County, who afterwards became the third President of the United States. This commission was issued from Richmond, then the Capitol of Virginia, appointing James Nourse, Moses Hunter, Robert Baylor, Robert Stewart, George Scott, James Wilson, and John Hearsley Justices of the Berkeley County Court. These, of course, were not all appointed at one time. There is one issued by Benjamin Harrison, for whom Harrison

County was named; one by Beverly Randolph, for whom Randolph County was named; James Wood, for whom Wood County was named; appointing Cato Moore Sheriff of Berkeley County, on Aug. 31, 1793; one by Robert Brooke, for whom Brooke County was named; appointing James Wilson Sheriff of the County, Aug. 29, 1795. Several are signed by James Monroe, afterward President of the United States and author of the famous Monroe Doctrine, and for which Monroe County was named, issued July 12, 1825, and appointing George North, Coroner; one by William H. Cabell, for whom Cabell County was named; one by John Tyler, for whom Tyler County was named, and who afterwards became President upon the death of William Henry Harrison. This commissioned as Justices, William Pendleton, Aaron Ferris, Joel Ward, George Woolf, Andrew Waggoner, Jr., Michael Rooney, William Rush, James Faulkner, and James E. Throckmorton. These Justices were appointed Jan. 23, 1810; one issued by James Barbour, for whom Barbour County was named; one by James P. Preston, for whom Preston County was named; one by James Pleasants, Jr., for whom Pleasants County was named; one by John Floyd, appointing Philip Nadenbousch, Sheriff of Berkeley County, Feb. 21st, 1831; one by Henry A. Wise, Virginia's "War Governor", appointing Charles Stucky and Robert Lemmon, Justices of the Peace for the Sixth District of Berkeley County, July 5, 1859; and one by James McDowell, for whom McDowell County was named. It is needless to say that these relics are highly prized by the County Clerk, Paul H. Martin, and his staff. Christian W. Doll filed these from among the records when he was Clerk of the County Court. All the above counties named are in West Virginia.

Thus it will be seen that all officers of the county up to the time of the formation of West Virginia were appointed by the Governors of Virginia. Only the Presidential, Congressional, State Senate, and Legislative Candidates were voted for by the people, and then the election franchise was granted to the land holders only. A land owner could vote in each county where his name was entered upon the Land Book, if he could reach a voting place within three days, for which time the polls were kept open. The system of voting was by *viva voce* or open spoken ballot.

The first marriage certificate issued and recorded in the Clerk's office was issued to Christopher Souders and Sally Butts on Dec. 15, 1788. A copy of a marriage license issued one hundred and twenty-eight years ago will be of interest to the public. It reads as follows:

"Berkeley, f.f.

"Know all Men by thefe Prefents:

That we, Elias Oden and William Orrick are held and firmly bound unto his Excellency J. Wood, Esquire, Governor of Virginia, in full fum of fifty pounds, current money to be paid to the said Governor or his succefsor to the which payment will and truly be made. We bind ourselves, our heirs, executors, and adminiftrators, firmly by thefe prefents.

Sealed with our feals, and dated this 4th day of May, 1799.

The condition of the above Obligation is fuch that whereas a Marriage is fuddenly intended to be folemnized between the above bound Elias Oden and Ann Shearer, both of this County.

NOW if there fhould be no lawful caufe to obstruct the faid marriage then the above obligation to be void, elfe to remain in full force and virtue in LAW.

 Sealed and signed   Charles Oden (L.S.)
 in the prefence of: · William Orrick, (L.S.)

Among these records is found the will of General Charles Lee, of Revolutionary War fame, and a resident at that time of Berkeley County, from which the following extract is taken:

"I desire most earnestly not to be buried in any church or church-yard or within a mile of any church or church-yard or within a mile of any Presbyterian or Anna Baptist meeting House.

For since I have resided in this country, I have kept so much bad company when living that I do not *chuse* to continue it when dead.

I recommend my soul to the Creator of all World's, and of all creatures who must from his visible attributes be indifferent to the modes of worship or creeds whether they be Christians, Mohammedans, or Jews, whether instilled by education or taken up by reflection, whether more or less absurd, as a weak mortal can no more be answerable for his persuasions or notions or even scepticism in religion, than for the color of his skin."

This will was recorded in 1782, and is in his own handwriting and was undoubtedly formulated by himself and is said to be peculiarly characteristic of the man.

CHAPTER X.

ESTABLISHMENT OF MARTINSBURG.

Martinsburg was laid out in October, 1778, and named in honor of Colonel T. B. Martin, one of the heirs of Lord Fairfax. General Adam Stephen named Martinsburg in compliment to Colonel Martin who founded a city farther up the Shenandoah Valley and named it Stephen City in honor of General Adam Stephen. Through the workings of fate or on account of environments, Stephen City never grew to be much of a town but Martinsburg expanded from the first. Both are situated in the Shenandoah Valley, separated only by a few miles of territory, with the same natural surroundings. Martinsburg had the advantage of water power in the form of the Tuscarora Creek which Stephen City lacked. Martinsburg has a population of some fourteen thousand inhabitants and many thriving industries, while Stephen City has a barely few hundred people.

The land on which Martinsburg now stands was, at an early period, the site of the principal village of the Tuscarora Indians. After the formation of Berkeley County, General Adam Stephen put forth every effort to have Martinsburg established and to make it the capitol or county seat of the county. Jacob Hite wished to make Leetown the seat of justice, but Adam Stephen prevailed upon the Virginia Assembly to establish the capitol at Martinsburg, advancing the argument that the capitol should be as near the center of the county as possible.

The following extract from the law enacted by the Virginia Legislature for the establishment of the town is as follows:

"Whereas it hath been represented to the Virginia Assembly that Adam Stephen Esq. hath lately laid off one hundred and thirty acres of land in the county of Berkeley, where the Court House now stands, in lots and streets for a town, etc. Be it enacted etc. that the said one hundred and thirty acres of land laid out into lots and streets, agreeable to the plan and survey thereof made containing the number of two hundred and sixty nine lots, as by the said plan and survey, relation thereunto being had, may more fully appear, be and the same is hereby vested in James McAlister, Joseph Mitchell, Anthony Noble, James Strode, Robert Carter Willis, William Patterson and William Pendleton, Gentlemen Trustees, and shall be established a town by the name of Martinsburg."

In the foregoing pages the term "Gentlemen Justices" and "Gentleman" is met with quite often. A word of explanation as to what that term implied might not be out of place here. "Gentlemen Justices" was a term of respect applied to members of the Court which presided over the county, or had jurisdiction over the entire county. This Court transacted the business of the county and took the place of the Circuit Court of the present day, it being "the court" as well as county commissioners. There was no

"Judge", they being the judge of all cases, both civil and criminal. The people of the county have always held the Court in reverence and the term "Gentlemen Justices" was applied to them as we apply the title of "Honorable" or "Esquire" in addressing a letter to a distinguished person.

The term "Gentleman" implied, in an individual, really more than the term "Gentlemen Justices". In "Ancient Virginia", as we might call it, there were five distinct classes of society: Planters, who were the wealthy class and were the governing class; Pretenders, who were on a level with the Planters in birth and culture, but inferior in means, Yeomen; the poor class, Indentured white Servants; or those who were bound to another person until a certain age, and Slaves or Negroes.

This distinction in classes of society existed in Berkeley County to a late date, but to a much lesser degree. Now, because society was thus organized, the class term "Gentleman" was in constant use and was even used in deeds of conveyance. The term later was applied to members of other classes of society and became so general that its use lost much of its dignity and in the course of time ceased to be used.

In theory, at least, the ancestors of the "Gentleman" had always been free. He had a coat of arms and could wear a sword, another insignia of honor. He was considered one of the "Big Bugs" or a "Member of the 400".

On the 28th day of August, 1779, Adam Stephen, the High Sheriff of Berkeley County, moved that the plat for Martinsburg be recorded, also the following restrictions to purchasers of lots:

"The purchasers of any of the lots in the above town is to build on the purchased lot a good dwelling house to be at least twenty feet long and sixteen feet wide with stone or brick chimney to same, in two years of the time of purchase, and on failure, the lot to return to the proprietor."

By the above agreement General Stephen was desirous of having the town grow, also to have the best possible houses built that the time afforded.

Martinsburg would have been established sooner, but General Stephen being in the Army of the Revolution, no steps were taken for the establishment of a town until his return in 1777. He then devoted his attention to the laying out and establishing it.

Jacob Hite, who entered an animated contest for the location of the county seat at his town, because his town did not win, became so disappointed that he disposed of his fine estate at Leetown and removed with his family to South Carolina. Here he opened a large retail store and traded with the Creek and Cherokee Indians. He had not been there long when he and his family were foully murdered by them. A man by the name of Parish, who had accompanied Mr. Hite, growing jealous of his popularity among the Indians, contrived to turn them against him. He made them believe that Hite was defrauding them, when, in truth, his dealings with them could not have been more honest and just. On the evening before the massacre an Indian squaw revealed the plot to Mrs. Hite which she immediately communicated to her husband. He scoffed the idea that the Indians would harm him. The next morning a party of Indians appeared and told Hite of their intentions. In vain he pleaded with them, declaring again and again his friendship for them.

They first attacked Hite, cutting him to pieces a joint at a time. While in the midst of this most excruciating torture, he was compelled to witness the murder of his wife and smaller children. After dispatching these they took the two older daughters—young women—and his slaves as prisoners and carried them off together with as much of his stock of goods, household and farm equipment as they could remove, setting fire to the remainder. Captain George Hite, an officer in the Revolution, the only child to escape, made a diligent search among the Creek nation for his two sisters but no trace of them was ever found. The only account ever heard from any of the captives was by a Colonel William Triplett of Wilkes County, Ga., who in traveling through the Creek country in 1809, came upon an old Negro man who told him he was one of Jacob Hite's slaves who had been carried away when his master and mistress were murdered in South Carolina; that there were about sixty descendants of the slaves carried away, at that time, living among the Indians in abject slavery.

Berkeley County is noted for being the home of three Revolutionary War generals at one time: General Adam Stephen, General Charles Lee and General Horatio Gates. General Stephen was dismissed from the army on the charge of unsoldierly conduct at the battle of Germantown, General Lee for insubordination at the battle of Monmouth, and General Gates for his inglorious retreat at the battle of Camden. Each owned farms in Berkeley County, to which each retired after dismissal. The three heroes would frequently meet at the home of General Lee. At these meetings, at which wine flowed freely, each would relate his experience as an army officer, and discuss at length the merits of the other as such. On one occasion, when the discussion was of longer duration and the spirits a little more ardent, General Lee remarked: "The county of Berkeley is indeed to be congratulated. She can claim three noted Major Generals of the Revolutionary War. You, Stephen, distinguished yourself by getting drunk when you should have remained sober; you, Gates, were cashiered for retreating when you should have been advancing, while your humble servant covered himself with glory and laurels and was cashiered for advancing when he should have been retreating."

General Gates, the "Conqueror of Burgoyne," was placed in supreme command of the American army at the South in 1780. The South hoped much from the coming of Gates, as he was considered the ablest General in the army at that time perhaps, with the exception of Washington. When he was on his way from his home in Berkeley to take command of the army, he had an interview with the eccentric ex-General Charles Lee, who gave him an ominous charge in parting: "Beware that your Northern laurels do not change to Southern willows." This very thing happened, for Gates was defeated at the battle of Camden, and that was the last of his military history.

Designing men tried to supercede General Washington with General Gates just after the surrender of Burgoyne, but without success. General Lee was also a candidate for the same position but failed. This led General Lee to hold a feeling of envy and hatred toward General Washington. The latter, wishing to make friends with Lee, notified him that he would on a certain day dine with him, if agreeable. Upon the date set, when Washington arrived at his home, found no one at home and fastened to the front door was this message: "No bread or bacon cooked today."

On the County Clerk's records under date of November 20th, 1776, of the proceedings of the Court, is the following extract:

"Proclamation being made for trial of a negro man belonging to General Horatio Gates, committed to the gaol of this county, for breaking open the cellar of the said Gates and feloniously taking from there a chest of money and clothes; who being brought to the bar and it being demanded of him whether he was guilty of the offence wherewith he stands charged, or not guilty, he says he is guilty. It is, therefore, the judgment of this Court that he be remanded back to the gaol from which he came, and there to continue till the third Friday in December next; then from thence to be taken and hanged by the neck till he is dead. It is the opinion of the said Court that the said slave is worth seventy pounds.*

A peculiar incident occurred at Martinsburg on the 21st of June, 1774. The members of the County Court or the Gentlemen Justices composing it went "on strike". The controversy arose over the fees of the Justices. The law for regulating the fees to be collected by these Justices having expired in the April previous, no fees were forthcoming, so the Court had the following admitted for record:

And it being weighed by the Gent. of the Barr, that the Court could not lay cost to Judgments granted since that time and the Court being of the Opinion, resolved unanimously, that they would not proceed with the business of the Dockett until same laws should be made for regulating the said fees."

Present:
R. E. Wells,   Goodwin Swift,   and   Gent.
Horatio Gates   John Cook,   William Patterson. Justices.
Signed by Samuel Washington.

Evidently the "laws" were made for we find the said Court doing business at the old stand on August 16th, 1774.

---

*The owner of a slave executed by the Court was recompensed by the State for the value of the slave set by the Court.

CHAPTER XI.

THE REVOLUTIONARY WAR.

It is not the intention of the author of this work to go into details or discuss in a broad sense, the history of the Revolutionary War. That is left for a much larger scope of American history, many of such works being available to the student, should he wish to pursue further the history of his country. Only the part played in this great war drama which pertains directly to the history of Berkeley County will be narrated here. A more detailed account can also be found in a chapter on the military history of the county.

At the outbreak of the Revolution only two counties in what is now West Virginia had an existence—Hampshire and Berkeley. The latter county responded liberally in men and means to the cause of Liberty, partly because of their hatred of anything savoring of English nobility, and partly because they had borne more than their just share in wrenching their land from the hand of the Indian and the detested Frenchman. Berkeley County contained few Tories—men who sided with the King. Another reason for their adherence to the American cause was the fact that George Washington was the leader of the American armies; one who had been their leader in their struggle against the savage, and one who was personally known to many of them. So, when a call came for a meeting of the people at Williamsburg to determine what action the Colony would take in regard to the acts of the British Parliament, Virginia, and especially the western section, resolved to stand by America in opposition to England.

Robert Rutherford and Adam Stephen were sent as delegates to represent Berkeley County in that Convention. They listened to the fiery eloquence of Patrick Henry; to the wise counseling of Thomas Jefferson, George Washington, and Richard Henry Lee. Needless to say that they voted to stand by the Colonies in their struggle for liberty.

Berkeley County furnished six distinguished officers in the Revolutionary War: General Horatio Gates, General Charles Lee, General Adam Stephen, General Daniel Morgan, General William Darke, and Colonel Hugh Stephenson, and many subordinate officers. All these were connected with the history of the county; all had their homes in the county. (A more extended account of their activities can be found elsewhere in this work.)

A provisional government, known as the Continental Congress, had been set up at Philadelphia (the Capitol) composed of members from the thirteen different colonies. This Congress directed the activities of the Revolution, but the real work of raising and equipping troops fell to the lot of the several States. Virginia bore her share of fitting out her quota of men, etc., and Berkeley County her share also in raising and equipping of troops.

from within her borders. Berkeley County alone furnished over six hundred men in this war. There were about thirty thousand white people—men, women and children—residing in what is now West Virginia during this war, and about twelve hundred in Berkeley County. According to this population, the county furnished one-half of its population as soldiers.

The Quakers, owing to their aversion to war, would not support either side. This brought down upon their heads the wrath of the Continental Congress and many of them were removed and placed in military camps and they were held there until the close of the war. One of these camps was at Staunton, Va. Hessian prisoners were confined in camps of like nature, at Winchester, Va., and at Fort Frederick, Maryland. King George employed these soldiers to fight the Americans in the War for Independence. It is a tradition that they brought in the straw used for bedding, an insect called the "Hessian Fly", which was spread over the entire wheat growing section of the United States. The larva of this insect feeds upon the stem of the wheat and causes it to become "straw fallen", that is, the stem of wheat attacked by it will fall to the ground and will not produce. Sometimes the ravages of this insect are so great as to cause an entire failure in the wheat crop. A remedy for it is said to be in the late sowing of the crop in the fall, as the egg depositing period of the adult takes place about the first of September in this section, and wheat sown later will escape the attack of the insect.

Under a resolution of the Continental Congress, Captain Hugh Stephenson raised a company of volunteers to serve one year in the Continental Army. Lieutenants in this company were: William Henshaw, George Scott and Thomas Hite. Among the privates were: Robert White, Abraham Shepherd, Nathaniel Pendleton, Henry Bedinger, Michael Bedinger, Samuel Findley, Joseph Swearingen, Isaac VanMetre and his son John. These men with Captain Hugh Stephenson at their head, assembled at Morgan Springs, at the site of Morgans Grove Fair Grounds, now in Jefferson County. At these springs are the ruins of the old church which was at that time a part of Nourborne Parish of the Episcopal Church. On the 17th day of July, 1775, the day of departure, they listened to a sermon, partook of a frugal meal, and "struck a bee line for Boston." Captain Stephenson reported his men "from the right bank of the Potomac". These soldiers were styled "The Border Riflemen of Virginia" and had for their emblem, or banner, the design of "The Culpepper Minute Men", a coiled rattlesnake with the words: *"The Minute Men"?* *"Liberty or Death"?* *"Don't Tread on Me"?* Each man carried a long rifle, a powder horn, a bullet pouch, and in their belt a tomahawk and a scalping knife. They wore buckskin suits, moccasins of the same material and coonskin caps with a bucktail on the side.

Daniel Morgan organized the second company of volunteers in the autumn of 1775, but most of these were from Frederick and Hampshire Counties. The remaining portion was from Berkeley County.

As the war of the Revolution continued it became necessary to raise money and men to prosecute it, therefore in 1780 a tax of one shilling was laid upon every glass window in Virginia and the assessors were required to count the same in making their annual assessments. In the same year requisition was made by the Continental Congress upon Virginia for 2000 troops. Berkeley County's quota was 68 men, also for 71 suits for the Continental troops. A suit consisted of two shirts of linen or cotton, one pair of overalls, two pairs of stockings, one pair of shoes, and one fur, felt hat or leather cap.

In 1776 Virginia was laid off into Senatorial Districts, Berkeley and Hampshire Counties comprising the 23d District.

The war ended with the capture of Cornwallis and his large army at Yorktown and our people, being permitted to resume their occupations, improved rapidly in commerce, agriculture and the mechanical arts. The French and English armies had left large sums of money in gold and silver coin in circulation and this had a happy tendency to drive out the worthless paper currency then in use. Continental paper money had so depreciated in value that during the second or third years of the war it became a common saying among the people in speaking of something of little value to use the phrase "not worth a Continental". To fully appreciate the worthlessness of this form of money it required $600 of it to purchase a pair of boots and $60 to purchase a dozen of eggs.. Immense quantities of French and British goods were imported and the colonists began to discard their plain home-made clothing for European goods, and to the plain, homely fare of former days were added luxuries of foreign countries. This caused the people to run into debt and the gold and silver to be removed to the other side of the Atlantic in payment of these luxuries, and a series of hard times and a scarcity of money ensued.

The country, not having a stable government, began to drift into anarchy. Many of the leading men wished for a firm government. After much delay, the Constitution was written and submitted to the several States for ratification or rejection. In 1788, delegates were selected to a convention at Richmond to determine whether Virginia would give her consent to the adoption of the Constitution or not. General Adam Stephen and General William Darke were chosen by the voters to represent Berkeley County. The convention was nearly equally divided on the question of adoption or rejection. The vote stood 89 for adoption and 79 against. Several votes were taken before it was finally adopted and Stephen and Darke voted for the adoption at all times. General Stephen delivered a speech in favor of the adoption of the Constitution at this convention, which did great credit to his ability, eloquence and patriotism. The Constitution was adopted by the States and the United States began its career as a sovereign nation.

General William Darke's next service to his country was in the war against the Indians in the Indian territory. He was a colonel commanding the Second Virginia Regiment under General St. Clair. A battle fought with the Indians on the St. Mary's River in that territory resulted in a complete route for the Americans. General Darke covered the retreat of St. Clair's broken and shattered army to Fort Jefferson, a distance of thirty miles, employing the same tactics Colonel Washington used at the retreat of Braddock at Fort Duquesne, thirty-six years before. In the next year he accompanied General Anthony Wayne (Mad Anthony) in a successful campaign against the same Indians, General Darke commanding the Virginians as before. In the battle of St. Mary's, among the fallen was Captain Joseph Darke, the youngest son of General Darke. Among the Virginians slain at this battle eighty are said to have been from Berkeley County.

Dueling was prevalent in those days. This seemed the right way to settle points of honor. The weapons used were the sword and pistol. In the case of the sword the first party to the duel to draw blood was considered the victor and his honor was appeased. The most noteworthy was between Alexander Hamilton and Aaron Burr—the former the first Secretary of the Treasury in President Washington's cabinet and the latter once Vice President of the United States. In this duel Hamilton lost his life. An amusing anecdote is related of an arranged duel between Major James Stephenson and General William Darke. They were to fight it with swords. Stephenson, who was a small man, appeared on the ground armed with a rapier. Darke, who was a man of gigantic proportions, came armed with a broad sword as large as an ordinary mowing scythe. When the seconds were about to place them in position for the combat, the difference in size of both the men and of their weapons was so irresistibly ludicrous that the seconds burst into uncontrollable fits of laughter, which soon communicated its effect to the principals. The duel was averted, all points of honor settled, and the two brave old soldiers shook hands and continued warm friends the rest of their lives.

CHAPTER XII.

AFTER THE ADOPTION OF THE CONSTITUTION.

The Federal Government at its beginning was greatly in need of revenue to carry on its affairs and to pay the tremendous war debt incurred by the Revolutionary War. In order to raise this revenue, among other things, a tax called the "Excise" was imposed on distilled liquors. Much dissatisfaction existed throughout the country against the imposition of this duty and especially in western Pennsylvania. Revenue officers sent to collect this tax were tarred and feathered, whipped, rode on a rail and subjected to other indignities. Many acts of violence were perpetrated, especially against those thought friendly to the Government. Lawlessness prevailed, armed bands of men were organized and openly defied the Government. President Washington issued a proclamation ordering the insurgents to disperse. As no attention was paid to this proclamation, the President issued a requisition upon the States of Pennsylvania, New Jersey and Virginia for 15,000 troops to crush the insurrection. Berkeley County furnished her quota with General Daniel Morgan in command of the Virginia troops. General Henry Lee, of Virginia, was placed at the head of this army. Alexander Hamilton left the Treasury Department and remained, during the expedition, at the headquarters of the commanding general. President Washington accompanied the troops as far as York, Pennsylvania, and expected to take command of the expedition, but Congress being in session at Philadelphia (then the Capitol) he returned thence. The appearance of this formidable array of the military brought the insurrectionists to their senses and they dispersed and no further violence was committed. The tax was collected and the people of the country were brought to see that open defiance of the Government would not be tolerated. This incident is known as "The Whiskey Rebellion", and was the first act of defiance of any importance to the authority of the Government.

In the year of 1801 Jefferson County was formed from Berkeley by a legislative act of the Virginia Assembly and Charles Town was named as the seat of justice for the county. Prior to this time, as Berkeley County included this county within her confines, many noted men from that section held responsible positions of honor and trust in the affairs of Berkeley County as is attested by the records.

Maryland had always contended that the South Branch of the Potomac should be the corner stone of that State instead of the headwaters of the Potomac at the "Fairfax Stone", its present south-west corner, and began a controversy in 1753 between that State and the State of Virginia by the Governor, Horatio Sharpe, appointing Thomas Cresap to make a map of that region. This controversy continued till 1830, when Governor Floyd of Virginia appointed Charles James Faulkner of Martinsburg to procure evidence to establishing Virginia's claim to this territory. The report of Mr. Faulkner was so complete and the evidence he obtained so convincing that Virginia's claim has been established to the territory in controversy. A full report of this claim can be found in another chapter in this work.

After the adoption of the Constitution of the United States, and the machinery of government had been set up, Virginia was laid off into ten Congressional Districts, Berkeley County with the counties of Hampshire, Shenandoah, Monongalia, Ohio, Hardy, Randolph and Frederick composed the First Congressional District of Virginia. Alexander White, a well known lawyer and resident of Berkeley County, represented this district in the First and Second Congresses (1789 to 1793). After the census of 1790 was taken and the ratio of representation had been established by Congress, it was found that Virginia was entitled to nineteen representatives in that body, and Berkeley and Frederick Counties were allotted to a district and constituted again, the First Congressional District of Virginia, and remained such until the new census of 1800 changed the ratio of representation. The following gentlemen, all from Berkeley County, represented the First District of Virginia in Congress for the first eleven Congresses, viz:

Alexander White (First and Second), 1789-1793.
Robert Rutherford (Third and Fourth), 1793-1797.
Daniel Morgan (Fifth), 1797-1799.
David Holmes (Sixth, Seventh, Eighth, Ninth, Tenth and Eleventh), 1799-1811.
John Baker (Twelfth), 1811-1813.
Edward Colston (Fifteenth), 1815-1817.

Nothing of importance transpired in the annals of Berkeley County until the outbreak of the Second War with Great Britain, other than that the people had grown prosperous and had recovered from the effects of the Revolutionary War. The county had increased in population and wealth, better homes had been established, larger tillable farms had been cleared of the forest and a general era of prosperity reigned. About this time, as the larger portion of the county's population was engaged in agricultural pursuits, many substantial houses were built. These were built of stone. On Tuscarora, eight of this type were erected, at present owned by George Walters, Wade Seibert, Homer Small, Charles Rousch, Arlington Roush, Senator Charles J. Faulkner, the Gotleib Noll house now owned by Mrs. George VanMetre, and the La Mar house. West of Arden near Apple Pie Ridge, the original Martin Pitzer home, now occupied by Kirk Smith; the original George V. Pitzer house, now owned by J. W. Spiker; the original James L. Campbell house, now owned by James Lyle Campbell; the original Samuel McKown house, now owned by James Horner. At Arden, the original James W. Chenoweth house, now owned by Robert G. Horner, Jr. On Back Creek, the James D. Stuckey property and the James B. Shipper property, also the Sylvester Jamison house, west of Tomahawk. On Dry Run, the

Hunter D. Sperow and Clarence Kilmer properties. On Warm Spring Road, the Shields Payne and the John Riner properties. At Spring Mills, the DuVall, the Luther Sperow and Riner Sperow properties. At this time, "Boydville", the present home of Senator Charles J. Faulkner was erected by General Elisha Boyd, a general in the Second War with Great Britain. All these properties, though built about 1800 or a little before, are still as substantial looking as if they had been recently erected and are able, no doubt, to withstand the ravages of another one hundred years of time. At a later date many houses were built throughout the county, some of brick, some of logs, which are still standing apparently none the worse for their century of usefulness.

CHAPTER XIII.

"BERKELEY COUNTY IN 1810."

Perhaps the people who now inhabit Berkeley County would like to know something of the condition of their county over one hundred years ago. The following chapter is taken from a rare old book or pamphlet written by Charles Varle in the year 1810 and describes the county as he knew it at that time. This work was kindly loaned the author by Hon. Charles J. Faulkner and is one of his cherished possessions. Such works should be passed on to posterity, hence the numerous sketches are copied *ver batim* for this work.

BERKELEY COUNTY.

"Lies between the 39th degree and 18 minutes North Latitude, and extends 20 miles in length and about 18 and 1-2 in breadth and is bounded to the north, inclining to the East by the river Potomac which divides the state of Virginia and Maryland; to the east inclining to the South by said river and Jefferson county; to the South inclining to the West by Frederick County, to the West inclined to the North by the county of Hampshire and the river Potomac. Martinsburg is the Capitol and the seat of justice of this county.

CONTENTS.

"It contains 484 square miles or 319760 acres.

PRODUCTIONS.

"The same as in Frederick County.

POPULATION.

"When the last census was taken in 1800, this county and Jefferson were but one; it then contained 15000 white inhabitants and 3600 slaves: suppose 1-3 of the white population has been taken to form the County of Jefferson 10000 would still remain to Berkeley. It is supposed that half the above number of blacks fell to Jefferson County although the division of the whites is not so equal. The next census will settle this point.
"There are now in this county 2100 tithables or males above 16 years of age, paying the poor tax.

THE MOUNTAINS IN THIS COUNTY ARE:

"*First*—The North Mountain: it is remarkable on account of rising immediately like a wall. It has a summit beautifully undulated in all its length. It might be computed to be about 500 feet perpendicular at its greatest height. It is not cultivated. The east side could be planted with vines. Mr. Edward Tabb living immediately under that side of the mountain showed me a European vine which has resisted the coldest winters and without either pruning or cultivation affords large quantities of luscious grapes every year.

"*Second*—The Third Hill and Sleepy Creek mountains are nearly joining, and both run parallel to the North Mountain. They are not cultivated except in the middle of the two, where issues a stream of water called Meadow Branch, and there the plantation of a huntsman is seen. The height of both mountains is about 700 feet from their base.

"*Third*—The Warm Spring Ridge is broken in several places, it is about 300 feet high. It divides Berkeley from Hampshire. These ridges succeed each other in the above order, running westerly from the North Mountain.

RIVERS.

"The Potomac is the only river in this County: it divides this state from Maryland.

CREEKS.

"The creeks are Opequon, Mill, Middle, Tuscarora, Back, Sleepy and the Warm Spring. The three first as well as part of the Warm Spring creek are never failing streams owing to the springs that feed them being in limestone land, which is deep and spongy, suffers the rain water to penetrate it: the water is therefore kept there as it were for the supply of the springs, while those creeks which have the head springs, on slate or rocky bottoms that does not permit the water to penetrate their substance become dry in the hot seasons of the year. This circumstance does not, I think, corroborate that system already spoken of respecting the springs receiving their supply from the sea by subterranean passages.

QUALITY OF THE SOIL.

"I have thought that in order to give an accurate idea of the qualities of the soil of this county, I ought to divide it into three parcels or valleys.

"*First*—The first parcel is nearly all limestone, of an excellent quality except on the ridge where I think that a mountain existed as spoken of in the article of Lithology of Frederick County, and where the sulphur springs are found. This ridge continues its course through this county but it has been washed by the rains more than in Frederick County and lies lower. The quality of the soil is good, and by means of clover and plaster of Paris, I think it will grow more valuable yet.

"*Second*—This parcel contains the valley of Back Creek and is watered by it. I will observe that there is a tract of land marked on the map with the sign of a hill on account of being higher than the other part of the valley and extends from Mr. Gaunt's mill to Mr. Robertson's mill on the Warm Spring road and on a breadth of about two miles, which is a good limestone land. The remainder of it is slate and mountain land except the bottom on the creek, which is loam. The whole is susceptible of great improvement and will become very valuable by attention to agriculture.

"*Third*—Is the Sleepy Creek watered by the said creek. Some part along the Warm Spring ridge is limestone, some bottoms on the creek are loam, the rest is slate and mountain land which however, improved by the plaster of Paris, and clover, would afford in my opinion, good crops of small grain.

LITHOLOGY.

"As a part of this county is limestone, marble will consequently be found in it sooner or later. I have seen spars of different kinds in the limestone land near Martinsburg, there are some in the form of a column, with sides and truncoted, white and transparent. On Apple Pie Ridge there are masses underground of those spars of different forms. The people on whose lands those stones are seen believing them of gypsum (Plaster Paris) had them ground and spread on their lands; indeed many bushels they said had been sold as such. I went to these places and obtained specimens of those stones and made a trial on them which is commonly used for detecting the true gypsum from the common stone: I put them in contact with fire and found after several experiments that the most intense heat had not the least immediate effect on them in causing them to lose their transparency or hardness and consequently I took them to be rather a carbonate of lime (of the nature of limestone) instead of being the sulphate of it, (of the nature of plaster) and in order to make the people on whose lands these stones are found, better acquainted with the nature of the true plaster of Paris, I shall extract a part of a chapter of Chaptal's on chemistry. He expresses himself himself thus: The plaister loses its transparency by calcination, at the same time that it becomes pulverulent and acquires the property of seizing the water of which it has been deprived, and resuming its hardness; it does not give fire with steel or effervesce with acids. He says further that 100 parts of gypsum contains 30 sulphuric acid, 32 calcarious earth, and 38 water; it loses nearly 20 per cent by calcination. It is soluble in 500 times its weight of water at the temperature of 60 degrees of Fahrenheit. When it is exposed to heat its water of chrystalization is dissipated; it becomes opaque, loses its consistance, and falls into powder. If it be moistened it becomes hard again but does not resume its transparency, a circumstance which appears to prove that its firm state is a state of crystalization; if it be kept in fire of considerable intensity it collects with powder of charcoal, the acid is decomposed, and the residue is lime, &c. Upon the principle above stated we learn that plaster and lime are both calcarious earth and we might draw a conclusion from them that if any virtue is attributed to the former in promoting the growth of clover and other plants, it is owing to the sulphuric acid that the plaster contains, and then both a pyretous and limestone ground is required for the formation of it. I will add for information also that as the plaster when calcinated, looks nearly as white as any other calcarious matter and in order that one may be known from the other, pour some drops of water on both, it will cause an immediate effervescence on the lime, while the plaster will receive no effect from it, besides, when the plaster after calcination, is pounded, pulverized and sifted, it can be formed with the addition of water into a paste which will grow solid by drying while it will not be so with any other calcarious substance.

"Near the mill of Mr. Stephen's on Tulliss branch I found a kind of soft limestone that the people also took for plaster of Paris, which being easily reduced to powder either by pounding or grinding, or made into lime by fire, may probably answer to improve lands. Another kind of limestone I found also at Mr. Samuel Hedge's in Sleepy Creek Valley, which would perhaps answer the same purpose as the above described. I have seen at Mr. Shearer's Mill on the Potomac, flag stones that he raised from the bottom of that river near his house, which surpass in color, beauty and size, any histus (slate stone) I have ever seen. Those slabs can be polished and sawed easier than marble and Mr. Shearer has used them in its stead to embellish his new house. When the navigation of this river shall be improved no doubt that they will be boated down to the cities below and will constitute a branch of commerce. These stones would be of great service in raising of dams and locks on this river for the improvement of navigation in the same manner as spoken of in the article of rivers in Frederick county.

MINERALOGY.

"On the banks of the Opequon near the house of Mr. John VanMetre, two or three miles from Martinsburg, is found a kind of sulphate of iron (copperas) which immediately turns leather black. It is found between the slates but not in abundance, however when a diligent search is made much may be found. Iron, copper as well as silver oars are found on Sleepy Creek mountain but the last oar is not found in quantities sufficient to be worthy of exploring; no search yet with a particular view to obtain those oars has been made by any chemist on these mountains. The waters of Sleepy Creek contain the iron in solution to such a degree that the stones on its bed are covered with the oxide of it.

NATURAL CURIOSITIES.

"There is a natural reservoir, bearing the name of Swan Pond in this county, the waters of which run off in a stream for some distance and then sink all at once and no more is seen of them until near the mouth of Opequon creek, where, in a hollow or pit of about 100 feet of depth and 300 feet of circumference you hear them pass under the rocks of the bottom of the pit and going undoubtedly to join the waters of Opequon creek.

MILLS.

"There is in this county upwards of 50 grist or merchant mills, as many saw mills, several fulling mills and oil mills and one paper mill.

MANUFACTORIES.

"A large and convenient stone merchant mill on Tuscarora and joining Martinsburg, has been bought lately from Mrs. Hunter by Messrs Hibbert and Gibbs for the purpose of establishing a wool and cotton manufactory: Mr. Hibbert is a fuller by trade—he has already erected all the apparatus for fulling, dressing and dyeing all sorts of clothes on a pretty large scale. Mr. Gibbs is an ingenious mechanic; he has moved from his cotton manufactory at Hagerstown, all his machinery for carding and spinning, both wool and cotton to place them in this building. Mr. Jonathan Wickersham, a fuller, the proprietor of a fuller mill and carding machine established on Middle Creek near the precincts of Bucklestown, has added lately to his factory, a genny of 50 spindles, to spin wool, and having at hand a number of capable weavers, he intends to carry on a complete factory of cloth. I hope these two manufactories may be encouraged so as to become permanent establishments and add to the stock of wealth of the county.

MINERAL WATERS.

"There are several of the sulphur kind on the Opequon in this county, but the most remarkable is the one occupied by Mr. Minghini about 8 miles from Martinsburg. His house is well fitted for accommodation and several hundred persons resort there every season. There is another also, about 2 miles distant from Martinsburg on which the citizens of Martinsburg have bestowed some trouble and expense to render it convenient and useful to visitors; they have put up a shower bath which is used by the neighbors and townsmen. The most conspicuous one is at Bath Town under the Warm Spring ridge, from the foot of which and by different channels issue a torrent of water capable to turn a mill. Water cannot be more limpid and beautiful than this is. This place, tho' agreeably ornamental, and capable of contributing to the pleasures of the gay and healthy as well as convenient and salutary to the sick and invalid might be greatly improved and embellished by taste and liberality, if the legislature of Virginia was disposed to encourage any practical scheme to raise money for that purpose. There are commissioners appointed by the state legislature for the regulation of this spring. I have given them last fall a plan for the embellishment of this town and spring and the ground adjacent to them, which if put into execution, will make this spot the handsomest watering place in the Union. Nature has been lavish of her favors to this spot of country for addition to those medicinal springs, she has showered her bounties upon the whole neighborhood by spreading over it a magnificent variety of the most finished and grand scenery. The soil around this place, as a mountainous country, has the appearance of sterility, but by proper attention to culture might be made productive and rich.

"I will not attempt to elucidate the properties of these waters. I will only say that the country in this valley looks barren and is uncommonly dry, and as under the surface of the earth there generally exists a hard rock which prevents the rain water from penetrating, so as to produce permanent springs: my curiosity was so much awakened as to induce me to look for the source of the springs and after much pains, I was informed by the neighbors that hunters living on the Ca-capon creek that the waters of that creek were sinking at about 10 miles from its mouth and formed a vortex. This spot lies to the south-west of Warm Spring Ridge, and of the Ca-Capon mountains and at a distance of about 9 miles in a straight line from Bath Town.

"This seemed to me the more probable as these springs are never influenced either in their temperature or quantity, by the warm or cold, or wet or dry weather, and probably after leaving, sojourned and passed through the mazes of the subterraneous cavities under the Ca-Capon mountain as well as under the valley which lies between the Ca-Capon mountains and the Warm Spring ridge, the soil of which is calcarious and having been in contact with the different pyrites, composing their bed receives by their decomposition the degree of heat that these waters contain as well as the gases with which they are impregnated and after a due filteration through the sandy rocks, of which the basis of that Warm Spring ridge is composed they arrive at this spot. These waters, when boiled, leave strong incrustions on the sides of the vessels, which plainly evinse that they are highly mineralized and consequently possessed of the virtues for which they have been so much extolled in relieving or removing complaints. I took with me last fall, some of these sediments to Philadelphia and gave them to Dr. Barton who as an eminent chemist, will give a full analysis of their contents. I have inserted this in order to counteract the opinion of those who, without taking any pains in the investigation or analysis of the waters have advanced, that they contain no minerals in solution, neither in a state of oxide nor gas and consequently are totally destitute of any properties whatever, more than common water.

MARTINSBURG.

"Is the Capitol of the county of Berkeley, it contains about 200 houses and nearly 800 inhabitants; it is the seat of justice and has for that purpose a handsome courthouse and jail of stone and a market house, well supplied with the necessarys of life. The situation of this town is remarkably pleasant and healthy on account of its standing on an elevated spot and for having the creek Tuscarora watering its precincts, which could be carried by pipes through the town for the convenience and comfort of the inhabitants, if desired. The streets are wide and partly planted with Lombardy poplars, and have a very fine appearance. Eight taverns are kept in this place, one of them has the reputation of being one of the best in the United States and is well known by those who resort to the Warm Springs. Here is kept a Coffee House where almost all the papers in the United States are read; 8 large stores, one printing office, there are also five public meeting houses for worship, one English Episcopalian, a Catholick, a German Lutheran, a Presbyterian, a Methodist, a Baptist, three English schools, several Manufactories, and every description of artificers and mechanics.

"Latitude North 39 degrees 32 minutes. It is 22 miles from Winchester, 20 miles from Hagerstown, 83 from Baltimore, 81 from the Federal City, 117 from Staunton, 171 from Philadelphia, 172 from Richmond and 16 from Charles Town.

MIDDLETOWN OR GERRARDSTOWN.

"Situated on a level soil, partly lime stone one mile and a half from Mill's Gap under the North Mountain to the east side of it and nearly at the head of Mill Creek. It contains about 40 families. A physician and a Presbyterian clergyman live here: several large stores are kept in this town for the supply of farmers around it, here are also a number of mechanics. There is in this place a handsome brick church, built by the Presbyterians. This town is 10 miles from Martinsburg and 15 1-2 from Winchester.

DARKESVILLE OR BUCKLESTOWN.

"Lies 7 1-4 miles from Martinsburg, on the road to Winchester, 15 miles from that place, and on Middle Creek, a never failing stream which crosses this place. There are 30 dwelling houses, 4 taverns, three stores, two blacksmiths, 2 weavers, one tailor, one cabinet maker, one wagon maker, one distillery of whiskey. A Methodist meeting house stands at the north end of this town.

BATH TOWN OR WARM SPRING.

"Situated immediately under the east side of the Warm Spring ridge, 6 miles from the Potomac in a narrow valley, watered by the stream which runs from the Warm Springs. Several years ago this town was handsome but the houses as being built with wood have decayed and on account of the celebrity of its waters was yearly visited by above 1000 of the *beau monde*. It has lost its reputation on account of some diseases which raged during one season occasioned by a pond where the waters were stagnating, but since the cause was removed, it has regained its character. Last year it was visited by above 500 and no doubt will increase each year. Here are five large and conservative taverns or boarding houses kept for the accommodation of visitors and invalids, 25 families are living in this place among the number various branches of mechanics. Here are several stores and manufactors of leather. I must not omit to for the information of the people who are to visit this watering place that besides the above springs there is a sulphur spring four miles distant from this place, near Sleepy Creek. It is but slightly impregnated with sulphur and no accommodation near it and a chahbiate spring on this ridge about half a mile from this town. It is 25 miles from Martinsburg, 35 miles from Winchester, 100 miles from the Federal City, 108 miles from Baltimore, 185 miles from Richmond and 195 miles from Philadelphia.

JAMESBURG (GANOTOWN).

"Is situated in Back Creek valley and has only the name of a town for it contains only a few scattering houses without regularity. It is about 13 miles from Martinsburg."

CHAPTER XIV.

WAR OF 1812.

At the close of President Jefferson's Administration it was evident that under the strained relationship between the United States and Great Britain war between these two nations would occur at any time. President Jefferson was a man of peace and his actions deferred hostilities to a later date. This climax was reached in the year of 1812, when the United States declared war on Great Britain on the 18th of June of that year. A year previous, a volunteer artillery company was organized of Berkeley County men. James Faulkner was elected Captain;* Robert Wilson, 1st Lieutenant; and William Long, 2nd Lieutenant. Among those who volunteered in this company were John R. Cooke, Edward Colston, John Alburtis, Alexander Stephens, William Campbell, James Newkirk, Tillotson Fryatt, Adam Young, Jacob Snyder, John Matthews, Jacob Poisal, Chas. Pendleton, James Shearer, and Nicholas Orrick. The *Martinsburg Gazette* of date of February 7th, 1812, published an address to this company by James Faulkner, as follows:

"You have upon two former occasions, volunteered your services to the Government, the Commander hopes your patriotic and military pride will not be damped by the circumstance that you have not been ordered into active service. He flatters himself that there is now every probability of a war that you will authorize him to offer your services to march whenever you may be required. He returns thanks to those patriotic young men not belonging to the Company who enrolled themselves to march with him on a former occasion and flatters himself that they and others who feel a desire to serve their country in the ranks of its defenders, will come forward and join the parade on Saturday, the 22nd inst., the anniversary of the immortal Washington."

JAMES FAULKNER,
Feb. 7th, 1812.   *Captain 1st, M. Artillery.*

As early as March, 1812, it was evident that the enemy was about to attack in the region of Portsmouth and Norfolk and General Orders were issued on the 24th of March for the assembling of the Virginia State Militia at those points. This volunteer company of Berkeley County assembled at Richmond. It was known then as Wilson's Berkeley Artillery in honor of First Lieutenant Robert Wilson who had been elected Captain in place of Captain James Faulkner, who had been, prior to this, commissioned the rank of Major of Artillery, and was ordered by Governor Barbour to report to him at Richmond and to take command of all the artillery companies then assembled.

During the summer of 1812, the engagements had taken place mainly on the Canadian border and with the allied forces of the Indians, of the

---
*See biography of James Faulkner in Biographical Notes.

Northwest under Tecumseh, their chief. These engagements had not all been victories for the American army. The men who had gone from Berkeley County to that section and who had served as officers were: Captain Lewis B. Willis, Captain Hiram Henshaw, Lieutenants John Strother and David Hunter, and General Elisha Boyd.

The first engagement in that war in which this entire company participated was at the attack on Craney Island by the British fleet under the command of General Sir Sidney Beckwith. On this island was a fortification defending the entrance to Portsmouth and Norfolk harbors. Major James Faulkner had entire command of this defense and so efficiently did he direct the defense that the enemy withdrew from the attack and those two towns were saved. Among the annals of heroic deeds of men from Berkeley County in that war was that of Major Andrew Waggoner, who was cited for bravery and soldierly conduct at the battle of Lundy's Lane, also a body of Minute Men raised largely from this county and adjoining counties in Virginia were the first to reach Washington after General Ross had burned the National Capitol.

For the prosecution of the war a direct tax was laid on the people of the various States for $3,000,000. Virginia's portion of this amount was $369,018.44, of which Berkeley County was required to pay $6,147.22.

CHAPTER XV.

PROGRESS OF THE COUNTY.

The first Constitution of Virginia was granted to that colony by King Charles II. in 1677, with instructions to the Colonial Governor to always be on the watch that the members of the Assembly should be elected only by the freeholders (or land owners) of the colony. This constitution was in force for ninety-nine years or until 1776, when Virginia framed another, the first of its kind in America. This constitution necessarily had some imperfections. It discriminated against the people of the western part of the State. That section grew in population to such an extent that by the year 1825 each of the counties of this section paid into the State treasury many times more taxes than some of the eastern counties, yet the representation in the Legislature for each section was the same. Taxation without representation was charged and great dissatisfaction prevailed among the people of the western section. Right here was sown the seed which contained the germ which eventually developed into the State of West Virginia and it only needed the opportunity to declare itself independent of the Mother State. That opportunity came in the advent of the Civil War. Popular demand caused the Virginia Legislature to pass an act providing for a vote on the question of a new constitution. It carried by an overwhelming majority. This convention met at Richmond on October 15th, 1829, and after due deliberation, adopted a new constitution for the State but this constitution did little to secure the rights of suffrage and representation in this section. The representatives in this convention from Berkeley County were Elisha Boyd and Philip Pendleton.

The agitation of this question of taxation without representation continued until the General Assembly of Virginia again passed an act to submit the question to a vote of the people whether to frame a new constitution or not. At this election the vote carried for a convention and on the 14th day of October, 1850, the convention met at Richmond, the Capitol, and after a thorough deliberation a third constitution was adopted which corrected many existing grievances, especially among the people of western Virginia. In this convention, Charles James Faulkner of Berkeley County, the "Champion of Western Virginia", took sides in favor of extending the right of suffrage and adjusting taxation on a more equitable basis. The office of Governor, heretofore elected by the Assembly, was made elective by the people of the State. This constitution continued in effect until after the Civil War.

For forty years after the close of the Second War with Great Britain, the people of our county lived in comparative quiet as far as hostilities were concerned. True, the Mexican War was fought to a successful close for the United States, but it affected Berkeley County but little, it being so far from the base of operations. A company of volunteers was raised after some soliciting. Among those who volunteered were Captain E. G. Alburtis, Daniel Poisal, Otho Harrison, William Sherrard, Samuel K. Stuckey, John Bear, John Gallaher, James Bear, John Ott, John Jamison, Wm. Keefe, John H. Hunter and others. This company rendezvoused at Fortress Monroe and served throughout the war. This time of comparative peace was given over to internal improvements in the county. In 1837 the surveying corps of the Baltimore and Ohio Railroad reached Martinsburg. This corps was surveying the route for that railroad through the county from Vanclevesville to North Mountain and Cherry Run, and in 1843 the road was completed to Martinsburg. In 1849, the Baltimore and Ohio Railroad began the erection of an engine and machine shops at this place. At this time the Martinsburg and Potomac Turnpike contract was let to contractors. It was the first turnpike built within the county. The money was raised by taxes for three-fifths and individual stock sales for the remaining two-fifths. Daniel Burkhart was the first president and John H. Likens the first secretary. The Martinsburg and Winchester Turnpike was built a few years later. The Chesapeake and Ohio Canal had been constructed a few years previous. This canal was begun by an appropriation of Congress for $1,000,000. The National Road from Washington to Cumberland, Md., had also been completed.

The canal mentioned does not touch any portion of the county proper, but is on the Maryland side of the Potomac River. Yet it was a great aid in developing this county for it furnished a mode of transportation for our flour, bacon and other farm products to eastern markets and caused numerous flour mills to be erected throughout the county, which in turn provided a ready market for the large quantity of wheat raised by the farmers. Likewise the National Road which passed through Hagerstown, although some distance to the north of the county limits, afforded a way of transportation by wagon for the county's products to eastern markets. This way led to the building of the Martinsburg and Potomac Turnpike to Williamsport, Md., to connect with the above canal and at Hagerstown, Md., with the National Road. This canal continued to carry produce until as late as the year 1925, when it was abandoned on account of the faster mode of transportation by express or truck and the heavier commodities by freight. These turnpikes have been turned into broad, well maintained highways and are entering their second stage of usefulness by the advent of the automobile and truck.

Many mills for the manufacture of flour were established during this period. All these were located on the streams of the county as water power was the only means of turning the machinery of them as steam engines were not perfected at this time. The farmers sold their wheat to the mills and as the mills were dependent solely upon the farmer for their raw material, the miller entered upon a system of "tolling", the miller taking the eighth bushel for grinding the farmer's product when he did not sell outright to the miller. The custom of the farmer putting enough wheat in the mill after threshing time to supply his needs until the next crop was gathered, gave rise to the axiom: "As good as old wheat in the mill." The wheat was made into flour and shipped in barrels. The standard flour barrel required five bushels and a peck of wheat to produce a barrel of flour when ground and ready for the market. This was the standard set by law although the manufacturer of flour today uses paper and cotton bags as containers, the barrel being discarded on account of the scarcity of timber for making it. This flour was hauled to eastern markets, Baltimore and Philadelphia, by four or six horse teams or conveyed to Williamsport, Md., and there loaded on canal boats and transported to Georgetown, D. C., thence by boats to the above named markets. When transported by wagon, the route was either by Williamsport or by Shepherdstown over the Old Pack Horse Road to Frederick City, Md., where the National Road was taken on into Baltimore. These trips by wagon usually consumed the best part of three weeks. On the return trip the teams would bring back a load of provisions, as tobacco, sugar, coffee, dry goods and such other materials as the stores of Martinsburg and the surrounding villages required, and in this way the trip was quite profitable.

Two of Berkeley County's famous men spent their early manhood as teamsters. One was Daniel Morgan, the Revolutionary War hero. He delighted in the management of his team and acquired throughout life the sobriquet of "Old Wagoner". Another one was David Crocket, afterwards the noted Indian fighter and scout and, the "Hero of the Alimo". When a young man he ran away from home and wandered into the confines of Berkeley County and was employed on the Gray farm (situated on the road leading from Horner's saw mill to the intersection of the Gerrardstown-Inwood road. "Davy" spent about three years on this farm. From this earliest youth, he had a desire to become President of the United States. After he had been working for Mr. Gray for some time, he took David along with him on one of his trips to Baltimore with a load of flour. Somewhere on the way the team ran away and David, who was riding on the wagon at the time, was in great danger of being crushed by the rolling and pitching of the flour barrels. He, however, escaped unhurt and afterwards remarked to Mr. Gray that "Any man who was cut out for President wouldn't be killed by the rolling of flour barrels."

Many mills were erected throughout the county on the larger streams. On Tuscarora, the Cushwa mill, and on that creek in Martinsburg, the Fitz mill and the one now owned by Alexander Parks, and the Flagg mill east of Martinsburg at Flagg's Crossing. On this stream were also located Kilmer's and Bender's mills. On Middle Creek was Throckmorton's mill west of Darkesville and Bryarly's and Thomas' mills at Darkesville. On Mill Creek (so named from its abundant water power) were the Henshaw mill west of Bunker Hill and the Cunningham and Lamon mills east of Bunker Hill and the Tate mill at Bunker Hill (burned by the soldiers during the Civil War). At Bedington was located Kennedy's mill, on the Opequon Snyder's and Billmyer's mills, and at Spring Mills the DuVall mill, and on Back Creek, Snyder's mill.

Another industry of those times was that of tanning hides for leather. Numerous tan yards were located throughout the county where farmers sold their hides or had them tanned for their own use in making boots, shoes and harness. This was quite an extensive business for considerable leather was consumed in making harness for farm work as well as driving horses for carriages. The bark of the chestnut oak was used almost exclusively and the bloom of the "sumac" was cut and dried and used for tanning, but the coming of the automobile and the growing scarcity of timber practically put the tanning industry out of business, and today no more tanneries exist. Another industry of considerable magnitude was the distilling of whiskey. Several of these existed throughout the county; at Flagg's, east of Martinsburg, Bryarly's, and Sencinciver's at Darkesville. The most noted one was the Hannis Distilling Company at Martinsburg, the makers of the famous Hannisville whiskey. This distillery continued to operate until 1920, when it closed its doors to the passage of the 18th Amendment to the Federal Constitution. Its immense plant was sold to the Cumberland Valley Fruit Products Company, which operates a vinegar plant there.

About this time the saw-mill for sawing lumber was brought into use. These mills were situated at the flour mills and operated by water power. These first saws were of the "up-and-down" variety. The saw, a straight blade, was fastened in a vertical frame. To the lower end of the saw was attached an arm which operated on a circular wheel not unlike the drive shaft on an engine. The revolving of this wheel caused the saw to move with an up-and-down motion. This kind of saw did not cut half so fast as the circular saw of a later date, but was a great improvement over the old method of cutting down a tree and hewing both sides with a broad-axe until the proper thinness was attained to obtain a board. The saw-mill business began to decline as the timber became scarce until at present hardly any saw-mills remain in the county, and not much timber any more, for that matter.

Travel was by horseback and the stage coach before the event of the railroad to Martinsburg. Four stages arrived and departed a day. One to Hagerstown, one to Winchester, one to Shepherdstown, and one to Bath, or Warm Springs (now Berkeley Springs). People traveling by stage coach were often required to alight and pry the stage out of mud holes in the road, especially in the spring time when the roads were made soft by the winter rains.

A market house has always been in evidence in Martinsburg since its first founding in 1778. For a number of years it fronted the Public Square. As the town grew and more country produce was raised, it became evident that a new market place was needed.

Therefore, on Monday, Oct. 13, 1845, three commissioners were appointed by the Board of Supervisors of Berkeley County to "adopt the size and plan and contract for and superintend the building of said market house", namely: Richard McSherry, Daniel Burkhart, and Lewis B. Willis (the latter declining to serve). This commission of two selected the present site and purchased the grounds for $187.50. It was afterwards agreed that a second story should be erected over the first for the use of the Odd Fellows and Free Masons as lodge rooms. William L. Boak was appointed as commissioner on the part of the Society of Odd Fellows and Anthony S. Chambers on the part of the Society of Free Masons. The societies were to build the upper story at their own cost and to keep the building under permanent roof. These contracts were adhered to and the building was erected in 1846. The town clock was erected upon it in the year 1847. This clock was long since removed from the market house and it was no doubt a mistake when this was done, for probably no town is complete without its town clock.

An amusing incident occurred about the year 1900 in regard to this clock. Candidates for mayor of the town, the Republican and the Democratic candidates, were nominated and the election was on. One enterprising candidate, not having any platform in particular to run on, proposed that if he was elected he would paint the town clock (it was sadly in need of paint). His opponent, not to be outdone, promised the people that if *he* was elected he would paint the band-stand. The latter was elected, the band-stand was painted, and the old town clock never received her promised coat of paint.

On December 16, 1872, the market house was conveyed by deed from the County Court to the Corporation of Martinsburg, to be used as a market house and a police station. If in the event of the Corporation of Martinsburg devoting said property to any other use than that of a market house, it was to provide at its own expense and keep up a market house at some point within the corporate limits of said town.

About 1880, the markets had outgrown the limited space within the building, and the corporation granted the use of the pavement immediately in front of the market house on Queen Street, on the west side, and the north side of Burke Street, on the south of it for a market and had a metal awning placed over it to protect against the elements. This awning was removed in 1920. In 1921, the Mayor and Councilmen removed the market from the west side of Queen Street and placed it on both sides of Burke Street between Queen and Church Streets. Several attempts have been made by the different Mayors and Councilmen to erect a suitable market house somewhere within the confines of the city, but as yet nothing has been accomplished on that project.

At the time of the laying of the Atlantic cable in 1858, public expectation was on tip-toe as to the success or failure of the project, as being the first message sent and received between the old and the new worlds. Ostensibly came two messages to Martinsburg by telegraph of congratulatory messages exchanged by Queen Victoria of England and President Buchannan of the United States. Everyone was so much impressed with the importance of the occasion that the Judge adjourned Court and the Mayor had the bells rung and issued a congratulatory proclamation and a wonderful time was had over the event, until it was discovered that the whole thing was a huge joke and the cable had not been completed at all.

The following are the messages:

(By Telegraph from England)

The Queen's Message.

London, Eng., Aug. 12, 1858.

To Hon. James Buchannan. P. U. S.:—
Come let us talk together. American genius and English enterprise have this day joined together the old and the new worlds. Let us hope that they may be as closely allied in the bonds of peace, harmony and kindred feeling. Victoria.

The President's Reply.

Bedford Springs, Aug. 12, 1858.

To Queen Victoria, Queen of England:
New England accepts with gladness the hand of fellowship proffered by old England, and if ever discord or diversity of interest should threaten this alliance, let our language be, "entreat me not to leave thee or return from following thee, for the interest of thy people shall be the interests of my people," and "Thy God shall be my God."
James Buchanan,
President of the U. S.

The perpetrators of the hoax were George Murphy, a young lawyer, Dr. J. P. McGary, Ben Chenoweth, and Charles Ways, a telegraph operator here. Judge Hoge read the message to the Court, coupled with some appropriate remarks, and, although the Judge afterwards professed to be in the secret, there was a thorough suspicion that he was as badly fooled as the balance. Mayor Chambers was so much incensed over the joke that he threatened to put the perpetrators in jail.

During this interval of peace the greater number of the inhabitants of the county were farmers, or directly or indirectly connected with agriculture. And as the farmer of that period bought little and sold much, many of them became wealthy. Many of the leading families of that day acquired large farms with fine residences and ample farm buildings. In some cases one man would acquire several farms. A father's ambition was to leave each of his children a farm at his death. The farm was a busy workshop for the entire family. The father usually sowed and reaped by hand. Most of his other activities on the farm were performed by hand. He raised his own livestock and produced his own material for his clothing. He sowed his grain by broadcast and plowed and harrowed it in, reaped it by either the sickle or the cradle and threshed it by flail or tramped it out by horses. In fact, he spent no money except for tobacco, coffee, teas, sugar and the like.

The housewife made all the cloth for the clothing for the family, spun and wove it. The spinning-wheel and loom were a part of the equipment of every household. She moulded the candles for lighting the household from tallow from the farmer's own animals, made all the soap for the family washing, raised geese to produce the feathers for use on the beds, besides did the cooking upon the open fire for large families for each family consisted of quite a large number of boys and girls.

People usually married when quite young. The first acquaintances ripened into speedy marriages. Divorces were seldom, as the homemakers had no time to brood over their misunderstandings.

The bride always possessed her "hope chest" well stocked with linens of every description for the bed, table, and clothing. She was early taught by her mother to bake, cook, wash, iron, sew, and keep house in general.

The male population usually had a trade which they had been brought up to, and their learning of this trade was very efficient. These trades consisted of farmers, merchants (a few), millers, masons, blacksmiths, tinkers, tanners, weavers, wagonmakers, distillers, fullers, tailors, shoemakers, and millwrights. The millwright was a person who built and repaired mills for grinding wheat, flour, corn and other grains. In the early days of this period, all weaving was done by the housewife, but before the Civil War factories for this business were located in the New England cities, and much of the goods for clothing were made in them and could be procured from the merchants. The shoemaker was the principal itinerant tradesman and would make his rounds before winter came and make shoes and boots for the family; the farmer usually having procured the leather by having a few hides tanned at the tannery for this purpose.

Travel at this time was by horseback, stage coach, and later by railroad. Berkeley County produced some of the best cavalrymen in the Civil War because they were accustomed to horseback riding, a habit of long standing. The best appearing men on horseback were Captain William Colston and Colonel John E. Boyd, men of that day who were always chosen to head a parade in Martinsburg during the latter days of the '90's. Colonel John W. Dodd was another, he having learned to ride horseback in his earlier days on the farm.

Many families in that day had their carriages, usually drawn by a pair of fine, prancing steeds with driver in livery. For social features, general muster days, Fourth of July, picnics, barbecues, public speakings, outdoor dancing, barn raisings, husking bees, quilting parties, and weddings were indulged in by everybody.

Almost every large community had its military company and once a year all the companies would meet for drills and maneuvers. On this occasion a whole ox or several pigs would be roasted in a pit. The day was generally spent in drilling the companies in the morning, barbecue at noon, and outdoor dancing in the afternoon, always interspersed with public speaking. This last accomplishment mentioned has apparently died out, as it seems as if it is not as popular as it once was, for if we at the present day could find anyone who could make a speech in public it would be hard to find an audience to listen to him.

Weddings were the most enjoyable events. The ceremony was usually performed at the bride's home at "High Noon", as the announcement proclaimed, immediately after which all sat down to an elaborate dinner. The bride's cake was cut by the bride, and a piece was given each unmarried lady present to be taken home and placed beneath her pillow to "dream on" for three successive nights. The man she dreamed of during these three nights was the one she was destined to marry. The bride would toss her bridal bouquet to her bridesmaids and the one catching it was destined to become a bride within a twelvemonth. A thimble and a ring were baked in the bride's cake and the lady finding the thimble within her slice was destined to become an old maid and the one receiving the ring was to become a bride. In some instances after the table was cleared away dancing would be indulged in and sometimes kept up until the next morning. Camp meetings were in vogue,, at which the family would bring a tent or erect a cabin and live in it during the entire protracted services.

No expensive machinery was required for harvesting the grain; the "cradle" was universally used to cut it. This implement consisted of a scythe attached to a frame of "fingers" and would lay the grain in neat swaths which was raked up and bound into bundles or sheaths by hand. At the harvest plenty of whiskey was drank but without much intoxication. The whiskey was produced at the distiller's at 25 cents per quart or exchanged for rye from the farmer. Hay was mown by scythe and thrown into swaths and raked by hand. The threshing was done on the large floor of the immense barn either by the flail or by tramping it with horses. It was winnowed by hand on windy days or separated from the chaff by "windmills", if the farmer was so fortunate as to possess one. Cooking was done on the open fire, cook stoves not coming into use until after the Civil War. Frying was done in long-handled skillets or frying pans; baking and roasting were resorted to in the "Dutch Oven", which was a flat iron pot about twenty inches in diameter with a depth of eight inches surmounted by an iron lid. It usually had three legs. Live coals of fire were kept heaped under, around and over it until the baking or roasting was ended.

If several families lived in close proximity, a large oven was built out of doors at some convenient place and on "bake days" each family would bake enough bread to last it a week. These ovens were usually constructed of brick, the arched-over oven surmounting the fire box. Each family would take its turn in heating the oven for baking, the heating being done with dry wood kept for that purpose. Wood was the universal fuel in the town and in the country, coal not being known and if known was unpopular. Even wood was used to fire the engines of the Baltimore and Ohio Railroad, which had just been constructed through Martinsburg, and as this railroad is celebrating its one hundredth anniversary this year (1927) at Baltimore, it might be well to state that teamsters returning from hauling flour to Baltimore brought back the news of the wonderful railroad being built between

Progress of the County

Baltimore and Ellicott Mills, of the amazing speed the trains made of *thirteen miles per hour* over wooden tracks, the engine fired with cord wood.

The leading families of that day: At Arden, the Chenoweths, Pitzers, Millers, Walkers, Gladdens, Lyles, Campbells, Tablers, Throckmortons, Ramsburgs and Bradys; at Darkesville the Thomases, Myerses, Bryarlys, Sencindivers, MacDonalds, Henshaws and Tates; on Tuscarora Creek, the Thatchers, Smalls, Nolls, Seiberts, Christys, Emmerts, Cushwas, Walters', Tabbs, Porterfields, Groves, Burkharts and Mongs; on Williamsport Pike, the Smalls, Harrisons, Turners, Reynolds, Lemasters, Hedges, McClearys, Porterfields, Le Fevres, Lights, Morrisons, Tablers and Ungers; along North Mountain, the Robinsons, Seiberts, Hedges, Wilsons, Wevers, Chriswells, Myers' and Robbins; along the Opequon Creek, the Willis', Masons, Hollidas, Van Dorens, Rushes, Van Metres, McGruders and McQuilkins; in the northern section of the county, the Ropps, Williamsons, Robinsons, Colstons, Prices, Wilsons, Smalls, Harleys, Lamons, Lights, Sperows, Emersons, Basores and Frenches; on Back Creek, the Barneys, Granthams, Robinsons, Suckeys, Keys (now spelled Kees), McKeevers and Shippers; at Bunker Hill, the Hensons, Henshaws, Gardners, Morgans, Wards, Stewarts and Swimleys; in Martinsburg, the Bakers, Shaffers, Conrads, Faulkners, Boyds, Harrisons, Turners, Gardners, Snodgrass's, Seiberts, McSherrys.

Many people are now living in the county who are descendants of these families, and many of them holding positions of trust and in every line of endeavor. It was from these people that the majority of our citizens have sprung, the small minority of our population having migrated here, being attracted by our healthful climate, beautiful surroundings and golden opportunities.

The original County Infirmary was located on West Race Street, now the Heiston property. At first it was called the parish, later the poorhouse, and then later the County Infirmary. Its close proximity to the railroad caused it to be overrun by tramps and hoboes. The rule of the County Court was that they were given a good supper, a good bed, and a good breakfast and sent on their way. This nuisance, with the added cost of maintaining this establishment so near the town, induced the County Supervosrs to purchase the present farm on Tuscarora Creek. The inmates were moved there in 1849, at which place the institution has been maintained to the present time. The proceeds of this farm are used to maintain the inmates and any deficiency is made up by the County Court from the county levy of taxes. The first Superintendent was James Moon. The proceeds from the farm generally defray the expenses of the institution with possibly the exception of the Superintendent's salary.

CHAPTER XVI.

"THE FAULKNER REPORT."

Maryland had always contended that a part of the northern section of what is now the State of West Virginia belonged to her by grant of Charles I., King of England, to Lord Baltimore in June, 1632. The circumstance upon which she based her claims laid in the dispute over which was the Potomac River. This river was the dividing line between that State and the State of Virginia throughout its entire length. Maryland claimed that what is called the South Branch in what is now the State of West Virginia and was then a part of Virginia was the real Potomac, and that what Virginia claimed was the real Potomac was the North Branch of that river; that there was no South Branch. This claim was pushed with so much earnestness by Maryland that Governor John Floyd of Virginia, in 1830, appointed Charles James Faulkner of Martinsburg a commissioner to collect and embody the necessary testimony to establish the claims of Virginia. The report of Mr. Faulkner was so thorough and convincing and so full of historical data in regard to this section that it is deemed advisable to reprint it in full in this work. The report follows:

REPORT OF CHARLES JAMES FAULKNER RELATIVE TO THE BOUNDARY LINE BETWEEN VIRGINIA AND MARYLAND.

Martinsburg, Va., November 6th, 1832.

Sir:—In execution of a commission addressed to me by your Excellency, and made out in pursuance of a joint resolution of the General Assembly of this State, of the 20th of March last, I have directed my time and attention to the collection of such testimony as the lapse of time and nature of the inquiry have enabled me to procure touching "the settlement and adjustment of the western boundary of Maryland". The division line which now separates the two States on the west, and which has heretofore been considered as fixed by positive adjudication and long acquiescence commences at a point where the Fairfax Stone is planted, at the head spring of the Potomac River and runs thence due north to the Pennsylvania line. This is the boundary by which Virginia has held for nearly a century; it is the line by which she held in 1786, when the compact made by the Virginia and Maryland commissioners was solemnly ratified by the legislative authorities of the two States.

An effort is now made by the General Assembly of Maryland to enlarge her territory by the establishment of a different division line. We have not been informed which fork of the South Branch she will elect as the new boundary, but the proposed line is to run from one of the forks to the South Branch, thence due north to the Pennsylvania terminus. It is needless to say that the substitution of the latter, no matter at which fork it may commence, would cause an important diminution in the already diminished territorial area of this State. It would deprive us of large portions of the counties of Hampshire, Hardy, Pendleton, Randolph and Preston, amounting to almost half a million acres—a section of the commonwealth which from the quality of its soil, and the character of its population, might well excite the cupidity of a government resting her claims upon a less substantial basis than a stale and groundless pretention of more than a century's antiquity. Although my instructions have directed my attention more particularly to the collection and preservation of the evidence of such living witnesses "as might be able to testify to any facts or circumstances in relation to the settlement and adjustment of the western boundary", I have consumed but a very inconsiderable portion of my time in labor of that sort, for who indeed, now living, could testify to any "facts or circumstances" which occurred nearly a century since? And if such individuals were now living, why waste time in taking depositions of those "facts" in proof of which the most ample and authentic testimony was taken in 1736, as the basis of a royal adjudication? I have consequently deemed it of more importance to procure the original documents where possible, if not, authentic copies of such papers would serve to exhibit a connected view of the origin, progress and termination of that controversy with the crown, which resulted, after the most accurate and laborious surveys, in the ascertainment of those very "facts and circumstances" which are now sought to be made the subject of discussion and inquiry. In this pursuit I have succeeded far beyond what I had any ground for anticipation; and from the almost forgotten rubbish of past years I have been enabled to draw forth documents and papers whose interest may survive the occasion which redeemed them from destruction.

To enable your Excellency to form a just conception of weight and importance of the evidence herewith accompanying this report, I beg leave to submit it with a succinct statement of the question in issue between the governments of Virginia and Maryland, with some observations showing the relevancy of the evidence to the question presented.

The territory of Maryland granted by Charles I. to Lord Baltimore in June, 1632, was described in the grant as "that region bounded by a line drawn from Watkins' Point on Chesapeake Bay to the ocean on the east; thence to that part of the estuary of Delaware on the north which lieth under the fortieth degree, where New England is terminated, thence in a straight line by the degree aforesaid, to the meridian of the fountain of the Potomac; thence following its course by its farther bank to its confluence".*

It is plain that the western boundary of this grant was the meridian of the fountain of the Potomac, from the point where it cut the fortieth degree of north latitude to the fountain of the river; and that the extent of the grant depended upon the question, what stream was the Potomac? So that the question now in controversy grows immediately out of the grant. The territory granted to Lord Baltimore was undoubtedly within the chartered limits of Virginia. (See 1st charter of April, 1606, sec. 4, and the 2nd charter of May, 1609, sec. 6, 1st of Hen. Stat. at Large, pp. 58-88.) And Marshall says that the grant "was the first example of the dismemberment of a colony, and the creation of a new one within its limits, by the mere act of the crown", and that the planters of Virginia presented a petition against it, "which was heard before the Privy Council (of England), in July, 1633, when it was declared that Lord Baltimore should retain his patent, and the petitioners their remedy at law. To this remedy they never thought proper to resort."

Whether there be any record of this proceeding extant, I have never been able to learn. The Civil War in England broke out about ten years after, and perhaps the record of the proceedings of the Privy Council were destroyed. Subsequently to this, we are informed by Graham, the planters,

---

*Marshall's Life of Washington, Vol. I., Chap. II., pp. 78-81, first edition.

"fortified by the opinion of eminent lawyers whom they consulted, and who scrupled not to assume them, that the ancient patents of Virginia still remained in force, and that the grant of Maryland, as derogatory to them, was utterly void, they presented an application to the Parliament complaining of the unjust invasion which their privileges had undergone." (Graham's History, Vol. 2, p. 12.) But as the Parliaments of those days were but the obsequious ministers of the crown, that application, it is presumed shared the fate of their former petition to the Privy Council.

The present claim of Maryland, then, must be founded on the supposition that the stream which we call the Potomac was not; and that the stream now called South Branch of the Potomac was in fact the Potomac intended in the grant to Lord Baltimore. I have never been informed which fork of the South Branch she claims as the Potomac (for there is a north and a south fork of the South Branch), neither have I been able to learn what is the evidence, or kind of evidence, on which she relies to ascertain that the stream which is now called the South Branch of the Potomac, but at the date of the grant to Lord Baltimore was not known at all, and when known, was known for many years only as the Wappocomo was the Potomac intended by Lord Baltimore's Grant. For this important geographical fact, I refer to the numerous early maps of the chartered limits of Virginia, some of which are to be seen in the public libraries of Washington and Richmond.

The question which stream was the Potomac is simply a question which of them, if either, bore the name. The name is a matter of general reputation. If there be any thing which depends wholly upon general acceptation, which ought and must be settled by prescription, it is this question, which of these rivers was and is the Potomac? The accompanying papers, it is believed, will ascertain this fact to the satisfaction of every impartial inquirer.

In the twenty-first year of Charles II, a grant was made to Lord Hopton and others, of what is called the Northern Neck of Virginia, which was sold by the other patentees to Lord Culpepper, and confirmed to him by letters patent in the fourth year of James II. This grant carried with it nothing but the right of soil and the incident of ownership; for it was expressly subjected to the jurisdiction of the government of Virginia. The original charter from James II. to Lord Culpepper accompanies this report, marked No. 1. They are both recited in the colonial statute of 1736. The tract of country thereby granted, was "all that entire tract, territory and parcel, of land, lying and being in America, and bounded by and within the heads if the rivers Tappahannock alias Rappahannock; and Quiriough alias Potomac rivers, the course of said rivers as they are commonly called and known by the inhabitants, and description of their parts and Chesapeake Bay."

As early as 1729, in consequence of the eagerness with which lands were sought on the Potomac, and its tributary streams, and from the difficulties growing out of conflicting grants from Lord Fairfax and the crown, the boundaries of the Northern Neck proprietary became a subject which attracted deep and earnest attention. At this time the Potomac had been but little explored; and although the stream itself above its confluence with the Shenandoah was known as the Cohongoroota, or upper Potomac, it had never been made the subject of any very accurate surveys and examinations, nor had it yet been settled, by any competent authority, which of its several tributaries was entitled to be regarded as the main or principal branch of the river. It became important, therefore, to remove all further doubt on that question.

In June, 1729, the Lieutenant-Governor of Virginia addressed a communication to the Lords Commissioners of Trade and Plantation Affairs in which he solicits their attention to the ambiguity of the Lord Proprietor's Charter, growing out of the fact that there were several streams which might be claimed as the head springs of the Potomac, among which he enumerates the Shenandoah, and expresses his determination "to refuse the suspension of the granting of patents, until the case should be fairly stated and determined according to the genuine construction of the Proprietor's Charter."

This was followed by a petition to the King in council, agreed to by the House of Burgesses in Virginia, in June, 1730, in which it set forth, among other matters of complaint, "that the head springs of the Rappahannock and Potomac are not yet known to any of your Majesty's subjects; that much inconvenience had resulted to grantees therefrom, and praying the adoption of such measures as might lead to its escertainment to the satisfaction of all interested." Lord Fairfax, who by his marriage with the only daughter of Lord Culpepper, had now succeeded to the proprietorship of the Northern Neck, feeling it likewise due to his grantees to have the question relieved from all further difficulty, preferred his petition to the King in 1733, praying that his Majesty would be pleased to order a commission to issue, for running out, marking and ascertaining the bounds of his patent, according to the true intent and meaning of his charter. An order to this effect was accordingly directed by the King, and three commissioners were appointed on behalf of the crown, and the same number on behalf of Lord Fairfax. The duty which devolved upon them was to ascertain, by actual examination and survey, the true fountains of the Rappahannock and Potomac rivers. To enable them more perfectly to discharge the important trust confided to them, they were authorized to summon persons before them, to take depositions and affidavits, to search papers, and employ surveyors, chain-carriers, markers, and other necessary attendants. The commissioners convened in Fredericksburg, on the 26th of September, 1736, and proceeded to discharge their duties, by taking depositions, appointing surveyors, and making every needful and requisite preparation for the survey. They commenced their journey of observation and survey on the 12th day of October, 1736, and finished it on the 14th day of December, in the same year, on which day they discovered and marked what they reported to be the first fountain of the Potomac River. Separate reports were made by the commissioners, which reports, with all the accompanying documents, papers, surveys, plans, etc., were on the 21st day of December, 1738, referred to the council for plantation affairs. That board, after hearing counsel, made a report on the 6th day of April, 1745, in which they state "that having examined into the several reports, returns, plans, and other papers transmitted to them by the commissioners, appointed on behalf of the crown, as likewise of Lord Fairfax, and having been attended in council on behalf of your Majesty, as likewise Lord Fairfax, and having heard all they have to offer thereon, and the question being concerning that boundary which ought to be drawn from the first head spring of the river Rappohanock to the first head spring of the river Potomac, the committee do humbly agree to report to your Majesty as their opinion, that within the words and meanings of the letters patent, granted by King James II, bearing date of the 27th day of September, in the fourth year of his reign, the said boundary ought to begin at the first spring of the South Branch of the river Rappahanock, and that the said boundary be from thence drawn in a straight line northwest to the place in the Allegheny Mountains where that Part of the Potomac River, which is now called the Cohongoroota, first rises." The Cohongoroota is known to be the stream which the Maryland writers term the North Branch of the Potomac, but which is recognized in Virginia, and described on all the maps and surveys which I have ever yet seen, as the Potomac River, from its fountain where the Fairfax stone is located, to its confluence with the Shenandoah River, there being, properly speaking, no such stream as the North Branch of the Potomac River. This report of the council on the 11th of April, 1745, and fully conformed by him, and a further order made, directing the appointment of commissioners, to run and mark the dividing line agreeably to this decision thus made. Commissioners were accordingly appointed, who having provided themselves with surveyors, chain-carriers, markers, etc., commenced their journey on the 18th of September, 1746. On the 17th of October they planted the Fairfax stone at the spot which had been described and marked by the preceding commissioners as the true head of the Potomac River, and which has continued to be regarded as from that period to the present time, the southern point of the western boundary between Maryland and Virginia. A joint record of these proceedings was made by the commissioners to the King, accompanied with their field notes; which report was received and ordered to be filed away among the records of His Majesty's Privy Council.. Thus terminated, after a lapse of sixteen years, a proceeding, which had for its object, among other matters, the ascertainment of the first fountain of the Potomac River, and which resulted in the establishment of that "fact" by a tribunal of competent jurisdiction. This decision has now been acquiesced in for nearly a century, and all topographical description and sketches of the country have been made to conform with it. I say "acquiesced in", for it is impossible to regard the varying, fluctuating legislation of Maryland on the subject, at one session of her Assembly recognizing the line as now established (see compact of 1785, Session Acts of 1803, 1818, and others), at another authorizing the appointment of commissioners to adjust the boundary, as a grave resistance of its conclusiveness, or such a continual claim, as under the usages of international law, would bar an application of the principals of usucapation and prescription. (See Vattal, p. 251, Grotius, lib. 2, cap. 4. Wolfius, Jus. Nat. par. 3.)

Jurisdiction in all cases relating to boundaries between provinces, the dominion of proprietary government, is by the common law of England exclusively vested in the King and council. (I Ves. Sen. p. 447.) And notwithstanding it may be a question of boundary between the crown and a lord proprietor of a province (such as that between Lord Fairfax and the crown), the King is the only judge, and is presumed to act with entire impartiality and justice in reference to all parties concerned, as well as those who are parties to the proceeding before him, as others not parties who may yet be interested in the adjustment. (Vesey, ib.). Such is the theory and practice of the English Constitution; and although it may not accord precisely with our improved conceptions of judicial practice, it is nevertheless the law which must now govern and control the legal aspect of the territorial dispute between Virginia and Maryland.

It does not appear by the accompanying papers, that Charles, Lord Baltimore, the then proprietor of Maryland, deputed an agent to attend upon his part in the examination and survey of the Potomac River. It is possible that he conceived his interests sufficiently protected in the aspect which the controversy had then assumed between Lord Fairfax and the crown. Certain it is, that it nowhere appears that he ever considered himself aggrieved by the result of that adjustment. That his government was fully apprised of what was in progress, can scarcely admit of a rational doubt. For it is impossible to conceive that a controversy so deeply affecting not only the interests of Lord Baltimore, but all who were concerned in the purchase of land in that section of the country, and conducted with so much solemnity and notoriety, could have extended through a period of sixteen years without attracting the attention of the government of Maryland—a government ever jealous because ever doubtful of the original tenure by which her charter was held. But had Lord Baltimore even considered himself aggrieved by the result of that settlement, it is difficult now to conceive upon what ground he would have excepted to its justice, or question its validity. Could he have said that the information upon which the decision was founded was imperfect? Or that the proceedings of the commissioners were characterized by haste, favoritism, or fraud? This, the proceedings of that board, still preserved, would contradict. For never was there an examination conducted with more deliberation, prosecuted with more labor, or scrutinized with more jealous or anxious vigilance. Could he have shown that some other stream should have been fixed upon as the true head spring of the Potomac? This, it is believed, is impossible, for although it may be true that the South Branch is a longer stream, it nevertheless wants those more important characteristics which were then considered by the commissioners, and have been subsequently regarded by esteemed geographers as essential in distinguishing a tributary from the main branch of a river. (See Flint's geography, Vol. 2, p. 88.) Lastly, would he have questioned the authority of the crown to settle the boundaries of Lord Fairfax, without first having made him a party to the proceedings? I have before shown the futility of such an idea. Besides, this would at once have been to question the authority under which he held his own grant, for Baltimore held by virtue of an arbitrary act of the second Charles. His grant was manifestly made in violation of the chartered rights of Virginia, and carried into effect not only without the acquiesence, but against the solemn and repeated remonstrances of her government. Was Virginia consulted in the "dismemberment" of her territory? Was she made a party to that proceeding by which, "for the first time in colonial history, one new province was created within the chartered limits of another by the mere act of the Crown?" But the fact is, that Charles Lord Baltimore, who lived for six years after the adjustment of this question, never did protest the proprietary of the boundary as settled by the commissioners, but from all that remains of his views and proceedings, fully acquiesced in its accuracy and justice. (See the treaty with the Six Nations of Indians, at Lancaster, in June, 1774).

The first evidence of dissatisfaction with the boundary as established which the researches of the Maryland writers, have enabled them to exhibit, are certain instructions from Frederick, Lord Baltimore, (successor of Charles), to Governor Sharp, which were presented here by the latter to his council in August, 1735. I have not been able to procure a copy of those instructions, but a recent historian of Maryland, and an ingenious advocate of her present claim, referring to them, says: "His instructions were predicated upon the supposition that the survey might possibly have been with the knowledge and concurrence of his predecessor, and hence he denies the power of the latter to enter into any arrangement of the boundaries, which could extend beyond his life estate, or conclude those in remainder." (See McMahon's History of Maryland, p. 53.).

What were the precise limitations of those conveyances made by the proprietors of Maryland, and under which Frederick, Lord Baltimore denies the power of his predecessor to enter into any arrangement as to the boundaries, which could extend beyond his life estate, I am unable to say—my utmost researches have failed to furnish me with a copy of them—but they were so far satisfactory to his lordship's legal conceptions, as to induce him to resist even the execution of a decree pronounced by Lord Hardwicke in 1750, (I Ves. Sen., p. 444-46), upon a written compact as to boundaries, which had been executed by his predecessors and the Penns, in 1732. To enforce the submission to that decree, the Penns filed a bill of reviver in 1754, and after an ineffectual struggle, of six years, Lord Baltimore was compelled with a bad grace to submit, and abide by the arrangement as to the boundaries which had been made by his predecessor. To this circumstance, in all probability, was Lord Fairfax indebted for his exemption from all further demands, of the proprietor of Maryland. For Lord Frederick no ways averse to litigation, had by this time doubtless become satisfied that the power of his predecessor did extend beyond his life estate and might even conclude those in remainder. Be that as it may, however, certain it is that the records of Maryland are silent upon the subject of this pretension, from September,

1753, to ten years subsequent to the compact between Virginia and Maryland in 1785.

An opinion prevails among our most distinguished jurists, resting solely upon traditionary information, that about 1761, Frederick, Lord Baltimore, presented a petition to the King and council, praying a revision of the adjustment made in 1745, which petition was rejected or after a short time abandoned as hopeless. If there ever was such a proceeding, I can find nothing of it in the archives of Virginia.

Be that as it may, it is certain that ever since 1754 Lord Fairfax claimed and held, and the Commonwealth of Virginia constantly has claimed and held to the Cohongoroota, that is by the Northern Branch, as the Potomac, and whatever Lord Baltimore or his heirs, and the State of Maryland, may have claimed, she has held by the same boundary. There was no reason that Lord Fairfax, being in possession, should have controverted the claim of Lord Baltimore, or of Maryland. If Lord Baltimore, or Maryland, ever controverted the boundary, the question must, and either has been decided against them, or it must have been abandoned as hopeless. If they never controverted it, the omission to do so, can only be accounted for, upon the supposition that they knew it to be hopeless. If Maryland ever asserted this claim,—seriously asserted it, I mean,—it must have been before the Revolution, or at least during it when we all know she was jealous of the extended territory of Virginia. *The claim must have had its origin before the compact between the two states, of March, 1785*, (I. Rev. Code, ch. 18). We then held by the same boundary by which we now hold, we held to what we called and now call the Potomac; she then held to what we call the Potomac. Is it possible to doubt that this is the Potomac recognized by the compact? That compact is now forty-seven years old.

I have diligently inquired whether as the Potomac above the confluence with the Shenandoah was called the Cohongoroota, the stream now called the South Branch of the Potomac, ever had any peculiar name known to and established among the English settlers, for it is well known that it bore the Indian name of Wappocomo. I never could learn that it was known by any other name but that which it yet bears, the South Branch of the Potomac. Now that the very name itself evinces, that it was regarded as a tributary stream to another river, and that that river was the Potomac; and that the river of which the South Branch was the tributary, was regarded as the main stream.

But let us for a moment concede that the decision of the King in council was not absolutely conclusive of the present question; let us concede that the long acquiescence of Maryland in that adjustment has not precluded a further discussion of its merits; let us even suppose that the compact of 1785 is thrown out of view, with all the subsequent recognition boundary, by the legislative acts of that state and the question between the two streams now for the first time as an original one of preference, what are the facts upon which Maryland would rely to show that any other stream than the one bearing the name is entitled to be regarded as the main branch of the Potomac? It were idle to say that the South Branch is the Potomac, because the South Branch is no longer or even larger stream than the North Branch by which Virginia holds. According to that sort of reasoning, the Missouri, above its confluence with the Mississippi, is the Mississippi, being beyond comparison the longer and larger stream. The claim of the South Branch, then, would rest solely upon its great length. In opposition to this, it might be said that the Cohongoroota is more frequently navigable—that it has a larger volume of water—*that the valley of the South Branch is, in the grand scale of conformation, secondary to that of the Potomac*—that the South Branch has not the general direction of that river which it joins nearly at right angles—that the *valley* of the Potomac is wider than that of the South Branch, as is also the river broader than the other. And lastly, that the course of the river and the direction of the valley are the same above and below the junction of the South Branch. (See letters accompanying this report No. 26). These considerations have been deemed sufficient to establish the title of the "father ot waters", to the name which he has so long borne. (See History, and Geography of Western States, Vol. 2, Missouri.) And as they exist in equal extent so should they equally conform to pre-eminence which the Cohongoroota has now for nearly a century so proudly and peacefully enjoyed.

The claim of Maryland to the territory in question is by no means so reasonable as the claim of the great Frederick of Prussia to Silesia, which that prince asserted and maintained, but which he tells us himself he never would have thought of asserting if his father had not left him an overflowing treasury and a powerful army.

With this brief historical retrospect, I will now lay before your Excellency in chronological order, a list of the documents and papers referred to in my preceding observations.

No. 1 is the original grant from King James II. to Thomas, Lord Culpepper, made on the 27th day of September, in the fourth year of his reign.

No. 2. Copy of a letter from Major Gooch, Lieutenant-Governor of Virginia, to the Lord's Commissioners for Trade and Plantations, dated at Williamsburg, June 29th, 1729.

No. 3. Petition to the King in council, in relation to the Northern Neck grants and their boundaries, agreed to by the House of Burgesses, June 30, 1730.

No. 4. The petition of Thomas Lord Fairfax to His Majesty in council, preferred in 1733, setting forth his grants from the Crown, and that there had been diverse disputes between the Governor and the council in Virginia and the petitioner and his agent, Robert Carter, Esq, touching the boundaries of the petitioner's said tract of land, and praying that His Majesty would be pleased to order a commission to issue for running out, marking, and ascertaining the bounds of the petitioner's said tract of land.

No. 5. A copy of an order of His Majesty in his Privy Council, bearing date, 29th of November, 1733, directing William Gooch, Esq., Lieutenant-Governor of Virginia, to appoint three or more commissioners (not exceeding five), who in conjunction with a like number to be named and deputed by the said Lord Fairfax, are to survey and settle the marks and boundaries of the said districts of land agreeably to the terms of the patent under which the Lord Fairfax claims.

No. 6. Copy of the Commission of Lieutenant-Governor Gooch to William Byrd, of Westover; John Robinson, of Piscataway; and John Grymes, of Brandon; appointing them commissioners on behalf of His Majesty, with full power, authority, etc....

(I have not been able to meet with a copy of the commission of Lord Fairfax to his commissioners—they were William Beverly, William Fairfax, and Charles Carter. It appears by the accompanying report of their proceedings that "his lordship's commissioners delivered to the King's commissioners an attested copy of their commission," which having been found upon examination more restricted in authority than that of the commissioners of the crown, gave rise to some little difficulty which was subsequently adjusted.)

No. 7. Copy of the instructions on behalf of the Right Honorable Lord Fairfax to his commissioners.

No. 8. Minutes of the proceedings of the commissioners appointed on the part of His Majesty and the Right Honorable Lord Fairfax, from the first meeting at Fredericksburg, September 25th, 1736.

No. 9. Original correspondence between the commissioners during the years 1736 and 1737, in reference to the examination and the survey of the Potomac River.

No. 10. The original field notes of the survey of the Potomac River and the mouth of the Shenandoah to the head spring of said Potomac River by Mr. Benjamin Winslow.

No. 11. The original plat of the survey of the Potomac River.

No. 12. Original letter from John Savage, one of the surveyors, dated January 17, 1737, stating the grounds upon which the commissioners had decided in favor of the Cohongoroota over the Wappocomo, as the main branch of the Potomac. The former, he says, is both wider and deeper than the latter.

No. 13. Letter from Charles Carter, Esq., dated January 20, 1737, exhibiting the result of a comparative examination of the North and the South Branch of the Potomac. The North Branch at its mouth, he says, is twenty-three poles wide, the South Branch sixteen, &c.

No. 14. A printed map of the Northern Neck of Virginia, situated between the rivers Potomac and Rappohannock, drawn in the year 1737 by William Mayo, one of the King's surveyors, according to the actual survey in the preceding year.

No. 15. A printed map of the course of the rivers Rappohannock and Potomac, in Virginia, as surveyed according to order in 1736 and 1737, (supposed to be by Lord Fairfax's surveyors).

No. 16. A copy of the separate report of the commissioners appointed on the part of the crown, (I have met with no copy of the separate report of Lord Fairfax's commissioners).

No. 17. Copy of Lord Fairfax's observation upon and exceptions to the report of the commissioners of the crown.

No. 18. A copy of the report and opinion of the Right Honorable the Lords of the Committee of Council for Plantation Affairs, dated 6th April, 1745.

No. 19. The decision of his Majesty in council, made on the 11th of April, 1745, confirming the report of the Council for Plantation Affairs, and further ordering the Lieutenant-Governor of Virginia to nominate three or more persons (not exceeding five) who, in conjunction with a like number, to be named and deputed by Lord Fairfax, are to run and mark out the boundary and dividing line, according to his decision thus made.

No. 20. The original commissioners from Thomas Lord Fairfax to the Honorable William Fairfax, Charles Carter, and William Beverly, Esqs., dated 11th June, 1745.

(Colonel Joshua Fry, Colonel Lunsford Lomax, and Major Peter Hedgeman were appointed commissioners on the part of the crown.)

No. 21. Original agreement entered into by the commissioners preparatory to their examination of the Potomac River.

No. 22. The original journal of the journey of the commissioners, surveyors, &c., from the head springs of the Rappohannock to the head spring of the Potomac, in 1746. (This is a curious and valuable document, and gives the only authentic narrative now extant of the planting of the Fairfax Stone.)

No. 23. The joint report of the commissioners appointed as well on the part of the crown as of Lord Fairfax, in obedience to his Majesty's orders, on 11th of April, 1735.

No. 24. A manuscript map of the head spring of the Potomac River, executed by Colonel George Mercer, of the regiment commanded in 1756 by General Washington.

No. 25. A copy of the act by the General Assembly of Maryland, passed February 19th, 1819, authorizing the appointment of commissioners on the part of the state to meet such commissioners of as may be appointed for the same purpose by the Commonwealth of Virginia, to settle and adjust by mutual compact between the two governments, the western limits of that state and the Commonwealth of Virginia, *to commence at the most western shore of the North Branch of the Potomac River, and to run a due north course to the Pennsylvania line.*

No. 26. Letters from intelligent and well-informed individuals, residing in the country watered by the Potomac and its branches, addressed to the undersigned, stating important geographical facts, bearing upon the present controversy.

There are other papers in my possession, not referable to any particular head, yet growing out of and illustrating the controversy between Lord Fairfax and the crown; these are also herewith transmitted.

There are other documents again not at all connected with my present duties, which chance has thrown in my way, worthy of preservation in the archives of the State. Such, for example, as the original plan of the line between Virginia and North Carolina, which was run in the year 1728, in the spring and fall, from the sea to Peter's Creek, by the Hon. William Byrd, William Dandridge and Richard Fitzwilliams, Esqrs., commissioners, and Mr. Alex'r Irvine and Mr. William Mayo, surveyors—and from Peter's Creek to Steep Rock Creek, was continued in the fall of the year 1749, by Joshua Fry and Peter Jefferson." Such documents, should in accord with the views of your Excellency, might be deposited with "the Virginia Historical and Philosophical Society," an institution of recent origin, yet founded upon the most expanded views of public utility, and which is seeking by its patriotic appeals to individual liberality, to wrest from the ravages of time the fast perishing records and memorials of our early history and institutions.

With sentiments of regard, I am, very respectfully, your obedient servant,

CHARLES JAS. FAULKNER.

To John Floyd, Esq., Governor of Virginia.

CHAPTER XVII.

SLAVERY.

Slavery began in this country in 1619, when a Dutch trading vessel landed and sold twenty African negroes to the Virginia planters at James-Town. In the early days, slavery existed in all parts of the country, but at the North it was unprofitable; the few held there in bondage were mostly house servants and the like, while at the South, where large plantations existed, it was profitable and came to be regarded as a necessity and, of course, as an institution. The North had gradually discarded its slaves by the individual freeing of them and by State Legislative acts prohibiting the holding of them.

That portion of Virginia lying west of the Allegheny Mountains, and usually spoken of as Western Virginia, did not take readily to the institution of slavery for slavery flourished in agricultural sections; and that portion of the State, engaged in other activities, never held many slaves. Berkeley County, being in an agricultural section, was possessed of many slaves and continued to hold them until the close of the Civil War.

The question of slavery might have been settled in a more amicable way had the South been left alone to settle it themselves for Charles James Faulkner when elected to the Virginia Legislature in 1832 submitted to that Legislature, a proposition for the abolishing of slavery upon the *post nati* principle,—all children of slave parents, born after July 1, 1840, were to be born free—had it not been, as Mr. Faulkner said on one occasion, "but for this impertinent and illegal intermeddling of Northern fanatics, emancipation would have become the predominating sentiment in Virginia and would have worked out its results without ruin and bloodshed."

The opening of the year 1833 was the beginning of the abolition movement in the North and from that time on, all sentiment for the emancipation of slaves ceased and the South regarded this movement as an encroachment upon her rights as states and the question was not settled in any other way than by "bloodshed".

In the days of slavery, slaves were bought and sold as we buy and sell farm animals or any other property. The circumstances which worked the greatest hardships upon them were in cases where the slaveholder became insolvent. In these instances they were generally sold to satisfy the creditors, and in most all instances of this kind whole families were parted, some going to one part of the country whilst others were taken to another part. Sometimes the infant was torn from the mother's arms and sold, the slaves being auctioned off to the highest bidder from the auction block in the market place. This was the evil side of slavery and the sad part of it was that the Government upheld this practice by upholding the institution. Slaves were rarely sold by their masters other than on these occasions and then the master could hardly help himself. Usually the master would give his slaves their freedom if they had been faithful—and they usually were—either by process of law, or after his demise, by will. A small piece of ground with a cabin upon it went with their freedom papers and there the faithful old slaves could spend their declining years in peace and security. They were forever free.

At this late day we stand aghast at the thought of buying and selling a human being, of one man leaving so many human creatures to another by will or otherwise as was frequently done, by observing the records at the Court House of that time, of rending asunder the ties of home and kindred, of parting fathers, mothers and children, but public sentiment has changed mightily within the last seventy-five or one hundred years.

The first laws on record relating to slavery date to April 17, 1772, when a commission to the first court of Berkeley County was sent to it relating to the governing of the slaves in the county and is of interest.

"Virginia, sct: John, Earl of Dunmore, his majesty's lieutenant and governor general of the colony and dominion of Virginia, and vice admiral of the same:

"To Ralph Wormley, Jacob Hite, Van Swearingen, Thomas Rutherford, Adam Stephen, John Neville, Thomas Swearingen, Samuel Washington, James Nourse, William Little, Robert Stephen, John Briscoe, Hugh Lyle, James Strode, William Morgon, Robert Stogdon, James Seton, Robert Carter Willis, and Thomas Robinson, gentlemen of the County of Berkeley, greeting: Whereas, pursuant to an Act of Assembly, made at a General Assembly begun and holden at the capitol, in the city of Williamsburg in the fifth year of his Majesty's reign entitled an act for amending the act entitled an act directing the trial of slaves committing capital crimes and for the more effectual punishment of conspiracies and insurrections of them, and for the better government of Negroes, Mulattoes, and Indians bound or free, the governor or commander-in-chief of this colony for the time being, is desired and empowered to issue commissions of Oyer and Terminer, directed to the justices of each county, respectively, empowering them from time to time, to try, condemn and execute, or otherwise punish or acquit all slaves committing capital crimes within their county.

"Know ye therefore, that I, the said John, Earl of Dunmore, by virtue of the powers and authorities to me given by the said act, as commander-in-chief of this dominion, do assign and empower you the said (the above named parties) or any four or more of you whereof any of you the said (the above named parties) shall be come justices in such manner, and by such ways and methods, as in the said acts of the General Assembly, are directed, prescribed and set down to inquire of and to hear and determine, all treasons, petit treasons, or misprisons thereof, felonies, murders or other offenses, or capital crimes whatsoever, committed or perpetrated or committed within the said county, by any slave or slaves whatsoever for the better performance whereof, you, or any four of you, as aforesaid are hereby required and commanded to meet at the court house of the said county, when thereunto required by the sheriff of the said county, for the trial of any slave or slaves, committing any of the above offenses mentioned, and any such slave or slaves being found guilty, in such manner and upon such evidence as the said acts of the General Assembly do direct, to pass judgment as the law directs, for the like crimes, and on such judgments to ward, extention or otherwise to acquit, as of right ought to be done, or to carry into execution any judgment by you given on such trials.

"Given under my hand and the seal of the colony, at Wiliamsburg, the 17th day of April, 1772, in the twelfth year of the reign of our *Sovereign Lord, George the Third.*

"*Dunmore.*"

The Court in question carried out the above instructions to the letter, for we find from the docket of the date of the 20th day of November, 1776, the following:

"Proclamation.

"Phil, Sambo, Joe, Will, Jack, Sam, Anthony, Ede, Hannah, Peggy, Betty, and Peg, negroes, belonging to Matthew Whiting, being bound to appear at this court for stealing hogs the property of John Cranes, appeared according to their Master's recognizance; on hearing the same, it is the opinion of the Court that the said Jack, Joe, Phill and Will are guilty of the said offense and it is ordered that the sheriff give them thirty-nine lashes on their bare backs, at whipping post, well laid on and that the others are not guilty; ordered that they be discharged."

"Another:

"At a court held in Berkeley County the 4th day of November, 1792, for the examination of Nell, a Mulatto woman slave, on suspicion of feloniously stealing from Amos Davis one muslin sheet, one white linen sheet, one girl's slipp, one flannel petticoat, one large shawl, one white linen handkerchief, ruffled, and one black lace tippett.

"Present: John Cook, David Hunter, James Maxwell, John Kerney, and Nicholas Orrick, Gentlemen Justices, The Prisoner being held to the bar, and it being demanded of her whether she was guilty of the facts wherewith she stood charged, or not guilty, said she was in no wise thereof guilty, whereof sundry witnesses were examined on consideration of whose testimony and the circumstances attending the same, it is the opinion of the Court that she is guilty of petit larceny only. Therefore it is ordered that the Sheriff do take her to the public whipping post and there give her thirty-nine lashes on her bare back well laid on, and then discharge her."

From the above incidents it must not be inferred that the slaves were cruelly mistreated. These are narratives of crimes committed against the law and punishment inflicted. All offenders were similarly dealt with whether slave or free. The whipping post was used until a late period and the pillory until some time later. The pillory was built above the whipping post to a height of ten feet from the ground with a small platform at its base for the culprit to stand upon. It was built in the form of a cross, the crosspiece consisting of two boards, one above the other and hinged at the middle where they came together. Holes or grooves were cut for the hands and the head to be thrust through. When this was locked, it left exposed on the front of the boards the hands and the head. It was considered great sport by the boys and sometimes the men to pelt the culprit with handballs of mud, rotting eggs and sometimes stones. Above the cross-piece, above mentioned, was a board upon which the name and crime for which the prisoner was accused was written. The prisoner was usually sentenced to stand in the pillory from one to three hours, according to the gravity of the crime committed. One sentence of this kind was usually enough to make him behave himself in the future, whether it made him a better citizen or not. But I am digressing. As has been stated, the agitation of the slavery question began in 1832. Then followed the "Missouri Compromise," the Mexican War, the Annexation of Texas, Clay's Compromise of 1850, the Kansas-Nebraska Bill, the Dred Scott Decision, all hinging on slavery. In 1860 Abraham Lincoln was elected President by the Republican party on a platform which, while leaving to each State the right to control its own domestic affairs, insisted that the normal condition was for freedom in all the territory of the United States.

The Southern States declared that the election of a President pledged to oppose the extension of slavery would be a violation of their Constitutional rights. In 1860 South Carolina seceded from the Union and was followed by Georgia, Mississippi, Alabama, Florida, Louisiana, Texas, Virginia, Arkansas, Tennessee, and North Carolina. In April, 1861, the conflict between the North and South began and lasted for nearly four years or until 1865, in which the North was victorious.

The slaves of Berkeley County were not freed by the famous Emancipation Proclamation of President Lincoln's, this proclamation pertained to States and parts of States in rebellion against the United States' authority at that time, for the part of the proclamation pertaining to Berkeley County read as follows:

" - - - - - - And Virginia (except the forty-eight counties designated as West Virginia and also the counties of Berkeley, Accomac, Northhampton, Elizabeth City, York, Princess Ann, and Norfolk, including the cities of Norfolk and Portsmouth), which excepted parts are for the present left precisely as if this proclamation were not issued."

The Thirteenth Amendment to the Constitution abolishing slavery within the territory of the United States freed all slaves. The Fourteenth Amendment made him a citizen, while the Fifteenth Amendment made him a voter.

When the Civil War began and as it progressed, many slaves escaped from their masters and to the Union lines. This was the first time in history where *property* of its own free will came to the enemy's hand, and to meet this emergency General Butler of the Union Army declared them "Contraband of War" and set them to work digging ditches and building forts.

This came, in time, to be the solution to the problem of what to do with the slaves. It struck a mighty blow at the South for the slaves had remained at home raising food while their masters fought in the army. President Lincoln issued the Emancipation Proclamation on September 22nd, 1863, to become effective 100 days after or on January 1st, 1864. For this reason the 22nd of September is observed by the negro race and is known as Emancipation Day.

Within the sixty years of freedom the negro race has made wonderful progress in Berkeley County. Many of them have achieved success as doctors, teachers, lawyers, and ministers, while others have entered the trades and occupations. For instance, of the 1436 farms of the county at present twenty-nine of them are operated by colored farmers.

CHAPTER XVIII.
THE FAULKNER DINNER.

At a public dinner given in Martinsburg, Virginia, on December 16th, 1852, by the Democracy of Berkeley County to the Honorable Charles James Faulkner, then Representative from the Tenth Congressional District of Virginia, the following was the order of proceedings: At a meeting of the Democratic party of the county of Berkeley held in the town of Martinsburg, on Monday, the 8th day of November, 1852, it being the first day of the Court, Alexander Newcomer was called to the chair and John H. Likens appointed secretary.

Allen C. Hammond, Esq., rose and stated the object of the meeting. He said he had mingled freely with the members of the party from all sections of the county, and he said that it was their desire that some manifestation of the grateful feeling for the noble and gallant services which he had rendered in the election just passed. This was the election of Franklin Pierce for President and William R. King for Vice President. All seemed to concur that the most appropriate ceremonial would be a public dinner. He said that a letter had been written and sent to Mr. Faulkner and, although no answer had been received from him, he would guarantee his acceptance of the honor proposed to be tendered to him. He said the letter of invitation had been signed by several gentlemen from adjoining counties but upon reflection it had been deemed advisable to strike their names from it as the Democrats of Berkeley County desired this dinner to be given exclusively by themselves.

He concluded by submitting the following resolution:

Resolved:—That the Democrats of Berkeley County will as some acknowledgement of the valuable services rendered by the Hon. Chas. Jas. Faulkner in the recent Presidential contest tender to him a public dinner; which resolution was unanimously adopted.

The following committees were appointed by the chair:

Committee of Arrangements: E. G. Alburtis, Wm. W. Walker, Geo. H. McClure, Philip Showers, Wm. H. Mong, John H. Likens, John P. Walters, John Billmire, G. A. Hamil, M. Locke, and Joseph C. Rawlins.

Committee of Invitation: A. C. Hammond, John E. Norris, John B. A. Nadenbousch, Thos. S. Page, and Vance Ball.

Finance Committee: Thomas G. Flag, J. W. Mason, Geo. W. Hollida, Geo. Sperow, James L. Cunningham, A. W. Porterfield, Jacob Hull, Chas. Stuckey, Jr., John Speck, Joseph Stuckey, Robert K. Robinson, Peter Everhardt, Wm. Barney, Casper Stump, Joseph Hollis, Lewis Fry, Col. Jacob Sencindiver, David Stewart, John B. Hoge, Henderson Lucas, Robert Stewart, Jr., Barnett Cushwa, Jacob A. Small, and Andrew Bowman.

Committee of Correspondence: Thos. S. Page, Jacob B. Small, Jacob Hull, Barnett Cushwa, Nathan D. Payne, R. D. Seaman, Geo. H. McClure, Thos. S. Flagg, Franklin Thomas, James W. Gray, L. B. Willis, Philip Showers, D. D. Murphy, J. B. A. Nadenbousch, Ezekiel Showers, Jacob Seibert, S. Eichelberger, John Blair Hoge, Allen Hammond, Samuel Alburtis, Geo. Daugherty, Robert Stewart, Jr., Lewis Fry, Alex. Newcomer, John Sencindiver, Meveralle Locke, Henry J. Seibert, Casper Stump, H. A. Hamill, John Burns, Jr., R. K. Robinson, Thos. J. VanMatre, Luther VanMetre, Wm. T. Seibert.

Over one thousand people attended this dinner, showing the esteem in which Mr. Faulkner was held by the people of the county. Many of the descendants of the above named gentlemen of committees are now living in the county. Many notables from all over the country were also present (the list being too long to be enumerated here).

The dinner was served by Joseph C. Rawlins, proprietor of the Hotel Rawlins. The tables seated in comfort five hundred guests at one time. The Cecilian Band of Martinsburg under the direction of Captain Blondell furnished the music for the occasion. Never before or since has such a demonstration of admiration and esteem been tendered a son of Berkeley by her citizens, and it is fitting that this incident be recorded in the annals of the history of the county.

CHAPTER XIX.

THE CIVIL WAR.

As early as 1831 agitation of the question of state's rights, slavery, and the tariff began, and as time went on different doctrines and views of men were set forth, dividing like a wedge, the country into two distinct sections; the North and the South. Among these might be mentioned: Abolition, Compromise of 1850, Harriet Beecher Stowe's "Uncle Tom's Cabin", Kansas-Nebraska Bill, the Dred Scott Decision, and the Lincoln-Douglas debates.

In a work of this kind it is impractical to discuss these measures further than as they affected the affairs and people of the county. Berkeley County, situated in the slave-holding part of Virginia and retaining many slaves at this time, did not altogether hold to the State's doctrine but sent delegates to the Convention at Richmond, Feb. 4th, 1861, which passed an Ordinance of Secession, and in turn sent delegates to Wheeling, May 13th, 1861, to a convention to take steps in the formation of a new State. Sentiment was therefore divided between the North and the South. This division of sentiments often extended to families, as often brother was found arrayed against brother and father against son.

Often one brother served with distinction in the Union Army while another brother served with equal distinction in the Confederate Army. All these questions were freely discussed by the people of the county, in the press, the pulpit, the stump and at the cross-roads store.

On October 19th, 1859, "Old John Brown of Ossawatama," captured the U. S. Arsenal at Harper's Ferry and the news reached Martinsburg that the citizens of the town were being shot down in the streets. Pleas for aid were also sent for armed men to suppress the insurrection and to defend the town. Word was soon sent out that a train of cars would be ready at the Baltimore and Ohio Railroad station and volunteers responded armed with such weapons as they had at hand. Captain E. G. Alburtis, a soldier of the Mexican War, was selected as leader. Other subordinate officers were selected and the train moved for Harper's Ferry accompanied by a large body of unarmed citizens. On arriving they were advised to repair to the western end of the Arsenal but being too impetuous they attacked the engine house where Brown and his men were entrenched and several men were wounded by Brown's men. Among the list were George Murphy, Prosecuting Attorney for Berkeley County; J. M. Hammond, Deputy Sheriff; George Wallett, and George Richardson. Brown and his men were captured the next day by one hundred United States Marines under the leadership of Colonel Robert E. Lee and Lieutenant J. E. B. Stewart, who were dispatched from Washington. Both of these officers became Generals in the Confederate service, the former being commander-in-chief of the Southern Armies while the latter became the celebrated cavalry leader for the same.

The Civil War

John Brown was tried for murder and treason at Charles Town and together with six of his companions were executed at that place on March 16th, 1860.

After the wounded men were brought to Martinsburg, and especially after this insurrection, great excitement prevailed in this town. The people, especially the adherents to the cause of the South, considered this as an act of invasion by the North, although it has been proven that the Northerners had no connection with the attack as Brown acted independently and his act is now considered the result of a crazed mind.

The Presidential election of 1860 resulted in the selection of Abraham Lincoln for President, the first Republican candidate to fill that office. He was selected on a platform excluding slavery from new territory while not interfering with it where it already existed, and granted certain States' rights but opposed secession. The result was that South Carolina seceded from the Union early in December of that year.

Early in 1861 Virginia in convention assembled passed an Ordinance of Secession. Berkeley County was divided on this question and when steps were taken for the formation of a new State from western Virginia she cast her lot with the western section.

Early in 1861, the Arsenal at Harper's Ferry was destroyed by Government troops stationed there as guards. This was done by orders from the War Department to keep the arms and ammunition stored there from falling into the hands of the South.

Immediately upon the news of John Brown's raid upon the Arsenal at Harper's Ferry, several military companies were raised in Berkeley County. The first one was organized October 31st, 1859, by Captain J. Q. A. Nadenbousch, known as the "Berkeley Border Guards", and was sent to Charles Town to be placed on duty to guard the prison containing John Brown and his associates confined there. This precaution was taken by the Commonwealth of Virginia on account of the persistent rumors afloat that an organized body of Northern sympathizers were to attempt the liberation of Brown and his followers. This attempt, however, never materialized.

This company afterwards became Company "D" of the Second Virginia Regiment, and was a part of the "Stonewall Brigade" and was made up entirely of Berkeley County men.

The second company was organized in November, 1859, which was also present at the execution of John Brown at Charles Town. It afterward became Company "B" Wise Artillery and was named such in honor of Governor Henry A. Wise, Virginia's "War Governor". Its captain was E. G. Alburtis, an old Mexican War hero. He resigned early in 1861 and Captain James G. Brown took his place.

The third company of men organized at Hedgesville in the fall of 1859 under the leadership of Captain M. C. Nadenbousch, who resigned shortly after and was succeeded by Captain Raleigh T. Colston. In 1862 this company became a part of the Second Virginia Regiment and a member of the Stonewall Brigade.

Another company was organized by Captain John Blair Hoge. This was a company of cavalry and served under the famous cavalry leader, General J. E. B. Stewart, and was known as the "Company "B", 1st Regiment, Virginia Cavalry. All were from Berkeley County and first saw service at "The Affair at Falling Waters". It also participated in the Chambersburg raid under that leader. Another cavalry company under the command of Captain G. W. Myers of Baltimore, Md., was organized in October, 1861. It became known as Company "A", Seventeenth Batallion, Virginia Cavalry. It was composed of men from Berkeley and surrounding counties and saw much service in the Shenandoah and around Richmond. It was known as the "Wild Cat Company". All the above companies were volunteers and served through the war for the Confederate cause.

For the U. S. Army a company of volunteers was organized at Williamsport, Md., May 17th, 1861, under the leadership of Colonel Ward H. Lamon. This was known as the Company "B", First Regiment, Virginia Volunteers, Berkeley County. It saw service at Harper's Ferry and participated in all the battles in the Shenandoah Valley and before Richmond.

The other company composed of men from Berkeley County became a part of the Third Regiment, West Virginia Cavalry, and known as Company "C". This regiment was organized at Charles Town, West Virginia, in December, 1863, by consolidating a number of companies that had already seen much service. The commander of the company was Captain Peter Tabler. It was afterwards transferred to the Middle Military Division and saw much fighting in the Valley of Virginia.

The spring of 1861 saw the beginnings of hostilities in Berkeley County. The South, anticipating an invasion from the North and supposing that invasion would come by Harper's Ferry and also desirous of obtaining the cannon and small arms of the latest improved type stored there, had collected a force of 1,200 Virginians and 400 Kentuckians in that place.

General Joseph E. Johnston was placed in command there with Colonel T. J. Jackson second in command (afterward General Stonewall Jackson). The Union forces did not attack from that quarter and the Confederates, after capturing the Arsenal, found nothing but the machinery; the cannon and the small arms having been destroyed by the Union troops when they evacuated that place. This machinery, however, was shipped to the South and used by them in the war.

General Johnston, finding it impractical to hold Harper's Ferry and receiving news that an army under General Patterson was advancing upon him by way of Williamsport, Md., and that another army under General Geo. B. McClellan was advancing by way of Romney, after destroying the remainder of the Arsenal and the wooden railroad bridge at that place, withdrew his army by way of Smithfield to Darkesville in Berkeley County. He sent Colonel A. P. Hill (afterwards General A. P. Hill) to intercept General

McClellan, and Colonel T. J. Jackson to support Colonel J. E. B. Stewart's cavalry with instructions to "resist the advances of any small body but to retire under the cover of the cavalry if the enemy appeared in force." Jackson, with one regiment of his brigade numbering three hundred and eighty men and one piece of artillery, advanced to meet Patterson's army. On July 1st, 1861, General Patterson's army forded the Potomac at Williamsport and advanced into Virginia (Berkeley County). His object was to operate against General Johnston, thus preventing him from joining McDowell in the defense of Richmond.

The advance skirmishers of each force met at Falling Waters. At this place General J. E. B. Stewart gave his first command in the war: "Aim low, boys, and may God have mercy on their souls." General Jackson was sitting on his horse by the side of the Williamsport Pike under an oak tree in front of what is now Hon. D. P. Lemaster's residence, when a bullet from the enemy cut a twig from a branch just over his head. He remarked: "They have gotten our range. I suppose we had better retire."

One instance of the quick courage of Colonel Stewart should be mentioned here: While operating with his army on the flank of Jackson's infantry, he rode along to a thick piece of woods to reconnoitre the enemy's position. He found himself suddenly confronted by a force of Union infantry with nothing but a fence between them. Not hesitating a moment, he rode towards them and ordered some of the men to throw down the fence. They quickly complied, probably mistaking him for one of their own officers. Stewart ordered them all to surrender. The boldness of the attack so surprised the men that they all surrendered to a single man. Colonel Stewart marched them through the gap in the fence and into his own lines. His followers were as delighted as the captured soldiers were dismayed at finding themselves in the enemy's hands on account of one man's bravery.

These forty-nine men belonged the Fifteenth Pennsylvania Volunteers and it was almost an entire company organization.

This, the first small battle at the beginning of the war, was mentioned in the dispatches of both commanders as the "Affair of Falling Waters". Several Union troopers were killed and captured and one Confederate was killed and several captured.

Colonel Jackson retired to Martinsburg and destroyed all the available Baltimore and Ohio engines and cars found there to prevent them from being used by General Patterson, and set fire to the beautiful colonade bridge built by the company over Burke Street and retired to the South of Martinsburg.

The destruction of the railroad property was a sad mistake on Jackson's part.

When at a later date the Confederates captured Martinsburg, these engines were provided with broad iron tires and hauled over the pike to Winchester and there repaired and used by them. The mistake was made in not taking them by rail by Harper's Ferry to Winchester. The Baltimore and Ohio Railroad was the route by which armies and provisions were transported from the west to the armies at Washington, and Jackson knowing that Patterson had a much larger force at hand than his own took the quickest way to strike a blow at his adversary.

So great was the weight of these engines that in several instances the tires cut through the solid stone road and to the hub and great difficulty was encountered in getting them to firm road again. Harrison Trigg, a member of Company "E", Second Regimant, Virginia Infantry, and a native of Berkeley County, was a driver on this expedition. Sometimes thirty-two horses were required to draw one engine.

On July 15th, General Patterson moved his army to Bunker Hill and on the 17th moved to Smithfield. This was the first movement of the troops in Berkeley County in the Civil War drama. Company "B", First Regiment, Virginia Cavalry, took part under Colonel J. E. B. Stewart.

The battle of Manassas was fought July 21, 1861. This was the first great battle of the war, and there was sorrowing in many a home throughout the county that night, for almost all of the first companies formed were in that battle. The southland won that battle but throughout the northland as well the people were amazed for a time at the mighty contest before them.

One of the saddest events of that battle and one that was felt with more sorrow perhaps by the people of Berkeley County was the death of two brothers, Holmes and Tucker Conrad, together with their cousin, Captain Peyton R. Harrison. All three were killed about the same time. They were brought home to Martinsburg in a spring wagon covered with oak boughs and were buried together in one tomb. The former were the sons of Holmes Conrad, a brilliant lawyer of Martinsburg who had formerly made a speech at the Court House favoring adherence to the Union. His two sons had left home and joined the Confederate Army without the knowledge of their father and the first news of their whereabouts was the notice of their death. Captain P. R. Harrison was the father of our present citizen, Peyton R. Harrison, and was killed when he, the son, was but four years old.

John T. Fryatt was also killed in action and at about the same time as the Conrads and Peyton R. Harrison.

They all lie buried in the Norbourne Cemetery. Peyton R. Harrison was a lawyer of promising ability and was but twenty-six years old.

As the railroad bridges of the Baltimore and Ohio had been destroyed by fire at Harper's Ferry, Opequon and Martinsburg by the Confederates, and considerable distances of the track had been torn up, the Federal army still had use of the Chesapeake and Potomac Canal which was situated on the left bank or north bank of the Potomac River, and they could still move large bodies of troops quickly to and from Cumberland, Md., to the National Capitol and they could transport large quantities of coal from the Allegheny Mountains to the furnaces making military supplies at Baltimore and Washington. General Jackson resolved to destroy this mode of transportation. The waters of the Potomac were raised to a sufficient height to allow them to flow into the canal by a series of dams placed across the channel at frequent intervals. The most important of these was Dam No. 5, built with a curve of the river north of Martinsburg and situated in the northern section of the county.

Jackson, in order to accomplish the destruction of this dam, marched to Martinsburg on December 10th. He had with him a part of his militia, cavalry, and the Stonewall Brigade and succeeded in demolishing Dam No. 5, although protested by Federal troops. It was necessary to descend into the icy waters of the river and to work at night on account of the close proximity of the enemy. A wide chasm was made in the dam, thus allowing the waters to flow back into their original channel, and destroying the usefulness of the canal to the Federals. General Jackson returned to Winchester on the 25th of December, having lost one man on this expedition. This was his second visit to Martinsburg but no fighting took place in Berkeley County at this time.

The next visit by General Jackson to Martinsburg, or rather to Berkeley County, was close on the heels of Generals Banks in his disastrous retreat, through the valley over the Martinsburg and Winchester Turnpike, to Williamsport. On this occasion his troops drove the Federal forces across the river into Maryland.

In June, 1862, General Robert E. Lee concentrated his army at Frederick City, Md., for the first invasion of the North. There was a considerable Federal force stationed at Harper's Ferry which General Lee anticipated would evacuate that place on hearing of the close proximity of the enemy, but it did not. Knowing it would be unsafe for his army to have an enemy force on its rear, he gave orders to General Jackson to capture or destroy these forces. General Jackson with his brigade on September 10th left Frederick City and by a circuitous route by Williamsport, Md., reached the vicinity of Martinsburg September 11th and captured considerable engines and cars of the Baltimore and Ohio ailroad to the north of Martinsburg and tore up the track. The Union garrison at Martinsburg, on finding Jackson's army so near, retreated to Harper's Ferry, thus delaying its capture a few days, for on the 15th Jackson captured that town and 1100 men, seventy-three pieces of artillery, 13,000 stands of small arms, large stores and munitions of war.

After the battle of Antietam on the 9th of October, eighteen hundred cavalrymen rendesvouzed at Darkesville. Six hundred of the best mounted and most reliable of these men were selected by Gneral J. E. B. Stewart. That commander issued them an address in which coolness, decision, bravery, implicit obedience to orders, without question or cavil, were stressed and strict order and sobriety were admonished. He pointed out that only strict adherence to these qualities would insure the success of the enterprise upon which they were about to embark. The destination of the expedition was to be known only to General Stewart and his officers: Brigadier-General Wade Hampton, Colonel W. H. F. Lee, and Colonel William E. Jones. Major John Pelham had command of four guns, which accompanied the expedition.

He indicated that if any man felt as if he could not comply with the terms thus set down he could retire to the barracks at once. Not a man moved.

On the 10th of October the expedition left Darkesville. Many knew the sagacity and daring of their leader and all felt safe in following. Hampton took the lead. The company reached Hedgesville that evening and camped there for the night, while General Stewart selected the place of crossing the Potomac in the morning. The place selected was McCoy's Ferry near Little Georgetown.

Thus began a cavalry expedition which for its boldness and quickness of execution has no parallel in history and is known as the "Chambersburg Raid". Many of the company were Berkeley County men.

Strict orders were given and carried out that no private citizen of Maryland was to be molested, and everything taken from them was to be paid for in full, but when the Pennsylvania line was reached the expedition was to be considered in the "enemy's country" and the command dispersed into bands for forage.

Chambersburg was captured by Stewart and the return to Virginia was begun. The Potomac was strictly guarded. On this memorable march General Stewart by forced marches outwitted General McClellan and crossed the river a few miles west of the Capitol at Washington. Within a week's time he had traversed one hundred and sixty miles of the enemy's territory and had destroyed two hundred and fifty thousand dollars of property of the Federal army stored at Chambersburg, had paroled two hundred and eighty sick and wounded Confederate soldiers, had captured about thirty government officials and prominent citizens to be sent to Richmond to be held as hostages for citizens of the Confederacy imprisoned by the United States authorities, had captured twelve hundred horses, had lost one man killed and his servant Bob, together with his two valuable horses—Lady Margrave and Shylark.

His motto, which might be mentioned here and which was characteristic of the man, was: "Trust in Providence and keep your powder dry."

General Stewart never visited Berkeley County again. On March 1st, 1862, Federal forces took possession of the city of Martinsburg and the County of Berkeley. They found the Court House and the County Clerk's office empty and abandoned and they immediately occupied them with their soldiers together with all the other public buildings of the city and county and continued to occupy them until July 3rd, 1862. The buildings were used as barracks. On several occasions during the war the cavalry of both armies used the basement of the Catholic Church as a stable for their horses. Many of the church buildings were used as hospitals for the wounded.

Immediately preceding this invasion of March, 1862, the Clerk of the Circuit Court and the Clerk of the County Court removed all the records and papers of their respective offices to Winchester and later to Lexington, Virginia. The two clerks and their deputies went with them to see to their preservation and safe-keeping. It is a good thing for posterity that these records were removed, and that they kept them safe, for they might have been destroyed and would have been gone forever. As it was, some half dozen were lost. They were subsequently returned in 1865. Ephraim G. Alburtis was Clerk of the County Court and his deputy was Joseph Burns. The people of the county owe a debt of gratitude to these faithful officers who stood by their posts during these trying times.

As in the case of all wars, and especially in a civil war, the people of Berkeley County suffered terribly during the struggle, and the effects of it were felt for years afterward. Business was at a stand-still, the mills for making flour erected throughout the county were idle, and some of them were destroyed. The few shops and small factories in Martinsburg had long ceased to operate. The only railroad in the county, the Baltimore and Ohio, was in a manner destroyed. The bridges between Kearneysville and North Mountain on this line had been burned and the track from Martinsburg to nearly to the vicinity of North Mountain had been torn up. In one instance a rail had been heated in the middle and while hot had been wrapped around a tree several times and remained there as a memento of its dstruction for several years after its clase. Farms were neglected because the men had been in the army, the slaves had gone, and no one was there to work them. Many a home was fatherless and many a home had a vacant place in the family circle. Those adhering to the Southern cause were the worst off, as they had to face defeat and were still considered enemies by those who had adhered to the North. The Confederate money was worthless and those who had sold what few commodities they could spare from their own use and who had accepted Confederate money in lieu thereof were in a bad way indeed, for they had lost commodities and money too. To show how this money had depreciated toward the close of the war may be illustrated by the fact that a Confederate soldier in one instance gave $800.00 for a pair of boots. Before the war many slaves had been owned by the people of the county, and these, of course, were now free, hence, each slave represented so much loss to the Southern soldier in money and in production.

The Civil War marked the turning point in the history of this country. Slavery was abolished; suffrage was extended to every citizen without regard to "race, color or previous condition of servitude", and by that act every man was free and equal; classes were broken up and the masses reached a social plane on an equality with them; the country entered upon a new era of progress; old ideas were swept away and new ideas took their places, and by the introduction of new ideas into every thought and activity, this county has become an industrial county whereas prior to the war, the activities of the people were confined to agriculture alone; a new State—the State of West Virginia, of which Berkeley County is a part—has been carved out of the body politic of the old—Virginia. The North and South are no more, but a united people, working together for a common cause. This was fully demonstrated in the World War when Berkeley County gave of her sons—sons and grandsons of the Blue and the Grey—to fight shoulder to shoulder under the flag of a united country.

CHAPTER XX.

RECONSTRUCTION.

Berkeley County was not included in West Virginia at the time of its admission into the Union, but on January 31st, 1863, the Assembly of Virginia, under the Reorganized Government, passed an act providing for an election to be held in it to determine whether a majority of the people were in favor of becoming a part of the new State or not. The majority was in favor of admission and, according to the Act, the Governor of the Reorganized Government of Virginia certified the result to Governor Arthur I. Boreman, and on August 5th, 1863, the Legislature of West Virginia passed an act admitting Berkeley County into the State of West Virginia. On December 8th, 1865, the Virginia Assembly repealed the act of 1863 by which the county became a part of West Virginia. Then the authorities of Virginia appealed to the 39th Congress and on March 2nd, 1866, that body declared this county to be a part of West Virginia, the same as if it had been a part of it at the time of its formation. Virginia then brought suit against West Virginia in the Supreme Court of the United States for its recovery. The case was argued in 1866 but no decision was reached until December, 1870, when the case was heard for the second time, and a decision rendered in favor of West Virginia—three of the judges of the Court dissenting.

Berkeley County, during the period of the formation of West Virginia, was made, as it were, a political football for the authorities at Wheeling, at Richmond and at Washington. It was bandied about from one government to another during those years—three separate and distinct governments claiming jurisdiction over it, some at one time and some at another, until poor old Berkeley scarcely recognized where she was "at". The government of West Virginia at Wheeling claimed it, the Reorganized Government of Virginia at Annapolis claimed it and the Confederate government at Richmond claimed it, and the question of to what State it did really belong was not settled until 1870, as above stated.

In 1864, the Legislature of West Virginia, sitting at Wheeling, the Capitol, enacted a law dividing the counties into townships, as they were called at that time. The counties had never been divided into districts before, not even by the old State of Virginia, the Board of Supervisors, or to be more explicit, the Justices Court holding jurisdiction over the entire county. The people now demanded a closer self-government which led to the formation of the district government. The following is the Proclamation of the Governor in regard to the formation of the township or district:

"The State of West Virginia:
"Executive Department.
"Whereas, an act of the Legislature of this State, entitled, 'An Act admitting the County of Berkeley into and making the same a "part of this State".
"8th. The Governor shall appoint one person for each magisterial district of the said County of Berkeley, Commissioners, to divide the same into townships under the provisions of an act passed at the present session of the Legislature entitled: 'An Act to provide for the divisions into townships of the several counties of the State.'
"Now, therefore, I, Arthur I. Boreman, Governor the State of West Virginia, by virtue of authority invested by the said VIII section of the act herein vested, do hereby appoint as Commissioners for the purpose therein named, William Miller, Elias M. Pitzer, Archibald Myers, Thomas Wandling, John W. Lamon, John Voorhees, William Wilan, and Jacob Ropp."
"Given under my hand and the Seal of the State at the City of Wheeling, this the 7th day of October, 1864.
"ARTHUR I. BOREMAN."
"(Seal of the State.)"

This committee met and divided the county into townships and submitted their reports to the Board of Supervisors, dividing the county into seven townships, namely: Martinsburg, Mill Creek, Gerardstown, Hedgesville, Falling Waters, Arden and Opequon. This report was submitted on December 26, 1864. David Pultz was the surveyor employed by the Board of Supervisors, who surveyed the lines which have remained intact with the exception of Martinsburg District which was enlarged from time to time by subsequent charters, taking territories from Arden, Opequon and Hedgesville Districts. The following are the confines of Martinsburg as laid off at that time—Beginning at the County Bridge on the Baltimore and Ohio Railroad; theice N. $11°$ E. 122 Poles, to a stake on the west side of a hill; thence in $15\frac{1}{2}°$ W. 104 Poles, to a stake on a hill; thence in $48_1°$ W. 222 Poles, to stake in a flat about 3 rods N. E. of railroad; thence S. $36\frac{3}{4}°$ W. 245.3, to a sake at the west end of King Street; thence S. $9°$ E. 176 Poles, to a stake about 2 rods S. W. of Faulkner's stone house; thence $72°$ E. 224 Poles, to the County Bridge, the place of beginning.

At an election held on the 3rd day of February, 1865, (the first election hald in the county after it became a part of West Virginia), the following were elected: Arden Township—Supervisor, Benjamin F. Brady; Township Clerk, Collins W. Thornburg; Justice of the Peace, Elias M. Pitzer; Constable, James MacDonald; Overseer of the Poor, James S. Pitzer; Inspector of Elections, Hiram H. Bohda and A. B. Bain.

Opequon Township—Justice of the Peace, Samuel Taylor; Constable, W. H. Taylor; Township Clerk, John L. Oliver; Overseer of the Poor, Geo. Nipe; Inspector of Elections, H. P. Tabler.

Mill Creek Township—Supervisor, Hiram McKown; Clerk, James N. Cledenning; Justice of the Peace, Levi Henshaw; Constable, John H. Lamon; Supervisor of Elections, William Hollida and John Graham.

Hedgesville Township—Supervisor, David Canby; Justice of the Peace,

George Ferrel; Constable, John McDaniel; Clerk, John B. Secrist; Overseer of the Poor, J. T. Johnson; Inspector of Election, Geo. Chrisman and J. H. Griffith.

Gerardstown Township—Supervisor, Geo. D. Miller; Clerk, A. J. Bowers; Justice of the Peace, John E. Brady; Constable, Benjamin F. Busey; Overseer of the Poor, W. Shuart; Commissioner of Election, William S. Miller and James Gordon.

Martinsburg Township—(Election contested.)

Falling Waters Township—Supervisor, Henry Riner; Justice of the Peace, William Ripple; Clerk, Cyrus Kershner; Constable, John A. French; Treasurer, John H. Miller; Overseer of the Poor, William Cole; Inspector of Election, William Jack and Robert Lamon.

The Board of Supervisors for the County met and appointed Jacob Ropp Treasurer.

As the election in Martinsburg Township was contested and no Supervisor was elected, the Justices of the Peace and Constables met and appointed Stephen B. Meade to fill the position for that township. (This was according to the Acts of the Legislature governing such cases.) David Canby was elected President of the Board of Supervisors and Joseph T. Hoke was elected Clerk.

In this year the Board of Supervisors granted thirty licenses to hotels, billiard and bowling alleys; fifteen of these licenses were granted to hotels. All sold liquor, wines and beer. In 1864 the county levy on real and personal was 20c on the $100.00 valuation.

The salaries of the variouds officers were as follows: Prosecuting Attorney, $600 per annum; Recorder, $100; Sheriff, $200; Clerk, $200; Jailer, $60; Clerk of the Board of Supervisors, $600; Township Clerk, each township, $50.

The first voting places established in the county were as follows: Hedgesville Township, Hedgesville; Opequon Township, Greensburg; Arden Township, Stanley's House (Darkesville); Gerardstown Township, Gerardstown; Martinsburg Township, Court House; Falling Waters Township, Hainesville; Mill Creek Township, Bunker Hill.

According to an act of the Legislature, each soldier from Berkeley County serving in the Union army was to receive $300 bounty from the county. On December 20, 1865, bonds bearing 6% interest payable semi-annually were issued to these soldiers.

The first Assessor elected from the county under the State of West Virginia was Elias M. Pitzer.

In 1867 lamps on posts, the same burning tallow candles, were in use. The Board of Supervisors, in that year, ordered that two be placed in front of the Court House, one at the entrance on King Street, and the other at the entrance on Queen Street. The covering for these candles was made of tin in the form of a hexagon, punched full of holes. The candles were one foot in length. These were lighted by the lamp lighter at dark. These candles were supposed to burn long enough to allow all honest people to be in bed. If from some reason a pedestrian was delayed he would be compelled to wade through mud on account of candle being burned out. In the same year the Board of Supervisors passed an order allowing the Town Council of Martinsburg to use the east front room of the second story of the Court House for their council meetings, no council chamber then being available at the City Hall or Market House. This room was jointly used by the Board of Education of the Martinsburg Independent School District, this Board having recently been created by an act of the Legislature.

In 1866 the Schoppert (Choppers) ford road was constructed from Martinsburg as far as Smoketown. In the same year the Bloomery and Martinsburg grade (Tuscorora Pike) was made a toll road, and constructed across the mountain as far as Shanghai. The first directors for the latter were William Smith and A. Myers. In 1868, by an act of the Legislature, prisoners convicted of misdemeanors were sentenced to work on the county road, either convicted by the Mayor of Martinsburg or any Justice of the Peace, They were to be in charge of the jailer and none were to be allowed to escape. The law relative to these prisoners is as follows: "It is further ordered that no such convict shall be employed by either the authorities of the town or by the jailer without having attached to his foot or leg a ball and chain sufficiently large and long to prevent the escape of any such convict so employed."

As the Baltimore and Ohio was the only railroad entering Martinsburg, the leading citizens of the town being desirous of getting another railroad to enter it, petitioned the Board of Supervisors to hold an election to see if the people of the county would be willing that this board subscribe stock in the proposed railway.

On December 13, 1869, the Board of Supervisors ordered that an election be held on Saturday, January 15, 1870, (this election was not held until May 21, 1870), by the legal voters of the county "to determine whether the county of Berkeley shall subscribe the sum of $200,000.00 to the stock of the Martinsburg and Potomac Railroad Company, the said to connect with the Cumberland Valley Railroad at some point on the Potomac River, and through the county of Berkeley touching at Martinsburg, the election is to be held and the returns thereof to be made in accordance with the general election laws of the State."

One-half of this amount was to go to the construction of the railroad to Martinsburg, the other half to the construction of a railroad to the Frederick line. Bonds were to be issued by the Board of Supervisors bearing 8% interest payable annually, the bonds payable in 1890 or after ten years extension, if the County Court so desired. The bonds were secured by the capital stock of the company. "No portion of the bonds to be used for the construction of the road from Martinsburg to the Frederick line until the road was completed to Martinsburg, or until that section of the road is commenced, nor then, if sufficient amount of money is not subscribed from other bonds." The vote was taken and the result was: For subscription, 1600; against subscription, 248, majority, 1352 in favor of issuing the bonds. In this way Martinsburg had the advantage of another railroad in its confines. This road was completed in 1871. It was not finished to the Frederick line, as was first proposed, until 1888. For many years it was known as the Cumberland Valley Railroad Company, until 1913, when the stock of this company was purchased by the Pennsylvania Railroad Company. Charles James Faulkner was the leading person to secure this railroad for Martinsburg and Berkeley County. He was elected its first president.

In 1871 the people of Back Creek Valley petitioned the Board of Supervisors for a bridge to cross that stream on the lands of Frederick and Gotleip Fuss. This petition was signed by J. Harley Miller of Hedgesville and 223 others. A committee was appointed to inspect the proposition and report. This committee was composed of Bernard Doll, Levi Henshaw, James Parke, Josiah D. Flagg, John W. Lamon, A. J. Thomas, and Henry Riner. This committee reported August 8, 1870. The matter came up before the Board of Supervisors and was settled on April 10, 1871, when it was decided to build the bridge, and the work was begun.

CHAPTER XXI.

FROM THE ADOPTION OF THE NEW CONSTITUTION OF WEST VIRGINIA TO THE PRESENT.

In 1872, the new Constitution of the State of West Virginia was adopted. This wrought many changes in the government machinery of the State. That part affecting the county the most was: The term of office of the members of the House of Delegates was increased from one to two years; the members of the Senate was increased from two to four years, and a system of county commissioners was inaugurated, discarding the old Board of Supervisors and substituting County Commissioners with terms of six years, and reducing the number to three instead of seven (one member for each township). The name "district" was substituted for "township".

THE BALTIMORE AND OHIO RAILROAD STRIKES AT MARTINSBURG.

At this place in the history of the county, an unhappy incident must be related—that of the great railroad strike at Martinsburg in July, 1877. The trouble between the railroad and the workmen began about April, 1877. John W. Garrett became president of the company in 1856. He came to this position when the stock was low, dividends small, if any, and the road in poor condition. But, by reason of excellent executive ability, he carried the railroad through the Civil War, extended the lines, and brought the railroad up to a paying basis, never before known in its history. Then came the era of hard times and severe business depression—the year of 1876. In that year thousands of employees were thrown out of work. They tramped the country spreading propaganda against all employers. The employees of this railroad had been getting good wages, but at a meeting of the executive committee it was found that the railroad in order to operate would be compelled to cut wages ten per cent. By an official circular issued to the workmen, the 16th of July was set as the day on which a new schedule of wages would begin. It was stated in this circular that as soon as the business of the road justified it, the old wage would again be adopted; that the earnings of the road were such that this reduction was absolutely necessary. Other roads like the Pennsylvania, Erie, New York Central, had made the same reduction and it had been accepted by the employees. The firemen decided to strike. They contended that they would not work for a less figure than they were formerly receiving. The Brotherhood of Locomotive Engineers and the Trainman's Union agreed to join them. On July 16th, early in the morning, a number of train hands left Baltimore and came to Martinsburg, while those idle from the west began to pour into the town. This news soon spread and hundreds of citizens began to collect. The engines were detached from the trains and run into the roundhouse. The police force of Martinsburg put in an appearance and sauntered around waiting to see if their services would be needed. The employees had collected in groups. A train filled with cattle and produce stood idly by with no engine to move it. The Mayor, Captain A. P. Shutt, was sent for and he held a conference with the railroad officials. He appealed to the strikers to proceed as heretofore and return to their work, but his advice was derided and ridiculed. He then ordered his police to arrest the ring leaders but they were powerless against the mob.

Nothing transpired until the next morning, when Thomas E. Sharpe, General Master of Transportation, appeared from Baltimore. He hastily viewed the situation and telegraphed the general office. The Baltimore officials telegraphed Governor Matthews, who promptly wired Colonel Chas. J. Faulkner, at Martinsburg, who had the command of a local company of State Militia, to call his men out and man the engines to proceed with the train. Colonel Faulkner did so and endeavored to unite an engine with the train and proceed. The strikers had turned a switch, thereby preventing the train from coming out upon the main track. A soldier, John Poisal by name, jumped from the moving engine to turn the switch, when one of strikers, Vandergriff by name, fired twice at him with a revolver, one bullet grazing his temple, the other flying wild. Poisal raised his gun and, taking direct aim, fired on Vandergriff. Another soldier also fired at the same time at him, both balls entering his body, one in the arm and another in the thick of the thigh. Poisal soon recovered, but Vandergriff lingered for several days suffering great agony. Everything was done for him that could be done, but on July 28th, ten days after the shooting, he died and was buried in Greenhill Cemetery.

Colonel Faulkner observed that his militia, however brave and trustworthy, under these circumstances, would not fire upon their relatives and friends. He informed Captain Sharpe of the situation and informed him of his intention of marching his men back to the Armory, which he did and then ordered them home, and left the road blocked up with loaded cars and the train in possession of the angry strikers. Colonel Faulkner had given his men no orders to fire and it was not his fault that these men had been wounded. His intentions were to move the train on without trouble, but his handful of men could do nothing against an infuriated mob of hundreds of strikers. He telegraphed Governor Matthews of this fact and the Governor dispatched the Matthews Light Guard from Wheeling under the command of Colonel Delplain, which arrived at seven-thirty o'clock Wednesday morning, July 18th. No further demonstrations were attempted by the strikers. The strikers visited the railroad shops on the 18th and ordered the men at work there to stop. But they refused to do so, stating that they had no part in the affair. Finally the cars loaded with cattle were shipped over the Cumberland Valley and Western Maryland roads. Governor Matthews telegraphed President Rutherford B. Hayes and after explaining the situation asked for United States troops. Brevet Major General W. H. French, Colonel of the Fourth U. S. Artillery, arrived from Washington with two hundred men armed as infantry. The President also issued a warning for the strikers to disperse on or before 12 o'clock M. on July 18th, and if this order was not complied with the U. S. soldiers were to act. This order was signed by the President and F. A. Stewart, Acting Secretary of State, with the stamp of the great seal of the United States attached.

This settled the strike so far as Martinsburg was concerned. The agitation spread all over the B. & O. line, but nowhere did it reach such proportion as at this place.

On May 27, 1873, an ordinance was passed the Council of Martinsburg by which a Water Board was created. This Board was to be appointed by the Mayor, and to consist of fifteen members, five of whom were to be members of the City Council. A new water system was to be installed and this Board was to superintend the erection of it, watch the construction, and inspect the material used. The Board was to report monthly to the City Council. Thus began the first system of water works of the town of Martinsburg. The mains were constructed of iron, the best that could be procured at that time, but these in course of time began to rust and it was necessary to adopt another system. The City Council used the springs at the southeast of the city at first but in 1902 it purchased the Kilmer springs, northwest of the city, and a modern water works plant was erected on the northwestern limits of the city. Up to the installing of the first water system the people of the town depended on "dug" wells located on the streets at convenient points and the natural springs on the southeast section of the town. The last of these wells with its pump made from a single piece of wood, the center bored out with a large auger and its long iron handle, stood on John Street between Maple Avenue and College Street.

On December 31, 1872, Council passed an ordinance substituting coal oil lamps for the tin lamps in use at that time. Each ward had a lamplighter whose duty it was to fill, clean and light the lamps in his district. These lamps were to be lighted upon moonless nights and cloudy nights. He was to receive as salary, $22.00 per month.

Maple Avenue was formerly called German Street. Church Street received its name from the first church, the Lutheran, of the town being located thereon. College Street its name from the fact of the Martinsburg Academy being located upon the southern end of it. Spring Street was named for a spring of pure water being located near its southern terminal. Water Street from the Water Works being located near its southern end. Liberty Street was at first called Tobin Street. A petition of the citizens of that section asked Council to change the name to Liberty Street, which was done March 4, 1873.

Martinsburg might have been the capitol of West Virginia. The Legislature of West Virginia began its work at Wheeling, which was made the capitol June 20, 1863. It remained the capitol until April 1, 1870, when it was removed to Charleston. This city was the capitol until February 20, 1875, when Wheeling again became the capitol and remained so until

May 1, 1885, when it was again removed to Charleston. This removal of the capitol so often produced so much dissatisfaction among the people of the State that the Legislature passed an act in February, 1877, submitting the question to a vote of the people. The question to be voted upon was whether the capitol should be permanently located at Clarksburg, Martinsburg or Charleston. Charleston won and the capitol hes remained there ever since (1885).

When this capitol was destroyed by fire in 1921, the old contention sprang up and there was some sentiment throughout the State for another removal to a more central location (preferably Clarksburg), but the Legislature of that year appropriated $4,000,000, to be expended for a new capitol building at Charleston. The newspapers of the State at that time jokingly suggested that the capitol be erected on wheels to facilitate its easier removal.

Then came the fire which destroyed the State House at Charleston and many valuable records beyond replacement were destroyed. Since that time a magnificent capitol building is in course of erection which, when completed, will be a source of pride to the people of the State. Another disastrous fire occurred while the capitol building was in course of construction, to the temporary quarters in which some of the departments were housed, notably the roads and automobile departments.

The objection to Martinsburg being the location chosen for the capitol was that it was too far from the center of the State.

As Berkeley County did not become a part of West Virginia until August 5, 1863, no Senators or Delegates from this county were elected to the First and Second Legislatures. At the convention of the Third Legislature, 1865, Berkeley County was included in the 10th Senatorial District. Hon. B. M. Kitchen, of Shanghai, was one of the two Senators from this district chosen to that Legislature. In 1872, by the new constitution, Berkeley County was transferred to the 12th Senatorial District. In 1880, on account of the increase of population, it was transferred to the 13th District and by the census of 1900 to the 15th Senatorial District.

Charles James Faulkner, of Martinsburg, was appointed a member of the Board of Regents of the West Virginia University at Morgantown in 1874-75. He made the principal address at the laying of the corner stone of the New University Hall on June 18th, 1874.

In 1891, the Legislature of West Virginia created the State Board of Agriculture. It consisted of five members, one from the then five Congressional districts of the State. Governor A. B. Fleming appointed Cromwell R. Sperow, of Berkeley County, a member from this Second Congressional District, a member of the first Board. Alexander Clohan was also appointed a member of this Board by Governor George W. Atkinson. This law was repealed in 1909, and a new law enacted creating a Commissioner of Agriculture. Governor William E. Glasscock appointed Charles P. Light, of Berkeley County, Commissioner. He was the first and only one to fill this position, as the Legislature at the next session repealed this law and enacted the present law

After the Adoption of the New Constituton of West Virginia

creating the Commissioner of Agriculture. This was made an elective office. The first person to fill this position was Howard E. Williams; the present incumbent being John W. Smith.

The four hundredth anniversary of the discovery of America by Columbus was celebrated at Chicago by a great World's Fair. On March 4th, 1891, the Legislature of West Virginia passed an act providing for the appointment of a Board of World's Fair Managers of West Virginia. Governor A. B. Fleming appointed Hon. George M. Bowers from Berkeley County one of the five members of this Board. This was Mr. Bowers' first appointment to an office of national importance, and ably did he fill the position. This anniversary was celebrated by the schools of the county, especially at Gerardstown. Apple Pie Ridge School and Union C orner School attended the exercises there, in wagons drawn by Mr. Smith M. VanMeter's traction engine. At Gerardstown, Mr. Hunter Markle drew the schools of that town through the streets by his traction engine. The parade, led by the Gerrardstown Band—then an organization of some twenty-five musicians which has since disbanded—marched through the principal streets, circled the Square, and repaired to the school house house, where the concluding exercises were held, conducted by Dr. G. W. Daniels of that place. Mr. James W. B. Evans had charge of the parade and Mr. D. Gold Miller, the instructor of the Gerrardstown band, composed a selection of band music for this special occasion, named "The Gerrardstown March," which was widely known throughout the county as a composition of extreme merit.

In the early spring of 1891, the Martinsburg Mining, Manufacturing & Improvement Company was organized with the following officers and directors: President, George M. Bowers; 1st Vice President, Dr. N. D. Baker; 2nd Vice President, H. C. Berry; Treasurer, John B. Wilson; Secretary, Stuart W. Walker; Directors, Stephen B. Elkins, Robert P. Porter, Chas. J. Faulkner, Thomas M. King, E. Boyd Faulkner, Geo. M. Bowers, George W. Buxton, Theodore K. Miller, John B. Wilson, Dr. N. D. Baker, H. |C. Berry, James F. Thompson. This company added that magnificent extent of territory known as "Boomland" to Martinsburg, which was the beginning of "Greater Martinsburg". At a later date, such men as Arlington Roush, W. B. Snyder, D. W. Snyder, Jr., M. L. Dorn and H. P. Thorn aided in adding that beautiful section of West Martinsburg known as "Rosemont" to the city's corporate limits.

For many years the stone property on the southeast corner of King and Spring Streets, Martinsburg, had been used as the county jail. In 1891, the Martinsburg Mining, Manufacturing & Improvement Company proposed to grant one acre of land of their holdings south of Martinsburg and adjacent to it, free of charge, for the purpose of erecting a new jail house thereon, if the County Court would erect a new jail house thereon as soon as convenient. There had been dissatisfaction on account of the jail being situated too close to the residential section of the town. The County Court, composed of B. M. Kitchen, G. P. Riner and Henry J. Seiber, accepted the proposition and the old jail property was sold to the King's Daughters Circle who, when it was vacated and made available, began a hospital there known as the King's Daughters Hospital.

The VanDorn Iron Works of Cleveland, Ohio, contracted to erect and complete a jail for $18,000 within 90 days. It was completed September 15, and the committee of citizens appointed to accept or reject the building was composed of H. T. Cushwa, Chairman, George Couchman, G. W. Buxton, and John Farren. Later, as the improved county road machinery was bought, the southern side of the jail-house lot was used for the erection of buildings for storing this machinery.

The West Virginia Historical and Antiquarian Society was re-organized January 29, 1890. In 1926 the Legislature of West Virginia passed a law greatly aiding this society and requiring the Governor to appoint one person from each county in the State as members, whose duty was to compile the history of the county. Hon. Charles J. Faulkner was appointed by Governor Howard M. Gore to represent Berkeley County. Mr. Faulkner is also Vice President of the State Society. In the fall of 1926 the Berkeley County Historical Society was formed. Willis F. Evans was the first President.

CHAPTER XXII.
MILITARY HISTORY OF BERKELEY COUNTY.

I deem it expedient at this place in this work to give the military history of the county. I had thought when contemplating the task of writing a history of the county, that it might be possible to eliminate, to a certain extent, at least, a large portion of the bloodshed and carnage of the story to give more attention to the civil and less to the military, but find it impossible to do so because in searching past records for historical data, I find that in time of peace the activities of our people are not chronicled as they are in time of war. I find within the three hundred and twenty years since the first English settlement in America until the present time, if we include all the Indian wars, a little over fifty per cent of that time has been spent in wars. Since the founding of Berkeley County in 1772 I find that over sixteen per cent of the time has been spent in wars, and of all of those years five have been spent in the most destructive wars known to mankind. Thus, if a nation must have wars, these wars must of necessity form a part of its history. A great English author has said, "Peace hath her victories no less renowned than war." This statement is true, but "peace victories" are not recorded as are "war victories". Perhaps people are prone to forget their activities unless impressed upon them by some calamity or when laboring under a great adversity. Let us hope the time will come when the affairs of a nation can be written without a war record.

From the first home building in Berkeley County by Morgan Morgan (1726) to within a year of the outbreak of the French and Indian War (1753), comparative peace reigned within the borders of the county. By the treaty with the Indians at Lancaster, Pennsylvania, all the territory from the Blue Ridge to the Ohio was ceded to the English, and at the treaty of Fort Stanwix, New York, a portion of this same territory was again purchased from the Indians. But the French, in 1752, by bribery and intrigue, induced the Indians to join them in making war on the white settlers on the frontier of Virginia. General Edward Braddock was sent with a force to Virginia in 1755. The Colony of Virginia, also having claims to the Ohio River valley, raised an army which joined General Braddock and proceeded against Fort Dukuesne at the forks of the Ohio. In this expedition were over a thousand men under the command of Lieutenant-Colonel George Washington, many serving from the region now comprising Berkeley County. This expedition ended in defeat for the English and Virginians and, as a consequence, this region was laid open to savage attacks and savage horrors. In consequence of these attacks and depredations Virginia recruited several companies of men for military operations against them. Their duty was to erect and garrison forts and hold the Indians in check, for had it not been for this, operating as they did, no doubt the whole region would have been

132   HISTORY OF BERKELEY COUNTY

completely denuded of white settlers. As it was, many of them were carried away as captives or murdered and their homes destroyed. One of these companies was Captain Robert Rutherford's Company of Rangers in service in 1758-59 and mentioned here because many of the soldiers were from the region of what is now Berkeley County. The following is a roster of the company of the men serving in it from Berkeley County:

OFFICERS.

Robert Rutherford, Captain
Edward Luce, Sergeant
John Rouse, Sergeant

William Darke, Corporal
Jonathan Seaman, Corporal

PRIVATES.

John Dastforan
Joseph Hedges
Walter Shirley

Thomas Bright
James Shirley
Richard Bowen
Jacob Rush

Jervice Rush
Alexander Lamon
Robert Buckles, Jr.

After the close of the French and Indian War until 1774, the outbreak of "Lord Dunmore's War", there was a period of ten years of peace and quiet in our section. Many of the old settlers who had been driven away by the dreadful years of 1754-1763 now returned, rebuilt their homes and were accompanied by new settlers. The section of what is now Berkeley County proper was never again molested by the Indians, but they began their depredations in western Virginia and along the Ohio River. Consequently when the call for troops to defend this section of Virginia came, Berkeley County responded. Lord Dunmore proceeded to organize an army, dividing it into two divisions. The Southern Division was placed under the command of Colonel Andrew Lewis, while Lord Dunmore took command of the Northern Division in person. Colonel Andrew Lewis' division was composed of regiments collected from the lower Shenandoah Valley. They were to proceed to the Ohio River by the Kanawha River valley and Dunmore by Fort Pitt (Pittsburg).

As the movements of Lord Dunmore mostly concern us, his division being composed of Berkeley County men, we will give an account of him. He dispatched Major Angus McDonald with four hundred men from the lower Shenandoah Valley by way of Wheeling against the Wakatomika and other Indian towns in the Muskingum Valley, northwest of the Ohio, as a preliminary movement, but he accomplished little. Meanwhile Lord Dunmore crossed the Blue Ridge and made his headquarters at "Greenway Court", the ancestral home of Lord Thomas Fairfax. Here a thousand men were collected—five hundred from Frederick County under command of Colonel Crawford and five hundred from Berkeley County commanded by Colonel Adam Stephen. Lord Dunmore assumed command of this force and proceeded to Fort Pitt. Here he was joined by the "West Augusta Battalion"

MILITARY HISTORY OF BERKELEY COUNTY 133

commanded by Major John Connolly. At Wheeling another hundred men joined him, increasing his force to thirteen hundred men. Dunmore proceeded down the Ohio to the mouth of the Hockhocking River where he erected a fort. In the meantime, Colonel (now General) Andrew Lewis had met the united tribes of the Indians under their leader Cornstalk at Point Pleasant and had defeated them after a hard battle. Seven days after this battle General Lewis with a thousand men crossed the Ohio and proceeded against the Indian towns on the Scioto. Governor Dunmore, hearing of his movement, proceeded to join him at the same point, but when General Lewis had marched eighty miles through the wilderness the Indians had sued for peace, whereupon Lord Dunmore recalled General Lewis and he marched his army back to Point Pleasant, and Lord Dunmore returned by way of Wheeling and thence to the Shenandoah Valley.

Strange to say, no rolls or musters of any of the companies with Major Angus McDonald or with Lord Dunmore from Berkeley County can be found. No mention of the officers or men can be found excepting that five hundred men in this expedition served under Colonel Adam Stephen, already mentioned elsewhere.

In the beginning of the Revolution in 1775, there were two counties in existence in what is now West Virginia—Berkeley and Hampshire—and the "District of West Augusta". Troops for the Continental Army raised from Berkeley County saw service on nearly every battlefield of that war from Cambridge to Yorktown. In all the ten calls for troops and equipment issued from the Virginia House of Burgesses, Berkeley County sent her full quota of men and arms excepting the fiirst in 1775, when no troops were asked from the county, and in the fifth call, 1779, when no troops were asked for, as in these two years men were collected for service against the western Indians from the western section of Virginia.

In October, 1776, the Virginia Assembly passed an act preparatory to raising six battalions of infantry on Continental Establishment, and by this act, Berkeley County was required to send one captain, one first lieutenant, one second lieutenant and two ensigns. It was further required that each captain should bring into the field twenty-eight men, each first lieutenant twenty men, each second lieutenant sixteen men, each ensign ten men. This totaled eight-four men from the county.

The third roll calle for soldiers from Berkeley County came in October, 1777, when the Virginia Assembly provided for speedily recruiting the Virginia regiments on Continental Establishment. The county furnished fifty-two men under this call.

The acts of the Virginia Assembly, in October, 1778, under the fourth call for troops required Berkeley County to send to the field, before the first of May ensuing, every twenty-fifth man of their entire enrolled militia. Each of these who would enlist for eighteen months was to receive a bounty of three hundred dollars and to all who enlisted for three years, or during the war, the sum of four hundred dollars.

The sixth call for troops occurred in 1779, when another Act was passed providing for the organization of four regiments, two for the defense of the eastern coast and two for the western frontier. Berkeley County was required to furnish one twenty-fifth part of their enrolled militia.

The seventh call for troops in May, 1780, required Berkeley County to furnish every fifteenth man of its enrolled militia between the ages of eighteen and fifty years. If these were not supplied within thirty days by volunteers, then any deficit was to be made up by draft.

When the eighth call came for troops in October, 1780, Berkeley County was required to send sixty-eight men into the field. These recruits were to be supplied by volunteers from the county.

The ninth call, in May, 1781, required that the Governor should immediately appoint a district officer in each county to recruit by voluntary enlistment soldiers for the term of two years or during the war, each soldier not to be less than five feet four inches, not a deserter nor subject to fits, but of able body and sound mind and fit for immediate service. For all such men enlisted, the recruiting officer was to receive twenty shillings each. The tenth and last call for men by General Assembly came in May, 1782. This was for the purpose of recruiting three thousand men to complete the State's quota on the Continental Line in the army of the United States. Berkeley County was required to furnish every fifteenth militia man who should be not less than five feet four inches in height, of able body, sound mind, and between the ages of eighteen and fifty years, whose term of service should be three years or during the war.

At the October session of 1780, an act was passed requiring Berkeley County to furnish her share of the clothing for the Continental Army. Every suit should consist of "two shirts of linen or cotton, one pair of overalls, two pairs of stockings, one pair of shoes, one wool, fur or felt hat or leather cap". Berkeley County was required to furnish seventy-one of these suits. Each county was divided into as many militia districts as there were suits to be furnished. It was further provided that each one of these "districts should furnish one good beef, weighing at least three hundred nett". Thus Berkeley County furnished seventy-one head of cattle. The county was also required on or before the first day of March ensuing, "to furnish and provide one good and serviceable waggon with a good cover and a team of four good horses and complete harness with driver who shall serve as driver for one month at the expense of each county respectively."*

As Berkeley County included all the present county of Jefferson, at the time of the Revolution, and includes the history of the latter county until 1801, the following extract from Lewis' Third Biennial Report of The Department of Archives and History is recorded here:

Under date of February 5, 1850, the Register then published by Hardy & McAuly at Shepherdstown, Jefferson County, West Virginia, printed under the above caption:

Henning's Statutes at Large.

"SHEPHERDSTOWN MEN IN THE REVOLUTIOARY WAR."

A lengthy article, giving the names of officers and privates, who served in the Revolutionary Army from Shepherdstown and its vicinity in Jefferson County. Their names with rank and memoranda in the said article appearing as it did sixty years ago were as follows.

William Darke—Brigadier General.
Colonel, afterwards General, served throughout the Revolution, both North and South, commanded the Virginia Regiment at St. Clair's defeat in the Northwest Territory, Nov. 4th, 1791. Died at Duffield's Station, in 1801.

Joseph Swearingen—Colonel.
Entered the Army as a Lieutenant in the fall of 1775, and was in active service throughout the Revolution. Promoted to a Captaincy for gallantry at the Battle of Brandywine, and at the close of the War had risen to the rank of Colonel.

John Morrow—Colonel.
Entered the Army at an early age to fight in the cause of liberty; a noble specimen of a soldier; no other man left his country's services more honored than he.

Henry Beddinger—Major.
Joined the Army when quite a youth and distinguished in several brilliant engagements. He died near Shepherdstown at an advanced age.

Dr. Nicholas Shell—Surgeon.
A native of Germany, emigrated to America before the Revolution, served as surgeon for six years. Died at Shepherdstown in 1803, beloved by all who knew him.

Charles Morrow—Captain.
Was an officer of high standing; served three years in the Southern campaign, with credit to himself and honor to his country.

Thomas Morrow—Captain.
Served two years in the Army of the North; taken prisoner at the Battle of Long Island, and, though exchanged, died soon after because of ill-treatment on board a British prison ship. He was the youngest of the "Three Morrows".

Abraham Shepherd—Captain.
A brother of the founder of Shepherdstown and an officer of high repute in the Revolution. When difficulties were apprehended with France in 1798, he raised a company of Jefferson County men in which James Glenn and Raleigh Morgan were Lieutenants. He died in 1825 and was buried with military honors.

Michael Beddinger—Captain.
A brother of Major Henry Beddinger; was a gallant and accomplished officer. Removed to Kentucky at the close of the war.

Christian Orndorff—Captain.
Distinguished himself in the Battle of Bennington and Skeensborough. Died on his farm near Shepherdstown.

James Glenn—Captain.
Volunteered as a private in the War of the Revolution and rose to the rank of Captain; was at St. Clair's defeat where he carried from the field his friend, Lieutenant Raleigh Morgan, of Jefferson County, who was fatally wounded.

William Morgan—Captain.
Distinguished for his bravery among distinguished comrades.

John Boyer (Byers?)—Captain.
Served in the Pennsylvania Line and died in York County, that State; he was physically powerful and a brave soldier.

Thomas Turner—Captain.
A brave soldier of the Revolution. It was he who afterwards did the work for James Rumsey in his experiments in steam navigation.

Ludwig Myers—Captain.
Served in the Revolution as Captain of Infantry; he was a brave soldier.

Burkett Riger (Regar?)—Captain.
Served in the Revolution under Colonel (afterwards General) William Darke.

Cato Moore—Lieutenant.
Born on the eastern shore of Maryland; came to Shepherdstown at an early age. Enlisted in the Continental Army and was so severely wounded at the Battle of Brandywine that he was forced to resign his commission.

Lemuel Riger (Reger?)—Lieutenant.
Was a brother of Burkett Reger and, like him, served under Colonel William Darke.

Jacob Eaty—Drummer. No memoranda.

Jacob Wysong—Drummer. No memoranda.

——————— Medler—Drummer. No memoranda.

Fayette Wysong—Fifer. No memoranda.

William Lucas—Private.
Known to his companions in arms as one of the bravest of the brave. He was the father of Hon. Robert Lucas, who was the Governor of Ohio from 1812 to 1836.

John Kearsley—Private.
A brave soldier once possessed of a spirit and determination that rendered him "fit for the emergency".

Michael Cookus—Private.
Served throughout almost all of the Revolutionary period.

James Peacock—Private. No memoranda.

Philip Robb—Private.
In service throughout almost all of the Revolutionary period.

Peter Stanley—Private.
In service in nearly all the years of the war.

Martin Ernst—Private.
Was a Hessian who deserted the British Army at the Battle of Princeton and joined the American Army. Settled at Shepherdstown and was a Revolutionary pensioner to the end of his life.

Henry E. Beller—Private.
Upwards of fifty years of age when he entered the army but served to the end of the war. Died about 1784, near Beddington in Berkeley County.

John Eckhart—Private. No memoranda.

Jacob Likens—Private. No memoranda.

John Randall—Private. Spent nearly all of the years of the war in the army.

Henry Unseld—Private. No memoranda.

George Shaver—Private. Was in the army almost constantly during the war.

William Wilson—Private. No memoranda.

Thomas Crockett—Private. No memoranda.

Peter Fisher—Private.
A veteran of the Revolution. Died in 1844 while serving as toll collector on the Smithfield and Shepherdstown Turnpike and was buried with military honors.

John Darnheffer—Private.
A good soldier of the Revolution and a soldier in Captain Glenn's Berkeley County company at St. Clair's defeat.

George Reynolds—Private.
Served throughout the Revolutionary period.

John Neal—Private.
Was a brave Revolutionary soldier and was a member of Captain Glenn's Company at St. Clair's defeat.

Michael DeCrock—Private.
A Hessian: deserted to Americans at the Battle of Princeton and proved himself to be a true and brave soldier in the American Army.

Daniel Folk—Private.
Was with Arnold at Ticonderoga and with General Montgomery at St. Johns, Montreal and Quebec. He died near Shepherdstown in 1838.

Robert Hoffman—Private.
A native of Shepherdstown; was in the front ranks of the American Army at the Battle of Germantown.

James Kretzer—Private. No memoranda.

Thomas Thornburg—Private. No memoranda.

Joseph Turner—Private.
A soldier of great strength, often carried the muskets and knapsacks of a wearied soldier in addition to his own.

Christy Young—Private.
Served with Gates and Green in the Carolina campaign.

Burrock Butt—Private.
Served with Gates and Green in the Southern campaign.

George Ox—Private.
A Hessian; deserted from the force under Kniphausen and enlisted under the banner of Pulaski. Followed the business of butcher in Shepherdstown after the war.

John Haynes—Private. No memoranda.

Thomas Johnson—Private. No memoranda.

John Loar—Private. No memoranda.

Philip Loar—Private. No memoranda.

Anthony Kearney—Private.

Adam Antler, Sr.—Private. No memoranda.

Adam Antler, Jr.—Private. No memoranda.

Philip Antler—Private. No memoranda.

Jacob Fachler—Private. No memoranda.

John Pearce—Private.
Was a member of Captain David Morgan's Company. Was with Arnold at Quebec and was taken prisoner while fighting within the ramparts of that city. He taught school in Shepherdstown for more than thirty years after the Revolution.

John Angell—Private.
Served in the campaign of Generals Gates and Green in the Carolinas and was a member of Captain Glenn's Company at St. Clair's defeat.

John Miller—Private. No memoranda.

Adam Mohler—Private. No memoranda.

George Powell—Private.
Was with "Mad Anthony" Wayne at the storming of Stony Point.

Lewis Ronemous—Private.
Served as a member of the body guard of General Horatio Gates.

Conrad Ronemous—Private.
A member of the body guard of General Gates.

Andrew Ronemous—Private.
A member of the body guard of General Gates.

Daniel Bedinger—Private.
Joined the army when sixteen years of age; taken prisoner at White Plains and suffered great privations.

Conrad Byers—Private. No memoranda.

It has been frequently asserted that Shepherdstown furnished more officers and soldiers to the Revolutionary Army than any other town in Virginia, and, from an examination of records, it appears that this assertion is founded in truth.

When the Revolution broke out a company of men was organized from Berkeley County and from the part comprising Jefferson County. This company was known as "Company of Berkeley County Riflemen". Hugh Stephenson was elected Captain. The men were dressed in homespun shirts made of "linsey woolsey", a kind of coarse cloth, fringed around the neck and down the front, leather leggings and moccasins, with deerskin caps and a bucktail at the side. They carried their bullet pouch strapped over one shoulder and a powder horn over the other in conjunction with their long rifles with a tomahawk and scalping knife thrust in their belts. There were over a hundred men in this company, all volunteers. They held themselves in readiness, waiting for the order to march. The order came on the 14th of June, 1775, when the Continental Congress ordered that two companies of expert riflemen should be raised in Pennsylvania, two in Maryland and two in Virginia. This company collected at Morgan Springs, near Shepherdstown, on the 17th of June following. They partook of a frugal meal, listened to a short sermon in the Episcopal Church hard by (the church is now in ruins) and struck a "bee line" for Boston, six hundred miles away. Not a man was missing. They reached Cambridge after a twenty-four days' march. When General Washington knew of their approach, he galloped away to meet them, dismounted and shook the hand of every man in the company. He knew many of them personally, having met them in his Indian campaigns, in the French and Indian Wars and on his surveying trips for Lord Fairfax. When the fiftieth anniversary of their departure from Morgan Springs occurred on July 17th, 1825, but four were living, Major Henry Beddinger of Berkeley County, Michael George Beddinger of Blue Licks, Kentucky, Peter Lauck of Winchester, Virginia, and William Hulse of Wheeling (now West Virginia).

The men of this company were expert rifle shots with their long rifles. At target practice one day, the outline of a man's face was drawn upon a board with a piece of white crayon and the test was to see how many men of the company could hit the "nose". In this contest *all* hit the target and ninety-eight out of the one hundred and four men of the company placed a ball in the coveted nose. When Benjamin Franklin heard of the incident he commenced on the extraordinary test of marksmanship in his newspaper and concluded with the admonition: "Now, General Gage, look out for *your* nose." The test was taken from a hundred yard distance—quite a feat, considering the low shooting power of the rifles of those days.

These men had for their banner the device of the "Culpepper Minute

140   HISTORY OF BERKELEY COUNTY

Men"—a coiled rattlesnake, ready to strike, with the motto: "Don't tread on me," with the words "Liberty or Death"—Patrick Henry's undying words.

NEARLY A COMPLETE MUSTER ROLL OF CAPTAIN HUGH STEPHENSON'S COMPANY OF RIFLEMEN OF 1775-1776.

(From Lewis's Report and Danske Dandridge's "Historic Shepherdstown".)
Shepherdstown".)

OFFICERS.

Hugh Stephenson, Captain.
William Henshaw, First Lieutenant.
George Scott, Second Lieutenant.
Thomas Hite, Third Lieutenant.
Abraham Shepherd, Fourth Lieutenant.
William Pyle (or Pile), Ensign.
Samuel Finley, First Sergeant.
William Kelly, Second Sergeant.
Josiah Flagg, Third Sergeant.
Henry Bedinger, Fourth Sergeant.
John Crawford, First Corporal.
David Miller, Second Corporal.
Henry Barrett, Third Corporal.
G. M. Bedinger, Fourth Corporal.
Garret Tunison, Surgeon.

PRIVATES.

William Shepherd,
Thomas Hutcheson,
William Anderson,
Duncan McFitrich,
David Gray,
William Blair,
William Hunter,
Richard Butcher,
William Green,
Thos. S. Williams,
Arther McCord,
Jacob Fink,
John Stewart,
Adam Sheets,
David Smith,
Henry McCartney,
John Bodine,
Benjamin Ardinger,
Michael Engle,
William Waller,
John McDead,
Charles Conner,

Philip Waggoner,
William English,
William Logan,
James Hamilton,
William Tabb,

Robert Howard,
Conway Oldham,
James Wallace,
Robert McCann,
Nicholas Makin,
George Tabb,
Joseph Swearingen,
William Hulse,
James Neilson,
James Wright,
Edward Bennett,
Benjamin Prime,
William McCue,
Francis Hickman,
Joseph Carter,
Nat Pendleton,
James Yancey,
George Benner,
Ebenezer Allen,
George Tayor,
David Stedman,
Stephen Varden
   (drummer boy),
Jacob Winn,
James Higgins,
Battail Harrison,
John McGarah,
John Keys,

John Curry,
Peter Hill,
Peter Mange,
Peter Hanes,
Patrick Vaugham,
Peter Sever,
Christian Brady,
William Davis,
Robert Eakins,
Thomas Steer,
John Beverley,
Thomas Nelson,
Josiah Swearingen,
Adam Rider,
Thomas Knox,
John Millikin,
Charles Murray,
James Roberts,
Robert White,
John Smoote,
John Cole,
Aaron Tullis,

Michael Tullis,
Richard Neal,
William Hickman,
John Medcalf
   (or Metcalf).

THE VIRGINIA RIFLE REGIMENT.

Riflemen from the wilderness sections of Virginia, Maryland and Pennsylvania were always popular with the Commander-in-Chief of the Continental

Military History of Berkeley County

Army, so he prevailed upon Congress to provide for the enlistment of companies from these sections. In 1776, Captain Hugh Stephenson returned from Boston and together with Captain Moses Rawlings, organized the Virginia-Maryland Rifle Regiment, of which he became Colonel and Rawlings Lieutenant Colonel. It was composed of men from Berkeley and Hampshire Counties and of men from Western Maryland. It consisted of eight companies: the 1st, 2nd, 5th, 6th and 7th from Virginia. The officers of the Virginia companies were as follows:

FIRST COMPANY.
Abraham Shepherd, Captain.
Samuel Finley, 1st Lieutenant.
William Kelly, 2nd Lieutenant.
Henry Bedinger, 3rd Lieutenant.

SECOND COMPANY.
Philemon Griffith, Captain.
Thomas Hussy Lucket, Lieutenant.

FIFTH COMPANY.
Thomas West, Captaini
William George, 1st Lieutenant.
Thomas Warren, 2nd Lieutenant.
Edward Smith, 3rd Lieutenant.

SIXTH COMPANY.
Gabriel Long, Captain.
Nathaniel Pendleton, 1st Lieutenant.
Philip Slaughter, 2nd Lieutenant.
James Hanson, 3rd Lieutenant.

SEVENTH COMPANY.
William Brady, Captain.
William Pile, 1st Lieutenant.
Christopher Brady, 2nd Lieutenant.
Battle Harrison, 3rd Lieutenant.

A list of officers and privates of the Company of Captain Abraham Shepherd of the Virginia Rifle Regiment raised in Berkeley County and being the first Company organized by Colonel Hugh Stephenson and, after his death, commanded by Colonel Moses Rawlings in the Continental service from July 1, 1776, to October 1, 1778:

OFFICERS.

Abraham Shepherd, Captain.
Samuel Finley, Lieutenant.
William Kelley, Lieutenant.
Henry Bedinger, Lieutenant.
John Crawford, 1st Sergeant.
John Kerney, 2nd Sergeant.
Robert Howard, 3rd Sergeant.

Dennis Rush, 4th Sergeant.
John Jeaburn, 1st Corporal.
Everet Hogland, 2nd Corporal.
Thomas Knox, 3rd Corporal.
Jonathan Gibbons, 4th Corporal.
Stephen Vandine, Drummer,
Thomas Cook, Fifer.

PRIVATES.

William Anderson,
Jacob Wine,
Richard Neal,
Peter Hill,
William Waller,
Adam Shirtz,
James Hamilton,
George Taylor,

John Nixon,
Charles Jones,
George Brown,
William Seaman,
John Blake,
James Brown,
Patrick Connell,
Isaac Price,

Nicholas Russell,
James Fox,
John Holmes,
Samuel Brown,
Patrick Murphy,
Thomas Pollock,
Conrad Rush,
William Wilson,

From Lewis' Report—by Hon. Braxton D. Gibson.

Adam Rider,	James Griffith,	Thomas Beattey,
Patrick Vaughn,	James Roberts,	Zachariah Butt,
Peter Hanes,	William Hickman,	Samuel Davis,
John Malcher,	Thomas Mitchell,	Gabriel Stevens,
Peter Snyder,	James Aitkin,	William Donnally,
Daniel Bedinger,	Moses McComesky,	Samuel Barnet,
John Barger,	Valentine Fritz,	William Bogle,
Bryan Timmons,	Charles Collins,	Christian Penninger,
David Harmon,	John Cummins,	Casper Myre,
John Wilson,	John Lewis,	Anthony Larkin,
John Gray,	John Cassady,	John Boulden,
WilliamMoredock,	George Helm,	Benjamin Hughes,
Conrad Cabbage,	Anthony Blackhead,	WilliamHix,
Michael Wolf,	William Case,	Thomas Mountsfield,
David Gilmore,	Benjamin McKnight,	John McSwame,
Peter Good,	Charles Snowden,	James Aitkens.

    Captain Hugh Stephenson was made Colonel of this Regiment with Colonel Moses Rawlings Lieutenant Colonel. Upon the death of Colonel Stephenson, in August, 1776, the command evolved upon Colonel Rawlings with the rank of Colonel. Colonel Stephenson died of disease at "Roxbury Camp", New England.

    The Roster of the recruits raised by Captain Henry Bedinger of Berekeley County, under the Acts of the General Assembly in October, 1780, for the State's quota of troops to serve in the Continental Army are as follows:

William Cruse,	Alexander Denny,	Thomas Williams,
Samuel Earle,	Lewis Wills,	John Bazil,
William Bedinger,	William Jacobs	George Bougher,
Thomas Matthews,	Joseph Whipple,	Walter Hooper.

    Pension Laws passed by Congress relative to soldiers serving in the Revolution. Act approved March 18, 1818.

    The first pension laws relative to all soldiers serving in the Revolution was passed in the above year. Previous to this time pension laws were passed for the relief of only the disabled officers and soldiers. The law of 1818 provided that any commissioned officer, non-commissioned officer, musician and private soldier who served in the war or the Revolution to the end thereof or who served nine consecutive months or longer, at any period of the War on Continental Establishment and who by reason of his reduced circumstances, should receive a pension from the United States Government. He must show, however, that he had served in the War of the Revolution to the end thereof: for a time of nine consecutive months or longer, at some period of the War on Continental Establishment; must be a resident of the United States, and be in such destitute circumstances in life as to need the aid of a pension.

    The above Roster from the original roll, loaned W. Va. Dept. Arc. & Hist. by Colonel Henry B. Davenport.

    Lewis' Report and by Hon. Braxton D. Gibson.

Act of May 1, 1820.

This act provided that no person should receive any further benefit under the law of 1818 unless he enter some court and make a schedule subscribed by him containing his whole estate and income. Many worthy men refused to comply with this law while others not so worthy complied, and the Secretary of War of that period called the attention of Congress to this discrimination, hence Congress in 1823, passed another pension law.

Act of March 1, 1823.

This act authorized the Secretary of War to restore to the list of pensioners the name of any person who may have been stricken therefrom if such person should furnish evidence that he was in need of assistance from the Government, or had not disposed of his property or any part thereof in order to obtain a pension. This was a more liberal act toward the deserving soldiers and many were restored to the list by its enactment.

Act Approved May 15, 1828.

This act was provided without regard to any "property qualification and being provided on the half-pay acts of the Contiental Congress and the Gratuity Act of May 15, 1778, no one could claim its pensions unless he was adjudged to be entitled to "commutation" per act of March 22, 1783, or to the gratuity of eighty dollars per act of May 15, 1778.

Act Approved June 4, 1832.

By this act any person who had served at one or more terms, a period of two years during the War of the Revolution and who were not entitled to any benefit under the Acts of May 15, 1828, should receive a pension in proportion to the length of term served, provided that no pension be paid to any person serving for less than six month. As the fiercest battles were fought at the end of the war, this debarred many who were entitled to a pension.

Act Approved July 4, 1836.

This act provided for the widows of the soldiers who had served in the Revolutionary War, provided the marriage took place before the expiration of the last period of his service.

Act of July 7, 1836.

This act provided "That if any person who served in the War of the Revolution in the manner specified in the act passed June 7, 1832, have died, leaving a widow, whose marriage took place after the expiration of the last period of his service, and before January 1, 1796, such widow shall be entitled to receive for and during the term of five years from the term of the 4th day of March, 1836, the annuity or pension which might have been allowed to her husband by virtue of the said act if living at the time it was passed; Provided: That in the event of the event of marriage of such widow, said annuity or pension shall be discontinued. All widows whose husbands served in the Revolutionary War, as stated in the act, and who were married after the last term of his service, and prior to January 1st, 1794, can claim pensions under this act, provided that they were widows at the passage thereof."*

Other pension acts were passed in 1843, 1844 and 1848, but were of minor importance.

Pensioners affected by these acts were as follows:

Placed on the Pension Roll by Act of March 18, 1818 (Berkeley County):

Jacob Anderson,	John Hixon,	John Kibler,
Thomas Russell,	David Spong,	Barrach Butt,
James Husband,	John Lessley,	William Somerville,
William Scott,	William Goodman,	Robert Johnson,
Peter Marlatt,	William Smith,	James Wilson.

Those receiving pensions prior to 1818 (Berkeley County):
David Blew,
Andrew McEver,
John Bayan,
James Campbell.

Those receiving pensions under Act of June 7th, 1832 (Berkeley County):

George Everhart,	John Stevens,	James Foster,
John Shober,	Alias Shover,	Erasmus Gantt,
Paul Taylor,	Isaac Krolson,	Charles Young.

Act of May 15, 1828:
Captain Henry Bedinger.

List of pensioners living in Berkeley County, 1840:
Charles Young. Age 84.
Catherine McKeven (idow). Age 84.
Erasmus Gantt. Age 81.
Paul Taylor. Age 90.
Basil Lucas. Age 83.
Henry Bedinger. Age 86.
Susan Shober (widow). Age 70.

Names of Berkeley County soldiers in the Revolution who received lands from Virginia, for services in the war, with amount of land and date of service.

Henry Bedinger, 5330⅓ acres. Served from Summer, 1775, to November, 1783.
Daniel Bedinger, 2666⅔ acres. Served three years.
William Darke, 8661 acres. Served February, 1776, to December, 1782.
Horatio Gates, 17,500 acres. Served May, 1776, to June, 1783.
Battle Harrison, 2666⅔ acres. Served for the war.
Abraham Shepherd, 4000 acres. Served three years.
Joseph Swearingen, 4000 acres. Served three years.
Joseph VanMetre, 2666⅔ acres. Served three years.
Andrew Wagoner, 1185 acres. Served sixteen months.

Henning's Statute at Large.

These "lands" were situated in the Ohio Valley in what is now the States of Ohio and Indiana. This territory, known as the North West Territory, had been won from the British by General George Rogers Clark.

In the year 1850, but two pensioners made application for pension, namely:

John Shimp, age 81.
Peter Shaffer, age 86.

THE INDIAN WARS AFTER THE REVOLUTION.

The surrender of Cornwallis at Yorktown did not guarantee peace on the border. The Indians continued to harass the settlements. The British continued to hold forts of importance in the "North West Territory"—that vast territory lying north of the Ohio River, extending from the Great Lakes to the Mississippi and claimed by Virginia. They were driven out of this territory by General George Rogers Clark. The Indians were victorious in all battles with the Virginians up to August 20, 1794, when General Anthony Wayne ("The Chief who never sleeps," so named by the Indians on account of his sagacity) defeated them with great slaughter, and compelled them to sue for peace. Prior to this event, General Arthur St. Clair was sent against them and on November 3, 1791, on the St. Mary's River, one of the bloodiest battles of the North-West was fought. St. Clair's army was rounted and had it not been for General William Darke, a soldier from Berkeley County, covering this retreat, the whole army would undoubtedly have been annihilated. At this battle 80 Berkeley County men were killed. To raise an army to drive the Indians out of this territory, likewise the British, the Virginia Assembly passed, at the October (1784) Session, the following law: "All free male persons (other than those excepted), between the ages of eighteen and fifty years, should be enrolled and formed into companies of three sergeants, three corporals, a drummer, a fifer and not less than forty nor more than sixty-five rank and file, and these companies into regiments of not more than one thousand nor fewer than five hundred men, if there be so many in the county.* Each company was to be commanded by a captain, lieutenant and ensign, and each regiment by a colonel, lieutenant-colonel and a major, and the whole by a county lieutenant. In all counties west of the Blue Ridge (Berkeley) the men were to be armed with rifles.

The regiments in Western Virginia counties were all in the Tenth and Thirteenth Brigades and in the Fourth Division. The military organization of Berkeley County was:

Berkeley County—Fifty-fifth and Sixty-seventh Regiments (completely organized); Sixteenth Brigade and Third Division; 2126 free white males of sixteen years and upwards. (*Henning's Statute at Large, Vol. III.*)

Colonel William Darke, of Berkeley County, was the hero of these Indian wars. He commanded the Second Virginia Regiment in the army of General

---

Henning's Statute at Large.

Arthur St. Clair. He commanded an expedition to Fort Pitt (Pittsburg), descended the Ohio to Fort Washington (Cincinnati), where an army was collecting for an invasion of the "North West Territory" under General St. Clair. On November 3, 1791, this army encamped on the St. Mary's River near the present boundary of the States of Indiana and Ohio. It was attacked the next morning at daybreak by a much larger force of Indians under the leadership of their chief, Little Turtle. The result of this battle is known as St. Clair's Defeat, and had it not been for Colonel Darke and his brave Virginians, or what was left of them, covering the retreat of the main army, it would have terminated into a massacre. Colonel Darke escaped with a slight flesh wound, although his clothes were pierced in many places by the bullets of the enemy. His youngest son, Captain Joseph Darke, was killed while leading a charge ordered by his father. General Darke always carried a broad sword larger than any other man, and as he was a man of gigantic proportions, the sword rightly fitted him. On this retreat, he happening to spy an Indian in the act of scalping a dead soldier, rushed to the spot and with one blow cleft the Indian's head into two halves as completely as if it had been sawed in two.

THE "WHISKEY REBELLION".

The next military movement in which Berkeley County participated was the "Whiskey Rebellion", as it was called, in Western Pennsylvania in 1794, also mentioned elsewhere in this book. After the National Government, and the State of Pennsylvania as well, had sent commissioners to Pittsburg to try to adjust matters between the "Insurgents" and the Government and had resulted in failure, President Washington immediately called or volunteers for an army from the States of Pennsylvania, New Jersey, Maryland and Virginia, as follows:

	Infantry.	Cavalry.	Artillery.
Pennsylvania	4500	500	200
Maryland	2000	200	150
New Jersey	1500	500	100
Virginia	3000	300	
	Total 12,950 men.		

Virginia complied by Acts of her General Assembly, passed December 2nd, 1793, providing for four divisions, the third of which embraced all the regimental organizations then existing in which is now West Virginia. Major General Daniel Morgan was placed in command of this division. This division was composed of seven brigades; the seventh of four regiments; the tenth of nine regiments; the thirteenth of nine regiments; the eighteenth of three regiments, and the nineteenth of five regiments. Of these regiments, the 55th and 67th were in Berkeley County. The 55th and 67th Regiments were in the Sixteenth Brigade, Brigadier General William Darke, commanding.

On the 15th of August, Governor Lee of Virginia, as Commender-in-Chief of the Military Establishment of that State, issued a "General Order", stating that the President of the United States had called upon the State for three thousand infantry and three hundred cavalry for immediate service. By this order these troops were to form a division commanded by General Daniel Morgan, and be divided into two brigades, an Eastern and Western. The Western was placed under the command of General William Darke of Berkeley County, the commandant of the Sixteenth Brigade of the Third Division.

When this formidable array of military power appeared before the misguided and excited farmers of Western Pennsylvania, they speedily came to their senses and dispersed and no blood was shed. Thus ended the "Whiskey Insurrection". Governor Henry Lee of Virginia issued an order for twenty-five hundred men under General Daniel Morgan to remain in the vicinity of Pittsburg during the winter of 1794-95. A portion of these men belonged to Brigadier General Darke's brigade and were from Berkeley County. No rolls or rosters seem to be in existence of these companies who served in this insurrection.

WAR OF 1812.

In the second war with England—the War 1812—Berkeley County furnished her full quota of troops levied by Acts of the General Assembly of Virginia, but no roster or roll of any company serving from this county appears to be inexistence, although "A Resolution, adopted by the General Assembly of Virginia, March 31st, 1851, directed the Governor to cause to be obtained authentic copies of all muster rolls of the Virginia Militia who served in the War of 1812, and in the War with Mexico, and that he caused five hundred copies to be printed". The only military data of that war is such as can be gleaned from other sources.

The first activities of Berkeley County people in that war were when James Faulkner, a young man of Martinsburg, in the mercantile business, organized a company of artillery to meet any of the probable demands of war. James Faulkner was elected Captain, with Robert Wilson as First Lieutenant and William Long, Second Lieutenant. Among those who volunteered as privates were John R. Cooke, Edward Colston, John Alburtis, Alexander Stephens, William Campbell, James Newkirk, Tillotson Fryatt, Adam Young, Jacob Snyder, John Matthews, Jacob Poisal, Charles Pendleton, James Shearer, Nicholas Orrick, and some fifty others. Was was declared on the 18th day of June, 1812, by the United States on Great Britain. On the 24th of March, 1812, general orders were issued for the assembling of a portion of the State Militia at Richmond. This company was accordingly ordered to that place. It was then known as Captain Wilson's Berkeley Artillery, Captain Faulkner having been promoted to the rank of Major of Artillery at Norfolk and Lieutenant Robert Wilson was promoted to the office of Captain of the Company. This company saw active service on the coast of Virginia and Major Faulkner as Major commanding the Artillery, gathered at Richmond, participated in the Battle of Craney Island, one of the positions defending Norfolk and Portsmouth. In this battle, he sunk the barges of the invading forces who sought to make a landing, and directed the attack of the Artillery so efficiently that the remainder of of the enemy raised sail and hurried away, and these two cities—Norfolk and Portsmouth—were not again molested. One instance of the coolness and courage of Major Faulkner in this battle is handed down to us and is recorded here: "Whilst the barges were approaching, Captain Emerson observed to Major Faulkner, 'Are they near enough to fire?' 'No, sir,' replied the commander of artillery, 'let them approach a little nearer.' In a few moments afterwards the word 'fire' was given, when our whole battery, except the disabled pieces, opened up on the nearest division of boats a brisk and heavy discharge of grape and canister."*

The names of the commanding officers, together with the number of the brigades, divisions and regiments, of the companies who participated in that war were: Colonel Elisha Boyd, Jr., with Major Andrew Waggoner Dougall Campbell, and Captain James Faulkner's Artillery Company, attached to the 67th Regiment of Berkeley County and estimated at 50 men. The county also furnished one colonel, one major, and a due proportion of captains, lieutenants, ensigns, non-commsisioned officers, musicians, &c, and allowing 60 men (officers (included) in one company.

The companies from Berkeley County were: Artillery Company No. 1, Captain Robert Wilson's Company No. 2, Captain Buckmaster's Light Infantry Company. Major James Faulkner was commander of the First Battalion, Light Infantry.

As has been stated above, the Virginia Assembly ordered the Governor to cause to be printed authentic copies of the rosters of the companies in the War of 1812, but from some reason the roster of the troops from Berkeley County who served at Norfolk and in the Northwestern Army under General William Henry Harrison were not included. There were several calls for troops as was indicated by the General Orders of the Governor.

In 1813, the Government of the United States, in need of money, passed an act entitled: "An act to lay and collect a Direct Tax within the United States", as follows: "Be it enacted by the Senate and House of Representatives of the United States of America in Congress assembled: That a direct tax of three million dollars shall be and is hereby laid upon the United States and apportioned to the States respectively." Further, the act apportioned this sum among the several States, then among the several counties composing each State. Virginia's share of this amount was: $369,018.44, of which amount $6,147.22 was allotted to Berkeley County.

THE WAR WITH MEXICO.

This war was fought over the admission of Texas into the Union. When the Mexican Minister at Washington notified Congress that if Texas

---

*From the report of Major-General Robt. B. Taylor, then the Commander-in-Chief.

MILITARY HISTORY OF BERKELEY COUNTY 149

should be admitted into the Union, war would follow, hardly any one paid attention to it. But when General Santa Anna raised and equipped an army and marched towards the Rio Grande, at the same time promising the excited populace of his Capitol that he would water his horse in the Potomac ere he returned, it began to dawn upon the American people the truth of the Mexican Minister's threat. Congress declared war upon Mexico May 13th, 1847. The act declared: "By an act of the Republic of Mexico, a state of war exists between that Government and the United States." President James K. Polk issued a call for troops and a requisition was made on Virginia for one infantry regiment of volunteers for immediate service and to be continued therein during the war with Mexico, unless sooner discharged. The regiment was to consist of field and staff—1 colonel, 1 lieutenant-colonel, 1 major, 1 adjutant (a lieutenant of one of the companies but not in addition).

Non-Commissioned Staff—1 sergeant-major, 1 quartermaster-sergeant, 2 principal musicians and 10 companies, each of which to consist of 1 captain, 1 first lieutenant, 2 second lieutenants, 4 sergeants, 4 corporals, 2 musicians and 80 privates. On the 18th of November, Governor Smith of Virginia issued a proclamation calling for ten companies of volunteers to constitute a regiment to meet the requirements of the President in his requisition. In the issue of the *Martinsburg Gazette* of November 26, 1846, there appeared a call for a meeting of the citizens of Berkeley County. The result of this meeting was that Captain Ephraim G. Alburtis, editor of the *Berkeley County Republican* and Captain of the "Independent Blues", offered the services of himself and his company to the Government and were promptly accepted.

The following is the roster of the company:

OFFICERS.

Ephraim G. Alburtis, Captain.
Otho B. Harrison, 1st Lieutenant.
David W. Gray, 2nd Lieutenant.
George W. Chambers, Jr., 2nd Lieutenant.
Edward W. Maxwell, 1st Sergeant.
John C. Reed, 2nd Sergeant.
Robert Pollock, 3rd Sergeant.

John Jamison, 4th Corporal.
Daniel Poisal, 1st Corporal.
William H. Page, 2nd Corporal.
Thornton Coontz, 3rd Corporal.
William Sherrard, 4th Corporal.
John W. Keef, Drummer.
Benj. W. Blondell, Fifer.

PRIVATES.

Bennett, Anderson
Beales, John A.
Blessing, John H.
Brown, John
Brown, Peter A.
Brown, William J.
Blakeney, George W.
Crowel, Jacob
Cain, William C.
Creamer, John Q.
Done, William D.
Duffey, Andrew

Heck, David
Hodges, George
Hood, John W.
Hunter, John H.
Harwood, James D.
Hoover, William
Hooser, Francis W. M.
Jones, John
Johnston, Joseph
Kissinger, Otho
Klein, Charles H.
Kimley, William

Ott, John H.
Prather, Socrates
Peare, James
Pentony, James
Peare, John
Rinor, John
Robbins, George T.
Reese, Jeremiah R.
Reamy, John T.
Shoemaker, William L.
Stewart, John P.
Shank, Jacob

150 HISTORY OF BERKELEY COUNTY

Dobb, Carlisle
Dunn, William W.
Evans, James
Erwin, Charles
Freer, Henry S.
Gordon, Aaron K.
Gainor, Robert
Grove, Lewis H.
Griffin, Andrew M.
Gallaher, John S., Jr.
Hagan, Arthur
Heilfeinstein, Jacob H.
Heller, Josiah

Loftin, Charles
Lewis, James
McCormack, Wm.
Mansfield, Robert
Miller, John M.
Mason, Thompson
McMinn, Joseph
Moore, Richard G.
Mimey, John
Magee, Bernard D.
Maguire, Patrick
McKorkle, Alexander C.
Mopie, William

Seigler, William
Stephens, Richard H.
Sorber, William
Vanhorn, John C.
Vanmetre, Abram G.
Vaden, Paskil
Vanlier, John
Weast, George L.
Wilhelm, Henry
Williams, John R.
Winter, Richard
Whiteman, Charles

On November 16, 1846, Hon. W. L. Marcy, Secretary of War, authorized Governor William Smith, of Virginia, to raise one regiment of infantry, and ordered that the place of rendezvous be at Guyandotte in Cabell County, now West Virginia. Governor Smith requested in writing of the Secretary of War that the place of rendezvous be changed to Richmond, Virginia. This request was granted and there the various companies of the State gathered and were mustered into the United States service by Captain Larkin of the Eighth Regiment, United States Infantry. The reason for this change of mobilization was the greater number of companies organized east of the Blue Ridge and that the bad roads and the deep snows of winter on the Alleghenies made marching almost impossible. On December 22, 1846, John F. Hamtramck, of Shepherdstown, Jefferson County, now West Virginia, was appointed colonel of the regiment by the Governor and Council of the State of Virginia. He arrived at Richmond on the 30th and took command amid a great public demonstration tendered the regiment by the populace of that city.

On January 3, 1847, the first battalion of five companies left Old Point Comfort. From here the regiment proceeded by sailing vessel to Port Isabel at the mouth of the Rio Grande, and from thence by steamboat up the Rio Grande to Monterey. From Monterey the march was continued by way of Santillo to Buena Vista. This regiment was in most of the engagements from Buena Vista to the Mexican Capitol.

THE CIVIL WAR.

The Civil War, fought between the United States and the Confederate States, 1861-1865, concerned the people of Berkeley County more than any other war of American history from the standpoint of sentiment and the actual number of its citizens engaged in it. Berkeley County was about evenly divided as to the number of men she furnished to either army. Berkeley County was a part of the State of Virginia, yet many of her sons joined the Union Army. In many cases even the family was divided, the father adhering to the Union while the sons gave their lives for the Confederate cause. In some instances, brother was arrayed against brother in battle. On account of her geographical position, many battles were fought on her soil and she was consantly subjected to invasions by either army, being situated on the line of movement of troops from the North to the South. On October 17, 1859, an event occurred which sent a thrill of terror through Virginia and roused the whole nation. This was the attack upon the United States Arsenal at Harper's Ferry by John Brown and a handful of followers. Brown was obsessed with the idea that the slaves of the country should be freed immediately. Virginia thought it was an attack upon her rights as a State, perpetrated and abetted by the North. Such was the feeling between the sections of the country, the North and the South, that the least provocation was destined to cause alarm, and, if needs be, to fly to arms. In the years intervening between the Mexican War and this time, Virginia had sanctioned the organization of companies throughout the State, members of the State Militia; no standing army in which every able-bodied man was to serve, but companies raised more for pleasure and parade than military action. These companies could be called into the service of the State at any time, to quell insurrections and the like; so, when the news was received that an attack had been made on the Harper's Ferry Arsenal, that the citizens were being shot down in the streets, and that a terrible Negro insurrection in which the slaves were rising and massacreing their masters, the whites, the Governor called out all the available companies. The companies of Jefferson and Berkeley Counties being closer to the disturbance, were the first to reach Harper's Ferry. The companies organized in Berkeley County at the time of the insurrection or shortly after were: "Berkeley County Company," organized at Gerardstown and commanded by Captain James W. Gray. The other companies, formed immediately after John Brown's Raid, were "The Berkeley Border Guards", Captain John Q. A. Nadenbousch, commanding, composed entirely of Berkeley County men, and were on duty at the trial and execution of Brown and his followers at Charles Town; Company "B", Wise Artillery, organized in November, 1859, and on duty at the trial and execution of Brown, Captain E. G. Alburtis, commanding, and Company "E", commanded by Captain Moses C. Nadenbousch. During the intervening time between the attack upon Harper's Ferry and the execution of John Brown and his cohorts, at Charles Town, seventeen hundred Virginia troops were on duty at Harper's Ferry and Charles Town at one time or another. The reason for this display of the military at these places was that the South feared other attacks upon its soil and persistent rumors of an attempt to rescue Brown by Northern sympathizers kept reaching the ears of the Virginia people. During this period there was a constant unrest felt by everyone, a constant feeling of uncertainty as to what would happen next. But no attempt at rescue happened and John Brown, with six of his followers were tried of treason, found guilty and executed; Brown on December 2nd, 1859; four on the 16th of the same month, and two on March 16th, 1860. Altogether from the insurrection to the hanging of Brown, 1800 troops were in camp at Charles Town.

On April 17, 1861, a convention at Richmond adopted an Ordinance of Secession. It was adopted by a vote of eighty yeas against a vote of fifty-five nays. The Ordinance declared "That the Ordinance adopted by the people of this State in convention on the 25th day of June, in the year on ethousand seven hundred and eighty-eight, where by the Constitution of the United States was ratified, is hereby repealed . . . . and we do further declare that said Constitution of the United States of America is no longer binding on any of the citizens of this State." Event followed event in quick succession; the people of Western Virginia took immediate action for the formation of a new State, the Confederate States of America was formed, President Lincoln called for troops "to put down the rebellion," the South marshalled its forces and the war was on.

The first military movement within the county was a skirmish with General Patterson's vanguard and Colonel Thomas J. Jackson's force, who had been sent against him by General Joseph E. Johnston, at the Porterfield farm near Falling Waters. This (the first skirmish of the Civil War) occurred on June 18th, 1861. Jackson fell back to Darkesville, four miles south of Martinsburg, and there joined the forces of General Joseph E. Johnston, who had evacuated Harper's Ferry on June 16th. Two days later General Johnston formed his line of battle at Bunker Hill, expecting an attack from General Patterson. Had the latter attacked him there would have been another "Battle of Bunker Hill" fought upon the soil of America; the one for the formation of the Union, the other for the preservation of the Union.

Another military movement which occurred in the county was the destruction of Dam No. 5, on the Potomac River, by Colonel (now General) Stonewall Jackson's men. By destroying this dam the Chesapeake and Ohio Canal was rendered useless to the Northern cause. because this dam fed the waters of the Potomac into this canal, and by its destruction, the canal was without water for several miles to the eastward. As General Jackson had destroyed the bridges, track and rolling stock of the Baltimore and Ohio Railroad in and around Martinsburg, the Federal Government was still using the Chesapeake and Ohio Canal to transport troops, munitions of war and large quantities of coal from the West to Washington and this route of transportation was not rendered useless without the destruction of the canal at this point.

The next military movement in the county was General Banks' retreat, May 25th, 1862, after his disastrous defeat at Winchester. On this retreat hundreds of wagons loaded with supplies fell into the Confederates' hands. The citizens, too, profited by this retreat, for large quantities of quartermaster's stores, medicines, etc., fell into their hands, being abandoned along the way in the hurry to get across the Potomac. These came at a time when food, clothing and blankets were scarce. One delighted citizen referred to this incident as "manna sent from heaven". Cavalrymen made their appearance first, as they had the fastest mode of transportation. They began to appear early in the morning and by noontime, four horse wagons, filled with infantry soldiers and runaway slaves, passed through Martinsburg at a full gallop. This was the worst defeat to the Northern troops administered at the hands of the dreaded Jackson. It was one of those disastrous retreats or panics with which groups of individuals are sometimes seized. The crowd is generally more excitable or inclined to be more panic-stricken by false alarms than the average individual. Banks' army imagined that they were being pursued by a relentless foe, when, in reality, Jackson had abandoned the pursuit at Winchester on account of the lack of fast moving cavalry. Had he been supported by this branch of the army, the entire force of Banks would undoubtedly have been captured.

When General Robert E. Lee crossed the Potomac on the 5th day of September, 1862, for his first invasion of the North, a considerable force of Federal troops under General Halleck was stationed at Harper's Ferry. General Lee surmised that his invasion of Frederick, Md., and other Northern cities would result in the peaceful evacuation of that place. But it did not, and as he could not afford to take the chance of having an army in his rear and possibly cut off his retreat, did he deem a retreat necessary, sent General Jackson to occupy that place and capture or destroy the army. General Jackson accordingly, with a large force marched to Williamsport, Mr., crossed the Potomac and arrived at Martinsburg. The small Union garrison stationed there speedily retreated to General Halleck's army at Harper's Ferry. Jackson, after tearing up the Baltimore and Ohio Railroad as far west as North Mountain, appeared before Harper's Ferry, invested the town, and captured the entire force of the Federals under Halleck, and joined Lee at Frederick City.

Another military movement, but without bloodshed, occurred in this war—that of the raid upon Chambersburg, Pa., by General J. E. B. Stuart. After the battle of Antietam, on the 19th day of October, eighteen hundred cavalrymen rendezvoused at Darkersville. Six hundred of the best mounted and most reliable men of this body were selected by General Stuart to accompany him on a proposed expedition. The officers chosen to accompany him were Brigadier-General Wade Hampton, Colonel W. H. F. Lee, and Colonel Jackson accordingly, with a large force, marched to Williamsport, Md., crossed the Potomac and arrived at Martinsburg. The small Union garrison stationed Wm. E. Jones. Major John Pelham commanded the four guns with the expedition. On the morning of the 10th, the expedition left Darkesville and that night camped at Hedgesville. They reached this place by way of Arden, Nollville and Butler's Chapel roads. By daylight the next morning, the expedition crossed the Potomac at McCoy's Ferry. This company raided Chambersburg, captured twelve hundred horses, destroyed two hundred and fifty thousand dollars worth of military stores for the Federals and captured thirty United States Government officials and citizens and had evaded two armies sent to capture it. Stuart had lost his valuable servant Bob and his two riding horses, Lady Margrave and Skylark.

Many times Martinsburg would change hands over night and several times during the day. On one time "Hampton's Brigade," under command of General "Jeb" Stuart, entered Martinsburg in the morning and were driven out by the cavalry of General Kilpatrick at noontime. That evening, the latter was dislodged and driven across the Potomac at Shepherdstown. After the important battles many sick and wounded were brought to our town and the churches were thrown open as hospitals. On one occasion, prisoners

History of Berkeley County

of war were held over night in the Clerk of the County Court's office, and it was used as a prison house many times during the war. The court house was considerably damaged by the prisoners and was unfit to hold court in for a while after the war. The basement of the Catholic Church was used to stable cavalry horses.

The following is a roster of the companies of soldiers who served in the Civil War, North and South, from Berkeley County.

Berkeley County—Company B, First Regiment, Virginia Volunteers, U. S. A.

OFFICERS.

Joseph Kerns, Captain.
James Fayman, 1st Lieutenant.
John Lowman, 2nd Lieutenant.
D. J. Weaver, 1st Sergeant.
William Smith, 2nd Sergeant.
Robert Lowery, 3rd Sergeant.

Jerome E. Pompell, 4th Sergeant.
M. H. Harman, 1st Corporal.
Robert Thompson, 2nd Corporal.
Harry Steansbaugh, 3rd Corporal.
J. Lewis Cleary, 4th Corporal.
Benjamin Lowery, 5th Corporal.

PRIVATES.

Ashkettle, J.
Adams, Friskey
Batch, C.
Bender, John
Bishop, John
Burriss, E.
Ball, John
Bateman, C.
Brown, William
Clevinger, R.
Coyle, James
Colbert, George
Cann, P.
Claspey, James
Dickerhoff, Isaac
Dailey, Arthur
Denan, A.
Ditman, John
Davis, Joseph
Davis, Samuel

Ebaugh, C.
Espehine, G.
Fahey, Thomas
Finigan, Patrick
Gagle, John
Giser, Christopher
Goodman, John
Grace, Israel
Grindes, R.
Harker, C.
Hipper, A.
Henry, R.
Harman, Hewett
Henlane, Henry
Ingless, Joseph
Ingram, John
Israil, Edward
Johnson, John
Jones, James
Johnson, William

Kilgore, C.
Korcross, John
Lincoln, C.
Lupman, Daniel
Lowery, Benjamin
Lowery, Robert
Murphy, Dennis
Matthew, Frank
Martin, John
Prescit, B. F.
Perkins, C.
Potter, R.
Shirk, John
Sadler, John
Smith, David
Sisco, John
Sisco, Joseph
Thompson, Daniel
Unger, John
VanMetre, Isaac

Berkeley County—Company C, Third Regiment, West Virginia Cavalry, U. S. A.

OFFICERS.

Peter Tabler, Captain.
John E. Bowers, 1st Lieutenant.
Albert Teets, 2nd Lieutenant.
James W. Kneedler, 1st Sergeant.
John Falkenstein, 2nd Sergeant.
Michael Ferrel, 3rd Sergeant.
Sylvester Ridgeway, 4th Sergeant.
Edmond Wagely, 5th Sergeant.
William Clendening, 6th Sergeant.
Levi J. Welshans, 7th Sergeant.
Edward N. Loy, 8th Sergeant.

Levi F. Miller, 1st Corporal.
Adam Wolf, 2nd Corporal.
James O. Ross, 3rd Corporal.
Alexander Horner, 4th Corporal.
Ulysses Davis, 5th Corporal.
William Deets, 6th Corporal.
Benj. F. Statter, 7th Corporal.
Franklin Spencer, 8th Corporal.
David Kiser, Bugler.
Alfred Potter, Bugler.

PRIVATES.

Anderson, Eli	Morgan, Enoch	Racy, William
Anderson, James W.	Myers, William C.	Ramsburg, Elijah
Allison, John	Myer, William	Reynolds, Elijah
Awman, Benjamin	Murphy, John W.	Roby, Middleton
Barnes, Lemuel	Murphy, James W.	Rude, George W.
Barthlow, Joshua	Myers, Enos	Shaffer, Balser
Butts, David	Myers, Samuel	Shaffer, David
Benson, Joseph A.	Myers, Jacob	Shrout, Andrew J.
Butler, Thomas J.	Novington, John W.	Shaw, William B.
Burch, George	Piles, Edgar C.	Siler, Philip
Barthlow, William	Perry, James S.	Smith, John
Brecker, Levi	Piles, Osborne H.	Smith, Mathias B.
Butts, William	Pitcher, John W.	Stanbury, H. B.
Colbert, Jesse	Pitcher, Charles W.	Stafford, John
Colbert, Clarkson	Prossman, William	Stoker, Thomas
Conger, Seymore B.	Pullin, William	Strawson, H. W.
Cross, John A.	Ridenour, James	Street, William J.
Cockran, Hiram	Ridenour, Charles	Stahl, Jonathan
Cockran, Charles C.	Hoffman, John E.	St. Clair, James P.
Crowe, James B.	Horner, Robert G.	Statler, Andrew J.
Curry, Alonza H.	Jenkins, George	Statler, Henry M.
Deen, Geo. W.	Johnson, Moses	Teets, Elisha
Dilly, John R.	Kines, W. E.	Teets, John
Deets, James	Kline, John W.	Tichnal, Samuel
Fravill, John	Kiser, Isaiah	Taylor, James
Fitzpatrick, David	Kiser, John	Taylor, Samuel H.
Fizer, John T.	Lamaster, Theodore	Taylor, Ephraim
Freshour, William A.	Lamaster, John H.	Vanansdal, Jerry
Fleming, William	Lazzel, William G.	Volgamott, Moses
Gardner, John W.	Light, Isaac J.	Wade, Alexander
Green, David S.	Long, George	Welsh, Patrick P.
Hart, Jacob H.	Mercer, Marshall	Welsh, Thomas S.
Hays, Joseph H.	McKinley, Alexander	Wise, Thomas
Hickman, Gilaspie	Miller, Isaac	Wister, Benjamin K.
Hower, Edmond	Mock, James M.	Yoho, Ezra

Berkeley County—Company D, Second Regiment, Virginia Infantry "Berkeley Border Guards", C. S. A.:

OFFICERS.

J. Q. A. Nadenbousch, Captain.
P. S. Cunningham, 1st Lieutenant.
Robert W. Hunter, 2nd Lieutenant.
Peyton R. Harrison, 3rd Lieutenant.
Israel Robinson, Major.
John A. Dugan, 1st Sergeant.
C. W. Welsh, 2nd Sergeant.
E. L. Hoffman, 3rd Sergeant.
H. S. Fowler, 4th Sergeant.

Holmes E. Conrad, 5th Sergeant.
E. Ryneal, 1st Corporal.
William Kline, 2nd Corporal.
T. Bentz, 3rd Corporal.
E. B. Hooper, Drum Major.
William Hayden, Asst. Drum Major.
E. G. Tabler, Musician.
Samuel Hutchinson, Musician.
Charles Shober, Musician.

PRIVATES.

Armstrong, John S.	Griffin, Michael	McCleary, Trip
Albin, William B.	Halem, M.	McGeary, William

Albin, James	Harrison, John	McWhorter, James W.
Austin, Thomas	Harman, William	Miller, Jonathan
Bales, Adam S.	Harrison, John S.	Muhlenburg, Charles
Barnett, A. J.	Hambleton, William	Nicholson, Thomas
Bell, Alfred	Harley, Patrick	Oden, Archibald
Blake, V. B.	Hedges, Owen T.	Painter, Joseph
Boyd, B. R.	Helferstay, John	Parker, Richard
Brady, Peter	Hill, Joseph	Piper, John R.
Brocius, William	Hollis, T. W.	Phillips, William
Buchannon, Thos.	Hodges, N.	Rust, William
Cage, James	Homrich, James M.	Sailes, Richard
Carlysle, James A.	Hollis, J.	Saville, Albert
Caskey, William	Hollis, T. P.	Scheig, George
Chambers, R. D.	Hunter, John C.	Sherrer, George
Chambers, John M.	Huff, Benjamin	Siler, John
Chevalley, James	Joy, J. F.	Simmons, W.
Cline, David A.	Kearfott, William P.	Smeltzer, C. W.
Conrad, H. Tucker	Kearfott, James L.	Smith, William
Copenhaver, T.	Kearnes, Joseph	Smith, John
Custer, Ephraim G.	Kilmer, Geo. H.	Staub, R. P. H.
Dalgarn, S. S.	Koiner, L. P.	Steward, T. W.
Dandridge, E. P.	Leathers, John H.	Staub, John F.
Day, James W.	Lewis, Lewis	Suiter, Charles
Diffenderfer, Wm.	Leshorn, James W.	Suddith, Joseph
Drebbing, C. L.	Larkins, Thomas	Thrush, John M.
Doll, R. M.	Lewis, Walter	Titlow, R.
Dugan, James A.	Light, William H.	Voorhees, George F.
Earson, Joseph	Manpin, T. A.	Weaver, Charles
Englebright, John	Matthews, Henry C.	Weaver, George
Fisher, James	Marikle, John B.	Webster, R. A.
Fisher, John L.	Marikle, Thos. T.	Weaver, John
Fravel, George	Marikle, Joseph S.	Whitson, George D.
Fryatt, John T.	Meachem, Richard	Wollf, C. A.
Gardner, Jarvus	McMullen, Charles	
Glass, G.	McIntire, John F.	

Berkeley County—Company E, Second Regiment, Virginia Infantry, C. S. A.:

OFFICERS.

Raleigh T. Colston, Captain.
David Manor, 1st Lieutenant.
Raleigh T. Colston, Jr., 1st Sergeant.

John T. Hull, 2nd Sergeant.
Charles W. Manor, 3rd Sergeant.
W. H. Lingumfelter, 4th Sergeant.

PRIVATES.

Bane, Newton	Hunter, John A.	Pryor, John
Basore, Emanuel	Jenkins, Asa	Riddle, John
Blamer, James	Johnson, William	Rockwell, George W.
Brown, Charles	Keischer, Newton	Sharff, Nicholas
Criswell, John L.	Keyser, John	Small, Reuben
Couchman, Geo. W.	Lanham, Jeremiah	Small, John M.
Dugan, James L.	Light, William E.	Snodgrass, Porterfield
Eversole, John W.	Merchant, Isaac N.	Sperow, Jacob
Eversole, Jacob H.	Miller, Geo. W.	Sperow, George
Eversole, Isaac	Miller, Harvey A.	Stuckey, Samuel A.

Military History of Berkeley County

Fiery, James V.
Guinn, James V.
Haines, John J.
Hill, Abraham
Hull, George W.
Hull, Dallas

Hunter, David
Merchant, W. S.
Myers, Cromwell
O'Connor, Michael
Perregory, William
Pike, Frank, Jr.
Porterfield, Milton

Porterfield, Alexander
Stuckey, John W.
Triggs, Harrison
Turner, William
Weddell, George W.
Wilson, Valerius

Berkeley County—Company B, Wise Artillery, C. S. A.:

OFFICERS.

E. G. Alburtis, Captain.
James S. Brown, 1st Lieutenant.
George H. Murphy, 2nd Lieutenant.
James Witherow, 3rd Lieutenant.
Frank Smith, 1st Sergeant.
Oliver King, 2nd Sergeant.
Robert Lowery, 3rd Sergeant.
John Maxwell, 4th Sergeant.
J. R. Couchman, 5th Sergeant.
Henry Wentz, 1st Corporal.

Barney Stewart, 2nd Corporal.
John Hines, 3rd Corporal.
John S. Robinson, 4th Corporal.
John H. Weddell, 5th Corporal.
Joseph Lantz, 6th Corporal.
J. C. Pelham, Lieutenant Instructor.
Dr. J. D. Newman, Surgeon.
Joseph Sherrer, Bugler.
John R. O'Neal, Ensign.

PRIVATES.

Alburtis, Samuel
Auld, Chas.
Armpriest, William
Bell, Harry
Beard, George
Blakeney, Edward
Blakeney, Harry
Blanchfield, John
Bowers, John
Britton, Edward
Causemenia, Charles
Chambers, Geo. W.
Clarke, William
Conway, James
Commiskey, Thomas
Cax, Samuel
Cunningham, David
Faulkner, E. Boyd
Feaman, James
Fiske, James
Frazier, James
Fultz, Thornton
Gruber, J.
Harley, James
Hazard, Charles
Hedges, B. S.
Harndon, Thomas
Helan, Patrick
Helferstay, William

Hess, A. T.
Hill, Christopher
Iradelia, Michael
Israel, Gilbert
Johnson, William
Kearnes, Cyrus
Kearnes, Robert
Keyes, John
Kisner, William
Kisner, Washington
Lantz, Christian
Landers, Michael
Lowman, James
Lowery, William
Lucas, Q. M.
Lucas, Benjamin
Lucas, Charles
Mahoney, Patrick
Markle, Samuel
McLaughlin, Franklin
Moore, J.
Moore, Andrew M.
Mooney, J. B.
Mulligan, Patrick
Murray, Patrick
Noland, William
Palmer, Kearney
Pendleton, P. C.
Prior, Thomas
Reed, J. F.

Reed, John
Reardon, John
Ridenour, Martin
Rose, A. P.
Ryneal, P.
Robison, Edgar
Schultz, William
Scheig, Adolphus
Seibert, Joseph
Shea, John
Sisco, John
Sisco, Peter
Strayer, A. P.
Strainey, Edward
Sullivan, Edward
Suter, T. C.
Tate, Robert
Tabler, Martin
Titlow, Robert
Thomas, B.
Vogel, John
Walker, E. M.
Walker, G. W.
Wann, John
Wastphall, Charles
Wert, H. T.
Whitehourst, James
Wallett, P.
Young, John

HISTORY OF BERKELEY COUNTY

Berkeley County—Company B, First Regiment, Virginia Cavalry, C. S. A.:

OFFICERS.

G. N. Hammond, Captain.
William K. Light, 1st Lieutenant.
William T. Noll, 2nd Lieutenant.
John B. Seibert, 1st Sergeant.
Charles Weller, 2nd Sergeant.

Robert H. Stewart, 3rd Sergeant.
James N. Cunningham, 1st Corporal.
Aquilla Janney, 2nd Corporal.
James W. Cushwa, 3rd Corporal.

PRIVATES.

Armstrong, Archibald
Auld, Thomas E.
Boley, Benjamin F.
Bowers, Richard H.
Boyd, John E.
Breathed, James W.
Bryarly, Robert P.
Buchannon, J. C.
Burkhart, R. C.
Carper, George W.
Catrow, John W.
Chapman, Jacob A.
Combs, J. L. E.
Couchman, David
Cunningham, Charles
Cunningham, W. L.
Cushen, R. D.
Cushwa, Daniel
Cushwa, David
Cushwa, Seibert
Frieze, A. J.
Frieze, George
Gageby, John N.
Gladden, George

House, Thomas
Janney, W. H. H.
Jefferson, Wm. M.
Kearfott, James
Kearfott, John P.
Kilmer, B. S.
Kilmer, Daniel
Kilmer, H. D.
Lemen, W. H.
Manning, Dennis
Lyle, R. G.
Marshall, Geo. W.
Marshall, Joseph
Mason, James A.
McClarey, Geo. W.
McKee, Maybury
Miller, Daniel
Mong, Wendall
Murphy, James B.
Murphy, Richard
Myers, W. H.
Payne, J. Tripp
Payne, Martin L.
Payne, O. F.

Rainer, George
Roberts, E. S.
Roberts, Geo. D.
Roberts, William
Roush, Charles
Seibert, Abraham
Seibert, Eli
Seibert, John B.
Seibert, Wendall
Shepherd, James
Showers, George E.
Silver, Frank
Silver, Henry
Small, David
Small, William
Strayer, D. J. R.
Strode, P. H.
Stump, John H.
Tabb, E. W.
Thatcher, Jacob
Thomas, Jacob
Weaver, Charles
Weaver, George

Berkeley County—Company A, Seventeenth Battalion, Virginia Cavalry, C. S. A.:

OFFICERS.

G. W. Myers, Captain.
George Wells, 1sst Lieutenant.

Henry Murray, 2nd Lieutenant.

PRIVATES.

Albain, John
Brittner, Thaddeus
Blondell, Charles
Bets, James
Butler, John
Carney, J. V.
Chapman, Thomas
Gorge, George

Hedges, Anthony
Kensel, John J.
Leech, Sidney
Miller, Harvey A.
Mingle, John
Patterson, Frank
McNemar, Michael
Ronk, Benjamin

Saderfield, Ephraim
Sayles, William
Seckman, T.
Seibert, J. B.
Strode, Joseph
Teack, S.
Turner, John A.
Wilson, J. L.

MILITARY HISTORY OF BERKELEY COUNTY 159

Berkeley County sent over 600 soldiers into the Civil War on both sides. As Virginia favored the Southern cause, and Berkeeley County was at that time a part that State, it naturally follows that more men served in the Southern army than in the Northern. Yet there were hundreds of soldiers of the county who fought under the Stars and Stripes. This is not a complete list of the men who went to this war from the county, but it is as near complete as can be obtained.. Of the six hundred soldiers who served in either army, only five are now living, W. R. Spiker, A. M. Graham, K. B. Creque, John Beard, J. R. Clifford, who wore the Blue, and five, Charles J. Faulkner, Dr. J. Whann McSherry, Thomas Austin, G. S. Brombaugh, R. C. Burkhart, of those who wore the Gray.

Twenty-three years of comparative peace had passed away until the United States entered into another military conflict—the war with Spain, or the Spanish-American War. This contest was fought mainly for the freedom of Cuba, from the tyranny of Spain. On Wednesday, April 2, 1898, Company E, First Regiment, West Virginia National Guards, left Martinsburg for Kanawha City, West Virginia, for this war. Previous to this time, Congress had declared war on Spain and President McKinley had requested the formation of a regiment of soldiers from this State as her quota. According to a call from the Governor—George W. Atkinson—compliance with the request of the President, so many young men from Berkeley County responded that more than enough to swell the regiment to a war footing offered their volunteer services and many had to be turned away. This declaration of war passed through the National House without a dissenting vote, without a roll call and without debate.

The following is the roster of the company from Berkeley County:

FIRST REGIMENT, WEST VIRGINIA NATIONAL GUARDS.

OFFICERS.

Albert J. Moore, Captain.   Howard M. Smith, 2nd Lieutenant.
John A. Weddle, 1st Lieutenant.

Sergeants.

Albert W. Weddle,   Elias P. Sharff,   W. Newton Finch.
William K. Shober,   Henry C. Dorn,

Corporals.

William L. Heiston,   Walter W. Clarke,   J. H. Grove,
W. S. Keiffer,   R. M. Wolf,   S. F. Guy.

PRIVATES.

Ambrose, Edward M.   Hasson, R. L.   Poole, J. W.
Arvin, R. L.   Hutzler, F. L.   Ramsey, Charles
Arvin, W. N.   Gross, D. E.   Rogers, L. T.

Blamer, C. E.	Kraus, Charles	Stewart, M. H.
Brenner, W. L.	Logan, Henry	Strickler, James
Blanchfield, H. L.	Martin, James A.	Turner, J. W.
Brown, T. D.	McCarroll, Chas. H.	Weddell, N. Baker
Brooks, C. E.	McKeever, Arthur B.	Williams, W. J. S.
Clark, Wesley W.	Myers, R. S.	Whittington, W. B.
Creamer, Chas. N.	Nickles, E. D.	Yeoder, N. G.
Criswell, Raleigh C.	Piper, T. H.	
Evans, Herman A.	Pitzer, T. H.	

The following volunteered but were not taken as they were not needed to bring the regiment up to a war footing. They were taken in the Second Regiment, West Virginia Volunteers, called later.

Bowers, Harry	Mansfield, N. W.	(Also served in the Philippine War)
Betz, Elmer	(Also served in the Philippine War)	Toup, William
Dunn, Daniel	Neville, Samuel	Watson, Michael
Foreman, P. J.	Plotner, T. H.	Whitemore, G. S.
Gaither, M. M.	Spring, Charles	Wolfe, R. M.
Hollish, Phil T.	Santman, J. M.	Wolfes, L. R.
Irvin, P. H.	Swope, Elmer	Weise, James E.
Keifer, William S.	Sellers, Eugene	Welling, Al. C.
Mullis, Van C.	Sullivan, H. E.	
Myers, John H.	Tobin, Geo. W.	
Marshall, J. W.		

On the south side of the monument erected to the World War soldiers of the county is the following inscription:

1917—1918

This Memorial is decilated as an enduring tribute to the patriotism of the citizens of Berkeley County who rendered loyal service to our country in the

GREAT WORLD WAR

And to honor the memory of those who made the supreme sacrifice in the Cause of Humanity.

Sponsored by
The American Legion Auxiliary

Florence M. Whitmore .... President
Sarah Alderson .... Vice President
Annabel P. Morrison .... Secretary
M. Eleanor Shade .... Treasurer
Ethel Sites .... Historian
Ella S. Gerhardt, Susan G. Hannis .... Hospital Corps

Erected 1925 by
The Berkeley County Memorial Association
with voluntary contributions made by the people of the county.

HONOR ROLL

"Lest we forget."

Adams, Thos. G.
Ashwood, Ernest
Bittinger, Harry
Bowers, Thos. V.
Butts, Earl E.
Carter, Chas.
Clapham, Henry L.
Cole, Paul F.
Cox, Charlotta A.
Crawford, Abey
Cromwell, Rudolph E.
Fritts, Chas. F.
Graves, Andrew J.
Henry, Roy O.

Holley, Lewis (Col.)
Hudgins, William B.
Hutzler, Adrian C.
Jones, W. Fitzgerald
Keyton, Levi M.
Lamp, Alvin C.
Lemaster, Homer W.
Lewis, Allen G.
Marshall, Calvin W.
Mason, Fred L.
Myers, Philip Clyde
Phoenix, Garrett (Col.)
Pitsnogle, Daniel H.
Porterfield, J. Myers

Price, Raymond W.
Shaffer, J. Guy
Shoap, Calvin Lee
Shriver, Boyd F.
Smurr, Harry F.
Snyder, John W.
Snyder, Luther
Spaulding, James H.
Stewart, S. Allen
Thompson, James E.
Wageley, Roy
Walker, Joseph E.
Williams, Allen P. Col.)

The following is a list of the soldiers who served in the World War from Berkeley County:

Those whose names are marked with a star (*) were wounded in battle.

Anderson, George F.
Anderson, Thomas R.
Anastos, Thomas J.
Anthony Edmund L.
Armbrester, Clarence W.
Armbrester, Wm. D.
Ashton, Fred
Ashton, Janney C.
Ash, George
Avey, Paul R.
Bacon, John B. F.
Bailey, Charles E.
Baird, Hobret E.
Baker, George T. H.
Baker, Gracien H.
Baker, Harry L.
Baker, Roy H.
Barrett, Fenton L.
Barrett, Stewart
Barbehen, Joel L.
Barry, Thomas H.
Bartles, Paul E.
Bartley, Harry
Bates Henry E.
Basore, Ernest R.
Bayer, Geo. Wm. G
Beall, C. Ralph, 2d Lieut.
Beard, Frank B.
Beard, James E.
Beard, John Wm.
Beard, Samuel T.
Beavers, Earl
Beckwith, C. L.

Bell, E. C.
Bell, Jesse L.
Bennett, Gabriel
Bentz, Ralph
Bentz, R. Lewis
Bibbee, Carl R.
Bishop, Charles R.
Bitner, Ernest H.
Bitner, Ralph W.*
Bitner, Raymond
Blackbur, S. C.
Blake, Edward I.
Blake, Maurice H.
Boak, Seibert D.
Bogert, Jackson L.
Bohrer, C.
Boltz, Howard W.
Boone, Luther C.
Booth, Georgte E.
Bowers, (George H.
Bowers, George M., Jr.
Bowers, Joseph F.*
Bowers Joseph Edward
Bowers, Raymond A.
Bowers, Robert N.
Bowers, Roy W.
Bowers, Stephen B.
Bowers, Walter F.
Bowers, Yost
Boyd, Elmer H.
Boyd, James Hunter
Brathwait, Paul R.
Breeden, George F.*

Breeden, L. C.
Breeden, David S.
Brewer, Eugene
Britchner, Bernard H.
Britt, Charles L.
Bromley, Bernie J.
Brookey, Roy F.
Brooks, Emory B.
Brooks, Robert D.
Brown, Angelo
Brown, Beecher
Brown, Fred M.
Brown, Howard K.
Brown, Lawrence V.
Brown, Lott D.
Brown, Loring T.
Brown, Marvin C.
Brown, Raleigh
Brown, Raymond M.
Brown, Roger M.
Brown, Preston C.
Brown, Yeakley A.
Broy, Lawrence L.
Burris, Wm. F.
Busey, Lacy W.
Busey, Oscar Gold.
Butler, Albert
Butler, Bernard G.
Butler, Charles C.
Butler, Floyd J.
Butts, Earl W.
Butts, Floyd
Butts, George W.

*Wounded.

Butts, Lester
Butts, Thomas Reed
Byers, David H.
Cappana, Antonio
Capini, Orebia
Carr, Leonard L.
Caldwell, G. S.
Carryer, Harry B.
Cashman, Matthew
Castleman, R. M.
Castleman, T. L.
Cave, Molder
Chamberlain, Charles
Chapman, Albert H.
Chapman, Arnold P.
Chapman, Robert I.
Chapman, Ryland P.
Chaise, H. G.
Chrisman, F. L.
Chrisman, R. C.
Christian, John
Church, W. G.
Clark, Ernest
Clark, W. B.
Clay, C. E.
Clapham, R. E.
Clemmons, E. H.
Clendenning, H. L.
Clendenning, R. M.
Cline, Edmund B.
Cline, Charles V.
Cline, Charles S.*
Cline, S. P.
Clohan, A. E.
Clowser, C. F.
Colbert, R. A.
Cole, J. B.
Coleman, Boyd
Coleman, C. E.
Collier, A. J.
Collier, Clinton
Colley, F. A.
Collis, A. W.
Collis, H. L.
Collins, J. F.
Cody, J. J.
Coffman, R. G.
Cohen, Lewis
Cohen, Sol
Comrey, A. L.
Conner, N. M.
Cook, H. M.
Cookus, Harry A.
Copenhaver, R. S.

Cowie, C. S.
Admiral, U.S.N.
Cowie, F. J.
Cowie, T. J.
Cox, Albert W.
Cox, Fabian C.
Cox, Foster N.
Cox, C. H.
Cox, G. W
Cox, Raymond
Cox, Roy C.
Coyle, Geo. S.
Crabb, W. W.
Crawford, Divid M.
Crawford, Douglas
Crawford, Hunter
Crawford, J. L. P.
Crawford, Gilbert
Creek, C. H.
Crim, C. E.
Crim, G. D.
Criswell, R. L.
Cross, James B.
Custer, A. W.
Custer, Leo
Dailey, Chas. S.
Dailey, Harry A.*
Dailey, Raymond B.
Daiuto, Frank B.
Daiuto, Joseph H.
Darr, Chas. L.
Darr, Claude E.
Davis, Charles H.
Davis, Charles E.
Davis, Francis M.
Davis, Fred
Davis, Newton B.
Dean, Charles A.
Dean, Julian
DeHaven, E. T.
DeHaven, Hunter
DeHaven, John W.
Delancy, Wm. R.
Dick, Homer E.
Dirting, Lewis R.
Dodd, David L.
Dodd, Donald S.
Dodd, Wm. Earl
Dodd, Maurice R.
Donaldson, Geo. F.
Driver, Wm. D.
  2nd Lieut.
Duke, Raymond A.
Dunham, Eugene C.
Dunham, Robert B.

Dunham, Wilbur
Dunn, Peter A.
Dudrow, Otis B.
Dutrow, H. R.
Dutrow, Lawrence E.
Duvall, Oscar J.
Edmonds, George E.
Edmonds, Raymond H.
Edwards, Collis C.
Eichelberger, Douglas C.
Elliott, Arthur C.
Elliott, John W.
Emmert, Allen R.
Engle, John R.
Eutsler, Keener W.
Everhart, Eugene
Everhart, Fred L.
Everhart, Guy L.
Evans, David F.
Evans, Frank
Evans, Roy L.
Eversole, Harry W.
Eversole, Virgil W.
Faircloth, Geo. A.
Faircloth, Jos. E.
Fairfax, Norman
Fanoras, Frank
Fansler, Hart G.
Fansler, William H.
Faulkner, Whiting C.
  1st Lieut.
Farnsworth, Harry S.
Fawver, Howard E.
Fawver, Wm. B.
Feller, C. Victor
Fetzer, Bernard J.
Fey, Arthur W.
Fiery, Benj. F.
Files, Carl R.
Files, Harry M.
Files, John T.
Files, Marvin H.
Fine, Harry C.
Fine, Nathan
Fischel, Charles O.
Fitz, H. S.
Flagg, Claud O.
Flick, Ashbey
Floyd, John W.
Flynn, David C.
Flynn, Jos. W.
Foley, John Wm.
Foley, Michael J.
Folk, Geo. Wm.
Ford, James W.

*Wounded.

Foreman, Ward T.
Fortney, Genton M.
Fortney, Harris J.
'Fortney, Dayton I.
Francis, John J.
Fowler, Grover C.
Franklin, Jesse
Franklin, Charles
Fravel, Fred C.
Fravel, Lewis A.
Fredinger, Raymond R.
Fry, Joseph Daniel
Fulk, Boyd W.
Fulk, Walter N.
Fuss Geo. B.
Fuss, Harry L.
Fuss, Howard
Fuss, Omer H.
Gain, John R. W.
Gain, Wilbur E.
Gaither, Geo. E.
Gaither, Oscar
Gambino, F. A.
Gaither, Wm. H.
Gambino, John W.
Gambino, Jos. F.
Gano, Richard McS.
Gates, Chester
Georgulius, Stecanos
Gerhardt, L. DeW., Jr.
  1st Lieut.
Gerhardt, Wm. Robert
  Captain
Gerling, J. Ferd.
Getts, Ellsworth
Gibbons, Lowell A.
Gibbs, Scott H.
Gilbert, Arthur M., Jr.
Glassford, Frank B.
Glassford, Wm. B.
Glenn, Jos. W.
Glessner, James B.
Glover, Arthur L.
Glover, John E.
Glover, Joseph A.
Glover, Victor L.
Good, Vernon L.
Gordon, Peter*
Gray, Richard D.
Grant, Lee S.
Gregoria, Tomaso
Gregory, Albert B. B.
Gregory, James W.
Gregory, Marshall
Greenfield, Lsaac M.

Griffith, F. Leith
Griffith, Harry S.
Grimes, Arthur C.
Grimes, Clarence B.
Grimes, Walter B.
Grimsley, James F.
Grove, Berkeley E.
Grove, C. W.
Grove, Gilbeft C.
Grove, Joseph L.
Grove, Lawrence E.
Grubbs, Bernard C.
Grubbs, Wm. David
Haas, Henry Jos.
Hamman, Harry C.
Hammond, Frank T.
Hannis, Herbert E.
  1st Lieut.
Hannis, Henry F.
  2nd Lieut.
Hausrote, Wm. C.
Harden, Ernest
Hardin, J. T.
Hardy, Bernard C.
Hardy, Marshall
Harmon, Edward N.
Harris, Milburn L.
Harrison, Wilbur
Hause, Arlington
Hause, Reno
Hayslett, Robert R.
Heironimus, O. R.
Henshaw, Newton L.
Hess, Ashbey A.
Hess, Charles B.
Hess, John M.
Hess, Robert T.
Hess, Walter T.
Hetzel, John J.
Hettenhouser, Lewis
Hesse, Henry
Hibbert, James F.
Hicks, Geo. E.
Hiett, H. Roy
High, Jennings B.
Hill, Alonzo
Hill, Elmer L.
Hinton, Edgar S.
Hinton, Stanley F.
Hite, John Dayton
Hobbs, J. Leonard
Hockinbury, Albert L.
Hoke, John Boyd
Hollida, Charles E.
Hollis, Clarence W.

Hollis, Charles L.
Hollis, James F.
Hollis, Jos. W.
Hollis, Roy W.
Horner, Albert Guy
Horner, D. Quincy
Horner, Geo. Wm.
Horner, Jos. B.
Horner, Charles
Horner, James Edw.
Horner, Jos. B.
Horner, Thomas B.
Hoiser, Charles Wm.
Houck, Berney J.
Houck, E. M.
Houck, John R.
Hughes, Chas. E.
Hull, Wm. G.
Hull, Robert B.
Hutton, Chas. M.
Hutzler, F. Leon
Hutzler, Geo. S.
Hutzler, Howard C.
Hyatt, Frank S.
Hyde, Richard E.
Ice, Will Creamer
Jacobs, Harry E.
James, Charles C.
James, Russell H.
James, James L.
Jenkins, Dan R.
Jenkins, Holmes E.
Jenkins, Wm. A.
Johnson, Earl H.
Johnson, Charles
Johnson, Samuel Ward
Jones, Harry C.
Jordon, Robert B.
Julias, Augustus G.
Julias, John, Jr.
Kackley, Charles M.
Katz, Allen B.
Kaufman, Robert L.
Keedy, Harold O.
Keefauver, Normon O.
Keesecker, Jesse L..
Keesecker, Palmer T.
Keesecker, Ward W.
Keller, Boyd M.
Keller, Hugh L.
Keller, Roy E.
Kennedy, Boyd C.
Keplinger, C. W.
Kerfoot, Allen M.*
Kericoff, Earl D.

---

*Wounded.

Kericoff, John R.
Kerns, George Nelson
Kerns, William
Kershner, Raymond E.
Kershner, Robert H.
Kettering, Bryan W.
Kettering, Isaac B.
Keyser, Edward L.
Keyser, Wilbur S.
Keyton, Brooke S.
Keif, David McI.
Kilmer, Chas. V.
Kilmer, Stuart H.
Kilpatrick, H. J.
Kitchen, Paul D.
    2nd Lieut.
Kline, C. Webster
Kline, John Wm.
Knadler, Harry E.
Knoggs, Howard H.
Kneisley, H. B.
Knipe, Joseph N.
Knipe, Wm. Paul
Knipple, Carl M.
Knode, John Stewart
Knode, Kenneth
Koontz, Frank J.
Kourelakos, Leonidas
Laise, Kenneth
Laise, Marion
Laign, Paul C.
LaMar, C. Roscoe
Lamon, Elmer M.
Landis, Golden A.
Langford, S. M.
    2nd Lieut.
Longhammer, Howard
Leach, Earl Lester
LeFevre, J. W.
Leggett, Clarence W.
Lemaster, Guy B.
Lemen, Daniel H.
Lemen, Shelby C.
Leonard, Frank E.
Lewis, Clyde J.*
Lewis, Edwin G.
Lewis, Frank M.
Lewis, Fred
Lewis, Ward Lee
Lewis, Willis B.
Leyburn, Boyd H.
Licklider, John D.*
    2nd Lieut.
Light, Bailey C.*
Light, Charles G.
Light, Edward T.

Light, Ely H.
Light, John C.
Light, Lewis McC.
Lingamfelter, R. L.
Linthicum, John E.
Locke, Ernest C.
Locke, Roger F.
Long, Clarence P.
Long, Lawrence H.
Lord, Allen P.
Lord, Charles P.
Louck, Barney J.
Lucas, Ward L.
Lupton, James McS.
    2nd Lieut.
Luttrell, E. L.
Lyeth, Ben. S.
MacDonald, Martin W.
Manford, Bernard H.
Mann, B. C.
Marker, Charles E.
Marker, Clyde D. G.
Marker, Edward L.
Marlett, George E.
Martin, Bernard C.
Martin, Geo. S.
Martin, Robert L.
Mason, Ellis V.
Mason, Elmer C.
Mason, Claud R.
Mason, Dennis A.
Mason, Harry S.
Mason, James Fred*
Mason, Robert F., Jr.
Mason, Robert K.
Matthews, Fred N.
May, Charles W.
May, Edward
Mayberry, Clarke E.
McCohan, Chas. P.
McCarty, Chas.
McCormack, Archie C.
McCormack, Frank W.
McDaniel, Benjamin F.
McDaniel, John
McDaniel, Raymond S.
McDonald, Robert G.
McDowell, Kenneth L.
McGower, T. B.
McIntire, Summers
McKee, Chas. J.
McKee, Herbert
McKown, Gilbert C.
McKown, Paul
McNoll, Roy D.

Meadows, Elmer M.
Meadows, John M.
Means, Beveridge E.
Melintz, Earl L.
Meshley, Paul S.
Michael, Harvey N.
Miles, Albert W.
Miller, Benjamin F.
Miller, Carrol R.
Miller, Chas. D.
Miller, Clarence A.
Miller, Dudley W.
Miller, Edwin W.
Miller, Frank W.
Miller, Geo. Wm.
Miller, Harry T.
Miller, Henry E.
Miller, Howard M.
Miller, Jacob G.
Miller, Jesse K.
Miller, John E.
Miller, John M.
Miller, Milton O.*
Miller, Oliver A.
Miller, Robert Lee
Miller, Willis J.
Miller, Arthur F.
Mills, Walter L.
Minghini, Goldie R.
Mish, Arnold F.
Mish, Geo. F.
Moler, Butler H.
Mongan, Melvin J.
Moran, Ernest W.
Morgan, Alva Rea
Morgan, Floyd H.*
Morgan, H. V.
Morris, Wm. G.
Morrow, Harry C.
Morrison, Garnett P.
    1st Lieut.
Morrison, Chas. W.
Morrison, Geo. L.
Mowery, Wm. H.
Murphy, Alonzo E.
Murphy, Edward A.*
Murphy, James R.
Murphy, William
Murry, James H.
Musser, Norman
Myers, Chas. B.
Myers, David E.
Myers, Edward Wm.
Myers, Harry M.
Myers, Howard F.

---

*Wounded.

Myers, Jacob H.
Myers, Willie H.
Myers, William Albright
Neville, Carter N.
Newcomb, Dayton
Newkirk, Geo. H.
Nicely, Chas. E.
Nicely, Geo. Howard
Nicely, Thomas S.
Nicodemus, Chas. M.
Noll, Albert M.
Noll, Chas. R.
Noll, Henry V.
Noll, Raymond
Noll, James McS.
Noll, Robert M.
Northcraft, Harry
O'Connor, Charles*
Oliver, Denton P.
O'Neal, Nelson B.
Onderdick, Howard W.
Organ, Chauncey B.
Orndorf, Nolan
O'Roke, Eber C.
O'Roke, Ward B.
O'Rourke, Paul L.
Orr, William F.
Osborne, J. Nelson
Owens, Holmes P.
Owens, Horace E.
Palmer, Chas. S.
Palmer, Harry P.
Palmer, Ray R.
Panniccia, Giovanni
Parker, Stacey C.
Paolo, Francisco*
Parkinson, John W.
Parkinson, L. A.
Parkinson, Wm. L.
Parks, John M., Major
Parson, Charles E.
Patterson, G. H.
Patterson, Wm. A.
Payne, Samuel S.
Pearrell, Allen E.
Perry, Marvin H.
Percy, Lee
Peters, Chas. M.
Petris, Frank*
Phillips, A. C.
   2nd Lieut.
Pine, Roland M.*
Pitsnogle, Perry M.
Pitzer, Ernest D.
Pitzer, Glenn M.

Pitzer, Homer S.
Pitzer, John
Pitzer, J. Hensel
Pitzer, Stuart J.
Plotner, Lawrence
Plotner, Herman D.
Plotner, Howard E.
Poffinberger, J. C.
Poisal, J. W.
Porterfield, M. H.
Powell, Elmer T.
Prather, Lemuel
Price, Harry
Price, Luther M.
Price, Samuel
Proctor, W. F.
Quaglio, Lario
Quenzel, Quay
Quick, Harry
Ramsburg, Geo. W.
Raney, Reginald
Wauch, William H.
Rawlings, Geo. R.
Reed, David A.
Reed, Henry
Reed, Richard
Reed, Russell F.
Reed, William C.
Reid, J. Thomas
Rhodes, C. H.
Rhodes, H. M.
Richards, John
Riekard, William H.
Rickel, Charles W.
Ridenour, Elmer J.
Ridings, N. B.
Ridings, Cleo E.
Ridings, R. H.
Ridings, Harry C.
Ridings, William Paul
Rife, Chas. L.
Riffle, Henry
Rind, Harry L.
Riordon, Edgar M.
Rittenour, C. A.
Rittenour, Henry F.
Roach, Claud J.
Roberts, Samuel R.
Robinson, Ruby B.
Rockwell, Wm. M.
Rockwell, F. M.
Rogers, A. Kenneth
Rogers, Robert L.
Rogers, Decatur H.
Roe, Owen R.

Romer, Edward L.
Rouark, Wm. H.
Ropp, Geo. Wm.
Rooney, Lee G.
Rowland, David M.
Russler, Harold S.
Runkles, Calvin F.
Runkles, Herbert H.
Rutherford, Andrew H.
Seafini; Giasfetto
Saville, John E.
Schneider, Albert A.
Schneider, Wm. Geo.
Schoppert, John L.
Schoppert, Wm. F.
Scott, Fred D.
Seibert, David H.
Seibert, Leslie M.
Seibert, Wm. C.
Sencindiver, Roy W.
Shade, Chester, S.
   2nd Lieut
Shade, Geo. A.
Shady, Ferris
Shaffer, Jacob A.
Shaffer, Jos. H.
Shaffer, Philip
Shanholtz, W. B.
Sheets, **David**
Shelly, Harry D.
Sherman, Walter A.
Shields, John D.
Shiflett, Edward
Shipe, Carter D.
Shipper, Thomas
Shipper, Geo. D.
Shirley, Ernest R.
Shriver, Harry R.
Shriver, Jos. W.
Shriver, Norman V.
Shriver, Wm. E.
Shroder, Chas. R.*
Sigler, Chas. M.
Sisk, Charles E.
Sisk, **Silas**
Sites, E. M.
Sibole, Eldridge
Skartelias, Conlstantine
Sloan, J. G.
Slonaker, Guy E.
Small, Fred P.
Small, Harvey G.
Small, Palham Lee
Small, W. Ernest
Smallwood, H. T.

*Wounded.

Smaltz, Andrew R.
Smeltzer, Harry
Smeltzer, Harlan
Smith, Albert K.
Smith, Arthur W.
Smith, C. G.
  2nd Lieut.
Smith, E. O.
Smith, Geo. A.
Smith, Norman W.
Smith, Stanley
Smith, Wm. F.
Smapp, C. M.
Snaidero, Renato
Snyder, Abraham
Snyder, Earl C.
Snyder, Isaac
Snyder, James E.
Snyder, John D.
Snyder, O. L.
Snyder, Perry L.
Snyder, Raymond M.
Snyder, R N.
Snyder, Robert S.
Snyder, W. S., Jr.
Snodgrass, C. S.
  Ensign
Snowdon, E. G.
Somers, H. L.
Sonner, Edward R.
Spaulding, Alva
Sperow, Chas. H. E.
Sperow, Elmer E.
Sperow, Harry
Sperow, Wilson P.
Spillman, H. I.
Sprecker, C. S.
Stuabley, L. H.
Stein, John R.
Stewart, Ralph W.
Stewart, Sheridan G.
Stewart, Spencer A.
Stilwell, Alex. W.
Stoliper, E. R.
Stotler, Geo. B.
Stout, Roy A.
Strode, J. T.
Stroop, R. B.
Strine, Elmer J.
Stuckey, Chas. L.
Stuckey, Harry J.
Stuckey, Lee F.
Stum, Robert C.
Stump, Ralph R.
Sullivan, Paul

Swartz, Fred F.
Swartz, Roy C.
Sweeney, Henty M.
Tabler, Carlton L.
Tabler, Duff H.
Tabler, Ernest R.
Tabler, Mark H.
Talbott, Holmes S.
Taylor, Charles
Taylor, John L.
Teal, Paul H.
Thompson, Chas. F.
Thompson, Chas. H.
Thompson, J. S. H.
Thompson, Hobert T.
Thornburg, David H.
Thurston, Ray C.
Tinsman, Harry D.
Tonkin, Dr. H. G.
  1st Lieut.
Toup, H. Clay
Trayer, Chas. S.
Triggs, Chas. B.
Trout, Edgar C.
Trump, Chas. S.
  1st Lieut.
Trump, Frank M.
Tucker, Harvey E.
Turner, Chas. McK.
Tyson, Gilbert M.
Tyson, James E.
Tyson, Robert G.
VanHohn, Daniel H.
VanHorn, Daniel H.
VanMetre, Lafayette
VanMetre, Robert S.
VanMetre, Thos. Earl
  Lieut. Com., U.S.N.
VanMetre, Thomas H.
Wageley, Arthur
Wallace, Edward F.
Walker, Frank W.
Walker, Noah
Walker, William B.
Wander, L. A.
Waters, Robert
Watson, Harry
Webb, James E.
Weigand, Herman E.
Weigle, Edward
Weigle, John M.
Weller, George
Wellinger, A. G.
Wellsh, Eddie
Welty, H. P.

Welty, Joseph
West, Garnet L.
West, J. I.
Westenhaver, J. D.
Wever, Geo. L., Major
Wharton, H. L.
Whetzel, J. C.
Whitacre, H. S.
Whitacre, S. E.
Whitacre, E. K.
White, C. C.
Whitlock, C. A.
Whitmore, G. F.
  Captain
Whittington, C. E.*
Whittington, Francis
Whittington, I. L.
Whittington, R. B.
Widmyer, R. S.
Widmyer, W. H.
Weist, C. W.
Willard, C. E.
Williams, H. R.
  2nd Lieut.
Williams, Lee
Williams, D. T.
Williams, J. E.
Williamson, J. E.
Wilson, E. A.
Wilson, C. M.
Wilson, Claude
Wilson, Howard
Wilson, C. L.
Wilson, R. H.
Wolford, A. G.
Wolford, C. F.
Wolford, E. A.
Wolford, J. R.
Wolford, Reginald
Wolford, R. G.
Wolford, E. B.
Wolford, J. C.
Wood, Howard
Wood, Cecil W.
Woore, A. M.
Wright, M. H.
Wright, R. S.
Wright, W. E.
Wyatt, E. V.
Wyndham, George
Wyndham, J. L.
Yost, C. C.
Zamarelly, Dominic
Zepp, James
Zepp, W. F.

*Wounded.

Zepp, W. J.
Ziler, W. C.

Ziler, W. J.
Zimmerman, E. J.
Zombro, G. B.

Zombro, R. B.
Ziler, J. W.

List of colored soldiers who served in the United States Army in the World War from Berkeley County:

Allen Hall
Ashbey, Lewis
Basey, Wilmon
Beaver, James
Blakeley, Vernon
Braxton, W. M.
Briscoe, W. M.
Brown, C. V.
Brown, E. W.
Brown, Howard
Brown, Randolph
Brown, Roy
Buesy, C. A.
Butler, W. F.
Cage, H. F.
Carpenter, Virgil
Carter, B. R.
Colston, W. L.
Cook, R. A.
Corsey, S. B. E.
Crissinger, G. N.
Earley, Robert
Evans, Lewis
Ford, Dunbar
Ford, J. M.
Ford, L. E.
Fox, H. L.
Gordon, C. A.
Gordon, D. D.
Green, C. G.

Green, Fulton
Green, J. H.
Green, R. J.
Harden, Jerry
Hughes, Stickley
Jackson, C. R.
Jackson, J. E.
Jackson, J. S.
Jefferson, S. H.
Johns, B. F.
Johns, Hicks
Johnson, A. J.
Johnson, George
Johnson, Henry
Jones, Jerry
Jones, John
Letfich, S. E.
Lewis, Richard
Lincoln, R. M.
Lucas, Albert
Mackey, J.W.
Marshall, J. H.
Mason, Marshall
Matthews, McK.
Mims, Sam
Minor, G. A.
Mosebey, L. W.
Mosebey, W. M.
Myers, Floyd
Myers, Harry

Myers, J. H.
Page, C. G.
Page, M. W.
Patterson, James
Perry, E. A.
Rideout, Timothy
Rideout, Edward
Robinson, J. H.
Rogers, Peyton
Schley, H. E.
Scott, J. E.
Shelton, E. S.
Shelton, J. W.
Shepherd, M. E.
Strain, George
Turner, Edward
Turner, J. F.
Veeney, A. I.
Walker, Caranda
Walker, E. W.
Walker, James
Walker, J. H.
Walker, Pernell
Wells, Edgar
Williams, A. T.
Williams, C. A.
Wilson, Stewart
Wright, Thomas

CHAPTER XXIII.
"BIOGRAPHY."

PAYNE.—Josiah Payne and Martha Shepherd Payne, his wife, migrated to America from England, about the beginning of the 18th Century, to New Garden Townshop, Chester County, Pennsylvania. They removed to Berkeley County just before the breaking out of the American Revolution, and settled in the vicinity of Hopewell Meeting House, now Hopewell, Va. The older members of the family were of the Quaker faith.

One of the descendents was Martin Luther Payne, ex-Confederate soldier and one of the Assessors of Berkeley County. His son, John D. Payne, has been filling the position of Magistrate for the Magisterial District of Mill Creek, Berkeley County, for a number of years.

WILLIAM GERHARDT—Removed to Berkeley County in 1863. He was a minister of the Lutheran Church. He was Principal of John Street School when all the children of school age in Martinsburg were gathered in one building on the present site of the John Street School. He continued in this capacity until the Martinsburg Grammar School was established, which was the forerunner of the old High School, and he was the first Principal. He lived to the age of one hundred years and four months. He was the oldest Odd Fellow in point of age in West Virginia at the time of his death. His wife was Lucinda (Riley) Gerhardt. From this union was born

LEWIS DEWITT GERHARDT—Lawyer. Graduate of Gettysburg College, Gettysburg, Pa., Degree of A.M. Practiced law in Martinsburg until 1897, when he was elected Clerk of the Circuit Court of Berkeley County, which position he now holds. He was elected to this position for five consecutive terms. He was director of the Martinsburg City Band for eight years. In 1887 he married Miss Ellen S. Rebert of Gettysburg, Pa. From this union was born three sons:

L. DEWITT GERHARDT, JR.—Deputy Clerk of the Circuit Court of Berkeley County for six years. World War veteran. Lieutenant, G2 (Training) G. H. Q. Service in the A. E. F. France.

HENRI K.—Deceased.

WILLIAM R. GERHARDT—Graduate West Point Military Academy, Captain in the Regular Army. At present, stationed at Boston, Mass.

GRAY SILVER—Son of Francis III. and Mary Ann (Gray) Silver. He was born on a farm near White Hall, Va., Feb. 17, 1870. He has always been interested in farm life. He is one of the largest commercial apple orchard in this section. He has been active in the affairs of Berkeley County, in West Virginia, and the nation. He has held the following positions of trust and responsibilities: Member of the National Park Board; president Grain Marketing Company (National Cooperative), Chicago, Ill.; director National Bureau Economic Research, New York City; member American Academy Political and Social Science, Philadelphia, Pa.; vice-president Federated Fruit and Vegetable Growers (National Cooperative), New York City; director Federated Growers Credit Association, capital $1,000,000, resources $10,000,000, headquarters New York City; decorated for Distinguished Service in Agriculture by the French Government, 1923; president Berkeley County Fruit Growers, Martinsburg, W. Va.; State Lecturer of the West Virginia State Grange, 1900-1902 member Sons of the American Revolution; member of the Sons and Daughters of The Pilgrims; Deputy Chieftain American Clem Greg Society. Political—Elected member of the West Virginia State Senate, 1907-15 president West Virginia State Senate, 1911-13;; minority floor leader of that body, 1907-10; appointed by Governor Howard M. Gore, member West Virginia Tax Commission, 1926-1927; member West Virginia State Tax Commissioner's Office.

The following is taken from "Who's Who in America": "Gray Silver— Farmer. Born Whitehall, Va., Feb. 17, 1870. Son Francis 3d and Mary Ann (Gray) Silver. Educated in public and private schools. Married Kate Bishop, Martinsburg, W. Va., Dec. 8, 1908. Children, Mary Gray, Gray, Jr., Anna Beall, Francis, Catherine du Bois. Engaged in farming in Shenandoah Valley, also in Illinois and Arkansas. Breeder Shorthorn cattle and Shropshire sheep. President John W. Bishop Co., Martinsburg, W. Va. Active in American Fram Bureau Federation and organizer of agricultural block in Congress. Member State Senate, W. Va., 1907-15. President Potomac Farm Loan Bank. Director Merchants and Farmers Bank, Martinsburg, W. Va. Member Martinsburg Fruit Exchange, National Bureau Economic Research, New York City. President Inwood Fruit Growers Club (Cooperative). Member Farm Bureau Group visiting Europe. Federal Fatt Finding Commission on Distribution Cost. National Improvement Conference (by appointment President Harding), Democrat, Presbyterian, Mason. Clubs—National Press, International Rotary. Home, Martinsburg, W. Va."

CAPTAIN WILLIAM MACKEY—To the right of "Boydville", in the Faulkner family's burial ground, you will find the grave of Captain William Mackey, an officer in the American Revolution, and the great-grandfather of ex-Senator Chas. J. Faulkner, the present owner of "Boydville". He was born near Belfast, Ireland, in 1738; came to America at the age of twenty-four and landed at Philadelphia. He afterward removed to the Cumberland Valley in Pennsylvania. When the Revolutionary War broke out he volunteered his services to the American cause as a private, but was speedily raised to the rank of captain. Was severely wounded at the Battle of Brandywine, so named from a small stream on which the battle was fought.

This battle was brought about by Generals Sir William Howe, Lord

Cornwallis, and General Kurypheusen endeavoring to capture Philadelphia, then the capitol of the Continental Congress or what afterwards became the United States of America, and by Generals Washington, Green, Wayne, Sullivan, and Stephens, defending it. The English had 18,000 well-equipped soldiers against the American force of 13,000, and a poorly-equipped army. The battle was lost by the Americans, Washington withdrawing the troops by a masterly retreat, leaving only the most severely wounded on the field. Among these was Captain William Mackey. After several months confined as a prisoner, he was exchanged and rejoined his regiment, though still suffering from his wounds, and continued to serve until the surrender of Cornwallis at Yorktown. Shortly after the war he moved to Berkeley County. He had two children: William Mackey, Jr., and Sarah Mackey, who married James Faulkner.

JAMES FAULKNER—Was the son of George and Rebecca Faulkner, who resided at Arnagh, Ireland, near Newry, where on April 2, 1776, their son James Faulkner was born. As will be noted, the name is of English origin, and retraced records show that the family ancestors had migrated to Ireland during the reign of William and Mary. At the age of ten years he was left an orphan. Richard McSherry, a friend of the family, had several years previous to the death of James Faulkner's parents, gone to the island of Jamaica. He had succeeded in a sugar plantation and had purchased a farm in the vicinity of Leetown, then in Berkeley County. He could not get immediate possession of it and in the interval decided to visit his old home in Ireland. He persuaded James Faulkner to accompany him to America. Young Faulkner was brought to Martinsburg and placed under the charge of Michael McKewan, an Irishman, who kept a retail store. He remained there until he was twenty-one years of age when he withdrew from the services of McKewan and purchased the property at the southeast corner of Queen and Burke Streets, (now owned by the People's Trust Company Bank), and began business for himself. On December 15, 1803, he married Sarah Mackey, the only daughter of Captain William Mackey.

But James Faulkner wanted to be a soldier. He spent much of his time in correspondence with Hon. James Stephens and Hon. John Morrow, the representatives in Congress from this district, and with Henry Dearborn, the Secretary of War, and President Jefferson, relative to procuring a commission in the army, but at that time the army was small, advancement was slow, and President Jefferson resolved upon a course of peace with all nations and young Faulkner was unsuccessful in obtaining a position in the army. But trouble was brewing. The Chesapeake had been fired upon; our seamen continued to be impressed and an intense war spirit was felt throughout the land.

Anticipating trouble with Great Britain, James Faulkner raised a volunteer artillery company in Berkeley County, of which he was elected Captain; Robert Wilson, First Lieutenant, and William Long, Second Lieutenant. Among those enlisting were John A. Cooke, Edward Colston, John Alburtus, Alexander Stephens, William Campbell, James Newkirk, Tillotson Fryatt,

Nicholas Orrick, James Shearer, Charles Pendleton, Jacob Poisal, Jacob Snyder, John Matthews, Adam Young and others. His company was the best drilled of any in the State of Virginia.

War was declared against Great Britain, June 18, 1812. In that year and in the Spring of 1813, miltary operations were in progress on our northwestern boundary and in Canada, but it was believed that a formidable array of armies and fleets of the enemy were to be gathered for an attack on the coast of Virginia, somewhere in the vicinity of Chesapeake Bay. Accordingly the State issued orders for all the military companies to be gathered at Richmond, and Wilson's Berkeley Artillery Company—by which name it was known, for Captain Faulkner had been promoted to the rank of Major of Artillery—was ordered to Richmond, also Major Faulkner was placed in command of all the companies stationed there.

Early in June, Admiral Warren with a large British naval and land force arrived in Chesapeake Bay. It was soon determined that he intended to attack Portsmouth and Norfolk first. Craney Island lay about four miles west of Norfolk and commanded the entrance to that horbor and also of Portsmouth. Major General Taylor, Commander-in-Chief, on the 13th of June, issued the following orders: "Major Faulkner of the regiment of artillery will tomorrow take command of all the artillery and fortifications of Craney Island. The Commander of Artillery will direct Captain Wilson's Company of Artillery to some place near the entrenchment in the rear of Fort Norfolk." On the 22nd of June the battle of Craney Island was fought and won by the artillery, and the force of three thousand British were repulsed, and the cities of Norfolk and Portsmouth were saved. The results of the battle were hailed with delight throughout the country.

On July 8th following Major Faulkner was placed in command of Forts Barbour and Tar and a mile of breastworks extending between the two forts with headquarters at Norfolk.

He was not a man of robust physique, and the low land climate of the coast, together with the strenuous military life, broke down his system and he continued an invalid until the end of the war and until his death, which occurred on April 11th, 1817, in the 41st year of his life. He was buried with military honors in the Norbourne Cemetery at Martinsburg. He left one son, an orphan, who was destined to become one of the most illustrious sons Berkeley County has ever produced—Charles James Faulkner.

CHARLES JAMES FAULKNER—His grandfather was Captain William Mackey, a commissioned officer in the American Revolution. His father, Major James Faulkner, was Major of Artillery in the Second War with Great Britain, and of Craney Island fame in that war.

Married Mary Boyd, daughter of General Elisha Boyd, an officer in the War of 1812, and was left an orphan at the age of eight years under the guardianship of Dr. Richard McSherry and Judge Pendleton of Martinsburg. He was placed in school and at the age of sixteen years was a graduate of Georgetown University. Began the study of the law at the famous law school of Chancellor Tucker, of Winchester, Va.; was never considered a brilliant student but by perseverance and hard stutdy graduated in less time than many other students of the same instituttion and admitted to the Berkeley bar. Charles James Faulkner's lot seemed always to be cast in rough places but these vicissitudes of fate seemed to be an asset to his career rather than a liability, for he said, in a speech in Martinsburg at a public dinner given in his honor by the citizens of Berkeley County December 16th, 1852:

"At the early age of eight years, as many of you well know, I was left an orphan boy, without father, without mother, brothers or sisters, and as far as I have any knowledge, the only surviving member of my family upon the wide continent of America. From the first moment that I am capable of reflection I saw that my reliance was wholly and exclusively upon myself, for whatever position or advancement I could achieve among my fellowmen. What others deem a misfortune, I sought to convert into a blessing. And I say it for the benefit of every orphan who may find himself in a situation similar to my own, that the very solitude of my situation in life has been worth more than the gold of Ophir. It guarded my habits against the influence of those temptations to which so many of the youths of our country fall a prey. It made me in an early period of my life habitually reflective upon every step which I took, for I well knew that if perchance I was misled into any serious error, I had no father under whose protecting arm I could seek refuge—I had no mother in whose sweet sympathies I could find consolation—I had no troop of relatives in whose banded influence and favor I could find countenance and support against the results of my own indiscretion and folly. I stood alone in the world, and I have no occasion to reproach my God for the loneliness of my condition."

The first public service for his state was to take sides for the adoption of the constitution of 1830, this constitution of the famous statesman, Watkins Leigh. Thomas Marshall of Kentucky, on a visit to his friends the Colston's, at the time the vote was taken for its ratification or rejection, bitterly opposed its adoption. Mr. Faulkner and Mr. Marshall met in joint debate. A great crowd gathered to hear it. Both were young men. Mr. Marshall carried the crowd by his wit and eloquence but Mr. Faulkner carried the election for its adoption in Berkeley County by dint of untiring energy and persuasion. He was elected to the Virginia House of Delegates in 1832. These were stirring times, and the Virginia Legislature and the National Congress composed of men of strong minds and stout hearts. John C. Calhoun was just putting forth his scheme of "Nullification". President Jackson had just issued his famous "Proclamation of Force"; Henry Clay his "Tariff Policy", and Daniel Webster his immortal "Liberty and Union, Now and Forever, One and Inseparable" oration. Mr. Faulkner presented to the Legislature a proposition for the gradual abolition of slavery by the *post nati* principle that all children of slave parents born after July 1st, 1840, should be born *free*. Many sections of the State received this principle with enthusiasm, but the slave-holding element, however, tried to defeat him in re-election in 1833, but without success, by making this subject a campaign issue. But he was returned by practically a unanimous vote. Once a year for many years afterward William Lloyd Garrison printed a speech, made on this subject by Mr. Faulkner in the Virginia Legislature, in full in the *Liberator* and circulated it widely throughout the North as evidence of the growing sentiment in the South against slavery. He declined a third term as a member of the Legislature of Virginia, whereupon Governor John Floyd appointed him a member of a commission to examine and report on the disputed question of the boundary line between Maryland and Virginia. He made his report which was favorably accepted by the Governor (this report is printed in full in another part of this work).

For the next fifteen years he devoted himself to the practice of his profession here, and at Richmond, which earned him a sustenance very valuable, as practice at the bar at that peridod was lucrative. In 1841, he was elected to the Virginia Senate; elected to the House of Delegates of Virginia again in 1848. Introduced a bill which was enacted into a law by both houses of the Legislature and transmitted to the Senators and Representatives of Congress which became the famous "Fugitive Slave Law", passed by Congress in 1850. Was appointed a member of the Reform Constitutional Convention in 1850. The call for this convention grew out of the controversy between the eastern and western sections of the State in regard to taxation and representation. Eastern Virginia had always borne heavily upon Western Virginia in taxation, in internal improvement. The eastern section, largely slave-holding, wished to count the slaves as population in representation but as chattel exempt from taxation in computing taxation. This gave the eastern section the advantage both ways. It gave them more votes in the Legislature, while the western section, not having as many slaves, had more taxation and less representation. Mr. Faulkner used all his influence for the rights and interests of Western Virginia while Henry A. Wise was the champion of Eastern Virginia. Mr. Faulkner won.

Elected to Congress in 1851 on an Independent ticket against Henry Beddinger of Jefferson County.

On August 2nd delivered a speech in Congress on "The Compromise—The Presidency—Political Parties". This speech was made the campaign document by the Democratic party during the next presidential campaign. One hundred and twenty-five thousand copies of this speech were printed and distributed and attracted national attention to Mr. Faulkner, and allied him with the Democratic party. (He was a Whig until the death of Henry Clay). He was elected to Congress for four consecutive terms, was made chairman of the Military Committee during his second term. While in this position he changed the custom of appointment of officers so that a private might gain a commission by merit and promotion. Member of the Democratic Convention which named James Buchanan for President in 1856; made chairman of the Democratic Congressional Committee for the conducting of the presidential campaign. Would have been appointed Secretary of War under President Buchanan had not the electoral college of Virginia recommended John B. Floyd.

Appointed Minister to France by President Buchanan in 1859. His first act after his presentation at the Court of Napoleon III was the right o fexpatriation being first admitted by that government and naturalized citizens of the United States given their right to visit their birth place without molestation or fear of military espionage. Although this right was opposed by M. Thouvenal, the French Minister of Foreign Affairs, it was satisfactorily concluded for the United States Government and the President thanked Mr. Faulkner in his annual message to Congress.

Relieved of his diplomatic duties in 1861 by President Lincoln appointing as his successor Hon. William L. Dayton from New Jersey. Returned to Washington to pay his respects to the President and Secretary Seward, settled all his and the Government's accounts, and was about to leave for his home in Martinsburg when he was arrested as a "distinguished citizen of Virginia" as hostages for James McGraw, State Treasurer of Pennsylvania, confined for one month in Washington. then transferred to Fort Lafayette. Soon after this he learned that Mr. McGraw had been set at liberty. He applied to Secretary of War Cameron for his release but was informed by that gentleman that he was now held as a prisoner of state. Soon after he was removed to Fort Warren in Boston Harbor. While he was confined there Mr. Ely, a Congressman from New York, who had been captured at Bull Run, where he had gone as a spectator to that battle, entered into a proposal to exchange Mr. Faulkner for Mr. Ely, but President Jefferson Davis, in his annual message to the Confederate Congress at Richmond, declared he would make Mr. Faulkner's arrest a ground of arraignment before the civilized world. After considerable delay it was decided that Mr. Faulkner should be granted a parole for thirty days, to go to Richmond, and effect, if possible, an exchange between himself and Mr. Ely. Finally President Davis reluctantly consented to the exchange and Mr. Faulkner returned to his home in Martinsburg. Within a few days after his return he was appointed Chief of Staff by General Stonewall Jackson with the rank of Lieutenant Colonel. He served in this capacity till the end of the war, when he returned a second time to his home in Berkeley County.

Defended West Virginia's claim in the Supreme Court of the United States to the counties of Jefferson and Berkeley in February, 1871, and won a decision in favor of West Virginia.

Appointed a member of the Constitutional Convention of West Virginia in 1872 and greatly aided in framing the second constitution of this State. In June, 1872, his political disabilities were removed by a special act of Congress, and in 1874 he was elected a member of the House of Rrepresentatives from West Virginia. Served on the important committees of Foreign Relations, also Education and Labor. Was a candidate for the office of United States Senator in 1876 but was defeated. Was mentioned as a candidate for Governor of West Virginia in 1880 but was unsuccessful.

His children were two sons and six daughters: Judge E. Boyd Faulkner, ex-Senator Charles J. Faulkner, Mrs. S. P. S. Pierce, Mrs. Thomas Bocock, Mrs. John P. Campbell, Mrs. Dr. W. S. Love, Mrs. Joel W. Flood, and Mrs. Dr. James W. McSherry. Died at "Boydville", his home at Martinsburg, November 1st, 1884. Three thousand people attended his funeral.

Buried in the private burying grounds of the Faulkners adjacent to Norborne Cemetery. During the latter years of his life he wrote and published a list of the prominent men and women of Berkeley County together with their activities in its affairs. This historical data which he marked "Memorabilia"—or "things to be remembered"—is of immense value to posterity, historical and otherwise.

DAVID DODD—Removed from the vicinity of Clearspring, Md., in 1851, to Berkeley County. The genealogy of the family has been traced to the time of the Crusades. The family resided in England near the boundary of Wales. Two brothers came to America in 1635 and settled in Franklin County, Pennsylvania.

David Dodd purchased what is now known as the old Dodd homestead one mile southwest of Falling Waters in 1851, and named the home "Stonington". He was a barn builder by occupation.

SAMUEL L. DODD, one of the sons of David Dodd, resides at Little Georgetown. His main occupation in former years was that of a farmer. In his time he also taught in the rural schools of the county, was County Superintendent of Schools, was Deputy Assessor of the county.

DAVID HENRY DODD—Was a teacher in the rural schools of the county, was Principal of the High Street School of Martinsburg for thirty-six consecutive terms—this position he still holds. Appointed to fill the unexpired term of Tucker Bowen (deceased) as County Superintendent of Schools of Berkeley County and was elected to that capacity for the following term. Was the author of the first Catalogue of Free Schools of the county. He, in conjunction with Willis F. Evans, organized the Berkeley County Teachers' Association (the first of the kind in the county), which functioned twelve years. This association was the forerunner of the Potomac Valley Round Table, a teacher's association on a large scale, which embraced the valley of the Potomac River in Berkeley, Jefferson, Morgan, Hampshire, Hardy and Mineral Counties in West Virginia, and Washington and Allegheny Counties, Maryland. This association merged into the Eastern Panhandle Teachers' Association, which is a large association of teachers. It meets annually and does much good for the teaching fraternity of this section. David Henry Dodd has two distinguished sons, William E. Dodd, practicing physician and surgeon, Rositer, Pa., and David L. Dodd, professor, Columbia University.

COLONEL JOHN W. DODD—Was another son of David Dodd. He was an auctioneer by profession and practiced in Berkeley County for forty years. He was the best auctioneer the county has ever produced. He had great ability as a public speaker. Was elected Assessor for two terms for the county, and while in this position put into operation a system of equal valuation which has been in use ever since. He was the Democratic candidate for Sheriff of Berkeley County against Hon. James H. Smith but was defeated by a small majority. Was proprietor of the Continental Hotel, a popular hostelry in the 90's, occupying the corner of the Public Square on the present site of the Old National Bank building, for several years. He married Miss Georgia Jefferson, a member of an old established family of the county. Mr. Dodd died in 1923.

Two daughters of David Dodd are Mrs. Ella Williamson of Harlen Springs, this county, and Mrs. Ada Dodd Poince of Dayton, Ohio, famous teacher, writer, lecturer and traveler.

S. LOWELL DODD, a son of Samuel L. Dodd, is connected with the extension work of the West Virginia Experimental Station at Morgantown, and D. E. Dodd, another son, with the Department of Agriculture of West Virginia at Morgantown. Both are grandsons of David Dodd, the head of this sketch.

NEWTON D. BAKER is one of Berkeley County's distinguished sons. He is the only one of her sons to hold a position in any of our President's Cabinets. He won universal praise in the capacity of Secretary of War in President Wilson's Cabinet in the manner in which he directed the affairs of that department in the World War. He was born at Martinsburg, W. Va., December 3rd, 1871. His parents were Dr. Newton Diehl and Mary (Dukehart) Baker. Was graduated from the Martinsburg High School, then attended the Episcopal High School of Virginia at Alexandria, and later John Hopkins University in Baltimore, from which he graduated in 1892. Returned there one year for post-graduate work and went to Washington and Lee University and took the two years law course in one year. Returned to Martinsburg and practiced law alone until about the first of January, 1896, when he went to Washington as private secretary to William L. Wilson, Post Master General of the second Cleveland administration. Returned to Martinsburg and became a law partner of the law firm of Flick, Westenhaver & Baker. Removed to Cleveland, Ohio, in January, 1899. About a year after he went there he met Tom L. Johnson at a political meeting. Johnson was then candidate for Mayor of Cleveland. Mr. Baker later became Director of the Law of the City of Cleveland (1893), which office he held until elected Mayor on the first of January. 1912. Mr. Baker knew President Wilson as a Professor at Johns Hopkins University. He, however, did not know Baker. He saw nothing more of him until he was a candidate for nomination for President, when Newton D. Baker went to Massachusetts at his invitation and made some campaign speeches with him in the primary campaign of that State. After he had been elected President, he invited Mr. Baker to occupy a seat in his Cabinet as Secretary of Interior, but as Mr. Baker had just been elected Mayor of Cleveland, he did not feel free to accept his invitation. In 1916, President Wilson appointed Newton D. Baker Secretary of War without any previous consultation with him on the subject or without his knowing he had any such intentions.

The following extract taken from "Who's Who in America", is worthy of note:

"Baker, Newton Diehl, ex-Sec. of War., b. Martinsburg, W. Va., Dec. 3, 1871, S. Newton Diehl and Mary (Dukehart) B.; B.A. Johns Hopkins, 1892; LL.B. Washington and Lee U., 1894. M. Elizabeth Leopold of Pottstown, Pa., July 5, 1902. Pvt. Sec. to Postmaster-General Wilson 1896-7; begun practice at Martinsburg, W. Va., 1897. City Solicitor of Cleveland, O., 1902-12; Mayor of Cleveland term 1912-1914 and 1914-16, and served until Mar. 4, 1921, Comm. Col. O. R. C. Mar., 1921. Member of law firm of Baker, Hostetler & Sidlo. Sos. of the Cincinnati. Clubs: Union, University, City, Chamber of Commerce (Cleveland) ; Army and Navy, University, Cosmos (Washington, D. C.). Home: 19200 S. Woodland Rd. Office: Union Trust Bldg., Cleveland, Ohio.

DR. NEWTON DIEHL BAKER—Born in Martinsburg, W. Va., on the 3rd day of October, 1841. His father, Elias Baker, was a saddler by trade, or at least he had been apprenticed to learn that trade. He married Mary Billmyer, whose family were large landowners in Jefferson County. Through this marriage he became a man of substantial property and after an unsuccessful adventure in lower Virginia, with an iron mill, he went to Martinsburg and then to Shepherdstown, having a general country store in each place in succession. At the age of nineteen, he entered the Confederate Army and remained in Stuart's Cavalry until the end of the war. His father, Elias Baker, was loyal to the Union and was appointed by President Lincoln postmaster of Shepherdstown, which office he retained throughout the whole period of the war. On his return from the war in 1865, Newton D. Baker went to Baltimore to study medicine in the University of Marylond. He had been one year at Wittenburg College at Springfield, Ohio, but he never completed his college work. In 1867, he graduated at the University of Maryland as a physician and came to Martinsburg, where he bought the house and practice of a Dr. Quigley, and from that time until his death, in 1909, he practiced medicine there. His home is now owned by Dr. James H. Shipper on East Burke Street.

D. C. WESTENHAVER—The following appeared in "Who's Who in the Buckeye State":

"Westenhaver, David C., Judge of U. S. Court, born Berkeley County, W. Va., January 13, 1865, son of David Westenhaver and Harriet (Turner) Westenhaver; educated public schools; Georgetown Univ. College Degree, LL.B.; LL.D. 1920. Married Mary C. Paull July 1, 1887. Engaged in practice of law, Martinsburg, W. Va., 1886-1903; removed to Cleveland, Ohio; resumed practice 1903. Pres. W. Va. State Bar Assn. 1898-1899. Appointed U. S. Dist. Judge Northern District of Ohio, February 19, 1917, and now serving in that capacity. Pros. Att'y Berkeley County, W. Va., 1902-1903. Member Board of Education, Cleevland, Ohio, 1912-1915. President of same, 1914-1915. Home address, 1944 East 93rd Street, Cleveland, Ohio."

GEORGE SEIBERT—Out the Tuscorora Pike, two miles west of Martinsburg, stands an old stone house of the design of the year of 1800, built by George Seibert, the father of Wendell Seibert and the grandfather of Hon. Cleveland M. Seibert of Martinsburg. George Seibert was one of the original settlers on Tuscorora Creek about the year 1763. The family originally came from Alsace-Lorraine, France, and migrated to New York State at the beginning of the eighteenth century. The name was originally spelled Seybert, as is attested by the old records of the county, but was changed to its present form about 1805. In Lewis' history of West Virginia can be found the account of Fort Seybert, a frontier post which stood twelve miles northeast of Franklin in Pendleton County. This fort was erected at that place by a relative of George Seybert's.

George Seibert left the following children: Wendall Seibert, Margaret A., who married Philip Showers, and was the grandmother of the present Showers family on Tuscorora Pike; Mary, who married William Mong, and was the grandmother of Carrie and Arlington Rousch; Otho W. Seibert, who was the father of George Seibert, who recently died on West King Street; Cromwell Seibert, and Louisa, who married Cromwell Curtis; Barnet C.

Seibert, who was the father of William Seibert, formerly of Arden; Fannie Noll, wife of Willis Noll; Otho Seibert and Albert Seibert, who went to Kansas, and Harriet, wife of Robert Miller, now residing in Maryland. The Seibert farm has been in the family name in an unbroken lineage for one hundred and thirty-six years, or since 1791. It was formerly a large farm of about 800 acres but tracts have been sold from it until it now contains 186 acres.

Wendall Seibert served with distinction throughout the Revolutionary War. The family have generally been farmers. Many grandchildren of Wendall Seibert are found residing throughout the county and in other States. The family has greatly aided in the building of Berkeley County.

CLEVELAND M. SEIBERT—Was educated in private schools, also Tinsley's Berkeley Military Academy of Martinsburg. Graduated in Law from West Virginia University at the age of 20 years. Was too young to be admitted to the bar and was not admitted to practice his profession until September, the following year, when he entered upon the practice of law at the Berkeley bar, in which he has been eminently successful.

Political Career—Elected to the West Virginia Legislature, House of Delegates, 1908; re-elected in 1911-1915. In 1911, while the youngest member of the Lower House in point of age, was made majority floor leader. From 1901 to 1903 was Mayor of Martinsburg, at which time the first sewerage and street paving program was put through. Procured from the B. & O. Railroad Company its consent to the building of the Queen Street Subway. Was nominated for Judge of the Circuit Court of the Twenty-third West Virginia Judicial District in 1926 but was defeated for the first time in his political career. In passing, it might be noted that Major General William Seibert, a relative of the Seibert family of Berkeley County, led the First Division of the American Army which landed in France upon the entry of the United States into the World War. He was also Chief Army Engineer with Colonel George W. Goethels in the building of the Panama Canal; was also Inspector of Munition Plants of the United States during the war.

HARRY ALLEN DOWNS—Charles Downs, great-grandfather of Harry Allen Downs, erected the first flour mill at Falling Waters, this county. The flour which he manufactured was transported to Williamsport, Md., thence by Chesapeak and Ohio Canal to eastern markets. Charles Downs was born the latter part of the eighteenth century not long after the Revolutionary War and was one of the largest landowners in Berkeley County. His son, Davenport Downs, was born at Falling Waters in the year 1826. He married Miss Ann LeFevre and moved to Iowa, Walpalls County. While residing there his only son, Joseph Allen Downs, was born. Upon the death of his mother, who died of childbirth, Joseph Allen Downs was brought east by his father and given to the care of Miss Mary Cookus, residing on a farm of a relative, Mr. Asahale VanMetre, in Berkeley County.

He was educated in the public schools of the county and at Hyde's Seminary, Martinsburg. Taught school in the country districts; was Principal of the Fifth Ward School of Martinsburg for fifteen years. He married Caroline

Jeanett Evans, a descendant of John Evans and Polly VanMetre Evans of French and Indian War fame at John Evans Fort on the Opequon Creek (mentioned elsewhere in this work).

To this union was born:

WILLIAM SMITH DOWNS—Who was educated in the Martinsburg schools, a graduate of the Martinsburg High School, class of 1901; was graduated from the West Virginia University, class of 1905, with the degree of B.S.C.E. After his graduation he was employed by the Bolivian Government of South America in railroad building for a period of two years. When he returned to West Virginia he located at Kingwood where he was engaged as engineer for the Pittsburg Hydro Electric Company in water-power enterprises; at present Division Engineer for the State Road Commission of West Virginia with headquarters at Morgantown.

Harry A. Downs, another son of Joseph Downs, was educated in the public Schools of Martinsburg. Graduated from the Martinsburg High School, class of 1905; graduated West Virginia University (Law Department), class of 1907, degree LL.B. Practiced law in Martinsburg. Elected to the West Virginia House of Delegates, 1920. Appointed Congressional Committeeman for Berkeley County for the Republican party, Second Congressional District. Candidate for Prosecuting Attorney of Berkeley County in 1912-1916, but was unsuccessful. Appointed United States Commissioner for the Northern District of West Virginia in January, 1913, by Hon. Alston G. Dayton, then Judge of the United States Court of that district, for four years; reappointed in 1917. Served in this capacity until 1921. Served as City Solicitor of Martinsburg under the administration of Mayor Dr. H. G. Tonkin and Mayor Cleveland M. Seibert. Re-appointed U. S. Commissioner in 1923, which position he now holds.

WILLIAM SMITH—Father of the Smith family on Tuscarora, together with George W. Horner, father of the Horner family in the vicinity of Arden, migrated from Adams County, Pennsylvania, in the year 1852 to Berkeley County. They traversed the Shenandoah Valley as far south as Staunton and in the vicinity of Richmond, looking for suitable locations to purchase homes. Not finding a location as well suited to their needs as the ones in Berkeley County, they returned, and William Smith purchased the present James H. Smith farm near Salem Church, on Tuscarora, and George Washington Horner purchased the present Robert G. Horner farm near Arden. William Smith, together with William Wilen, the father of Undertaker John Wilen of Martinsburg, were elected to the West Virginia Legislature as members of the House of Delegates, at Wheeling (then the Capitol of West Virginia), January 17, 1865. These two gentlemen have the distinction of being the first Delegates to represent Berkeley County after it became a part of West Virginia.

William Smith also represented Berkeley County in the Fourth and Fifth Legislatures.

JAMES H. SMITH—Son of William Smith, the subject of the above sketch, together with I. B. Snodgrass, represented Berkeley County in the

Seventeenth Legislature of West Virginia at Wheeling, January 14, 1885. He served as Deputy Sheriff under Charles H. Miller for two years. Was elected Sheriff of Berkeley County 1896-1900. Was appointed a Member of the Board of Equalization at its formation and held that office continuously until July 1st, 1926, when he resigned on account of ill health, having held the office under four different Governors, showing with what high esteem his sound judgment in the true valuation of real estate property was held by them. This Board was created by the Legislature in 1902 and had for its purpose a more equitable assessed valuation of the real estate throughout the county, and Mr. Smith, while a member of this Board, had instituted a system by which all real estate valuation was placed on the same footing. He married Miss Emma Thatcher, a member of a prominent family of Tuscarora, and to this union were born:

HENRY LOTT SMITH—Educated in the rural schools, in the Martinsburg High School and West Virginia University (Agricultural Department). Lott Smith, together with Rev. Charles Beard, served the county in the Thirty-seventh Legislature, and with James S. Dailey in the Thirty-sixth Legislature at Charleston. The latter convened January 10, 1923, and the former in January, 1925. He succeeded in getting several important bills enacted into laws; one, the elimination of the cedar trees, known as the Cedar Rust Law, on account of the damage done the apple industry from the cedar rust fungi; the other, a law creating an apple inspection commission to inspect apple packing locally to see that the pack confirms to the West Virginia standard pack. Under the old system the inspection was done when the shipment arrived at its destination, thus working a hardship on the grower for, in many instances, the shipment did not conform to the standard required by the law of the State to which the shipment was made and the grower was compelled to sell at a loss. Under the present system the shipment is accepted at its face value, provided it bears the inspector's stamp.

JOHN W. SMITH—The younger brother, resides at his farm near the old Smith homestead and is actively engaged in apple culture.

CHARLES M. LAMAR—Thomas LaMar, the great-grandfather of this sketch, was a native of France. He removed to England and became a naturalized Englishman. He married there and migrated to America in 1653 and settled in Prince George County, Maryland, on a grant of land he had obtained from the King of England; a grant for one thousand acres. Afterwards his son migrated to Martinsburg vicinity and bought a farm near the North Mountain near the Jonathan Thatcher homestead. The family finally moved to Martinsburg.

Charles M. Lamar was a Member of the City Council of Martinsburg for two terms while Dr. James W. McSherry was Mayor. He was Chairman of the Republican City Executive Committee while Hon. Alexander Clohan was Chairman of the Republican County Executive Committee. He was at one time a candidate for Sheriff of Berkeley County but lost the nomination to the late Kensey B. Creque, Jr.

His brother, E. Holmes Lamar, was a prominent educator in the schools of the county, holding the Principalship of the Hedgesville High School for a number of terms. He was a graduate of Dickenson College, Carlysle, Pa. Mr. Charles M. Lamar is at present extensively engaged in the culture of apple orchards in the county.

F. M. WOODS, D.D.—This eminent divine has been the pastor of the Presbyterian Church of Martinsburg for forty-eight lears, having been appointed to that charge in 1879. He took charge of the Tuscarora Presbyterian Church in the fall of 1889 and had charge of that church until 1913 also. Where the Presbyterian Church now stands on Tuscarora Creek was the first place where the gospel was publicly proclaimed west of the Blue Ridge Mountains.

His advanced age together with having served his people so long and faithfully caused him to tender his resignation as pastor of the church September 1, 1926, but at this time (1927) he is still their pastor, the people loathing to give him up. He is a gentleman of the "old school", universally loved by all, whether of that denomination or not. He was Moderator of the Synod of Virginia in 1897. He has three distinguished sons, two ministers and one a lawyer. The first of the former is David J. Woods, D.D., a Presbyterian minister, stationed at Clinton, S. C.,; the second, Andrew H. Woods, M.D., stationed at Peking, China, connected with the Rockefeller Foundation and Professor of Neurology, Peking Union Medical College; the latter, Judge J. M. Woods, Judge of the Twenty-third Judicial Circuit of West Virginia from 1913 to 1925, when he resigned to practice his profession in Charleston, W. Va.

PERCEY W. LEITER—Is a native of Washington County, Md. He came to Martinsburg in 1874. He was elected Mayor of Martinsburg one term and Recorder five terms or eleven years. While Mayor, he instigated the bond issue for the present sewage system and the subway on North Queen Street. Mrs. P. W. Leiter is the daughter of H. N. Deatrick, a former merchant of the city. Mr. Leiter was a groceryman for five years and a wholesale produce merchant for three years in Martinsburg. At present he is connected with the Old National Bank as trust officer.

ALEXANDER PARKS, SR.—Was a member of the West Virginia Senate, 1903, and as such member was the first Chairman of the Committee on Labor of that body. He also introduced the bill creating the State Board of Agriculture, of which Hon. C. R. Sperow of Hedgesville District was one of the first members. He married Miss Mary Ella Nadenbousch, daughter of Colonel J. Q. A. Nadenbousch of Civil War fame. He was a member of the City Council three terms, at which time he held the office of City Treasurer. When he became City Treasurer, the finances of the city were in bad condition and he, by good business methods, placed them on a solid footing. The people of the county, recognizing his ability to handle the affairs of a municipality, elected him a member of the County Court of Berkeley County in 1909. He was president of that body for six years. While a member of the Court, he inaugurated the new road building system which was the elimination of the old antiquated system of free road labor and appointed road overseers over various sections of the county. He operated for a number of years the Equality Flour and Feed Mill on Commerce Street. He has large farm holdings throughout the county.

ALEXANDER B. PARKS—Son of Alexander Parks, Sr., and Mary Ella (Nadenbousch) Parks. One of the foremost men to promote an interest in aviation in this section. Founder of the Berkeley Aviation Club of Martinsburg and Berkeley County. His first experiments in this field was with kites, next with gliders flown from the top of Berkeley Place (then known as the Old Fair Ground), east of the southern part of the town. These gliders were of a crude character. He has been fortunate in not having any serious accidents with these but many slight ones. In 1916, he learned to pilot planes at Halethorp, Maryland. This was in the early days of flying in this country. He has written many articles on aviation for various magazines of national circulation and assisted in establishing landing fields on the airways, sending sketches and description in to the then, Air Service—now Army Air Corps. All of this type of work, including traveling and other expenses, were borne by himself without compensation. As a reward of his interest, time and energies for work of national and local character, he was notified from Washington by Captain St. Clair Streett (who acted recently as escort to Lindburg) that he was made a member of "A.H.F." (Aeronautical Hall of Fame), a most coveted honor and international in character, whose membership list contains many of the notables of America, Europe, Japan and Australia, as the Prince of Wales, Captain Charles A. Lindburg, Commander Richard F. Byrd, Lieutenant Maitland and some two hundred others. Mr. Parks was made the first President of the Berkeley Aviation Club and has held the same position since its organization. Besides these activities, he has been associated with his father, Hon. Alexander Parks, in the milling business at Parks' Mill.

JOHN N. PARKS—Son of Hon. Alexander Parks and Mary Ella (Nadenbousch) Parks and was a member of the West Virginia Legislature at the outbreak of the World War. Notwithstanding his connection with that body, he volunteered his services in 1917, but could not be accepted on that account. Finding this to be the case, he offered his resignation as a member of the Legislature, but it was not accepted. He entered the war any way and was commissioned Captain in the fall of 1917. Later he was promoted to the rank of Major in the 99th Division, in which capacity he served until the end of the war. He was instrumental in getting the first post of the American Legion established at Martinsburg, and has a letter on file from the late Colonel Theodore Roosevelt commending him highly for his work of organizing this post.

JACOB HESSE—Ludwig Hesse, his father, came from Hanover, Germany, about 1850 to Martinsburg and established a meat market on Liberty Street. Jacob Hesse removed to the vicinity of Jones Springs and later to Baxter in Back Creek Valley. He was elected County Commissioner of Berkeley

County from 1918 to 1924. He was President of this Court for four years. At the time he was a member of the Court he operated extensive apple orchards in Back Creek Valley. When he became a member of the County Court the county owned only one old dilapidated truck, and he immediately began to build up the present fine system of road machinery with which the County Road Department is at present supplied.

GEORGE MEADE BOWERS—Was born in Gerardstown, Berkeley County, Virginia (Berkeley County then being still a part of Virginia), on September 13, 1863, and was the son of John S. Bowers and Mary E. (Stump) Bowers. He was educated in the Gerardstown schools and the Martinsburg Grammar School. At the age of seventeen, he operated the flour mill for his father, known as the Bowers Mill. When he became of age his father having died, he administered the estate with singular dispatch. At this early age he was elected a member of the Board of Directors of the National Bank of Martinsburg (The Old National Bank), and was later elected to the Board of Directors of the Peoples National Bank of Martinsburg (The Peoples Trust Company). In 1911, he was elected President of this bank and held the office until his death in 1926. He cast his first vote for James G. Blaine for President. In 1884 he was Chairman of the Berkeley County delegates at the Republican State Convention at Parkersburg. In 1885 he was elected a member of the House of Delegates from Berkeley County. In 1889 he was the Republican nominee for State Auditor of West Virginia but was defeated. In 1890 he was appointed by President Harrison Supervisor of the Census for northern West Virginia. In 1892 he was a delegate to the Republican National Convention at Minneapolis. In 1893 he was made a member and the Treasurer of the World's Fair at Chicago. In 1896 he was appointed by President McKinley U. S. Commissioner of Fish and Fisheries. This bureau had just been formed by the National Government to propagate and promulgate the culture of fish, as several species of fish were in danger of becoming extinct. Mr. Bowers, with his usual energy and sound judgment, took hold of the work and in a short time had built up his department to such an efficiency that he received the commendation of Congress and the President. He did not know much about fish when he first entered upon his duties, but in less than three months after his appointment he was the best informed man on that subject in the country. He was re-appointed to this position by three Presidents successively, McKinley, Roosevelt and Taft, and served in all fifteen years or until 1913.

In 1914 he was elected to the 64th Congress to fill the unexpired term of Hon. Wm. G. Brown (deceased) of the Second Congressional District of West Virginia. He was elected to the 65th Congress by a majority of 860 votes, to the 66th Congress by a majority of 2360 votes, and to the 67th Congress by a majority of 10,342 votes. While in the 65th Congress he voted for the United States to enter the war against Germany. While in Congress he was a member of the important Ways and Means Committee. On November 18, 1884, he married Bessie C. Gray of Gerardstown. They have four children living: George M. Bowers, Jr., Stephen E. Bowers, Eleanore (Bowers) Grove and Jeane Daugherty. Congressman Bowers died

December 8th, 1925, and was buried in the Presbyterian Cemetery at Gerardstown. In 1924 he was the largest individual owner of apple orchards in Berkeley County. George M. Bowers was one of the prominent citizens of the county in his time and did much for its welfare, but the greatest and best thing that can be said of him is he was a friend of man.

The following is taken from the "Congressional Directory" of the 65th Congress, Second Session, April, 1918:

"Representatives. West Virginia—Second District—Counties: Barbour, Berkeley, Grant, Hampshire, Hardy, Jefferson, Mineral, Monongalia, Morgan, Pandleton, Preston, Randolph and Tucker (13 counties). Population (1910), 211,690.

"George M. Bowers, Republican, of Martinsburg, W. Va., was born September 13, 1863, at Gerrardstown, West Virginia, in the heart of the Shenandoah Valley; was a member of the West Virginia Legislature at the age of 23; a candidate for Auditor of the State in 1888; Census Superintendent in 1890; Treasurer World's Fair Managers in 1893; appointed by President McKinley Commissioner of Fisheries in February, 1898, and reappointed by President Roosevelt and President Taft; resigned April 16, 1913. Elected at a special election held in the Second Crongressional District of West Virginia on May 9, 1916, to fill the vacancy caused by the death of Hon. William G. Brown; was nominated on June 6. 1916, by a majority of nearly 10,000 votes, and re-elected November 7, 1916, to the Sixty-fifth Congress."

PEYTON R. HARRISON III—Father was Lieutenant Peyton R. Harrison of Company D, "Berkeley Border Guards," C. S. A. Killed at the first battle of Manassas, July 21st, 1861, when Peyton R. Harrison III was but two years old. After the close of the Civil War, his mother, Sarah F. Harrison, in conjunction with Miss Betty J. Hunter, established the Norbourn Female Seminary at the old Norbourn Hall, then situated on West Race Street where the Heiston property now stands. Educated at the Virginia Military Institute at Lexington, Va. Was Mayor of Martinsburg two terms. Elected Magistrate of Martinsburg at Cleveland's first election. Elected in 1924 to the same position, which he now holds. Appointed Commissioner in Chancery and has held this same office for the puast quarter of a century. Appointed and continued to hold the office of Secretary of the Board of Education of Arden District for fourteen consecutive years. Married twice—First wife was Miss Lilian Gorham of Rockford, Ill. Second wife was Mrs. Nannie Spottswood Boyd, daughter of E. Holmes Boyd of Winchester, Va., and a grand-daughter of General Elisha Boyd of "Boydville". There have been four Peyton R. Harrisons in direct line of descent: Peyton R. Harrison I, Presbyterian Minister, Martinsburg; Peyton R. Harrison II, Lawyer, Lieutenant in the Confederate Army, killed in action at the first battle of Manassas, July 21st, 1861; Peyton R. Harrison III, subject of this sketch, and Peyton R. Harrison IIII, student at Washington and Lee University of Virginia, Law and Literature. The Peyton R. Harrison family were Confederates and lived in the property (Norbourn Hall) owned by James L. Randolph, who was a relative of theirs and a Union man. In this way their home during the Civil War was free from destruction by fire or any other incursions by either army.

DAVID HUNTER STROTHER (*"Port Crayon"*)—In Norbourne Cemetery are six little graves, all children of David Hunter Strother who died in infancy. Born at Martinsburg, Virginia, September 26, 1816, and died at Charles Town, Jefferson County, March 8, 1888. One of the most widely known authors of the United States. One of his first teachers was Samuel F. B. Morse, inventor of the electric telegraph. Studied art for two years in Rome, Italy. Returned home and adopted the nom-de-plume of "Port Crayon"., under which he wrote "The Virginia Caanan", which made him famous. Served in the Federal Army during the Civil War and rose to the rank of Briegadier-General. Consul-General to Mexico in 1877; appointed by President Hayes. Filled this position for seven years.

Was war correspondent for Harper's Magazine during the Civil War. His sister was Mrs. James L. Randolph, whose husband was James L. Randolph, Chief Civil Engineer for the Baltimore and Ohio Railroad for a number of years and mentioned in the biographical sketch of Peyton R. Harrison III (this work).

While traveling in France, he saw a cemetery laid out to suit his artistic taste, and, making a sketch of it, when he returned to Martinsburg he devised the plans of the present Green Hill Cemetery precisely as he saw the one France. He, together with the surveyor, John P. Kearfott, laid off the grounds. As everyone knows, this cemetery covers a knoll, the mausoleum in the center with the lots, walks and drives arranged around it in a circular shape. This is the most beautiful cemetery in this country on account of its taste in arrangement.

JOSEPH D. SMITH—Magistrate for Arden District. Was appointed in 1904 and elected at the ensuing term and continued in office for twenty years. Was defeated in the election of 1920. Was appointed by the County Court of Berkeley County to fill the unexpired term of Noble B. Kilmer, resigned. Was elected in the fall 1926 and serving at the present time. Was born in Jefferson County. Was educated in the rural schools. Was a volunteer in the "Flue" epidemic in Berkeley County in 1918. Has four brothers: Dr. E. L. Smith, D.D.S., at Martinsburg, who was educated at the University of Maryland, Baltimore; T. G. Smith and Harry Smith, Photographers, Martinsburg, and E. L. Smith, deceased.

HAROLD H. KEEDY—Assistant Clerk of the County Court of Berkeley County from January 21 1921, to the present. Appointed by Paul H. Martin, Clark. Chairman of the Republican Executive Committee of Berkeley County from 1921 to the present. Soldier in the World War, with position in the Ordnance Department stationed at Camp Hancock, Ga. Military Instructor, 1918 to the end of the war. At present holds a commission as First Lieutenant in the Officers' Reserve Corps of the Army of the United States.

JACK O. HENSON—Lawyer, Martinsburg, W. Va. Father was John O. Henson. Born at Bunker Hill, W. Va., in 1890. Educated in the rural and village schools of that place. Graduate of the Law Department of West Virginia University, class of 1908, with the degree of LL.B. Assistant Attorney General under William G. Conley for West Virginia, 1910 to

1913. present holds the position of Commissioner, State Board of Law Examiners, to which office he was appointed by the State Supreme Court in 1919. Holds position as City Attorney for the City of Martinsburg, having been appointed by Mayor Geo. W. Applebey. President, The Peoples Trust Company Bank, to which position he was elected in 1926, upon the death of Hon. George M. Bowers.

WILLIAM R. SPIKER—One of the five remaining veterans of the Union Army still living in Berkeley County. Retired farmer. Farmed for many years the "Runnymeade" farm in Berkeley County, situated near the Frederick County, Va., line, south of Gerrardstown. Union soldier in the Civil War. Enlisted February 4th, 1864, at Logansport, Indiana, in the 73rd Indiana Regiment. Transferred to the 29th Indiana Regiment, and was assigned to duty under General Thomas' Brigade, w.th which he served till the close of the Civil War. Born in Shenandoah County, Va. Father of Arthur L. Spiker, residing at the Spiker farm at Horner Sawmill on the Arden road; J. W. Spiker, west of Arden; Edward Spiker, farmer, at Bunker Hill; Amos W. Spiker, at Arden; Mrs. Carter Coe, at Tablers; and Mrs. Geo. William Pitzer, at Pitzer's Chapel.

JAMES W. MCDONALD, SR.—Was large landowner in the vicinity of Darkesville. Prominent in the affairs of that town until his death in 1918. Father of Ernest F. McDonald, large landowner and orchardist near Darkesville, also in Pennsylvania; James W. McDonald, Sheriff of Pima Cote County, Arizona; Bruce E. McDonald, farmer, at the McDonald homestead at Darkesville; Mrs. E. N. Zeilor, Frederick County, Maryland; Mrs. Mazie Miller, wife of former Sheriff H. S. Miller of Berkeley County, and Roy McDonald of Wichita, Kansas. Grandfather of James E. McDonald, prominent fruit grower of Arden, graduate of West Virginia, class of 1922, with degree of B.S.Agr.; First Lieutenant, O. R. C., United States Army, Headquarters 100th Division at Huntington, W. Va.; connected with the Extension Department, West Virginia University; also of Richard C. McDonald, graduate West Virginia University, class of 1923, degree of B.S.Agr., Field Agent of the Chilian Nitrate Company, Valparaiso, Chili.

JAMES B. FISHER—Father was a man of considerable means in Fulton County, Pennsylvania, but lost all his wealth by endorsing notes for his neighbors. He, together with his wife and daughter and son James, came to Berkeley County in 1875. Father only lived two years after moving to this county. The family drove here by wagon, rented the farm of the late James M. Vanmetre, east of Martinsburg. A long illness, causing a large doctor's bill together with the family expenses, consumed all the possessions of the family, which left the mother and sister wholly dependent upon young Fisher, a lad of 16 years. He moved the family to Martinsburg and secured a position as clerk in the store of C. P. Herring for five dollars per month and board. Shortly afterwards he received $20 per month by boarding with his mother. He remained in this position for two years, and then went to Pittsburgh, Pennsylvania, and worked for forty dollars per month. Came back to Martinsburg and clerked for Eugene Herring, a brother of C. P.

Herring, who conducted the "Blue Front" (on account of the frontage of the store being painted with a bright sky-blue color), a general store. Remained there six months and accepted a position with John W. Bishop, wholesale grocer, as traveling salesman for the smaller towns in this section and as far west as Keyser, W. Va. Remained in this capacity for ten years, his salary being advanced from time to time until reached the mark of $1000 per year.

Started in business for himself in 1885 in the Myers building on North Queen Street, now occupied by the Sites hardware store, under the head of James B. Fisher, Dry Goods, &c. Remained in this building 24 years, when he disposed of his store and fixtures to Miss Ida Beck. After retiring from this business he purchased the farms of E. Mong Pitzer on the Arden road, which he still owns, and the Captain E. L. Hoffman farm on the Arden-Darkesville road. The latter he sold to James E. Butler in 1920. Was a candidate for the Legislature in 1913, again a candidate for the office of County Commissioner in 1917, but was defeated for both offices by small majorities. As chairman of the Roads Committee of the Business Men's Association of Martinsburg, he helped to build the Arden-Darkesville road and the Shoppert Ford road in the county. He is an Elder in the Reformed Church of Martinsburg and has also held the office of Treasurer in that church for twelve years. His only child, J. Carl Fisher, was a soldier in the World War in the Bureau of Standards in Washington, D. C., and is at present connected with the Consolidated Gas and Electric Company of Baltimore City.

MILTON S. MILLER—Deputy Sheriff and Jailer under Sheriffs E. S. Tabler and Harry S. Miller. Member of the Arden Board of Education with Geo. D. Pitzer and David Hudgel—these three who brought the efficiency of that district up to the present high standard by wisely locating and building eight new school houses throughout the district. This building program extended over a number of years and the taxpayers realized no burdensome taxation by this policy. His father, Geo. W. Miller, was a large landholder east of Pikeside near Opequon Creek. His grandfather, Samuel Miller, came to this section and bought a large tract of land about the beginning of the nineteenth century. When Milton S. Miller was a lad of seven years, a Confederate soldier drew his musket and was going to shoot his grandfather, Samuel Miller, who was an aged man, because he did not vote for the secession of Virginia at the beginning of the Civil War (he thinking it was not right). The grandfather told him to shoot, as he would not deprive him of many more years of life. This bold affront on the part of his grandfather probably saved his life for the soldier lowered his gun and walked away. Young Milton was compelled to stand by, a trembling witness to this attempt on his grandfather's life. His father, Geo. W. Miller, volunteered to serve in the Confederate Army but was rejected on account of physical disability. During the Civil War there was no undertaker at Martinsburg. An epidemic carried off a number of the inhabitants of that section. George W. Miller offered his services to bury the deceased there. At one time he swam the Opequon at Boley's Ford, the waters of that creek being too high to cross with a team on account of hard rains, with a coffin under one arm to bury Benjamin Boley, grandfather of Frank E. Boley, the hardware merchant of Martinsburg.

Brother to R. Seaton Miller, the merchant on North Queen Street and at one time a farmer east of town.

MAURICE FITZGERALD—Foreman, Interwoven Mills. His father, Michael Fitzgerald, was a soldier in the Union Army during the entire war. He was a private soldier attached to General Lew Wallis' command and his first visit to Berkeley County was when this command encamped for several days on Berkeley Place at one time during the war. He liked the appearance of the county so well that when the war was over he came here and settled in Martinsburg. He knew Major McKinley (afterwards President) at the battle of Anteitam. The night of President Lincoln's assassination he was detailed to guard duty at the White House. Volunteered for service at Indianapolis, Indiana, in the spring of 1861.

CHARLES E. DICK—Elected County Commissioner for Berkeley County in the fall of 1924. His great-grandfather, Peter Dick, migrated to America from Bavaria, Germany, to Pennsylvania, about 1780; thence to Winchester, Va., 1790, and thence to Back Creek Valley in the vicinity of Jones Spring in 1792. His grandfather, Peter Dick, was reared a "bound boy", that is, he was placed in charge of a man who reared him until he became 21 years of age, at which time he was his own man or "Free". He was known as "The Wagoner", as he was one of the best manipulators of a team of horses, two, four or six, in that section. Charles E. Dick, the subject of this sketch, is an adept as a teamster also. In those days when wood and timber was plentiful a wagoner or teamster, if he was a good one, was one to be envied, but the position has fallen into disuse and has been superceded by the "truck driver". Robert W. Dick, the father of Charles, was born at Ganotown in 1853 and died at Jones Spring in 1919. Mr. Dick has proven himself to be an efficient member of the County Court, looking after the business of the county in a businesslike manner.

JOHN SHIMP—Came from Pennsylvania with Peter Dick in 1780. Was a soldier in the American Revolution, serving the entire period of the war. One of the earliest settlers in Back Creek Valley near Jones Spring. Left three sons: Jonas, John and Jacob. The latter was a Methodist minister. Jonas S. Shimp purchased the Dick homestead in 1823 and the property has been in the Dick and Shimp family for 104 years. Nathan Shimp, about the only blacksmith left in the county, is located on the Warm Spring road at John Riner's Crossroads. He has worked at his trade for thirty years.

OSCAR B. MILLER—Assistant Jailer for former Sheriffs E. H. Tabler and H. S. Miller. Deputy Sheriff under the present Sheriff, J. C. McKown. Appointed City Sergeant of Martinsburg by Mayrs G. B. Wiltshire and Cleveland M. Seibert. Son of Milton S. Miller. His wife, Mrs. Oscar B. Miller, is a teacher of prominence in the Pikeside Graded School.

VERNON B. GARTON—Assistant editor and reporter for the *Martinsburg Evening Journal*. Came to Martinsburg in 1909 and entered upon his duties with that paper which connection he has held for eighteen years. His home was formerly in Winchester, Va. His father was a soldier in the Union Army in the Civil War, connected with Cole's Cavalry. His editorials in the *Journal* are read by thousands and are a great factor in moulding public sentiment in this section of the State and surrounding States. His reporting is of a high order, clean cut and to the point.

J. C. MCKOWN—Sheriff of Berkeley County; elected in the fall of 1924. Married Miss Martha Zimmerman of Louisville, Ky. He has a daughter, Charlotte Campbell McKown, member of the Martinsburg High School, class of 1927. Has son, Gilbert C. McKown, also member of the Martinsburg High School, class of 1930. Secretary Cumberland Fruit Exchange, the original fruit exchange of the Cumberland-Shenandoah apple section. Chairman Finance Committee, Shenandoah Valley Bank and Trust Company. Business Manager Agent for John M. Miller since 1918. Interested in 1140 acres of apple orchards in this section. Handles from 500 to 1100 carloads apples yearly for the Cumberland Fruit Exchange.

RAY SEVERS—Deputy Sheriff under Sheriff J. C. McKown. Formerly engaged in the apple barrel industry at Inwood priod to his appointment.

HARRY F. SMITH—Originally from Washington County, Maryland. Manager Western Union Telegraph Company at this place for twenty years. Elected Chairman Republic City Executive Committee and under his supervision the Mayor, Geo. W. Appleby, and City Council was elected in 1925. Appointed Deputy Assessor by Assessor Harry E. Johnson in 1924. Extensively engaged in small fruit culture at his farm on the Dry Run road.

WILLIAM C. MORGAN—County Surveyor. Born in Clarke County, Virginia, and came to Berkeley County in 1892. Was opponent of George W. Vanmetre for this position at every election from that time until Mr. Vanmetre's death in 1919. Since that time has been elected County Surveyor without opposition.

GEORGE RYNEAL, JR.—Father, George Ryneal, Sr. Born in Switzerland in 1798; came from there to Martinsburg; established a bakery; embarked in the mercantile business which he continued until his death which occurred in 1879. During the Civil War was a Union supporter. Having the interests of the soldiers at heart, did everything he could to better their condition. In acknowledgment of these services he was presented with a testimonial by one of the regiments, as follows: "Presented to George Ryneal, Sr., by Company A, Eighteenth Connecticut Volunteer Infantry, for his manifestations of loyalty, true patriotism and faithfulness to the United States Government in preserving their efforts from falling into the hands of the enemy during the recent invasion of Maryland"; signed by Lieutenant R. Kerr and forty-two others. He left the following distinguished sons: O. F. Ryneal, Principal Third Ward School at one time, and George Ryneal, Jr., connected with the *Martinsburg Herald* at one time, a newspaper of prominence, published at Martinsburg. Born at Martinsburg March 24, 1838; accepted a clerkship in a store at St. Louis, Mo. (1857); was clerk in a pharmacy at Pocahontas, Arkansas; removed to Washington, D. C. (1862); held a clerkship in a store there, and in 1865 launched in business for himself, dealing in paint, oils and artists' supplies; continued there until 1894, when he turned his business over to his three nephews who were his clerks at that time. Accumulated large holdings in Washington (D. C.) real estate; became President of the Independent Roller Milling Company of North Mountain; Director of the Peoples Trust Company Bank of Martinsburg; President of the Franklin Insurance Company of Washington, D. C.; and President of the North Mountain Brick Works. In 1905 he presented Martinsburg with a modern fire engine with complete equipment. The company organized soon after took the name of Ryneal Hose Company, of which he was made honorary president; helped materially in the financing and building of the Y. M. C. A. building on West King Street; one of the builders of the Lutheran Memorial Church in Washington, D. C.; treasurer of the church for twenty-two years. Bought and repaired the fine old colonial mansion on the Potomac River near Dam No. 5, in the northern section of the county. This is known as "Honeywood," the ancestral home of the Colston's. Was elected to the Legislature of West Virginia in 1907. Died at Martinsburg.

WILLIAM T. NOLL—The Noll family dates back to the reign of Henry VIII of England. At that time the name was written Knoll, later as Knollys, Noel and Nolle, and were large landholders in England. During the reign of Queen Mary, on account of the family adhering to the Church of England, the property of the four brothers was confiscated by the Crown and two of them sent to the block, the other two escaping to France. Here their case was almost as bad as it was in England and the family were reduced to the direst poverty and they were compelled to keep continually in hiding. One of the sons returned to England during the reign of Queen Elizabeth and was given a small share of the once princely estate. He married there, reared a family, and one of his grandsons migrated to Virginia in the good ship "Due Return" on one of her voyages to America. The name was changed to Noll, and from there one of the sons migrated to Berkeley County and settled at the headwaters of the Tuscarora—Gottleib Noll by name. William T. Noll was a member of Company B, First Regiment, Virginia Cavalry, C. S. A. He entered as Second Lieutenant at the time of its organization (1860) and was afterwards promoted to First Lieutenant; wounded at Gettysburg, July 3, 1863; served throughout the war from 1860 to 1865, until the surrender at Appomattox. Was Deputy Sheriff of Berkeley County under Sheriff Robert H. Lamon.

ALLEN B. NOLL—Born in Gerardstown District, Berkeley County; educated in the rural schools and Martinsburg High School; graduated with honors from the West Virginia University, class of 1896, degree LL.B.; began the practice of law in the law firm of Flick, Westenhaver & Noll.

Mr. Flick died in 1904, when the firm became Westenhaver & Noll. In 1903 D. C. Westenhaver moved to Cleveland, Ohio, and became United States District Judge of the Northern District of Ohio, and Mr. Noll continued under the firm name of Allen B. Noll, Attorney-at-Law. He was three times elected Prosecuting Attorney of Berkeley County, and during the "Flue" epidemic at Martinsburg was appointed Chairman of the Welfare Committee, and, although a sick man himself, remained at his post until the ravages of that dread disease had spent itself. At one time he served as doctor, nurse and undertaker, all in one.

CHARLES STEWART—Charles Stuart, as the name was once spelled, migrated to the Colony of Jamestown and became a tobacco planter. He came from England and was a staunch supporter of the English throne at that time. After building a home on the James River, he sent to England for his young wife who had been left behind until he could be located in the New World. William S. Stewart, a descendant of Charles Stuart the Cavalier emigrant to Jamestown, was born in Martinsburg, Virginia, in 1844. At first he was engaged in agricultural pursuits but later turned his attention to banking and became a successful and widely known financier; built "Aspen Hall", a large country residence in the suburbs of Martinsburg (Boyd Avenue). His son, William T. Stewart, married Miss Amelia L. E. Emmart.

JOHN W. STEWART—Educated in the public schools of Martinsburg, University of West Virginia, and University of Maryland; entered the real estate and insurance business; later founded the American Horticultural Distributing Company at Martinsburg, and, together with Nat T. Frame (at present connected with the West Virginia Extension Department), patented and manufactured the celebrated "Target Brand" insecticide spray material for the eradication of sucking insects and fungi, injurious to fruit trees. Developed the large "Protumna Orchards" at Tablers, Berkeley County; also manufactured the Stewart Spraynig Outfit at Tablers, a machine for spraying fruit trees for large commercial orchards, operated and transported by its own power. Had Mr. Stewart lived to complete this invention it would have revolutionized the spraying part of the fruit industry. He died in 1921, and in his death Berkeley County lost one of its most useful young men. Another son of William T. Stewart and Amelia (Emmart) Stewart, was:

ROBERT H. STEWART—Born at Martinsburg, W. Va., July 13, 1879. Educated at Fishburn Military Academy, Waynesboro, Va., West Virginia University and University of Maryland, graduating from the latter in 1900 with distinction in scientific agriculture which he applied to fruit growing; purchased five hundred and seventeen acres of land which he planted in apple trees. This orchard is known today throughout the country. The photographic views of this model orchard in its various phases of development were exhibited at the Pittsburg Land Show and were highly appreciated by the orchard owners of the country. Married Elizabeth Boak, daughter of S. D. Boak of Martinsburg.

CASKEY—The name dates back to the time of the conquest of England by William the Conqueror. When William the Norman invaded England, Jean Casque, one of his most trusted captains, was at the head of a trained body of troops. Jean Casque married an English maid and settled near London. After a time the French name became Angelicised into Caskey. In 1624, Richard Caskey, the lineal descendant of Jean Casque, came to the Colony of Virginia; became a tobacco planter; took up a large tract of land on the James River above Wyenoke; married a maid who came from England; built a log house in the midst of a clearing. The family consisted of several children. His eldest son, Richard, and several companions, on returning from a hunting expedition, found their parents and brothers and sisters massacred by the Indians and their houses burned. Two members of the family, John, a boy of fourteen, and Esther, a girl of twelve, were missing., and it was later discovered that they had gone down the river in a canoe that morning to visit friends. Richard took them to Jamestown and placed them among friends and set himself to the task of exterminating the Indians. Right well did he accomplish this for he became known throughout that region as an Indian scout. From these two brothers descended the Caskeys of Berkeley County.

JOHN C. CASKEY—A descendent of Jean Casque of Normandy and of Richard I. and Richard II. of Virginia, was born in Berkeley County. He was a planter. Married Mary Schoffstall. To this union was born:

WILLIAM CASKEY—Born in Berkeley County, Va. Enlisted in the Confederate Army, Company D, 2nd Reg. Va. Inf. Volunteers (Berkeley Border Guards), 1860. Taken ill at the end of the war and died in a short time. Married Mary Ann Palmer.

WILLIAM P. CASKEY—Born in Martinsburg, Va., November 9th, 1849; was at first a farmer, then employed at the Hannis Distilling Company from 1880 to 1883; was First Sergeant, Martinsburg Artillery Company No. 3, J. L. Nadenbousch, Captain; from 1883 to 1886 Second Sergeant of the Berkeley Zouaves; in 1913 elected Captain of Ryneal Hose Company No. 1 of Martinsburg. Married Miss Rebecca Seckman. To this union was born:

JOHN WILLIAM RUFUS CASKEY—At Martinsburg, W. Va., February 18, 1874. Educated in the Berkeley County public schools, first at Three Runs School, next at Hooge Street School and at the Martinsburg High School. In 1900, Mr. Caskey established the Caskey Baking Company with a branch factory at Hagerstown, Md. Member of the City Council from June 1, 1907, to June 1, 1909. Mayor of Martinsburg from June 1, 1910, to June 1, 1912. President of the Board of Education, Martinsburg schools. February 12, 1908, married Miss Dora Matthaei, who was a teacher in the schools in Martinsburg. They have two children: Margaret Rebecca, born December 8, 1908, and a graduate of the Martinsburg High Schol, class of 1926, and a student in Goucher College, Baltimore, and William Rufus, born March 15, 1915.

MORGAN MORGAN—The founder of this family was Colonel Morgan Morgan I., a native of Wales and an ordained clergyman of the Church of England; educated in London during the reign of William the Third; emigrated to America during the reign of Queen Anne; settled in Delaware Colony; commenced business on the present site of Christiana; married Catharine Garretson, "a respectable lady of Delaware"; moved to the Valley of Virginia and established a church (Episcopal) at Winchester, where he was a pastor for many years. His son, Morgan Morgan II., built the first cabin home in what is now the State of West Virginia, on Mill Creek, in Berkeley County in 1726. From one branch of this family many settlers by the name of Morgan settled in what is now northern West Virginia, and a descendant of these founded Morgantown. Another descendant of these was the famous Indian fighter and scout, Zackwell Morgan. Still another descendant was Daniel Morgan of Revolutionary War fame; another, B. S. Morgan, at one time State Superintendent of Free Schools of West Virginia, and Ephraim B. Morgan, Governor of West Virginia. Of the Morgans who remained in Berkeley County there is a direct line of Morgan Morgan's for seven generations. Dr. Morgan Morgan of Martinsburg is the VI. and his son, a lad of 14 years, is the VII.

HENSHAW—This family originally came from Gloucster, England, and has been traced back in an unbroken line to the time before the coming of William the Conqueror. The family eventually migrated to America, and wherever it has settled it has been famous for its noble men and women, famous for their intense patriotism, high moral courage and brilliant minds.

JOSHUA HENSHAW—The founder of the American branch of the family, was born in England probably about 1670. He was one of two boys placed under the care of Rev. Richard Mather, one of the eminent Puritan divines of Dorcester, Massachusetts, by a dishonest executor of the Henshaw estate, after which he announced to the friends of the family that the boys were at school in London, thus trying to defraud them of their property left them by their father.

JOHN HENSHAW—Born in 1680; engaged in business in Dorchester; later removed to Philadelphia and raised a large family there. With his son, Nicholas, migrated to the Colony of Virginia, purchased an estate from Lord Fairfax; erected the house which became the old Henshaw homestead on Mill Creek in Berkeley County. His son Nicholas, mentioned above, was born in Philadelphia. His will, one of the few probated in 1772, the year Berkeley County was formed, is one of the first on record in the Clerk of the County Court's office in Martinsburg.

WILLIAM HENSHAW—Was born and reared on the old homestead on Mill Creek. In 1775, when Captain Hugh Stephenson raised a company of volunteers for one year's service in the Continental Army, William Henshaw volunteered his services and was commissioned an officer in the company as Lieutenant. He served throughout the Revolution and his name is connected with much of the history of that war. Tradition has it that he never accepted any pay for his services.

LEVI HENSHAW—Was born on Mill Creek at the ancestral home, July 22, 1769; a prominent and influential man of that section; elected Justice of the Peace 1810; elected a member of the Virginia Assembly 1821-22-30-31; Sheriff of Berkeley County in 1840; vestryman of the Protestant Episcopal Church at Bunker Hill for many years. Levi Henshaw II.; born at the Henshaw homestead, July 15, 1815; engaged in the milling business at the Henshaw Mill on Mill Creek, near the Henshaw homestead; removed to Hedgesville, Berkeley County, and lived there till the day of his death, February 21, 1879. Married Sarah Ann Snodgrass, of Tomahawk Springs (Tomahawk). Children of this union were: Lily Snodgrass, married Dr. M. S. Butler, a physician of Hedgesville; Annie Laurie, married Edward Cleggett Williams, pharmacist and druggist of Martinsburg.

EDGAR C. HENSHAW—Postmaster of Martinsburg; Postmaster of Hedgesvi'le; Collector of Internal Revenue, Martinsburg; horticulturist; owner of several large commercial orchards; Vice-President Peoples Trust Company Bank; State Food Distributor for Berkeley County during the World War. He was one of the men who lent a helping hand to struggling youth to get a start in life. Mr. Henshaw organized the Henshaw, Hollis & Company as president; a firm dealing in orchard supplies at Martinsburg, of which he was the president and his son, Edgar L. Henshaw, is general manager, and his son-in-law, M. Trammell Hollis, is a large stockholder. Edgar L. Henshaw married Miss Florence Langford. Trammell Hollis is a member of the family of Hollis of Gerardstown. He is now engaged in the garage business at Martinsburg.

EVANS—There were three men in direct descent in the Evans family by the name of John. The ancestor of the family in this county was John Evans I., who migrated to New Jersey from Wales and settled near Burlington. His son, John Evans II., migrated to the Valley of Virginia about the year 1740, bought land of the VanMetres on Opequon River (Creek). When trouble with the Indians was apparent in 1753, he hastily constructed a stockade fort two miles southeast of where Martinsburg now stands. This came to be known as John Evans Fort and was a refuge for the settlers of that region. He had previously married Polly VanMetre, who was the defender of the fort on several occasions when the men were away. This fort was visited by General Braddock on his way through Berkeley County to the Monongahela campaign in 1755, for from *Seaman's Journal*, doubtless written by Lieutenant Spendalowe of the detachment of Marines sent by Commodore Kepple of the British fleet, for he says: "May 1st—At 5 we went with our people, and began ferrying the army into Virginia, which we completed by 10 o'clock and marched in our way to one John Evans (Fort), where we arrived at 3 o'clock—17 miles from Connecocheig, and 20 miles from Winchester. We got some provisions and forage here." The army spent a little time here, for he says further: "On the 2nd:—As it is customary in the army to halt a day after three days' march, we halted today to rest the army." From the union of John Evans and Polly (VanMetre) Evans was born Johns Evans II. The families of Evans and VanMetre married and intermarried in several instances. In one instance, Abraham VanMetre married Isabel Evans. Of this line is descended James M. VanMetre (deceased) and Isaac D. VanMetre of the Arden District. On another occasion John Evans III. married Margaret VanMetre. Of this line descended Tillotson Evans, the youngest of eight sons (no daughters). Tillotson Evans was a farmer who resided west of Arden in Gerrardstown District. He married Mary Ann Orr. Of this union was born JAMES W. B. EVANS, who was a teacher in the public schools of the county for 43 years. Mr. Evans was a Democrat of the old school. He always cherished a desire to hold public office but lacked the abilities of the politician to succeed in that line. He was a candidate on several occasions; for the West Virginia State Senate in 1896, a candidate for County Superintendent of Schools in 1892, a candidate for Assessor of Madison County, Ohio. President of the Board of Education of Gerrardstown District. He held two appointive offices, President of the Board of Education of Gerrardstown District under John W. Shirley, County Superintendent, and Deputy Sheriff of Berkeley County under Sheriff H. S. Miller, 1916. Was serving in that capacity when his death occurred on November 30, 1918. The State Tax Commissioner's audit of his books showed not one cent deficit during the three years of his office and the Commissioner verified this by a letter of commendation to Mr. Evans, stating that his books were in the best shape of any in the State.

WILLIS F. EVANS—Son of James W. B. Evans. Been engaged in the school work of the county for thirty-six years as teacher and County Superintendent; also in organizing teachers' clubs and associations. Educated in the rural schools, Shepherd College State Normal School and Shenandoah Normal School at Reliance, Va. Taught thirty-two years in the rural schools of the county, in eight different schools. Was County Superintendent of Schools of the county for four years. Helped to organize the Berkeley County Teachers Association, organized the Berkeley County School Improvement League, and was the first president. Procured the present County Superintendent's office in the Court House at a time when the statute did not exist compelling the County Court to establish and maintain such an office. Has thirty-two graduates to his credit from the schools that he has taught. Has taught 1540 boys and girls in the county, and among these are citizens holding high positions of trust, some in this county and some in other States. Taught the first soldier in the World War, to be wounded, from Berkeley County—Peter Gordon—in that conflict. Favorite books: Franklin's Autobiography, Bible, Three Histories of the United States, Lewis' History of West Virginia, and Prescott's Conquest of Mexico, and other books of travel and biography. Has always been a great reader and has read over three hundred books of the classics and fiction. His favorite study is geology and history. In 1926 organized The Berkeley County Historical Society with headquarters in the County Court House, Martinsburg. Was its first president. Has served on the State Grading Board at Charleston, for the grading of teachers' examination papers. Besides these has been a market gardener to Martinsburg for 21 years. Has developed several small fruit and apple orchards in the county. In 1924 began the research for the material for a history of Berkeley County. Member of the Eastern Panhandle Teachers Association, the State Educational Association, and the State Historical Society. Motto: "Hustle while you wait." On December 30, 1902, married Mabel Claire Townsend. From this union was born Arlington Wesley, a graduate of the Martinsburg High School, class of 1924, who taught school in the rural districts after receiving his certificate from Shepherd College; Mary Ann, graduate of Martinsburg High School, class of 1927, and a student in the Nurses' Training School, Emergency Hospital, Washington, D. C.; and Helen Orcutt, a graduate of Martinsburg High School class of 1928.

CHARLES J. FAULKNER—Son of distinguished father, Charles James Faulkner, who took prominent part in the welfare of two States, Virginia and West Virginia. Educated in the village schools. When fifteen years of age entered the Virginia Military Institute at Lexington, Va. Served with the Cadets at the Battle of New Market, where he was distinguished for his ardor and daring. Attended schools of Switzerland and Paris, having accompanied his father thither when he was Minister to France. Returned to America in August, 1861, and was with his father at the time of his arrest in Washington, the story of which has become a matter of national history. Served as Aide on the Staff of General J. C. Breckenridge until he (Breckenridge) was made Secretary of War; afterward appointed Aide to General Henry A. Wise, and surrendered with him at Appomattox; returned home and began the study of law; graduated from the University of Virginia in June, 1868. Admitted to the bar September following, having just attained his majority. Elected Judge of the 13th Judicial Circuit, 1880, at the age of 33 years, being one of the youngest Judges of the State. He presided over this Court with credit to himself and to the universal satisfaction of the people, who witnessed the impartial justice which he meted out to all alike. Elected to the United States Senate in 1887, while holding the position of Judge. Resigned as Judge to accept the high honor conferred upon him by the Legislature of the State (the U. S. Senators then being chosen by the Legislature). He served with credit in the halls of Congress; secured for Martinsburg the magnificent edifice which stands on the corner of Maple Avenue and West King Street, known as the United States Court House and Postoffice of Martinsburg. Appointed by President McKinley as a member of a commission—the Anglo-American Commission—to promote a closer relationship between the Governments of the United States, Great Britain and Canada. Although 79 years of age, he still practices his profession and also takes great interest in the preservation of the county's history for future generations, having been appointed by Governor Howard M. Gore of West Virginia a representative of the State Historical Society, to represent Berkeley County in that body.

Received his rank of Lieutenancy on the Staff of General Breckenridge in the Civil War, as follows: At the Battle of New Market, May 15, 1864, the Confederates, sorely pressed for want of men, called to the colors the entire force of the Virginia Military Institute at Lexington, Va., to defend that section against the Federal forces. These were mere boys, ranging in ages from fourteen to nineteen. Young Faulkner was one of these cadets. But these behaved themselves like veterans and under a withering fire of artilery and musketry from the Federal batteries drove the enemy from their position in confusion across the river. In this advance, Cadet Faulkner found himself somewhat in advance of his comrades and suddenly in the presence of a small force of Union soldiers. Knowing that he would be captured if he hesitated a moment, he decided to try a ruse which worked admirably. He called upon them to surrender: "It is no use, boys. You may as well surrender, as the rest of us are just over the hill back there." The entire twenty-two men threw down their arms and surrendered on the spot. Cadet Faulkner was marching them all to the rear of his own army when he happened to meet General Breckonridge. "Where did you get those?" asked the General. "I captured them just over the hill, sir," replied young Faulkner. "How?" demanded the astonished General. "I don't know, sir," answered Faulkner, "I just surrounded them." "How could you surround them? Were you alone?" "Yes, sir," answered young Faulkner. "I just surrounded them and took them." The General then asked him his name and when on being told, exclaimed: "Are you a son of Charles James Faulkner?" "Yes, sir," was the reply. "Well, take these men back to the prison camp and report to my headquarters at 6 o'clock." The amusing part of this incident was that Cadet Faulkner did all this with a musket which had been put out of commission just before this incident occurred; the barrel, having been hit by shrapnel, was bent so that the ramrod would not go into it to ram the load home, thus rendering the gun useless, he not having time to get another. Imagine the chagrin of these twenty-two captives when the truth was known. Cadet Faulkner reported at headquarters at the appointed time and General Breckonridge appointed him a member of his Staff then and there. He served in this capacity until General Breckonridge was made Secretary in President Davis' Cabinet, when he was transferred to the Staff of General Henry A. Wise.

In the Senate he served on many important committees, as Claims, Pensions, Appropriation, District of Columbia, Emigration, Pacific Railroad, Territories and Judiciary. At the session of Congress, 1888-1889, framed and secured the passage of a bill to prevent the adulteration of foods and drugs—being the father of the "Pure Food Law"; framed and secured the passage of a bill regulating the railroad systems; one of the leaders in the contest in which the famous "Force Bill" was defeated, holding at one time continuously for a period of twelve hours the floor of the Senate.

Prominent Mason; in 1889, held the chair of the Grand Master of the Grand Lodge of West Virginia. Was appointed by the Senate in 1898 as a member of the joint commission of the two houses to investigate the receipts and expenditures of the Post Office Department. Has always taken a great interest in the civic welfare of the county and city. Has headed all the commissions appointed for the betterment of the community; has lent many a helping hand to struggling and deserving youth in securing a foothold in the uphill start of life. He is rightly and truly styled "The Grand Old Man of Berkeley County."

Some of the activities of Charles J. Faulkner's life in later years: Permanent chairman (1888) and temporary and permanent chairman (1892) of the Democratic State Convention of West Virginia; chairman of the Democratic Congressional Campaign Committee, 1894 and 1896; member of the American Bar Association; member of the Bar Association of Berkeley County and president of same; member of Society of International Law; one of the organizers and an original member of the American Law Institute; member of the National Geographical Society; member of a Commission of 100 of the American Association to Advance Science; trustee of the Alumni Endowment Fund of the Association of the University of Virginia; member of the Berkeley County Historical Society and vice-president of the West Virginia Historical Society.

W. H. H. FLICK—Born in Cuyahoga County, Ohio, February 24th, 1841; educated in the country schools, one term at Garfield School at Hiram, Ohio; entered the Union Army of the Civil War, July, 1861, 41st Ohio Regiment; wounded at Shiloh, April 7, 1862. Taught school and earned enough money to study law. Graduated from Cleveland Law School, 1865. Removed to Moorefield, W. Va.; practiced law there two years; moved to Pendleton County, W. Va.; served two terms in the Legislature from that county. Appointed to fill the unexpired term of Prosecuting Attorney of Grant County, W. Va. Removed to Martinsburg in 1874. Candidate for Congress, Second Congressional District, W. Va., in 1886; made a strong run, being defeated by ninety votes in the district. Practiced his profession in Martinsburg until his death.

GENERAL WILLIAM DARKE—Hero of many battles between the Virginians and the Indians. Formed the covers for the retreat of two armies, thus saving them from utter rout or massacre—Braddock's and St. Clair's. Born near Lancaster, Pennsylvania, 1763. When but five years of age accompanied his parents to the Shenandoah Valley and settled near Shepherdstown, Virginia; grew up on the border; nearest neighbors were Thomas Shepherd, founder of Shepherdstown, and Robert Harper, after whom Harper's Ferry was named; rough in manners, strong in mind, of herculean frame, frank and fearless. Early learned woodscraft and how to take care of himself anywhere; became a hunter, scout and Indian fighter. Joined General Edward Braddock in his expedition to the forks of the Ohio in 1755; helped to cover the retreat of that army after the disastrous defeat at the Monongahela River. Associated in the Indian wars with George Washington, George Rogers Clark, William Clarke, Arthur St. Clair and Andrew Lewis. Volunteered in the Army of the Revolution on the Continental side; speedily rose to the position of Captain, later to Lieutenant, then Major General; was at the surrender of Cornwallis at Yorktown, October, 1781. Returned to Berkeley County, where he engaged in farming. Elected a Delegate with Brigadier General Adam Stephen to represent Berkeley County in the Constitutional Convention of 1788; voted to ratify the Federal Constitution.

Commanded the right wing of the American Army at St. Clair's defeat in the North-West Territory by the Indians. Again covered the retreat of that shattered army back to Fort Jefferson. Elected to represent Berkeley County in the Virginia Assembly almost continuously till his death in 1801. Buried at Duffields, Jefferson County, W. Va. Darkesville, Berkeley County, was named for him, also Darke County, Ohio.

COLONEL EDMOND P. HUNTER—Lawyer. Admitted to the Berkeley Bar in 1831. Born in Martinsburg (now West Virginia), March 24, 1809. Educated at Jefferson College. Editor and proprietor of the *Martinsburg Gazette*, 1832 to 1845. In May, 1832, was appointed as a member of the "Young Men's Convention", in Washington, D. C., at which meeting Henry Clay was the chief speaker. General Elisha Boyd, having held the office of Prosecuting Attorney of Berkeley County for forty years, resigned in March, 1838. Edmond Hunter and David Holmes Conrad were aspirants for the position. The County Court then had the power to appoint to fill the vacancy. After a full Court had voted on the two men, Mr. Hunter received the majority of the votes and was declared elected; was re-elected to the same position several terms and filled it with ability and justice to all. Elected to the Virginia House of Delegates in 1834-35-39 and '41. Received the title of Colonel as an officer of the 67th Regiment of Virginia Militia. Member of the Masonic Order. Member of the Episcopal Church. Died in the cholera epidemic of 1854, aged only forty-five years.

ANDREW HUNTER—Lawyer. Born at Martinsburg, Berkeley County, Virginia, in 1804. Appointed by Governor Wise of Virginia to assist Charles W. Harding in the prosecution of John Brown and his associates at Charles Town (1859). John Brown was tried for treason for raiding the United States Arsenal at Harper's Ferry of that year. John Brown and six of his companions were found guilty and hanged there December 2, 1859.

GENERAL HORATIO GATES—Appointed by the Continental Congress in 1775 as Major General in the Continental Army in the Revolution. Born in England; purchased a farm in Berkeley County after Braddock's defeat at the Monongahela; severely wounded there; in conjunction with Daniel Morgan and Benedict Arnold, captured Burgoyne's army at Saratoga, October 17, 1777, for which he received a vote of thanks and a gold medal from Congress. Aspired to Washington's place as Commander-in-Chief of the American Army. Happily, Congress did not remove General Washington and appoint General Gates in his stead, for on August 16, 1780, he was badly defeated by Lord Cornwallis at Camden, S. C.; was superceded by General Green after this battle but was in 1872 restored to his old command. After the war he retired to his Berkeley County farm home which he had named "Travelers' Rest". Died at New York City, April 10, 1806.

JOHN Q. A. NADENBOUSCH—Soldier in the Confederate Army. Father of Mary Ella (Nadenbousch) Parks, who married Hon. Alexander Parks, Sr.

Organized the "Berkeley Border Guards", the first military company organized in Virginia to serve in the Civil War, and was elected Colonel of the Regiment composing the famous "Stonewall Brigade" and served throughout the war. As Captain of the Berkeley Border Guards, was ordered by Governor Henry A. Wise to Harper's Ferry in 1859 to quell the insurrection of John Brown at that place. Assisted in the capture of Brown and was on duty at the execution of him at Charles Town; called into service as Colonel of the Second Virginia Regiment of Infantry at the Battle of Manassas; brought home the bodies of Holmes and Tucker Conrad and Captain P. R. Harrison, Martinsburg soldiers killed at that battle, in a spring wagon and buried them himself at night in the Old Norbourn Cemetery. These three young men were members of his Company and were killed at that battle July 21, 1861. He saw hard fighting and distinguished himself at Fredericksburg and Chancellorsville. Born in Berkeley County October 31, 1824, and was always prominent in the affairs of the county, before and after the war, until his death.

In the possession of his grandson, Hon. John N. Parks, is a sword presented to him by the men of his Company, which shows the love and esteem by which he was held by his soldiers. The sword bears the following inscription:

Presented to
Captain J. Q. A. Nadenbousch
By his Company the "Berkeley Border Guards"
as a token of esteem for him as an
Officer & Gentleman
March 10, 1860

CHARLES S. TRUMP, D.D.—Minister of the Lutheran Church of Martinsburg for many years or from 1888 to his death in 1916; was greatly loved and esteemed by every one; family originally came from Holland.

CHARLES S. TRUMP, JR.—Son of Rev. Charles S. Trump. Lawyer. Educated in the Martinsburg schools. Graduate of Martinsburg High School and a graduate of West Virginia University. Enlisted in the United States service in the World War; stationed at Camp Benj. Harrison, Indiana, with the rank of Second Lieutenant of the 83rd Division, 1917; saw much service overseas; wounded at the Battle of Mont Fancon, France; recovered and served until the Armistice was signed, November 11, 1918.

WILSON P. SPEROW, A.B.—Teacher. Third gaandson of George O. Sperow. Born at Bedington, W. Va. Great-grandson of George Sperow who originally came from Pennsylvania and lived in Hedgesville District, Berkeley County. Came of a line of expert agriculturalists, of which there is no better class farmers in the county. Graduated from Shepherd College State Normal School, Shepherdstown, W. Va., class of 1914, with degree of A.B. Taught in the Martinsburg High School. Enlisted in the World War, 1917; stationed at Camp Meade, with rank of Sergeant. Elected Principal Bunker Hill High School, from 1919 to 1926. Past Moderator of the Potomac Valley Round Table, a teacher's organization. Is Principal of the Boonesboro, Md., High School. Stands high in the teaching profession.

JOHN W. SPEROW—Farmer and business man. Father of Prof. Sperow mentioned in above sketch. Member of the West Virginia House of Delegates 1911-12. Barkeley County Road Engineer 1913-15.

F. VERNON ALER—Corporation lawyer, author, orator. Born at Martinsburg, W. Va., April 29, 1868. His father, Samuel Aler, was draughtsman for the Baltimore and Ohio Railroad Company for a number of years and was closely associated with John W. Garrett. At the outbreak of the Civil War, Samuel Aler was placed in charge of the United States Arsenal at Harper's Ferry, Quartermaster Department, and while serving as such was detailed to Frederick, Md., to dismantle several locomotives that were in danger of capture by the Confederates. He with a small force of companion workmen, took the locomotives apart and secreted the dismantled parts, thus making them useless to the enemy. All this had to be done under cover of darkness and at great peril of capture, but he accomplished the task without mishap. In 1891, Senator Stephen B. Elkins secured for him a position in the Navy Yard at Washington, D. C.

His son, F. Vernon Aler, worked on the *Martinsburg Independent* (a newspaper published for a number of years at Martinsburg) at the age of twelve years; studied law and was admitted to the bar at the age of twenty-two; formed a partnership with Judge Daniel B. Lucas soon after being admitted; promoted and financed corporations representing $12,000,000, all in Berkeley County, of which four are brick plants. Is president of the Eastern Clay Products Company, located at Flagg's Crossing east of Martinsburg; has long been a member of the West Virginia Historical and Antiquarian Society. In 1888, he wrote and published a thorough and comprehensive history of Berkeley County—the first of its kind—copies of which are in the largest libraries of the world, a copy being filed in the Library of Edinburg, Scotland.

FREDERICK NADENBOUSCH—Born in Berkeley County, October 14, 1778. Resided in the neighborhood of Hedgesville. His son, Moses T. Nadenbousch, was born at Hedgesville, April 1, 1827. Sheriff of Berkeley County. Had two sons, John T. Nadenbousch, born at Martinsburg. Appointed by his father Deputy Sheriff of Berkeley County at the age of sixteen, which position, though so young in years, he filled with credit to himself and the county. Afterwards employed by the old Adams Express Company at Martinsburg. When the Merchants and Farmers Bank was organized—the first State Bank in this section—he was elected as assistant cashier. Became cashier of this bank in 1875, and has filled the position ever since, a period of thirty-two years. In all that time he has never been tardy and never lost a day from being away from his job. His son, J. Roy Nadenbousch, is engaged in the insurance business at Martinsburg and is one of the city's leading young business men.

ADRIAN C. NADENBOUSCH—Brother of John T. Nadenbousch. Lawyer; orator; active in all public enterprises for the uplift of the county and city; has served as Judge of the Judicial Circuit of this section; consulted in all important questions in law; was one of the "four-minute-men" who volunteered in the World War to put Liberty Loans for the Government across in Berkeley County, and through his efforts, it went "over the top" in every loan launched during that time.

WILLIAM S. BERT—President Board of Education of Martinsburg, W. Va., 1920; president of a Sunday School class of 200 at the First Methodist Episcopal Church, that city; elected member of the City Council, Martinsburg, for two years, beginning in 1910; elected again in 1916, at which time he was City Treasurer for two years; long connected with the Royal Woollen Mills Company at a branch in Martinsburg, of which he was General Manager.

HON. E. BOYD FAULKNER—Born at "Boydville" at Martinsburg, Va., July 24, 1841. Educated in private schools, Winchester Academy, Georgetown College and University of Virginia. Attended lectures on constitutional law in Paris, France; attached to legation of the United States at that place while his father, Charles James Faulkner, was United States Minister to France. Lawyer. Resided in Kentucky from 1867 to 1872, leaving West Virginia on account of the "test oath" required to be taken at that time. Returned to Martinsburg in 1872; elected to the West Virginia House of Delegates in 1876 and to the West Virginia Senate in 1878; declined presidency of the Senate; appointed a member of the Revising Committee by the Legislature to revise the laws of the State; defeated for the nomination for Governor at the Democratic State Convention at Wheeling in 1884; was tendered during President Cleveland's administration the office of Consul General and Agent at Cairo, Egypt (1885), also Minister to Persia, but declined both; appointed Judge of the Thirteenth Judicial District of West Virginia and re-elected three terms with little opposition, serving in all twenty-one years.

War Record.—Volunteered, 1861, Confederate Army; first entered Wise Artillery; second, the Rockbridge Artillery; third, appointed on the Staff of Governor Letcher of Virginia; fourth, appointed Captain in the Confederate Army; captured at the battle of Piedmont, June, 1864, when General W. E. Jones was killed; confined a prisoner on Johnson's Island one year; received wounds in the ear at the first battle of Manassas from fragment of bursting shell; fought throughout the war. The most important engagements in which he participated were Manassas (first) and Cedar Creek, February 11, 1863. Married Miss Susan Hopkinsville of Kentucky. Judge Faulkner died in 1917, one child succeeding him, Mary Buckner Faulkner, an industrious worker in the First Baptist Church of Martinsburg, also in charities and all uplift movements for the betterment of society.

PHILIP HETZEL—The founder of the family in this county was Joshua Philip Hetzel, born at Wurtemburg, Germany; was an agitator against the wrongs of the common people of that country and was compelled to flee his native land on account of his writing and speaking; came to America with other patriots, like Carl Schurz, Franz Sigel, and others; settled at Cumberland, Md.; helped nurse through a cholera epidemic there in 1885, fortunately not contracting the dread disease; a successful business man there and a member of the Lutheran Church.

JOHN J. HETZEL, SR.—Was born in New York City, February 1, 1849; came to Cumberland, Md., with his parents; educated in the German Lutheran Parochial School; attended Allegheny Male and Female Seminary at Rainsburg, Pennsylvania; after completing his general education, clerked in a general store at Bloody Run (now Everett) Pennsylvania; in 1875 engaged with the firm of J. B. Hoyt & Company, the largest leather manufacturers in the United States at that time; auditor of the company for several years, afterwards general manager of their fourteen tanneries; removed to Martinsburg, W. Va., in 1901; purchased the wholesale grocery concern of Evans, Shaffer Grocery Company of Martinsburg; reorganized it under the name of the National Commercial Company as president; organized the Bank of Martinsburg in 1902; elected president for a number of years; organized the Bank of Morgan County, located at Berkeley Springs and became its first president; built the Berkeley Springs Telephone Company system in 1904; organized the Romney Wholesale Grocery Company of Romney, W. Va., of which he was president and general manager; represented Morgan County in the State Legislature, 1882-3; received 187 votes of the 190 cast at his home precinct of Paw Paw; was a worker in the Methodist Episcopal Church and the Young Men's Christian Association; was prominent in Good Templars, an organization which brought about the expulsion of the liquor traffic from the United States. In 1871 he married Anna Barndollar of Danville, Pa.

STEWART W. WALKER—His emigrant ancestor was Thomas Walker, who came from London, England, in 1623, and landed in the Colony of Jamestown. The name of Walker can be found among the Indian fighters of early times, with George Washington in his campaigns against the Indians and French, with distinguished jurists, with representatives in the State and National congresses and wherever leaders were needed. Colonel Stewart W. Walker was born in Berkeley County, 1862; educated in the district schools, the Berkeley Academy, Washington and Lee University at Lexington, Va.; graduated in law at the latter and began the practice of his profession at Martinsburg bar; associated with Hon. Charles J. Faulkner; later Hon. J. M. Woods of Martinsburg was associated with them under the firm name of Faulkner, Walker & Woods. Mr. Walker was appointed United States District Attorney for the Northern District of West Virginia by President Wilson in 1916, in which capacity he served until the year 1920. During that time the ability of Colonel Walker was taxed to the utmost, as the United States was at war with Germany, and many cases of violation of the sedition laws added to the already overburdened business, of his office, but Mr. Walker handled all business that came before him with energy and dispatch, characteristic of the man. He was one of the most able lawyers of the Berkeley bar. In 1913 he built for himself and his wife a fine colonial mansion on Rosemont, a suburb of Martinsburg. Was a candidate for Congress against the late Hon. Alston G. Dayton, but was defeated. He was a member of the West Virginia Legislature and when serving in that capacity married Annette Thayer of Charleston, W. Va. He died in 1923, leaving a widow but no children. His brother, A. Hunter Walker, was a prominent farmer residing on the Dry Run road. In 1922 he was elected president of the Board of Education of Hedgesville District, and was the "father of the new Hedgesville High School, a new $75,000 school building finished in the fall of 1926. He died in that year but needs no greater monument to his memory.

ALBERT D. DARBY—His father, Ezra Darby, came from Devonshire, England, to the Virginia Colony of Jamestown in 1626; engaged in the raising of tobacco, a most lucrative occupation of that time. Came to Berkeley County after the Civil War. Albert D. Darby was born in Martinsburg, January 22, 1868. On leaving the public schools he filled his first position with the Old National Bank as clerk; was assistant cashier of the Peoples Trust Company, and later, when the Bank of Martinsburg was organized in 1902 by the late John J. Hetzel, he was elected cashier of that institution. He was active in organizing the Adamantine Clay Products Company works at North Mountain; was always a faithful worker in the Methodist Episcopal Church and Sunday School.

ROUSH—Conrad Roush; born in Pennsylvania; came to Martinsburg when a young man and engaged in the hat manufacturing business; later in farming; married Sarah Randall. George Roush, son of Conrad and Sarah (Randall) Roush, was a farmer; married Margaret Walter. Of this union were born Charles and George S. Roush.

George S. Roush—Successful farmer. As the town of Martinsburg extended westward he sub-divided his farm, known as "Rosemont", into city lots and became an extensive real estate operator. His son, Arlington Roush, carried on the operations of his father and became a director in the Roush-Bowers Real Estate Company, which company built up that section of Martinsburg known as "Rosemont".

Enlisted in the Confederate Army as private in Company B, First Virginia Cavalry, and in conjunction with his brother, Charles Roush, served throughout the war. George S. Roush was instrumental in establishing and building the Methodist Episcopal Church South, the corner stone of the present structure on West Martin Street, laid September 19, 1885, and was completed in October, 1887. Married Anna E. Mong, daughter of William H. Mong. To this union was born Arlington and Carrie Roush, the former a prominent business man and the latter a prominent church worker.

HON. WILLIAM E. MONG—Born on Tuscarora in the stone house of the Mong family erected by them about 1800 and still standing. Was engaged in farming all his life. Was a member of the County Court of Berkeley County for a number of years. Justice of the Peace for Arden District and elected to the Virginia Legislature in 1860. Loyal to the South in the Civil War.

WENDALL SEIBERT—Berkeley County farmer; volunteered as a private in Company B, First Virginia Cavalry, under General J. E. B. Stuart; promoted to Fourth Corporal (1861); taken prisoner and held for twenty-four hours at Hedgesville prison when he effected his escape. Served with distinction throughout the war.

W. E. MINGHINI, D.D.S.—Dr. Minghini was born at Middleway, Jefferson County, W. Va., June 5, 1867. Son of Joseph L. and Lydia (Sencindiver) descendant on the father's side of Italian ancestors. His great-grandparent was an Italian nobleman, an officer in the Italian Army and personal friend of General Charles Lee of Revolutionary War fame. His father, Joseph L. Minghini, was a cabinet maker and undertaker. Enlisted in Company D, Twelfth Virginia Cavalry, C. S. A. Was a scout for General J. E. B. Stewart. In service at Chancellorsville, Kelly Ford, Fredericksburg and Mine Run. Was ordered to burn Hall's rifle factory at Harper's Ferry. At the Battle of Kelly's Ford, where Major John Pelham was wounded, he carried that officer off the field and remained with him until he died. Dr. Minghini was educated in the public schools of Jefferson County; graduate of the University of Maryland, class of 1893, degree of D.D.S. Came to Martinsburg upon his graduation and has engaged in his profession since that time. In 1899 was appointed a member of the West Virginia State Board of Dental Examiners, and has filled every office of that body, president, secretary and treasurer. Elected Mayor of Martinsburg in the election of 1904 by a large majority over his Republican opponent. He owned the first automobile in Berkeley County; organized the Martinsburg Auto Club. On October 3, 1899, married Viola Marie Pitcher of Baltimore, a descendant of Roger Williams and Mollie Pitcher of the Battle of Bennington fame (Revolution).

SNODGRASS—William Snodgrass left Scotland in 1700 during one of the Scottish feuds and finally settled on Back Creek in Berkeley County; was a farmer and a Presbyterian by faith; buried in the Mount Zion churchyard at Hedgesville. William II., grandson of William Snodgrass I., married Nancy Fryatt, a descendant of Archbishop Tillotson of Canterbury, England. Her parents were wealthy in England and brought much silver plate and other valuables to America. William Snodgrass II. owned a large estate in Berkeley County. The most of the family were buried in their own burying grounds. Some of their library is in possession of the various descendants. Among these are many volumes of sermons of Archbishop Tillotson. The family were members of the Church of England. John Fryatt Snodgrass, son of William II. and Mary Snodgrass, was born March 4, 1802, in Berkeley County. When a young man he removed to Parkersburg and began the practice of law; was a brilliant lawyer, successful in business, social and political life; built the house now used by the Blennerhassett Club House for a home for his family, one of the finest homes in the western part of the State at that time. As there were no railroads, every summer he drove his own coach to White Sulphur Springs, where he and his family were social leaders. Delegate to the State Constitutional Convention in 1850, which revised the Constitution of the State of Virginia. Elected to the Thirty-third Congress as a Democrat. Descendants of the family are found in that part of the State at the present time. Another member of the family, Philip Snodgrass, left Derbyshire, England, in 1656, and with several companions, all young men, came to the New World in search of adventure. They landed at Jamestown, Virginia. Philip located on the James River in the Piedmont section of the State and took up land; in the course of time became the owner of a large tobacco plantation, cultivated small grains in conjunction and erected a primitive mill for the purpose of grinding it, which was the first of its kind in that section. He built a dwelling house of logs and stone, placed a well in the center of it and thus was able to withstand all of the sieges of the Indians, which were many and frequent. His descendants moved north and west and one locating in Berkeley County established the old Snodgrass homestead known as "Wheaton". Here Elisha Kelly Snodgrass was born December 25, 1878. He studied civil engineering and at the end of twelve years formed a partnership with Messrs. Hebard and Bailey under the firm name of the Albott Construction Company.

CHARLES WILLIAM LINK, D.D.S.—Born in Duffields, Jefferson County, W. Va., February 6, 1868. Educated in the district schools of that county, Charles Town Academy, West Virginia University, class of 1892, University of Maryland, class of 1895, with degree of D.D.S. Practiced his profession in Martinsburg. In 1903 married Margharetta Hetzel, daughter of Hon. John J. Hetzel.

ALEXANDER CLOHAN—Family of Scottish descent; first to come to America was William Clohan, a coal miner of Scotland, in 1849; came to Preston County, Virginia; followed mining there for five years, thence removed to Wheeling, Ohio County; engaged in the trade of coal operator; became prominent in that county; many years a Justice of the Peace in Webster District, Ohio County; president of the Board of Registration of Wheeling during the Civil War; married Agnes Anderson of Scotland, sister to Rev. William Anderson of Old Calabar, Africa, who served there fifty years as a missionary. Alexander Clohan was the youngest of six children. His oldest brother, William, enlisted in Company B, First Virginia Loyal Regiment, being three-monthed time men under Colonel B. F. Kelly. After serving his time, Mr. Clohan re-enlisted, this time becoming a member of Company G, First Virginia Regiment, under Colonel Joseph Thoburn. Was promoted to Company K as First Sergeant. Killed at Kernstown, near Winchester, Sunday, March 23, 1862. His body was sent back to Wheeling where it was buried with military honors, he being the first Wheeling soldier to give his life for the Union cause.

Alexander Clohan of Berkeley County was born at Hollytown, Scotland, April 8, 1846; came to Preston County with his parents when three years old. When a young man, engaged in the coal business with his father; entered the employ of the laBelle Iron Works as a puddler and later in a position with the Bellaire Iron Works. Came to Berkeley County in 1878, he, his wife and eldest son William, a child of two years, in a two-horse wagon. Purchased the Clohan farm in Gerardstown District and engaged in farming and truck gardening. In 1906 organized the Highland Orchard Company as president; organized the Hart-Clohan Company on Opequon Creek (fruit and truck raising) as president; also the Gold Orchard Company, the Tomahawk Orchard Company, the Cherry Run Orchard Company. Elected president of the West Virginia State Horticultural Society, which office he held for nine years ,1899. President of the Berkeley County Horticultural Society. Appointed by Governor William A. MacCorkle, member of the State Board of Agriculture in 1885. Member of the Eastern Fruit Growers Association in 1888. Delegate to each Republican State Convention for ten years or since 1888. Appointed Deputy Sheriff of Berkeley County (1893) by Sheriff L. C. Gerling. Appointed Postmaster of Martinsburg in 1898 by President McKinley and twice by President Roosevelt, serving in all twelve years. Mr. Clohan married 1872, Celia, daughter of Enos R. Crouch of Wheeling. To this union were born William (deceased), Herbert (deceased), Robert, Chief Postal Clerk in the Martinsburg Postoffice, Louis (deceased), Lucy, married William S. Cline of Martinsburg, Bessie, maried Prince Dunn of Martinsburg, Archie A., soldier in the World War, and Elsie of Washington, D. C.

Mr. Clohan died at Martinsburg. He was a friend to all, especially to young people struggling to get a start in life, and scores of people of Berkeley County can today look back to the time when Alexander Clohan lent them a helping hand to start them on their way to competency and usefulness.

THE VANMETRE LINE—The name has been spelled in a large number of ways: Van Metren, Van Metre, Van Meter, Van Matre; at present the style most popular is Vanmetre. In the early history of the county the spelling of the name was Van Matre. Enough research has been made into the history of this family to establish the fact that Emanuel Van Meteren was the Dutch Consul in London, England, in the early seventeenth century; he was an historian and an acquaintance of Hendrick Hudson, the explorer. The arms of the Dutch Van Metern family are; quartered: first and fourth of silver with a fleur-de-lis, gules; with second and third of gold, with two feses ;gules accomplished with eight martlets of the same color arranged in orle. Crest; a fleur-de-lis. It is said that the name is derived from Metern, a town of Guerlderland, Holland. If this be true, the correct spelling of the name should be Van Meter. There are two early settlers from whom the Virginia pioneer family has been supposed to have come:

(1). Jan Joosten, the founder of this family, arrived at New Amsterdam (now New York City), September 12, 1662, coming from Tiederwelt, with his wife and five children ranging in age from two to fifteen years; removed to Wyltrick, Kingston, New York, same year. In 1663 the Minnisik Indians raided and burned Wyltrick and carried off his wife and two children but these were rescued. Was a schephan at Wiltwick; was elected (1667) a deacon in the Dutch Reformed Church. In 1673 was one of the four magistrates of Hurley and Marbletown, New York; swore allegiance to the English in Ulster County, New York, 1689; in 1695 purchased five hundred acres of land in Burlington County, New Jersey, on the Delaware River on the present site of Burlington, New Jersey; bought a large acreage of land in Somerset County, New Jersey, and died near Raritan, New Jersey; married Machyken Hendrickson of Meppelen Province of Dreuthe, Holland.

(2). Joost Janse, son of Jan Joosten and Machyken Hendrickson; born in Europe about 1656; son Jan, baptised October 14, 1683; settled somewhere on the Raritan River in Somerset County, New Jersey; thence removed to Maryland and settled on the Monocacy River; in 1726 received a grant of land in Frederick County at the mouth of Metre's Run, which empties into the Monocacy. When Governor Gooch of Virginia was giving away large tracts of land in the Shenandoah Valley, he advised his sons John (Jan) and Isaac Van Matre to avail themselves of this opportunity to get a large tract of land for a little or nothing. Their father, John Van Matre, had visited this region a few years before on a trading expedition with the Indians. John and Isaac Van Matre received 40,000 acres of land in this grant, much of which is now in Berkeley and Jefferson Counties. Many descendants of these men are still living in Berkeley County, among which are Isaac Van Metre of Kearneysville and Floyd and Allen Van Metre on the Arden road; George W. Vanmetre (deceased), for many years County Surveyor of Berkeley County; E. W. Vanmetre, Washington, D. C., and James Henry Vanmetre of the county.

C. NEWTON STUCKEY—County Road Engineer of Berkeley County for the past seven years. The originator of this family in this county, Jacob Stuckey, came to the county in company with John Cushwa, the originator of the Cushwa (then written Gushwa) family, on Tuscarora Creek. They originally came from Pennsylvania. They were both of German descent. Jacob Stuckey bought a large tract of land on Tuscarora and John Cushwa bought a large tract on Back Creek in the vicinity of Jones Springs. On being informed that Back Creek occasionally raised and overflowed its banks far and wide, John Cushwa proposed a trade of the tracts of lands owned by him on Back Creek for the tracts of lands owned by Jacob Stuckey on Tuscarora. The trade was effected and Jacob Stuckey went to Back Creek, while John Cushwa came to Tuscarora. Samuel Stuckey, a son of Jacob Stuckey, was a soldier in the War of 1812, and was the grandfather of Dr. James H. Shipper of Martinsburg, also of Mrs. S. S. Felker of that same place. Jacob H. Stuckey, a son of Samuel's, was elected County Commissioner of Berkeley County. He died before he could take his seat, and his brother, Charles W. Stuckey, was appointed to fill the unexpired term. At the next election Charles W. Stuckey was elected to succeed himself as Commissioner.

Carlton B. Stuckey, a son of C. Newton Stuckey, was appointed by the County Court as road machinist for the county in 1923, which position he now holds.

ROBERT C. BURKHART—Veteran of the Civil War. Volunteered in the Confederate Army in 1861 and surrendered with that army at Appomattox in 1865. Member of Company B, First Virginia Cavalry; had command of fifteen scouts as Chief of Scouts under General Fitz Hugh Lee. He informed General Early of the absence of General Phil Sheridan from his army upon a visit to Washington, D. C., where he was called to a conference with the War Board and President Lincoln. Upon this information, Early attacked Sheridan's troops at Cedar Creek, Virginia, and had them on the rout. General Sheridan arrived from Washington in time to hear the thunder of Early's cannon. He was at Winchester, "twenty miles away," and immediately mounted "his coal black steed" and galloped to his retreating army, arriving there in time to turn rout into victory.

The ride of Sheridan from Winchester to the scene of battle has been immortalized by Thomas Buchanan Reed's poem: "Sheridan's Ride." Two nights before this battle General Sheridan and his staff spent the night at Martinsburg in the old Everett House, a hostelry of importance at that time. This building is still standing at the southwest corner of Burke and Queen Streets; the lower part of this building is now occupied by Spillman brothers' grocery. He came by Martinsburg on his way to Winchester from the conference at Washington.

Mr. Burkhart witnessed the ride of General Sheridan down the Valley Pike but did not recognize him as the general until he was too far away to intercept him. Had he and his scouts recognized him and succeeded in stopping his flight, history might have had another tale to record. Mr. Burkhart was born at Darkesville October 8th, 1839. He was the father of the truck-raising industry of the county, operating a large truck farm at Burkhart's Flats, at Pikeside. He served a term as State Senator from this district in the West Virginia Legislature. He was the father of a large family of boys and girls, most of whom located in Berkeley County after marriage, and are holding responsible positions in the various callings they have chosen.

HARRY S. CUSHWA—One time member West Virginia Legislature from Berkeley County. Descendant of John Gushwa (Cushwa), Bucks County, Pennsylvania. Jonathan Cushwa settled on Tuscarora Creek. One of his sons, Barnet Cushwa, and an uncle of H. S. Cushwa, was nominated for Sheriff on the Democratic ticket. Alexander Newcomer was nominated on the Independent ticket. The election was very close, Mr. Cushwa receiving a majority of seven votes. The election was contested before the County Court, which decided that no one was elected; another election being held, Mr. Cushwa received sixty-seven votes majority. This election was also contested on the charge of irregularity, but the dread disease of cholera having become an epidemic before the Court could convene, the law gave the office to Mr. Cushwa. He proved a most efficient county officer. H. S. Cushwa, at the age of eighteen, formed a partnership with his brother, Harvey C. Cushwa, as carpenters and contractors. Later they engaged in the hardware business under the firm name of H. T. Cushwa & Bro. After the death of Harvey in 1902, Mr. Harry Cushwa continued the hardware business in his own name. He has conducted the business in the same place for forty years.

W. S. MILLER—Father of the apple industry in Berkeley County; first planted sixteen acres of orchard on the old Miller homestead near Gerardstown in 1851. His neighbors predicted failure, that it would never amount to anything. When the Civil War broke out, Mr. Miller had on hand a large number of peach, apple, pear and plum nursery trees which he had budded himself. As he had no sale for them at that time, he set them out on his own land. At the close of the war he had 4,000 bearing trees; continued to set out nursery stock until he had 6,500 planted—2,500 peach and 4,000 apple. From this humble beginning sprang the commercial apple industry of Berkeley County. Needless to say, Mr. Miller made good, made money, sold his crop each fall, and induced others to venture in the business. He was the father of several boys who became large orchard planters. One, John M. Miller, the largest apple grower in Berkeley County. His other sons, D. Gold Miller, of Gerardstown, Harry P. Miller, Port Miller, and Gilbert P. Miller, of Paw Paw and Romney, are owners of large commercial orchards of apple and peach.

CHARLES W. RUBLE—Father was Matthias Ruble, who came from Frederick County, Virginia, to Berkeley County 55 years ago. Charles Ruble bought the farm he now operates at Marlowe in December, 1907. Was active in securing the Marlowe Consolidated School, at which place most of the scholars of Falling Waters District are transported by truck to this central place. This school was the first of its kind in the county. Was president of the Board of Education of Falling Waters District for eight years; had been a director of the Williamsport Turnpike Company for eight years, until it was taken over by the State Road Commission; a director in the Shenandoah Valley Bank and Trust Company of Martinsburg. At present is a member of the Board of Equalization. He has been a farmer by occupation.

E. A. HOBBS—Came to Berkeley County January 1st, 1896. Born in Wheeling, West Virginia. Elected Clerk of the County Court of Berkeley County for two terms, 1909-1922. His father, M. R. Hobbs, enlisted in the Union Army of the Civil War. Was a member of the Army Band at Fort Delaware, New Jersey. John Leonard Hobbs, son of E. A. Hobbs, enlisted in a Harrisburg (Pennsylvania) Company, and served on the border of Mexico against Villa under General Pershing, and in the World War. Served in the occupation of the Rhine, after the close of that war. While thus in service he met a German girl, married her and brought her home with him when his regiment was disbanded. Mary Hobbs, a daughter of E. A. Hobbs, is bookkeeper for Merchants and Farmers Bank of Martinsburg and is a graduate of the Martinsburg High School.

GEORGE F. WHITMORE—His father was John C. Whitmore, who came to Berkeley County from Maryland. Occupation, a carpenter.

GEORGE F. WHITMORE—Was a Corporal in Company M, Second Regiment West Virginia Volunteer Infantry in the Spanish-American War. In June, 1909, helped to organize Company F, First Regiment West Virginia National Guards, stationed at Martinsburg, all Berkeley County men. Served as First Sergeant in this Company from June, 1909, to May, 1911, then commissioned as Second Lieutenant. Served in the Paint Creek and Cabin

Creek labor trouble. In the summer and fall of 1916, engaged in recruiting for the Second West Virginia Regiment. On duty on the Mexican border. On March 28, 1917, the Company was ordered to mobilize at Martinsburg and on April 2nd joined the Regiment in the mobilization camp at Camp Cornwall, Fairmont, W. Va. Promoted to Captain and assigned to command of Company F, First West Virginia National Guards; June 1st, 1917, left Camp Cornwall and removed to Camp Shelby, Miss; September 18th, assigned to command of Company B, Motor Battalion 113th Ammunition Train; embarked for France October 5th, 1918; landed there October 11th, 1918. Returned to the United States July 20th, 1919; landed in New York City, July 31st, 1919, and mustered out of service August 21st, 1919. Has held a position as Superintendent of Mails in the Martinsburg Post Office since June 1st, 1920.

Miss Edna Fellers, a niece of Mr. Whitmore's, won the first prize for the best essay on the subject "Stonewall Jackson" sponsored by the local chapter of the U. D. C. in January, 1927. The contestants were from the Martinsburg High School and the Saint Joseph's Catholic School.

JOSEPH WHITMORE—Was in business in Martinsburg from 1906 to 1912 under the firm name of Dean-Whitmore-Drewry—Men's Clothing. Appointed Deputy Assessor, under John Riner, Assessor, 1920-24.

JOHN L. WHITMORE—Another brother; in real estate business at Miami, Florida. Was a candidate for the West Virginia State Senate from the 15th Senatorial District. He being the Republican nominee and the district overwhelmingly Democratic in sentiment, he was defeated by less than 300 votes.

ED. C. BROWN—Rural mail carrier for Route No. 6, out of Martinsburg, for twenty-five years. His twin brother is John H. Brown, of Arden District, a school commissioner of that district and a candidate for the office of County Commissioner in the August primary of 1926 but was defeated by a small majority. Mr. Ed. Brown began life in a very lowly position, working for a farmer when he was ten years old for a dollar a month and his board.

E. B. KETTERING—His father, Adam Kettering, in company with Daniel Long, Therman Long and James Hogue, migrated by "prairie schooner" to Back Creek Valley fifty-two years ago, in the vicinity of Ganotown, from Indiana County, Pennsylvania. James Hogue returned but the other three remained. They bought about 250 acres of land there. Daniel Long brought the first threshing outfit to Berkeley County. It was called a "shaker", and left the grain, straw and chaff all in one pile, after the sheaves were run through it. The straw and chaff were winnowed from the grain by throwing it into the air on a windy day. This was a decided step for improvement in threshing by flail. Adam Kettering served in the Union Army under General Banks. His sons were Albert, Ephraim and Isaac. Ephraim Kettering was elected Sheriff of Berkeley County 1908-1912; had served as Deputy Sheriff under Sheriffs C. L. Stuckey, 1900-1904, and under E. D. Gardner,

1904-1908. He died at Martinsburg, December 12th, 1921, and was buried at Ganotown. One son, Bryan Kettering, served in the World War as Volunteer Engineer at Fort Benj. Harrison, Indianapolis, Ind., as a member of the 49th Division. Another son, Walter Kettering, was appointed to fill the vacancy of his brother, Harrison Kettering (deceased), as Deputy Sheriff of Berkeley County.

DAVID CROCKETT—Noted Indian fighter and scout; ran away from home when a boy of twelve and wandered into the confines of Berkeley County. Worked on a farm owned by John David Gray, situated on the road leading from Arden to the intersection of the Gerardstown-Inwood road. Lived there about three years, afterward returned to his home in Tennessee and became reconciled to his father. Elected to Congress from that State. In this campaign many amusing incidents occurred. His opponent was a brilliant, youthful lawyer. At one place Crockett and his opponent met. In his speech his opponent never alluded to Crockett at all. While he was making his speech a guinea fowl perched on the limb of a tree close by kept up such a chatter that he sent and had the guinea driven away. When it came Crockett's turn to speak he mounted the stump and began his speech by saying that his opponent never once alluded to him, but had to have the guinea driven away because it kept "hollerin 'Crocket! Crocket!' " so much that it interfered with his speech. At these "stump speeches" the candidate would mount a stump in a newly-made "clearing" and would make his speech from this sort of platform. He never was without an audience for the backwoods people would travel for miles to be present at a "stump speech." This custom gave rise to the term, in politics, "stump the state". After the candidate would speak for a while the audience would become dry, when a bottle would have to be produced (by the candidate, of course,) and passed around, then the speaker would proceed until the audience would become dry again, when another bottle would have to be produced. Some of these stump speeches would last for days or weeks. (Reference, the Lincoln-Douglas debates.)

David Crockett was uneducated but was honest and fearless and the people trusted him. He lost his life at the Alamo, fighting for Texas independence, thinking, doubtless, that this action would strengthen his chances for the Presidency. He always had an ambition to become President of the United States. At one time, when he was a candidate for Congress, a constituent interviewed him and asked him how he stood on the "Judiciary". Crockett replied that it would be a good thing, but soon escaped from his interviewer for he did not know what the "Judiciary" meant, and might be called upon to explain. One more instance of his life while living in Berkeley County might be mentioned here. Mr. Gray, mentioned above, was a farmer and raised a large quantity of wheat. He had this wheat ground at Throckmorton's mill and hauled the flour in barrels by wagon to Baltimore, Md. On one of these trips young Crockett accompanied him. While well on his way to Baltimore in passing down a steep grade the brake broke and the team ran away. "Davy" was riding among the barrels. He was thrown out and several barrels upset in close proximity to him. After the team had stopped, Mr. Gray came back to see what had become of him, and found David up and smiling and unhurt. Mr. Gray asked him if he was not afraid of being killed, and David remarked that any "man that was cut out to be President of the United States would never be killed by a flour barrel." His motto, as every schoolboy, knows, was: "Be sure you are right then—go ahead."

NELSON B. O'NEAL—Banker and business man. Educated in the Martinsburg schools. Began his career as bookkeeper for the National Commercial Company, once located on West Race Street. Was a clerk for the Old National Bank for eleven years. At the end of this period entered the United States Army in the World War in the Medical Department. Was commissioned Second Lieutenant in the Sanitary Corps, stationed at Camp Meade, Md. Was later transferred to Washington, D. C., in the same capacity in the Surgeon General's Office. After his honorable discharge from the Army, accepted a position with the Riggs National Bank of Washington, D. C., as assistant auditor. After two years of service there, came to Martinsburg as cashier of the Bank of Martinsburg. Brought this bank to a high standing as a banking institution. Remained with that corporation for three years and a half, then returned to Riggs National Bank as assistant cashier.

WILLIAM H. KIBLER—Born in Luray, Va. Soldier in the Civil War, C. S. A., Company K, Infantry, Captain Parks commanding. His son, William Walter Kibler; born in Frederick County, Va.; came to Martinsburg in 1887; has been a machinist in the Middlesex Mill, Martinsburg, since 1891; Past Great Sachem of Improved Order of Red Men of West Virginia; member of Tuscarora Tribe No. 50, Imp. O. R. M., at Martinsburg, W. Va. His son, Calvin H. Kibler; graduate of M. H. S., class of 1922; clerk at B. & O. freight office at Martinsburg. His son, Charles E. Kibler, is a graduate of the Martinsburg High School, class of 1927. Walter Kibler is the oldest employe of the Interwoven Mills, Inc., of Martinsburg in point of service.

H. L. SNAPP—Three brothers by the name of Snapp came from Scotland and located in Shenandoah County, Va. One of these men, named Joseph, was the grandfather of H. L. Snapp. The family were farmers. Joseph W. Snapp came to Berkeley County in 1870 and located on a farm. H. L. Snapp opened a store at Inwood at the time of the founding of this town. Here he dealt in everything a general country store handled from a toothpick to a threshing machine. The post office at this place was located at this store and Mr. Snapp was Postmaster of Inwood for seventeen years. Sold his store and having purchased a farm at Pikeside, resided there for a number of years, dealing in live stock. Located the Peoples Meat Market on East Burke Street in 1925. Resold the store and removed to Pikeside in 1927 and resumed the occupation of a stock dealer. His son, G. M. Snapp, is a graduate of the Martinsburg High School, class of 1921. Another son associated with him is Fred D. Snapp, also a graduate of this institution, class of 1922. Another son is Raymond Snapp, a graduate of Rinker Business College, and is at present located at Rippon, Jefferson County,

W. Va., where he conducts a large general store. A daughter, Katharine, is a member of the High School of York, Pennsylvania.

MARTIN QUINN—Chief of the Martinsburg Fire Department and president of the Cumberland Valley Volunteer Fireman's Association. Has been long associated with the Martinsburg Fire Department, having joined the volunteer forces during the year 1904, and appointed a paid fireman January 17, 1906. Appointed chief July 1st, 1913; attended the New York Fire Department in 1924; celebrated his 20th anniversary as a paid fireman. Has seen the department grow from the hand-drawn reel to motor-driven apparatus, and modern fire station. In 1926 wrote a history of the Martinsburg Fire Department for the Silver Anniversary of the Cumberland Valley Volunteer Fireman's Association at their convention at Martinsburg, August 11, 12 and 13, 1926, which is given *verbatim* in another place in this work.

DR. J. WHANN MCSHERRY—Father was a lawyer and lived at "Wizard Clipp", Jefferson County, W. Va. Richard McSherry, born July 28th, 1747, was a soldier and physician and surgeon in the War of 1812, and was a relative of Dr. J. Whann McSherry. The doctor was born in Martinsburg, December 7, 1833, and is the oldest physician in Berkeley County, the oldest living member of the West Virginia Medical Association and the oldest banker in West Virginia. Educated at the Martinsburg Academy, St. Mary's College of Baltimore, Md., and a graduate of the University of Maryland, Baltimore. Was a soldier in the Civil War. Captain of Company B, 36th Virginia Regiment Infantry Volunteers, in the Confederate service. Was appointed Captain by Governor Henry A. Wise. After peace he came to Martinsburg but was not allowed to practice his profession on account of his having been a "rebel". Removed to Baltimore and remained there until 1869, when he returned to Martinsburg, the "Flick Amendment" having been passed allowing all who served in the Southern cause to take the oath of allegiance to the United States Government. Dr. McSherry was allowed to practice in West Virginia. Was elected Mayor of Martinsburg two terms; was also a member of the City Council. Married the daughter of Charles James Faulkner on June 3rd, 1876. Was a banker connected with the Old National Bank, but when the Citizens National Bank was organized was elected president of that institution and has held that position to the present time excepting two years. Although nearly a hundred years old, he still attends the bank meetings of that institution. He helped to organize the bank with a capital stock of $100,000.

D. N. KEES—Of Jones' Springs. Celebrated his 90th birthday April 12th, 1927. Born, reared at his home place at Jones' Springs. Father of Joseph Ed. Kees, a commercial man of Philadelphia, Pa. His son, Robert L. Kees, resides at home and occupies the farm of his father. He is also father of Mrs. Matilda Wheeler of the same place, and grandfather of Victor Wheeler, assistant cashier of the Shenandoah Valley Bank & Trust Company of Martinsburg. In all old records the Kees family name is spelled Keys. This is an old family, the ancestors having migrated to this country along about the beginning of the Revolution and have always resided in Back Creek Valley.

WILLIAM CODY—Grandfather of the famous Indian fighter and scout, William F. Cody (Buffalo Bill). Tradition has it that he once lived in Back Creek Valley and hunted and trapped over the mountains and along the streams of Back Creek, Sleepy Creek and Meadow Branch, also along the banks of the Potomac, in that section of Berkeley County which is now included in Morgan County. Whether this is correct or not, it is recorded that that much of traditional history may not be lost.

COLONEL HUGH STEPHENSON—Born in Berkeley County. When the Continental Congress met in Philadelphia in June, 1775, and passed a resolution calling upon Virginia to place soldiers in the field to fight for American liberties, Colonel Stephenson raised a company of volunteers to serve one year in that army. William Henshaw, Geo. Scott, and Thomas Hite were chosen lieutenants. Among the privates in this company who afterwards arose to prominence were: Robert White, afterwards a Judge of the General Court of Virginia; Joseph Swearingen, Justice of the Court of Berkeley County; General Samuel Findlay, Major Henry Bedinger, Major Michael Bedinger of Revolutionary War fame, Nathaniel Pendleton, Esq., and Lieutenant Abraham Shepherd. Lieutenant Hite resigned his commission and Abraham Shepherd was unaniously elected to fill his position in this company. Afterwards raised a regiment of riflemen. Hugh Stephenson was appointed colonel with John Rawlins as lieutenant-colonel. Colonel Stephenson died at "Roxbury Camp, New England." Half brother of Colonel William Crawford, whose death at the hands of the savages on the Sandusky River in 1782 was the most revolting in savage warfare.

JOHN STROTHER—Born in Berkeley County, 1792; deputy Clerk of the County Court of that County at the age of thirteen; served in the defense of Norfolk in the War of 1812, with Captain Faulkner's company of artillery, with the rank of Second Lieutenant; afterwards appointed Lieutenant of the 12th Infantry, in camp at Fredericksburg, Virginia; resigned his commission in the State Company; was succeeded by Edward Colston, also of Berkeley County; joined his regiment on the Canadaian border under Wilkenson, against Montreal, and at Chrisler's Field; pronmoted to Adjutant of the Regiment. After the war, returned to Martinsburg; married Elizabeth Pendleton, daughter of Philip Pendleton, Esq.; elected Clerk of the County Court of Berkeley County in 1829 and served till 1833. In 1832, appointed Clerk of the Supreme Court of Law and Chancery by Judge Richard Parker for the County of Berkeley; was connected with the clerkship of the county for forty-five years; erected a hotel at Berkeley Springs in 1845. Took sides with the North in the Civil War; had one son in the Union Army; died at Berkeley Springs, January 16th, 1862, and was buried at Martinsburg with Masonic and military honors. No other man has so long been connected with the Clerk's office as has he.

LIEUTENANT JACOB S. BOAK, C. S. A.—Born in Berkeley County,

Virginia (W. Va.), in 1839. Was a Lieutenant of the Jackson Horse Artillery. Eentered the Confederate service in 1861 as Corporal, promoted to Orderly Sergeant, later to Third Lieutenant; served till the surrender at Appomattox, 1865. Was in engagement of Two-Mile Creek, near Charleston Cross Lanes, Big Sewell Mountain, Carnifax Ferry, and Fayetteville. Captured at Fort Donaldson and held at Camp Douglas, Illinois, for eight months; afterward exchanged. Was at the battles of Gettysburg, Atlea's Station, near Richmond. At Fisher's Hill his horse was shot under him and eight bullet holes were found in his clothing, several inflicting slight wounds. After the close of the war he studied dentistry and followed that profession at Martinsburg until his death. He married Miss Kate A. Davis of Maryland in 1873. Eight children were born to this union. Dr. Boak had three brothers in the Confederate Army.

CAPTAIN WILLIAM B. COLSTON, C. S. A.—Born in Berkeley County; a direct descendant of the Colston's who owned "Honeywood", a fine estate overlooking the Potomac in the northern section of this county. Was always prominent in the affairs of Berkeley County. Born at "Honeywood" in 1836. Educated at the Episcopal High School, near Alexandria, Va., and at the University of Virginia. Joined a company of volunteers raised at Hedgesville in 1859 as a private. This company was known as "The Hedgesville Blues" and was recruited of young men from the northern section of the county and from around Hedgesville. This company became Company E, Second Virginia Infantry, Stonewall Brigade. Captain Colston became Orderly Sergeant; in 1862 was elected First Lieutenant, and in the spring of 1863 was made Captain, which position he held throughout tne war. Wounded twice, once at the Battle of Kernstown, again at the Battle of Fredericksburg. From this last wound he was confined to the hospital for eight months. Again took the field and was in the Battle of Nine Runs, at which place his brother, Raleigh T. Colston, of Berkeley County was killed. Assigned to post duty at Charlottesville. This forced inactivity did not appeal to Captain Colston's nature and he applied to General Clermont A. Evans, commanding a division of Stonewall's Brigade. On his way to Charlottesville to procure a horse was captured at Farmville and was paroled. In 1863 was elected by the soldiers from Berkeley County, then in the hands of the enemy, as a representative in the Virginia Legislature, and served in that capacity for two years. Engaged in farming after the close of the war in Berkeley County until 1872, then removed to Martinsburg. Elected Magistrate in 1880. Appointed Postmaster of Martinsburg in 1885-1889 by President Cleveland. Elected Clerk of the Circuit Court 1890-1896. Editor of the *Martinsburg Statesman*, 1883-1889. In 1866 married Miss Minnie Summers. From this union were born four children: Susan, Jane, Elizabeth and Sophia. Another brother of Captain Colston's to serve in the Confederate Army was Edward, a private in the Second Virginia Cavalry, who lost an arm at Appomattox, 1862. Is now a prominent attorney at Cincinnati, Ohio.

CANTAIN JAMES N. CUNNINGHAM, C. S. A.—Born in Berkeley County, 1863. A member of John B. Hoge's Cavalry, a company organized of

Berkeley County men. Was Corporal in this company, which joined the Confederate Army April 19th, 1861, and became Company B, Frist Virginia Cavalry, Stewart's Bridgade. Elected First Lieutenant 1862. While conducting 317 Federal prisoners to prison camp, was met near Beaver's Dam Station by Sheridan's command, overpowered, and the prisoners released. He and most of his men, however, escaped capture. The following day at the Battle of Yellow Caverns, Captain Hammond of Company B was killed and Lieutenant Cunningham was promoted to Captain in his stead. Continued in this position until the end of the war. Was in numerous engagements throughout the war:, viz: first Battle of Manassas, Chancellorsville, Gettysburg, Sharpsburg, Tom's Brook, Fredericksburg, Spottsylvania, Wilderness, Beaver's Dam, Brandy Station, Yellow Tavern, Woodstock and Front Royal. Captain Cunningham had two brothers in the Confederate Army, James L., wounded and captured at Gettysburg, and Charles A., killed at the Battle of Winchester, September 19, 1864.

JACOB GASSMAN—Inhabitant of Berkeley County since 1879. Born in Hagerstown, Md., in 1852; was a veteran of the 7th Virginia Cavalry, C. S. A., which he joined at Romney (W. Va.) in 1861. Was in many battles for the South, the most important ones being Kernstown, Winchester, Front Royal, and with Stuart's command at Second Manassas, Sharpsburg and Gettysburg. At the latter place was shot through the neck and in a fall from his horse his collar bone was broken; recovered and joined his command and was again wounded so severely at Moorefield (W. Va.) that he was unable to do any more fighting during the remainder of the war. Engaged in farming in Berkeley County from 1888 to the end of his life.

G. B. WILTSHIRE—Born at Leetown, Jefferson County, Virginia, July 3ad, 1861; father was a farmer; married Miss Lorena Flick, daugter of Judge W. H. H. Flick. Elected a member of the City Council of Martinsburg two terms, in which he helped to put forward the project of new street paving. Elected Mayor of Martinsburg: treasurer and deacon of the building committee of the First Baptist Church, which rebuilt the present edifice on West King Street. They have three children: Harrison, educated at Mercersburg Academy, Mercersburg, Pa., and at Princeton University; is with Armour & Co., in an important position; Elizabeth, married C. Bruce Flick, now residing in Berkeley, Calif., graduate of Martinsburg High School, class of 1922, also educated at Wilson College; G. B. Wiltshire, Jr., graduate of Martinsburg High School, class of 1926, president of the class for three terms, now attending Washington and Lee University.

PETER HESS—Father of the large Hess family, descendants of which are still prominent in the vicinity of Salem and Needmore. Was steward of the Berkeley County Infirmary at Salem after the close of the Civil War. Was the father of George, Solomon, Balem, and the grandfather of Lewis and William T. Hess, the latter a merchant in the vicinity of Needmore.

ZACHARY T. GROVE—Merchant of Martinsburg during the latter part of the nineteenth century; father of Philip Grove, who is now in the employ of the Nelson Hardware Company of Roanoke, Va., the leading wholesale hardware firm of the South. Philip Grove married Eleanor Bowers, daughter of the late George M. Bowers. To this union was born George Bowers Grove, graduate of the M. H. S., class of 1923, at present a student of Roanoke of Salem, Va., and Philip Ryneal Grove, a graduate of the M. H. S., 1928. Mrs. Philip Grove was educated at the Martinsburg High School and the Mary Baldwin Seminary, Staunton, Va. She is a sister of Jean B. Daugherty, who married Draper M. Daugherty, son of Harry M. Daugherty, who was Attorney-General of the United States in President Harding's Cabinet.

JOSEPH THOMPSON—The progenitor of that family in Berkeley County was an officer in the Orange Army in the Orange Rebellion in Ireland. The rebellion was unsuccessful, the property of Joseph Thompson was confiscated for the English, or, properly speaking, the Ireland branch of it by the Duke of Antrim. After this catastrophe, Joseph Thompson fled to America and landed in Baltimore. Later he came to Kearneysville, Jefferson County. He was overseer of the "Bowery", the home of the Dandridges on the Opequon. His son Samuel Thompson, the founder of the Thompson family in Berkeley County, a family which is today one of the prominent ones in the business annals and the upbuilding of the county and city. Jospeh Thompson came to America from Ireland in 1790 and settled at Dandridge's. Married a lady by the name of Mary Brown. His occupation was a weaver. To this union was born a family of nine children, five boys and four girls. Soldier in the War of 1812 and helped defend Fort McHenry, Baltimore, against the British fleet on the memorable night that Francis Scott Key wrote his immortal "Star Spangled Banner". Samuel J. Thompson, his son, was a conductor of a wood train which supplied the various engines of the Baltimore and Ohio Railroad with fuel, coal not then being thought of as a fuel for railroad engines. In this capacity he came to Martinsburg where the family has been resident ever since. He was a father of a family of thirteen children, all of which, the boys at least, have been connected with the business of Martinsburg, as follows:

JAMES F. THOMPSON—A clothing merchant (deceased), started in business as a clerk in a store of the late David Weil, in Martinsburg. After clerking for some time in this store, he formed a partnership with Maybury G. Tabler under the firm name of Thompson & Tabler. The firm prospered and Mr. Tabler, wishing to withdraw, the partnership was dissolved and Mr. Thompson opened a store for men's furnishings under the firm name of J. F. Thompson & Bro. The "Bro." was J. Frank Thompson. James F. Thompson was a director of the Peoples Trust Company of Martinsburg. A daughter, Anna Lee Alonzo Ryneal, was principal at one time of the Third Ward School.

JOHN W. THOMPSON—Who connected a meat market at Thomas, W. Va., for several years, eventually moved to Martinsburg and located on East Martin Street in the business of a grocer and butcher shop combined.

CHARLES E. THOMPSON—Who conducts a shoe store on Queen Street also has large holdings in the county. His two sons are Charles, in business with his father, graduate of the Martinsburg High School, class of 1924, and Downey, assistant cashier of the Bank of Martinsburg, also a graduate of the same school, class of 1925.

ROBERT S. THOMPSON—Hardware merchant of Martinsburg.

H. S. THOMPSON—Elected Magistrate for Martinsburg District for three terms and in the insurance business.

J. FRANK THOMPSON—One time in business with his brother, James F. Thompson. Postmaster of Martinsburg for two terms, 1912 to 1920, having been appointed by the late President Wilson.

LOUIS H. THOMPSON—Men's clothing merchant, associated with his brother Ben under the firm name of Thompson & Thompson; member of the City Council one term; president of the Shenandoah Valley Bank and Trust Company; president of the Shenandoah Hotel Corporation; president of the local baseball club, during which time the club won the penant three times of the Blue Ridge Baseball Association.

BEN J. THOMPSON—Conducted a men's furnishing establishment under the name of "Just Ben" for a few years on North Queen Street. Is now associated with his brother Louis H. Thompson in the clothing business. When a very young man was the fastest bicycle racer in this section, winning many races· at Martinsburg, Shepherdstown and elsewhere in the valley. Virginia, a daughter of Samuel J. Thompson, married Boyd Lambert, a large livestock dealer for this section. J. Frank Thompson was chairman of the Democratic Congressional Committee for a number of years. Louis H. Thompson was elected a member of the Democratic National Committee and a delegate to the Democratic National Convention at New York City which nominated John W. Davis for President in the 1924 convention.

CHARLES RALPH BEALL—Lawyer. Born at Hedgesville, Berkeley County, W. Va., April 23, 1895. Son of Edward and Laura (Marsh) Beall; graduate of Washington and Lee University in 1915, with the degree of LL.B.; admitted to the Martinsburg Bar, 1917; on May 8, 1923, married Virginia Emmart, daughter of Frank S. Emmart, noted business man of F. S. Emmart & Son. Associated with the law firm of Martin & Seibert in the general practice of law. Entered the World War as First Lieutenant, 1917, at Fort Benjamin Harrison Camp and Perry's Camp Custer, 45th Division.

HARRY H. BYRER—Lawyer. Born at Philippi, Barbour County, W. Va., April 20th, 1877. Son of Frederick and Isabella (Woods) Byrer. His grandfather, Samuel Woods, was a former member of the Supreme Court of Appeals of West Virginia; admitted to the bar at Philippi, W. Va. (1902), and practiced there in the State and Federal Courts until 1919, when he moved to Martinsburg and formed a partnership with Hon. Stuart W. Walker. Wade C. Kilmer became a member of the law firm in 1922. Upon the death of Mr. Walker, the firm name continued as Kilmer & Byrer. Was Assistant United States District Attorney for the Northern District of West Virginia, 1914-1922. Prosecuting Attorney for Barbour County, W. Va., 1909-1913. Member of the Berkeley Bar Association and the West Virginia State Association. Director of the Y. M. C. A. Member of the Chamber of Commerce.

REUBEN FINE—Lawyer. Born at Martinsburg, W. Va., March 6, 1892. Son of Louis and Julia (Wolf) Fine. Graduate West Virginia University, class of 1913, with degree of LL.B. Admitted to the Bar in 1913 and is a member of the American Bar Association and of the Berkeley Bar Association. Practices in all the courts.

WADE C. KILMER—Lawyer. Son of John D. and Anna (Cushwa) Kilmer. Graduate of the West Virginia University with degrees of A.B. and LL.B. Admitted to the Bar, 1899. Member of the law firm of Walker, Kilmer & Byrer; practices in all the courts; was appointed a member of the Public Service Commission of West Virginia, 1913-1915; director of the Citizens National Bank of Martinsburg; was former Captain of Company F, First West Virginia National Guards, U. S. A.

THOMAS DAVIS, M.D.—Born in Kentucky. Removed to Berkeley County in 1820; practiced medicine for ten years in Martinsburg but gradually allowed his practice to lapse, devoting his time to literature and history. Went to Natchez, Tennessee, in 1845, but the epidemic of yellow fever broke out there and he succumbed to its ravages. Founded the Martinsburg Library and supported it with his able means for many years. Representted Berkeley County in the Virginia Legislature one term (1831).

JOHN BAKER—Lawyer. Born in Berkeley County, Virginia, 1769. Educated at Liberty Hall Academy, Rockbridge County, Virginia; began the practice of his profession at Shepherdstown. Member of the Federalist party. Elected to Congress from the district comprising then the Counties of Berkeley, Hampshire and Jefferson (1811-13). Favored a bill in that Congress pensioning survivors, officers and soldiers of the Revolution. Voted against the War 1812 and was one of the 34 members of Congress who published an elaborate defense of their opposition to the war; presented a petition to Congress asking that body to make improvements near Georgetown that would give the farmers of that section a choice of markets for their flour. The improvmeents were made. It was stated that 300,000 barrels of flour were annually shipped over the Potomac in boats. Such an immense amount of flour shipped in a single year showed to what extent this industry of wheat growing and flour milling had grown throughout this section at that time (1812). Died at Shepherdstown on August 18, 1823, of a violent bilious epidemic which visited that section, carrying off hundreds of citizens of that town.

"BIOGRAPHY" 221

ALEXANDER WILSON—Writer, poet, student; born in Paisly, Scot and July, 1766; came to the United States; settled in Berkeley County, Virginia; by trade was a weaver. (In those days most everybody was bought up to some trade or another, regardless of his other qualifications, a commendable practice.) Spent his life here in writing books on Natural Science, which reduced him to dire poverty. He completed the seventh volume of his work on ornithology and was engaged in collecting material for the eight volume when he died, August 23, 1813.

RICHARD MCSHERRY, M.D.—Born at "Retirement", a homestead near Leetown, Jefferson County, then within the confines of Berkeley County, May 28, 1792. Son of Richard and Anastatia McSherry. Received his education at Fredericktown Academy, Frederick, Md., at Hagerstown and at Georgetown College, D. C. Studied medicine under Dr. Samuel J. Creamer, a physician at Charles Town. Graduated from the University of Pennsylvania in Medicine, 1816. Joined a company from Jefferson County in the War of 1812. Upon the death of the medical officer of the company was commissioned in his place and served as a surgeon in the army until the end of the war. Began the practice of medicine at Martinsburg and held an extensive and lucrative practice until 1871, when he retired. In January, 1817, he married Miss Ann C. King, daughter of George King of Georgetown. Was a physician who by constant study kept well in advance of medical science. Was a student all his life in history and general literature.

GENERAL ELISHA BOYD, U. S. A.—Born in Berkeley County, October 6, 1769. Son of John Boyd, one of the early emigrants to the county. Attended the country schools of that time, hence his early education was limited. In 1785, entered Liberty Hall Academy, which was the nucleus of the great Washington and Lee University. Studied law in the office of Colonel Philip Pendleton. Elected to the Virginia House of Delegates, 1796, with William Lamon as his colleague, and in 1797 with Richard Baylor as his colleague. Chosen attorney for the State by the County Court of Berkeley County and filled this position for forty years. Married Mary, daughter of Major Andrew Waggoner of Revolutionary War fame. They had one child, a daughter, Sara Ann Boyd, who married Philip C. Pendleton. Some years after the death of his first wife, he married Ann Holmes, daughter of Colonel Joseph Holmes and sister of Governor Holmes of Virginia and Major Andrew Hunter Holmes. Four children were born to this union, Ann Rebecca Holmes, John E. Boyd, Rev. Andrew H. H. Boyd, and Mary, who married Charles James Faulkner.

Served in the War of 1812 with the commission of Colonel of the 4th Regiment of Virginia Militia and was engaged in the second defense of Norfolk and Portsmouth against a British attack of land and naval forces. For his services in the defense of Virginia, the General Assembly elected him a Brigadier-General. (The United States Army was then composed of States Militia.) Was a member of the Convention of 1830 which amended the Constitution of Virginia. Elected in 1832 to a seat in the Senate of Virginia. Commissioned a Magistrate of the County of Berkeley in 1838. Was an advocate of a reform of the "Old Constitution" of Virginia and was elected chairman of the county meeting held here and a delegate to the State Reform Convention. Helped to establish Martinsburg Academy which functioned for many years as a seat of learning for youth in this section. Built "Boydville", the home of the present owner, Charles J. Faulkner; bequeathed it to his daughter Mary. Was married a third time to Elizabeth Byrd of the Westover family, who died on the 16th of November, 1839. General Boyd died October 21, 1841, and was buried in the family burying ground at Norborne Cemetery.

MOSES T. HUNTER—Born in Berkeley County, 1790; the son of Moses Hunter, one of the Clerks of the Court of Berkeley County and one of the Presidential electors who cast the vote of Virginia for George Washington. Lawyer of brilliant oratorical powers and sound reasoning. Inherited the famous "Red House", one mile north of Martinsburg, which was known as the birthplace of Berkeley County. Here the first session of the Court of Berkeley County was held May 19, 1772. Mr. Hunter, having spent his money lavishly, decided to recuperate his fortune by the practice of law. He had for his circuit the Counties of Berkeley, Jefferson, Morgan and Frederick; also the District Court of Chancery held at Winchester which had jurisdiction over some fifteen or twenty counties. His practice immediately became lucrative. In April, 1827, Edward Colston, a Federalist, and Moses T. Hunter, a Democrat, were elected to the House of Delegates of Virginia without opposition, all the voters of the county voting for these two men. Berkeley County then as now being entitled to two members of the House of Delegates. He made some speeches in this body which were highly commended by his constituents, but he fell into habits of dissipation in Richmond which impaired his health and he died at Winchester at the home of his brother-in-law, Chemcellor Tucker, on June 4, 1829, in the 39th year of his life.

DAVID HOLMES, U. S. A.—Born in Winchester, Virginia; son of Colonel Joseph Holmes of Frederick County, Virginia; brother of Major Andrew Hunter Holmes, distinguished in the War of 1812, who was killed at the Battle of Mackinaw on August 4, 1814, and a sword was voted to his heirs by the Legislature of Virginia; also brother to Judge Holmes, who occasionally resided in this district, and a brother to Anne Holmes, who married General Elisha Boyd of this county. Was a member of the 5th, 6th, 7th, 8th, 9th, and 10th Congresses from this district. Appointed by President Madison Governor of the Mississippi Territory and when that Territory was admitted as a State was elected its first Governor. Elected a Senator from that State in 1820. When elected to the 5th Congress he was a resident of Shenandoah County. In 1799, having removed back to Winchester, he was elected from the District of Frederick and Berkeley. When the district was rearranged, after the census of 1800, he represented Frederick and Shenandoah Counties from 1793 to 1809, thus consecutively representing three distinct districts of the State within the twelve years he was a member of that body.

GENERAL DANIEL MORGAN, U. S. A.—Born in New Jersey, 1737. At the age of eighteen worked for a farmer by the name of Roberts in Berkeley County; was an experienced teamster or wagoner, which was the only mode of freight transportation in those days (1755). Some of these drivers became expert in that line. General Morgan was one of these. He was one of the drivers of the teams in transporting General Braddock's munition wagons on that memorable march to Fort Duquesne. He acquired the sobrioquet of "Old Wagoner". Entered the Continental Army with the position of Captain of Infantry; aided in the capture of Burgoyne's Army at Saratoga, October 17th, 1777; defeated Tarleton at Cowpens, for which action the Continental Congress voted him a gold medal; for this service he was commissioned as Brigadier-General; had command of the Virginia Militia during the "'Whiskey Rebellion" in western Pennsylvania and was detailed for some time in that affected region to see that the agitation did not start again. Under President John Adams' administration, when the prospect of a war with France seemed imminent and a provisional army was organized, the President strongly advocated Daniel Morgan as Commander-in-Chief, but General Washington favored the appointment of Alexander Hamilton, to which President Adams assented but with reluctance. General Morgan was elected from the district composing the Counties of Berkeley and Frederick to a seat in the 5th Congress. But he was a better soldier than statesman. He was a rough, uneducated man, and strictly honest, knew how to vote if he did not know how to make a speech, and always adhered to the principles of his party. Bought a farm in Frederick County, Virginia, to which place he retired after a strenuous life used in making his country free. No other American is held in greater esteem by his countrymen save Washington. Died in Winchester, Virginia, July 6, 1892, age sixty-five years.

JOHN MYERS—Hunter and trapper. His home was in the mountainous section of the county. Received the name of sobrioquet of "Hunter John Myers". His descendants still live in that section and for a number of years John Myers, his grandson, lived on Meadow Branch and was the sole inhabitant of that valley. He reared a large family and at one time there were seventeen children living there and Mr. Myers built a house and employed a private teacher to teach his children. Hunter John Myers lived by his rifle, was an unerring shot and would often be seen with deer and bear meat and numbers of wild turkeys for sale. He was a tall, well-built man, six feet four inches in height. His strenuous life in the open enabled him to live to a good old age and he died in the year 1835.

LIEUTENANT DAVID HUNTER, U. S. A.—Born in Berkeley County; son of Colonel Moses T. Hunter. Joined the United States Army in the War of 1812. Was assigned to duty in the Northern section; was killed leading his troops in the assault of Williamsburg on the St. Lawrence in 1813.

CHARLES D. STEWART—Has the distinction of holding the office of Deputy Sheriff of Berkeley County longer than any other man which office he held for forty-eight years. Few men in this day and time succeed themselves in office and it is a tribute to his sterling qualities that he was selected to fill the office for so long a period. Died in 1854.

RALEIGH COLSTON—Born in England. Married Elizabeth Marshall, sister of Chief Justice John Marshall, distinguished jurist. She lies buried at "Honeywood", the ancestral home of the Colstons in the northern section of the county. Purchased an estate overlooking the banks of the Potomac River and erected a fine mansion thereon know today as "Honeywood". Was a man of literary tastes and devoted to the cause of religion. His distinguished son was Edward Colston, who represented this district in Congress.

ALEXANDER WHITE—First lawyer commissioned to practice law in this county. Heads the list of Prosecuting Attorneys for the county. When Berkeley County held its first court, on May 19th, 1772, Mr. White presented his qualifications and from the record of that court is taken the following extract: "Alexander White having produced a commission from the Attorney General of this State, appointing him deputy attorney for this county, the same be read, he having taken the usual oath, and sworn Deputy King's Attorney for this county."

Elected a member of the First Congress from this district under the present Constitution of the United States and was the only member of Congress from Virginia present on the first day of the first session (1789). Re-elected to the Second Congress in 1791. Appointed a Magistrate for the county 1798. Elected to the Virginia House of Delegates from Berkeley County in 1799. At the time of his first election to Congress, Virginia was, by the United States Constitution, entitled to ten members in the House of Representatives. Therefore, the Legislature of Virginia laid off the State into ten districts, making the Counties of Berkeley, Hampshire, Frederick, Randolph, Shenandoah, Hardy, Ohio and Monongalia the First District. Mr. White was the *first* representative of the *first* district to sit in the *first* session of Congress of the United States, and the *first* member to be at his post of duty from Virginia. After the first census of 1790, Congress fixed the ratio of representation at nineteen members for Virginia. The first district then composed the Counties of Berkeley and Frederick.

ROBERT RUTHERFORD—Elected from Berkeley County to a seat in the Third Congress in 1793 from the First District composing the Counties of Berkeley and Frederick. Re-elected to the Fourth Congress in 1795. Was defeated in the next election by Daniel Morgan. Contested the election of Morgan before the House, but Morgan won.

MAJOR HENRY BEDINGER, U. S. A.—Born at Little York, Pa., October 16th, 1753. His father afterwards removed to Berkeley County at Shepherdstown, now in Jefferson County. Joined the company of volunteers for the Continental Army, raised by Captain Hugh Stephenson, as a private. At the end of one year this company was disbanded but immediately Colonel Hugh Stephenson organized a rifle company for service in this war, and young Bedinger was commissioned as Third Lieutenant. His commission was signed by John Hancock, President of the Continental Congress. In 1777 he was captured by the British at King's Bridge and confined in a British prison until 1781; was afterward exchanged and returned to the army and was made a Captain of the Fourth Virginia Regiment. Elected Clerk of the County Court of Berkeley in 1798, when he returned to Martinsburg. He served one term as a member of the House of Delegates of Virginia. Bought a fine estate five miles south of Martinsburg (at Tablers, William T. Stewart's "Protumna" orchards). Lived to the good old age of ninety, his death ocurring on the 14th day of May, 1843.

EDWARD COLSTON—Son of Raleigh Colston, of whom mention has been made in an above sketch. Born at "Honeywood" in Berkeley County (1788). Was graduated from Princeton College, New Jersey (1806); took up the study of law; was a Federalist adherent. At the age of twenty-five was elected to represent Berkeley County in the Legislature of Virginia, and when twenty-nine was elected a member of Congress from this district, then composing the Counties of Berkeley, Hampshire, Hardy and Jefferson. Married Jane Marshall, daughter of Charles Marshall of Fauquier County, Virginia, a lady of many lovely traits of character. She died March 5th, 1815, when but twenty-one years of age. While in Congress he met in debate many of the leading men of that time, as Henry Clay, William Henry Harrison (afterwards President), John Floyd, Henry Baldwin, Philip R. Barbour, etc., and maintained and defended his opinion with the best of them. Made many memorable speeches in that Congress: "Commutation of Soldiers' Pay," "The Reduction of the Staff of the Army," "Migration of Slaves," etc. As his father, Raleigh Colston, was growing old, he was compelled to return to "Honeywood", and give his attention to the affairs of that estate. Was elected to the Virginia House of Delegates in 1823 and 1824, and was a candidate for Congress in 1825, but was defeated by Hon. William Armstrong of Hampshire County. This defeat was brought about by the disrupting of the Federalist party. In 1826 he was elected a member of the Virginia Legislature by a unanmious vote in Berkeley County. Was again re-elected in 1827, 1833, and 1834. Met, in Richmond, and married Sarah Jane Brockenbrough; was commissioned a Magistrate in 1818; volunteered in the War of 1812 in the Faulkner Artillery Company of Martinsburg and rose to the rank of Lieutenant and aided in repulsing the British in their attack on Portsmouth and Norfolk. Died April 23, 1851.

MAJOR-GENERAL ADAM STEPHEN, U. S. A.—Probably the one man who did the most for the establishing of Berkeley County. He purchased the land where Martinsburg now stands and considerable more surrounding it from Colonel T. B. Martin, who had purchased the last remaining portion of the once princely estate of Lord Fairfax. By the order of Lord Dunmore, Colonial Governor of Virginia, issuing a Commission of Oyer and Terminer to certain Gentlemen Justices for the formation of Berkeley County, we find Adam Stephen's name among them. He was also commissioned the first Sheriff of the county. He founded the town of Martinsburg by laying off one hundred and thirty acres of land into lots and streets. After the Virginia

Assembly had learned what Sheriff Stephen had done, it promptly established the town of Martinsburg, October 18th, 1778. Other towns were competing for the honor of being made the county seat of Berkeley County, but Adam Stephen, by persuasion and the use of sound judgment, contrived to have the capital of the county placed as near the center of it as possible; which place it then held as it does now, Jefferson County and the largest portion of Morgan County being within the boundaries of Berkeley. Adam Stephen raised a company of infantry from this section when the French and Indian War broke out and was ordered by Colonel Washington to appear in Winchester, Va., which he did on the twelfth day of March, 1754, and there started for the frontier. By the death of Colonel Fry, the command fell to Washington and Stephen was made a Major. On August 14th this regiment, to which Major Stephen belonged, was reorganized, Washington being made Colonel, Stephen Lieutenant-Colonel, and Andrew Lewis as Major. At Great Meadows, this army surrendered Fort Necessity but the army marched back to Fort Cumberland. Here Colonel Stephen was placed in command, it being the farthest western outpost of the time. Was at the defeat of Braddock and helped to cover the retreat of that shattered army. Was present at the final capture of Fort Duquesne. Fought against the Creek Indians in the South (1757). Aided in defending the Virginia frontier against the Indians (1763-68)). Had been commissioned a Brigadier-General in the State Militia (1769). Colonel Stephen was placed in command of Fort Loudon at Winchester, from which place he still continued to protect the Northwestern frontier against further depredations by the Indians. It was at this time that the State of Virginia gave him his commission of Brigadier-General, that State fully recognizing his ability as a soldier, he having, up to this time, spent fourteen years of continuous service in the defense of the frontiers of that State's western territory.

When the Revolutionary War began in 1775, Stephen was placed by the Virginia Legislature as one of its regiments. Isaac Read was commissioned Lieutenant-Colonel and Robert Lawson was made Major. February 13, 1776, was transferred to the Continental Line. On September 4th, 1776, was commissioned by Congress a Brigadier-General in the Continental Army, and on February 9th, 1777, was promoted to the rank of Major-General. Fought with Washington at Trenton and Princeton and was in the retreat through the Jerseys, a retreat of ninety miles. At the Battle of Brandywine General Stephen was charged with "unofficer-like conduct" and "intoxication," was found guilty and dismissed from the army.

History has proven that General Stephen contributed in nowise to the disaster met by the Americans on that day; that he was too harshly dealt with; that Washington wished for an opportunity to place his friend and favorite, the Marquis de Lafayette, to a position as an officer in the American Army. However this may be, Washington wrote to the President of the Congress asking that authority be given him to appoint Lafayette to a division of the army. This was granted and Lafayette was appointed to the position recently vacated by General Stephen.

General Stephen was appointed by Lord Dunmore one of the Justices of the first Court of Berkeley County. Martinsburg was then a cluster of houses occupying the site of the Indian village of the Tuscaroras, and was known as Morgan's Springs. It was at the house of Edward Beesom, situated on the farm of George Tremble, Esq., and is known as the "Red House", still standing and in good repair, that the first Court of the county was held. He was elected a delegate with General William Darke to the Virginia convention to ratify or reject the Constitution of the United States in 1788. A letter written by General Stephen prior to the Revolutionary War, setting forth and vindicating the stand taken by the colonies, expresses fully his views on that subject. Needless to say, when General Stephen had the opportunity of creating a new government he voted for the adoption of that Constitution. Made a speech in that convention favoring the adoption of a new Constitution which, for patriotism and eloquence, was not surpassed by any other made..

General Stephen died at Martinsburg in 1791 and was buried on the present estate of ex-Senator Charles James Faulkner. A monument, a rectangular pyramid with a base of twenty feet, the altitude from the vertex to the base, nine feet, marks the spot of his grave. It is situated on the right of South Queen Street at the northeast corner of the new Martinsburg High School grounds. The large stone used in the construction, the largest of them twelve feet in length, are of hard silicious mountain stone and are not native to this section, but must have been transported from a distance. This monument was thrown down and destroyed at one time until its altitude was left to the height of only four feet, but the D. A. R. had it restored to its original height, the top being surrounded by a pyramid of cannon balls from the Civil War. Who first erected the monument is not known as records shed no light upon the subject but it is hoped that the work was accomplished by his grateful and appreciative countrymen.

THOMAS MASLIN—Born at Gerardstown, Berkeley County, October 28th, 1808. Began his business career as clerk in a store at Harper's Ferry, later removed to Moorefield, Hardy County (now W. Va.), continued in business there for thirty years. Was very successful. When the Bank of the Valley established a branch there (1853), he became a director and was made president, which position he held until the Civil War period closed most of the banks of this section. In 1837 was commissioned a Magistrate by the Governor of Virginia for Hardy County and was made Presiding Justice of the County Court of that county; elected by the people of his county to represent them in the Virginia State Convention at Richmond in 1861. In 1872, helped to frame a new State Constitution of West Virginia, representing Hardy and Grant Counties in that convention. Held other offices of trust in Hardy County, being treasurer of one turnpike company and president of another. Died at Moorefield in 1878; was the son of William and Ann Maslin of Gerardstown.

DANIEL BEDINGER—Born in Berkeley County (now Jefferson), near Shepherdstown. When 16 years of age ran away from home and joined a company of volunteers in the Revolutionary War. Captured at the Battle of Brandywine (September 11, 1777), and was held a prisoner until the next year, when he was exchanged and rejoined the army. Held the rank of Ensign and was appointed Navy Agent at Gasport, Va., by President Jefferson. When the old frigate "Constitution" was dismantled he purchased the masts and used them as pillars in the portico of his house which he built at Shepherdstown, which house was burned on the order of General Hunter during the Civil War in retaliation of the burning of the Governor Bradford home in Maryland by the Confederate forces.

CAPTAIN ABRAHAM SHEPHERD—Volunteered in the Berkeley Company raised by Captain Hugh Stephenson for the Revolutionary War. Elected Lieutenant in place of Lieutenant Thomas, who declined the commission. Marched with that company to Boston in July, 1775; served one year with that company. When his time of enlistment had expired, he returned to Berkeley County and organized a new company which became a part of the Virginia Rifle Regiment, Captain Hugh Stephenson in command. Was sent to the northern section in 1776, at Bergen Point, opposite New York, Colonel Rawlings in command, Colonel Hugh Stephenson having died. For three days, November 12th-14th, was employed in severe skirmishing with the enemy at King's Ridge. On November 16th engaged in severe action in which Colonel Rawlings and Major Williams were severely wounded and had to be removed from the field when the command fell to him. Finding himself overwhelmed by superior numbers, he slowly retired to Fort Washington, half a mile distant, where all were captured and made prisoners. Captain Shepherd remained a prisoner there for nearly a year. Was released and returned home. He became superanuary by the action of Virginia reducing her fifteen regiments to eleven. Captain Shepherd never entered the Colonial service again. He died September 7th, 1822, age sixty-nine years.

ANDREW H. H. BOYD, D.D.—Eminent divine. Born at Martinsburg (1814). Second son of General Elisha Boyd. Educated at Martinsburg Academy. At the age of fourteen entered the Junior Class of Jefferson College; graduated therefrom in 1830; joined the Presbyterian Church; attended Yale College two years; decided to enter the ministry and completed a regular course in theology at Princeton University. Visited Europe and attended lectures delivered by Dr. Chalmers and Sir William Hamilton in Edinburgh, Scotland. First charge in the Presbyterian Church was at Leesburg and Middleburg (1838), Harrisonburg, Va. (1840), Winchester (1842). During the Civil War resided within the Confederate lines; was captured as a hostage and held as such in retaliation for the arrest of prominent citizens adhering to the Union. Health was endangered by this confinement, which he never regained, and he died after a long illness at Winchester, Va., December 16, 1865. Was a sincere Christian gentleman. Was well versed in literature and science and highly esteemed by all who knew him.

JOHN S. HARRISON, M.D.—Born on West River, Anne Arundel County, Md. Educated at St. John's College, Annapolis, Md. Spent four years in study in the medical and surgical institutions of France and England. In

1805 he married Holland Williams Stull, niece of the General Otho Holland Williams of Revolutionary War fame, after whom she was named. Came to Martinsburg (1806) and soon built up a large and lucrative practice in Martinsburg and the country surrounding. Appointed a Justice of the Peace of the County Court of Berkeley County (1818) and continued in this office for ten years. Died in 1838, leaving a large family of children, some of which descendants are still living in the county.

JOHN MORE—Born in Berkeley County in 1788. Was a representative in Congress from Louisiana, 1841 to 1843, and from 1851 to 1853.

ALONZO SORTWELL—Principal of the Martinsburg Academy for many years. Born in the New England section; was a profound scholar and a thorough educator, and the youth of the county who received their instruction under him were well prepared to enter higher schools of learning.

JOHN FRYATT SNODGRASS—Lawyer. Born in Berkeley County, Virginia, March 2, 1804. Removed to Parkersburg, Virginia, and practiced law there. Member of the Virginia Convention which met at Richmond in 1850 to revise the Constitution of that State. Represented this district in Congress, 1853, and until his death while trying a case in the Parkersburg Court.

COLONEL WILLIAM CRAWFORD—Ensign in the French and Indian War. Born in Berkeley County. Was half-brother to Colonel Hugh Stephenson. At the outbreak of the Revolution raised a regiment of Berkeley County men by his own exertions and was commissioned a Colonel in the Continental Army. Was sent to destroy the Wyandott and Moravian Indian towns on the Muskingum River in Ohio territory. While engaged in this expedition he was captured and put to death by most horrible tortures. Dr. McKnoght, who was a fellow prisoner, who later escaped, and was an eye witness to these tortures, relates: "He was stripped naked, severely beaten with clubs and sticks and made to sit down near a post which had been planted for the purpose and around which a fire of poles was burning briskly. His hands were then pinioned behind him and a rope attached to the band around his wrist and fastened to the foot of a post about fifteen feet high allowing him liberty only to sit down or walk once or twice around it and return the same way. His ears were then cut off and while the men would apply the burning ends of the poles to his flesh, the squaws threw coals and hot embers upon him. For three hours he endured these excruciating agonies with the utmost fortitude. When faint and exhausted he commended his soul to God and laid down on his face. He was then scalped and burning coals being laid upon head and back by one of the squaws he again attempted to walk but strength failed him and he sank into the welcome arms of death. His body was thrown into the fire and consumed into ashes.

MAJOR SAMUEL BRADY—Among the celebrated scouts and Indian fighters who formed a strong defense against the savage hordes who spread death and devastation along the frontier of our section none rendered greater service than Major Samuel Brady. He was born in Berkeley County (now

Jefferson County) near Harper's Ferry about 1735. Grew to manhood among the confines of the forest; became a hunter and trapper. After witnessing the destruction of his youthful home and the murder of his younger brother and a sister, he resolved to devote his life to the extermination of the redskin. This destruction occurred when he was away on a hunting expedition over the North Mountain. When he returned he found the home in ashes, the two above mentioned lying dead and scalped near the destroyed home and his father and mother carried away captives by the Indians. He thought that by hunting Indians that he might be able to learn of the fate of them but he never did. He joined Washington and William Darke in their expeditions but was mostly employed as a scout to lead expeditions, warn settlers of attacks, etc., rather than as a soldier in the ranks and in this capacity rendered valuable service both to these commanders and to the early settlers. He had many hairbreadth escapes but managed to retain his scalp and died at last in his old home of old age, surrounded by his family and secure in the peace he had helped to establish. Many of his descendants are now living in Berkeley and Hampshire Counties, West Virginia, and the name is a familiar one around the village of Arden in Berkeley County. He is classed with the famous frontiersmen and scouts such as William Crawford, Daniel Boone, John Stuart, Andrew Poe, Lewis Wetzel, Ebenezer Zane and Samuel McCollough.

PHILIP NADENBOUSCH—Born in Bedford County, Pennsylvania, October 20, 1777. Came to Berkeley County in 1799. Was commissioned a Magistrate for Berkeley County in 1807 and was twice appointed Sheriff of the county. Was a Presiding Justice of the Court for twenty years. Died in 1863.

JOEL WARD—Born in Berkeley County near Bunker Hill, May 4, 1881. Was for many years one of the most influential citizens and Magistrates of the county. Elected to the Virginia House of Delegates, 1819-20-28. Died at Bunker Hill, February 17, 1937.

REV. BERNARD C. WOLFF, D.D.—Born in Martinsburg, Va., 1795. Was the son of George Wolff, a Magistrate for a number of years for Berkeley County. Decided to become a minister at the age of 36 years. Entered the theological Seminary of the German Reformed Church of York, Pa. Pastor of that church at Easton, Pa., for nine years. In 1845 took charge of the Third Reformed Church of Baltimore. Became professor of Dogmatic and Pastoral Theology at Mercersburg Seminary (1854), and in 1864 removed to Lancaster, Pa., and devoted his attention to the interests of Franklin and Marshall College. Died October 31, 1870.

THOMAS WORTHINGTON—Born in Berkeley County, 1766; emigrated to Ohio and settled in Ross County, 1798; represented his State in the Constitutional Convention, also in Congress, 1803-1807 and in 1810-1814. Elected Governor of Ohio, 1814; was a member of the first Board of Canal Commissioners of that State and served till his death in 1827.

THOMAS VAN SWEARINGEN—Born in Berkeley County. Represented this Virginia district in Congress from 1819 to 1821.

CAPTAIN NAPOLEON B. HARRISON, U. S. N.—Born in Martinsburg, Virginia, February 19, 1823. Youngest son of Dr. John S. Harrison and Holland Williams (Stull) Harrison. Entered the naval service as Midshipman, February 28, 1838. Saw his first service in the West Indies, Brazil, Coast of Africa and with the Pacific Squadron. During the Mexican War was promoted to the rank of Passed Midshipman. Under Commodore Stockton, helped to rescue General Kearney's command from a desperate position. In that war volunteered to carry a message in a open boat to a distant command, but encountering a terrific storm, his boat was carried far out to sea and was unable to land for five days, but he finally brought his boat and crew safely to its destination. In 1850, was on duty at the Washington Observatory. In 1853, promoted to Lieutenant and was made Naval Storekeeper in the East Indies, Japan and the Coast of Africa. In 1862, was placed in command of the gunboat "Cayuga", attached to the Mississippi Squadron under command of Commodore Farragut. The Commodore, in forcing the passage of the Mississippi arranged his fleet in three divisions. Captain Baily, the Division Commander, made Lieutenant Harrison's "Cayuga" his flagship, and just before daybreak on April 23, 1862, Lieutenant Harrison led the advance of the Federal fleet, and, although his vessel was one of the lightest, he rushed into the thickest of the fray and fought bravely for half an hour. She received forty shot-holes in her hull and rigging and had only six men wounded, having maintained her position with all the larger vessels. She next covered the encampment of the Chalmette Regiment with her guns and forced its surrender with six thousand men. The next day she attacked the Chalmette Batteries and sustained the attack until the Hartford came up, when the batteries were surrendered. For his bravery during these engagements, he was promoted to the rank of Commander on the July 15, 1863. Was soon after ordered to the "Makaska" of the James River fleet and assisted General McClellan in his operations at Harrison's Landing. Late in the same year was attached to the North Atlantic Squadron as Commander of the "Minnesota", and assisted in the evacuation of Charleston, South Carolina. At the close of the war, Commander Harrison had charge of the Navy Yard at Portsmouth, New Hampshire, till 1868. On April 28th of this year he was commissioned Captain and ordered to duty at Annapolis Naval Academy as Commandant of Midshipmen. In 1869 was ordered to the command of the "Congress", flagship of the North Atlantic Squadron. While at Key West, his vessel encountered a terrific storm, in which Captain Harrison duly exposed himself and from which he died two days later. His remains were interred in Oak Hill Cemetery, Georgetown, D. C.

CHARLES ROBERTS—Probably the longest-lived person in the county. Born at Oxfordshire, England. He resided in Berkeley County for eighty years. Died February 17, 1796, aged 116 years. Another aged man, resident of Berkeley County, was Andrew McKown, great-great-great-grandfather of Sheriff J. C. McKown, who lived to be 114 years old.

MAJOR ANDREW WAGGONER, JR.—Son of Major Andrew Waggoner of Revolutionary War fame. Born at Bunker Hill, Berkeley County, Virginia, October 24, 1779. Elected a member of the House of Delegates, 1811. When the War 1812 began he volunteered as a private but was soon promoted to Captain, then as Major of Infantry. Was with his Regiment at the Battle of Craney Island, but was not called into action there, the Artillery under Major James Faulkner being efficient there in repelling the combined attack of the combined land and naval force of the British. After the war, he returned to his home in Berkeley, but later removed to Point Pleasant, Mason County, Va., in 1836, to take possession of some valuable land there which had been granted to his father for his Revolutionary War services. Elected from that county a member of the Virginia House of Delegates in 1836. He was killed on March 30, 1863, by the fire of a detachment of Federal soldiers stationed there as he was passing from the town to his farm.

WILLIAM ALBURTIS—Born in Martinsburg, 1806. Commissioned Second Lieutenant in the Regular Army of the United States, March 8, 1827. Was engaged against the Seminole Indians in the Seminole War, in Florida, at Fort Brooks on Orange Creek of that State, March 2, 1841. Made a Captain in 1842, and was killed in action on March 11, 1847, at the storming of Vera Cruz.

COLONEL DAVID HUNTER—Born in York, Pennsylvania, May 3, 1761. When a boy his parents removed to Martinsburg vicinity and purchased the "Red House" farm, so conspicuous in the annals of Berkeley County. Received his education in a log school house which stood at the corner of Queen and Burke Streets, walking the whole way from his father's house (about a mile to the north of Martinsburg, and, as he expressed it, "through unbroken forest"). Made Deputy Clerk of the County Court of Berkeley County, under his brother, Moses Hunter, 1835 to 1848. Went to England on some business for his family in 1787, and upon his return, married Elizabeth, eldest daughter of Philip Pendleton. After the death of his brother, Moses Hunter, he competed for the office against Major Henry Bedinger, who was elected by the vote of the Magistrates. Irregularities were charged by Colonel Hunter, and, after several years of litigation, his case was sustained and he was made Clerk in 1803, which office he held until 1813.

MAJOR-GENERAL THOMAS SIDNEY JESSUP—Born in Berkeley County in 1788. Entered the United States Army, 1808, as Second Lieutenant of the Seventh Infantry. Made a Brigade Major in 1812, acting as Adjutant-General to Brigadier-General Hull. Major of the 19th Infantry, 1813; transferred in 1814 to the 25th Infantry as Brevet Lieutenant-Colonel for distinguished services at the Battle of Chippewa, July 5, 1814; was brevetted Colonel for gallant conduct at the Battle of Niagara, July 25, 1814. Was retained as Lieutenant-Colonel of the Third Infantry in 1817. Appointed Adjutant-General with the rank of Colonel in 1818, and was made Quartermaster-General with the rank of Brigadier-General, and breveted Major-General in May, 1828, for ten years' meritorious service. Assigned to the command of the army against the Creek Indians in Alabama in 1836 and succeeded General Call in Florida in 1836. Was wounded in action against the Seminole Indians near Jupiter Inlet, January, 1838. Was succeeded by General Zachary Taylor in May, 1838. Was head of the Quartermaster's Department of the United States until his death, June 10, 1860. Was engaged in active service in the Army of the United States for more than fifty years.

JOHN R. COOKE—Lawyer. Born in Bermuda Islands; a son of Dr. Stephen Cooke and Catherine (Eston) Cooke. Settled in Martinsburg in 1810 and practiced his profession. Elected to represent Berkeley County in the Virginia House of Delegates in 1814. Removed to Winchester, thence to Baltimore, thence to Richmond. Elected a member of the Constitutional Convention of Virginia in 1830. Writer of some note. In 1825, published "The Constitution of 1776"; in 1827, "The Convention Question"; in 1828, 'An Earnest Appeal to the Friends of Reform". These were published in pamphlet form but attracted the whole attention of the State to him and largely contributed to the passage of the law organizing the Constitutional Convention of 1830. Died in Richmond in December, 1854, at the age of 67 years.

MAGNUS TATE—Born in Berkeley County in 1760. Was a farmer by profession and was a man of superior intelligence, as was shown by the many positions of trust which he held during his lifetime. Elected to the Virginia House of Delegates in 1797 and again in 1798. Received his commission as Magistrate of Berkeley County, 1799. Commissioned Sheriff of the county in 1819 and again in 1820. Elected to the Virginia House of Delegates in 1803-1809-1819. Was a lover of dogs and horses and the fox chase. In January, 1815, asked the voters of Berkeley, Jefferson, Hardy and Hampshire Counties (then composing the Congressional district for this section) the nomination for Congress, and was elected by an overwhelming majority. Below is given his appeal to his constituents, and for its straightforwardness and ability to express himself, might be taken as a model by candidates at this day and time:

"*To the Freeholders of the District composed of the Counties of Berkeley, Hampshire, Hardy and Jefferson:*—

"FELLOW CITIZENS:—I offer myself to your consideration as a candidate to represent you in the next Congress of the United States. It is possible the curious may be disposed to inquire why I have become a candidate without the sanction of a committee. To this interrogatory I answer that the recent manner of nominating candidates by committee, however highly I might incline to appreciate the practice, is, nevertheless, as it seems to me, no way preferable to the ancient custom which everyone understands. Again, I have been induced to declare myself at this time and in this way by the requests of my friends, who think with me it is the wish of a majority of the freeholders of the district. If, however, we should be mistaken in this particular, whatever the result may be, I will cheerfully submit to when fairly ascertained on the day of election. All I desire is to give the people an opportunity of making a selection, and all I ask is an unbiased expression of public opinion. This manner of proceeding appears perfectly congenial with the first principles of our government, with all our political institutions, and consequently can be be liable to no rational objection. Here, perhaps, it may not be improper to premise that I trust my deportment on this occasion will be found fair and manly, and that if I should meet with an opponent he shall receive from me all the politeness and decorum due from one gentleman to another. To those gentlemen in the upper parts of this district with whom I have not the pleasure of a personal acquaintance, I am persuaded I shall be exonerated from the charge of egotism and of complimenting myself when they are informed I am a farmer in the middle walks of life, and that if honored with their suffrages my circumstances are such that I will neither be driven from the path leading to the posterity of our country by want or poverty, nor allured from it by avarice or ambition.

"Citizens of the district, if an ardent attachment to my native soil, if many friends and relatives whom I esteem and venerate; if a numerous progeny entertwined with every moral perception of my heart; if either or all of these considerations firmly combined can rivet a man to his country and to liberty—these motives, these inducements, which, in my estimation, are the most powerful that can operate on the human mind, shall be left by me, as pledges."

Sat in Congress with such men as Henry Clay, John C. Calhoun, Daniel Webster, John Randolph, William Gaston, Philip P. Barbour, and Henry St. George Tucker, all distinguished men in their day and generation, and met them on the same intellectual footing, also served on the most important committees with them. He lived on the Walker farm, as it is now known, on the Dry Run road, about three miles northwest from Martinsburg. Left a large family. Died March 30, 1823.

JOHN BOYD—Born in England. One of the earliest settlers of the county. Acquired large holdings at the eastern base of the North Mountain near where the County Infirmary is now located. Was an Indian fighter as all early settlers were required to be on account of the frequent incursions of the savages, and always came off victorious in his many encounters with them. Was the father of General Elisha Boyd of the Second War with England. Was the ancestor of Colonel John E. Boyd, a noted soldier in the Civil War, of which Sheridan remarked, "He would hang him as high as Haaman", but did not quite get the opportunity, and of Robert H. Boyd, a distinguished attorney of the Berkeley Bar. He left a large family: Charles, Margaret, Fulton, John, William, Rachael, Bailey, Elijah, Mary, Munford and Elisha. With the exception of Elisha, the children were among the earliest emigrants to Kentucky. Hon. Lem Boyd, of Kentucky, for several years Speaker of the House of epresentatives, was a descendant of his.

JOHN S. GALLAHER—Born in Martinsburg, Berkeley County, Virginia, December 1, 1796. His early life was connected with the newspapers of Martinsburg and Charles Town. His educational schooling was limited but he learned much more in the school of experience and adversity. Was first employed by John Alburtis, editor of the *Berkeley and Jefferson Intelligencer,* afterwards the *Martinsburg Gazette.* He began this work in 1809, at the age of twelve. Later worked upon Nile's *Register* in Baltimore. In August, 1814, was in charge of the *Farmers' Repository,* printed in Charles Town. Joined the Volunteer Rifle Company of Captain George W. Humphreys, and served one month. Engaged during that month in action at the White House Bluff on the Potomac, in which Commodore Porter undertook to stop the British vessels then descending that river laden with flour and other stores captured at Alexandria. Mr. Gallaher next worked on the *National Intelligencer,* published by Gales and Seaton. In 1821 he and his younger brother began the publication of the Harper's Ferry *Free Press,* known as the *Virginia Free Press.* Also published a literary paper called *The Ladies' Garland.* In 1827 he purchased the *Farmers' Repository* at Charles Town and merged it with the *Free Press.* In 1830 elected a member of the Virginia House of Delegates. His colleague was the famous Daniel Morgan. The amended constitution of 1828 being adopted, the election of delegates was set aside and in October, 1830, John S. Gallaher and Edward Lucas were chosen. Re-elected for four consecutive terms without opposition. In the year 1835 he removed to Richmond and became chief manager of the *Richmond Compiler.* Appointed by Governor John W. Floyd of Virginia to serve on a committee to settle the boundary dispute between the State of Maryland and the State of Virginia, the other members of the commission being Charles James Faulkner of Berkeley County and John B. D. Smith of Frederick County. In January, 1837, Mr. Gallaher purchased the one-third interest in the *Richmond Hawk* and conducted that paper for three years in conjunction with John Hampden Pleasants and Alexander Moseley. In 1840 he sold out to his partners and published the *Yeoman,* a campaign paper in support of Harrison and Tyler. In 1841, Mr. Gallaher returned to Charles Town and began work on the *Free Press.* Was elected to the Virginia House of Delegates and served two terms (1842). Was elected State Senator for Virginia by a majority of 62 in a strong Democratic district. In the same election Polk carried the district by a majority of one vote. In 1848 was again a candidate but was defeated by a majority of 22. The reason of this was on account of a school bill which he carried through both Houses and had enacted into a law. This law put into effect the free school system of Virginia. When he retired from active service, twenty-seven free schools were placed upon a firm basis in his county (Jefferson) at that time and continued to exist despite the opposition. He was the father of the Free School System of the State of Virginia and later West Virginia. Mr. Gallaher on October 22, 1849, was appointed by President Tyler as Third Auditor of the Treasury to succeed Peter Hagner, who resigned on account of ill health, he having held the position for thirty-two years. Mr. Gallaher held this position through President Tyler's and President Filmore's administrations and was removed by President Pierce for Francis Burt of South Carolina, a friend of Jefferson Davis, then Secretary of War. He afterwards accepted a position in the office of the Quartermaster-General. Died at Washington, D. C., at his home there on February 4, 1877, and was buried in Edge Hill Cemetery at Charles Town.

FELIX GRUNBY—Born in Back Creek Valley, September 11, 1777. His father was born in England and migrated to America and settled on Back Creek. Did not remain there long, and when little Felix was three years of age the family removed to Kentucky. Here amid scenes of savage warfare and suffering he grew up. By dint of many self-denials on the part of his widowed mother, Felix received quite a liberal education at Bardstown Academy. Next took up the study of law and it is an assured fact that he did not waste his opportunities. Began public life at the age of twenty-two. Elected seven years a member of his State Legislature. In 1805, elected one of the Judges of the Supreme Court of Kentucky and was soon afterwards made Chief Justice. Moved to Nashville, Tennessee, in 1807. From 1811 to 1814, represented his district in the Congress of the United States, and during his incumbency the question of the War of 1812 came up. Many people opposed it at that time. That was the one war which the people of the United States fought half-heartedly, and, in a direct way, gained nothing. Mr. Grunby gave such ardent support to President Madison's war measures that he was known as the "War Hawk" of Democracy. Was United States Senator from 1829 to 1838. In 1838 was appointed by President Van Buren to a place in his Cabinet as Attorney-General of the United States. In 1840 he resigned this position and was again elected to the Senate. He died at Nashville, Tenn., December 19, 1840.

While he was in the United States Senate and while Charles James Faulkner was in the House of Representatives, he in company with the latter paid a visit to his birthplace on Back Creek but found nothing but the foundation and a dilapidated stone chimney remaining of his cabin home.

CAPTAIN JOHN KERNEY—Born in Berkeley County. Volunteered in the Virginia line as First Sergeant to a company, July, 1775, in Colonel Hugh Stephenson's Regiment of Infantry. Was taken prisoner at Fort Washington and held for a long period. Was afterwards released and continued in the American Army. Appointed a Lieutenant in a Virginia Regiment commanded by Colonel Joseph Crockett. Later succeeded to the captaincy of his company, and served until the regiment was disbanded. Was a distinguished and brave officer in the Continental service. After his war services, he returned to Berkeley County and held the position of Magistrate and member of the County Court of Berkeley County until 1805, when he emigrated to Kentucky. Died and was buried in that State.

WILLIAM CREIGHTON—Born in Berkeley County, Virginia, October 29, 1778. Graduated at Dickenson College. Studied law and was admitted to the bar at the age of twenty. In 1798 removed to Chillicothe, Ohio. Continued in the practice of the law. Was the first Secretary of State of the State of Ohio. Elected to the House of Representatives of that State, 1813 to 1817, and again from 1827 to 1833. Died at Chillicothe, Ohio, October 8, 1851.

JOHN MILLER—Born on Tuscarora Creek, Berkeley County. Was an officer in the United States Army, War of 1812. After the close of that war was appointed Register of the Land Office in Missouri; later elected Governor of that State. Was a representative in Congress from that State from 1837 to 1843. Died near Florissant, Missouri, March 13, 1846.

JAMES STEPHENSON—Born in Berkeley County, March 20, 1764. His first military experiences were with General St. Clair in his defeat on the St. Mary's River, near the boundary of Indiana and Ohio. At this battle thirty-eight officers and five hundred and ninety-three men were slaughtered by the Miami Indians and twenty-one officers and two hundred and forty-three men were badly wounded. Helped to overcome the "Whiskey Rebellion" in Western Pennsylvania, and was made Brigade Inspector. Represented Berkeley County in the Virginia House of Delegates, 1800, 1801 and 1802. Was a representative in Congress from this district 1803-1805-1809-1811 and again in 1822-1825. Died at Martinsburg in 1833.

NATHANIEL WILLIS—Born in Massachusetts, 1773. Came to Martinsburg when twenty-one years of age and founded the first newspaper in Berkeley County and in what is now West Virginia—*The Potomack Guardian*. The *Berkeley Intelligencer* was started about 1799, the *Potomack Guardian* two years earlier. Early in 1927, Hon. Clifford Myers, State Historian and Archivist, purchased one each of the copies of the first editions of these papers. They were found in a little curio shop in an Indiana town, and as soon as Mr. Myers found out about them, he purchased them by wire for the department at Charleston, just barely purchasing them in time for the large Library of New York City was arranging to purchase them when Mr. Myers obtained possession of them. Both copies were sent to W. G. Burnett at Key's Ferry and had been kept intact by his descendants all these years. Mr. Willis continued to edit the *Intelligencer* until 1803, when he sold it to John Alburtis and left Martinsburg and removed to Maine and established the *Eastern Argus*. He was an active journalist for many years. He was the father of the distinguished poet, Nathaniel Parker Willis. He died at Boston May 26, 1870, in the eighty-ninth year of his age.

MICHAEL ROONEY—Born in Ireland. Was a seaman in the British Navy and had the reputation of being an expert sailor and a skillful navigator. Was well educated for his day. Emigrated to Berkeley County about 1800 and purchased a large body of land on Cherry Run in Back Creek Valley. Was commissioned a Magistrate for Berkeley County and continued to hold that position for a number of years. When Morgan County was formed in 1820 from parts of Berkeley, Mr. Rooney lived on the western bank of this stream and this threw his new residence in the new county. He promptly removed to the eastern side of the stream that he might still be a resident of Berkeley County. He held his court at the old Robert Snodgrass tavern on Back Creek and dispensed justice and decided cases in law. This place became so much noted for his trials that it received the name of "Mike Rooney's Court" by the inhabitants for miles around. He was elected Sheriff of Berkeley County one term, which office he handled with the same dspatch that he had handled his Magistrate's Court. When he died he left a will emancipating his slaves and providing means for their transportation to the colony in Liberia, Africa, but the slaves, though grateful for their freedom, refused to be transported to their ancestral home. Descendants of Michael Rooney, of which Lewis Rooney is one, still live in Back Creek Valley.

GEORGE PORTERFIELD—Born in Berkeley County in 1790. When a small boy he witnessed the killing of his brother Charles by the Indians, who had the previous day attacked Neely's Fort on the Opequon River., massacred the inmates and carried off several prisoners, George Porterfield being among the number. He managed to escape, however. Was commissioned a Magistrate, which body then constituted the County Court. Sheriff of Berkeley County in 1808 and in 1810 was elected to the Virginia House of Delegates. In 1814 he was elected chairman of the meeting for the organization of the Berkeley County Bible Society.

I. L. BENDER—Born at Bendersville, Pennsylvania, in 1850, a town founded by two of his ancestors. Removed to Martinsburg in 1876 and bought a third interest in the lumber business of Mosser and Company. A few years later he and his brother, Lee M. Bender, formed a partnership trading under the firm name of I. L. Bender & Bro., thereby acquiring the entire business. This business prospered and in 1896, when I. L. Bender was elected Clerk of the County Court of Berkeley County, he sold his share to his brother, Lee M. Bender. Mr. I. L. Bender was elected a second term but by a small majority of four votes, and at that time occurred the celebrated Doll and Bender contest. Mr. Frank W. Doll, his Democratic opponent, contested the election and it was a case of litigation in the Courts for a number of months. The case was finally settled in favor of Mr. Bender, he, in the meantime, holding the office. In 1908, Mr. Bender died and his son, Harold H. Bender, was appointed to fill the unexpired term to January 1, 1909. Mr. I. L. Bender was among the pioneers of the apple industry of the county, he and his brother, Lee M. Bender, being among the first to plant large commercial apple orchards in the Shenandoah Valley in Berkeley County.

LEE M. BENDER—Born at Bendersville, Pennsylvania, in 1854. He removed to Berkeley County and with his brother, I. L. Bender, established the firm of I. L. Bender & Bro., dealers in lumber, coal and wood, and when his brother, I. L. Bender, was elected Clerk of the County Court of Berkeley County he acquired the share of his brother and conducted the business in his own name for a number of years. He was one of the builders of Greater Martinsburg, having built numbers of houses throughout the town, which he sold to home seekers at a nominal profit and on long terms. He was a constant worker in the Methodist Episcopal Church, having been a deacon of that church for many years and an organizer of the Berkeley County Sunday School League which has a large membership at the present day.

HAROLD H. BENDER—In writing the biography of Harold H. Bender nothing could be more appropriately said than to quote from "Who's Who in America". He is truly one of Berkeley County's noble sons.

"Bender. Harold H., philologist; born Martinsburg, W. Va., April 20, 1882; son of I. Lewis and Margaret Eleanore (Kline) Bender; A.B. Lafayette College, 1903; Ph.D. John Hopkins, 1907; University of Berlin, 1907-08; Phil. L.D. University of Kovno, Lithuania, 1922; Litt.D. Lafayette College, 1924; married Amelia Oshcom Hetzel of Martinsburg, September 3, 1910; one son, John Lewis, University Fellow in Sanskrit and Comparative Philology, Johns Hopkins, 1906-07; instructor in Modern Languages, 1908-12; assistant professor and preceptor in Modern Languages,

1912-18; professor of Indo-Germanic Philology, 1918—; chairman of the Department of Oriental Languages and Literatures, 1927—Princeton University. Member of American Philological Association, American Oriental Society (director 1923-26), Modern Language Association of America, Modern Humanities Research Association, Gesellschaft fur Deutsche Philologie (Berlin), American Association of University Professors (member of council 1923-26), Oriental Club of Philadelphia (president 1923-24), Baltic American Society (director and member of executive committee), American Association for the Advancement of Science, Linguistic, Society of America (foundation member), Altorientalalische Gesellschaft (Berlin), Phi Beta Kappa, Phi Delta Theta, Sons of the American Revolution. Clubs: Nassau (Princeton), Princeton (New York), Contributor to American and European Philological journals, various articles on grammar, syntax, accent and etymology. Author, The Suffixes Mant and Vant in Sanskrit and Aveston, 1910; German Short Stories, 1920. On the Lithuanian Word-Stock as Indo-European Material (in Studies in Honor of Maurice Bloomfield), 1920; A Lithuanian Etymological Index, 1921; The Tome of the Indo-Europeans, 1922; The Selection of Undergraduates, 1926. Address: 120 Fitz Randolph Road, Princeton, N. J.; (Summer) King's Highway Orient, Long Island, N. Y.

J. P. FITZGERALD—Employe of the Baltimore and Ohio Railroad as Freight Conductor for many years. Member of the Holy Name Society of the Catholic Church. His father, Michael Fitzgerald, was a Union soldier who served throughout the Civil War; belonged to the 11th Indiana Regiment; fought under General Lew Wallace. He came from Ireland direct to America in Indiana and took up government land and was a farmer when President Lincoln's first call for volunteers came. Like Israel Putnam, he left his plow in the furrow and hastened away to join his company. He was a scout after the Civil War and did scout duty in the Black Hills and in the far west. He personally knew General George A. Custer and warned him of the close proximity of the Indians and of their large number before the Little Big Horn massacre. Had General Custer listened to his warning that massacre might not have happened.

GENERAL LEW WALLACE—Soldier and an officer in the Union Army during the Civil War. He encamped with his entire command on the site of the Old Fair Grounds, southeast of Martinsburg for a period of two weeks, also spent about a week with his command just below the present site of the new Hedgesville High School at Hedgesville. This was during the latter years of the war—he working in conjunction with General Phil Sheridan in driving the Confederates out of the Shenandoah Valley. Many years after the war he wrote "Ben Hur", which became a popular novel.

J. C. WOLF—Veterinary Surgeon. Came of a long line of veterinary surgeons. His father, Jacob Wolf, and his grandfather, Michael Wolf, were veterinary surgeons and practiced in Berkeley County. The family originally came from York, Pennsylvania. J. C. Wolf served as jailer under Sheriff E. D. Gardner, also Deputy Sheriff under Sheriff E. H. Tabler. Was elected Constable of Martinsburg District. Was elected Justice of the Peace of Martinsburg District in 1915, and his popularity was asserted in 1919, when he was the only Democrat elected to any office in the county. He is serving his twenty-fourth year in office, having held elective and appointive offices for continuous service for that time.

G. S. BRUMBAUGH, C. S. A.—Confederate soldier, serving throughout the Civil War. Was born in (Dunmore) (Shenandoah) County, Va., in 1843. Enlisted in Company K, 7th Virginia Cavalry in Aster's Brigade. Was captured at where Pikeside now stands, this county, and confined at Fore McHenry and Point Lookout, Md. Was on the last boat that went up the James River prior to the surrender of General Robert E. Lee in 1865. He is one of the three Confederate soldiers survivors of the Civil War living in the county at the present, Mr. Brumbaugh, Dr. J. Whann McSherry and Colonel Charles J. Faulkner.

HENRY J. SEIBERT—Served as a member of the first County Court of Berkeley County. Was elected for the short term in 1880. Prior to this date the county was governed by a Board of Supervisors, one man from each district, seven members for the county. Henry J. Seibert was re-elected for the long term—six years—in 1890. The first County Court under this system was composed of Blackburn Hughes, Jacob Miller and Henry J. Seibert.

CHARLES L. STUCKEY—His grandfather, Jacob Stuckey, came from Bedford County, Pennsylvania, about the year 1800. Tradition relates that Jacob Stuckey and George Gushwa (now written Cushwa) came to Berkeley County together. Jacob Stuckey bought land on Tuscarora and George Cushwa bought land on Back Creek. Neither being satisfied with his location, one traded the other farms and George Gushwa removed to Tuscarora at where the Cushwa mill now stands and Jacob Stuckey removed to Back Creek near Jones Spring vicinity. Jacob Stuckey was a soldier in the War of 1812. Jacob Stuckey's son, Daniel, married Elizabeth (Grantham) Stuckey. From this union was born three children, Charles L. Stuckey, David H. Stuckey and Mrs. Anna McKune. Charles L. was first elected to West Virginia Legislature. Again he was elected Sheriff of Berkeley County in 1900. He was a candidate for County Commissioner in the fall of 1926 and received the nomination but was defeated at the polls.

Lewis Grantham, a grandfather by marriage on his mother's side, was elected a member of the Virginia Assembly. Daniel Stuckey, his father, was a Captain in the Confederate Army, Captain of Company B, Stonewall Brigade. He served in the Shenandoah Valley with Jackson. At the Battle of Cedarville he became rheumatic, resigned his commission and came home.

DAVID H. STUCKEY—Was elected Assessor of Berkeley County, 1880. He filled the office of Deputy Sheriff under his brother, Charles, who was High Sheriff; also was appointed to take the census of 1880.

WILBUR H. THOMAS—Lawyer. Born near Tomahawk Springs, Berkeley County, August 8, 1876. Son of the Rev. P. H. Thomas and Martha (Hedges) Thomas. Educated in the public schools—Dayton, Virginia, Shenandoah Valley Academy and the West Virginia University, graduating in the Law Department in 1903. Public school teacher for four years in the schools of the county. Admitted to the bar in 1903. In 1920, candidate for Judge of the 23rd Judicial District, comprising the Counties of Berkeley, Morgan and Jefferson, and as this district is overwhelmingly Democratic, Mr. Thomas was defeated by a few votes over one hundred. Was appointed United States Commissioner by the late Judge Alston G. Dayton, which office he held from 1905 to 1913. Resigned to take up the position of Referee in Bankruptcy for the Northern District of West Virginia (1913), which position he has held since that time. Has large orchard interests in the county. Was a director in the Peoples Trust Company of Martinsburg for ten years, which office he resigned to organize the Shenandoah Valley Bank and Trust Company in the summer of 1920, at which time it opened its doors for business with Wilbur H. Thomas as president and a member of the Board of Directors. Is a deacon in the Presbyterian Church in Martinsburg. In 1906, married Millicene R. Cootes of Dayton, Va. From this union one son was born, Douglas Graham, who is now a student in Washington and Lee University, at Lexington, Va.

NOAH KIRSON—Born in Kovno, Russia, in 1848. Came to America and direct to Martinsburg in 1885 and remained two years. During this period he raised enough money $25.00) to outfit a pack which was in the form of a large chocolate drop strapped to his back and weighed, when full, about one hundred pounds. These pack peddlers usually carried needles, combs, knives, shoestrings, handkerchiefs, etc., and sometimes dry goods, and would range the country, making periodical visits to every family in the neighborhood. Pack peddlers were known before Revolutionary War days as they are portrayed in characters in many old novels, as Washington Irving's "Rip Van Winkle", and was known to have been a favorite disguise for a spy during Revolutionary War days. The pack peddler became such a nuisance in this State that the West Virginia Legislature in 1886 passed a law requiring a peddler to procure a license of $100 per year to carry a pack. This law put a stop to this business for a pack peddler could hardly afford to pay such a license fee to conduct his business. Noah Kirson, after remaining two years in this country, went back to Russia and brought his wife to this country and went into the second-hand furniture store business on West Race Street near Queen. After conducting this business for a few years he sold and opened a clothing store on Queen Street in the Wilan building. He had several sons and daughters. Mary (Mrs. Theodore Birnbeck) conducts the Kirson Women's Store on North Queen Street. Wolf Kirson is in business in Martinsburg and conducts the Kirson Men's Store on North Queen Street. Dan and Max conduct clothing stores in Hagerstown, Md. Wolf Kirson is president of the Jewish Synagogue on East Liberty Street, which was the original United Brethren Church of Martinsburg.

JAMES H. C. DAILEY—Born in Berkeley County in 1865. By trade he was a boiler maker for the Baltimore and Ohio Railroad Company at their shops in Martinsburg. Married Anna Gertrude Baker. From this union were born James S. Dailey: elected a member of the West Virginia Legislature in

1922, and at present connected with the sales department of Trammell Hollis, automobile business.

Christopher H. Dailey. Elected a member of the Martinsburg City Council from the Fifth Ward in 1925.

J. H. Dailey, Druggist. Connected with Snodgrass Drug Store on Queen Street.

Raymond B. Dailey, Clerk in the Citizens National Bank, Martinsburg.

B. H. FELLERS—Member of the 8th New York Cavalry in connection with General George B. Meade and saw service in the Battle of Gettysburg under that General. He served with distinction throughout the Civil War. He entered the scout service of that army. He was present the night General Philip Sheridan stopped in Martinsburg at the Everett House, a famous hostelry in those days, and notified Sheridan that he was wanted at his army headquarters at Winchester as his army was in danger. It is a singular coincidence that two Berkeley County soldiers serving in different armies and each in the scout service should have been the means of bringing about the Battle of Cedar Creek, Robert C. Burkhart being the one to advise General Early to make the attack and B. H. Fellers being the one to inform General Sheridan of the danger of his army. Mr. Fellers was born at Vanclevesville and Mr. Burkhart was born at Darkesville.

JAMES WILLIAM DEAN—Born in Virginia. Came to Berkeley County in 1864 from Maryland where he engaged in farming. Helped to build the stone bridge over Burke Street for the B. & O. Railroad, after the Civil War, which had been destroyed by the Confederates. Later in life worked in the Baltimore and Ohio machine shops at Martinsburg as a boilermaker. In 1873 he married Emily Snideal. From this union was born:

JOHN W. DEAN—Educated in the ward schools of the city. When he was in the junior year of the Martinsburg High School his father died and he was compelled to quit school to help support the family. He was a clerk for twenty-nine years. During this time he was traveling salesman for J. H. Miller & Son., wholesale grocers, for about twelve years. Started in business for himself on the Blondell Corner, corner of Queen and Martin Streets, under the firm name of Dean-Whitmore-Drewry Company, clothiers. Eventually he acquired the entire business and purchased the building. He was Deputy Assessor under Otho Williams, Assessor for Berkeley County. February 28, 1901, he married Daisy May Schill, daughter of George W. Schill, who came from Maryland, and was a business man in Martinsburg for a number of years. Their son, John W. Dean, Jr., is a graduate of the M. H. S., class of 1924. Is at present a student of Carnegie School of Technology, of Pittsburg, Pa. Another son of James William Dean was:

WILLIAM DEAN—Sheriff of Berkeley County, 1920-1924. Another son is George R. Dean, in the automobile business in Brooklyn, N. Y., and still another is J. E. A. Dean, a shoe merchant of Pittsburg, Pa.

MICHAEL W. RIORDON—His experiences have been thrilling and variable. Was a member of the Martinsburg police force under Mayor W. E. Minghini. He carries the scars of four bullet wounds, one of these bullets never having been extracted. He received these on two different occasions, two when he was on the police force and two when he was detective for the Baltimore and Ohio Railroad Company. He was a B. & O. Railroad detective for twenty years. In 1878 he received word that some party or parties were robbing box cars at the west end of the B. & O. freight yard. He with another detective, Christopher Lance, were detailed to try to capture the thief or thieves if possible. Between one and two o'clock at night they saw two men enter a car. They rushed to the scene when a pitched battle with revolvers at close range ensued between the detectives and the robbers. Lance was wounded severely and died the next day. Mr. Riordon, though shot twice, succeeded in capturing one of the offenders but the other got away. Both were negroes. The one that was captured proved to be Marshall Smith, who afterwards reformed and entered the ministry, and is now the pastor of the largest negro congregation of Washington City. The other, who escaped, was afterward drowned in the James River, having fallen from a barge upon which he was working.

JAMES H. SHIPPER, M.D.—Born at the old Shipper homestead near Tomahawk Springs, in Back Creek Valley, in 1864. Was the son of James B. Shipper and Hester Virginia (Stuckey) Shipper. Educated in the country schools, Molton High School, Molton, Iowa, and the University of Baltimore. Has been a practicing physician for thirty years, twenty-two years in Gerardstown and eight in Martinsburg. Was County Infirmary Doctor for twenty-five years. Parish physician for Berkeley County and for Martinsburg City Schools for the past four years. Was appointed a member of the State Board of Health for four years by Governor Henry D. Hatfield.

E. E. CHURCH—Teacher. Principal of the Martinsburg High School since 1923. Born at Rutan, Green County, Pa., October 19, 1897. Was the son of James Church and Jennie (Riley) Church. He received his education as follows: Valley Schools; graduate of Center Township High School, class of 1914; Waynesburg College, Waynesburg, Pa., with an A.B. degree; West Virginia University, class of 1926, A.M. Was principal of Claysville School, 1919. Taught Social Studies in the Fairmont High School. Came to Martinsburg in 1923 as principal of the Martinsburg High School. He is president of the Secondary School Principals Association of West Virginia, 1926-27. Member of the Presbyterian Church of Martinsburg. Married Mary Noble. Mr. Church has taught in Shepherd College State Normal School summer school, also did Teachers' Institute Work throughout the State.

RICHARD HAMMERSLA—Son of J. A. Hammersla, a volunteer in the Union Army during the Civil War. Richard Hammersla was one of the founders of the Independent Roller Milling Company of North Mountain, founded in 1900. Mr. Hammersla has been superintendent of the plant since its erection and under his efficient charge it has grown to be one of the most successful flour mills in the county. Mr. Hammersla was superintendent of the Potomac Pulp Mill at Dam No. 5 on the Potomac River until the Johnstown flood which occurred in 1889. This flood did considerable damage to the plant, washing away thousands of dollars worth of material.

GILBERT MCKOWN—The originator of the McKown family in Berkeley County was Gilbert McKown, who was a native of Ireland. He married a beautiful Irish girl by the name of Jane Crawford. On account of religious persecution there he fled with his young bride to America, settling in Adams County, Pa. Hearing of a settlement of Baptists from New York at Middletown or Gerardstown, as it is now called (about the year 1743), he came to Berkeley County and purchased the McKown estate at the latter place from Lord Fairfax. This property has been in the McKown family ever since. In the year 1745 Gilbert McKown removed his family to his new home, having reared his cabin on the little stream which is the headwaters of Mill Creek. The family name was formerly spelled McCowen. Gilbert McKown, after he had become firmly established in his forest home, sent to Ireland for his aged father, Andrew McKown. The latter, who lived to be 114 years of age, and lies buried in a clump of trees at the old Busey homestead on the Gerrardstown-Inwood road, east of Gerrardstown. In direct descent was Samuel McKown, whose descendants were Hunter and Gilbert McKown, the latter the father of J. C. McKown and Gilbert C. McKown, editor of the *Martinsburg Evening Journal*. The family were earnest Christian characters of the Presbyterian faith. In those days churches were "few and far between", yet the family was accustomed to attend church services at the old log Presbyterian Church at Tuscarora, seven miles away. This church had just been established, and, to show the present generation something of the privations and poverty which those early settlers had to endure, it might here be noted that the entire family would walk the entire distance to and from church, allowing their horses a day of rest over Sunday to be ready for the arduous work of the week following, and that the family would carry their shoes and stockings and walk barefooted to within sight of the church and then put them on, then on returning home the same process would be continued. Money was scarce in those days and a family to get on in the world were compelled to practice the most rigid economy. The present generation has many, many things to be thankful for which those early pioneers did not have, yet I wonder if any of us give it a passing thought.

The McKowns have always been prominent in the upbuilding of the county, for we find in the list of trustees for the government of the town of Gerrardstown, the name of Gilbert M'Kewan (McKown). John McKown was one of the founders of the Presbyterian Church at Gerrardstown. Gilbert McKown was one of the pioneers in the apple industry of Berkeley County, and his son, Sheriff J. C. McKown, is continuing the business on a larger scale than his father. Hunter McKown is also one of the pioneer orchard men of the county, having held, at one time, a large acreage of apple orchards. He was educated for the ministry but was compelled to retire owing to ill health. Though well on in years, he still takes an active interest in the affairs of the county. John McKown was a member of the County Court of Berkeley County.

HOLMES TALBOTT—Soldier in the World War. Volunteered December 8, 1917, and was assigned to Quartermaster Corps, Motor Transport Company No. 444. Served with Corps at Columbus Barracks, Columbus, Ohio, at Camp Johnson, Jacksonville, Fla., and at Camp Wadsworth, Spartansburg, S. C. Member of the American Legion. At present in the grocery business at Arden. His father, Robert Talbott, is a farmer residing at Vanclevesville. His grandfather was a Confederate soldier and served with Lee at Gettysburg.

SAMUEL S. HARRISON—Farmer and orchardist living at Arden. His grandfather, Jacob Harrison, was a soldier in the War of 1812. At the conclusion of that war he settled at Marlowe, this county. His father, William J. Harrison, was Steward of the County Infirmary for eight years from 1857 to 1865. When Samuel Cox, the first Steward, had charge of the Infirmary, Mr. Harrison was employed by him. He afterward married his employer's daughter and succeeded him as Steward. Two sons were born to this union, Samuel S. Harrison and Robert L. Harrison. The former married Anna Pitzer and to this union were born Ernest T. Harrison, a minister of the gospel of the M. E. Church South, who was educated at Front Royal Academy at Ashland, Va., and Randolph-Macon College. He is stationed at Vienna, N. J. Elmer S. Harrison, another son, is a member of the Citizens Military Training Camp at Camp Knox, Ky., and a member of the Cadet Corps. This part of the Military Service of the United States Government was created by law of Congress and passed in 1921 and is for the training of youthful soldiers for military duty. The following were members of this camp from Berkeley County: 1924—George R. Burkhart, Paul F. Burkhart, Elmer S. Harrison, Rumsey Newbraugh, George S. Speilman, Jr., Harvey L. Weller, David Horner.

THE PITZER FAMILY—This family has always been prominent in the affairs of the county since its first coming to the county, about the beginning of the nineteenth century. At that time three brothers, Martin, Jacob and John, came from Ireland to the vicinity of Gettysburg, Pa. They did not tarry long there but came to Berkeley County in search of homes. Martin and Jacob purchased about 800 acres of land in the vicinity of Arden and the North Mountain, but the third brother returned to Gettysburg and purchased a farm there. On this farm the fiercest part of the Battle of Gettysburg was fought, known as "Wheat Field Fight". It was said that this field of wheat was ready to cut and that Mr. Pitzer was to begin harvesting on the morning of the first day's fight, but after the battle was over not a spear of wheat was left standing, so utterly had it been destroyed.

The descendants of Martin Pitzer were John W. Pitzer, who was the first Sheriff of Berkeley County after it became a part of West Virginia.

Elias M. Pitzer, the first Assessor of the county after it became a part of West Virginia, and a member of a commission appointed by Governor

Arthur I. Boreman, first Governor of West Virginia, to lay off the county into townships, and a member of the County Court.

Mrs. William T. Noll, wife of Lieutenant William T. Noll, a celebrated officer in the Confederate Army and Deputy Sheriff of Berkeley County and father of Allen B. Noll, prominent attorney and Prosecuting Attorney for Berkeley County for several terms; Mrs. Benjamin F. Busey, mother of Rev: B. P. S. Busey, a prominent minister of the United Brethren Church; Mrs. James Walker, mother of the prominent educator, E. M. Walker, who was County Superintendent of Schools of Berkeley County; and Mrs. Anthony Turner, mother of Thomas W. Turner, at one time Mayor of Martinsburg.

Three of the sons of John W. Pitzer were William A. Pitzer, principal of the Burke Street School, also secretary of the Board of Education of Martinsburg for many years; U. S. Grant Pitzer, lawyer and Prosecuting Attorney for Berkeley County for a number of terms, and Charles W. Pitzer, veteran baseball player and a member of the first baseball league of Martinsburg and mail carrier for Martinsburg for a number of years.

The sons and daughters of Jacob Pitzer were George V. Pitzer, father of George W. Pitzer, a member of the Gerardstown Board of Education for many years; Harrison Taylor Pitzer of Tabler, manufacturer of apple by-products at that place; Mrs. Frank Noll of Tuscarora, Mrs. S. S. Harrison of Arden, Mrs. Eliza Rench of Martinsburg, Mrs. Preston Lewis of Tablers, Mrs. Harry S. Catrow of Arden and Miss Ida Pitzer of Martinsburg.

Michael K. Pitzer of Arden, whose son, George D. Pitzer, was a member and president of the Arden Board of Education for a number years; Mrs. George R. Sperow of Dry Run, Mrs. Lida Snook of Frederick, Md., and Mrs. Smith M. Vanmetre of Martinsburg; Charles L. Pitzer (deceased), County Commissioner of Berkeley County, and Glen M. Pitzer, also County Commissioner and World War veteran. Other descendants of Michael K. Pitzer were Mrs. George D. Miller, wife of George D. Miller, at one time County Commissioner for Berkeley County; Mrs. Benjamin F. Brady, wife of Benjamin F. Brady, County Commissioner and a member of the West Virginia Legislature; Mrs. Washington Bender, Mrs. William Couchman and Mrs. Barnet Seibert.

CHRISTOPHER GAIN—Was the head of the Gain family of Berkeley County. He came from Ireland and settled in Back Creek Valley about 1800 at Jamesburg (Ganotown). Among his descendants are to be found many educators, as follows: Lucy B. Gain (Hiett) and John C. Gain, who taught in the schools of Berkeley County; Josiah W. Gain, graduate of the Martinsburg High School, Shepherd College State Normal School, and John Hopkins University. He was a teacher in the schools of the county. Charles G. Gain, a teacher in the county schools, principal of the Romney High School for several terms, a teacher in Shepherd College Summer School, and at present a member of the faculty of the Martinsburg High School. A daughter of Jacob Gain, Blanche, is a graduate of Shepherd College and a prominent teacher in the county schools.

KENSEY B. CREQUE, SR.—One of the four surviving soldiers of the Union Army now living in Berkeley County. His original home was in Bucks County, Pa. He went to Ohio and remained one year, then removed to Grand Rapids, Michigan. When the Civil War broke out he volunteered his services, just being 17 years of age. He joined Company K, Michigan Volunteers. In the fall of 1862 was transferred to the 1st New York Lincoln Cavalry as Sergeant. Was detailed on Detach Service (Scout Service) in the 18th New York Regiment in the Valley of Virginia under General Milroy and General Philip Sheridan. He liked the valley, as many other Northern soldiers had done who saw it, so after the war spirit had subsided he returned a second time to the Valley of Virginia, settled at Martinsburg and has made his home here ever since. He served on the police force of Martinsburg as Chief Sergeant under Mayor William Logan and held the position of Deputy Sheriff and Jailer under Sheriff George Chrisman. Has been a director of the Old National Bank for a number of years.

JOSEPHUS BISHOP—Was the father of Charles and Thomas Bishop, who settled on Back Creek at the old Bishop homestead at Shanghai. Thomas J. Bishop was a soldier in the Confederate Army and was a farmer living in the upper regions of Back Creek Valley in Berkeley County. Charles Bishop was the owner of the old Bishop house which stands one mile north of Shanghai and is said to be the oldest house still standing in that valley.

JAMES CAMPBELL—The first James Campbell originally came from Scotland and left there on account of the religious Presbyterian persecution. He and his family fled to Ireland and came to America in the seventeenth century and settled in Pennsylvania. There is a direct line of descent by the name of James Campbell to the sixth generation. James Campbell VI. is two years old. Three brothers came to Pennsylvania, one remained there, one went to Lexington, Va., and the other, James, came here. The James Campbell I. was a member of the County Court of Berkeley County and a member of the Virginia Legislature for two terms. James Campbell II. was commissioned an officer in the Revolution and James Campbell III. served in the War of 1812. James Campbell IV. was a soldier in the Confederate Army in the Civil War, having volunteered early in the war but was discharged on account of ill health. James Campbell was a candidate on the Democratic ticket for County Commissioner of Berkeley County in the fall of 1918. He resides on the old Campbell homestead near Gerardstown and is extensively engaged in the culture of apples. His brother, Ned B. Campbell, is a Presbyterian minister stationed at Pumplin City, Va. For many years he was stationed in Monroe County, W. Va.

W. E. LANGFORD, D.V.S.—Born at Granton, Province of Ontario, Canada, in 1860. Graduate of Ontario Veterinary College. Removed to Newark, N. Y., 1889. Came to Martinsburg in 1905. Practiced his profession here until 1917, when he removed to Keyser, W. Va. Enterprises: Chief of the Martinsburg Fire Department; took great interest in the agricultural fairs of the county; was interested in harness horses.

SAMUEL M. LANGFORD, D.V.S.—Son of Dr. W. E. Langford. Born in 1889 at Newark, N. Y. Educated at Ontario College, Ontario, Canada, from which he graduated, class of 1912. Came to Martinsburg in 1905, and practiced his profession with his father until the United States entered the World War, 1917. Volunteered for service. Commissioned First Lieutenant, Veterinary Corps, 14th Field Artillery, stationed at Fort Sill, Oklahoma, June 12, 1917. Received his honorable discharge from the army in April, 1919. Was appointed by Hon. Howard E. Williams, Commissioner of Agriculture of West Virginia, as Consulting State Veterinarian. Held same position under Hon. John W. Smith, Commissioner of Agriculture of West Virginia, until he was appointed Recorder of the City of Martinsburg by Mayor George W. Appleby, Jr., June 1, 1926.

JOHN WOLFORD—Chief of Police of the City of Martinsburg under Mayor George W. Appleby, Jr. Son of Thomas Wolford, a soldier in the Union Army of the Civil War, who was a member of the First Maryland Regiment. John Wolford was appointed Chief of Police June 1, 1926. The Wolford family came to Berkeley County from Adams County, Pennsylvania. Thomas Wolford was Steward of the County Infirmary for four years. He had four sons: Harry, farmer of the county; John, the subject of this sketch; Emory, in the mercantile business at Jones Spring, and R. G. Wolford, a soldier in the World War; severely wounded in the Argonne, France. Chief John Wolford was elected a member of the City Council of Martinsburg for three terms.

GEORGE L. WEVER—Soldier in the Spanish-American War. Commissioned First Lieutenant, Company F, West Virginia National Guards, a company of soldiers from Berkeley County comprising sixty-five men; also served this company as Captain on the Mexican border in the trouble with "Villa", the Mexican bandit, under General Pershing. Served in the World War. Was elected a member of the Board of Education of Martinsburg District, which placed on foot the movement for the new Martinsburg High School. This board consisted of President W. R. Caskey, George L. Wever, W. S. Bert, Charles E. Siler and Mrs. Carrie Hess Hinkle with Lee Siler as secretry. Was connected with the Merchants and Farmers Bank of Martinsburg as clerk for a number of years prior to entering upon his World War record.

DANIEL BURKHART—Came to Martinsburg about the year 1810. Married Miss Ruth Flagg. Sheriff of Berkeley County. Organized the Berkeley Savings Bank, the first bank operated in the county. This institution flourished until the breaking out of the Civil War, when, for fear of robbery or burglary, Daniel Burkhart, the president, took all the money, $60,000, to his farm house on Tuscarora (farm now owned by his grandson, John D. Burkhart, Jr.) and buried it secretly at night. One batch, $20,000, in gold and silver currency, was buried in the garden; another batch, $20,000 in U. S. money (green backs), was placed in a satchel and secreted in the hollow of an old tree on this farm; a third batch, $20,000, was placed in an iron box and was buried in the cow stable in a pit three feet deep at the same homestead. This lay secreted until after Civil War closed, when it was brought to Martinsburg and applied towards starting another bank called "The Bank of Berkeley". Daniel Burkhart was president; his son, Dr. William Burkhart, was cashier, and the venerable banker, George S. Hill, began his career as a clerk in this institution.

In the law office of W. W. Downey stands the "safety" vault of the first bank of Martinsburg, a very meager protection against burglary compared to the modern safety vault of the banks of the present day. Daniel Burkhart was the great-grandfather of Harwood Burkhart, Deputy Sheriff under Sheriff J. C. McKown. John D. Burkhart II. and John D. Burkhart III. live on this farm on Tuscarora.

NELSON CLIFFORD CALDWELL—N. C. Caldwell, familiary known as "Cliff" Caldwell, has been prominent in the affairs of the county, having been connected with the Sheriff's office in the capacity of jailer of the county. He was born in Berkeley County. From 1897 to 1899 he was Baltimore and Railroad detective, resigning this responsible position to accept the position of jailer and Deputy Sheriff of Berkeley County under Sheriff Charles L. Stuckey, 1901 to 1905. In 1924, Sheriff J. C. McKown appointed him to the same position, which office he is filling at the present time.

CAPTAIN E. L. HOFFMAN, C. S. A.—E. L. Hoffman enlisted in the Confederate Army at the outbreak of the Civil War as a member of Captain John Q. A. Nadenbousch's "Berkeley Border Guards" with the position of Third Sergeant. Was on duty at John Brown's raid; was wounded at the Battle of Kernstown, March 23, 1862. He fought in all the important batltes in which the Stonewall Brigade participated in in that war. After the Battle of Kernstown he was promoted to the rank of Captain.

H. GLENVILLE TONKIN, M.D.—Born at Concord, N. H., 1881. Married; no children. Graduate of the University of Maryland, 1908. Came to Martinsburg to practice medicine. While a student of medicine played professional baseball and distinguished himself as a pitcher of the Martinsburg Baseball Club, season of 1907. Was elected Mayor of the City of Martinsburg, 1918-1920. Enlisted as Captain in the World War while Mayor, 1918. Was later elected Mayor, 1922-1924. During his term as Mayor many modern improvements were inaugurated, including the sewage of streets, sewage disposal plant and starting of the new paved streets, the new B. & O. subway and the new water commission. Has enjoyed a large practice in his profession. His parents were from England and came to this country in the early '70s. Dr. Tonkin has repeatedly been spoken of as Congressional timber.

ALBERT J. CLENDENING—Ancestors came from Scotland and settled in Loudon County, Va. Moved west of the Blue Ridge Mountains about 1800. His grandfather, Andrew Clendening, was a soldier in the Mexican War. His father, William Clendening, served in the Union Army in the Civil War under General Sheridan in the Valley of Virginia. He had an uncle, Abram Clendening, who served in the Union Army and was killed in the storming of Chattanooga, Tennessee. His father, William Clendening, was a school commissioner of Mill Creek District for a number of years.

GLENN M. PITZER—Appointed a member of the County Court of Berkeley County April 13, 1927, to fill the unexpired term of the late Charles L. Pitzer. Engaged in the culture of apple orchards in the county. World War record: Entered the army April 2, 1918, at Camp Lee, Virginia, as private in 36th Company, 9th Training Battalion, 155th Depot Brigade. Was made a Corporal April 17, 1918, of this company, and Sergeant May 5, 1918. Mustered out of service of Officers Training School, Camp Lee, Va., November 22, 1918.

LEE SILER—Parents were George and Isabelle Siler. Was educated in the Martinsburg High School, class of 1887, and the Independent Normal School of Virginia. Was a teacher in the schools of the county, having taught at the Dry Run School for six years continuously until coming to Martinsburg, where he has been engaged in teaching as principal of the John Street School for thirty-four years. Has held the position as secretary of the Martinsburg Board of Education for a number of years.

JUDGE J. M. WOODS—Lawyer; now located at Charleston, W. Va., as a member of the law firm of Price, Smith & Spilman. Was educated in the Private Academy of the late John Diffenderfer of Martinsburg, W. Va.; in the Martinsburg High School; Pantop's Academy, Charlottesville, Va.; Washington and Jefferson College; Washington and Lee University. Graduated from the latter in law, class of 1892. Was Prosecuting Attorney for Berkeley County from April to November, 1902, serving out the unexpired term of U. S. G. Pitzer (deceased). Was elected Judge of the Thirteenth Judicial District of West Virginia for twelve years or two terms and was serving his second term when he resigned to practice his profession at Charleston, W. Va. During his office as Judge he was asked to try the case of the Armed March of the Union Miners, at Charles Town. Some two or three hundred of these marchers were indicted in the Circuit Courts of Logan and Kanawha Counties—some for treason, some for murder and for several other offenses. A change of venue was granted to Jefferson County. Four cases were tried there. The first trial was that of William Blizzard, one of the officials of the United Mine Workers, on an indictment for treason. His trial began on the 24th day of April, 1922, and terminated in a verdict of acquittal on the 27th day of May, 1922, the trial lasting exactly five weeks. The next man tried was Rev. J. E. Wilburn on a charge of murder. He was convicted of murder in the second degree and sent to the penitentiary. The next man tried was John Wilburn, son of Rev. J. E. Wilburn, and he was also convicted of murder in the second degree and sent to the penitentiary. In both of these cases applications were made to the Supreme Court of Appeals for writs of error but these writs were denied. The next trial was that of Walter Allen on an indictment for treason, and he was convicted and sentenced to the penitentiary, but admitted to bail pending his application to the Supreme Court of Appeals for a writ of error. Allen forfeited his bail and has never been heard from since. When the case against Frank Keeney, President of District No. 17 of the United Mine Workers, was called an application for a change of venue was made and granted, and the trial removed to Morgan County. But when called for trial there in 1923, the State was allowed to enter a *nolle prose qui* and that case was dropped. By consent of counsel for the State and for the miners, the cases were all then transferred to Greenbrier County. These were perhaps the most important cases Judge Woods had to try during his incumbency and it brought him into prominence throughout the State and the Nation. In all his long term as Judge of this District he was respected by all who knew him for his unbiased judgment and his dealing justice to every one.

ALMON W. SMITH—County Commissioner of Berkeley County, West Virginia. Born at Gloucester City, New Jersey, February 22, 1865. Came to West Virginia (Berkeley County) in 1879. He was educated in the public schools of New Jersey and West Virginia and at Randolph-Macon College, Ashland, Va. He is a member of the Methodist Episcopal Church, South, of which denomination he was ordained to the ministry. He held the position of minister for several years but was compelled to give it up on account of ill health. He then began teaching and for ten years was a teacher in the public schools of this State and Maryland. He spent some fourteen years in the U. S. Railway Mail Service, retiring from that occupation in 1913 to take up the growing of small fruits and vegetables. In 1920 he was chosen County Commissioner of Berkeley County, and served the full term of six years, being re-elected in 1927 for another six year term. He overcame the strenuous and determined opposition in this campaign as the people saw his worth as Commissioner. He is now serving the third year as President of the Court. When he became a member of the County Court the road machinery of the county was very inefficient, but he, together with Jacob Hesse, another member of the Court, instituted a system of building up that department of the county's operation. This was added to gradually until now Berkeley County has one of the best equipments for road work in the State of West Virginia. This was accomplished with a small increase of taxes each year and by extending it over a period of several years, the cost of this department was not felt by the taxpayer. Hon. Chas. L. Pitzer (deceased) was the third member which aided in this improvement. When Mr. Chas. F. Dick became a member of the Court, in 1922, he carried on and aided in the work begun by these two members of the Court mentioned above.

WILLIAM DEAN SMITH—Father of Almon W. Smith, County Commissioner of Berkeley County, was born at Stockport, England, in 1828, and died in Berkeley County in 1917. When but a young man he migrated to the United States, becoming a naturalized citizen in the early 50's. At the outbreak of the Civil War, he enlisted from Gloucester City, New Jersey, from Company D, in the Sixth New Jersey Volunteers in the Army of the Potomac, and served actively until the Battle of Gettysburg, where he lost a limb, incapacitating him for further duties as a soldier. He was a member of the G. A. R. In 1879 he removed to Berkeley County, W. Va., and resided there until his death. He was a citizen highly esteemed by all who knew him.

ANDREW M. GRAHAM—Born at Greencastle, Pa. Came to Berkeley County August 28, 1869. He was a soldier in the Union Army. Belonged to Company F, 8th Maryland Infantry. He was discharged as 2nd Lieutenant of Company F. Served for three years under Generals Meade, Grant, and G. K. Warren. He was never wounded. He was in every engagement from the time that General Grant took command of the Army of the Potomac until Lee's surrender. He then came to Berkeley County and engaged in teaching. He taught in the rural schools of the county for forty years. He was Secretary of the Board of Education of Gerardstown and a member of the same. He was elected Magistrate of Gerardstown District and served for four years, 1873-1877. Married Belle Breneizen from Lancaster County, Pa. From this union five girls and one boy were born. Several of them were teachers, Loula, Nan, Sally, Sebina. John K. Graham was a lumber inspector at Dallas, Texas, for Government ship timbers during the World War.

Mr. A. M. Graham is one of the four Union soldiers still living in Berkeley County. He is a good mathematician, and has often asserted, and proved it, that he could find the solid contents of a brushpile. This is found in the following manner: Put the brush in a cylindrical vessel, then fill the vessel to the top with water; pour the water into another vessel and measure the solid contents of the water. The difference between the solid contents of the water and the solid contents of the first vessel will be the solid contents of the brushpile. He was the third free school teacher in the county; Andrew J. Bowers was the first, and Dr. G. W. Daniels was the second. All three resided in Gerardstown, and all three taught in the stone building which still stands in the Presbyterian Cemetery at that place, which is said to be the oldest schoolhouse standing in the State of West Virginia.

CHRISTOPHER COLUMBUS TABLER—Was thirty-three years a teacher in the country schools of the county, twenty-seven of which were passed in teaching in one school—North Mountain—now known as Columbus School of Hedgesville District. He has devoted one-third of a century to the advancement of education in this county, being teacher, Secretary of the Board of Education and County Superintendent of Schools during that time. When C. C. Tabler was twenty-one years of age he took charge of the Fearno School, Morgan County; the next year he taught North Mountain School. He was educated in the common schools of Welltown and Little Georgetown, Berkeley County, and in Shepherd College State Normal School. He took a course in telegraphy at the Valentine College of Telegraphy, Oberlin, Ohio, in 1882, and a business course in the Elliott Business College in Wheeling, West Virginia, in the summer of 1902. In January, 1907, Mr. Tabler left the Columbus School to run a telegraph school in the City of Martinsburg, and in two years made 43 operators for the B. & O. Railroad. His telegraphic career occupied two years and his school was in the second story of the Katz building, corner of Queen and Martin Streets, then occupied by the Martinsburg Business College. The school was in a room 18x18 and started with two day students and an equipment of ten learners' instruments and one switchboard. By February 1, 1908, twenty pupils had enrolled and the room was enlarged and equipped with twenty-five learners' instruments and two switchboards, the railroad train wire and the block wire. This department was open day and night, five days each week, giving six hours practice days and three hours nights. In 1892, the old schoolhouse at North Mountain was sold and a more commodious building erected three-quarters of a mile south of it on a one-acre lot. Mr. Tabler was teaching there at the time, and named the new schoolhouse for himself, "Columbus." In the dedication of the new schoolhouse, a flag 5x8 was raised over it. This was the first schoolhouse in Berkeley County over which Old Glory flew. This flag was later replaced by a new one, which is in service yet. It contained but forty-five stars. His father's name was Adam Malachai Tabler and his mother was Elizabeth Green Claybourne Tabler, nee Butts. Both lived to a good old age.

HARRY P. HENSHAW—State Senator of West Virginia for the 15th Senatorial District. This district comprises the four counties of Jefferson, Berkeley, Morgan, and Hampshire. He was elected a member of the House of Delegates of West Virginia, 1917-18. As State Senator has been active in establishing the county basis of pro-rating the fund of the State Road Commission. His father was Edwin S. Henshaw and his mother was Mary (Campbell) Henshaw.

B. M. DEHAVEN—His ancestors, Samuel, Peter and William, came to America with General LaFayette in the Revolutionary War. They loaned the American Government at that time $400,000. General Washington's records show this. His direct ancestor was William DeHaven, who came to Frederick County, Virginia. His father's name was Jackson DeHaven. His uncle, Alex. DeHaven, was a soldier in the Confederate Army. Bennett M. DeHaven has been in the mercantile business and is now a contractor. He married Miss Daisy Bishop. From this union was born five children. Two of them are teachers in the public schools: Sula DeHaven and Virginia (DeHaven) Stuckey. Elizabeth is a student at Shepherd College. His two sons: Leslie is with the O. M. Ramsey Furniture Company and Levi is with the Ford Sales Company of Martinsburg.

FRANK A. MINOR—Merchant of Martinsburg. Began business on Queen Street in what is now the Ripple building in 1896. He now owns two grocery stores, one at 219 West King Street and one at 105 Queen Street. His father was R. T. Minor, a soldier in the Confederate Army. Came from Fredericksburg, Virginia, and storekeeper for a number of years on the corner of Queen and Burke Streets, now occupied by the Bank of Martinsburg. Mr. Frank A. Minor was born in Martinsburg. He was Superintendent of the Sunday School of the M. E. Church South for twenty years. He has been in continuous business for thirty years.

JAMES W. ARMBRESTER—Family first settled in Back Creek Valley near Shanghai. Was elected School Commissioner of Hedgesville District and together with A. Hunter Walker and James W. Dillon planned and executed the erection of the new high school building at Hedgesville. Was appointed Deputy Assessor for Hedgesville District by Assessor H. E. Johnston in 1924.

I. D. VAN METRE—Son of James M. Van Metre; farmer, dairyman, stockman. The farm on which he resides, "Old Stone House Farm," is very productive as is indicated by the fact that it produced a ton and a quarter of milk per day during the World War, along with other productions in proportion. Mr. Van Metre is a member of the Board of Directors, Maryland-Virginia Co-operative Milk Producers Association, with headquarters at Washington, D. C. He has two daughters, Katherine and Bessie, the former a graduate of the Martinsburg High School, class of 1928, the later a Junior in the same institution; and two sons, James and I. D., Jr., both members of the 4-H Calf Club of Berkeley County, and, as members of this club with John DeBaugh, these boys at the ages of 11, 12, and 12, respectively, won the largest number of points of any county of the State at the West Virginia State Fair at Wheeling, September, 1926, for training, showing, and judging Jersey cattle, and demonstrating modern milking equipment and sanitary condition of milk.

Mr. Van Metre lives in a historic neighborhood. His home he now occupies was the home of General Adam Stephens, a soldier of the Revolutionary War. It was called the "Old Stone House Farm" when General Stephen resided there. The house was built in 1727. This farm joins the "Old Spaws Springs" farm. At this spring was located an old Indian fort which was destroyed by the Indians during the French and Indian War. Just a mile east of the Van Metre home, where Thos. K. Campbell now resides, was the home of General Horatio Gates, another general in the Revolutionary War. General Gates named his residence "Traveler's Rest". South three miles from this residence is the town of Leetown, named in honor of General Chas. Lee, another general in the American Revolution, who also resided there. About three miles east of Leetown on the road leading from Charles Town to Middleway stands the old mansion named "Harewood", which was the home of Martha Dandridge Curtiss, the wife of General George Washington, a widow who had two children, a boy and a girl. She was a Dandridge, of Dandridge's Ford, "The Bower" on the east bank of the Opequon.

"Killdare", the ancestral home of Haunce Van Metre, is situated on the State highway, one mile north of the Stone House Farm. He was an Indian fighter. His son, Jacob Van Metre, and his grandson, James LaRue Van Metre, were born at this place. This place is now owned by Mrs. Mary C. Copenhaver.

CHARLES H. MILLER—Son of W. S. Miller, pioneer apple grower of the county, was elected Assessor and again Sheriff of the county. Planter of numerous orchards throughout the county. Organized a cannery company and began business on Winchester Avenue, Northwest Martinsburg, canning corn, beans, tomatoes, peaches, etc. This establishment prospered until destroyed by fire. This was the forerunner of the Rockwell-Lovet Cannery Company, which is now the Gatrell-Yearick Company, ice plant and cold storage, situated in Southwest Martinsburg. Charles H. Miller was instrumental in getting additional territory added to Martinsburg through the Martinsburg Mining, Manufacturing and Improvement Company, of which firm he was one of the chief promoters.

ROBERT H. BOYD—Attorney. Educated in the city schools and a graduate of the Martinsburg High School, class of 1898. Graduate of West Virginia University, class of 1902, degree of A.B.; class of 1903, LL.B. City Attorney under Mayor P. W. Leiter.

GEORGE W. BUXTON—Connected to the end of his life with the fire brick industry of Berkeley County, owning and operating the first brick plant at Martinsburg. Was a member of the West Virginia House of Delegates and connected with the various enterprises of Martinsburg, the main one being the developing of "Greater Martinsburg" by the addition of the Boom Land. Was a Civil War veteran. Fought in the Union Army and volunteered in a Pennsylvania Regiment at the beginning of that war. Saw service in and around Martinsburg, and was so well pleased with its locality that he removed here after the war and made it his permanent home.

COLONEL JOHN E. BOYD—Soldier in the Civil War, C. S. A., with the rank of Colonel in the scout service of General Early's command at Winchester. Captured by the Union forces, operating in the Shenandoah Valley, at Bunker Hill, 1864, and sentenced to be shot as a spy. It is not often that a person is allowed the opportunity of witnessing the digging of his own grave and the placing of the coffin therein, but such was his privilege. When he was confined at Winchester as a prisoner he watched a squad of soldiers digging a grave and placing a coffin in it through the bars of the back window grating of his prison cell. The custom was to dig the grave, fix the coffin, and stand the culprit to be shot so that the body would fall directly into the grave. Colonel Boyd asked the guard what grave they were digging. The guard replied, "Some d——d rebel spy," he supposed, neither of them knowing it was being made for Colonel Boyd. Valuable information of the Union forces was found upon his person when he was captured, purporting that he was a dangerous spy. He was captured about ten o'clock in the morning and taken to Winchester and confined there, and was sentenced to be shot two days later at sunrise. Through the intercession of Colonel Ward Hill Lamon, who was in command of the Union forces in the Shenandoah Valley, and a friend of Colonel Boyd's, with President Lincoln, his death sentence was commuted and changed to solitary confinement in prison. He lived to be an old man and died at Martinsburg, esteemed by all. He was a farmer after the war, later entered the mercantile business and later was connected with the Merchants and Farmers Bank of Martinsburg. He was so active and cunning in getting information of General Philip Sheridan's movements that that General threatened to "hang him as high as Haaman".

J. A. THROCKMORTON, D.D.S.—Practicing dentist at Sidney, Ohio; soldier in the Civil War, Union Army, and was a scout in the cavalry service under Generals Sheridan and Geo. W. Custer. After the Civil War was aide-de-camp on the staff of the commander of the G. A. R. On March 7, 1909, he made his famous long-distance ride of 126 miles, continuously in 12 hours and 36 minutes on horseback, and that record stands good today. He made the ride to show that he was as good a horseback rider as Colonel Roosevelt. Dr. Throckmorton was the son of Job Throckmorton, who operated Throckmorton Mill west of Darkesville for many years.

JOSHUA FLAGG—Sixth in descent from Thomas Flegg (as the name was originally spelled), ancestor of the Flagg family, who came from Norfolk County, England, under Richard Carver, who became Governor of Massachusetts Bay Colony, in 1637. Josiah Flagg inherited the grant of land situated at "Flagg" Mill, at Flagg's Crossing, east of Martinsburg, from his wife Margaret, who was the daughter of John Shively, who obtained this land from Thomas, Lord Fairfax of Greenway Court, in 1755. Josiah Flagg operated a mill located on Tuscarora Creek one mile east of Martinsburg for many years. It was built in 1800. At one time a large distillery and barrel plant was also operated here. Hon. Alexander Parks, of Martinsburg, operated this mill for several years under the name of the Enterprise Mills. He bought this property from the Flagg estate in 1885. On October 13, 1926, he sold this site with some fourteen acres of land adjacent, to the Baltimore and Ohio Railroad Company, which immediately began the demolition of this once important plant.

The brick in the old Flagg family home at this place, now owned by Josiah Flagg's great-grandchild, Mrs. Sally B. Harrison, were brought from England as ballast in ships, and was used in the building of this home. It is a coincidence that a better grade of brick is now being made within a few hundred feet of this home by the Eastern Clay Products Company.

PAUL H. MARTIN—Lawyer by profession. Clerk of the County Court of Berkeley County since January 1, 1921. Born at Kingwood, Preston County, West Virginia. Educated in the public schools of that city, a preparatory school and the West Virginia University, class of 1907, with the degree of L.L.B. Father was J. Ani Martin, of Preston County. His people were the pioneers of that county. Paul H. Martin, after his graduation from the University of West Virginia, located in Martinsburg ond continued the prectice of law until he was appointed Assistant Clerk of the County Court by Hon. E. A. Hobbs, the clerk at that time. Was City Attorney, 1914-1917, under Mayors Thomas W. Turner and Percey W. Leiter.

OTHO MOSEBY RAMSEY–OSCAR MAHONE RAMSEY—Twin brothers. Born April 11, 1871, Steel's Tavern, Augusta County, Va. Sons of D. C. Ramsey and Vervenia (Fauver) Ramsey. Their father was a soldier in the Civil War, C. S. A. The Ramsey brothers came to Martinsburg in 1903 and organized the firm of O. M. Ramsey & Company, House Furnishings. This business was located on West King Street in the Smith building. In

1905 they purchased the property where they are now located and have been in business there since that time. Otho M. Ramsey is a director of the Shenandoah Hotel Corporation and is interested in large orchard holdings in the county.

REV. ROY C. SCHMUCKER—Pastor of the Winchester Avenue Christian Church for the past 13 years. Previous to this time he had been stationed at Downs, Md., for three years, and seven years at Gore, Frederick County, Va. In this interval he had married 1000 and had baptised 1300 people. His father, Morgan Schmucker, died in his 81st year. He had been a Confederate soldier, and had been Assessor of Shenandoah County for two terms. The Schmucker family migrated from Germany to Pennsylvania 150 years ago. They afterwards removed to Shenandoah County, Va., and had been engaged in farming for one hundred years. Rev. Schmucker is a descendant of Rev. S. S. Schmucker, Professor of the Lutheran Theological Seminary at Gettysburg, Pa. He was an extensive writer of books on Theology.

JOHN E. HELSLEY—Born in Morgan County, W. Va., near Unger's Store, August 22, 1869. His parents were George W. Helsley and Catherine (Hoil) Helsley. His father was a Civil War veteran, C. S. A., under the command of Captain Chew at Charles Town at the time of the execution of John Brown. John E. Helsley was a teacher in the schools of Berkeley County, Gerrardstown District, for 18 years. In 1910, was a candidate for County Commissioner against Hon. Charles W. Stuckey, but was defeated by only six votes. He never contested the election. He removed to Berkeley Springs in 1914 and engaged in the mercantile business. Since that time he has been elected Mayor of Berkeley Springs for six consecutive terms, a member of the City Council three terms, and in 1926 was elected President of the Bath District Board of Education.

WILLIAM H. SCHILL—State Prohibition Officer for the Eastern District of West Virginia. Appointed 1924 by J. H. Gadd, Federal Prohibition Director for the United States Government. Held this position until March 31, 1927, when he was appointed to his present position by Ross G. Wells, State Prohibition Commissioner.

JOHN L. WEVER—Born in Martinsburg. Is a machinist by trade at the B. & O. Railroad Shops at that place. Has been a candidate for the Legislature from Berkeley County for several terms but has been unsuccessful. His daughter, Anna Lee (Wever) Hammersla, is a teacher in the public schools of the county. His father, Hon. Charles Albert Wever, was a member of the West Virginia Legislature, State Bank Examiner under Governor William A. MacCorkle, President of the Bank of Martinsburg, and an extensive farmer and banker.

ROY E. HARRISON—Banker. Son of Robert L. and Ella (Crimm) Harrison. Educated in the city schools. Clerk in Minor's grocery store for a number of years. Messenger for the Bank of Martinsburg, Assistant Cashier of that institution. When the Shenandoah Valley Bank and Trust Company was organized in 1920, he was elected Cashier and has since held that position. Trustee of the First Methodist Church, ex-Superintendent of the Sunday School. Clubs: Member of the Masonic Club; Treasurer Kiwanis Club; Treasurer Chamber of Commerce of Martinsburg.

W. H. HEISTON—Born at Luray, Page County, Va. Educated in the schools of that city. Came to Martinsburg in 1887. Occupation, Millwright. Has erected mills in Ohio, Indiana and Kentucky. When the draft of 1860 came it caught him and he was connected with the Signal Corps of the Confederate Army from Richmond to the Potomac River. Been engaged in erecting hydro-electric power and water wheels. In this capacity has erected over one thousand water wheels throughout the county. Established the business in Martinsburg known as the W. H. Heiston Construction Company. Mr. Heiston bought out the other members of the firm and organized the firm under the name of W. H. Heiston & Son, Mill Supplies. Built and owned a mill at Smithfield, Jefferson County, W. Va., 1876, 1877 and 1878. In all these years of dealing with men he has never had a lawsuit, always having the mill he was constructing running on the day set forth in the contract.

ANDREW JACKSON—Hero of New Orleans and twice President of the United States. Dandridge's History of Shepherdstown gives the following interesting account of the Strode family:

"Near Fort Evans (John Evans' Fort) lived Captain James Strode, a wealthy gentleman, who had a large estate in Berkeley County. Having been warned of the approach of the savages, the family ran to the fort for protection. The home and everything that they possessed was destroyed except an iron kettle which is still preserved by a descendant in Charles Town. Captain Strode had three beautiful daughters who were descended through their mother from the Duke of Hamilton. Eleanor Strode married Captain Abram Shepherd, Phoebe married Captain Joseph Swearingen and Rachael married Captain Henry Bedinger.

"The Strode place is memorable as the birthplace of Andrew Jackson, whose parents, poor Irish emigrants, lived on the plantation for a few years in the employ of Captain Strode before they moved to the Waxhaw Settlement in North Carolina. During this time, about 1765, Andrew Jackson was born. When the Jacksons moved, the Strode girls, having no brother, begged their father to let them keep little Andrew. Mr. Strode consented but the child's parents would not give him up. . . . . . They then followed the moving family and made an attempt to steal the child but were unsuccessful and went home in tears."

WASHINGTON IRVING'S ACCOUNT OF BERKELEY COUNTY—Washington Irving, the noted writer and historian, after a visit to Berkeley County as a guest at a wedding, gives his impressions of the county in his "Life of Washington":—

"It was in the month of March, 1748, just after he had completed his sixteenth year, that Washington set out on horseback on a surveying expedition in company with George William Fairfax. . . . . . . They entered the great Valley of Virginia where it was about twenty-five miles wide, a lovely and temperate region, diversified by gentle swells and slopes admirably adapted to cultivation. The Blue Ridge bounds it on the one side, the North Mountain, a ridge of the Alleghenies, on the other; while through it flows that bright and abounding river which, on account of its unsurpassing beauty, was named by the Indians, the Shenandoah, that is to say, the 'Daughter of the Stars'."

ROBERT L. CRISWELL—World War soldier. Volunteered in the 368th Aero Squad, Langley Field, Va. Saw service in France. Was Army Field Clerk, G. H. Q., Chamont, France. Expert horticulturist. Has gardens at Arden, Berkeley County. One of his ancestors, John Shober, born August 17, 1759, was made Clerk of the County Court or Gentlemen Justice Court of Berkeley County in June, 1827.

JAMES T. GANO—Merchant at Tablers (W. Va.). The family's name was formerly Gerneaux. Frances Gerneaux was a member of the sect of Huguenots or French Protestants who were so bitterly persecuted in that country. In 1685, Frances Gerenaux, after his family was destroyed, contrived to reach the Island of Guernsey and by friends there was secreted in a shipping hogshead for a fortnight awaiting the departure of a sailing vessel bound for America. In due course of time he reached Boston harbor. He proceeded to New Rochelle, N. Y., where there was a colony of Huguenots. When upon reaching that settlement he exclaimed, "I have been expelled from my birthplace and my property has been taken from me for one aggression—a love for the Bible and its teachings. Let my name change with the circumstances." He adopted the name of Gano, the English pronunciation of Gerneaux, which has been used by the family ever since.

One of the descendants of this man, James Gano, emigrated to Back Creek Valley and married Catharine Kitchen, sister to Congressman Bethuel M. Kitchen. From this union was born, sons: Joseph, Daniel and John. Joseph was the father of James T. Gano at Tablers (W. Va.), who has been located there for thirty-eight consecutive years in the employ of, first, the Cumberland Valley, and second, the Pennsylvania Railroad Companies. He has conducted a general store at that place during this time. He also served as agent and postmaster. He conducted a branch general store at Arden for a number of years. His son, Marion E. Gano, is in the employ of the Merchants and Farmers Bank of Martinsburg as Assistant Cashier.

Another son of Joseph Gano was Richard Gano, father of Roland and Richard Gano of Pikeside, farmers and market gardeners. They own the old Tillotson Fryatt homestead at that place. Richard Gano was a successful farmer in the county all his life.

Another son of Joseph Gano was Daniel Gano, who was the father of William Gano, the originator of the famous Gano apple. William Gano found this apple, a seedling, growing on his farm in the Ozark region, Missouri, and saw at once that he had discovered a new variety of superior qualities, hence he began its propagation and has added another to the long list of excellent varieties of apples. This apple grows to perfection in Berkeley County and has added fame to one of her illustrious sons. Daniel Gano was the grandfather of Algernon, John, Berkeley and Liston of the County.

THATCHER—Samuel Thatcher, the ancestor of the Thatcher family in Berkeley County, came to Tuscarora in 1700 and purchased two tracts of land, the one of which is still in the family under the name of The J. N. Thatcher Company Corporation. These tracts were purchased from Lord Fairfax, which deed is in the possession of the family. It is written on "sheep-skin parchment" and bears the signature "Fairfax".

The family were of Quaker descent and originated the old Quaker burying ground on the Tuscarora pike near the farm of Mr. George B. Walters. On one occasion, the wife of Stephen Thatcher, residing at the La Mar near the Thatcher homestead, was scalped and left for dead by the Indians. She recovered, however, and lived to be an old woman. She was compelled contiuously to wear a turban to disguise her disfigurement.

The Thatcher family of Berkeley County are descendants of Rev. Peter Thatcher, a theologian of New England in the early 1600's. His son was Jonathan Thatcher, whose son was Jonathan W. Thatcher,, whose son was Jonathan Newton Thatcher.

JONATHAN N. THATCHER—Left the farm in 1876 and removed to Martinsburg and engaged in the farm implement business on West Martin Street on the present site of the H. A. Hammann and Son plumbing establishment. Later he and his brother, James, built the Martinsburg Skating Rink on the site of what was the Central Opera House and is now occupied by the Shenandoah Hotel. Later Mr. Thatcher moved to where the late T. P. Licklider and the Berkeley Farmers Exchange is now located at the Pennsylvania Depot. He operated, in conjunction with his implement business, the grain elevator at that place.

When the Cumberland Valley Railroad was built from Martinsburg to Winchester, in 1888, he, in partnership with John Staub, operated the grain elevator at Inwood. Mr. Thatcher was desirous of establishing a post office at Inwood. The original name of this place was Gerrard, in compliment to Gerrardstown, four miles west, which had been an established post office for a long time. The post-office authorities at Washington informed him that they would establish a post office there if he could find another name for it rather than Gerrard, as that name was too conflicting with the name of Gerrardstown. Mr. I. B. Thatcher, of Inwood, Cal., a cousin of Mr. Tatcher's, on a visit to the latter's, home showed him a letter with his home address upon it, "Inwood, California". The incident suggested a name for the village to Mr. Thatcher, who immediately wrote to the post-office department and the post office was named Inwood. Mr. Thatcher was the first postmaster when the town was established.

CHARLES W. THATCHER—As traveling agent for the Walter A. Wood Mowing and Reaping Machine Company, he visited Christchurch, New Zealand; Honolulu, Hawaii; Hayti, Samoan Islands. He was engaged in this capacity for four years. Saw Queen Lilluokalani imprisoned in Honolulu when that ill-fated Queen was deposed as Queen of the Sandwich Islands.

Elected County Commissioner of Berkeley County, 1910-1916. President of the County Court, 1914-1916. Chairman of the Local Draft Board

"BIOGRAPHY" 261

for Berkeley County during the World War. This Board was composed as follows: Charles W. Thatcher, Dr. W. T. Henshaw, Dr. S. N. Myers and Paul H. Martin as Clerk. While a member of the County Court, built the Arden road with convict labor from the penitentiary.

HARLAN C. THATCHER—Put across five apple canivals for Berkeley County, and it was by this act that the wonderful impetus was given to the apple growing industry in the county. At present he resides at the old Tatcher homestead, engaged in the growing of apples. Is the junior member of the J. N. Thatcher Orchard Company.

HARRY FLOOD BYRD—Few of our people know that the present Executive of Virginia, H. F. Byrd, was born in Berkeley County. The circumstances pertaining to his birthplace were accidental, perhaps, but that does not disguise the fact that we can claim him as one of Berkeley County's illustrious sons. While his mother was on a visit to Dr. James McSherry's, at Martinsburg, Harry Flood Byrd was born, for he once said in a letter to a friend, "I was born at Martinsburg, W. Va., at Dr. McSherry's in the house next to Newton Baker's."

He was State Senator of Virginia, 1915-19-23. Was elected without opposition, either in the primary or in the election. Was elected Chief Executive of the State, 1924

While Senator was one of the two patrons of a bill to appoint a commission of several members to establish a state highway system and a member of the commission. Patron of a bill establishing a State Highway Commission, which led to the establishing of a system of State roads, none better in the Union. Was a member of the Senate Committee on Roads, the Finance Committee, the Steering Committee, the Committee on Privileges and Elections. Was a member of the Committee of Schools and Colleges. Advocated a tax on gasoline as a fair method of raising revenue for road construction.

On February 2, 1923, was sued by the Virginia Highway Contractors Association for $100,000 because he said their activities by combination and agreements might be very detrimental to the State. The Court dismissed the suit, stating that the criticism was legal, imposing all cost upon the association. The Highway Contractors Association then gave up their charter and dissolved their corporation.

Was Fuel Commissioner for the State of Virginia during the World War, being appointed by President Wilson and serving without compensation. Is now, perhaps, the largest individual orchardist east of the Mississippi. Owns 60,000 trees which produced 225,000 bushels of apples (1926), 500 car loads, one-twenty-fifth of the entire output of Virginia. President of the Winchester Cold Storage Company, the largest storage specializing for apples, in the world (capacity, 300,000 barrels). Director of the Farmers and Merchants National Bank of Winchester, the National Fruit Products Company, and manager of the *Harrisonburg Daily News-Record* and vestryman in the Episcopal Church.

Began to work for his living at the age of fifteen as manager of the *Winchester Star*. Started the *Martinsburg Evening Journal* and in three years the *Journal* was on a prosperous basis, when he sold it to Martinsburg interests.

JUDGE DECATUR H. RODGERS—Judge of the Judicial Circuit of West Virginia, comprising the Counties of Jefferson, Berkeley and Morgan. Born August 13, 1890, at Taxahaw, Lancaster County, South Carolina. Father was James S. Rodgers, M.D.; afterwards removed to Kentucky, taking young Rodgers along, 1895. Lived there until he came to Berkeley County, 1918.

Mother was Mary Hedges, daughter of Decatur Hedges, a Confederate soldier in the Civil War. Educated in the public schools of Bowling Green, Ky., and Berkeley County. A.B., Ogden College, Bowling Green, Ky., class of 1910. Graduate of the University of Virginia, class of 1913; degree of L.L.B. Admitted to the Bar in Martinsburg, 1913, practicing in all the courts. Assistant Prosecuting Attorney for Berkeley County from 1921 to 1924. Upon the resignation of Judge J. M. Woods was appointed by Governor Howard M. Gore of West Virginia until the next general election to fill the office in April, 1925. At the general election in November, 1926, was elected to fill the unexpired term of Judge J. M. Woods.

World War Record—Volunteered, although exempt from service, September 7, 1918, in the Infantry Officers Training Camp, Camp Lee, Va., 22nd Co. C. Q. T. S. Discharged November 23, 1918.

H. P. THORN—Came from Gettysburg, Pa., to Martinsburg, 1897, and engaged in the lumber business under the firm name of H. P. Thorn, Lumber. This business began in a very small way and Mr. Thorn built it up until, when he sold the business to the Thorn Lumber Company, it was the leading lumber business in the City of Martinsburg and in the Shenandoah Valley. Mr. Thorn has been one of the builders of "Greater Martinsburg". During the thirty years of his residence here he has erected and sold over 600 homes to home owners, erecting the home and letting the purchaser have it on a long time payment plant and at a small advance of the cost price. Altogether he has erected over 1600 houses and buildings in the county and Martinsburg. He is interested in a fine bearing, commercial orchard in Hedgesville District, consisting of 120 acres. He recently purchased the George M. Bowers farm on the Arden road and has erected an up-to-date dairy barn upon it, one of the largest and best equipped in the county. He spent two years of the thirty mentioned above in Florida in the lumber business.

CLYDE C. BORUM—Father was Richard Borum, born at Strausburg, Va., and moved to Berkeley County in 1872 and purchased the Borum farm at Arden and was a successful farmer there until his death. He was a soldier in the Civil War, C. S. A., volunteering early in the war and serving until its close. His son, C. C. Borum, succeeded his father in the farm and is one of the largest growers of apples in the county.

WOMEN.

MARY BOYD FAULKNER—General Elisha Boyd purchased the location of "Boydville" from General Adam Stephen, the founder of Martinsburg. The family moved into it August, 1812. At the death of General Boyd, this property, with a large farm adjoining it, was devised by him to his daughter, Mary, who married Charles James Faulkner, and it has been occupied by the Faulkner family since the death of General Boyd in 1844, and since the death of Mary Boyd Faulkner, in 1894, has been occupied by her son, Senator Charles J. Faulkner.

In July, 1864, during the Civil War, the home was occupied by Mrs. Faulkner. Her husband, Charles James Faulkner, was a prisoner of State of the United States Government, confined in prison in the North; her two sons, Charles and Boyd, were in the Confederate Army, and Mrs. Faulkner was the sole protector of the home. General Hunter, who then commanded the Federal forces in the Valley of Virginia, ordered Captain Martindale, of a New York Cavalry Company, to proceed to burn the home of his uncle, Andrew Hunter, of Charles Town; the home of A. R. Butler, of Shepherdstown, and "Boydville". After the burning of the two former places, refusing to allow anything except the personal clothing of the inmates to be removed, early in the morning, July, 1864, General Averill, who was then in command of the forces at Martinsburg, notified Mrs. Faulkner that Captain Martindale, with a squad of cavalrymen, was on his way to carry out the orders of General Hunter as to "Boydville" and that all articles that were absolutely essential to their comfort should be removed from the house. Nothing was done, however, by Mrs. Faulkner in accumulating their articles and about 9 o'clock, after two hours of the most painful suspense, Mrs. Pierce, who was on the front porch, noticed a body of cavalrymen riding up the lawn drive from the street. When this body reached the point of fifty yards frm the house it was halted and two of the men dismounted, one of them being Captain Martindale. When he reached the porch he asked whether that was Mrs. Faulkner and was informed that it was not, but her daughter, he replied: "I want to see Mrs. Faulkner." The Captain was then shown into the drawing room and when Mrs. Faulkner appeared, Captain Martindale remarked that "This is a fine old place." Mrs. Faulkner replied, "Do you wish to see me, Sir?" He replied, "I have called to inform you, Madam, that I have orders from General Hunter to burn 'Boydville' to the ground." Mrs. Faulkner replied, "Will you let me see your orders?" "No, Madam, my order is a sealed one." "Perhaps you will, however, let me see it." The Captain then took the order from his pocket and read: "You are ordered to burn the property of Charles J. Faulkner to the ground and everything in it. "Give me one hour's notice," Mrs. Faulkner replied. "This is not the property of Mr. Faulkner and neither you nor General Hunter will dare to put a torch to this house. It was given to me by my father, General Boyd, who was an officer in the War of 1812." At this moment, two of Mrs. Faulkner's nephews, Judge Edmond Pendleton, and Dr. E. Boyd Pendleton, walked into the room and had an interview with Captain Martindale. Both of these gentlemen were Union men. When the contents of the order of Captain Martindale became known in the town, great sympathy was expressed by the people of Martinsburg, and an indignation meeting was held to protest against the execution of the order. Through the influence of General Averill, the matter was suspended for a short time and with the assistance of Mrs. Faulkner's nephews, and others, a telegram was sent by the kindness of General Averill to Hagerstown, by courier, addressed to General Cullum, Chief of General Hallock's staff, and an old friend of the family, requesting him to lay the subject before President Lincoln, with the request that the order of General Hunter be countermanded.

Suspense of the family during the intervening between the sending of the message and the reply to it was exceedingly painful. About the hour when, under the orders of Captain Martindale, the torch was to be applied, all were anxiously watching the entrance to the lawn for the return or the courier with a reply which would save the home or lay it in ashes. When the soldiers had commenced their preparations to burn the building, the anxious eyes that were watching the entrance to the lawn saw a man riding rapidly towards the house holding in his hand an envelope. On reaching the pavement that led down to the driveway, he dismounted and came rapidly to the porch and presented Mrs. Faulkner with an envelope addressed to Captain Martindale, which she turned over to him and, when opened, contained the following message from the President:

"The property of Charles J. Faulkner is exempt from the order of General David S. Hunter for the burning of the residences of prominent citizens of the Shenandoah Valley in retaliation for the burning of the Governor Bradford's house in Maryland by the Confederate forces.
"(Signed) ABRAHAM LINCOLN."

Captain Martindale raised his cap in salutation and walking down to where he had left his men, gave orders which put them in their saddles and in a moment he and his men were clattering down the avenue to the street.

The carved mantels and doorways of her home, "Boydville," and the locks were brought from England. When the house was first built, the grass plot on each side of the brick pavement in front were surrounded by a high fence of old English brick—later these were taken down and replaced by hedges of box-wood which very unfortunately were killed by the zero weather of the severe winter of 1914. A high brick wall also enclosed the grounds in front of the entrance on the street. The garden walls, six feet in height, are standing to-day in perfect condition as originally built in 1812.

Many distinguished guests have been entertained at "Boydville", among them being Henry Clay, who held in his arms and blessed the present owner, former Senator Charles J. Faulkner, when a babe of five months; also Mr. Bancroft, the historian, and two Vice-Presidents of the United States, Adlai E. Stevenson of Illinois and Charles W. Fairbanks of Indiana. In 1898, the Anglo-American Commission, of which Senator Faulkner was a member, was entertained by him at "Boydville". Sir Wilfred Laurier, Sir Louis Davies and Sir Richard Cartwright were among those who represented Great Britain on the Commission. There were other distinguished Canadians and Americans—among the latter were Hon. John W. Foster, former Secretary of State; Hon. Nelson Dingley, Chairman of the Ways and Means Committee of the House of Representatives, and the eminent divine, T. DeWitt Talmage, who accompanied the guests and added very much to the occasion, and Charles W. Fairbanks, Senator from Indiana, and afterwards Vice-President.

Mary Boyd Faulkner died in 1894 and was buried beside her illustrious husband, Charles James Faulkner, in the private bury grounds adjoining Norborn Cemetery. Many people of Berkeley County had cause to mourn her loss for she was a friend to the lowly as well as the mighty. Truly, she was one of whom the poet spoke when he said:

"Let me live in a house by the side of the road,
And be a friend to man."

ADAH DODD POINCE—Daughter of David Dodd and a distinguished daughter of Berkeley County. Taught in the rural schools of the county several terms. In 1892, she married John William Poince of Ohio and began her married life in Dayton, which is her present home. She always had a desire for public life and to accomplish this desire she went to Boston and entered Emerson College of Oratory. She caught something of the magnificent ideals set forth by its President, Charles Waldo Emerson, and from that day to this has striven earnestly to advance education, to purify politics, and to establish higher standards of living, and to promulgate the teachings of the Christian religion. In order to accomplish this she has lectured in eleven States in the Union. She has toured Europe five times, visited Canada and Mexico, and seen much of Africa and the Near East. Has "stumped" Oregon and Ohio for Woman's Suffrage, and has been a campaign speaker in every State and National election for the last ten years. At present, she is the Hostess of the Ohio Senate. For three years—1920-1923—she was Assistant State Fire Marshal of Ohio and traveled constantly over the State speaking in schools, colleges, churches and before men and women clubs on Fire Prevention.

She has visited every European country. She has contributed many articles to Ohio and West Virginia magazines and her editorials have appeared in many newspapers. Her lectures are: "To Him Who Hath"; "The Under Dog in the Fight"; "Vision, Voice and Victory"; "The Who and Why of the European War". Travelogues: "From the City of Commerce to the City of Silence"; "From the Eternal City to the Moslem Center"; "In the Palaces of the Kings"; "Through El Portal to Wonderland"; "Where Geysers Leap and Chaos Reigns"; "Alaska, the Land of the Weird"; "Up the Danube and Down the Rhine".

MARIA COOPER—Was a lady of great intellectual and brilliant conversational powers. In the fall of 1854, when the cholera pestilence visited this section she fell victim to its ravishes. A few years before her death, she published a small work composed of original and selected matter. She left a will bequeathing a large portion of her estate to charitable institutions, among them a fund for founding an academy at Martinsburg and an institution was incorporated under the name of the Martinsburg Cooper Academy, but the Supreme Court of Appeals of West Virginia declared the bequest invalid, hence the institution was lost to the city. Her death was lamented by the entire community as no one was more universally loved than she.

MABEL HENSHAW GARDNER—Graduate from the New Windsor College of Maryland with degree of Mistress of Polite Literature. Student of the West

Virginia University; teacher of History, Shepherd College State Normal School, Shepherdstown; member of the American Historical Association. Married Dr. I. H. Gardner. Of this union one child was born, Anna Henshaw Gardner, student Massachusetts General Hospital, Boston, Mass. Her sister, Frances L. Henshaw, was a teacher in the schools of Berkeley County for a number of years.

HATTIE L. ZEPP—Born in Berkeley County. Is holding the position of Sergeant of Accounts of the City of Martinsburg. Was appointed by Dr. H. G. Tinkon (Mayor), July 1, 1922, and has served continuously under three Mayors—Dr. H. G. Tnkin, Albert A. Smallwood, and George W. Applebey, Jr.

MARY ETHEL (DOWNS) SITES—Graduate Martinsburg High School, class of 1913, and Randolph-Macon Woman's College at Lynchburg, Va., with degree of A.B. Prominent club woman, D. A. R., Woman's Club of Martinsburg, and a historian of much repute.

BERTHA M. MOCK—Miss Mock has been office Deputy Assessor for Berkeley County under three different Assessors—John W. Dodd, John H. Riner and Harry E. Johnson. She was born in Loudon County, Virginia. Her efficiency as a stenographer attracted the attention of the Draft Board of Berkeley County in the World War and was detailed to do stenographic work for that Board. The Board consisted of Charles W. Thatcher, President; Dr. William T. Henshaw and Paul Martin. During the "Flu" epidemic she was the only stenographer to remain at her post of duty around the Court House, she fortunately escaping the attacks of that dread disease.

POLLY (VANMETRE) EVANS—In the corner of a field to the right of the State Road leading from Martinsburg to Charles Town and on the east side of Opequon Creek and adjoining the old bridge across that stream is a scattered pile of stone which is all that remains of John Evans Fort, and Polly Vanmetre Evans was its heroic defender. This was a stockade fort, which was really two forts in one. The outer defense was a stockade, the inner a block house type, built of logs with a stone foundation. This fort was substantially though hastily constructed in the late spring of 1755, after the outbreak of the French and Indian War, by John Evans II., and was a refuge for the settlers of this region when attacked by the Indians. Polly Vanmetre was the daughter of Abraham VanMetre, and when quite young had married John Evans II., a young man of that region. They lived quietly and peacefully, tilling their farm on the Opequon River and had reared a family of boys and girls when the French and Indian War suddenly burst upon them with all of its relentless fury. Polly Evans had learned to use the rifle quite as well as her father, Abraham VanMetre, who was a hunter as well as a farmer, she accompanying him on several occasions on his hunting expeditions when she was a young girl. She owned her own rifle but had laid it aside for the more peaceful occupation of rearing her family. But when the Indian hostilities began she again took it up in the defense of her home and carried it for a number of years strapped to her shoulder. Tradition relates that when she was prepared for burial her attendants found a depression in the skin across her shoulder caused by the constant wearing of the strap of her rifle. In those days nurses were unheard of and doctors were so few and so far away that it was almost impossible to procure their services in case of sickness, so Polly Evans was the doctor and nurse of the region. She nursed the sick and attended most of the new-born babies of that community. She owned a large dog of the Great Dane breed, who always accompanied her on her expeditions. He could "smell Injun" for a great distance if one happened to be in the vicinity, and would indicate the fact by his incessant restlessness and loud barking.

The above fort was visited by General Edward Braddock on his march to Fort Duquesne and he remained here the better part of two days, as was indicated by his sceretary's account of that expedition (see account of Lieutenant Spendelow's "Seaman's Journal" of General Braddock's march through this section in another chapter).

On one occasion none but the women and children of the neighborhood were at the fort when it was suddenly attacked by the Indians. Polly Evans made the women load rifles and she did the shooting from one port hole after another and kept up such a raking fire on the Indians that they abandoned the attack, supposing, from the incessant firing from the fort, that it was heavily garrisoned.

On another occasion she was returning to the fort from visiting a sick neighbor, when a large savage warrior suddenly darted from behind a tree and grabbed both arms around her and started to carry her off, deciding, no doubt, to capture a valuable prisoner alive. The dog, from some reason had not accompanied her on this visit. She immediately began calling for him. He suddenly came bounding through the forests and attacked the warrior with such vicious onslaughts that he was obliged to let his captive go in order to defend himself against the dog. This gave Mrs. Evans the opportunity to unsling her rifle, when she shot the Indian dead.

Many a savage warrior boasted that her scalp, with its long tresses, would dangle from his lodge pole, but it never did. She was dreaded by the Indians, yet was respected by them. They gave her the name of "Wa-hon-da," which signified in the Shawnee language, "Squaw Chief". This fort was attacked several different times by the savages—on two occasions led by a white man, supqposedly a Frenchman, but were driven off each time. She, together with her husband, were buried within a short distance of the fort. For many years their graves were undisturbed, but were at last desecrated by the plow, and now no mark remains as the resting place of the builder of this fort or its faithful defender.

BESSIE D. KILMER—Has the distinction of being the first woman in Berkeley County to hold a political office. She was elected County Superintendent of Schools in 1922 and re-elected in 1926. She was a teacher in the county, country and city schools before she became County Superintendent. Educated in private schools in West Virginia and the New Summer School, Norfolk, Va. Taught in Southern Virginia for six years; was District Supervisor in Arden District for three years. She is a member of the National Educational Association; the State Educational Association, and President of the Eastern Panhandle Teachers' Association. Her sister, Rebecca Kilmer, was a teacher in Berkeley County; stenographer and clerical assistant to Hon. George M. Bowers of Berkeley County during his six years in Congress from this District. She now holds the position of Secretary in the Chamber of Commerce, Martinsburg. Miss Kilmer's brother, H. Raymond Kilmer, a civil engineer for the United States Government is with the Geological Survey, residing in Washington, D. C. Her father, H. D. Kilmer, was a farmer and merchant. Was a soldier in the Civil War, C. S. A., private in J. B. Stewart's Cavalry. Was captured in that war and retained prisoner in New York City.

BELLE BOYD—A noted Confederate spy. Was so enthused with the cause of the South that she donned male attire and scouted for the Confederate forces in the Shenandoah Valley and other places during the entire war between the States. Was never captured as she had the advantage of disguise. Rendered valuable aid to the Southern armies. Some say that she was a myth and never existed at all. She was a relative of Colonel John E. Boyd and Attorney Robert H. Boyd.

BETTY DANDRIDGE—Cousin of Colonel John E. Boyd and a daughter of President Zachary Taylor. Lived at Dandridge's Ford, "The Bower," near the Berkeley and Jefferson Counties' line.

MARIE (BUXTON) MARTIN—The wife of the Clerk of the County Court, Paul H. Martin, and daughter of the late Geo. W. Buxton, of Martinsburg. She is an authoress of note, having written and published in 1926 a literary work entitled, "Within The Rock". She has also contributed magazine articles for the *West Virginia Review*. She is a graduate of the Martinsburg High School and West Virginia University.

NOTA K. WEVER—No other woman, perhaps, has compiled so much historical material of the county than has this inestimable woman. By years of diligent research and by delving into the dusty and musty records of the county's past records, she has collected a vast fund of valuable information, which, if it was published, would add untold wealth to the great store of knowledge of the happenings in the county's history. Quiet, unassuming, she has worked, considering this effort not as labor, but as a pleasing pastime. She is a member of the D. A. R. (Shenandoah Chapter), the U. D. C. and a Colonial Dame.

LYDIA BOGGS—Daughter of Captain John Boggs; was born in Back Creek Valley February 26, 1766. Her father and grandfather, William Boggs, Sr. and Jr., came to America in 1750 and obtained a grant of land from Lord Fairfax, situated on the State Road leading from Hedgesville to Berkeley Springs, on the west border of Back Creek. Her father was a captain in "Lord Dunmore's War" and was stationed at Cat Fish Camp, 25 miles from Wheeling (now Little Washington, Pa.).

Lydia Boggs removed with her family to Chartiers Creek in Western Pennsylvania, and her father, Captain John Boggs, was stationed at Cat Fish Camp. Although very young, Lydia remembered perfectly when her father was in command of this camp and of seeing Lord Dunmore and his army when they stopped at Cat Fish Camp.

In 1871, Captain Boggs and his family were living on Buffalo Creek in what is now Ohio County, W. Va., when the father and daughter were captured by the Indians but made their escape. On account of the unprotected situation, Lydia and her family removed to Wheeling. At the second siege of Fort Henry, when she was but sixteen years of age, she was with her father in the fort and assisted in molding bullets until her arms and hands were blistered, making ammunition and relieving the handful of wearied men who so courageously defended it. With her at the time was Elizabeth Zane, of whom the world knows, and Moses Shepherd. Here an acquaintance sprang up and ripened into love and she afterwards married Moses Shepherd.

Moses Shepherd was born at Shepherdstown and when he was but seven years old removed with his father to his plantation between Big and Little Creeks, near Wheeling, W. Va. Colonel David Shepherd, his father, later built Fort Shepherd, near this place. When Moses was fourteen, the Dunmore War was in progress and the fort was destroyed with all the buildings except the mill, which was spared by the Indians, as this afforded them much pleasure to see the wheel run. Colonel David Shepherd then took command of Fort Henry and successfully defended it against the Indian and British attack.

Lydia (Boggs) Shepherd on the death of Moses Shepherd, later married General David Cruger of New York State. She inherited considerable wealth from her first husband, Moses Shepherd, including "Shepherd Hall", which stood upon the old site of Fort Shepherd. Here she spent her later years, "in the stone mansion, managing her extensive plantation and large business interests." Many noted people visited her in this home: Major S. A. Duke of Arkansas, who wrote an extended article of her home and her dress; Senator Benton and family and Mrs. Rebecca Harding Davis wrote a magazine article that included a description of her.

She spent her winters in Washington, D. C., and when there met and talked with Benton, Clay and Webster, then political leaders, and spoke of them as "those young men promising but crude, crude." She entertained all the notables of her day, Lafayette, Henry Clay, Calhoun, Andrew Jackson, and James K. Polk. She lived to be 102 years of age.

FREDERICK RANDOLPH RAMER—Born at Martinsburg, W. Va., January 1, 1869. Attended the public schools of that city. Graduated from Storer College High and Normal, (........). Began teaching in Sumner School, 1889, when it had but two teachers. Taught there two years; resigned to learn the barber trade. Worked at this trade for three years with the following well-known shop owners: Samuel Hopewell, Monroe Taylor, and Lewis Lambert. Left Mr. Lambert to accept a position as laborer in the United States Senate. This gave him an opportunity to attend night schools. Served as employee of U. S. Senate six years (1893-99), and was privileged to listen to the debates and to witness the stirring scenes incident to the repeal of the purchasing clause of the Sherman Act. Heard Senator Allen make his seventeen hour speech and listened to Senator Thurston's appeal for Cuba, now a classic. During this period many men now famous in history were in the Senate: Allison, Hoar, Hale, Lodge, Gorman, Hill of New York, Blackburn, Faulkner, Bailey, Butler, Jones of Nevada, Jones of Arkansas, Mark Hanna, Matt Quay, Harris, Morgan, Cockerill, Pettus, Tillman, Vest, Voorhees, and others who have left enduring records. To have listened to these men and to have imbibed that atmosphere was in itself a liberal education. Ramer worked in the daytime and attended school at night. He was graduated from Howard University 1899 with the degree of L.L.B., and was presented his diploma by the late President McKinley. Taught in the rural schools of Berkeley County for several years. Clerk in Steam Engineering Department of the Norfolk Navy Yard (1907). Resigned to take up teaching again. Served some time in the United States Fish Commission. Instructor in first Summer School for Colored Teachers at Institute, West Virginia. Further prepared himself for his chosen profession by attendance upon Summer School at the University of Pittsburg. Took correspondence and extension courses from International Correspondence Schools of Scranton, Pa., and the West Virginia Collegiate Institute. By continued attendance upon summer schools was able to win his Bachelor's degree in Education. He is a member of the Alpha Phi Alpha, Greek Letter fraternity, Masons, Odd Fellows, Knights of Pythias, Elks, Trustees Sons and Daughters of Enoch Hall, Trustee of Mount Hope Cemetery, member and Trustee Mount Zion Methodist Episcopal Church, member of the Potomac Valleys Teachers' Association, West Virginia Teachers' Association, National Education Association, National Association of Teachers in Colored Schools, National Sociological Society. During the World War he served as a "Four Minute Man" among the colored soldiers and civilians, helping to put over the various governmental programs; instructor in Teachers' Institute of Mercer. County, 1925. Twice married; two children by first marriage and one by a second. At present Principal of Sumner Junior High School, where he has served acceptably for the past sixteen years. He has raised Sumner from a little three room, three teacher, tumbledown shack to a fine ten room, ten grade Junior High School, with four standard normal and four college graduates as teachers. Always intensely interested in the social sciences, he is now conducting extension classes in Social Psychology for the West Virginia Collegiate Institute.

JAMES W. WALKER—Teacher. Born in Frederick County, July 11, 1867. Graduated at Storer College, Harper's Ferry, West Virginia, May 3, 1887, also at Virginia Normal Industrial Institute, Petersburg, Va., May, 1892. Has taught in the rural schools of Virginia for five years; in the rural schools of West Virginia for thirty-five years. Parents, William Frances Walker, born in Warren County, Virginia, of free parents, in 1840, beneficiaries of the last will and testament of one Constance Carter, a slave holder.

BENJAMIN F. BRISCOE—Was the leader of a colony of colored people who first settled at Mount Pleasant, two miles south of Gerrardstown. This colony consisted of about fifty of that race gathered from the western section of Virginia 1866. Was the founder of the Mt. Pleasant school at that place. This school-house is also used as a church for the Colored Methodist Episcopal Church.

J. FRANK BRISCOE—Educated at Mount Pleasant school only, but the education he received from the contact of the world made him an unusual man in intellectual affairs. Was a "Four Minute Man" in the World War to the colored race. He was Assistant Food Administrator and a member of the State Auxiliary Council. Appointed by Governor John J. Cornwell of West Virginia. Served in the U. S. Fish Commission under Commissioner George M. Bowers at Woodshole, Massachusetts. Organized a colored Elk Club, Martinsburg. Member of the Mount Pisda Lodge (Masons), also a member of the Knights of Pythias. Secretary and Treasurer of the Board of Mount Zion Church (colored). Supervisor of the Employers at Hotel Berkeley for 37 years, under six different proprietors.

PERRY SCOTT—Born in Berkeley County. Was a horse dealer, being one of the best judges of horse flesh in the county. Died at Martinsburg in January, 1921. Had three sons, Harry, Sydney and James, who under the firm name of Scott Bros. Taxi Company, operate the best transfer line in the city. Perry Scott, Jr., another son, is a gardner at Washington, D. C.

DR. GEORGE W. BAYLIS—Colored practicing physician of Martinsburg. Born in Faquier County, Virginia. Educated in the rural schools of that county and Union University, Richmond, Va. Practiced in the county for fifteen years. During the "Flu" epidemic in Berkeley County worked night and day but did not contract the disease. Member Knights of Pythias and Masonic Lodge. Master of Finance, K. of P. Treasurer Blue Ridge Lodge No. 31.

J. R. CLIFFORD—Lawyer. First colored lawyer admitted to the bar in West Virginia. Educated Chicago High School. Graduated at Storer College, 1875. Has diploma, degree of A.M., Shaw University, Raleigh, N. C. Principal Sumner School, Martinsburg, ten years. Taught in Keyser and Williamsport, W. Va., Grant County, and Moorefield, Hardy County, W. Va. Founded and published the "Pioneer Press" at Martinsburg for 36 years. This was the first colored newspaper published in West Virginia and the oldest in the country at the time of its discontinuance. It was devoted to the uplift of that race.

Soldier in the Union Army of the Civil War. Member of Company F, 13th U. S. Heavy Artillery, with the rank of Corporal. Saw service in Kentucky, Tennessee and Eastern Virginia under General Grant. Volunteered at Chicago, Ill., and served in the war for three years.

Is a 33d Degree Mason, colored; Lecturer for the State of West Virginia; Past Grand Master of West Virginia, colored; First Vice President of the American Negro Academy. In 1881, was a member of a Committee of the "Wise Men", an organization, met at Atlanta, Ga. J. R. Clifford made a speech at this meeting at the Capitol building and was presented with a gold headed cane, which he now has, by that convention. Governor Colquitt of Georgia took an active part in getting this cane.

REV. W. E. JEFFERSON—Pastor of the Mt. Zion Methodist Episcopal Church of Martinsburg. Educated at Hampden Institute. Lodges: A. F. and A. M., Mount Zion No. 18. Specialized in Sunday School work among the members of the colored race in Pennsylvania. At present District Sunday School Superintendent of West Virginia (colored), in the auspices of the Council of Education, Charleston District.

MRS. MABEL B. JEFFERSON—Educated at Washington, M. St. High School. Teacher in the rural schools of Maryland, Virginia and West Virginia. Also specializes in Sunday School work among the colored race in Western Pennsylvania. At present is Superintendent of the Sunday School Teacher Training of Charleston, W. Va., District.

JOHN W. CORSEY—Born at Bunker Hill, (W. Va.), June 22, 1859. Educated at Storer College, Harper's Ferry, graduating from that institution, class of 1887. Has been a teacher in the colored schools of the county for a number of years. Principal of Sumner School, Martinsburg, three terms. Douglas Grove, a school for colored children, located in the Arden District, east of Pikeside, was named by him. Through his activities Sumner School was increased from a one room to a three room building. Was a delegate to the Republican Congressional Convention at Parkersburg in 1888. Was chairman of the Colored Republican rally at Martinsburg in the second McKinley campaign, at which meeting Hon. John C. Dacy was orator.

MATTIE E. CORSEY—Teacher in the colored schools of the county for 31 years. Educated at Storer College. She has taught 23 years in the Sumner School in Martinsburg.

CHAPTER XXIV.

OFFICERS OF THE COUNTY.

A list of the officers of Berkeley County from the formation of the county, 1772, to the present:

SHERIFFS.

Adam Stephen,
Samuel Washington,
Cato Moore,
James Wilson,
John Kearsley,
James Campbell,
John Davenport,
William Porterfield,
Nicholas Orrick,
John Turner,
Andrew Wagoner,
James Stephenson,
Charles Orrick,
William Riddle,
James Anderson,
Magnus Tate,

George Porterfield,
Erasmus Gantt,
Jacob Wever,
George Harris,
Philip Nadenbousch,
Joel Ward,
George Wolff,
Anthony S. Chambers,
Levi Henshaw,
William Gregory,
Edward Colston,
Benjamin Comequy,
Silas Harlan,
Daniel Burkhart,
Tillotson Fryatt,
Jacob Van Doren,

Barnet Cushwa,
Daniel LaFevre,
John W. Pitzer,
A. J. Thomas,
Moses C. Nadenbousch,
George A. Chrisman,
Robert Lamon,
Charles H. Miller,
L. C. Gerling,
James H. Smith,
E. B. Kettering,
E. D. Gardner,
E. H. Tabler,
Harry S. Miller,
William Dean,
J. C. McKown.

SURVEYORS.

Robert Cockburn,
John Turner,
David Hunter,
Josiah Swearingen,

James Maxwell,
John B. Kearfott,
David Pultz,
J. Baker Kearfott,

James W. Robinson,
George W. Vanmetre,
I. W. Wood,
William C. Morgan.

PROSECUTING ATTORNEYS.

Alexander White,
Elisha Boyd,
David N. Conrad,
Edmond P. Hunter,
John E. Norris,
George H. Murphy,
Joseph T. Hoke,
J Nelson Wisner,

H. H. Blackburn,
Edmond Shaw,
Reuben Price,
Luther M. Shaffer,
W. H. H. Flick,
Perry A. Roherbaugh,
Wm. S. Henshaw,
Alex. S. Hughes,

George W. Feict,
U. S. Grant Pitzer,
D. O. Westenhaver,
Ward B. Lindsey,
Allen B. Noll,
J. M. Woods,
W. W. Downey,
Herbert E. Hannis.

CORONERS.

Robert Worthington,
David Shepherd,
Gorge North,
William Riddle,
George Wolff,

Conrad Hogmire,
Anthony S. Chambers,
Frank D. Stehley,
H. N. Deatrick,
George Izatte,

William McKee,
Jacob Sites,
Dr. H. G. Tonkin.

JUDGES OF THE CIRCUIT COURT.

Robert White,	L. P. W. Balch,	Joseph H. Duckwall,
Wm. Brockanbraugh,	Ephraim B. Hall,	E. Boyd, Faulkner,
John Scott,	Joseph Chapman,	J. M. Woods,
Richard E. Parker,	John Blair Hoge,	Adrian C. Nadenbousch,
Isaac R. Douglas,	Chas. J. Faulkner, Jr.	Decatur H. Rogers.
John W. Kennedy,	Frank Beckwith,	

CLERKS OF THE CIRCUIT COURT.

Obed Waite,	Joseph Barnes,	W. B. Colston,
John Strother,	John Canby,	L. DeWitt Gerhardt.
Israel Robinson,	E. S. Troxall,	
John Dunn,	H. S. Martin,	

CLERKS OF THE COUNTY COURT.

William Drew,	Norman Miller,	Christian W. Doll,
Moses Hunter,	Jacob VanDoren,	I. L. Bender,
Henry Bedinger,	E. G. Alburtis,	Harold H. Bender,
David Hunter,	James W. Robinson,	E. A. Hobbs,
John Strother,	Seamon Gerard,	Paul H. Martin.
Harrison Waite,	Bernard Doll,	

ASSESSORS.

Christopher Hill,	David Dodd,	Otho Williams,
Charles Hill,	Charles H. Miller,	Martin L. Payne,
W. B. Colston,	Henry S. Butts,	Ellis Ellis,
Thornton Henshaw,	John D. Gordon,	John W. Dodd,
David Stuckey,	Collins L. Niceley,	Harry E. Johnson,
James T. Guinn,	James A. Gageby,	John H. Riner.

COUNTY AGRICULTURAL AGENTS.

Paul H. Teal,	E. G. Deagan,	Joseph D. Eckhart.

TRAFFIC OFFICER.

William H. Barber.

PRESIDENTS OF THE COUNTY COURT SINCE 1873.

M. S. Grantham,	B. M. Kitchen,	Alexander Parks,
A. W. McClary,	G. P. Riner,	Charles W. Thatcher,
C. W. Thornburg,	D. P. Lemaster,	Jacob Hesse,
Blackburn Hughes,	John H. Lamen,	Almon W. Smith.
Jacob M. Seibert,	John Grosinger,	

COUNTY SUPERINTENDENTS OF SCHOOLS.

J. Canby,	S. L. Dodd,	John W. Shirley,
E. S. Lacy,	Henry S. Butts,	Edward H. Tabler,
J. S. Heilig,	E. S. Tabler,	Willis F. Evans,
W. S. Penick,	David H. Dodd,	E. N. Zeilor,
J. P. Stump,	P. T. Keesecker,	Charles W. Crowell,
M. T. Bowen,	C. C. Tabler,	Palmer T. Keesecker,
E. M. Walker,	James Snyder,	Bessie D. Kilmer.

OFFICERS OF THE COUNTY 275

MAYORS OF MARTINSBURG.

A. S. Chambers,
James Matthews,
J. W. Abel,
A. P. Shutt,
W. T. Logan,
C. O. Lambert,
Dr. J. Whann McSherry,

John B. Wilson,
Dr. W. T. Henshaw,
George F. Evans,
W. E. Minghini,
P. R. Harrison,
Charles G. Cushwa,
P. W. Leiter,

G. B. Wiltshire,
C. M. Seibert,
Thomas W. Turner,
Dr. H. G. Tonkin,
Albert A. Smallwood,
George W. Appleby, Jr.

COMMISSIONERS OF ACCOUNTS.

John T. Picking,
William B. Colston,

C. W. Doll,
Adrian C. Nadenbousch,
C. J. Simpson,

U. S. G. Pitzer,
L. DeW. Gerhardt.

COUNTY COMMISSIONERS.

NOTE—When the county was formed the Governor of Virginia appointed Gentlemen Justices, as they were called, who acted in the capacity of the present County Court, the Circuit Court and Judge. The Gentlemen Justices were numerous, and were appointed for one year. For instance, Lord Dunmore, Colonial Governor of Virginia, appointed eleven men Gentlemen Justices as members of the first County Court of Berkeley County. Their salaries were meager, they receiving a small fee from the State for all cases wherein the person was convicted of crime, and in case of civil suit, the loser in the suit had this fee to pay. Oftentimes these men could not agree, and some of them would resign with indignation. The practice of appointing Gentlemen Justices continued until West Virginia became a State, or until Berkeley County became a part of the State of West Virginia, when the first Constitution required one commissioner to be elected from each magisterial district of the county, or townships, as they were designated at that time, and this body comprised the Board of Supervisors. This practice continued until the revision of the Constitution of West Virginia, in 1872, when, after that time, three men were elected from the county as a whole, and comprised the County Court of Berkeley County. The County Board of Supervisors were elected for two years, and the members of the County Court are elected for six years.

Ralph Wormley,
Jacob Hite,
Van Swearingen,
Thos. Rutherford,
Adam Stephen,
John Neaville,
Thos. Swearingen,
Samuel Washington,
James Nourse,
William Little,
Robert Stephen,
John Briscoe,
Hugh Lyle,
James Strode,
William Morgan,
Robert Stogdon,
James Seaton,
Robert Carter Mills,
Thomas Robinson,

John Puckett,
George Porterfield ,
Erasmus Gantt,
Jacob Wever,
Philip Nadenbousch,
Joel Ware,
George Wolff,
Michael Rooney,
Thomas Robinson,
Douglass Campbell,
Levi Hanshaw,
William Gregory,
Edward Colston,
John S. Harrison,
William Morrison,
Edward Gibbs,
Benjamin Comequy,
William Campbell,
Gantt VanDorn,

James L. Campbell,
Louis B. Weller,
Betheul M. Kitchen,
Thomas J. Harley,
James L. Cunningham,
William Dorsey,
Daniel H. Dodd,
John McKown,
Lewis Fry,
George W. Hollida,
Andrew W. McClary,
John A. Voorhees,
George F. Hollida,
A. R. McQuilkin,
Owen T. Hedges,
Charles Downs,
Richard Bodine,
Henry J. Seibert,
Lewis Grantham,

Robert Tabb,
John Throckmorton,
Thomas Lowery,
Horatio Gates,
Goodwin Swift,
John Avis,
William Patterson,
Morgan Morgan,
John Cooke,
Henry Whiting,
Robert Worthington,
William McGaw,
John McAllister,
Anthony Noble,
John Morrow,
Robert Throckmorton,
John Gantt,
Walter Baker,
George Grund,
George Cunningham,
Moses Hunter,
Robert Baylor,
Robert Stewart,
George Scott,
James Wilson,
John Kearney,
John Davenport,
William Porterfield,
Joseph Sweringen,
John Turner,
William Henshaw,
James Maxwell,
Andrew Wagoner,
Alexander White,
William Darke,
Adam Sheppard,
James Stephenson,
Winn Winslip,
Richard Baylor
Charles Orrick,
William Alexander,
Charles Cranmer,
George Hite,
William Riddle,
James Anderson,
George North,
Daniel Collett,
Abraham Davenport,
Smith Slaughter,
Morganus Tate,
John Hunter,
Van Rutherford,
Isaac E. Houser,
Martin Lupton,
B. J. Speck,
W. D. North,
J. P. Musseter,
B. F. Harmison,

Silas Harlan,
Isaac S. LeMarr,
William Granthum,
Daniel Burkhart,
Tillotson Fryatt,
Archibald Shearer,
Robert V. Snodgrass,
John Lamon,
Thomas Davis.
Francis Silver,
Philip C. Pendleton,
Conrad Hogmire,
Samuel Balser,
Edward Winning,
William L. Boak,
Alexander Oden,
Thomas S. Page,
Richard McSherry,
William Maslin,
Jacob Hamm,
Stephen R. Snodgrass,
Robert K. Robinson,
Jacob Myers,
Daniel B. Morrison,
James W. Newkirk,
James H. Robinson,
Alfred Ross,
Hiram McKown,
David Canby,
A. J. Bowers,
Henry Riner,
Jonathan Strine,
William Sigler,
Samuel R. Powell,
George D. Miller,
James M. Vanmetre,
Harrison Tabler,
Samuel Gold,
William N. Riddle,
Joseph H. Barnett,
William Sperow,
Robert Lamon,
John E. Barney,
Thornton Henshaw,
Joseph Fiscus,
Richard J. Thomas,
John W. Hollida,
Alexander Parks,
John H. Lamon,
Charles W. Stnckey,
Thomas Kearns,
Jacob Stuckey,
William McKee,
Charles Stuckey,
E. C. Williams,
A. B. Stismitz,
Joseph Alexander,
Jacob Strine,

Philip Everhart,
Casper Stump,
George R. Wysong,
William Jack,
Stephen B. Meade,
Alfred Ross,
Israel Robinson,
Joseph W. Hollis,
Joseph C. Rawlins,
Thomas G. Flagg,
William H. Mong,
Joseph Stuckey,
Martin H. Payne,
John W. Kendrick,
Samuel Taylor,
George Ferrel,
William Ripple,
Andrew J. Brown,
William R. Parkinson,
D. P. Lamaster,
Moses S. Grantham,
C. W. Thornburg,
Blackburn Hughes,
Jacob M. Seibert,
John Grozinger,
Charles W. Thatcher,
Jacob Hesse,
Joseph DeHaven,
D. S. Eichelberger,
John E. Boyd,
Alexander Newcomer,
George Doll,
George H. McClarey,
Barnet Cushwa,
Barnett Doll,
S. J. Williamson,
Joseph Hoffman,
F. S. Dellinger,
Joseph W. Hollida,
Ezekiel Showers,
William Miller,
Elias M. Pitzer,
Archibald Myers,
Thomas Wandling,
John W. Lamon,
William Wilan,
Jacob Ropp,
David Thompson,
Benjamin F. Brady,
J. B. A. Nadenbousch,
William Leith,
William J. Hensel,
A. J. Bowen,
G. P. Riner,
Almon W. Smith,
Charles L. Pitzer,
Glenn M. Pitzer,
Charles E. Dick.

MEMBERS OF THE WEST VIRGINIA SENATE AND HOUSE OF DELEGATES.

NOTE—When the First and Second Legislatures of West Virginia met, Berkeley County was not a part of that State. Therefore, there is no record of Representatives in that body from this county. The same rule, of course, applies to the State Senators. The number after each individual name indicates the Legislatures of which each was a member. Berkeley County has always been entitled to two Delegates in the House of Delegates of the West Virginia Legislature.

Senators.

Behtuel M. Kitchen (3)
E. Boyd Faulkner (14-15)
Samuel Gold (9)
Moses S. Granthum (12-13)
George A. Blakemore (10)
Alexander Parks (21)

D. W. Shaffer (23)
Robert C. Burkhart (24-25)
Gray Silver (28-29-30-31)
A. C. McIntyre (30)
Harry P. Henshaw (35-36-37-38)

House of Delegates.

William Smith (3-4-5)
William Wilen (3)
Abraham R. McQuilkin (4-5)
Samuel Gold (6-7)
Levi J. Tabler (6-7)
John W. Lamon (8)
Jacob Ropp (8)
Moses C. Nadenbousch (9-10)
John E. Stehley (9)
G. W. Legg (10-11)
Eli Fleming (11)
J. H. Gettinger (12)
Adam Small (12)
E. Boyd Faulkner (13)
E. L. Hoffman (13)
D. F. Billmyer (14)
B. M. Kitchen (14)
Benjamin F. Brady (15)
George Ferrel (15)
George F. Evans (16-23)
Marion L. Henshaw (16)
James H. Smith (17)
George M. Bowers (18)
C. H. Ropp (18)
George W. Braxton (19)
Joseph G. Kitchen (19)

C. A. Wever (20)
Robert Lamon (20)
E. S. Tabler (21)
James Blakemore (21)
H. S. Cushwa (24)
William T. Henshaw (25)
Jacob Sites (25)
John Hunter (26-27)
W. W. Westphall (27)
George Ryneal, (Jr. (28)
I. W. Wood (28)
Dr. G. W. Daniels (29)
C. M. Seibert (29-30-31)
John W. Sperow (31)
W. B. Ligamfelter (31)
Charles Beard (32 to 38)
S. S. Cline (32)
Harry P. Henshaw (33)
John N. Parks (33)
Roy C. Grove (34)
Theodore F. Imbach (34)
H. A. Downs (35)
M. K. Butts (35)
James S. Dailey (36)
H. Lott Smith (36-37)
H. L. Alexander (38)

NOTE—From 1873, Berkeley County was included in the Seventh Delegate District, and the following served as members of the House of Delegates from the county:

Chas. L. Stuckey (22)
John Henshaw (23)

R. W. Morrow (24)
Stuart W. Walker (25)

H. T. Cushwa (26)
A. W. McDonald (27)

MEMBERS OF THE VIRGINIA LEGISLATURE FROM BERKELEY COUNTY WHEN THAT BODY WAS TERMED "THE VIRGINIA HOUSE OF BURGESSES"—1754 TO 1775.

What is now West Virginia was not included in the first grant to the Virginia Company (1606); in fact, at that time nothing was known of the region west of the Blue Ridge and hardly that far west, for after the settlement of Jamestown Captain John Smith, of that Colony and "Governor of Virginia", made extensive explorations of the rivers of that section running in from the west in hopes of finding a waterway "through" America which was then considered a narrow peninsula. These explorations of Captain Smith's extended to the foothills of the eastern base of the Blue Ridge plateau, which was then styled "The Great Western Mountains".

In the second chartered limits (1609), which improved and enlarged the first, the limits of Virginia were set as follows, to include:: "all those lands, countries, and territories situate, lying, and being, in that part of America called Virginia, from the point of land, called Cape or Point Comfort, all along the sea-coast to the northward two hundred miles; and from the said point of Cape Comfort, all along the sea-coast to the southward two hundred miles, and all that space and circuit of land, lying from the sea-coast of the precinct aforesaid, up, into the land throughout from sea to sea west and northwest."

For ten years the Jamestown Colony was governed by the Royal Governor and his Council; the Governor being appointed by the King and the Council by the Governor. Then, in 1619, the Colony having spread along the James River, the settlements were divided into eleven sub-divisions called "boroughs" and each borough was instructed to elect representatives called "Burgesses" to constitute a legislative body—the first elective body in America—called the Houses of Burgesses. There was no Senate or Upper House, the Governor and his Council performing that duty. This continued to be the law-making body of Virginia until the Revolution.

In 1645, Virginia was divided into eight counties or shires, similar to those in England. In 1734, there had been thirty-two of such counties formed in Virginia, all east of the Blue Ridge. In 1738, Augusta and Frederick Counties were the first two counties laid off west of those mountains. The only two counties laid off by that body in what is now West Virginia were Hampshire and Berkeley. Thus it will be seen that our county was formed by the oldest law-making body in America—The Virginia House of Burgesses. On May 6, 1776, Virginia cast off the old order of the Colonial System and came forth a sovereign state and its law-making body became known as the General Assembly of Virginia.

Below is given the roster of the men who represented Berkeley County in these law-making bodies:

MEMBERS OF THE HOUSE OF BURGESSES—Robert Rutherford, Thomas Hite (1772-1775).

MEMBRES OF THE GENERAL ASSEMBLY:

Senators (1777-1864)—Robert Rutherford, Hugh Holmes, Elisha Boyd, Charles James Faulkner, Moses Grantham, Andrew Hunter.

Delegates (1777-1864)—Philip Pendleton, Thomas Hite, James Nourse, Moses Hunter, Adam Stephen, Dolphin Drew, James Campbell, Thomas Rutherford, Joseph Swearingen, Andrew Waggener, Robert Throckmorton, David Hunter, Henry Bedinger, Elisha Boyd, Richard Baylor, William Lemon, John Dixon, Magnus Tate, Alexander White, Jr., James Stevenson, Matthew Ranson, Samuel Boyd, Aaron Faris, Philip R. Wilson, George Porterfield, Thomas Shearer, Andrew Waggener, Jr., Edward Colston, George Newkirk, John R. Cook, Archibald Shearer, Israel Robinson, Archibald S. Porterfield, Joel Ward, John Porterfield, Levi Henshaw, Richard Cleggett, William Good, Moses T. Hunter, Thomas Davis, Charles James Faulkner, Edmond P. Hunter, Robert V. Snodgrass, Tillotson Fryatt, Jacob Myers, Jacob Vandoren, James M. Newkirk, William T. Snodgrass, Edmond Pendleton, William L. Boak, Adam Small, James E. Stewart, Thomas Brown, Allen C. Hammond, Lewis Grantham, James W. Gray, George H. McClure, Henry J. Seibert, R. D. Seaman, John Blair Hoge, William M. Mong, R. K. Robinson, Robert W. Hunter, William B. Colston.

THE FAMOUS VIRGINIA CONVENTION AND THE DELEGATES TO SAME FROM BERKELEY COUNTY.

On May 24, 1774, the House of Burgesses, then sitting at Williamsburg, the Capitol, received the news of the closing of Boston Harbor against commerce by the British—Boston Port Bill. That body passed resolutions denouncing that action. Lord Dunmore, the Colonial Governor of Virginia, became so incensed by this act of the House of Burgesses that he dissolved it and many Delegates left for their homes. Twenty-five remained at Williamsburg and all these united in a call upon all the Burgesses to re-assemble, which they did on August 1, 1774, claiming that Lord Dunmore usurped his power in dissolving this convention. Robert Rutherford was one of the twenty-five who remained.

The object of the second convention was to determine whether Virginia should stand by Massachusetts or Great Britain. The members of this convention resolved to cast their lot with the rebelling Northerners and took steps to get rid of his Lordship.

The members of this convention from Berkeley County were Robert Rutherford and Thomas Hite.

The members of the convention which framed the first Constitution of Virginia from Berkeley County were William Drew and Robert Rutherford.

The members of the convention which ratified the Federal Constitution from Berkeley County were William Darke and Adam Stephen.

The members of the convention assembled at Richmond for the purpose of amending the first Constitution of Virginia (1829) from Berkeley County was Elisha Boyd.

The members of the convention which met at Richmond to adopt a new Constitution for Virginia (1850) from Berkeley County were Charles James Faulkner and Dennis Murphy.

The members of the convention which met at Richmond and adopted the Ordinance of Secession, (1861), from Berkeley County were Allen C. Hammond and Edmund Pendleton.

The members of the first convention at Wheeling (1861) to take steps to form a new State from Berkeley County were A. R. McQuilkin, John W. Dailey and J. S. Bowers. This was the last convention to which Berkeley County sent delegates until after the Civil War.

OFFICERS OF BERKELEY COUNTY AT PRESENT.

United States Senators—M. M. Neeley, Guy D. Goff.

Member of Congress—Frank L. Bowman.

U. S. District Judge—W. E. Baker.

Judge of the Circuit Court—Decatur H. Rogers.

Sheriff—J. C. McKown; Deputies: N. Cliff Caldwell, (Jailer) Ray Severs, Harwood Burkhart, Oscar B. Miller.

Prosecuting Attorney—Herbert E. Hannis; Assistant, Charles N. Campbell.

Clerk of Circuit Court—L. DeW. Gerhardt; Assistant, L. DeW. Gerhardt, Jr.

General Receiver Circuit Court—Edward Rutledge.

Chancery Commissioners—A. C. Nadenbousch, R. H. Boyd, A. C. McIntyre, P. R. Harrison.

Clerk County Court—Paul H. Martin; Assistant, Harold H. Keedy; Stenographers, Rae Hammon, Ruth Farnsworth.

Assessor—Harry E. Johnson. Deputies—John E. Armbrester, Harry May, Harry F. Smith, Reva Mock.

State Senator—Harry P. Henshaw.

House of Delegates—Charles Beard, Herbert L. Alexander.

County Superintendent of Schools—Bessie D. Kilmer.

County Agricultural Agent—Joseph D. Eckhardt.

County Commissioners—Almon W. Smith (President), Charles E. Dick, Glenn M. Pitzer.

County Board of Equalization—J. R. Catrow, John H. Lamon, Charles Ruble.

Surveyor—Wm. C. Morgan.

Agent Board of Children's Guardians—Kathleen Welton.

Humane Officer—L. G. Harper.

Probation Judge—E. J. Fulk.

Coroner—Dr. H. G. Tonkin.

County Road Engineer—C. Newton Stuckey. Deputies—Abe Reed, John C. Speck, Lemuel Files, Carlton B. Stuckey, Jacob Gain.

Janitor Court House—A. W. Neer.

Berkeley County has produced mighty men in the affairs of the State and Nation, some of whose names and positions are mentioned here:

Members of Congress—Bethuel M. Kitchen, John R. Cooke, Charles

James Faulkner, Thomas Van Swearingen, Edward Colston, George M. Bowers, Daniel Morgan, John Baker.

Members of Congress from Other States, but Born in Berkeley County—Felix Grunby, Tennessee; William Creighton, Ohio; John Moore, Louisiana.

United States Senators—Charles James Faulkner, West Virginia; Felix Grunby, Kentucky.

Commanders in the United States Navy—Napoleon B. Harrison, Admiral Stribling, Stribling Snodgrass.

Member of President's Cabinet—Newton D. Baker, Secretary of War under President Wilson.

Ministers to Foreign Countries—Charles James Faulkner, Minister to France under President Buchannon; David Hunter Strother, Consul General to Mexico under President Hayes.

United States Fish Commissioner—George M. Bowers.

Attorney General, United States—Magnus Tate.

Major Generals United States Army—Adam Steven, Charles Lee, William Darke, Horatio Gates, Thomas Sidney Jessup.

Four Governors of Ohio—Edward Tiffin, Thomas Worthington, Robert Lucas, Jeremiah Morrow, and Harry F. Byrd, Governor of Virginia.

Member American Federation Farm Bureau—Gray Silver.

Names of men who have held Positions of Trust in the State of West Virginia from Berkeley County—Dr. James H. Shipper, member State Board of Health; Dr. William T. Henshaw, State Health Commissioner; John D. McCune, State Inspector of Sand Mines; Charles P. Light, State Commissioner of Agriculture; Jack O. Henson, Assistant Attorney General State of West Virginia; Wade C. Kilmer, member State Public Service Commission; Harry H. Byrer, Assistant District Attorney for the Northern District of West Virginia; Charles N. Campbell, Assistant District Attorney for the Northern District of West Virginia; Harry P. Henshaw, Commissioner to Adjust Revenue; Gray Silver, Commissioner to Adjust Revenue; C. R. Sperow and Alexander Clohan, members of the State Board of Agriculture.

CHAPTER XXV.

TRANSPORTATION, AVIATION, COMMUNICATION.

TRANSPORTATION AND ROADS.

The first mode of travel in this section was afoot. The Indian used this method for centuries before the coming of the white man. True, he had the birch bark canoe which he used on the larger streams and rivers, but as these streams lead in an eastern and western direction, and as it cost considerable labor and not a little skill to fashion the canoe, the majority of the Indians, for the most part, preferred to travel on foot. This fact is attested by the well defined trails in use by the red men which were found traversing the section of the country which is now Berkeley County by the first explorers. One of these, the "Indian Road", traversed this valley, north and south. It was known at where Harrisburg, Pa., now stands and was still continuing in the vicinity of Lexington, Virginia, and is now followed almost identically by the Williamsport, Winchester and Valley Pikes. Another well defined Indian trail was found leading from where Shepherdstown now stands across the Shenandoah Valley to Mills Gap, two miles west of Gerardstown, where it crossed the North Mountain and extended on west across Back Creek Valley in the neighborhood of Glengary and Mount Carmel. This was the mode of transportation used by the early explorers, John Lederer, John Howard and his son, and John VanMatre. They carried the long rifle, ammunition, a bag of parched corn and depended on wild game for their meat. They also carried a generous supply of glass beads, shining trinkets of brass and gewgaws which were the delight of the Indian and were used to compensate him for their trespass of the Indian lands or as presents to them to keep them in a friendly mood.

When the setlters began to arrive, they, with a little labor, put these trails into passable condition for the pack horse, which was the mode of travel used by them. Oftentimes, three and four horses were brought together, one tied behind the other by a halter, sometimes tied to the leader's tail, sometimes led by the settler astride of the leader. Each was laden with a pack-saddle—a large affair, made of leather with two enormous pockets, hanging down on either side of the horse, the whole securely fastened to the animal by a wide belt of leather or girth, passing around its body. In these pockets were carried powder, lead, salt, iron, an ax and a grubbing hoe, a few household articles or keepsakes from the old home, and not infrequently the children; the mother perched upon the back of one of the pack-horses. This mode of transportation was used for many years in traveling from the new settlements to the old. Often pigs and poultry were conveyed from the old home to the new in like manner. Periodical visits were of necessity made to the older settlements to renew the supply of provisions not to be obtained in the new settlement. At this time the whole male population and sometimes the women and children would travel in what they called "a caravan"—that is, all traveled in a body by pack-horse. In these times the Indians were friendly and no apprehension on the part of the whites were felt from molestation of their property until their return.

After the settlers became pretty numerous in this valley, better facilities for travel began to come into use. The first one was the wagon drawn by a yoke of oxen. Later these were supplemented by the horse team, sometimes two, sometimes four or even six horses hitchd to a wagon was used. At the event of the coming of the wagon, the roads were widened and some of the hills were cut down to insure the passage of the wagon over them. As most of the first settlers of our county came from the north of us, mainly from Pennsylvania, New Jersey and Maryland, they came by way of the "Old Pack Horse Road" by way of what is now Shepherdstown, or by way of the old "Indian Road" by way of what is now Williamsport.

The wagon continued to be almost the main mode of travel until the completion of the Chesapeake and Ohio Canal, from Cumberland, Md., to Georgetown, D. C. Before this event, the farmers of Berkeley County had their wheat ground into flour at the numerous mills in this section and hauled it to Baltimore by way of Shepherdstown or Williamsport and to this city and to other eastern markets. On the way back they would bring a load of provisions for the stores scattered among the larger villages. After the completion of this canal, the distance was much shortened and most of the flour, pork and other farm products were hauled to Williamsport or Shepherdstown and loaded on the canal boats there and transported on to market. Thus these two places became flourishing towns. This canal was projected by the leading citizens of Baltimore, who prevailed upon Congress to build it. There had always been a sharp rivalry between Baltimore and the larger cities to the northward, and when Governor DeWitt Clinton of New York finished the Erie Canal, thus connecting New York City with the Mid-West by an all water route, Baltimore took steps for a canal route connecting with the same region. But Baltimore's objective was the Ohio River, hence the canal received, like the railroad which came later out of Baltimore, the name of Chesapeake and Ohio Canal. Although the canal was not swift moving as the railroad which came later, yet it was a decided step in improvement, both in time and comfort of travel. And, although this canal did not touch any of the territory of what is now Berkeley County, it had a decided influence on the progress of our county. This canal continued in use until 1925 when it was abandoned.

The stage coach had been in use for a considerable period prior to this time and people could travel quite conveniently in this manner. These stages had a fairly good schedule of time between various points and made very good time in transit. Along about the year 1836 four stages arrived and departed from Martinsburg, one to Winchester, one to Shepherdstown, one to Hagerstown and one to Warm Springs (Berkeley Springs). These stage coaches were lumbering affairs, usually drawn by two horses. The passengers rode inside and sat facing each other on a seat at the front and rear. They usually carried eight passengers without crowding and in case of too many, one and sometimes two could ride on the driver's seat. The top of the stage coach was surrounded by a low railing to keep the freight and baggage from falling off, this material being carried there. On the rear was strapped trunks, boxes and any other freight to be transported. The coming of the railroad gradually put a stop to the use of the stage coach in this section, but one continued to ply its trade between Martinsburg and Winchester until about 1890, but it hauled freight only and was at last discontinued, the railroad freight train driving it out of business.

In 1837 the surveying corps of the Baltimore and Ohio Railroad Company came to Martinsburg for the purpose of surveying a route through the town to the Ohio River. In the month of May, 1843, the first steam railroad engine reached Martinsburg. From that time on regular trains were run from Martinsburg to Baltimore and the railroad as a means of transportation had begun. The engines were fired with wood, the material being obtained from the farmers along the right of way. This wood was placed at convenient intervals along the track and gathered up along the track and hauled where needed by the "wood train". At first tickets were not sold at a ticket office but fare was paid to the conductor of the train. In September-October, 1927, the Baltimore and Ohio Railroad celebrated its one hundredth anniversary of the opening of that road at Baltimore. It is the oldest railroad in the United States and began its career in 1827 with 21 miles of road from Baltimore to Ellicott's Mills. Martinsburg did not "happen" to be located on the line of this railroad. The old spirit of rivalry between Baltimore and New York City was renewed and the people of Baltimore realized that to hold her place with that city, she had to reach the mid-west by other means than the National Road with its slow moving wagons.

About this time experiments had begun with "steam wagons", principally in England. A number of the leading citizens of Baltimore conceived the plan of building a road to the Ohio River for the use of these "wagons", and as Martinsburg lay in the direct route from Baltimore to the Ohio River at Wheeling, the road was built through this town. This road helped wonderfully in the upbuilding of Martinsburg and vicinity, and without the aid of this enterprise would not have become the town of importance that it now occupies in the Shenandoah Valley.

The carriage was in use during all these years but it was nominally a vehicle of pleasure rather than a necessity. Only the well-to-do could afford to own one and this condition was not conclusive to the upbuilding of the county. Later the "buggy", a light four-wheeled vehicle, came into use and the price was such as to be in the reach of all and travel and transportation took a decided step forward. In about the year 1896 the bicycle came into use and later when the "safety" bicycle was invented travel by this mode became almost universal.

After the bicycle, came the automobile, or, as it was first called, the "horseless carriage". The discovery of gasoline brought about the advent of the motor engine, without which the automobile, the motor truck and the areoplane would be useless. The motor transport business has grown by leaps and bounds within the last ten years, and this advent has brought about a system of hard surfaced State and county road building never before witnessed. The invention of the flying machine had introduced a new mode of transportation which is just in its infancy and bids to be one of the best modes of transportation yet known.

Martinsburg and Berkeley County has always kept up to the procession in the use of modes of transportation. It has owned the first in all these improvements from the pack-horse to the areoplane and with her countless garages, repair shops filling stations and, with her miles of hard surfaced roads, will continue to keep the lead which she has attained.

ROADS.

The Old Pack Horse Road was the first road built in the county. It begun in 1727-28 by the German emigrants from the vicinity of York, Pennsylvania, who founded New Mecklenberg (Shepherdstown). Later it was extended to Romney, in Hampshire County. It began at Shepherdstown and extended westward a little to the south of Martinsburg, crossed the Opequon Creek at where the residence of Benjamin H. Snyder is now located, crossed the North Mountain at Mills Gap, two miles west of Gerrardstown, thence to the foot of this mountain in the direction of Shanghai, thence across Back Creek at the place where the home of Peter Mason now stands, thence in a southwesterly direction to Mount Carmel. Parts of this old road bed are county roads, other parts are closed but the marks of this ancient road are still to be seen, especially from the top of North Mountain to Glengary. At first this road was a mere Indian trail, but in the advent of the wagon it was widened and used by emigrants passing to new settlements or travelers passing back and forth from one settlement to another. This road aided greatly in the settlement of our county. Another road of importance to our county was the "Great Winchester Road", as it was called. It extended from Echel's Ferry (Williamsport) to Winchester, Va. It traversed the entire length of Berkeley County from north to south. Later this road from Williamsport to Martinsburg was called the Williamsport Pike. In 1832, citizens of the county in conjunction with the County Board of Supervisors rebuilt this road between the above named places and made it a toll road, charging the sum of two cents a mile for vehicles passing over it. About the same time the Winchester Pike was rebuilt from Martinsburg to Winchester. Toll to the same amount was charged on this road also. Much dissatisfaction prevailed on account of charging for travel on a road owned by the county and especially in the advent of the automobile. So, in the year 1918, the County Court of Berkeley County bought the share holdings of these roads, abolished the system of toll and took the roads under their charge. When the $50,000,000 West Virginia road bond issue was voted by the people of this State, these roads were taken over by the State Road Commission and are now in first class condition and are maintained by the State. This road figured prominently in the time of the Civil War as a thoroughfare for the transportation of troops from the north and south by both armies. It is now the prominent highway for tourists traveling from the south to the north or from the north to south.

Another road of importance and one built at an early period was one leading from Shepherdstown to Bath (Berkeley Springs). It passed through Berkeley County by way of Hainsville, North Mountain and Hedgesville. After Martinsburg became a town, this road was changed to its present site. It has always been known as the Warm Springs Road. It received its name from the mineral springs located at Berkeley Springs and was built that the people of Virginia and States east might reach this noted resort. There was formerly more travel over this road than at present, for people were in the habit of repairing there to drink of the waters and bath in them.

The Berkeley and Hampshire Grade was a title conferred upon the road now known as the Tuscarora Pike. This road was built in 1810; began at Martinsburg and extended direct west across the North Mountain to Shanghai, in Back Creek Valley and on across the Back Mountain to the western confines of Berkeley County but now Morgan County. The object of these roads was to direct trade to Martinsburg and give the people of Berkeley County a convenient way of communication with each other. Martinsburg has always been the metropolis of the Eastern Panhandle, and, after Morgan County was laid off in 1820, and Berkeley Springs was made the county seat of it. the people of that section naturally traded there, and that road ceased to be used longer and was abandoned west of Back Creek Valley. In 1840, the part known as Tusacrora Pike was rebuilt and made a toll road and was the last road in Berkeley County upon which toll was charged. The toll gate for collecting the toll was situated on Rosemont, West King Street, but when the corporate limits of Martinsburg were extended, this toll house was removed to near the foot of Red Hill, west of town, just outside the corporate limits. Mr. Kennedy Avey was the last toll-gate keeper on this road.

It might not be amiss here to explain this system of toll roads, as many of the younger generation know nothing of it. At an early date the people of the county were poor compared to the present time. Taxes were low, valuation of property was low, hence a small amount of taxes were raised each year for road purposes. The maintenance of the roads were mostly from free or voluntary labor upon the part of the inhabitants. There was a law upon the statute books requiring every able bodied male citizen between the ages of twenty-one and fifty to work two days on the road at free labor. This forced labor, together with the meager sum received from the county treasury, was all the road system of the county had for its upkeep. Occasionally public spirited men would give several days free labor with their teams for grading and hauling stone to fill mud holes, that the road might be kept in passable condition. Therefore, some system of getting more money for road building had to be devised, and the Legislature of Virginia passed a law enabling the County Board of Supervisors (as it was then called) to form a company and sell stock, the county subscribing three-fifths of the stock and individuals the remaining two-fifths. Officers of the company were elected and the County Court, holding the controlling interest in the enterprise, would appoint directors to look after the road and keep it in repair, etc. The only compensation the director received was free toll for himself and his family's teams. Occasionally designing persons would try to evade the payment of toll by representing his team as belonging to the director, but the toll-gate keeper was a pretty wise old bird and usually knew all the teams in the country and the toll was collected. A "gate" would be erected directly across the road. This consisted of a long piece of timber, 6 x 6 inches at the larger end and tapering at the smaller end to about 4 x 4 inches. The larger end was fastened to a post by a huge bolt about four or five feet from the end, upon which a weight was fastened to allow the "gate" to swing up or down upon a pivot, thus describing a quarter circle upon being raised or lowered. The "gate" occupied the center of the road, either side of it being fenced to compel persons traveling in wagons to pass through the gate. A small shanty was built by the side of the road by the company, to shelter the toll-gate keeper from inclement weather or a house would be built along side the road in which he and his family lived, rent free. The keeper's wages were very small and usually some elderly person was hired who had passed his years of usefulness as a day laborer, to collect the toll. The rate established by law was two cents a mile round trip for toll for each vehicle drawn by one horse; a two-horse team, three cents, and a four-horse team, five cents. This toll, though comparatively small, amounted to a considerable sum in the course of a year, and the stock of these companies usually sold above par and paid a handsome dividend after the expenses of maintaining the road were deducted. This system of toll roads began about the year 1832 and continued through all the years to 1918, when the people, refusing to pay the toll or tax, the County Court bought the stock of the individual share holders at par and the system was abolished. Different roads were established throughout the county from time to time, an attempt to give a full history of each would be almost impossible and the reading of such would be tiresome.

In 1922 a system of roads called "Class A" roads was inaugurated in West Virginia and this system is maintained by a special levy upon the property of the county. This tax is used to maintain certain main roads of the county according to the standard prescribed by the State Road Commission for such roads and the County Court builds a few miles of this type of roads in the county each year. The roads of Berkeley County are in good condition in general and are kept in efficient repair notwithstanding the enormous amount of travel over them by automobiles and heavy laden trucks.

AVIATION.

Berkeley County has kept abreast of the development of the areoplane through the energies of a few young men, such as Alexander B. Parks, A. C. Burns, Edgar L. Henshaw, Edgar Sites, Alexander Shepherd and a few others. These were the ones who interested and attracted aviators to this locality, and it was through the constant portraying of the possibilities of Martinsburg as a link in the great chain of landing fields throughout the country that finally secured for us one of the best fields (Shepherd Landing Field), situated about two miles south of Martinsburg in a direct line. In 1916, Alexander B. Parks learned to pilot planes at Halethorp, Maryland. Prior to this time, he had been experimenting with kites and gliders, put off from the top of Berkeley Place, a suburb of Martinsburg. He became interested in the number of areoplanes seen passing east and west between Washington, D. C., and Dayton, Cincinnati and St. Louis and intervening points, and after a careful survey by him and his friends interested in aviation, it was found that the greater number of planes passed over points between Pikeside and Tablers. Before this time, several fields had been designated as a landing field around Martinsburg, in case passing planes were forced to land, such as the Kunkle field and the Patterson field, north of town, and the VanMetre field to the southeast on the Charles Town road.

Then, in 1923, the office of the Dayton-Washington Model Airway at Washington, D. C., urged the Civic Aviation Committee, as the aviation club of Berkeley County was then called, to secure, if possible, a suitable place for such a landing field. At this point Alexander Shepherd came forward with a proposition that his field was available without cost of leasing and purchase. The various activities to put the field in shape—such as leveling, scarifying, and the erection of a wind cone (an instrument to indicate the direction of the wind) was looked after by a committee under the direction of Edgar L. Henshaw. The farmers of the vicinity readily lent their aid with plows, harrows and mowers; the County Court, composed of Almon W. Smith, Jacob Hesse and Charles L. Pitzer, assisted by putting the county road to the field in first class condition; the firm of Henshaw, Hollis & Company allowed the large sign, reading "Martinsburg, W. Va.," to be printed on both sides of the roof of their large building in the western section of the city, the City Council, with Mayor Albert A. Smallwood, bearing the greater portion of this expense. The limestone companies, the Kiwanis and Rotary Clubs also lent their aid gratis.

June 17, 1923, was the date upon which the local club was to have the field inspected by the Government officials, to see if this spot met their approval or not. Captain St. Clair Streett, together with Sergeant Hooe, made a careful inspection of the field and stated that it compared favorably with the conditions laid down by the Air Service. The club was reorganized and the name changed to the Berkeley Aviation Club. Alexander B. Parks was made President, Edgar M. Sites was made Secretary, and J. Roy Nadenbousch was chosen Treasurer. On April 9, 1923, the first landing was made. In the summer of that year, officers and men of the 99th Aero Squadron and the 3d Photo Section under command of Captain C. R. Reynolds, regularly stationed at Boling Field, Washington, D. C., arrived at the field preparatory to a twelve day summer camp. The location of the landing field and its condition signally attest to the importance of it from a Governmental standpoint when it was chosen one of the many for a summer camp for this squadron. The location of this aerial site is further attested to by the fact that it is the natural western boundary for ordinary flying from Washington, the chief center of the aeronautical activities of the nation. To the westward, extending beyond Cumberland, Md., is a mountainous district overhung by cloud banks, which is very hazardous to flyers. Shepherd Field is logically situated for a landing place for the U. S. Mail flyers should they be forced to land from some unforeseen cause. It is on the direct route of this service from Washington, D. C., to Dayton, Ohio, and Detroit, Mich.

Many notables have visited this field by plane, such as Major General Mason M. Patrick, Chief of the Air Service; Brigadier General Fetchet, Assistant Chief.

Some of the "stunts" performed was one in which Captain C. R. Reynolds in company with Lieutenants Murry and Jones, using one of the older models heavy type observation plane (they weigh 3900 lbs.), flew it within a few feet of the top of St. John's Lutheran spire, following Queen Street north, occasionally just grazing the top of some of the tallest buildings. Lieutenant Norland, doing photographic work, apparently just passed the spire of St. Joseph's Catholic Church.

The first plane owned by a Berkeley County man up to this time is George A. Kershner. In the summer of 1924 a plane crashed to earth at Ridgeway. It was almost a total wreck. The pilot was not injured, as this plane fell in a field belonging to a Mr. Snapp. It was stored in his large barn awaiting the return of the aviator. He did not return and Mr. Kershner bought it at auction for $25.00 when it was sold for storage. He brought it to Martinsburg to his garage on West King Street. He repaired it and sold it to Herbert Fahy, a commercial aviator of Washington, D. C. Mr. Fahy stated that this plane was a twin to one he had flown for some time and was the only one in existence exactly like his. The owner of the plane which fell at Ridgeway was a noted and wealthy aviator, Lawrence Sperry, head of the Sperry Aircraft Corporation of Long Island, N. Y., and son of the great inventor, Elmer Sperry. Lawrence Sperry was on his way to Florida in this plane, called a "Camel", when the accident happened. He was killed about eighteen months afterward when he tried to fly from London to Paris in a tiny "Sperry Messenger". The plane was found in the English Channel, but nothing was heard of Sperry afterwards.

COMMUNICATION.

In Colonial days and in the Piedmont section of Virginia, the plantations were far apart, and the visiting was done at frequent intervals, but in this region not much time was given to this pleasure. Occasionally the "circuit rider" would arrive among the settlements with his fund of "news" of the happenings of distant localities. After the postal system had been established friends did little correspondence on account of the large postal charge on letters. The postage was paid by the recipient of the letter and as that charge was around forty cents a person would rather that a friend would think of them often and write seldom. About the beginning of the 1800's the postage was greatly reduced and letter writing became popular. The mail was carried by men on horseback in "saddle-pockets" and after the advent of the railroad was carried to remote parts in this way. Even as late as 1885 a respected and venerable employe of the Government Mail Service, a Mr. "Johnny" Kees, carried the mail from Gerrardstown to Shanghai in a "dog-cart" drawn by a mule. He made a round trip each day and never missed a mail, winter and summer, for many years.

In 1897, Perry S. Heath, then Assistant Postmaster General of the United States, originated the system of rural free delivery. Shortly after this, under the lead of Postmaster Alexander Clohan of Martinsburg, a route was established in Berkeley County, leading out of Martinsburg out Tuscarora Pike, south over the Mountain road, around by Arden and back into Martinsburg. This was designated as R. F. D. No. 1 and was the first practical route established in the State of West Virginia and the first in the county. Golden E. Hess was the first carrier, at a salary of $75.00 per month. He carried the mail on horseback. Today every section of the county is visited by a rural carrier, there being twelve well defined routes in the county.

In 1835 Samuel F. B. Morse invented the electric telegraph. The invention was used by the railroads at first and a line reached Martinsburg in the summer of 1845, being used by the Baltimore and Ohio Railroad. Messages other than those used by the railroad in dispatching trains could be sent over this line and the citizens of the county made use of it at this early date.

In 1925 the radio began to be used by many people and lines and radios were installed in their homes, and today, after a short period of two years, there is hardly a community in the county that does not possess one or more instruments.

THE TELEPHONE.

The first telephone service established in Berkeley County was at Martinsburg by a company known as the Exchange and Electric Telephone Company in 1885. This company was incorporated March 23 of that year, the charter to extend for a period of fifty years (1935). The incorporators were Newton D. Baker, later Secretary of War in President Wilson's Cabinet; John Fitz, proprietor of the Fitz Foundry and Machine Shops, Martinsburg; J. Nelson Wisner, attorney and editor of the *Martinsburg Independent;* J. S. Boak, dentist, Martinsburg; John B. Wilson, cashier of the Peoples National Bank (The Peoples Trust Company), and W. L. Jones, jeweler. There are only three of the six incorporators living: Newton D. Baker, Cleveland, Ohio, John B. Wilson of Texas and W. L. Jones of Martinsburg. The charter was granted under the laws of West Virginia by Henry S. Walker, then Secretary of State of West Virginia.

The first year of its incorporation $600 worth of capital stock was subscribed and $60.00 was paid in on subscription for the purpose of constructing and maintaining magnetic telegraph and telephone lines and lines for the use of electric light or electric uses, both underground and overhead. There were very few subscribers the first year of incorporation. Among these were W. L. Jones, jeweler; Dr. J. Whann McSherry, physician and first president of the Citizens National Bank; Charles J. Faulkner, attorney, and at that time Judge of the District Court and later United States Senator from West Virginia; Alexander Parks, now a retired business man and miller; the two banks then in existence in Martinsburg, The Peoples National Bank and the National Bank of Martinsburg; the County Court House, the jail and the Mayor's office. This company had its exchange on the third floor of what is now the Peoples Trust Company Bank building. L. DeWitt Gerhardt, the present Clerk of the Circuit Court, was one of the operators. Service was magneto, grounded circuits wall type instruments known as Emmner telephones; in fact, a Mr. Emmner of Washington, D. C., superintended the erection of their lines, installing the exchange and their instruments. Rental for service was $12.00 per year. The population of the town at that time was between six and seven thousand. There was quite a bit of opposition on the part of residents having poles erected in front of their properties and business places and stringing wires through their shade trees, but by persuasion and tactful handling of the situation on the part of the management this difficulty was overcome and the line was completed about the town. In September, 1886, this company was granted a franchise to erect poles over any of the county roads for the purpose of connecting Martinsburg up with the line of Jefferson County, Darkesville, Gerardstown, Bunker Hill, and the old Frederick County Virginia State line, also with Hedgesville, North Mountain and Williamsport, Md. No rural sections were built by this company. In October, 1887, the Exchange and Eelectric Telephone Company sold out to the Chesapeake and Potomac Telephone Company of New York for $1,000. Transfer was made by H. T. Cushwa, president, and John W. Bishop, secretary, both now deceased. At this time the company had only 75 subscribers.

Electric arc lights did not appear in Martinsburg until several years later (1893). The C. & P. Company operated the old Electric Exchange switchboard, etc., until 1898, when the exchange was moved to the Little building on Queen Street and in 1912 to the *Journal* building on West King Street, the present location. In 1898 Martinsburg was connected by wire with Hagerstown, Md., the first outside connection. On November 4, 1897, a franchise was granted the Winchester Telephone Company by the City of Martinsburg. There were two companies operating in the city until 1922, when the Chesapeake and Potomac Company purchased this line, thus eliminating the installation of two telephones by subscribers who wished for convenience to reach different sections or who were compelled by necessity to have the use of an exchange at Inwood. This was installed in the home of Mr. D. B. Shickel.

In 1902 the Winchester Telephone Company extended its service to Hedgesville, a distance of seven miles. In 1904 the Chesapeake and Potomac Telephone Company extended its line to Hedgesville, putting an instrument in the store of C. W. Hess at North Mountain (the first one at that place). Mr. Hess is conducting the same business at the same place and has been a constant subscriber from that time to the present. This company had six subscribers at Hedgesville the first year. On October 17, 1912, an exchange was installed in the home of the Misses Alice and Mary Ronk, who are still operators there. From this time the company entered upon a system of extension of lines to every section of the county and there is no part of it that does not now have the use of phone service. The manager of the telephone company, Mr. R. W. Stake, has brought the company's system up to its present high standard of efficiency by applying sound business principles to it.

Recently he has installed a new operating practice, "A Board," operating and the "combined line and recording" system of completing toll calls. This system is the simplifying of the handling of out-of-town calls to make them more like local city calls, thus enabling anyone, anywhere at any time to pick up a telephone and talk anywhere in this country clearly, quickly and at a reasonable cost. To show the magnitude to which this branch of communication has grown since 1885, the year in which two operators handled all the business of the Martinsburg Exchange, it is worthy of note that it takes ten operators continuously to do the same work at present. At least 300 out-of-town calls are handled daily besides the thousands of local city calls by these courteous operators under the management of Mr. Stake. Miss Elizabeth Grozinger has charge of the long-distance calls at this office.

CHAPTER XXVI.

SCHOOLS AND CHURCHES.

SCHOOLS.

The magnificent public school system of our county at the present day is of recent origin, and one passing through it and observing "a school house upon almost every hill top" could scarcely realize that "three score and ten" years ago there were no free schools within the county confines. Our forefathers are not to blame for this condition, but the authorities sent from the mother country to be their rulers were responsible.

Sir William Berkeley, Colonial Governor of Virginia, in making his report to the Privy Council of the King in the year 1671, said: "I thank God that there are no free schools or printing presses and I hope there will be none these hundred years, for learning has brought disobedience and heresy and sects into the world and printing has divulged these and other libels." The tyrannical and bigoted Sir William fully had his wish for instead of "these hundred years" one hundred and twenty-five years had passed away from this utterance (1796) before Virginia made a law having the semblance of a public school system and this law was ineffective until fifty years later (1846), and was amended in 1848. This amendment gave the counties the power to take advantage of it if they saw fit. Unfortunately, Berkeley County did not, but her neighbor, Jefferson, did, and in 1847, and at the beginning of the Civil War she had twenty-seven free schools in the county.

It must not be construed that the people of Berkeley County in those early times did not want educational facilities for their children. Quite the contrary! But they met no encouragement from the State authorities, until the year 1863, when Arthur I. Boreman, first Governor of West Virginia, in his annual message to the Legislature called especial attention to the constitutional provision for a free school system. The Legislature speedily enacted a school law for the State. During these early times the people of the county had excellent free schools established at Martinsburg, but they were kept up by popular subscription, and only sons and daughters of the well-to-do were able to get an education.

In order to understand why free schools were not popular in Virginia until a late period it might be well to review the economical and political conditions which existed there. In the first place, this was an agricultural region in the extreme. The farms were large, consisting often of hundreds of acres. The farmer, or "planter", as he loved to designate himself, lived upon his plantation. This necessarily caused the homes to be widely separated, and towns or hamlets were not popular. Even at a late date, when the plantations were cut up into smaller farms, the owner naturally built his home far back from the road, sometimes a mile away. Then near his home he built his barns and outbuildings, not neglecting his "slave quarters" wherein dwelt his slaves. These houses were generally built near the "great house" to be close and handy to the beck and call of their "Mars'er and Missus". Many of this kind of houses are still standing, particularly in the Shenandoah Valley section of Berkeley County, and may be seen as the traveler "whizzes" by in his high-powered automobile on the Winchester Pike.

In the second place schools for the poor or common people were scarce as the legislative body was made up almost wholly from the landed class, and they were, of course, adverse to enacting laws that would tax themselves to support free schools to educate the poorer children. The rich planter usually sent his children to private schools for which he could readily afford to pay handsomely, while the poor class could ill-afford to go to the expense of sending their children to a private school on the daily wage which they received.

Thirdly: The different classes which then existed in Virginia, the master and the slave, greatly added to the ostracism of the third or middle class. If a parent happened to be born of common people he was looked upon as an underling by the master and as common clay by the slaves themselves, the latter designating them as "po' white trash". It might be said that the slaves themselves, outside of the custom of buying and selling them, were much happier than the common laboring white man.

All these conditions extended to Berkeley County, and this is the real reason of the tardy establishment of free schools throughout the county.

About 1800, or perhaps earlier, a system of schools was inaugurated throughout the country known as the "Academy", at which schools the academic course was taught. This system had been advocated by Benjamin Franklin, and, while it developed to a surprising degree throughout the New England and Middle Atlantic States, it extended to this section of Virginia. One was established at Martinsburg, known as the Martinsburg Academy, and was located at the Old Norbourne Cemetery. One was located at Shepherdstown and one at Charles Town. These schools were maintained by popular subscription, and while they served the purpose of educating the sons and daughters of the well-to-do, the great body of the masses were not benefited.

Another factor which caused the speedy establishment of free schools in the county, after it became a part of the State of West Virginia, was the fact that many Union soldiers with their families migrated to the county. These had mostly seen service in the army in this valley and were so thrilled with the beauty and charm of the valley and the fertility of the soil that they returned after the war and purchased homes here. I might enumerate among these the Spikers, Horners, Smiths, Lords, Creques, Westphalls, Catrows, Sherards, McBrides, and a host of others which constitute the leading families of the county today. These came from a section in which free schools had long been established, and were the first to take advantage of the legislation relative to free schools.

As has been stated, the early settlers were the tutors of their children. Happily these were mostly Germans and Quakers from Pennsylvania, and were educated to the extent of reading and writing. But they had little time for the instruction of their youth. One part of their education was not neglected; that was the strict religious training, constituting of repeating verses of scripture and memorizing little prayers, poems, etc.

As time went on and the settlements became more numerous, the "circuit rider", who was a minister, would make occasional visits to the neighborhood and preach for the older folks and relate Bible stories to the children. Later on several settlers would band together and build a school house. To these houses would be gathered the youth of the neighborhood for sometimes a radius of four or five miles, the young men and young ladies in the winter and the younger in the spring and fall months. The teacher was often a stranger from parts unknown, who would announce that he would "take up" school at the school house. The tuition was two dollars a week for the pupil, the teacher "boarding around", that is, he would board two weeks with each pupil. This board was furnished free.

The teacher would instruct the pupils in the three "R's", "Readin', 'Ritin', and 'Rithmetic". Mathematics were taught to the rule of three, simple proportions, the textbook containing the fundamentals, Addition, Multiplication, Subtraction, Division, long and short, and simple proportion.

The textbook on reading consisted of short stories concluding with a moral, fables, and religious teachings. The textbook on spelling commenced with the "Abs", and generally ended with words of three syllables, diacritical markings, and phonics. For a writing exercise, the teacher "set copies", wrote a copy at the top of a page of "foolscap" which the pupil copied upon the lines below. All writing was done with a quill-pen, the boy or girl bringing the tail feathers of a hen, turkey or goose from home. The teacher would make the pen by sharpening the quill end of the feather in a shape not unlike the steel pen of the present day and they were usually expert in this line. Many of the youth became expert in the use of the pens, as can be verified by looking over the early records at the Clerk's office in the County Court House. The quill pen was universally used, steel pens not being invented until after the Civil War.

The furniture consisted in early times of slabs with six holes bored through them through which legs were thrust. Before sawmills came into use, boards were hewn flat on one side and the legs were thrust in on the other side. The teacher's desk was usually placed at the end of the room facing the door. By his side was placed the water bucket and the long-handled dipper from which all drank. These water buckets were handmade usually from mulberry wood, with handmade hoops and handle. The individual drinking cup did not come into use until about fifteen years ago when the State Legislature passed a law prohibiting the use of the common drinking cup in the schools of West Virginia. At first no blackboards were used, later boards planed to smoothness were set up and painted with black paint. These were followed by the heavy slate blackboard which cost more to install than the material itself on account of the weight, later by the composition blackboard in use to-day.

Later the pupils' desks were made of board, often an inch and a half to two inches in thickness, securely nailed to the walls and floor. These were followed by the double "patent" desk, and then by the individual desks.

The first of the schools of this description was erected at Apple Pie Ridge, or Ridge, in Gerardstown district, about the year 1842. Fifty dollars in money was raised by popular subscription, and each prominent farmer in the neighborhood furnishing free labor and the building was completed in two days. Those contributing to its erection were: W. S. Miller, Abishe VanMetre, Martin and Jacob Pitzer, William Bender, Daniel Stuckey, Tillotson Evans, George Brady, William Gladden, James Chenoweth and others. This school accommodated the pupils for miles around. The pupils thought nothing of walking five miles to and from school. It might be stated in passing that excellent work was accomplished there, for out of this school has come—

Four Sheriffs of Berkeley County; viz., John W. Pitzer, James H. Smith, Chas. L. Stuckey, Harry S. Miller.

Two Assessors: Elias M. Pitzer, David H. Stuckey.

Three members of Legislature: Chas. L. Stuckey, Benjamin F. Brady, James H. Smith.

Two County Superintendents of Schools: Willis F. Evans, E. M. Walker.

Two County Commissioners: Chas. L. Pitzer, Benjamin F. Brady.

Two Prosecuting Attorneys: Allen B. Noll, U. S. Grant Pitzer.

One Mayor Martinsburg: Thomas M. Turner.

One Minister of the Gospel: B. P. S. Busey.

Twelve Teachers in the County Schools: W. A. Pitzer, Willis F. Evan. Madeline Miller, Arlington W. Evans, Mabel E. Seibert, Clarence Townsend, Ella Lord, Mabel C .Evans, J. W. B. Evans, Ella Brady, Margaret Burkhart, Paul Turner, Frank Townsend.

Shortly after the time of the founding of the Apple Pie Ridge School a similar school was established at Three Runs, now in Mill Creek District one at Gerardsawn, and one at Hedgesville. These were practically the only schools established in Berkeley County, except in Martinsburg, prior to the Civil War.

When the first Constitutional Convention of West Virginia met, the Committee on Education put forth every effort to have a clause in it pertaining to the free school system. In this they were successful, and, with a few changes in their report, it became Article X. of the first Constitution. At the adoption of the present Constitution, the part pertaining to the free school system became Article XII.

The public school system as it now exists includes the eight grades in the country schools, and in the cities the eight grades in the ward schools. By examination the pupil is admitted to the High Schools, a course comprising four years; then if the pupil wishes to fit himself to teach, his diploma admits him to the State Normal School; if he wishes to fit himself for other professions or vocations, he is admitted to the State Preparatory Schools, of which there are two in number: one at Keyser, Mineral County, and one at

Montgomery, Fayette County. It takes two years time to complete this course and two years attendance at the West Virginia University. A diploma from this institution admits him to any college in the country. Taking into consideration that the free schools of the State are only sixty-four years old and observing the efficiency of the system and the work done by these schools, from the grade to the college, the people of West Virginia have a school system of which they might rightly be proud.

Berkeley County has a number of citizens now filling every vocation of life who have completed these courses and it is a rare instance to find within its boundaries one who has reached the age of twenty-one years and who cannot read or write.

From about the year 1872, with the liberal patronage of the State, many schools were established throughout the county. This system has grown until at the present time there are individual schools employing 175 teachers, there are eleven grade schools, two district high schools, and one secondary high school. All these are equipped with modern appliances, and the term is of eight months duration. An efficient compulsory school law compels each pupil within the county to attend some school between the ages of six and sixteen years. The largest proportion of teachers are graduates of Normal Schools or are students at them.

The school system of Martinsburg is composed of the grades or ward schools, of which there are six in number: Winchester Avenue School, Burke Street School, High Street School, Hoge Street School, and Sumner School (colored). Graduates of these schools are admitted to Martinsburg High School except the latter, whose graduates are admitted to Storer College at Harper's Ferry. This is a State institution for colored students supported by the State.

In 1884 the present High School was established on South Queen Street. It was made a high school in 1902, being formerly designated as a "Grammar School". In that year it underwent extensive improvements. Owing to the overcrowded condition of the building, the people of the city by an overwhelming majority voted a bond issue of $310,000.00 and a new high school building is in the course of construction on South Queen Street on the historic grounds purchased by the Board of Education from the estate of Hon. Chas. J. Faulkner.

THE HEDGESVILLE HIGH SCHOOL.

The first building was built in 1866. It was a one-room log building costing in the aggregate $1500.00. It was built to accommodate the children of the town of Hedgesville proper, although children from afar attended this school. The President of the Board of Education of Hedgesville District at that time was R. Bodine. The Commissioners were Jacob French and T. L. Harper. James Robinson was Clerk. The amount of salary paid the Principal (one teacher) was $40.00 per month.

In 1884 the old building was torn down and a new building was erected of brick. This was a four-room graded school; two rooms were added later, and in 1888 two more rooms were added and the school was made a first class high school with the grades added. The members of the Board of Education at that time were as follows: President, Wm. H. Kilmer; Commissioners, Wm. J. Cunningham and Wm. G. Siler, and Secretary, Geo. W. McAllister.

In 1925 the people of the district, by a majority of popular vote, voted a seventy-five thousand dollar bond issue. The building was completed in the fall of 1926. The members of the Board of Education at that time were: President, A. Hunter Walker; Commissioners, James Dillon and J. W. Armbrester. The corps of teachers consisted of four grade teachers and three high school teachers. All the buildings mentioned above have occupied the same site. It is the best location for a school in the county. It occupies one of the foothills of North Mountain and overlooks the beautiful Shenandoah Valley.

The present and first principal to occupy the new high school building is R. L. Rice. He is a graduate of West Virginia University with the class of 1925, and has the degree of A.B.

Notes on Hedgesville District Schools.—Dr. Thomas J. Harley, Jacob Ropp and Thomas L. Harper, School Commissioners for Hedgesville District, met in the village of Hedgesville, April 16, 1866, and organized the schools of the district by establishing schools in nine sub-divisions, viz.: Hedgesville, Little Georgetown, Johnsontown, Silers, Tomahawk, Ptzier's Mill, Dry Run, Welltown and North Mountain. George W. McAllister was Clerk of the Board. Out of Little Georgetown School has come twelve teachers, Samuel L. Dodd, David Henry Dodd, Christopher C. Tabler, Ella Dodd Williamson, Adah Dodd-Poince, Robert LeFevre, Harry Faulkwell, Richard Hammersla, Rose Hammersla, Hester Dugan Davis, Esther V. Tabler and Helen I. Tabler-Gletner; three County superintendents, S. L. Dodd, C. C. Tabler and D. H. Dodd; and one novelist, Adah Dodd-Poince.

Below is an official directory of the school system of the county, 1927-1928, which consists of extracts taken from a pamphlet entitled "School Directory, Berkeley County, W. Va.", printed and published by Bessie D. Kilmer, County Superintendent of Schools of Berkeley County:

County Superintendent—Bessie D. Kilmer.

Council of Education—Bessie D. Kilmer, Robert Allison, A. L. Rodgers, A. N. Burgess, Sadah Miller, Mary Needy, Katharine Nihion, Katharine Brady, Carrie M. Barnhart, Ella Strong.

ARDEN DISTRICT.

Board of Education—President, Henry J. Seibert; Commissioner, G. Oliver Noll; Commissioner, John Brown; Secretary, Edith Miller.

Schools and Teachers—Pikeside Consolidated, Margaret Burkhart, Edna Seibert, Mrs. Oscar B. Miller, Edith Miller; Baker, Clara D. Smallwood; Fairview, Katharine Nihion, Lucy Miller; Forest Hill, Minnie M. Pownall; Green Hill, Helen Cushwa; New Haven, Mildred Tabler; Tuscarora, Mildred Zeilor; VanMetre, Blanch G. Files; Vanclevesville, Virginia Blue; Douglas Grove, Estelle Shepherd.

SCHOOLS AND CHURCHES 299

FALLING WATERS DISTRICT.

Board of Education—President, C. M. Solenberger; Commissioner, Frank LeMaster; Commissioner, William Miller; Secretary, W. H. Keller.

Schools and Teachers—Marlowe Junior High, A. H. Burgess, Ara Keesecker; Marlowe Graded, Sarah Burdette, Caroline Branham, Amanda Bane, Rachael Needy, Rineal Hammersla, Clara Harris; Spring Mills, Eleanor Light; Beddington, Bess Miller; Knipetown, Jean Harlan.

GERARDSTOWN DISTRICT.

Board of Education—President, J. C. Aikens; Commissioner, G. W. Pitzer; Commissioner, Carl Slonaker; Secretary, Katherine S. Brady.

Schools and Teachers—Gerardstown Graded, Elizabeth Smith, Irma McBride; Shanghai, Mabel C. Evans, Carrye M. Barnhart; Jones Spring, Hilda Beall; Glengary, Nora Whitacre; Ganotown, Bessie Hite; Mt. Carmel, Ella Brady; McCubbin, Elizabeth Lewis; Buck Hill, Willis F. Evans; Smith, Bertha Carter, Corrine Eversole; Needmore, Cora B. Luttrell; Ridge, Madaline Miller; Union Corner, Katherine Brady; Cedar Hill, Ruth Cooper; Mt. Pleasant, James W. Walker.

HEDGESVILLE DISTRICT.

Board of Education—President, Cecil W. Woods; Commissioner, Arthur Stuckey; Commissioner, J. W. Armbruster; Secretary, George Kilmer.

Schools and Teachers—Hedgesville High, A. L. Rodgers, Ruth McCombs, Joseph Prettyman; Hedgesville Graded, Jane, Riner, Eliza Branhan, Naomi Landis, Maggie Riner; Cedar Hill, Katherine Holly; Little Georgetown, Rosa L. Hammersla; Johnsontown, Flora M. Barnes; Mingo, Kathleen Johnson; Greenwood, Willard Coffinbarger; Welltown, Oscar Butts; Columbus, C. C. Tabler; Locust Grove, Charles W. Stuckey; Dry Run, Virginia Sperow, Emma Fishel Armbrester; Tomahawk, Edgar Saville, Retha Edwards; Good Hope, Hilda Lemaster; Baxter, William B. Rooney; Cross Roads, Dorothy M. Nelson; Oak Grove, Nelson F. Kees.

MILL CREEK DISTRICT.

Board of Education—President, L. C. Hoffman; Commissioner, Dr. Edgar LeFevre; Commissioner, Morris Snapp; Secretary, Anna Mary Henshaw.

Schools and Teachers—Bunker Hill High, Robert E. Allison, Orin J. Beard, Elizabeth Trump; Bunker Hill Graded, D. M. Hook, Esther Homer, Leona Thatcher, Mildred Bowers; Inwood Graded, Ella Strong, Julia Staub, Virginia Stuckey; Ridgeway, Gladys Pitzer; Pine Grove, Sabine Lewis; Cedar Grove, A. F. Newbraugh; Fairview, Virginia Gould Clendenning; Darkesville, Cora Lee Ford.

OPEQUON DISTRICT.

Board of Education—President, Thomas Sine; Commissioner, Maud Welshans; Commissioner, Rev. Hesse; Secretary, J. H. Myers.

Schools and Teachers—Newtown, Eleanor Williams; Greensburg, Leota Whiting; Smoketown, Gertrude Jones; Fairview, Susan Staley; Ridenour, Genie Banks; Oak Grove, Elizabeth Sperow, Martha Grubbs; Scrabble, Adna Bender; Eagles, J. W. Eversole; Mt. Airy, Mary Needy; Friendship, Virginia Newkirk; Blairton, Rachael Caskey, Isabelle Payne; Berkeley, Quay Keesecker, Irine Lemaster Riser; Blairton (col.), Daisy Taylor Baitty.

MARTINSBURG PUBLIC SCHOOLS.

Board of Education—President, John L. Schroder; Vice-President, James S. Shipe; Commissioner, T. W. Martin; Commissioner, J. R. Poland; Commissioner, J. R. Heck; Secretary, Lee Siler.

Administration and Supervision—Superintendent of Schools, L. W. Burns; Art Supervisor, Alice K. Ort; Music Supervisor, Grace M. Oliver; Attendance Officer, E. J. Fulk; Secretary to Superintendent, Mary Moran.

High School Faculty—E. E. Church, Margaret E. Baker, Elizabeth A. Battle, Helen Bryan Bentz, Lelia M. Bitner, Vannetta Chambers, Charles G. Gain, Lois Latham, Adelyn I. Miller, Katharin H. Miller, G. D. Mullin, Nellie Offutt, Mrs. A. C. Phillips, Lena M. Reed, L. A. Ruckman, Duane D. Smith, Elena E. Spielman, Edna Stevens.

Burke Street School—O. L. Snyder, Principal; Mollie E. Trout, Della B. Hill, Lorena J. Mason, Helen M. Ellis, Florence M. Curtis, Minnie G. Chamberlin, Alberta Chambers.

High Street School—D. H. Dodd, Principal; M. Adah Mason, Beatrice R. Locke, Lillian M. VanMetre, Elizabeth Chambers, Ruth M. Pitzer, Helen M. Smith, Kathryn Williams, Ella E. Swartz.

Hooge Street School—J. B. Martin, Principal; Elsie Quigley, Ruth Ridgeway, Josina T. Showers, Lille D. Mullen, Zella I. Shade, Mollie E. Martin, Ethel Hollida.

John Street School—Lee Siler, Principal; George N. O'Brien, Katharine R. Laise, Grace E. Lindsey, Frances L. Henshaw, Ruth K. Kilmer, Jessie B. Smith, Sara E. Kidwell, Alice Bowers, Dora E. Wolfensberger, Maude G. Kuykendall.

Winchester Avenue School—Paul E. Sherard, Principal; Virginia A. Beckert, J. C. Kidwiler, Helen Little, Sula M. DeHaven, Virginia Koonce, Margaret Ropp, Hilda Doggett, Helen Matthews, Maude Hollida, Louise Griffith, Lillie Karnes, Frances Ramsburg, Sue E. Henson.

Sumner School (Colored)—Fred R. Ramer, Principal; M. F. Griggs, Marion G. Scott, Tanner L. Johnson, Juanita A. Ramer, Matilda S. Green, Sadie B. Crane, Mattie E. Corsey.

CHURCHES.

The first emigrants to our section of the Valley of Virginia were from Pennsylvania, Maryland and New Jersey and were adherents to the religious sects of Lutherans, Catholics, Mennonists (Mennonites), Quakers and a few Tunkers (Dunkards). The settlers were deeply religious notwithstanding the fact that no churches were built till later. They held their religious services at some of the homes of these, where "circuit riders" would make priodical visits and preach for the people, baptize, and read burial services of those who had died in the interval since his last visit.

These forms of religious gatherings were in vogue long before the first churches were established. But as soon as communities began to grow a little, churches began to be founded. These were erected in the woods by logs procured from the surrounding forest and built by free labor; all the community helping, the men erecting the house, the women furnishing the food for the laborers.

The first church erected west of the Blue Ridge Mountains was the old Presbyterian Church built on Tuscarora Creek about 1750, a quarter of a century after the building of the first cabin home in Berkeley County. It is still used as a public place of worship and the burying ground for burial purposes. The present edifice is of stone and replaced the first log structure. People of that faith attended that church from a long distance as is shown by the McKowns who attended it and lived at Gerardstown. (See Biography of Samuel McKown.)

Another of the early church edifices was a Baptist Meeting House near the Opequon Creek. The spot where it stood is at the top of the long hill on the State Road leading from Martinsburg to Charles Town just beyond the bridge which crosses that stream. The only mark to show where it once stood is a few scattered grave stones. This building was erected in 1754 through the efforts of Rev. John Gerard, a Baptist minister, who came from New Jersey.

The Quakers settled in the southern part of the county at an early period but did not erect any church until 1781, when one was built at Arden which was the first of that denomination built in the county. Hedges Church (or chapel) on Back Creek near Jones Spring is another early church, probably the oldest in that valley. Tradition relates that George Washington attended this church while on surveying expeditions at what is now Berkeley Springs.

St. John's Lutheran Church—The Lutheran Congregation was one of the oldest in the Lower Shenandoah Valley and the largest. Baptist congregations were established before this one but they were small. The Lutheran congregation was founded in 1775, and ten years later a regular pastor took charge. Rev. Christian Streit also took charge of a circuit embracing the Counties of Frederick, Jefferson and Berkeley. He served as Bishop over the circuit until 1790.

In Martinsburg, the first church for this congregation was located on the northwest corner of Church and John Streets and was used jointly by the Lutheran and Reformed congregations. This building was first erected for a tavern by Jacob Shortel but was afterwards purchased by these congregations and jointly used as a house of worship by them. The two lots extending from John to King Streets were also purchased at the same time and used as a burying ground by these two congregations. On June 10, 1832, the corner stone of a new edifice was laid. This was located at the present site of the Lutheran Church, southwest corner of Queen and Martin Streets, the lot having been purchased from Jacob Shoppert. This building was erected at a cost of $3,786.50. This church was improved in 1854 and a large bell placed in the belfry. This church was used as a hospital for both armies in the Civil War and was, in consequence, considerably damaged. It was again remodeled in 1884—this cost being $10,000. In the first building the plastering laths were riven out by an instrument called a "fro" and were fastened to the walls by grooves cut in the logs. The first pipe organ used in this church was worked by ropes and weighted down by stones.

Trinity (Episcopal) Church—The original Norbourn Parish included the County of Frederick, which at that time included the Counties of Jefferson, Berkeley and Morgan (W. Va.). There were three churches within the limits of this parish: the one at Bunker Hill and founded by Morgan Morgan—a minister of that church—in 1740, and the first Episcopal church west of the Blue Ridge; the one built shortly afterwards at Hedgesville and the one founded at Mecklenburg (Shepherdstown), built by Van Swearingen. In 1769, Norbourn Parish was taken from the Frederick Parish, and when Jefferson County was formed in 1802, that part was taken from Norbourn Parish.

The first Episcopal church in Martinsburg was built shortly after the close of the Revolutionary War at the entrance of Norbourn Cemetery. This cemetery, with lands for the church grounds, was laid out by General Adam Stephen and established by law in 1778. It was built by Philip Pendleton, Esq. This building continued in use until 1835, when the old building, becoming unsafe, steps were taken to erect a new church in the town. The lot upon which the present building now stands on West King Street being donated, a new edifice was erected thereon and in 1843 it was dedicated. This church also was used as a hospital for wounded soldiers for both armies in the Civil War and was damaged to such an extent that repairs were necessary before the builIding could be used for public worship. In 1848, Norbourn Parish was divided and included Mt. Zion Church at Hedgesville, Calvary Church, Back Creek, and Trinity Church, Martinsburg.

First Baptist Church, Martinsburg—This church was organized in 1858 with ten members. The first pastor was Rev. J. W. Jones. The congregation used the stone building which was formerly the Martinsburg Academy, which stood near the Norbourn Cemetery, for the first two years of its existence. In 1859, the lot upon which the church now stands on West King Street was purchased with the intention of erecting a church building thereon but the Civil War scattered the members and nothing was done until after the war, or 1869, when, in the spring of that year, a building was begun on this lot. In the interval of the Civil War, preaching was occasionally held at the Reformed and Lutheran Churches. The first pastor to preach in the new church was Rev. W. S. Penick, who also served a term as County Superintendent of Schools of Berkeley County. In May, 1870, the Sunday School was organized. The cost of this building and furniture was $7,364.43. In 1921, the present commodious building was opened for service.

Presbyterian Church, Martinsburg—This church was organized from the congregation of the old Tuscarora Presbyterian Church on Tuscarora Creek in April, 1825. The present manse on South Queen Street was built at a cost of $6,000. The first pastor of this church was Rev. John Matthews (1827). He also preached at Charles Town and Shepherdstown jointly before he came to Martinsburg. Rev. Matthews and all the succeeding pastors have had the old mother church at Tuscarora in charge. Rev. F. M. Woods was the pastor in charge for nearly half a century (1879 to 1926), resigning this position then on account of old age infirmities.

Catholic Church—The first services of this denomination was held at the home of John Timmons on West Race Street in 1810. This continued to be the meeting place of this sect until 1830, when a small building was erected at St. Joseph's Cemetery. This was built on grounds donated by Richard McSherry at a cost of $4,000. The stone work of the present church was begun by Father Plunkett, but had to stop on account of funds. Rev. Andrew Talty, his assistant, afterwards raised the money to finish it. There were a pair of wooden stairs in front of the building but Rev. J. J. Kain afterwards had them removed for the present stone ones. The present building stands on South Queen Street and is an imposing edifice. The exterior is of brick walls with a massive stone frontage. Inside it contains a beautiful marble altar. This building was greatly damaged during the war as the Jessie Scouts used it for a stable for seventy horses and used the Sacristy rooms as prisons. Captain Kyd Douglass was imprisoned here for six months. This edifice cost altogether about $40,000 and required about ten years in building.

The St. Joseph Parochial School was taught for a long time in the basement of the church, when, in 1883, the congregation purchased the Judge Hall property on East Stephen Street. In 1900 this was enlarged until this school is one of the largest in the county. The Sisters of Charity from Emmittsburg, Md., took charge in 1883.

Reformed Church—This congregation was founded by German emigrants to the Shenandoah Valley from Pennsylvania. They worshipped in connection with the Lutherans in the building of that denomination on the corner of Church and John Streets until in 1846, the congregation becoming too large, the Reformed congregation purchased the lot on East Burke Street, where the present edifice now stands, and erected a church for $5,000. The services were formerly conducted in the German language but has been supplanted by the English on account of the younger members not being familiar with the German. It owned the first church bell of any denomination in the county, having been purchased and placed in the belfry in 1808.

Methodist Episcopal Church—The first Methodist Episcopal Church west of the Blue Ridge was erected on East John Street south of where the King's Daughters Hospital is now located (1789) and the first sermon preached by that denomination west of the Blue Ridge was delivered by Rev. Bishop Francis Asbury at the Market House in Martinsburg on Sunday, June 2, 1782. The congregation was called together by blowing a tin horn, they being opposed to the ringing of church bells. The ritual of the church opposed slavery and this led to a division of the church in 1846, those favoring slavery withdrawing and forming a separate branch known as the Methodist Episcopal Church South. The Methodist denomination grew steadily, being popular with the people on account of making no distinction in the social standing of its members, and was at one time termed "the church of the common people". During the Civil War the congregation was scattered and no services were held as a body except at irregular intervals, when some traveling preacher held services. In 1863 the old church edifice on John Street being partially destroyed, the lot on the corner of German Street (Maple Avenue) and Burke Street was purchased and the present edifice erected. The original church contained one of the tallest spires in the city, but this being thought unsafe, was torn down to the roof of the church building and a dome placed over this part and the necessary repairs made.

Methodist Episcopal Church South—In 1866 this society was organized by Rev. David Short and John A. Kearn. Their first place of worship was on King Street in a small school building. The membership was fifteen. In 1867 they erected an edifice on Maple Avenue for $3,500 and worshiped there until the year 1886, when they purchased the present site on West Martin Street from Frederick Becker.

United Brethren Church—This church was founded by William Otterbein and Martin Boehm. William Otterbein was a minister in the German Reformed Church and Martin Boehm a member of the Mennonite Church. They wished to promote a church in which the cold formalities of their mother churches would be eliminated and to promote spiritual membership. These two earnest, Christian men were first brought together at a great union meeting of the churches held in Isaac Long's barn in Lancaster County, Pennsylvania. Mr. Boehm preached a powerful sermon and so stirred Mr. Otterbein that he arose at the close of the discourse and embraced Mr. Boehm and exclaimed, "We are brethren." The multitude, stirred by this demonstration of Christian fellowship and good will, adopted the name "United Brethern" for their new denomination was here organized. The words, "In Christ',, were afterwards added to distinguish it from the Moravian United Brethren. In 1774 the first organization of a church was made at Baltimore, Md. In 1856 the congregation of Martinsburg was organized, and in 1857 the first U. B. Church was erected. It was located on Penn Avenue. The old church building was badly damaged during the Civil War. Since that time a much larger edifice has been erected and it contains one of the largest congregations of any church in the city.

The Second Baptist Church is located on North High Street and contains a large congregation.

Mount Zion Baptist Church—This church, located near Kearneysville, in Berkeley County, was erected in 1838, the land having been deeded to the Baptist denomination, June 11, 1836. The first trustees were Josiah Gorrell, Abraham VanMetre, Jacob Walters, John Burns and Benjamin F. Burns. The congregation becoming small, the church was closed, but the burying grounds are still used for that purpose.

Winchester Avenue Christian Church—The present church building was erected in 1901 on the corner of Winchester Avenue and Stephen Street. The first Christian Church, or Disciples of Christ, was founded at Johnsontown in Back Creek Valley. Later churches of this denomination were located at Tomahawk, Martinsburg and at Vanville, east of Darkesville. Tomahawk Church was erected in 1913 and Vanville Church in 1918. The present pastor, Rev. Roy C. Schmucker, has been the pastor of these churches for the last thirteen years.

Free Will Baptist Church (Colored)—This church was built after the Civil War by the Home Mission Society under the supervision of Miss A. S. Dudley, of Maine, a general missionary among the negroes of America. The Rev. M. C. Brackett and A. H. Morrel assisted the church in its early struggles. This church was built on North Raleigh Street at a cost of $2,500 and a parsonage built with it for $500.

The Methodist Episcopal Church (Colored)—This congregation was founded after the Civil War. The first edifice was erected on the present site of the church on West Martin Street. It was torn down and the present new brick building erected in its place.

From these above denominations have sprung other churches throughout the county—these have mostly been built to accommodate the people in which community they stand. At Spring Mills, a Presbyterian Church; at Johnstown, a Dunkard Church; at Providence, a U. B. Church; at Jones Springs, a Methodist and a U. B. Church; at Shanghai, a Presbyterian Church; Central, United Brethren; Ganotown, Methodist; at Mt. Carmel, United Brethren; at Buck Hill, Union; at Gerardstown, Presbyterian, two Methodist and Lutheran; at Needmore, Lutheran; at Mountain Chapel, Presbyterian; at Salem, United Brethren; at Arden, Methodist; at Pitzer's Chapel, Methodist; on Tuscarora, Presbyterian; at Marlowe, Methodist; at Falling Waters, Presbyterian; at Berkeley, Presbyterian and Methodist; at Scrabble, Presbyterian; at Blairton, United Brethren; at Vanclevesville, Dunkard; at Mt. Zion, Baptist; at Tablers, Presbyterian; at Pikeside, United Brethren; at Pleasant Plane, United Brethren; at Vanvllie, Christian; at Darkesville, Methodist and Methodist (Colored); at Inwood, United Brethren; at Bunker Hill,

Methodist, Episcopalian and Presbyterian; at Ridgeway, Methodist; at Payne's Chapel, Methodist; at Butler's Chapel, Methodist; at Beddington, Methodist; at Swan Pond, Presbyterian.

The Jewish Synagogue is located on East Pennsylvania Avenue. It was formerly the United Brethren Church, but when that denomination erected its present edifice the Jewish congregation purchased this edifice and now use it for church purposes.

The Quaker Church at Arden—In the year 1779, Benjamin Thornburg gave a deed for one acre of land at this place to Jacob Moon, James Mendenhall, Anthony Lee and Stephen Thatcher in trust, "for the erection of a church for the worshipping of God, the education of the Youth and the burial of the Dead, as may be found necessary." This plot of ground was given to the religious sect commonly called Quakers, although no mention of that fact was made in the deed. A church was erected there the next year and continued to be used by that denomination until 1873 when the Methodist Episcopal Church South purchased the building and they continued to use the old building until 1915 when the present commodious building was erected. In view of the fact that the deed for the ground upon which the church stood was to be used "for the education of the Youth" and that the Quakers "were no respectors of persons", in 1880, the colored people of Arden vicinity asked that a school house be erected there for the education of their children. This was not granted. However, a brick building was erected by the Arden Board of Education near here on the Arden-Tabler road for their use and is known as Locust Grove School of that District.

CHAPTER XXVII.

THE "FLU" EPIDEMIC.

Below is given a history of the "Flu" epidemic which swept the country in the fall of 1918, and was very severe in Berkeley County. This description was given the author by Hon. Allen B. Noll, who was appointed by the County Court of Berkeley County to take charge of the situation in the county during that malady. Mr. Noll was Prosecuting Attorney of the county also. His description of that scourge and how he handled the situation is given in his own words.

I was among one of the first victims and had partially recovered when the big battle started. I shall detail chronologically what happened in order that it may be better followed. It may appear to you that I am more or less personal but from the statements and facts which will hereafter appear, you will understand why this is more or less necessary.

This dreadful scourge struck this county about the ending of the Federal Court at the September Term 1918. Over one hundred Federal prisoners, in addition to our own prisoners, were crowded into our county jail, several times over its capacity and creating a condition that was very dangerous to the inmates. I had occasion, before these prisoners were removed, to go to the jail, accompanied by Mr. R. H. Boyd, and the coughing we heard upon that occasion was so unusual it caused me to inquire of Mr. M. S. Miller, the jailer, what was the matter and he replied that they were all sick and I asked if he had gotten a doctor and he said "Yes". In a day or two they were removed to various jails in the State and several died before they reached Keyser. We had a prisoner in jail, by the name of Hovart, who was represented by R. H. Boyd. His trial was set for the 27th of September, 1918, and he was brought to the court room and arraigned. He was a very ill man and Mr. Boyd asked for a continuance, to which I agreed as I, at that time, was ill with the "flu" myself. However, Hovart would not agree to it and wanted to go to trial. The case consumed practically all day and after the verdict he was sentenced. That was a sad day for Berkeley County but we did not know it at that time. Behind Hovart sat Edmund P. Hunter, a most competent attorney, a likeable fellow and a gentleman. In three or four days he died. State Senator Williams from the Eastern Shore of Maryland, who represented a client awaiting trial to follow the Hovart case, went home and in three or four days he died. D. C. Casto, a resident of Parkersburg, W. Va., another attorney who volunteered to assist Mr. Boyd in the defense of Hovart, went home and in three days he was dead. These men were apparently in elegant, physical condition. The Honorable J. M. Woods went down and it was his last appearance on the Bench during that term, except by Special Judges, also, Mr. L. D. Gerhardt, Clerk, both of whom were very ill. Mr. E. L. Luttrell, who was Assistant Prosecuting Attorney in the Hovart trial, went home and his wife and all of his children went down. Just how many did carry away from the court room this contagious disease no one can tell, but I am safe in saying from the date of the Hovart trial it spread all over the City of Martinsburg and into the county.

Conditions became so bad that the business men held a meeting and appointed Mr. Frank C. Foreman to wait upon the County Court and the Y. M. C. A. likewise held a meeting and appointed Mr. Walter Trout to join with the business men's association to take action. They met the County

Court on the afternoon of the 8th of October, 1918, and I was sent for. I reported and expressions of fear and doubt over the situation were very freely expressed and discussed. The Court finally appointed a committee of three, consisting of Messrs. Walter Trout, Frank C. Foreman and myself, to deal with the situation. I complained to the Court, at the time, that I was ill and someone else should have charge of the work. They stated to me that all I would have to do would be to look after the expenditure of the money. I finally consented to do that much and they entered an order directing me to spend $1,000.00 in any way I saw fit.

The committee met together immediately and discussed the situation. First of all, we determined to ascertain what the situation was. We decided to divide up the drug stores and find out from them what they were doing. I, personally, was assigned to West King Street, where the drug stores of Messrs. Kogelschatz and Martin were located. I approached Mr. Kogelschatz's store first and there I found a line of twenty to twenty-five waiting to have prescriptions filled. I broke through the line and reached the window and asked Mr. Kogelschatz what it meant. He was haggard, worn out and could hardly stand upon his feet. His reply was, "I do not know but something terrible has happened." I left and went to Martin's store and there I found the same conditions to exist. Meeting the committee, at the appointed hour, the reports were that the same conditions existed in all the drug stores in town. We then began to realize, for the first time, just what a fight we had ahead of us and determined to call all the doctors together in consultation. We summoned them to appear October 8th at 12 o'clock at night at the Mayor's office, and everyone was there, except those who had gone down. This was a memorable conference and expressions were freely made by them to the effect that they did not know what it was nor how to treat it. The general consensus, however, was that heart stimulants, perspiration and fresh air were the best they could do. We decided the town should be divided into zones and physicians assigned to them and the calls to come in to headquarters and to be transmitted by headquarters to the physician in charge. This plan was adopted and afterwards carried out with much success. I might say, in this connection, that many stricken families would call a half a dozen physicians. One would finally respond, then another one would go, only to find that a doctor had already been to see them. The zone proposition was meant and intended to avoid the overlapping and centralize the work of the physician. For example, I went to Dr. Tonkin's office to inspect his calls, just for the information it would give me, and the young lady showed me his list, which, at that time, was near seventy-five. No doctor, of course, could possibly meet such a mass of unfinished business, however urgent it might be. Other doctors were in the same predicament, hence, the zone proposition, which was a great success.

I now pass into another stage of this great battle. We immediately charted the town into zones, opened headquarters and put Mr. Baker Sefton in charge, with orders to employ such help as he needed to carry on his work. The newspapers were advised of our action and calls immediately began to come in through headquarters. Upon a large sheet of paper each call was registered, in its respective zone, and the physician notified. In the meantime, people were dying everywhere. We closed down all places of public amusement and schools. Mr. Trout's brother, Horace Trout, went down and we lost the valuable services of Mr. Walter Trout, when we needed him most. He did everything he could to save his brother, who was a stalwart young man, but it could not be done. The deaths became so numerous and the question of digging graves so serious that Mr. Foreman took charge of that end of the work. He was then building an addition to the Berkeley Woolen Co., and not being able to secure men to dig graves, he closed down his work and used his entire force, all that were left of them, for the work, and in this connection I want to say they did not cost Berkeley County a cent, and the citizens of Martinsburg owe Mr. Foreman a debt of gratitude which they can never pay, and I might add here, with all the force he was able to muster, at times he would be behind as many as twenty-five bodies a day, so you can see what a job he had on his hands.

The chief work assigned to me was to look after the organization of the hospitals and do general utility work. Four or five of our most active doctors went down and were of no service to us. The nurses in the hospitals went down and volunteers had to be furnished. Many could have been found under ordinary conditions, but when they had sickness in their own homes, without a physician, they were hard to get. It became my duty to furnish volunteer nurses for each hospital every night and to report at 4 o'clock in the morning to look the situation over. I kept in touch with the number of deaths in the hospitals and made my reports through the newspapers, which were meant and intended to quiet the public as we did not dare let them know how much sickness and how many deaths there really were. We took a further precaution to advise ourselves of the conditions by thoroughly canvassing the First and Fourth Wards. This was done from house to house and a report was made and, by estimation, there were six thousand cases in Martinsburg at that time. This was done early in our fight and we well knew the terrible consequences that were bound to come but we did not let the public know it.

Conditions did not improve but went from bad to worse. We appealed to the Government for medical assistance and they did send us one doctor, who was a lady. I have forgotten her name but she was most efficient and a hard worker. We wired all over the country for nurses and finally landed three in Wheeling, W. Va., one of whom reported. She went to work and lasted about one day, when she went down and became a serious liability instead of an asset. We were running short of caskets and Mr. Foreman handed Mr. H. M. Cole $600.00 in cash and told him to go to the cities and buy caskets. He left and, after a day and night trip to Washington, Baltimore, Philadelphia and New York, returned with four caskets, which was the best he could do. We then decided we would have to make our own caskets and that perhaps the Auburn Wagon Company could make them. We sent for Mr. Bradford and he came to my house, while I was taking my afternoon rest. There he agreed to build all we needed, provided the Government would release him from the work in which he was engaged, permit him to use Government material and we would furnish him a pattern. I left my home in search of Joseph Artz and, as luck would have it, I found him on the street near the Berkeley Hotel. He agreed to build a form for the Auburn Wagon Company to go by and immediately set to work to do it. It took him several hours to complete his work. In the meantime, I wired the War Department for permission to use the Auburn Wagon Company and its material for the purpose of building caskets and they wired back to proceed, without further notice. We inspected the caskets, which were built out of kiln-dried, white oak and, I should say, the best material that ever went into a casket in Berkeley County. I wish to say, in this connection, when I came to pay the bill, the average cost was $24.50. Our rough boxes were built by the Berkeley Lumber Company and, if my recollection serves me rightly, cost us about $9.00 each.

The situation, by this time, was very acute and became most alarming. There was nothing to do but the best we could, under the circumstances. The veterinary surgeons, Drs. J. C. Wolf, Geo. W. Wolf, E. T. Hott and Roy S. Proctor, went to work and deserve honorable mention for their services. With their help we were not able to do the work, so we called in the dentists, who were assigned to various zones to answer the calls that came to headquarters. Without them, we would have failed utterly. They worked night and day. We ran out of medicine and we sent Mr. Kogelschatz to Baltimore for a supply. He had hardly arrived here until it was all gone and then we had to dispatch another messenger. The drug store of W. H. Hague had gone into the hands of a receiver and we forcibly entered it and took all the medicine we could find that would help us, which, of course, was carefully inventoried and paid for afterwards. The dentists, in the Mayor's office, on a table in the rear room, filled the general prescription which we had. This was on the eve of "Black Friday" when we lost one hundred souls, but the crest was broken and the tide began to subside.

And now, to give you some idea of what happened and the things with which we had to contend, I wish to relate one or two instances that should not go unnoticed.

Mr. Z. T. Brantner met me one morning on the street and told me of a family at Bedington where Rev. Steelman had gone to preach a funeral. Upon arriving there, the neighbors told him not to go near the house as they were suffering with a very contagious disease and he thought I ought to know it. I told him I certainly did want to know it and would look into the matter at once. I sent for Harry S. Miller, Sheriff, and told him what I had heard and asked him to investigate the case and he said he would. He took two men with him and drove to the home of a Mr. Price, at Bedington, entered the house and found the father, the mother and two half-grown children all dead. Again, I was stopped by Mr. McIntyre, the painter, who advised me he thought something was wrong in a cabin at the Kelly Island Quarry and it ought to be investigated. I again sent for the Sheriff and he went out. He found both the father and mother dead in bed and a new-born babe, also dead, on the top of a dresser. These were awful things to occur in a civilized community but we were powerless to prevent them. I might as well say, here and now, that the work of Harry S. Miller, who threw away his mask, was most efficient and consistent and the people of Berkeley County owe him a debt of gratitude they will never be able to pay.

There were many other incidents which I could relate but I cannot refrain from indulging one other. We were compelled to secure a morgue, which we did, across College Alley from the Berkeley Hotel stable. We placed four bodies in this morgue and assigned Mr. Miflin Pyles to look after them. We were using the mausoleum in Green Hill but we had it filled and outside accommodations had to be secured. We obtained the caskets necessary to dispose of the bodies in the morgue. I went with Mr. Pyles one morning about 10 o'clock to look after the matter. He unlocked the door and the odor that struck me hurled me across College Alley until I hit the wall of the stable. Anyone who has not experienced it cannot realize what it was like. I finally got my breath and I said to Pyles, "Didn't I tell you to put those windows up?", and he replied, "They are nailed down and I can't do it." I said, "Get something and break every window at once." He put his mask on, grabbed a piece of board and did as I directed. The bodies were then removed and buried. I wish to say, in this connection, that Mr. Pyles was a good man, worked hard and deserves honorable mention.

The most serious part of my work was providing nurses for the hospitals. This had to be done by 10 o'clock at night and 9 o'clock in the morning and was practically all volunteer service. Great credit is due to George W. Wolf, Samuel Young, J. E. Roderick, Charles L. Davidson, Bruce Engle, Mrs. Guy Felker and a half a score of others who assisted and worked practically night and day in the hospitals. The importance of the work they did cannot be overestimated. For example, we had planned to manage the City Hospital with an additional force of four men and they reported but not one of them stayed. Interviewing one of them, as he was leaving, he frankly stated it was work he could not do and would have to quit and he did. It was that night that George W. Wolf and Mrs. Calvin Heberlig had charge of twenty-four patients in one ward. The men they had to assist them left and the two undertook to fight it out themselves. When the morning came they had lost six, four of whom, Mr. Wolf told me, he thought he could have saved had he the necessary help. He explained the situation to me in this way, that the patients would reach a point where they were semi-delirious and could not be kept in their cots. If two of them would quiet down, a half a dozen would be prowling around in the ward and it was impossible to keep them in their beds. I went to the City Hospital one evening to see George W. Wolf and I inquired of a nurse where he was and she told me he was up on the roof garden, so I went up. There I found him caring for my good friend, Calvin Weidman, and his son. On the other side was Mrs. Carmichael, who was attending a young woman. I asked George what he could do for Weidman and he said, "Nothing but moisten his lips with the tip of my fingers, he and his son will soon be gone." I asked Mrs. Carmichael how about her patient and she said nothing could be done and she was doing the same thing. I turned and walked away.

In the meantime, I had been summoned by the County Court to furnish a report. I gave it to them as best I could, told them I was about out of money, in fact, had already spent more than the amount appropriated. They, thereupon, ordered me to spend any amount of money necessary, in my judgment, to stamp out the disease. We had cots, blankets and sheets to buy, masks to build and many other necessaries to equip the hospitals to meet the overflow work. Eventually, the ravages of the disease began to wane and one night about 11 o'clock, after our work had been completed, Mr. Sefton, on his way home, called at my house and we were discussing the situation when the phone rang and the King's Daughters Hospital had to have a special nurse at once. We decided to go down and help them out and we started. I became dreadfully nauseated walking around the street but I kept on going. Fortunately, we met Dr. Bruce Engle, who had been relieved for the night, and, upon request, he decided to go back on duty again. We went to the hospital and looked his patient over, who was very delirious, but Bruce decided to take the job and he did. I think the poor fellow died that night. Nevertheless, I went home and retired for the night and that was my last active participation in the "flu" fight. I expected to die and nothing but a good heart and skin and about eighteen glasses of water saved me. At this time, Mr. Trout got back in the line and the situation passed along very well.

I got over my attack in a few days and met the Government doctor in my office and I again asked her what the Government knew about the "flu." She told me she was not able to give me any information whatever that could be relied upon nor could she prescribe any definite treatment other than what we had given our patients.

The evil effects of this scourge will be felt for many years to come. We lost five hundred souls, many of whom lie in nameless graves, without markers. We had very few funeral services and often the members of the family were too ill to attend the burial of their kin-folk. This had to be, however regretable.

The night the doctors met in the Mayor's office we were greatly alarmed about it spreading among the colored people. We had in the field Dr. J. R. Clifford, who deserves great credit, two or three preachers, a doctor and several other volunteers. They were instructed to give the colored population quinine and salts, throw open the windows and require the ones who were not sick to take treatment as well as those who were sick. Strange to say, results were most gratifying and, while I cannot say accurately, I am sure we did not lose over a dozen in the whole county. This is a fine showing compared to what occurred in Charles Town among the same race.

I am reminded of the inquiry, by the Government, as to how many persons in the city were carrying on their usual vocation. We conferred together and wired the War Department that only twenty per cent were at work. This was true. Those who were not ill were very busy taking care of those who were and the situation was desperate. You might not believe it but it is true that a man went to Dr. Tonkin's office, drew a revolver and threatened to kill him if he did not come at once to the assistance of his ill wife, and the Doctor, appreciating the seriousness of the situation, and with cool, level-headed judgment, went with him and the matter was ended. It is hard for anyone to realize just what our Doctors had to contend with. They did, as the rest of us, the best they could and worked hard and long to save human lives.

The treatment of the "flu" was something new to the medical fraternity. They did not know then, nor do they know now, its cause or proper manner of treatment and perhaps never will know. I made, as nearly as I could, a special study of it as we went along and all I can tell you, so far as treatment is concerned, is what happened to me to obtain the best results. I have told you previously that the use of heart stimulants, together with phenacetine, acetanilid and their derivities, meant and intended to produce perspiration, was the best treatment we could give. It may be true that alcoholic spirits were very helpful, chiefly, however, as a preventive. We became convinced that once a patient had gone down it was a failure, although, in some cases, it may have been very useful. I recall that onion plasters were very successful, as was the eating of raw onions, the drinking of hot lemonades and anything that induced perspiration. What would help one would not help another, which was very often the case. No one has yet been able to explain the toxic condition of the patient, nor did we understand it. It was indeed a strange disease. The stronger the patient was physically the more likely he was to die. A vicious phlegm, which formed in the throat and bronchial tubes, broke down the "resistance" of the patient and he would be unable to throw it off.

I need only mention to you a few names of those who passed away to give you some idea of the class of men who lost their lives:—Harvey Bush, reporter for the *Evening Journal;* M. L. Wachtel, professor of the Martinsburg High School; Mr. Coppersmith, manager of the Norwalk Motor Company; Edgar A. Hollis, head watch repairer of Bentz's Jewelry Store, and scores of others whose names I could mention but space will not permit. These men were vigorous and physically fit for anything but they could not successfully meet this dreadful disease This is the mysterious part about it. You would have thought, knowing them as we did, if they could not successfully fight it, who could?

The passing of the "flu" was an epoch in the history of Berkeley County never to be forgotten. It left in its wake a path of sorrow and broken hearts. Let us hope it will never visit us again. We cannot say too much in commendation of the faithful men and women who stood up and fought. I recall that nearly nine years have passed away and I have forgotten the names of many who assisted but I could not call this a completed paper if I did not refer to Miss Carrie M. Roush, who finally assumed control of the King's Daughters Hospital, and Mr. S. V. Fiery, who worked in the City Hospital. They fought night and day and went as far as their strength would let them go. God bless them and all the others who assisted in the great work.

And now, in conclusion, with commendable pride, the committee points to the fact that it only expended a little over $3,000.00, as shown by the records. The use of money was not "unstinted," and yet, at the same time, not extravagant. Much of our service was voluntary, for which we were very thankful. If you will compare the two small-pox epidemics, when only six or eight lives were lost, you will find the records show the cost to the county was something over $10,000.00. We feel we are justified in going before the citizens and taxpayers of Berkeley County and claiming credit for the way the situation was handled.

Respectfully yours,
ALLEN B. NOLL.

CHAPTER XXVIII.

MISCELLANEOUS.

NEWSPAPERS.

Martinsburg has the honor of being the place where the first newspaper was published within the State of West Virginia. The first one was *The Potomack Guardian and Berkeley Advertiser*, founded in 1789 by Dr. Thomas Henry, a physician of Martinsburg. The second was *The Martinsburg Gazette*, established in 1789 by Nathaniel Willis, father of the distinguished poet, Nathan Parker Willis. The third was *The Intelligencer and Northern Neck Advertiser*, in 1800, by John Alburtis. These were all weeklies, and wielded great influence among their readers from every standpoint.

In those days all papers were printed by hand labor. The type was set by hand, and the paper was printed by running a sheet over rollers and printing one page at a time. This work was laborious, the printing presses were run by man power, one man running out the papers by a hand crank. Daily papers were unheard of, and it is likely that none would have wanted them except the city people, the country people then having no daily rural delivery, they only getting their mail once a week or thereabout when they attended the postoffice, and it would have been impossible to get out a daily edition from lack of quick facilities.

Among old newspapers, fortunately filed with the Clerk of the County Court, are the following: How these newspapers happened to be filed as above mentioned is interesting. The Legislature early enacted a law compelling the County Board of Supervisors to make a financial statement of its assets and liabilities, levies and settlements at the end of each year. For future reference copies of all newspapers published in Martinsburg were also required to be bound and filed in this office. Hence the Legislature and the Board have perhaps unwittingly preserved these old files, which will be of immense historical value to future generations. Hon. Christian W. Doll, for many years Clerk of the County Court of this county, did much more than the law required in this line, digging up old records of a legal nature and any other records which he compiled and placed in vaults there which add greatly to the records of this office. Such men as these, doing more work than is actually required, are the ones who aid most in the making of a community.

Among these papers are to be found copies of the following papers together with place of publication: *The Martinsburg Gazette*, May 9, 1840, Martinsburg, Va., Edmond P. Hunter, editor; *The Berkeley American*, May 30, 1855, Martinsburg, Va.; *Virginia Republican*, June 11, 1855, Martinsburg, Va., Samuel Alburtis, editor; "*The American and Gazette*, June 22, 1859, Martinsburg, Va.; *South Branch Intelligencer*, May 22, 1857, Romney, Va.; *Virginia Argus and Hampshire Advertiser*, May 22, 1857, Romney, Va.; *The Enterprise*, May 14, 1857, Bath, Va.; *The Berkeley*

American and Martinsburg Gazette, May 13, 1857, Martinsburg, Va., A. T. Maupin, editor; *Berryville Gazette*, June 5, 1857, Berryville, Va.; *The Democratic Mirror*, March 30, 1859, Leesburg, Va.; *The Berkeley Union*, Feb. 24, 1866, Martinsburg, W. Va., published by Hope, Robinson & Co.; *The Valley Star*, Oct. 6, 1869, Martinsburg, W. Va.

The first newspaper established in Martinsburg after the Civil War was the *Berkeley Union*, of which mention has already been made. J. Nelson Wisner, a lawyer of large practice in the county, was editor until 1873. The *New Era*, a Democratic newspaper, was started by Hon. Chas. James Faulkner, but was acquired by Schaffer and Longan. It closed its career in 1873. That year the two newspapers, *Berkeley Union* and *New Era* was consolidated and a new sheet appeared, *The Martinsburg Independent*, until the early part of 1876. It was published daily and weekly. This was the first daily newspaper published in Martinsburg. From that time until 1876 it was controlled by the Independent Printing Company, when Messrs. Wilson, Wisner, and Logan acquired the entire plant. It continued until 1885, when Mr. Logan retired on account of ill health and Mr. Wisner purchased the interest of Mr. Logan. Mr. J. Nelson Wisner continued to publish this paper for a number of years.

The *Martinsburg Statesman* began its career under the name of the *Valley Star*, with James W. Robinson as editor. In 1869 Mr. D. S. Eichelberger purchased this paper and changed its name to the *Martinsburg Statesman* and it continued under that title for a number of years, under the editorship of such men as Captain W. B. Colston, John S. Robinson and C. W. Boyer. It closed its period of usefulness upon the death of Mr. C. W. Boyer in 1908. The *Martinsburg Herald* began publication in 1881 by A. S. Golden and John T. Riley. It continued its career under this management until 1885, when Hon. Geo. F. Evans purchased the interest of Mr. Golden, and it continued thus until 1890, when A. B. Smith became the editor and proprietor.

About 1888 Mr. F. Vernon Aler started a newspaper called the *Berkeley Democrat*. This afterwards merged into the *Martinsburg World*, a daily and weekly paper under the ownership of W. E. Hoffheins & Company, Publishers. This paper was eventually acquired by the *Martinsburg Evening Journal*, which was started by H. F. Byrd of Winchester, Va., who later sold his interest to Hon. H. C. Ogden, of Wheeling, W. Va. It is the only newspaper published at this time.

J. R. Clifford, a prominent colored attorney-at-law of Martinsburg, established (1883) a newspaper which he called the *Pioneer Press*. It was Republican in politics, and greatly aided the advancement of the colored race. Beginning with a circulation of one hundred, it increased to a thousand in a short while. This paper was printed in the *Independent* office until 1888, when Mr. Clifford purchased the outfit of the *Hardy Express* of Moorefield, W. Va., after which he printed his own paper for a number of years.

The *Gerardstown Times* was established in 1870 by J. B. Morgan at Gerardstown, W. Va. It was a weekly, published every Saturday. It was a four column quarto and was well edited. Its politics were neutral. Its columns were given to publishing the local news in and around Gerardstown and had a large circulation. It was discontinued at the death of James B. Morgan and was never revived.

About the year 1880 the Independent Order of Good Templars, an organization which had for its object the correction of intemperance, was at its height in this county. The *West Virginia Good Templar*, a paper devoted entirely to the order, was also published by Mr. James B. Morgan at Gerardstown. It continued to flourish until the order ceased to exist.

HISTORY OF THE MARTINSBURG FIRE DEPARTMENT.

The following history of the Martinsburg Fire Department was from data gleaned from the *Souvenior Program* of the Cumberland Valley Volunteer Firemen's Association and from Martin Quinn's *History of the Martinsburg Fire Department*, loaned the writer of this work, extracts of which are given here:

"One of the most authentic references in city records to the firemen is under the date of Feb. 7, 1823, when the Town Trustees appointed Jacob Bishop and Edwin Gibbs a committee to buy four long and two short ladders and twenty fire buckets for the use of the town, and to deposit them at the Market House. Tradition has it that residents found these ladders very handy about the house and would borrow them, sometimes keeping them indefinitely. To curb this practice the Town Trustees passed an ordinance, effective March 1, the same year, forbidding the removal of any ladder unless for use at a fire and imposing a penalty of not less than $1.00 nor more than $10.00 for each offense. This limited apparatus sufficed for but a few years. On Nov. 9, 1825, attention of the Town Trustees being called by the destruction by fire of two houses the previous evening, the question of securing a (hand) fire engine was discussed, and Conrad Hogermine, John Strothers, and Jacob S. Lauck were named a committee to procure the same. The treasurer was authorized to pay $500.00 for the same out of money that might come into his hands. Presumably these moneys came into hand slowly, for there is no record of the hand engine being purchased until June 13, 1829, from Merrick & Agnew, of Philadelphia, for $500.00. John Doll and John Strother were the purchasing committee.

"This engine was shipped over the railroad to Baltimore from Philadelphia and had to be hauled from the latter city to Martinsburg over the pike. June 5, 1830, Michael Anderson was paid $12.50 for the task. Nearly thirteen years afterward, on March 11, 1843, the Trustees ordered the payment of $19.47 to William Hayden for repairs to the engine. Another note in the city records, dated Oct. 26, 1831, orders the building of a cistern in front of the County Court House for use in case of fire.

"August 29, 1846, it was decided to build a new market house and engine house, the city to stand part of the expense. It was thought $100.00 a fair price for the Trustees to pay, and on March 12, 1847, the amount was paid and Peter Gardner and Patrick Cunningham were appointed a committee to have the engine room and cupalo finished. Ten years later, on June 5, 1857, Council ordered a shed built on the Market House lot to place ladders and hooks in to protect them from the weather.

"May 12, 1859, John H. Blondell was instructed to make a thorough examination of the fire engine of the First Baltimore Hose Company, and, if he found it desirable and could make proper terms, to purchase the same and hose. Seven days later the committee reported that the engine had been purchased for $762.50, and arrangements were made to borrow $600.00 to complete payments from the Bank of Berkeley.

"Undoubtedly this aroused interest in firemanic affairs, for on June 9, 1859, Council was petitioned by John Q. A. Nadenbousch and others for permission to use the engine and apparatus and form a fire company. This was granted, but Council retained control and reserved the right to rescind its action at any time it saw fit. On July 21, 1859, John Weller was instructed to make application to the County Court for use of ground at the west end of the Market House, on which to build an engine house and for other purposes, and at the August 4th meeting Council appropriated $30.00 annually as the salary of the superintendent of the fire company, payable quarterly. The new organization was named 'Mechanical Fire Company.'

"It required nearly ten more years for expansion, and on March 9, 1868, Council subscribed $500.00 to the purchase of a ladder truck for the Hook and Ladder Company, the company agreeing topay the balance Sept. 22, 1870. Council appointed J. Q. A. Nadenbousch, W. D. Burkhart, Louis Schew, Howard Gettinger, Wm. Logan, F. Gerling, Levi Kapp, Wm. Wilen and David Schaffer of First Ward, A. Kogelschatz, Chas. E. Diffenderfer, Geo. Blocker, J. Baker Kerfott, Chas. Keefer, John Fellers, A. Blondell, H. C. Robinson, Henry Kratz and F. H. Flaging of Second Ward a committee to organize a fire company.

"This action followed the arrival in Martinsburg of the first steam engine ever owned by the city. The previous July 22, on motion of H. M. Couchman, Council purchased a steam fire engine and two reels with hose from the Sibley Company of Seneca Falls, N. Y., at a cost of $8,175.00. In August, Frederick Spillman and Jacob Schaffer, both long since dead, were appointed as temporary engineers. September 1st the steamer was officially tested, and only six minute elapsed from the time of striking the match until steam was up and water thrown. This was attested to by the following committee: J. Q. A. Nadenbousch, Wm. Riddle, Wm. Dorsey, Wm. Wilen, Henry Kratz, A. Kogelschatz, J. H. King, J. S. W. Baker, August P. Shutt and Wm. Edwards.

"The Martinsburg Fire Company was duly organized Dec. 12, 1870, with Colonel J. Q. A. Nadenbousch as marshal. From thence to the present day the evolution of the fire department is faithfully recorded for nearly twenty-seven years, until the department was sub-divided into five other companies, of which the active survivors are Ryneal and Hose Company No. 5 with their handsome fire house, while No. 3 is technically out of service until the realization of its fire house to be erected on Winchester Avenue, and No. 4's dream of a hose house on North High Street materializes. The volunteer arm of the service now revolves around the paid fire department and Chief Martin Quinn, with the confidence of his associates, the city authorities, and the public in general, is proving equal to the task in guiding the department on to a higher state of efficiency."

HISTORY OF THE MARTINSBURG CHAPTER OF THE AMERICAN RED CROSS.

On April 19, 1917, the President of the Community Club of Martinsburg called a general meeting of the women of the town for the purpose of considering the organization of a local Chapter of the Red Cross.

Responsive to their country's need and eager to serve in the great work of the American Red Cross, many answered the call. At this meeting plans for organization were discussed; temporary officers were elected, and a petition asking for authority to organize were sent to national headquarters at Washington.

Permission was granted and on April 28, 1917, the Martinsburg Chapter of the American Red Cross organized with their jurisdiction extending over Berkeley County. There were fifty-two members when they first organized. The following officers were appointed:

    Mrs. Virginia F. Faulkner............................Chairman
    Mrs. H. S. Shade............................Vice Chairman
    Mrs. G. J. E. Sponseller............................Treasurer
    Miss Nota K. Wever............................Secretary

The first meeting of the Chapter was held in the rooms of the Young Women's Christian League. At this meeting an executive committee was appointed. Soon after the headquarters of the Chapter were moved to a vacant store room on King Street. The only equipment that they had was one borrowed sewing machine, a table and some chairs.

On September 17, 1917, the People's Trust Company furnished the Chapter rooms in their building. From these rooms were shipped during the war:

    70,000 Surgical Dressings,
    1,050 Hospital Shirts,
    985 Prs. Pajamas,
    904 Sweaters,
    342 Prs. Socks,
    106 Other Knitted Garments,
    812 Miscellaneous Garments and Supplies,
    200 Xmas Packages.

From June 18 to June 25 a drive was made and $3,000 was raised. Auxiliaries organized were (July 31, 1917):

The Bunker Hill Auxiliary, The Gerardstown Auxiliary, The Hedgesville Auxiliary, The Opequon Auxiliary, The "Crepsus Attucks" Auxiliary (Colored), and The D. A. R. Naval Auxiliary. All these did general Red Cross work, with the exception of the D. A. R. Naval Auxiliary, which concentrated its activities in knitting garments for the sailors of the Destroyer "Stribling," which ship is named for one of Martinsburg's distinguished citizens, Admiral Stribling. On April 13, 1918, the following officers for the ensuing year were elected:

    Mrs. C. W. Link............................Chairman
    Mrs. G. B. Wiltshire............................Vice Chairman
    Mrs. Gilbert McKown............................Secretary
    Mrs. Bernard Myers............................Treasurer

In 1918, two drives for old clothes for French and Belgian refuges resulted in the shipping of 4,870 pounds of clothing to this worthy cause; 345 books were collected and sent to the soldiers; 1800 pounds of peach seeds for use in the manufacture of gas masks were collected, chiefly by the school children of the city and county. For the latter six months of 1918 the following report was done: 55 families were under care 31 having been

MISCELLANEOUS 319

given material relief, and 24 helped with advice; sum spent in relief work, $346.11. During the Spanish influenza, 56 families were cared for, 42 of which were given material help at a cost of $171.38. Broths were made at the Young Woman's Christian League and sent out to the sick.

During the influenza epidemic, the two local hospitals were presented with 200 dressing pads besides a small number of small dressings. After the signing of the Armistice, Nov. 11, 1918, the need for surgical dressings was over, and early in December this department closed after twenty months of efficient and faithful work. In November, 1918, the official name was changed to the Berkeley County Chapter". The November election of officers resulted as follows:

Mrs. C. W. Link, Chairman.
Mrs. G. B. Wiltshire, Vice Chairman.
Mrs. S. V. Fiery, Secretary.
Mrs. G. C. McKown, Assistant Secretary.
J. M. Woods, Treasurer.
Director of Chapter Productions, Mrs. G. B. Wiltshire.
Supervisor Surgical Dressing, Mrs. W. C. Kilmer.
Supervisor Hospital Garments and Supplies, Miss May E. Faulkner.
Supervisor of Knitting, Mrs. Gamble, Miss Ramer.
Chairman Workroom Committee, Mrs. Abram Horsfall.
Chairman Publicity Committee, Mrs. A. C. Irons.
Chairman Committee on Supplies, Miss Mary C. Stribling.
Chairman Home Service Section, Rev. A. M. Gluck.
Chairman Shipping Commission, Mrs. G. W. F. Mullis.
Chairman of Junior Red Cross, Miss Lucetta Logan.
Treasurer Junior Red Cross, Mrs. Hattie Geyer.
Many noble works were carried on by the Chapter.

The above was taken from the sketch of the activities of the local Red Cross Chapter during the World War, compiled by Mrs. C. J. Faulkner and Miss Mary Calvert Stribling and placed on file in the Clerk's office of the County Court as a permanent record of the county.

MARTINSBURG KIWANIS CLUB.

The name "Kiwanis" is a coined name. The first club in the United States started at Detroit thirteen years ago (1914). From this beginning of five members, Kiwanis has grown until it has taken the title "International" with 100,849 members.

The first West Virginia State Convention was held at Charleston on July 16-17, 1920. The Berkeley County Kiwanis Club was organized at Martinsburg (the Hotel Berkeley), Sept. 19, 1921. Mayor Cleveland M. Seibert was the first President. At first it held its dinners at the Episcopal Parish House, the Y. M. C. A. and at Hotel Berkeley, until 1924, when it adopted as its dinner headquarters, the dining rooms of Nurses' Home, King's Daughters Hospital. These dinners are held at 6:30 on Tuesday evenings.

The motto of the organization is: "We Build." The objects of the organization are crystallizing community sentiment for municipal improvement, pure politics, develop leaders, urge harmony in business, advocates honesty and integrity in all dealings, furnishes a forum for the discussion of all fair and interesting questions, promulgates the advancement of public welfare, morals, health, charities, better citizenship, civic improvement and obedience to law and all the tenets of proper living.

In its six years of existence in Berkeley County it has advocated and carried forward a movement for a new high school building for Martinsburg. This building is now in the course of erection on South Queen Street in a 23-acre park and at a cost of $310,000. Another project is their annual Blue and Gray Nights, when all the available veterans of the Civil War, on both the Union and Confederate sides, are gathered together. On May 30th, Decoration Day, 1922, there were thirty-nine present; on Decoration Day, 1926, there were six present, showing how fast the old heroes are responding to their last reveille. The club has played an important part in the development of aviation in this section through Kiwanians Alexander Parks, Edgar Henshaw, and Richard Fellers. The club has helped in the financing and otherwise of outings, camps, and special training for the youth, equipment for the Boy Scouts, sending underprivileged children to summer camps, providing a milk and ice fund for hot months.

This club has a membership of 70, from all walks of life: farmers, physicians, clergy, business men, etc.

The officers of the club are:
President—E. E. Church, Principal Martinsburg High School.
Vice President—Albert R. Coudhman, Limestone Operator.
Secretary—Edgar M. Sites, Hardware Merchant.
Treasurer—Roy A. Harrison, Banker.
General Chairman State Convention Committee—Dr. A. Bruce Eagle, Physician.

THE FRUIT INDUSTRY OF BERKELEY COUNTY.

This county is well known the world over for its fruit, apples and apple products. Even as far back as 1740, one hundred and eighty-seven years ago, Apple Pie Ridge was then a producer of fine apples, for, as has been stated in another section in this work, it received its name from a casual remark made by a Quaker minister at a Quaker meeting on the Opequon at that time.

The pioneer in the apple industry was William S. Miller of Gerrardstown, who set the first commercial orchard in the county, consisting of sixteen acres of orchard on his farm, in 1851. His neighbors predicted failure. The Civil War came and he had on hand a large number of budded nursery stock, and as he could find no sale for them (everyone then being engaged in some way in the war), he set them on his own land. At the close of the Civil War he had 4000 bearing trees. He continued to plant until he had 6500 trees planted. From the humble beginning of sixteen acres, the commercial apple industry has gone on apace until Berkeley County is the banner county in this industry in the State. Long before this event, nearly every large farm owner had apple trees planted at his homestead for the use of his own family.

On the J. N. Thatcher orchard, on Tuscarora, are two apple trees of the Grindstone-Vandever variety which were known to have been bearing one hundred years ago, and are producing abundant crops still. On the James L. Campbell farm are a few trees of the Bellflower variety still producing, which is the remnant of a large orchard for that day, which orchard was just coming into bearing one hundred years ago.

The second large planting of orchards in the county was by J. N. Thatcher about 1868, when he proceeded to buy out the remnant of a nurseryman going out of business at Greencastle, Pa. Mr. Thatcher proceeded to purchase the entire remaining stock for about $17 and brought it home in a four-horse wagon. The nature of the stock was, of course, a conglomeration of odds and ends of left-overs, but of excellent condition.

Some of the varieties were: Early Harvest, Early Ripe, Maiden Blush, Spice, Red Astrakhan, Smoke-House, Bellflower, Vanderver, Albemarle Pippin, Rumbo, Smith Cider, P. W. Sweet, Talahapahawkin. About 1890, apples that year bringing $3 per barrel, lent a great impetus to the planting of large orchards. Among these planters were Alexander Clohan, James H. Smith, J. T. Catrow, Jonathan Newton Thatcher, John M. Miller, D. Gold Miller, G. C. McKown, Hunter McKown, Gilbert P. Miller, and I. L. Bender. Incidentally, all these plantings were on Apple Pie Ridge.

The fact must not be left unmentioned that about the year 1889 Mr. S. S. Felker of Martinsburg bought the first car-load of apples ever shipped from Berkeley County. Some of these found their way to English tables and then and there the fame of Berkeley County apples was established as far as the English epicures were concerned. In the fall of 1895, the first apple carnival was held in Martinsburg. This added greatly to the advancement of the apple industry of the county. Miss Sue E. Henson was the first "Queen of the Apple Carnival". This carnival was put across by Alexander Clohan, Nat T. Frame, J. W. Stewart, D. Gold Miller, H. L. Smith, E. C. Henshaw, John T. Janney, Edward Lupton, Harlan Thatcher, R. C. Burkhart and others.

The Berkeley County Horticultural Society was formed in 1894 and held its first apple show in Fellers Hall, corner of Queen and Race Streets. About this time the Horticultural Society, working in conjunction with the West Virginia Experimental Station at Morgantown, began the systematic combatting of the San Jose scale and other fruit tree pests by the use of sprays, the power sprayer just beginning to come into use.

The planting of the apple tree has increased to the astounding figures of 312,789 young trees and 567,348 bearing trees (1927) with a total of over 880,000 trees in the county and with an output of 695,150 bushels of apples in a single year. About 17,600 acres of the county are planted to orchards which is about 11% of the tillable land of the county.

The largest individual owners of orchards in the county are: American

Fruit Growers, Dr. A. B. Eagle, X. Poole, J. C. McKown, Thomas S. Brown, John M. Miller, D. Gold Miller, E. L. Henshaw, H. H. Rutherford, Wilbur H. Thomas, Dr. T. K. Oats, Geo. M. Bowers, Emory F. Thomas, Dr. E. B. LeFevre, James L. Campbell, Vernon Shade, R. G. Horner, Ernest McDonald, Glenn M. Pitzer, North Valley Orchard Company, John H. Zirkle. H. D. Sperow, Harry A. Hammann, Harlan Thatcher, Homer C. Small, C. J. Seibert, C. C. Borum, Cecil W. Wood, John Porterfield, W. A. Catrow, Charles W. Sperow, H. P. Thorn.

In 1920, through the efforts of Hon. Roy C. Grove, a delegate to the 34th Legislature of West Virginia, the State Demonstration Packing Plant was located at Inwood for the demonstration of the packing and shipping of apples. This is the only one of its kind in the world. Here thousands of boxes and barrels of apples are packed for the growers and sent out over the country. At Inwood is also located the Musselman plant for the canning of apples, and at this plant thousands of dollars of apples are used which would otherwise be a loss to the grower.

HOTELS.

HOTEL BERKELEY—At present there are two principal hotels in Martinsburg. The oldest one is Hotel Berkeley, which was and is yet, one of the famous hostelries in the Shenandoah Valley. In 1843, Archibald Oden remodeled his property (his dwelling house, located where this hotel now stands) and opened it as a hotel. It immediately became the leading hotel of the town and was known far and wide as a hotel that was more like a home than a hotel. At the time of the opening of this hotel, there were six others open in the town—Everett House, Globe, Claycomb House, Gardiner House, Kelley House and "Old Tammany" House. Why so many hotels could exist at that time was that the Baltimore and Ohio Railroad was then in the course of construction and many of these made their homes at these hotels, and, although the rates were much lower then than now, each conducted a bar in connection and all did a flourishing business.

This hotel continued under the management of Mr. Oden for a number of years, till it was remodeled and its name changed to the St. Clair. In 1917 Thomas W. Martin became proprietor and the building was again remodeled and the name changed to Hotel Berkeley. Mr. Martin continued to conduct the establishment until 1924, when he sold the equipment to Peyton H. Ramer and Harry O. Evans, who are the proprietors at the present time. Many hotels have come and gone in the town of Martinsburg, but this popular hotel has continued to exist and is as well patronized now as in the days of the stage coach.

SHENANDOAH HOTEL—In 1925, the American Hotels Company began a campaign for the subscription of stock for the erection of a new hotel in Martinsburg. This stock was sold and the erection of the commodious building on Queen and Martin Streets corner was begun. It opened its doors to business in 1927 and has been successful from the start. This hotel is owned

MISCELLANEOUS 323

by practically all Berkeley County stockholders and speaks admirably for the prosperity and business acumen of the leading citizens of the city and county.

CITIES AND TOWNS.

BATH (BERKELEY SPRINGS)—Situated in what is now Morgan County, W. Va., at the famous "Warm Springs of Virginia". These springs were known to the Indians and they made use of them, for when they were first discovered by George Washington on a surveying expedition for Lord Fairfax, well defined Indian trails led to them. These springs were included in the grant of King Charles II. to Lord Fairfax (1680), but, of course, were not known to him. When his surveyors found them he denoted and set apart forever these springs, the same for the public use and benefit, the same to vest in the Colony of Virginia. In 1776, the General Assembly of Virginia, among its first acts, was to establish a town by the name of "Bath", at the Warm Springs. The place was known before this event as Bathtown. The first trustees were Bryan Fairfax, T. B. Martin, Warner Washington, Rev. Charles Mynn Thurston, Robert Rutherford, Thomas Rutherford, Alexander White, Philip Pendleton, Samuel Washington, William Ellzay, Van Swearingen, Thomas Hite, James Edmondson and James Nourse. These gentlemen had charge of the springs, which were made suitable for bathing, trees planted and walks laid out. It became a favorite resort for the sick as well as a resort for the well almost at once.

A road was built from Shepherdstown through Berkeley County by way of Bedington, Hainesville and Hedgesville and was known as the Warm Springs Road.

No other trustees were appointed for thirty years, when it was found that several members of the old board were dead and others had resigned long since. The Legislature of Virginia, in 1808, appointed a new Board of Trustees for the "Warm Springs". This board consisted of Hugh Holmes, Henry St. George Tucker, Alfred Powell, Henry Turner, John Baker, Stephen Dandridge, Philip C. Pendleton, Elisha Boyd, David Hunter and Ralph Colston, the latter four being from Berkeley County.

After the Civil War these springs became the property of West Virginia, and a Board of Trustees was appointed for their supervision consisting in part, five men from Berkeley County: D. Darby, Esq., Bethuel M. Kitchen, Dr. E. Boyd Pendleton, Dr. John S. Wilson, and Commodore Charles Boreman. The name of Bath was changed to Berkeley Springs from the fact that these springs were so long included in Berkeley County.

This town has made wonderful progress in home building. The industries are the great sand mines and apple culture. The plain, substantial "tomato" has made Morgan County famous the country over, as nowhere else does this vegetable grow to such perfection as in this section.

NEW MECKLENBURG (SHEPHERDSTOWN)—This is the oldest town in West Virginia. Where Bunker Hill now stands was the place where the first home was erected, 1726-27, but it did not get the resemblance of a town until many years later. Thirty-five years later, or in 1762, the Virginia House of Burgesses established the town and changed its name to Shepherdstown, in honor of Captain Thomas Shepherd, who had laid off a large portion of his land at this place into town lots. Two miles below on the Potomac River is a ford, which at low water in the Potomac can be crossed with ease with teams, known as "The Old Pack-Horse Ford", over which crossing many of the settlers of Berkeley County came in their wagons and ox-carts. At this place began "The Old Pack-Horse Road", mentioned elsewhere in this work.

This town is noted as the place where James Rumsey built the first steamboat in the world. In 1788 Mr. Rumsey perfected a boat which was propelled by steam and which moved against the brisk current of the Potomac at this place. His mortal remains lie buried in Westminster Abbey, England— the only West Virginian with that honor. It is a "college town" and is ideally situated as such, being the seat of Shepherd College State Normal School.

CHARLES TOWN—Founded in 1786 and named in honor of Charles Washington, a brother of General George Washington. It is the county seat of Jefferson County. It is noted among other things as the place where the imprisonment, trial and execution of John Brown and his followers for his attack on the United States Arsenal at Harper's Ferry. It is situated in a rich farming section, and is a thriving town.

HARPER'S FERRY—Named in honor of Robert Harper, an Englishman who was a carpenter and mill-wright residing at Philadelphia. In 1747 he was employed by the Quakers to build a church on the Opequon Creek, and, coming by the way of "The Hole" as the present site of Harper's Ferry was then called, was so much pleased with the place that he purchased the dwelling of Peter Stevens, the only man then residing there, and, after purchasing a large section of the surrounding territory from Lord Fairfax, brought his family here and made it his home for the rest of his life. He died in 1782 and his remains are interred in an old church yard on a hill west of the town. In 1761, the Virginia House of Burgesses established a ferry across the Potomac at that place and it has been known as "Harper's Ferry" ever since. In 1794, Congress established an arsenal and gun factory at that place. This arsenal was captured by John Brown on October 17, 1859. At this town is located Storer College, a school for negroes, one of the best schools of its kind in the South. The historical points of interest are Jefferson's Rock, situated and overlooking the Shenandoah and Potomac Rivers, and "John Brown's Fort," which stands on the campus of Storer College.

THE "RED HOUSE".

Among the historical residences of Berkeley County is one which stands about a mile north of the present County Court House and is still known as the "Red House" on account of its having been painted a dark red or crimson color and was about the first in Martinsburg to receive a coat of paint, that commodity not then being much used. Surrounding it and extending north and northwest to about where the Baltimore and Ohio Railroad and the Warm Spring State Road intersect, was a large farm of some 300 acres and known as the "Red House Farm". This farm, or estate, was purchased by the father of Col. David Hunter, who emigrated from York, Pennsylvania, about 1760. The present "Red House" was built about ten years later (1770), over 150 years ago, and stands today apparently awaiting another 150 years of usefulness and is in as good a state of preservation as when first built. It is partly erected of stone and partly of logs, weather-boarded.

At this house, then occupied by Edward Beeson, the first Court of Berkeley County was held (May 19, 1772) and here the county began her existence. At that time there was no Martinsburg, but the small cluster of houses around the springs, now known as the Old Water Works, was known as Morgan's Springs. This building continued to be the court house for the county until by writ obtained by General Adam Stephen, when it was removed to the latter Springs. This house was built in the forest, heavy timbered woodland extending from there to the present site of the County Court House.

THE MARTINSBURG STREET RAILWAY COMPANY.

In 1892, this company, with John B. Wilson at the head as President, laid a street car railway connecting the southern limits of the town with the northern. This was long before the advent of the automobile and at a time when the electric street railways were in demand. This company flourished for awhile but fell into disuse owing to the fact that Martinsburg at that time was not large enough to support a street car railway system. Mr. Wilson lost heavily by this enterprise but it was by such projects as these that he was one of the builders of "Greater Martinsburg".

PROMINENT PEOPLE WHO HAVE VISITED OUR CITY.

William Jennings Bryan—four times—in 1896 on his memorable speaking tour of the country when he was a candidate for President the first time; in the capacity of lecturer, once at the First U. B. Church and twice at the First Methodist Church, the first when he delivered his famous lecture, "The Prince of Peace," and the second, when he spoke in the interest of prohibition.

Dr. T. DeWitt Talmadge, the eminent divine, and George Bancroft, the historian; guests of Charles J. Faulkner, when Mr. Faulkner and they were members of the Anglo-American Commission.

Queen Marie, of Roumania, visited this town on the occasion of her visit to the United States in 1925. On this occasion she left her private train at Martinsburg and traveled to Winchester, Va., by automobile, the party passing over the Winchester Pike to the latter city. From there she motored to Harper's Ferry, at which place she again entrained for Washington, D. C.

Martin VanBuren paid a visit to Martinsburg in the summer of 1830, while he was Secretary of State under President Jackson. His visit was purely one of recreation. The trip was made by stage-coach, as this was seven years before the surveying corps of the Baltimore and Ohio Railroad reached Martinsburg. He incidentally visited Bath—Berkeley Springs—to enjoy its waters.

Henry Clay spent several days at Martinsburg in July, 1827, when he was Secretary of State under President John Q. Adams. He also visited the Berkeley Springs on this occasion. On another occasion, in January, 1848, he spent nother short period of time here as the guest of Charles James Faulkner.

William Howard Taft, while in President's Cabinet as Secretary of War, spoke on the political issues of the day in the Apollo Theater then called Thornwood Hall in honor of H. P. Thorn, a lifelong resident of Maritnsburg, who had erected the building. Hon. George M. Bowers was chairman of this meeting and in a prophetic address introduced Mr. Taft as "the next President of the United States," which literally came true.

Colonel Theodore Roosevelt, on the occasion of his candidacy for the Presidency on the Progressive ticket. He spoke from the Band Stand in the Public Square to a large concourse of people. During this campaign it will be remembered that President Taft was the nominee of the regular Republican party, the "Old Guard," and Mr. Roosevelt that of the Progressive Republican or "Bull Moose" party. This split the Republican party into two factions and Woodrow Wilson was elected President.

President Woodrow Wilson, on a campaign tour in the fall previous to his second election, passed through Martinsburg and spoke from the rear end of a Pullman at the B. & O. Station to a large gathering of people.

Vice-President Thomas R. Marshall made the principal address at the corner-stone laying of the Second United Brethren Church at Martinsburg when he was Vice-President of the United States. This was on a bright, summer, Sabbath afternoon. On this occasion, he spoke to a tremendous concourse of people.

BANKS OF MARTINSBURG.

THE OLD NATIONAL BANK—On August 12, 1865, a few months after the close of the Civil War, this bank opened its doors in the corner room of the Daniel Burkhart property on the north-east corner of the Public Square, now known as the Downey and Henson building, under the name of The National Bank of Martinsburg. The first President was George R. Wysong; first Cashier was Dr. William D. Burkhart, son of Daniel Burkhart, President of the Bank of Berkeley, which flourished prior to the Civil War. The first Board of Directors was J. H. King, Jacob Miller, Jacob Ropp, John S. Bowers, Colonel John W. Stewart, James W. Robinson, John W. Able. In 1867, George W. Hoke became President, Mr. Wysong resigning.

On Feb. 1, 1866, George S. Hill was appointed bookkeeper. He served with this bank as Cashier and First Vice-President for 59 years, or until 1920, when on account of old age infirmities, he retired as Cashier and W. F. McAneny was elected Cashier. Mr. Hill still holds the position as First Vice-President, but does not take an active part in the business of the institution.

Presidents of the Bank in rotation: Geo. R. Wysong, 8 years; John N. Able, 7 years; William T. Stewart, 33 years; H. M. Emmert, to present. The Bank was located for three years in the Burkhart building; then removed to the present Kilmer building, North Queen Street, until 1907, when it purchased the old Continental Hotel property. This property was purchased from Joseph H. Shaffer and David Shaffer. The Bank erected the present commodious building in 1907. The motto of the Bank is "On The Square." Officers: H. H. Emmert, President; George S. Hill, First Vice-President; William W. Westphal, Second Vice-President; W. F. McAneny, Cashier; R. Lewis Bent, Assistant Cashier; A. W. Miles, Assistant Cashier; P. W. Leiter, Trust Officer; Herbert A. Avey, Teller; John N. Caldwell, Note Teller; Rebecca T. Doll, Manager Savings Department; Ernest O. Siler, Bookkeeper; P. L. Sharff, Bookkeeper; Raymond J. Horner, Assistant Bookkeeper; Edward Fox, Custodian.

Board of Directors—C. G. Smith, F. C. Foreman, G. S. Hill, Jacob H. Miller, K. B. Creque, Sr., J. W. Smith, Boyd E. Hollis, J. L. Campbell, Dr. J. B. Chamberland, G. H. Shaffer, Daniel E. Dennis, H. H. Emmart, W. W. Westphal, Earl F. Gardner, C. J. Thornton.

THE SHENANDOAH VALLEY BANK AND TRUST COMPANY—Organized in the summer of 1920 in the Daniels building, southwest corner of the Public Square. This institution is the newest in the City of Martinsburg. It continued to operate in this building and it had purchased the property on the west side of North Queen Street, adjoining the County Court House, and erected a new building, equipped with the necessary modern banking facilities. This Bank was organized by Hon. Wilbur H. Thomas and he became the first President of the institution. The following are the officers: Lewis H. Thompson, President; John M. Miller, Vice-President; J. R. Poland, Second Vice-President; Roy A. Harrison, Cashier; Earl C. Weller, Assistant Cashier.

THE PEOPLES TRUST COMPANY—Organized in 1873 under the name of the Peoples Deposit Bank of Martinsburg. The banking room was in the Deihl building, located on the northern side of East Martin Street near Queen. In 1874, the name of the bank was changed to The Peoples National Bank of Martinsburg. In 1882, the institution purchased the present location, southeast corner of Queen and Burke Streets, known as the Scheu building. In 1898, the bank was reorganized under a State charter with the name of The Peoples Trust Company. The first President was Samuel Busey; the first Cashier, John B. Wilson. In 1875 Major E. S. Troxell was elected President; in 1883, A. J. Thomas; in 1898, Henry J. Seibert; in 1910, F. E. Wilson; in 1914, George M. Bowers; in 1925, J. O. Henson.

Since its organization, in 1873, it has had but three Cashiers: John B. Wilson, F. E. Wilson and Dudley Harley. In 1927, the building was remodeled, both interior and exterior, and made a modern improved banking institution in every respect.

THE BANK OF MARTINSBURG—The Bank of Martinsburg was organized on June 3, 1902, with John J. Hetzel as its first President and A. D. Darby as the first Cashier. The first Directors of the Bank were: John J. Hetzel, M. L. Dorn, H. H. Rutherford, C. G. Grove, Geo. F. Evans, A. T. Hess, G. B. Hedges, Lee M. Bender O. S. Rigsby.

The first location of the Bank was in the Wilen building on the same street. On March 8, 1922, this Bank moved into its own home, corner of Queen and Burke Streets. This corner had been purchased previously to this and remodeled and fitted up as a modern banking building in every respect. Since that time it has been located here. The officers of the Bank at present are: W. T. McQuilkin, President; M. G. Schneider, Cashier; W. W. Downey, Vice-President.

CHAPTER XXIX.

BERKELEY COUNTY AT PRESENT.

BOUNDED: North, Morgan County and Potomac River; East Jefferson County; South, Frederick County, Va.; West, Morgan County.

MOUNTAINS: Old North Mountain runs north and south through the county, a little to the west of the center; Back Mountain runs north and south through the county near the western part; and Sleepy Creek Mountain is on the extreme western boundary. The highest elevation is Round Top, 1,000 feet. The other lesser elevations are Buck Hill and Cannon Hill, in Back Creek Valley, and Apple Pie Ridge, which extends north and south and parallel to North Mountain, and east of it. Elevations of these three, about 500 feet. The mountainous section of the county is in the western section. Traveling eastward, the Apple Pie Ridge section is met, famous for apple growing. Eastward of this section is the limestone section, a great agricultural region and famous for its quarries of the best grade of limestone in the world. On the extreme east is the section known as the "Pine Hill" region, where some of the best shale is obtained for making brick, pottery, etc., in the country. Many plants for the manufacture of this product are located in this region.

STREAMS: The Potomac River is on the north and is the largest stream. The Opequon Creek flows in a northerly direction through the eastern section of the county. Its tributaries are the Mill Creek, Middle Creek, Tuscarora Creek. In Back Creek Valley, Back Creek, with its many smaller tributaries, flows in a northern direction through this valley. Between Back and Sleepy Creek Mountains, Meadow Branch, a small stream, traverses this valley in a northerly direction. The county is well watered. The larger portion of Berkeley County is in the Shenandoah Valley. This valley is twenty-five miles wide at this section. Berkeley County occupies the western portion of it, and extends about eight miles in an easterly direction from North Mountain. It is about 16 miles from the Frederick (Va.) line to the Potomac River on the north. Back Creek Valley is about five miles in width and 16 miles long, extending in a northern and a southern direction from the Frederick line to the Potomac River. It lies between North and Back Mountains.

The Potomac River is the only one that touches Berkeley County and it belongs to Maryland to low water mark on the West Virginia side. It marks the northern boundary of the county. Its ancient name was "Co-hon-go-ru-ta," an Indian name signifying "River of the Wild Goose," "Cohonk" or call of the wild goose suggesting the name to the Indian.

Note—This river is not now nor was it at that time infested or inhabited by wild geese. In their annual or semi-annual migrations that fowl does not alight on any rivers in this section, yet occasionally a stray one will be forced to alight on account of sleet or high winds. Just such an incident as this may have led the Indian to give the name to the river.

Potomac is of Indian original also, meaning "They come and go," in an allusion to the Spaniards who, at the close of the sixteenth century, made trips from Florida to the Potomac to trade with the Indians, but made no settlements. The ancient name was spelled "Po-to-mack" and has been corrupted to its present form. It is one of the historic rivers of the nation. It marks the boundary between the grants of Lord Baltimore (Maryland) and Lord Fairfax (the Northern Neck of Virginia), for such the northern portion of the Colony of Virginia was at that time considered. It marks the boundary of the States of Maryland, Virginia and West Virginia. It was the dividing line between the United States and the Confederate States during the Civil War. All territory south of this river is considered "Dixie". It was on this river, at Shepherdstown, that the first steamboat in the world was launched by James Rumsey. On this river the Nation's Capitol is situated, also the home of George Washington and his tomb.

The towns of the county are:

MARTINSBURG—The capitol of the county, a busy city of 15,000 inhabitants, founded in 1778 by General Adam Stephen, an officer in the American Revolution. It occupies the sites of the ancient town of the Tuscarora Indians. It contains the Interwoven Mills, Inc., the largest hosiery mills in the world; two large woollen mills for the manufacture of woollen cloth—The Berkeley Woollen and Dun Woollen Company. Near this town are extensive quarries— The Kelley Limestone Company, The Baker Limestone Company, The Standard Limestone Company, also a plant for the manufacturing of "Amiesite", a material for building roads, and the Baltimore and Ohio Railroad workshops and two large plants for the making of brick and clay products. It has six flourishing banks—The Bank of Martinsburg, The Peoples Trust Company, The Old National Bank, The Merchants and Farmers, The Shenadoah Valley Bank and Trust Company and The Ctizens National Bank. It contains 18 churches and a splendid school system, extending through all the grades up to the Grammar School and the High School, a building in the course of construction to cost $310,000. It has paved streets, a splendid sewage system and disposal plant. It contains a large United States Government building in which the Martinsburg post office and the Federal Court and other government officials are housed.

HEDGESVILLE—Founded and named by Joshua Hedges, whose residence, a log house, stood on the site of the present home of Thomas Speck, Esq., at the eastern foot-hills of North Mountain, to the left of the State Road leading from Martinsburg to Hedgesville. During "Lord Dunmore's War", Josiah Hedges built a stockade fort at the site where the home of Mr. J. B. Branham is now situated. This was for protection against Indian attacks for the settlers of that region, and was known as Hedges Fort. At the present residence of Mr. G. W. Fuss, at the Back Creek bridge, Robert Snodgrass, Sr., built a tavern in 1740, to accommodate travelers over the Warm Springs road on their way to and from Bath (Berkeley Springs). It was known as the Sondgrass Tavern and continued a famous hostelry for many years. General Washington, when he was President of the United States, paid a visit to Bath in the summer of 1790, making the trip from Mount Vernon in his own private "coach and four". He spent the night at Snodgrass Tavern. Hedgesville is an incorporated town, having been made such by Act of the Virginia Legislature March 1, 1854. The incorporated area contains 60 acres, three roods and twenty-three square poles. The corporate name was "The Town of Hedgesville. Seven trustees compose the Council (four can act) and are elected for a term of one year. Said election is held the first Monday in May. The first town lots were laid off on the land of John Westenhaver. General J. E. B. Stuart encamped here on the night of the 9th of October, 1862, on his memorable raid upon Chambersburg. Mount Clifton, a famous summer resort before the advent of the automobile, is located here. The Hedgesville District High School, the largest in the county, is located here.

GERARDSTOWN—A town of perhaps 400 population, situated in the southwestern section of the county. It was founded at the headwaters of Mill Creek—one of the first towns in the county settled by emigrants of the Baptist faith from New Jersey, 1742 or 1743. There were fourteen families in this body. In 1754, Rev. John Gerrard, a Baptist minister, came to Opequon River (creek) as a pastor of a congregation of that faith. He also preached to the Baptists located at Middletown, as it was then called. In October, 1787, Rev. David Gerrard, a brother of the other Gerrard, enlarged the town by laying off an additional one hundred lots to be sold to settlers. For this act, the Legislature of Virginia established a town there and named it Gerardstown in honor of him. The first trustees appointed for the town by the Legislature were William Henshaw, James Haw, John Gray, Gilbert McKewan (McKown), and Robert A. Allen. It now contains a Presbyterian, two Methodist and one Lutheran churches and an excellent graded school, built in 1924. The members of the Board of Education who erected the building were A. H. Griffith, George W. Pitzer and Carl Slonaker. This town is the center of the apple industry of the county, situated on Apple Pie Ridge, is almost surrounded by apple orchards. Two newspapers were published here in the 80's by James B. Morgan, the *Gerrardstown Times* and the *West Virginia Good Templar*.

In the Presbyterian churchyard are buried Ward Hill Lamon, the law partner of President Lincoln when he practiced law at Springfield, Ills., an organizer of a company of Union troops from this county; also Grady Lewis, who lost his life as one of the Word War soldiers on the firing line in France. It was the birthplace of Hon. George M. Bowers, who was nationally known as head of the U. S. Bureau of Fisheries under three Presidents—McKinley, Roosevelt and Taft; also a member of Congress.

At the early date of 1755, Gerrardstown clustered around a stockade fort, situated over the spring on the property recently owned by the late Dr. G. W. Daniels. When this fort was hastily constructed it was found that the north side of the fort was all in forest, which extended up to within a few yards of the fort, from which the Indians might fire directly into it from the tall tree tops. A day was accordingly set upon which the entire community met and cleared off this hill-side, cutting the trees and burning them in great heaps. The women and children assisted by cooking food and carrying water for the laborers. Often this place was attacked by the Indians in the French and Indian wars, as Gerrardstown was situated only two miles from Mills Gap, a favorite place for the Indians to cross North Mountain from the west. In the spring of 1756 a party of twenty Indians came into this vicinity and attacked a family by the name of Kelly, murdered him and his entire family. This occurred within a few steps of the present home of Mr. Marion Hollis, about one-half mile of the fort to the west. So sudden was the attack that Mr. Kelly had no warning of the approach of the Indians and thus had no time to escape with his family to the fort.

At the beginning of the Civil War Captain James W. Gray organized a company of volunteer soldiers called "The Berkeley Guards," which hastened away to Harper's Ferry to help put down John Brown's insurrection. Near this town was born William S. Miller, pioneer orchard man of Berkeley County; also Gray Silver, who is also a national figure as the head of the American Farm Bureau at Washington, D. C., also State Senator for West Virginia for a number of terms.

INWOOD—On the Winchester Pike and the Pennsylvania Railroad, nine miles south of Martinsburg. It is a thriving town. It began its existence when the Cumberland Valley Railroad line was built past that place on to Winchester, Va., in 1884. This company erected a grain elevator there for the loading of wheat which greatly aided the town. Mr. H. L. Snapp conducted the first store there for a number of years. This town grew steadily. It was the seat of Inwood Park which was a noted summer resort. The Inwood Fair Association was formed and held a fair in the park for many years. This park was located in the woods on the south-west side of the station. It was noted for several camp meetings held there, both white and colored. At the white gathering, Rev. Sam P. Jones and Rev. Sam Small, noted evangelists, have preached. After this park ceased to be used, the buildings and timber were sold (the grounds belonging to Mr. J. W. Strong), and the grounds laid off into building lots. Shortly after the lots were sold, the Musselman Fruit Products Company erected a modern plant for the canning of apples, etc. This plant gives employment to hundreds of people, and being situated in the center of the apple-shipping district of the county, gives an output for hundreds of dollars worth of apples which would otherwise waste. This is one of the manufacturing plants of the county which materially aids in the advancement of it. At this place is also located the State Demonstration School for instruction in grading and packing apples— the only one of its kind in the world. Here thousands of boxes and barrels of apples are packed and shipped to all parts of the country. These apples are packed under the famous trade mark, "Johnny Appleseed."

The town contains two large cooperage factories for the making of apple barrels. In 1925, a modern four-room consolidated school was established here. The United Brethren Church is located here. The Butler Lumber Company has offices here. Stewart Sherard, a large buyer of apples, has his headquarters here. R. S. Whiting has charge of the large grain elevator at this place. The town has a population of about four hundred.

BUNKER HILL—Situated on Mill Creek at the junction of that stream and the Winchester Pike. The Pennsylvania Railroad line runs through the town. At this place Morgan Morgan built the first house in what is now Berkeley County and West Virginia (1725). It is an old village, having seen much of the destruction wrought by both armies during the Civil War. Formerly it was an industrious center for grinding flour, as Mill Creek received its name from the abundance of water power which it furnished to the numerous flour mills erected along its course. It, however, keeps abreast of the times, having a branch of the Perfection Garment Company of Martinsburg located here. The Baker Quarries are situated east of the town. This is a village of about four hundred inhabitants. It contains the Mill Creek District High School and the Bunker Hill Consolidated School of that district. It contains two churches—the Episcopal, the first built of logs by Morgan Morgan (1730), who founded the town. A large granite monument, commemorating the building of the first home in West Virginia by Morgan Morgan, stands along the Winchester Pike where the road crosses Mill Creek. It was dedicated in 1921.

DARKESVILLE—On Middle Creek and Pennsylvania Railroad intersection. Was formerly known as Bucklestown for General Buckles of the Revolutionary War. Made a town by the Virginia Legislature 1797. Named for General William Darke, Indian fighter and Revolutionary War hero. Has not progressed as have its neighbor towns, Inwood or Pikeside. Many of the residences show style of architecture prevalent in 1800. Many of these were shell, torn and bullet pierced during the Civil War. Its long central street (the Winchester Pike) resounded to the tread of armies during the struggle, under the leadership of Stonewall Jackson, Patterson, Banks and Kilpatrick. Has two Methodist Churches, one colored church and one colored school. George Pine has conducted a blacksmith shop continuously for forty years in the same place. Harry May operated a factory for making hickory chairs at this place. The oldest residences are Bruce McDonald's home, Harry Bryarly's mill and the old store room of A. D. Tate, now owned by William Wright.

PIKESIDE—A village of recent origin on the Winchester Pike. It is situated at Big Spring, famous for an Indian attack on the home of Jacob Evans in the French and Indian War. Contains a beautiful four-room consolidated school building, at which place the pupils of Pikeside, Darkesville and Tablers are transported by truck to that place. The town was started by Alexander Clohan, Charles J. Faulkner and George M. Bowers, laying off a large number of building lots. Home of the noted Confederate Scout and ex-Senator, Robert C. Burkhart. Contains a large United Brethren Church, built in 1925-26.

NOLLVILLE—On the Tuscarora Creek and the old Berkeley and Hampshire Grade (1832). Was started by E. C. Henshaw laying off the first one hundred lots. Was named for James W. Noll, who conducted a machine shop and cider mill there. It is near the spot where the old Presbyterian Church was built (1750), the first church west of the Blue Ridge Mountains.

CUMBO—At the intersection of the Pennsylvania and the Baltimore and Ohio Railroads, five miles west of Martinsburg. The name was "coined" by taking the first three letters of the name of the Cumberland Valley Railroad (Pennsylvania), "Cum", and attaching the initials of the Baltimore and Ohio Railroad, "B. O."—these combining, make the name "Cum-bo". The town is of recent origin (1914.) Many residences are built here and the place is a beehive of industry.

BERKELEY—Thriving town four miles north of Martinsburg, on the Pennsylvania Railroad and Williamsport Pike. The plant of the Security Lime and Cement Company is located here. That company operates large limestone quarries. It contains, two two-room graded schools, the one on the east of the village, Berkeley, and the other on the west, Oak Grove. It contains two churches, Presbyterian and United Brethren.

BLAIRTON—This village is on the B. & O. Railroad, three miles east of Martinsburg. It has been built up around the Blair Limestone Company's plant at that place. It contains a school and a United Brethren Church.

BEDINGTON—Situated on the Pennsylvania Railroad and William port Pike, six miles north of Martinsburg. It was started when the Martinsburg and Potomac Railroad (Pennsylvania) was built through that place. Contains famous "Sulphur Lot", a summer resort in former years; also the old Kennedy Mill, one day famous for making a high grade flour. Near to it to the west is the village of Hainesville, much older. These villages were on the Warm Spring Road leading from Shepherdstown to Bath (Berkeley Springs).

RIDGEWAY—A thriving town in the southern section of the county, on the Pennsylvania Railroad and Winchester Pike. Named for Charles J. Ridgeway, who has conducted a large general store there for a number of years. It is in an agricultural section. The Methodist parsonage is located here.

MARLOWE—On the Williamsport Pike, nine miles from Martinsburg. Has the first consolidated school to be established in the county, at which place nearly all the children of Falling Waters District are taught. This is also a Junior District High School. It is near the large Nessel Quarry.

NORTH MOUNTAIN—A thriving town on the line of the Baltimore and Ohio Railroad, north-west of Martinsburg. Is the shipping point for Back Creek Valley and the north-west section of the county. Contains a large brick plant and a large roller flour mill.

TABLERS—A village on the Pennsylvania Railroad, four miles south of Martinsburg. Great quantities of apples are loaded on trains here. Was founded when the Cumberland Valley (Pennsylvania) Railroad was built through that place (1884). Contains two apple barrel factories and a cider mill. Has one church, Presbyterian. The factory for the making of the Stewart spraying machine was located here by the late John W. Stewart. At this place is the celebrated "Protumna" orchard, which produced 29,000 barrels of apples in 1925.

ARDEN—An old village founded 1775 by Jacob Moon, a Quaker, who had fled from England on account of religious persecution. It was named for the village in England from which he fled. The name means "Quiet Pastoral scene".

TOMAHAWK or TOMAHAWK SPRINGS—Situated in Back Creek Valley; was once noted for the charm of its scenery and its pure water. The springs—three in number—give it its name from their arrangement in the form of a tomahawk.

SWAN POND—Situated in the northern section of the county. Named for a large pond which rises there, runs for a short distance through the channel of its stream and disappears in the direction of the Potomac River. It is not found again, its waters probably following some subterranean cavern for which that particular section is noted. It contains a few dwellings, a colored school and a church, Presbyterian.

Population:

Martinsburg (1926)	13,544
Outside of Martinsburg	12,458
Total, County	26,002

Valuation:

Martinsburg—	
Real Estate	$ 8,257,800
Personal	4,452,108
Arden District—	
Real Estate	1,846,910
Personal	523,543
Falling Waters—	
Real Estate	1,049,250
Personal	342,810
Gerardstown—	
Real Estate	1,175,610
Personal	396,550
Hedgesville—	
Real Estate	1,364,340
Personal	476,714
Mill Creek—	
Real Estate	1,031,725
Personal	272,853
Opequon—	
Real Estate	1,317,565
Personal	323,736
Total, County	$22,831,514

Public Utilities:

Hedgesville	$2,512,612
Opequon	1,280,426
Arden	947,579
Martinsburg	1,203,162
Mill Creek	310,306
Falling Waters	799,715
Hedgesville, Municipal	6,942
Gerrardstown	8,7.72
Total	$7,069,514

Berkeley County:

Land area .... 208,000 acres
Tillable .... 154,473 acres
Untillable (not worthless, but including timber lands, mountain lands and waste lands) .... 53,527 acres
showing that practically three-fourths of the area of the county is under the plow.

Number Farms—White, 1,047; Colored, 29.

Farms operated by owners, 890; managers, 114; tenants, 432.

Crop Lands—77,677 acres. Harvested, 64,061 acres; failures, 1,025 acres; idle, 12,591 acres; pasture, 40,987 acres; plowable, 31,025 acres.

Woodland, 5,474 acres; other lands, 4,488 acres; woodland not pastured (mostly mountain land), 588 acres.

Value of Farm Lands and Buildings	$10,914,340
Land alone	7,259,885
Buildings	3,654,455

Live Stock—

Horses	3,890
Mules	349
Cattle	7,473
Beef Cattle	859
Dairy Cows	4,086
Other Cattle	1,661
Swine	7,763

Crops—

Corn	13,678 acres.	201,850 bu.
Oats	1,056 acres.	23,030 bu.
Wheat	16,602 acres.	187,372 bu.
Hay	14,582 acres.	16,623 ton

Fruit Trees—

Young apples	212,789
Bearing trees	567,348
Bushels	695,150
Automobiles	4,093
Dogs—Male .... 2,040 Female	253

FULLNAME INDEX

ABEL, J W 275
ABLE, John N 327 John W 326
ACTS OF CONGRESS, 143
    Revolutions And Pensions 143-145
ADAMS, Friskey 154 John 223
    John Q 326 Pres 223 Thos G 161
ADOPTION, Of Constitution (U.S.) 75-77
AFFAIR, At Falling Waters 114
AGNEW, 316
AIKENS, J C 299
AITKENS, James 142
AITKIN, James 142
ALBAIN, John 158
ALBERTIS, Ephraim G 63 William 63
ALBIN, James 156 William B 155
ALBURTIS, E G 88 110 112-113 151 157 274 Ephraim G 119 149 John 85 147 234 237 314 Samuel 111 157 314 William 232
ALBURTUS, John 170
ALDERSON, Sarah 160
ALER, F Vernon 201 315 Samuel 201
ALEXANDER, H L 277 Herbert L 280 Joseph 276 William 276
ALLEN, 251 Ebenezer 140 Hall 167 Robert A 331 Sen 270 Walter 250
ALLISON, 270 John 155 Robert 298 Robert E 299
AMBROSE, Edward M 159
AMERICAN, Red Cross 317
ANASTOS, Thomas J 161
ANDERSON, Agnes 206 Eli 155 George F 161 Jacob 144 James 273 276 James W 155 Michael 316 Thomas R 161 William 140-141 206
ANGELL, John 138
ANNE, Queen Of 193
ANTHONY, Edmund L 161

ANTLER, Adam Jr 138 Adam Sr 138 Philip 138
ANTRIM, Duke Of 218
APPLE, Pie Ridge 23 76
APPLEBEY, Geo W 186 George W Jr 266
APPLEBY, Geo W 189 George W Jr 248 275
ARDINGER, Benjamin 140
ARMBRESTER, Clarence W 161 Emma Fishel 299 J W 298 James W 254 John E 280 Wm D 161
ARMBRUSTER, J W 299
ARMPRIEST, William 157
ARMSTRONG, Archibald 158 John S 155 William 225
ARNOLD, 137-138 Benedict 199
ARTZ, Joseph 309
ARVIN, R L 159 W N 159
ASBURY, Francis 304
ASH, George 161
ASHBEY, Lewis 167
ASHKETTLE, J 154
ASHTON, Fred 161 Janney C 161
ASHWOOD, Ernest 161
ASSESSORS, 274
ATKINSON, George W 128 159
ATTORNEY-GENERAL, (U.S.) 281
AULD, Chas 157 Thomas E 158
AUSTIN, Thomas 156 159
AUTOMOBILE, 336
AVERILL, Gen 263-264
AVEY, Herbert A 327 Kennedy 286 Paul R 161
AVIATION, 287
AVIS, John 276
AWMAN, Benjamin 155
BACK, Creek 79 329
BACON, John B F 161 Nathaniel 61
BAILEY, 270 Charles E 161 Mr 206
BAILY, Capt 231
BAIN, A B 121
BAIRD, Hobret E 161
BAITTY, Daisy Taylor 300
BAKER, 95 330 333 Newton Diehl 176 Anna Gertrude 241 Elias 176-177 Elizabeth 176 George T H 161

BAKER (cont.)
  Gracien H 161 Harry L 161 J S
  W 317 John 76 220 281 323
  Margaret E 300 Mary 176-177
  Mr 176 N D 129 Newton 261
  Newton D 176-177 281 290 Roy
  H 161 W E 280 Walter 276
BALCH, L P W 274
BALDWIN, Henry 225
BALES, Adam S 156
BALL, John 154 Vance 110
BALSER, Samuel 276
BALTIMORE, And Ohio R R 88 103
  105 125 284 Lord 24 28 53 96-
  98 100-102 330 Lord Charles
  100-101 Lord Frederick 101-102
BANCROFT, Mr 264
BANE, Amanda 299 Newton 156
BANK, Of Martinsburg The 327
BANKS, 153 326 333 Gen 117 152
  211 Genie 300
BANROFT, George 325
BAPTISTS, 21
BARBEHEN, Joel L 161
BARBER, William H 274
BARBOUR, Gov 85 James 65
  Philip P 234 Philip R 225
BARGER, John 142
BARNDOLLAR, Anna 203
BARNES, Flora M 299 Joseph 274
  Lemuel 155
BARNET, Samuel 142
BARNETT, A J 156 Joseph H 276
BARNEY, 95 Jacob 58 John E 276
  Wm 110
BARNHART, Carrie M 298 Carrye
  M 299
BARRETT, Fenton L 161 Henry
  140 Stewart 161
BARRINGER, Widow 51
BARRY, Thomas H 161
BARTER, 33
BARTHLOW, Joshua 155 William
  155
BARTLES, Paul E 161
BARTLEY, Harry 161
BARTON, Dr 82
BASEY, Wilmon 167
BASORE, 95 Emanuel 156 Ernest
  R 161
BATCH, C 154
BATEMAN, C 154

BATES, Henry E 161
BATT, Thomas 63
BATTLE, Elizabeth A 300
BAYAN, John 144
BAYER, Geo Wm G 161
BAYLIS, George W 271
BAYLOR, Richard 221 276 279 Robert 64
  276
BAZIL, John 142
BEALES, John A 149
BEALL, Anna 169 C Ralph 161 Charles
  Ralph 219 Edward 219 Hilda 299
  Laura 219 Virginia 219
BEAR, James 88 John 88
BEARD, Charles 180 277 280 Frank B
  161 George 157 James E 161 John
  159 John Wm 161 Orin J 299 Samuel
  T 161
BEATTEY, Thomas 142
BEAVER, James 167
BEAVERS, Earl 161
BECK, Ida 187
BECKER, Frederick 304
BECKERT, Virginia A 300
BECKWITH, C L 161 Frank 274 Sidney
  86
BEDDINGER, Henry 135 139 173 274
  Michael 135 Michael George 139
BEDINGER, Daniel 139 142 144 227 G
  M 140 Henry 72 140-142 144 215 224
  232 258 279 Michael 72 215 Rachael
  258 William 142
BEDINGTON, 334
BEESOM, Edward 227
BEESON, Edward 61-62 325
BELL, Alfred 156 E C 161 Harry 157
  Jesse L 161
BELLER, Henry E 137
BENDER, 89 Adna 300 Amelia Oshcom
  238 Harold H 238 274 I L 238 274
  321 I Lewis 238 John 154 John Lewis
  238 Lee M 238 328 Margaret
  Eleanore 238 Mr 238 Mrs
  Washington 246 William 296
BENNER, George 140
BENNETT, Anderson 149 Edward 140
  Gabriel 161
BENSON, Joseph A 155
BENT, R Lewis 327
BENTON, Sen 269
BENTZ, 312 Helen Bryan 300 R Lewis
  161 Ralph 161 T 155

Index

BERKELEY, 334 And Hampshire Grade 286 Border Guards 113 151-156 County 60-66 71-72 78 128 329 County Court 57 County Historical Society 321 County Horticultural Society 321 County In 1810 78-84 John 9 Lord 24 Norborne 61 Springs 83 323 William 17 61 293
BERRY, H C 129
BERT, W S 248 William S 202
BETS, James 158
BETZ, Elmer 160
BEVERLEY, John 140
BEVERLY, William 103-104
BIBBEE, Carl R 161
BILLMIRE, John 110
BILLMYER, 90 D F 277 Mary 177
BIRNBECK, Mary 241 Theodore 241
BISHOP, Charles 247 Charles R 161 Daisy 253 Jacob 316 John 154 John W 169 187 291 Josephus 247 Kate 169 Thomas 247 Thomas J 247
BITNER, Ernest H 161 Lelia M 300 Ralph W 161 Raymond 161
BITTINGER, Harry 161
BLACKBUR, S C 161
BLACKBURN, 270 H H 273
BLACKHEAD, Anthony 142
BLAINE, James G 183
BLAIR, 334 William 140
BLAIRTON, 334
BLAKE, Edward I 161 John 141 Maurice H 161 V B 156
BLAKELEY, Vernon 167
BLAKEMORE, George A 277 James 277
BLAKENEY, Edward 157 George W 149 Harry 157
BLAMER, C E 160 James 156
BLANCHFIELD, H L 160 John 157
BLESSING, John H 149
BLEW, David 144
BLIZZARD, William 250
BLOCKER, Geo 317
BLONDELL, A 317 Benj W 149 Capt 111 Charles 158 John H 316
BLOOMERY, And Hampshire Grade 123

BLOOMFIELD, Maurice 239
BLUE, Virginia 298
BOAK, Dr 216 Elizabeth 191 J S 290 Jacob S 215 Kate A 216 S D 191 Seibert D 161 William L 91 276 279
BOARD, Of Supervisors 124
BOCOCK, Mrs Thomas 174
BODINE, John 140 R 297 Richard 275
BOEHM, Martin 304 Mr 304
BOGERT, Jackson L 161
BOGGS, Capt 269 John 268-269 Lydia 268-269 William Jr 268 William Sr 268
BOGLE, William 142
BOHDA, Hiram H 121
BOHRER, C 161
BOLEY, Benjamin 188 Benjamin F 158 Frank E 188
BOLTZ, Howard W 161
BOONE, Daniel 230 Luther C 161
BOOTH, Georgte E 161
BORDEN, John 63
BORDS, 64
BOREMAN, Arthur I 120-121 246 293 Charles 323
BORUM, C C 262 322 Clyde C 262 Richard 262
BOUGHER, George 142
BOULDEN, John 142
BOUTETORT, Baron Of 61
BOWEN, A J 276 M T 274 Richard 132 Tucker 175
BOWERS, A J 122 276 Alice 300 Andrew J 252 Bessie C 183 Eleanor 218 Eleanore 183 Geo M 129 322 George H 161 George M 129 184 186 218 262 268 271 277 281 326-327 331 333 George M Jr 161 183 George Meade 183 Harry 160 J S 280 Jean B 218 Jeane 183 John 157 John E 154 John S 183 326 Joseph Edward 161 Joseph F 161 Mary E 183 Mildred 299 Mr 129 183 Raymond A 161 Richard H 158 Robert N 161 Roy W 161 Stephen B 161 Stephen E 183 Thos V 161 Walter F 161 Yost 161
BOWMAN, Andrew 63 110 Frank L 280 George 19
BOYD, 95 Andrew H H 221 228 Ann 221 Ann Rebecca Holmes 221 Anne 222 B R 156 Bailey 234 Belle 268 Charles 234 Col 255 E Holmes 184 Elijah 234

BOYD (cont.)
  Elisha 57 77 86-87 171 184 199
    221-222 228 234 262 273 278-
    279 323 Elisha Jr 148 Elizabeth
    222 Elmer H 161 Fulton 234
    Gen 222 263 James Hunter 161
    John 20 57 221 234 John E 93
    158 221 234 255 268 John W
    276 Lem 234 Margaret 234
    Mary 171 221-222 234 263 Mr
    307 Munford 234 Nannie
    Spottswood 184 R H 280 307
    Rachael 234 Robert H 234 255
    268 Samuel 279 Sara Ann 221
    William 234
BOYDVILLE, 57 77 283
BOYER, C W 315 John 136
BOYLES, Stephen 63
BOYT, J B 203
BRACKETT, M C 305
BRADDOCK, 53 74 199 226
  Edward 50 198 267 Gen 33 50-
  52 55 59 131 194 223 267
BRADFORD, Gov 228 264 Mr 309
BRADOCK, Edward 131
BRADY, 95 Benjamin F 121 246
  276-277 296 Christian 140
  Christopher 141 Ella 296 299
  George 296 John E 122
  Katharine 298 Katherine 299
  Katherine S 299 Mrs Benjamin
  F 246 Peter 156 Samuel 229
  William 141
BRANHAM, Caroline 299 Eliza 299
  J B 330
BRANTNER, Z T 310
BRATHWAIT, Paul R 161
BRAXTON, George W 277 W M 167
BREATHED, James W 158
BRECKENRIDGE, Gen 196
BRECKER, Levi 155
BRECKONRIDGE, Gen 197 J C
  196
BREEDEN, David S 161 George F
  161 L C 161
BRENEIZEN, Belle 252
BRENNER, W L 160
BRENT, George 62
BREWER, Eugene 161
BRIGHT, Thomas 132
BRISCOE, Benjamin F 270 George
  62 J Frank 271

BRISCOE (cont.)
  John 61 107 275 W M 167
BRITCHNER, Bernard H 161
BRITT, Charles L 161
BRITTNER, Thaddeus 158
BRITTON, Edward 157
BROCIUS, William 156
BROCKANBRAUGH, Wm 274
BROCKENBROUGH, Sarah Jane 225
BROMBAUGH, G S 159
BROMLEY, Bernie J 161
BROOKE, Robert 65
BROOKEY, Roy F 161
BROOKS, C E 160 Emory B 161 Robert
  D 161
BROWN, Andrew J 276 Angelo 161
  Beecher 161 C V 167 Charles 156 E
  W 167 Ed 211 Ed C 211 Fred M 161
  George 141 Howard 167 Howard K
  161 James 141 James G 113 James S
  157 John 113 149 151 199-200 249
  257 298 324 332 John H 211
  Lawrence V 161 Loring T 161 Lott D
  161 Marvin C 161 Mary 218 Old John
  112 Peter A 149 Preston C 161
  Raleigh 161 Randolph 167 Raymond
  M 161 Roger M 161 Roy 167 Samuel
  141 T D 160 Thomas 279 Thomas S
  322 William 154 William G 184
  William J 149 Wm G 183 Yeakley A
  161
BROY, Lawrence L 161
BRUMBAUGH, G S 240 Mr 240
BRYAN, William Jennings 325
BRYARLY, 89-90 95 Harry 333 Robert P
  158
BUCHANAN, James 173 Pres 173
BUCHANNAN, James 92 Pres 91
BUCHANNON, J C 158 Pres 281 Thos
  156
BUCKLES, Gen 333 Robert 19 Robert Jr
  132
BUCKMASTER, Capt 148
BUESY, C A 167
BUNKER, Hill 58 95 291 333
BURCH, George 155
BURDETTE, Sarah 299
BURGESS, A H 299 A N 298
BURGOYNE, 70 199 223
BURKHART, 95 Daniel 88 91 248-249
  273 276 326 George R 245 Harwood
  249 280 John D II 249 John D III 249

INDEX 341

BURKHART (cont.)
  John D Jr 248 Margaret 296
  298 Mr 209 242 Paul F 245 R C
  158-159 321 Robert C 208 242
  277 333 Ruth 248 W D 317
  William 249 William D 326
BURNETT, W G 237
BURNS, A C 287 Benjamin F 305
  John 305 John Jr 111 Joseph
  119 L W 300
BURR, Aaron 74
BURRIS, Wm F 161
BURRISS, E 154
BURRY, John 63
BURT, Francis 235
BURTON, Catharine 64 Joseph 64
BUSEY, B P S 246 296 Benjamin F
  122 Lacy W 161 Mrs Benjamin
  F 246 Oscar Gold 161 Samuel
  327
BUSH, Harvey 312
BUT, Barrach 144
BUTCHER, Richard 140
BUTLER, 270 332 A R 263 Albert
  161 Bernard G 161 Charles C
  161 Floyd J 161 Gen 109 James
  E 187 John 158 Lily Snodgrass
  194 M S 194 Thomas J 155 W F
  167
BUTT, Burrock 138 Zachariah 142
BUTTS, David 155 Earl E 161 Earl
  W 161 Elizabeth Green
  Claybourne 253 Floyd 161
  George W 161 Henry S 274
  Lester 162 M K 277 Oscar 299
  Sally 65 Thomas Reed 162
  William 155
BUXTON, G W 130 Geo W 268
  George W 129 255 Marie 268
BYERS, Conrad 139 David H 162
  John 136
BYRD, Elizabeth 222 H F 261 315
  Harry F 281 Harry Flood 261
  Richard F 182 William 103 105
BYRER, 220 Frederick 219 Harry
  H 219 281 Isabella 219
C, & P Telephone Co 291
CABBAGE, Conrad 142
CABELL, William H 65
CABOT, John 5 Sebastian 5
CAGE, H F 167 James 156
CAIN, William C 149

CALDWELL, Cliff 249 G S 162 John N
  327 N C 249 N Cliff 280 Nelson
  Clifford 249
CALHOUN, 269 John C 172 234
CALL, Gen 233
CAMERON, Secretary 174
CAMPBELL, 95 Charles N 280-281
  Dougal 63 Dougall 148 Douglass 275
  J L 327 James 63 144 247 273 279
  James I 247 James II 247 James III
  247 James IV 247 James L 76 275
  321-322 James Lyle 76 James Vi 247
  Mary 253 Mrs John P 174 Ned B 247
  Thos K 254 William 85 147 170 275
CANBY, David 121-122 276 J 274 John
  274
CANN, P 154
CAPINI, Orebia 162
CAPPANA, Antonio 162
CARLYSLE, James A 156
CARMICHAEL, Mrs 311
CARNEY, J V 158
CARPENTER, Virgil 167
CARPER, George W 158
CARR, Leonard L 162
CARRYER, Harry B 162
CARTER, B R 167 Bertha 299 Charles
  103-104 Chas 161 Constance 270
  Joseph 140 Robert 103
CARTWRIGHT, Richard 264
CARVER, Richard 256
CASE, William 142
CASEY, Peter 56
CASHMAN, Matthew 162
CASHWA, Barnet 273
CASKEY, Dora 192 Esther 192 John 192
  John C 192 John William Rufus 192
  Margaret Rebecca 192 Mary 192
  Mary Ann 192 Mr 192 Rachael 300
  Rebecca 192 Richard 192 Richard I
  192 Richard II 192 W R 248 William
  156 192 William P 192 William Rufus
  192
CASQUE, Jean 192
CASSADY, John 142
CASTLEMAN, R M 162 T L 162
CASTO, D C 307
CATROW, 294 J R 280 J T 321 John W
  158 Mrs Harry S 246 W A 322
CAUSEMENIA, Charles 157
CAVE, Molder 162
CAX, Samuel 157

342 INDEX

CHAFIN, Carol 13
CHAISE, H G 162
CHALMERS, Dr 228
CHAMBERLAIN, Charles 162
CHAMBERLAND, J B 327
CHAMBERLIN, Minnie G 300
CHAMBERS, A S 275 Alberta 300 Anthony S 91 273 Elizabeth 300 Geo W 157 George W Jr 149 John M 156 Mayor 92 R D 156 Vannetta 300
CHAPMAN, Albert H 162 Arnold P 162 Jacob A 158 Joseph 274 Robert I 162 Ryland P 162 Thomas 158
CHAPTAL, 80
CHARLES I, King Of England 28 96-97
CHARLES II, King Of England 21 24-25 28 61 87 98 101 323
CHARLES TOWN, 151 324
CHARTER, 8
CHEAGLES, John 20
CHENOWETH, 95 Ben 92 James 296 James W 76
CHERRY, Run 88
CHESAPEAKE, And Ohio Canal 88
CHEVALLEY, James 156
CHEW, Capt 257
CHOPPERS, 123
CHRISMAN, F L 162 Geo 122 George 247 George A 273 Jacob 19 R C 162
CHRISTIAN, John 162
CHRISTY, 95
CHRISWELL, 95
CHURCH, E E 243 320 James 243 Jennie 243 Mary 243 Mr 243 W G 162
CHURCHES, 301-306
CITIZEN'S, National Bank 290
CIVIL, War 57 112-119 150 159
CLAPHAM, Henry L 161 R E 162
CLARENDEN, Lord 28
CLARK, Ernest 162 George Rogers 145 198 W B 162 Wesley W 160
CLARKE, 56 Walt 159 Wm 157 198
CLASPEY, James 154
CLAY, 109 C E 162 Henry 172-173 199 225 234 264 269 326
CLAYBOURNE, William 9
CLEARY, J Lewis 154
CLEDENNING, James N 121
CLEGGETT, Richard 279
CLEMMONS, E H 162
CLENDENING, Abram 250 Albert J 249 Andrew 249 William 154 249-250
CLENDENNING, H L 162 R M 162 Virginia Gould 299
CLERK'S, Office 62 274
CLEVELAND, 176 Pres 202 216
CLEVINGER, R 154
CLIFFORD, J R 159 271 311 315 Mr 315
CLINE, Charles S 162 Charles V 162 David A 156 Edmund B 162 Lucy 207 S P 162 S S 277 William S 207
CLINTON, Dewitt 283
CLOHAN, A E 162 Agnes 206 Alexander 128 180 206-207 281 290 321 333 Archie A 207 Bessie 207 Celia 207 Elsie 207 Herbert 207 Louis 207 Lucy 207 Mr 206-207 Robert 207 William 206 206-207
CLOWSER, C F 162
COCKBURN, Robert 273
COCKERILL, 270
COCKRAN, Charles C 155 Hiram 155
CODY, Buffalo Bill 215 J J 162 William 215 William F 215
COE, Mrs Carter 186
COFFINBARGER, Willard 299
COFFMAN, R G 162
COHEN, Lewis 162 Sol 162
COHONGOROOTON, River 17 50
COLBERT, Clarkson 155 George 154 Jesse 155 R A 162
COLE, 189 H M 309 J B 162 John 140 Paul F 161 William 122
COLEMAN, Boyd 162 C E 162
COLLETT, Daniel 276
COLLEY, F A 162
COLLIER, A J 162 Clinton 162
COLLINS, Charles 142 J F 162
COLLIS, A W 162 H L 162
COLQUITT, Gov 272
COLSTON, 95 172 190 Capt 216 Edward 76 85 147 170 215-216 222 224-225 273 275 279 281 Elizabeth 216 224 Jane 216 225 Minnie 216 Raleigh 29 224-225 Raleigh T 113 156 216 Raleigh T Jr 156 Ralph 323 Sarah Jane 225 Sophia 216 Susan 216 W B 274 315 W L 167 William 93 William B 216 275 279

INDEX 343

COLUMBUS, 129 Christopher 5
COMBS, J L E 158
COMEQUY, Benjamin 273 275
COMMANDERS, U. S. Navy 281
COMMISKEY, Thomas 157
COMMUNICATION, 289
COMPANIES, Of Civil War 113-114 151 154-158
COMREY, A L 162
CONGER, Seymore B 155
CONGRESSIONAL, Districts 75
CONLEY, William G 185
CONNELL, Patrick 141
CONNER, Charles 140 N M 162
CONNOLLY, John 133
CONOCOCHEAGUE, Creek 16
CONRAD, 95 David Holmes 199 David N 273 H Tucker 156 Holmes 116 200 Holmes E 155 Tucker 116 200
CONTINENTAL, Congress 71-72 Currency 73
CONWAY, James 157
COOK, H M 162 John 70 108 John R 279 R A 167 Thomas 141
COOKE, Catherine 233 John 276 John A 170 John R 85 147 233 280 Stephen 233
COOKUS, Harry A 162 Mary 178 Michael 136
COONTZ, Thornton 149
COOPER, Maria 265 Ruth 299
COOTES, Millicene R 241
COPENHAVER, John 63 Mary C 254 R S 162 T 156
COPPERSMITH, Mr 312
CORNWALLIS, 27 73 145 198 Lord 169-170 199
CORNWELL, John J 271
CORSEY, John W 272 Mattie E 272 300 S B E 167
COUCHMAN, David 158 Geo W 156 George 130 H M 317 J R 157 Mrs William 246
COUDHMAN, Albert R 320
COUNTY, Court 91 275 Infirmary 95 Jail 129-130 Officers 1928 280 Officers From 1772 To Present 273-281
COWIE, C S 162 F J 162 T J 162
COX, Albert W 162 C H 162 Charlotta A 161 Fabian C 162

COX (cont.)
  Foster N 162 Friend 51 G W 162
  Raymond 162 Roy C 162 Samuel 245
COYLE, Geo S 162 James 154
CRABB, W W 162
CRANE, Sadie B 300
CRANES, John 108
CRANMER, Charles 276
CRAWFORD, Abey 161 Col 132 Divid M 162 Douglas 162 Gilbert 162 Hunter 162 J L P 162 Jane 244 John 140-141 William 52 215 229-230
CREAMER, Chas N 160 John Q 149 Samuel J 221
CREEK, C H 162
CREIGHTON, William 236 281
CREQUE, 294 K B 159 K B Sr 327 Kensey B Jr 180 Kensey B Sr 247
CRESAP, Thomas 75
CRIM, C E 162 G D 162
CRIMM, Ella 257
CRISSINGER, G N 167
CRISWELL, John L 156 R L 162 Raleigh C 160 Robert L 259
CROCKET, David 89 Davy 89
CROCKETT, David 212 Davy 212 Joseph 236 Thomas 137
CROMWELL, Rudolph E 161
CROPS, 336
CROSS, James B 162 John A 155
CROUCH, Celia 207 Enos R 207
CROWE, James B 155
CROWEL, Jacob 149
CROWELL, Charles W 274
CRUGER, David 269
CRUSE, William 142
CULLUM, Gen 264
CULPEPPER, Catherine 25 Catherine Daughter Of Lord Alexander 24 Lord 24-25 98-99 Lord Alexander 24 Lord Thomas 103
CUMBERLAND, Valley R R Co 124 260
CUMBO, 334
CUMMINS, John 142
CUNNINGHAM, 89 Capt 217 Charles 158 Charles A 217 David 157 George 62 276 James L 110 217 275 James N 158 216 Lt 217 P S 155 Patrick 316 W L 158 Wm J 298
CURRY, Alonza H 155 John 140
CURTIS, Cromwell 177 Florence M 300 Louisa 177

CURTISS, Martha Dandridge 254
CUSHEN, R D 158
CUSHWA, 95 Anna 220 Barnet 209 276 Barnett 110-111 Charles G 275 Daniel 158 David 158 George 240 H S 209 277 H T 130 277 291 Harry 209 Harry S 209 Harvey C 209 Helen 298 James W 158 John 208-209 Jonathan 209 Mr 209 Seibert 158
CUSTER, A W 162 Ephraim G 156 Gen 239 Geo W 256 George A 239 Leo 162
DACY, John C 272
DAILEY, Anna Gertrude 241 Arthur 154 Chas S 162 Christopher H 242 Harry A 162 J H 242 James H C 241 James S 180 241 277 John W 280 Raymond B 162 242
DAIUTO, Frank B 162 Joseph H 162
DALGARN, S S 156
DANDRIDGE, 218 254 258 Betty 268 Danske 140 E P 156 Stephen 323 William 105
DANIELS, 327 G W 129 252 277 331
DARBY, A D 328 Albert D 204 D 323 Ezra 204
DARKE, 56 Col 146 Gen 74 147 Joseph 74 146 William 52 71 73-74 132 135-136 144-147 198 227 230 276 279 281 333
DARKESVILLE, 57 83 114 117-118 333
DARNHEFFER, John 137
DARR, Chas L 162 Claude E 162
DASTFORAN, John 132
DAUGHERTY, Draper M 218 Geo 111 Harry M 218 Jean B 218 Jeane 183
DAVENPORT, Abraham 276 Henry B 142 John 273 276
DAVID, Pres 197
DAVIDSON, Charles L 310
DAVIES, Louis 264
DAVIS, Amos 108 Charles E 162 Charles H 162 Francis M 162 Fred 162 Hester Dugan 298 Jefferson 174 235 John W 219

DAVIS (cont.)
Joseph 154 Kate A 216 Newton B 162 Pres 174 Rebecca Harding 269 Samuel 142 154 Thomas 220 276 279 Ulysses 154 William 140
DAY, James W 156
DAYTON, Alston G 179 203 241 William L 174
DEAGAN, E G 274
DEAN, 211 Charles A 162 Daisy May 242 Emily 242 George R 242 J E A 242 James William 242 John W 242 John W Jr 242 Julian 162 William 242 273
DEARBORN, Henry 170
DEATRICK, H N 181 273 Miss 181
DEBAUGH, John 254
DECELORON, Bienville 49
DECROCK, Michael 137
DEEN, Geo W 155
DEETS, James 155 William 154
DEHAVEN, Alex 253 B M 253 Bennett M 253 Daisy 253 E T 162 Elizabeth 253 Hunter 162 Jackson 253 John W 162 Joseph 276 Leslie 253 Levi 253 Peter 253 Samuel 253 Sula 253 Sula M 300 Virginia 253 William 253
DEIHL, 327
DELANCY, Wm R 162
DELLINGER, F S 276
DELPLAIN, Col 126
DENAN, A 154
DENNIS, Daniel E 327
DENNY, Alexander 142
DICK, Charles 188 Charles E 188 276 280 Chas F 251 Homer E 162 Mr 188 Peter 188 Robert W 188
DICKERHOFF, Isaac 154
DIFFENDERFER, Chas E 317 John 250 Wm 156
DILLON, James 298 James W 254
DILLY, John R 155
DINGLEY, Nelson 264
DINWIDDIE, Gov 49 Robert 49
DIRTING, Lewis R 162
DISTINGUISHED, Berkeley County People 280
DISTRICTS, 16 121-123
DITMAN, John 154
DIXON, John 279
DOBB, Carlisle 150
DODD, Ada 175 Adah 265 D E 176 D H 298 300 Daniel H 275 David 175-176

DODD (cont.)
  265 274 David H 274 David
  Henry 175 298 David L 162 175
  Donald S 162 Ella 175 Georgia
  175 John W 93 175 266 274
  Maurice R 162 S L 274 298 S
  Lowell 175 Samuel L 175 298
  William E 175 Wm Earl 162
DODD-POINCE, Adah 298
DOGGETT, Hilda 300
DOGS, 336
DOGWORTHY, John 53
DOLL, Barnett 276 Bernard 124
  274 C W 275 Christian W 65
  274 314 Frank W 238 George
  276 John 316 R M 156 Rebecca
  T 327
DONALDSON, Geo F 162
DONE, William D 149
DONNALLY, William 142
DORN, Henry C 159 M L 129 328
DORSEY, William 275 Wm 317
DOUGLAS, 112 212 Isaac R 274
DOUGLASS, Kyd 303
DOWNEY, 62 326 W W 249 273
  328
DOWNS, Ann 178 Caroline Jeanett
  178-179 Charles 178 275
  Davenport 178 H A 277 Harry
  A 179 Harry Allen 178 Joseph
  179 Joseph Allen 178 Mary
  Ethel 266 William Smith 179
DRAPER, Linnen 64
DREBBING, C L 156
DRESS, 32
DREW, Dolphin 279 William 62
  274 279
DREWRY, 211 242
DRINKING, 47
DRIVER, Wm D 162
DUBOIS, Catherine 169
DUCKWALL, Joseph H 274
DUDLEY, A S 305
DUDROW, Otis B 162
DUFF, William 19
DUFFEY, Andrew 149
DUFFIELD, 135
DUGAN, James A 156 James L 156
  John A 155
DUKE, Raymond A 162 S A 269
DUKEHART, Mary 176
DUNBAR, Col 50 53 Thomas 50

DUNHAM, Eugene C 162 Robert B 162
  Wilbur 162
DUNMORE, 108 Earl Of 58 Gov 133
  John Earl Of 64 107 Lord 56 59 61-62
  132 225-226 268-269 275 279 330
DUNN, Bessie 207 Daniel 160 John 274
  Peter A 162 Prince 207 William W
  150
DUQUESNE, Marquis 49
DUTROW, H R 162 Lawrence E 162
DUVALL, 77 90 Oscar J 162
EAGLE, A B 322 A Bruce 320
EAKINS, Robert 140
EARLE, Samuel 142
EARLEY, Robert 167
EARLY, 209 Explorers And Settlements
  17 Gen 208 242 255 Settlers 30-45 45
  47
EARSON, Joseph 156
EASTERN, Panhandle 17
EATY, Jacob 136
EBAUGH, C 154
ECKHARDT, Joseph D 280
ECKHART, John 137 Joseph D 274
EDMONDS, George E 162 Raymond H
  162
EDMONDSON, James 323
EDWARDS, Collis C 162 Retha 299 Wm
  317
EICHELBERGER, D S 276 315 Douglas
  C 162 S 111
ELIZABETH, Queen Of England 6 190
ELKINS, Stephen B 129 201
ELLICOTT, 95
ELLIOTT, Arthur C 162 John W 162
ELLIS, Ellis 274 Helen M 300
ELLZAY, William 323
ELY, Mr 174
EMERSON, 95 Capt 148 Charles Waldo
  265
EMMART, Amelia 191 Amelia L E 191 F
  S 219 Frank S 219 H H 327 Virginia
  219
EMMERT, 95 Allen R 162 H H 327 H M
  327
EMMNER, Mr 291
ENGLE, Bruce 310-311 John R 162
  Michael 140
ENGLEBRIGHT, John 156
ENGLISH, William 140
ENOCH, Henry 51
EPISCOPAL, Church 72

ERNST, Martin 137
ERWIN, Charles 150
ESPEHINE, G 154
ESTON, Catherine 233
EUTSLER, Keener W 162
EVANS, 15 203 Arlington W 296 Arlington Wesley 196 Caroline Jeanett 178-179 Clermont A 216 David F 162 Frank 162 Geo F 315 328 George F 275 277 Harry O 322 Helen Orcutt 196 Herman A 160 Isaac 63 Isabel 195 J W B 296 Jacob 333 James 150 James W B 129 195 John 20 50-52 54 179 194-195 258 266 John I 194 John II 55 194-195 266 John III 195 Joseph 63 Lewis 167 Mabel C 296 299 Mabel Claire 196 Margaret 195 Mary Ann 195-196 Mr 195 Mrs 267 Polly 55 194-195 266-267 Polly Vanmetre 179 266 Roy L 162 Squaw Chief 267 Tillotson 195 296 Wa-hon-da 267 Willis F 130 175 195 274 296 299
EVERETT, 209 242
EVERHARDT, Peter 110
EVERHART, Eugene 162 Fred L 162 George 144 Guy L 162 Philip 276
EVERSOLE, Corrine 299 Harry W 162 Isaac 156 J W 300 Jacob H 156 John W 156 Virgil W 162
FACHLER, Jacob 138
FAHEY, Thomas 154
FAHY, Herbert 289 Mr 289
FAIRBANKS, Charles W 264
FAIRCLOTH, Geo A 162 Jos E 162
FAIRFAX, 48 Bryan 323 Denny 29 George William 258 Land Grant 28 Lord 17 23-29 45 57 67 98-105 139 193 225 244 260 268 323-324 330 Lord Thomas 103-104 132 256 Norman 162 Stone 75 William 25 103-104
FALKENSTEIN, John 154
FALLING, Waters 299
FANORAS, Frank 162
FANSLER, Hart G 162 Wm H 162
FARIS, Aaron 279
FARNSWORTH, Harry S 162 Ruth 280

FARRAGUT, Commodore 231
FARREN, John 130
FAULKNER, 95 121 270 Boyd 263 Capt 147 171 215 Charles 263 Charles J 57 76-78 130 159 174 196 198 203 222 240 263-264 290 325 333 Charles James 76 87 96 106 110 124 128 171-172 196-197 202 214 221 227 235-236 263 265 278-281 326 Charles Jas 105 Chas J 126 129 169 297 Chas J Jr 274 Chas James 315 Chas Jas 110 Col 126 Dinner The 110-111 E Boyd 129 157 174 202 274 277 George 170 James 65 85-86 147-148 170-171 232 Judge 202 Maj 147-148 171 Mary 171 221-222 263 Mary Boyd 262-263 265 Mary Buckner 202 May E 319 Mr 76 96 106 110-111 130 172-174 263 325 Mrs 263-264 Mrs C J 319 Rebecca 170 Report The 96-105 Sara 170 Sen 264 Susan 202 Virginia F 318 Whiting C 162
FAULKWELL, Harry 298
FAUVER, Vervenia 256
FAWVER, Howard E 162 Wm B 162
FAYMAN, James 154
FEAMAN, James 157
FEIDT, George W 273
FELKER, Guy 310 Mrs S S 208 S S 321
FELLER, C Victor 162
FELLERS, B H 242 Edna 211 John 317 Mr 242 Richard 320
FERREL, George 122 276-277 Michael 154
FERRIS, Aaron 65
FETCHET, Brig Gen 289
FETZER, Bernard J 162
FEY, Arthur W 162
FIERY, Benj F 162 James V 157 Mrs S V 319 S V 312
FILES, Blanch G 298 Carl R 162 Harry M 162 John T 162 Lemuel 280 Marvin H 162
FILMORE, Pres 235
FINCH, W Newton 159
FINDLAY, Samuel 215
FINDLEY, Samuel 72
FINE, Harry C 162 Julia 220 Louis 220 Nathan 162 Reuben 220
FINIGAN, Patrick 154
FINK, Jacob 140
FINLEY, Samuel 140-141

INDEX 347

FISCHEL, Charles O 162
FISCUS, Joseph 276
FISHER, J Carl 187 Jacob 55
 James 156 186 James B 186-
 187 John L 156 Peter 137
FISKE, James 157
FITZ, 89 H S 162 John 290
FITZGERALD, J P 239 Maurice
 188 Michael 188 239
FITZPATRICK, David 155
FITZWILLIAMS, Richard 105
FIZER, John T 155
FLAG, Thomas G 110
FLAGG, 89-90 Claud O 162 Joshua
 256 Josiah 140 Josiah D 124
 Margaret 256 Ruth 248 Thomas
 G 276 Thos S 111
FLAGING, F H 317
FLEGG, Thomas 256
FLEMING, A B 128-129 Eli 277
 William 155
FLICK, 176 190 Ashbey 162 C
 Bruce 217 Elizabeth 217
 Lorena 217 Mr 191 W H H 198
 217 273
FLINT, 101
FLOOD, Mrs Joel W 174
FLOYD, Gov 75 John 65 96 105 173
 225 John B 173 John W 162
 235
FLU, Epidemic 307
FLYNN, David C 162 Jos W 162
FOLEY, John Wm 162 Michael J
 162
FOLK, Daniel 137 Geo Wm 162
FOOD, 31
FOOLS', Gold 27
FORD, Cora Lee 299 Dunbar 167 J
 M 167 James W 162 L E 167
FOREMAN, F C 327 Frank C 307-
 308 James 19 Mr 308-309 P J
 160 Paul 19 Ward T 163
FORESTER, Thomas 19 William 19
FORT, Duquesne (pitt) 49
 Frederick 53-54 56 72 Necessity
 49 Neely 55
FORTNEY, Dayton I 163 Genton M
 163 Harris J 163
FOSTER, James 144 John W 264
 William 19
FOUR, Governors Of Ohio 281
FOWLER, Grover C 163 H S 155

FOX, Edward 327 H L 167 James 141
FRAME, Nat T 191 321
FRANCIS, John J 163
FRANKLIN, 195 Benjamin 39 46 139 294
 Charles 163 Jesse 163
FRAVEL, Fred C 163 George 156 Lewis
 A 163
FRAVILL, John 155
FRAZIER, James 157
FREDERICK, County 19 60 Of Prussia
 103
FREDINGER, Raymond R 163
FREER, Henry S 150
FRENCH, 95 And Indian War 48-56 60
 And Indian War To The Revolution
 57-59 Jacob 297 John A 122 W H 126
FRESHOUR, William A 155
FRIEND, Israel 19
FRIEZE, A J 158 George 158
FRITTS, Chas F 161
FRITZ, Valentine 142
FRUIT, Industry The 320 Trees 336
FRY, Col 226 Joseph Daniel 163 Joshua
 104-105 Lewis 110-111 275
FRYATT, John T 116 156 Nancy 205
 Tillotson 57 85 147 170 259 273 276
 279
FULK, Boyd W 163 E J 280 300 Walter N
 163
FULTZ, Thornton 157
FUSS, Frederick 124 G W 330 Geo B 163
 Gotleip 124 Harry L 163 Howard 163
 Omer H 163
GADD, J H 257
GAGE, Gen 139
GAGEBY, James A 274 John N 158
GAGLE, John 154
GAIN, Blanche 246 Charles G 246 300
 Christopher 246 Jacob 246 280 John
 C 246 John R W 163 Josiah W 246
 Lucy B 246 Wilbur E 163
GAINOR, Robert 150
GAITHER, Geo E 163 M M 160 Oscar
 163 Wm H 163
GALES, 235
GALLAHER, John 88 John S 234-235
 John S Jr 150 Mr 235
GAMBINO, F A 163 John W 163 Jos F
 163
GAMBLE, Mrs 319
GANO, Algernon 259 Berkeley 259
 Catharine 259 Daniel 259

GANO (cont.)
    Frances 259 James 259 James
    T 259 John 259 Joseph 259
    Liston 259 Marion E 259
    Richard 57 259 Richard Mcs
    163 Roland 57 259 William 259
GANOTOWN, (jamesburg) 83
GANTT, Erasmus 144 273 275
    John 276
GARDNER, 95 Anna Henshaw 266
    E D 211 239 273 Earl F 327 I H
    266 Jarvus 156 John W 155
    Mabel Henshaw 265 Peter 316
GARRETSON, Catharine 193
GARRETT, John W 125 201
GARRISON, William Lloyd 172
GARTON, Vernon B 189
GASSMAN, Jacob 217
GASTON, William 234
GATES, Chester 163 Gen 69-70 138
    199 254 Horatio 52 64 69-71
    138 144 199 254 276 281
GATRELL, 255
GAUNT, Mr 79
GENERAL, Assembly Of Virginia 8
    10 16 87 107 120 133 299 331
GENTLEMAN, Justices 61-62 64
    67-68 107-108
GEORGE III, King Of Great
    Britain 61 64 72 108
GEORGE, William 141
GEORGULIUS, Stecanos 163
GERARD, John 21 301 Seamon 274
GERHARDT, Ella S 160 Ellen S
    168 Henri K 168 L D 307 L
    Dew 275 280 L Dew Jr 163 280
    L Dewitt 274 291 L Dewitt Jr
    168 Lewis Dewitt 168 Lucinda
    168 William 168 William R 168
    Wm Robert 163
GERLING, F 317 J Ferd 163 L C
    207 273
GERNEAUX, Frances 259
GERRARD, David 331 John 331
GERRARDSTOWN, 15 291
GETTINGER, Howard 317 J H 277
GETTS, Ellsworth 163
GEYER, Hattie 319
GHOST, Stories 43
GIBBONS, Jonathan 141 Lowell A
    163
GIBBS, Edward 275 Edwin 316

GIBBS (cont.)
    Mr 81 Scott H 163
GIBSON, Braxton D 141-142
GILBERT, Arthur M Jr 163
GILMORE, David 142
GISER, Christopher 154
GIST, Christopher 26
GLADDEN, 95 George 158 William 296
GLASS, G 156
GLASSCOCK, William E 128
GLASSFORD, Frank B 163 Wm B 163
GLENN, Capt 137-138 James 135-136
    Jos W 163
GLESSNER, James B 163
GLOVER, Arthur L 163 John E 163
    Joseph A 163 Victor L 163
GLUCK, A M 319
GOETHELS, George W 178
GOFF, Guy D 280
GOLD, Samuel 276-277
GOLDEN, A S 315 Mr 315
GOOCH, Gov 19 23 25 208 Maj 103
    William 103
GOOD, Peter 142 Vernon L 163 William
    279
GOODMAN, John 154 William 144
GORDON, Aaron K 150 C A 167 D D 167
    James 122 John D 274 Peter 163 195
GORE, Howard M 130 169 196 262
GORGE, George 158
GORHAM, Lilian 184
GORMAN, 270
GORRELL, Josiah 305
GRACE, Israel 154
GRAHAM, 97-98 A M 159 252 Andrew M
    252 Belle 252 John 121 John K 252
    Loula 252 Nan 252 Sally 252 Sebina
    252
GRANT, Gen 252 271 Lee S 163
GRANTHAM, 95 Elizabeth 240 Lewis
    240 275 279 M S 274 Moses 278
    Moses S 276
GRANTHUM, Moses S 277 William 276
GRAVES, Andrew J 161
GRAY, Anna 169 Bessie C 183 Catherine
    169 David 140 David W 149 James W
    111 151 279 332 John 142 331 John
    David 212 Mary Ann 168-169 Mr 89
    212-213 Richard D 163
GREAT, Winchester Road 19 60 285
GREEN, C G 167 David S 155 Fulton 167
    Gen 138 170 199 J H 167

INDEX 349

GREEN (cont.)
　Matilda S 300 R J 167 Robert
　19 William 140
GREENFIELD, Lsaac M 163
GREENVILLE, Richard 6
GREENWAY, Court 25-27 29 132
GREGORIA, Tomaso 163
GREGORY, Albert B B 163 James
　W 163 Marshall 163 William
　273 275
GRIFFIN, Andrew M 150 Michael
　155
GRIFFITH, A H 331 F Leith 163
　Harry S 163 J H 122 James 142
　Louise 300 Philemon 141
GRIGGS, M F 300
GRIMES, Arthur C 163 Clarence B
　163 Walter B 163
GRIMSLEY, James F 163
GRINDES, R 154
GROSINGER, John 274
GROSS, D E 159
GROVE, 95 Berkeley E 163 C G
　328 C W 163 Doughlas 298
　Eleanor 218 Eleanore 183
　George Bowers 218 Gilbeft C
　163 J H 159 Joseph L 163
　Lawrence E 163 Lewis H 150
　Mrs Philip 218 Philip 217-218
　Philip Ryneal 218 Roy C 277
　322 Zachary T 217
GROZINGER, Elizabeth 292 John
　276
GRUBBS, Bernard C 163 Martha
　300 Wm David 163
GRUBER, J 157
GRUNBY, Felix 235 281 Mr 236
GRUND, George 276
GRYMES, John 103
GUINN, James T 274 James V 157
GUSHWA, 208 Geo 240 John 209
GUY, S F 159
HAAS, Henry Jos 163
HAGAN, Arthur 150
HAGNER, Peter 235
HAGUE, W H 310
HAINES, John J 157
HALE, 270
HALEM, M 155
HALKET, Peter 50-51
HALL, 205 Ephraim B 274 Judge
　303

HALLECK, Gen 153
HALLOCK, Gen 264
HAMBELTON, William 156
HAMIL, G A 110
HAMILL, H A 111
HAMILTON, Alexander 74-75 223 Duke
　Of 258 James 140-141 William 228
HAMM, Jacob 276
HAMMAN, Harry C 163
HAMMANN, H A 260 Harry A 322
HAMMERSLA, Anna Lee 257 J A 243 Mr
　243-244 Richard 243 298 Rineal 299
　Rosa L 299 Rose 298
HAMMON, Rae 280
HAMMOND, A C 110 Allen 111 Allen C
　110 279 Capt 217 Frank T 163 G N
　158 J M 112
HAMPSHIRE, County 19 60 71-72
HAMPTON, Wade 117 153
HAMTRAMCK, John F 150
HANCOCK, John 225
HANDSHEW, William 62
HANES, Peter 140 142
HANNA, Mark 270
HANNIS, 90 Henry F 163 Herbert E 163
　273 280 Susan G 160
HANSHAW, Levi 275
HANSON, James 141
HARDEN, Ernest 163 Jerry 167
HARDIN, J T 163
HARDING, Charles W 199 Pres 169 218
HARDWICKE, Lord 101
HARDY, 134 Bernard C 163 County 19
　Marshall 163
HARKER, C 154
HARLAN, Jean 299 Silas 273 276
HARLEY, 95 Dudley 327 James 157
　Patrick 156 Thomas J 275 298
HARMAN, Hewett 154 M H 154 William
　156
HARMISON, B F 276
HARMON, David 142 Edward N 163
HARNDON, Thomas 157
HARPER, L G 280 Robert 19 198 324 T L
　297 Thomas L 298
HARPERS, Ferry 17 19 113-114 151 324
HARRIS, 270 Clara 299 George 273
　Milburn L 163
HARRISON, 95 235 Anna 245 Battail
　140 Battle 141 144 Benjamin 64 Capt
　231 Commander 231 Ella 257 Elmer
　S 245 Ernest T 245

HARRISON (cont.)
  Holland Williams 229 231
  Jacob 245 John 156 John S 156
  228 231 275 Lilian 184 Lt 231
  Mr 245 Mrs S S 246 Nannie
  184 Napoleon B 231 281 Otho
  88 Otho B 149 P R 116 200 275
  280 Peyton R 116 155 184
  Peyton R I 184 Peyton R II 184
  Peyton R III 184-185 Peyton R
  IIII 184 Pres 183 Robert L 245
  257 Roy A 320 327 Roy E 257
  Sally B 256 Samuel S 245
  Sarah F 184 Wilbur 163
  William Henry 65 148 225
  William J 245
HART, Jacob H 155
HARWOOD, James D 149
HASSON, R L 159
HATFIELD, Henry D 243
HAUCHER, William 63
HAUSE, Arlington 163 Reno 163
HAUSROTE, Wm C 163
HAW, James 331
HAYDEN, William 155 316
HAYES, Pres 185 281 Rutherford B 126
HAYNES, John 138
HAYS, Joseph H 155
HAYSLETT, Robert R 163
HAZARD, Charles 157
HEARSLEY, John 64
HEATH, Perry S 290
HEBARD, Mr 206
HEBERLIG, Mrs Calvin 311
HECK, David 149 J R 300
HEDGE, 95 Samuel 80
HEDGEMAN, Peter 104
HEDGES, Anthony 158 B S 157
  Dacatur 262 Fort 55 58 G B 328
  Hezekiah 58 Joseph 132 Joshua
  330 Josiah 330 Martha 240
  Mary 262 Owen T 156 275
HEDGESVILLE, 291 297 299 330
HEILFEINSTEIN, Jacob H 150
HEILIG, J S 274
HEIRONIMUS, O R 163
HEISTON, 95 Mr 258 W H 258
  William L 159
HELAN, Patrick 157
HELFERSTAY, John 156 William 157

HELLER, Josiah 150
HELM, George 142
HELSLEY, Catherine 257 George W 257
  John E 257
HENDRICKSON, Machyken 208
HENLANE, Henry 154
HENNIPEN, Father 48
HENRY, Patrick 64 71 140 R 154 Roy O
  161 Thomas 314 Viii King Of
  England 5 190
HENSEL, William J 276
HENSHAW, 89 95 Anna Mary 299 Annie
  Laurie 194 E C 321 333 E L 322
  Edgar 320 Edgar C 194 Edgar L 194
  287-288 Edwin S 253 Florence 194
  Frances L 266 300 Harry P 253 277
  281 Henry P 280 Hiram 86 John 193
  277 Joshua 193 Levi 121 124 194 273
  279 Levi II 194 Lily Snodgrass 194
  Mabel 266 Marion L 277 Mary 253
  Mr 194 Newton L 163 Nicholas 193
  Sarah Ann 194 Thornton 274 276 W
  T 261 275 William 72 140 193 215
  276 331 William T 266 277 281 Wm S
  273
HENSHEW, Levi 58
HENSON, 62 95 326 J O 327 Jack O 185
  281 John O 185 Sue E 300 321
HERRING, C P 186-187 Eugene 186
HESS, A T 157 328 Ashbey A 163 Balem
  217 C W 291 Charles B 163 George
  217 Golden E 290 John M 163 Lewis
  217 Mr 291 Peter 217 Robert T 163
  Solomon 217 Walter T 163 William T
  217
HESSE, Henry 163 Jacob 182 251 274
  276 288 Ludwig 182 Rev 300
HESSIAN, Fly 72
HETTENHOUSER, Lewis 163
HETZEL, Amelia Oshcom 238 Anna 203
  John J 163 204 206 328 John J Sr
  203 Joshua Philip 202 Margharetta
  206 Philip 202
HIBBERT, James F 163 Mr 81
HICKMAN, Francis 140 Gilaspie 155
  William 140 142
HICKS, Geo E 163
HIETT, H Roy 163 Lucy B 246
HIGGINS, James 140
HIGH, Jennings B 163
HILL, 270 A P 114 Abraham 157 Alonzo
  163 Charles 274

HILL (cont.)
  Christopher 157 274 Della B 300 Elmer L 163 G S 327 George S 249 326-327 George W 157 Joseph 156 Mr 326 Peter 140-141
HINES, John 157
HINKLE, Carrie Hess 248
HINTON, Edgar S 163 Stanley F 163
HIPPER, A 154
HITE, 48 Bessie 299 George 69 276 Isaac 61 Jacob 19 67-69 107 275 John 58 John Dayton 163 Joist 19 25-26 Lt 215 Mr 68 Mrs 68 Thomas 72 140 215 278-279 323
HIX, William 142
HIXON, John 144
HOAR, 270
HOBBS, E A 210 256 274 J Leonard 163 John Leonard 210 M R 210 Mary 210
HOCKINBURY, Albert L 163
HODGES, George 149 N 156
HOFFHEINS, W E 315
HOFFMAN, E L 155 187 249 277 John E 155 Joseph 276 L C 299 Robert 137
HOGE, John B 110 216 John Blair 111 114 274 279 Judge 92
HOGERMINE, Conrad 316
HOGLAND, Everet 141
HOGMIRE, Conrad 273 276
HOGUE, James 211
HOIL, Catherine 257
HOISER, Charles Wm 163
HOKE, George W 326 John Boyd 163 Joseph T 122 273
HOLLEY, Lewis 161
HOLLIDA, 95 Charles E 163 Ethel 300 Geo W 110 George F 275 George W 275 John W 276 Joseph W 276 Maude 300 William 121
HOLLIS, 288 Boyd E 327 Charles L 163 Clarence W 163 Edgar A 312 J 156 James F 163 Jos W 163 Joseph 110 Joseph W 276 M Trammell 194 Marion 332 Roy W 163 T P 156 T W 156 Trammell 194 242
HOLLISH, Phil T 160
HOLLY, Katherine 299
HOLMES, Andrew Hunter 221-222 Ann 221 Anne 222 David 76 222 Gov 221 Hugh 278 323 John 141 Joseph 221-222 Judge 222
HOME, Building 30
HOMER, Esther 299
HOMRICH, James M 156
HOOD, John W 149
HOOE, Sgt 288
HOOK, D M 299
HOOPER, E B 155 Walter 142
HOOSER, Francis W M 149
HOOVER, William 149
HOPE, 315
HOPEWELL, Samuel 269
HOPKINSVILLE, Susan 202
HOPTON, Lord 24 28 98
HORNER, 89 294 Robert G Jr 76 Albert Guy 163 Alexander 154 Charles 163 D Quincy 163 David 245 Geo Wm 163 George W 179 George Washington 179 James 76 James Edw 163 Jos B 163 R G 322 Raymond J 327 Robert G 155 179 Thomas B 163
HORSFALL, Mrs Abram 319
HOSTETLER, 176
HOTEL, Berkeley 322
HOTT, E T 309
HOUCK, Berney J 163 E M 163 John R 163
HOUSE, Of Delegates 277-279 Thomas 158
HOUSER, Isaac E 276
HOVART, 307
HOWARD, John 17-18 25 282 Robert 140-141
HOWE, William 169
HOWER, Edmond 155
HUDGEL, David 187
HUDGINS, William B 161
HUDSON, Hendrick 207
HUFF, Benjamin 156
HUGHES, Alex S 273 Benjamin 142 Blackburn 240 274 276 Chas E 163 Stickley 167 William 64
HULL, Dallas 157 Jacob 110-111 John T 156 Robert B 163 Wm G 163
HULSE, William 139-140
HUMPHREYS, George W 234
HUNTER, Andrew 199 263 278

HUNTER (cont.)
  Betty J 184 Col 232 David 86
  108 157 223 232 273-274 279
  323 325 David S 264 Edmond
  199 Edmond P 199 273 279 314
  Edmund P 307 Elizabeth 232
  Gen 228 263-264 John 276-277
  John A 156 John C 156 John H
  88 149 Moses 64 222 232 274
  276 279 Moses T 222-223 279
  Mr 199 222 Mrs 81 Robert W
  155 279 William 140
HUNTING, 44-45
HUSBAND, James 144
HUTCHESON, Thomas 140
HUTCHINSON, Samuel 155
HUTTON, Chas M 163
HUTZLER, Adrian C 161 F L 159 F
  Leon 163 Geo S 163 Howard C
  163
HYATT, Frank S 163
HYDE, Richard E 163
ICE, Will Creamer 163
IMBACH, Theodore F 277
IMPLEMENTS, 94
INDIAN, Cornstalk 58-59 133
  Crane 14 Kill-buck 56 Killbuck
  56 Opecancannough 10
  Powhatan 10 Road 60-61
  Tecumseh 86
INDIANS, 12-16 48-49 52 55
INDUSTRIES, 81 90 322
INGLESS, Joseph 154
INGRAM, John 154
INSTRUCTIONS, To Gov Wyatt 8-9
INWOOD, 260
IRADELIA, Michael 157
IRONS, Mrs A C 319
IRVIN, P H 160
IRVINE, Alex'r 105
IRVING, Washington 241 258
ISRAEL, Gilbert 157
ISRAIL, Edward 154
IZATTE, George 273
JACK, William 122 276
JACKSON, 51 240 Andrew 258 269
  C R 167 Col 115 153 Gen 115-117 152-153 J E 167 J S 167
  Pres 172 325 Stonewall 52 114
  152 174 333 T J 114-115
  Thomas J 54 152

JACOBS, Harry E 163 William 142
JAMES, Charles C 163 James L 163
  Russell H 163
JAMES I, King Of England 6 8
JAMES II, King Of England 49 98-99 103
JAMISON, John 88 149 Sylvester 76
JANNEY, Aquilla 158 John T 321 W H H
  158
JEABURN, John 141
JEFFERSON, 27 County 17 75 Georgia
  175 Mabel B 272 Peter 105 Pres 85
  170 228 S H 167 Thomas 64 71 W E
  272 Wm M 158
JENKINS, Asa 156 Dan R 163 George
  155 Holmes E 163 Wm A 163
JESSUP, Thomas Sidney 232 281
JEWISH, Synagogue 306
JOB, 57
JOHN, Evans Fort 50-52 54
JOHNS, B F 167 Hicks 167
JOHNSON, A J 167 Charles 163 Earl H
  163 George 167 Harry E 189 266 274
  280 Henry 167 J T 122 John 154
  Kathleen 299 Moses 155 Robert 144
  Samuel Ward 163 Tanner L 300
  Thomas 138 Tom L 176 William 154
  156-157
JOHNSTON, Gen 114-115 152 George 62
  H E 254 Joseph 149 Joseph E 114
  152
JOLIET, 48
JONES, 15 240 270 Charles 141 Gertude
  300 Harry C 163 J W 302 James 154
  Jerry 167 John 149 167 Lt 289 Sam P
  332 W E 202 W Fitzgerald 161 W L
  290 William E 117 Wm E 153
JORDON, Robert B 163
JOY, J F 156
JULIAS, Augustus G 163 John Jr 163
JUNIOR, High Schools 299
KACKLEY, Charles M 163
KAIN, J J 303
KAPP, Levi 317
KARNES, Lillie 300
KATZ, 253 Allen B 163
KAUFMAN, Robert L 163
KEARFOTT, J Baker 273 James 158
  James L 156 John B 273 John P 158
  185 William P 156
KEARN, John A 304
KEARNES, Cyrus 157 Joseph 156 Robert
  157

INDEX 353

KEARNEY, Anthony 138 Gen 231
  John 276
KEARNS, Thomas 276
KEARSLEY, John 136 273
KEEDY, Harold H 185 280 Harold
  O 163
KEEF, John W 149
KEEFAUVER, Normon O 163
KEEFE, Wm 88
KEEFER, Chas 317
KEENEY, Frank 251
KEES, 95 D N 214 Johnny 289
  Joseph Ed 214 Matilda 214
  Nelson F 299 Robert L 214
KEESECKER, Ara 299 Jesse I 163
  P T 274 Palmer T 163 274 Quay
  300 Ward W 163
KEIF, David Mci 164
KEIFER, William S 160
KEIFFER, W S 159
KEISCHER, Newton 156
KELLER, Boyd M 163 Hugh L 163
  Roy E 163 W H 299
KELLEY, 330 William 141
KELLY, B F 206 Mr 332 William
  140-141
KENDRICK, John W 276
KENLEY, Col 54
KENNEDY, 89 334 Boyd C 163
  John W 274
KENSEL, John J 158
KEPLINGER, C W 163
KEPPLE, Commodore 194
KERCHEVAL, 21
KERCHIVAL, 14
KERFOOT, Allen M 163
KERFOTT, J Baker 317
KERICOFF, Earl D 163 John R 164
KERNEY, John 108 141 236
KERNS, George Nelson 164 Joseph
  154 William 164
KERR, R 189
KERSHNER, Cyrus 122 George A
  289 Mr 289 Raymond E 164
  Robert H 164
KETTERING, Adam 211 Albert
  211 Bryan 212 Bryan W 164 E
  B 211 273 Ephraim 211
  Harrison 212 Isaac 211 Isaac B
  164 Walter 212
KEY, Francis Scott 218
KEYES, John 157

KEYS, 95 214 John 140
KEYSER, Edward L 164 John 156
  Wilbur S 164
KEYTON, Brooke S 164 Levi M 161
KIBLER, Calvin H 213 Charles E 213
  John 144 Walter 213 William H 213
  William Walter 213
KIDWELL, Sara E 300
KIDWILER, J C 300
KILGORE, C 154
KILL-BUCK, 56
KILMER, 89 327 Anna 220 B S 158
  Bessie D 267 274 280 298 Chas V 164
  Clarence 77 Daniel 158 Geo H 156
  George 299 H D 158 268 H Raymond
  268 John D 220 Miss 268 Mrs W C
  319 Noble B 185 Rebecca 268 Ruth K
  300 Stuart H 164 Wade C 220 281
  Wm H 298
KILPATRICK, 333 Gen 153 H J 164
KIMLEY, William 149
KINES, W E 155
KING, Ann C 221 George 221 J H 317
  326 Oliver 157 Thomas M 129
  William R 110
KINGS, Daughters Hospital 311
KIPPEL, Commodore 50
KIRSON, Dan 241 Mary 241 Max 241
  Noah 241 Wolf 241
KISER, David 154 Isaiah 155 John 155
KISNER, Washington 157 William 157
KISSINGER, Otho 149
KITCHEN, B M 128-129 274 277 Behtuel
  M 277 Betheul M 275 Bethuel M 259
  280 323 Catharine 259 Joseph G 277
  Paul D 164
KIWANIS, Club (martinsburg) 319
KLEIN, Charles H 149
KLINE, C Webster 164 John W 155 John
  Wm 164 Margaret Eleanore 238
  William 155
KNADLER, Harry E 164
KNEEDLER, James W 154
KNEISLEY, H B 164
KNIGHTS, Of The Golden Horeshoe 18
KNIPE, Joseph N 164 Wm Paul 164
KNIPHAUSEN, 138
KNIPPLE, Carl M 164
KNODE, John Stewart 164 Kenneth 164
KNOGGS, Howard H 164
KNOLL, 190
KNOLLYS, 190

KNOX, Thomas 140-141
KOGELSCHATZ, A 317 Mr 308 310
KOINER, L P 156
KOONCE, Virginia 300
KOONTZ, Frank J 164
KORCROSS, John 154
KOURELAKOS, Leonidas 164
KRATZ, Henry 317
KRAUS, Charles 160
KRETZER, James 137
KROLSON, Isaac 144
KUNKLE, 288
KURYPHEUSEN, Gen 170
KUYKENDALL, Maude G 300
LACY, E S 274
LAFAYETTE, 269 Gen 253 Marquis De 226
LAFEVRE, Daniel 273
LAIGN, Paul C 164
LAISE, Katharine R 300 Kenneth 164 Marion 164
LAMAR, 76 C Roscoe 164 Charles M 180-181 E Holmes 181 Thomas 180
LAMASTER, D P 276 John H 155 Theodore 155
LAMBERT, Boyd 219 C O 275 Lewis 269 Mr 269 Virginia 219
LAMEN, John H 274
LAMON, 89 95 Alexander 132 Elmer M 164 John 276 John H 121 276 280 John W 121 124 276-277 Robert 122 273 276-277 Robert H 190 Ward H 114 Ward Hill 255 331 William 221
LAMP, Alvin C 161
LANCE, Christopher 243
LAND, Area 336
LANDERS, Michael 157
LANDIS, Golden A 164 Naomi 299
LANGFORD, Florence 194 S M 164 Samuel M 248 W E 247-248
LANHAM, Jeremiah 156
LANTZ, Christian 157 Joseph 157
LARKIN, Anthony 142 Capt 150
LARKINS, Thomas 156
LASALLE, Robert Cavalier 17 49
LATHAM, Lois 300
LAUCK, Jacob S 316 Peter 139
LAURIER, Wilfred 264
LAWSON, Robert 226

LAZZEL, William G 155
LEACH, Earl Lester 164
LEATHERS, John H 156
LEDERER, John 17 282
LEE, 57 245 252 Anthony 306 Charles 66 69 71 205 281 Chas 254 Fitz Hugh 208 Gen 69-70 117 153 Gov 146 Henry 29 75 147 Richard Henry 71 Robert E 112 117 153 240 W H F 117 153
LEECH, Sidney 158
LEFEVRE, 95 Ann 178 E B 322 Edgar 299 J W 164 Robert 298
LEGG, G W 277
LEGGETT, Clarence W 164
LEIGH, Watkins 172
LEITER, Mr 181 Mrs P W 181 P W 255 275 327 Percey W 181 256
LEITH, William 276
LEMARR, Isaac S 276
LEMASTER, 95 D P 115 274 Frank 299 Guy B 164 Hilda 299 Homer W 161
LEMEN, Daniel H 164 Shelby C 164 W H 158
LEMMON, John 63 Robert 63 65
LEMON, John 19 William 279
LEONARD, Frank E 164
LEOPOLD, Elizabeth 176
LESHORN, James W 156
LESSLEY, John 144
LETCHER, Gov 202
LETFICH, S E 167
LEWIS, 50 134 140-141 177 195 Allen G 161 Andrew 59 132-133 198 226 Clyde J 164 Col 59 Edwin G 164 Elizabeth 299 Frank M 164 Fred 164 Gen 59 133 Grady 331 James 150 John 142 Lewis 156 Mrs Preston 246 Richard 167 Sabine 299 Walter 156 Ward Lee 164 Willis B 164
LEYBURN, Boyd H 164
LICKLIDER, John D 164 T P 260
LIGAMFELTER, W B 277
LIGHT, 95 Bailey C 164 Charles G 164 Charles P 128 281 Edward T 164 Eleanor 299 Ely H 164 Isaac J 155 John C 164 Lewis Mcc 164 William E 156 William H 156 William K 158
LIGHTS, Electric Arc 291
LIKENS, Jacob 137 John H 88 110
LILLUOKALANI, Queen Of Sandwich Islands 260

Index

355

LINCOLN, 112 212 Abraham 109 113 264 C 154 Pres 109 152 174 177 188 209 239 255 264 331 R M 167
LINDBURG, Charles A 182
LINDSEY, Grace E 300 Ward B 273
LINGAMFELTER, R L 164
LINGUMFELTER, W H 156
LINK, Charles William 206 Margharetta 206 Mrs C W 318-319
LINTHICUM, John E 164
LITTLE, Helen 300 William 62-63 107 275 Wm 61-62
LIVE, Stock 336
LOAR, John 138 Philip 138
LOCKE, Beatrice R 300 Ernest C 164 M 110 Meveralle 111 Roger F 164
LODGE, 270
LOFTIN, Charles 150
LOGAN, Henry 160 Lucetta 319 Mr 315 W T 275 William 140 247 Wm 317
LOMAX, Lunsford 104
LONDON, Company 7 49
LONG, Clarence P 164 Daniel 211 Gabriel 141 George 155 Isaac 304 Knives 21 Lawrence H 164 Therman 211 William 85 147 170
LONGAN, 315
LONGHAMMER, Howard 164
LORD, 294 Allen P 164 Charles P 164 Ella 296
LOST, Colony Of America 6
LOUCK, Barney J 164
LOVE, Mrs W S 174
LOVET, 255
LOWERY, Benjamin 154 Robert 154 157 Thomas 276 William 157
LOWMAN, James 157 John 154
LOY, Edward N 154
LT, Gov Gooch 103
LUCAS, Albert 167 Basil 144 Benjamin 157 Charles 157 Daniel B 201 Edward 19 235 Henderson 110 Q M 157 Robert 136 281 Ward L 164 William 136
LUCE, Edward 132
LUCKET, Thomas Hussy 141
LUNDY, 86
LUPMAN, Daniel 154
LUPTON, Edward 321 James Mcs 164 Martin 276
LUTTRELL, Cora B 299 E L 164 307
LYETH, Ben S 164
LYLE, 95 Hugh 61 107 275 R G 158
M, & P Telephone Co 88 95
M'KEWAN, Gilbert 244
MACCORKLE, William A 207 257
MACDONALD, 95 James 121 Martin W 164
MACGILL, John 62
MACKAY, Robert 19
MACKEY, J W 167 Sarah 170 William 169-171 William Jr 170
MADISON, Pres 222 236
MAGEE, Bernard D 150
MAGUIRE, Patrick 150
MAHONEY, Patrick 157
MAITLAND, Lt 182
MAJ-GENERALS, 281
MAJOR, Generals 281
MAKIN, Nicholas 140
MALCHER, John 142
MANFORD, Bernard H 164
MANGE, Peter 140
MANN, B C 164
MANNING, Dennis 158
MANOR, Charles W 156 David 156
MANPIN, T A 156
MANSFIELD, N W 160 Robert 150
MARCY, W L 150
MARIE, Queen Of Roumania 325
MARIKLE, John B 156 Joseph S 156 Thos T 156
MARKER, Charles E 164 Clyde D G 164 Edward L 164
MARKET, House 90-91
MARKLE, Hunter 129 Samuel 157
MARLATT, Peter 144
MARLETT, George E 164
MARQUETTE, 48
MARSH, Laura 219
MARSHALL, 97 Calvin W 161 Charles 225 Elizabeth 224 Geo W 158 J H 167 J W 160 James 29 Jane 225 John 29 224 Joseph 158 Mr 172 Thomas 172 Thomas R 326
MARTIN, 219 Bernard C 164 Col 29 67

INDEX

MARTIN (cont.)
  Denny 28-29 Geo S 164 H S 274
  J Ani 256 J B 300 James A 160
  John 58 154 Marie 268 Mollie E
  300 Mr 308 322 Paul 266 Paul
  H 65 185 256 261 268 274 280
  Philip 29 Robert L 164 T B 67
  225 323 T W 300 Thomas
  Bryan 29 Thomas W 322
MARTINDALE, Capt 263-264
MARTINSBURG, 16 58 61 67-70 83
  95 115 125-129 153 330 And
  Potomac R R Co 123-124 And
  Winchester Turnpike Co 88
  Evening Journal 261 291 Fire
  Department 316 Gazette 85 Ind
  School District 123 Public
  Schools 300 Street Railway Co
  325
MARY, Queen Of 170 Queen Of
  England 190
MASLIN, Ann 227 Thomas 227
  William 227 276
MASON, 95 Claud R 164 Dennis A
  164 Ellis V 164 Elmer C 164
  Fred L 161 Harry S 164 J W
  110 James A 158 James Fred
  164 Lorena J 300 M Adah 300
  Marshall 167 Peter 285 Robert
  F Jr 164 Robert K 164
  Thompson 150
MATHER, Richard 193
MATTHAEI, Dora 192
MATTHEW, Frank 154
MATTHEWS, Fred N 164 Gov 126
  Helen 300 Henry C 156 James
  275 John 85 147 171 303 Mck
  167 Rev 303 Thomas 142
MAUPIN, A T 315
MAXWELL, Edward W 149 James
  108 273 276 John 157
MAY, Charles W 164 Edward 164
  Harry 280 333
MAYBERRY, Clarke E 164
MAYO, William 104-105
MAYORS, Of Martinsburg 275
MCALISTER, James 67
MCALLISTER, Geo W 298 George
  W 298 John 276
MCANENY, W F 326-327
MCAULY, 134
MCBRIDE, 294 Irma 299

MCCANN, Robert 140
MCCARROLL, Chas H 160
MCCARTNEY, Henry 140
MCCARTY, Chas 164
MCCLAREY, Geo W 158 George H 276
MCCLARY, A W 274 Andrew W 275.
MCCLEARY, 95 Trip 155
MCCLELLAN, Gen 114-115 118 231 Geo
  B 114
MCCLURE, Geo H 110-111 George H 279
MCCOHAN, Chas P 164
MCCOLLOUGH, Samuel 230
MCCOMBS, Ruth 299
MCCOMESKY, Moses 142
MCCORD, Arther 140
MCCORMACK, Archie C 164 Frank W
  164 Wm 150
MCCOWEN, 244
MCCOY, 118
MCCUE, William 140
MCCUNE, John D 281
MCDANIEL, Benjamin F 164 John 122
  164 Raymond S 164
MCDEAD, John 140
MCDONALD, A W 277 Angus 58 132-133
  Bruce 333 Bruce E 186 Col 58 Ernest
  322 Ernest F 186 James E 186 James
  W 186 James W Sr 186 Mazie 186
  Miss 186 Richard C 186 Robert G 164
  Roy 186
MCDOWELL, 115 James 65 Kenneth L
  164
MCEVER, Andrew 144
MCFITRICH, Duncan 140
MCGARAH, John 140
MCGARY, J P 92
MCGAW, William 276
MCGEARY, William 155
MCGOWER, T B 164
MCGRAW, James 174 Mr 174
MCGRUDER, 95
MCINTIRE, John F 156 Summers 164
MCINTYRE, A C 277 280 Mr 310
MCKEE, Chas J 164 Herbert 164
  Maybury 158 William 273 276
MCKEEVER, 95 Arthur B 160
MCKEVEN, Catherine 144
MCKEWAN, Gilbert 331 Michael 170
MCKINLEY, 272 Alexander 155 Maj 188
  Pres 159 183-184 188 196 207 270
  331
MCKNIGHT, Benjamin 142

INDEX 357

MCKNOGHT, Dr 229
MCKORKLE, Alexander C 150
MCKOWN, Andrew 231 244
  Charlotte Campbell 189 G C
  321 Gilbert 244 331 Gilbert C
  164 189 244 Hiram 121 276
  Hunter 244 321 J C 188-189
  231 244 249 273 280 322 Jane
  244 John 244-245 275 Martha
  189 Mrs G C 319 Mrs Gilbert
  318 Paul 164 Samuel 76 244
  301
MCKUNE, Anna 240
MCLAUGHLIN, Franklin 157
MCMAHON, 101
MCMINN, Joseph 150
MCMULLEN, Charles 156
MCNEMAR, Michael 158
MCNOLL, Roy D 164
MCQUILKIN, 95 A R 275 280
  Abraham R 277 W T 328
MCSHERRY, 95 Anastatia 221
  Ann C 221 Dr 214 261 J Whann
  159 214 240 275 290 James 261
  James W 180 Mrs James W 174
  Richard 91 170-171 214 221 276
  303
MCSWAME, John 142
MCWHORTER, James W 156
MEACHEM, Richard 156
MEADE, Gen 252 George B 242
  Stephen B 122 276
MEADOWS, Elmer M 164 John M
  164
MEANS, Beveridge E 164
MECHANICAL, Arts 40
MEDCALF, John 140
MEDICINE, 41
MEDLER, 136
MEEKS, Guy 58
MELINTZ, Earl L 164
MEMBERS, Of Cabinets 281 Of
  Congress 280-281 Of
  Federation Farm Bureau 281
  Of Virginia Legislature 278-279
MENDENHALL, James 306
MERCER, Edward 19 George 105
  Marshall 155 Richard 19
MERCHANT, Isaac N 156 W S 157
MERRICK, 316
MESHLEY, Paul S 164
METCALF, John 140

METERN, 207
MEXICAN, War 87
MICHAEL, Harvey N 164
MILES, A W 327 Albert W 164
MILITARY, History 131-167
MILLER, 95 Adelyn I 300 Arthur F 164
  Benjamin F 164 Bess 299 Carrol R
  164 Charles H 180 254-255 273-274
  Chas D 164 Clarence A 164 D Gold
  129 210 321-322 Daniel 158 David
  140 Dudley W 164 Edith 298 Edwin
  W 164 Frank W 164 Geo D 122 Geo
  W 156 187 Geo Wm 164 George D
  246 276 George W 187 Gilbert P 210
  321 H S 186 188 195 Harriet 178
  Harry P 210 Harry S 187 273 296 310
  Harry T 164 Harvey A 156 158 Henry
  E 164 Howard M 164 Isaac 155 J H
  242 J Harley 124 Jacob 240 326
  Jacob G 164 Jacob H 327 Jesse K 164
  John 58 138 236 John E 164 John H
  122 John M 150 164 189 210 321-322
  327 Jonathan 156 Katharin H 300
  Levi F 154 Lucy 298 M S 307
  Madaline 299 Madeline 296 Milton O
  164 Milton S 187-188 Mr 209-210
  Mrs George D 246 Mrs Mazie 186
  Mrs Oscar B 188 298 Norman 274
  Oliver A 164 Oscar B 188 280 R
  Seaton 188 Robert 178 Robert Lee
  164 Sadah 298 Samuel 187 Theodore
  K 129 W S 209 254 296 William 121
  276 299 William S 122 320 332 Willis
  J 164
MILLIKIN, John 140
MILLS, Robert Carter 275 Walter L 164
MILROY, Gen 247
MIMEY, John 150
MIMS, Sam 167
MINGHINI, Dr 205 Goldie R 164 Joseph
  L 205 Lydia 205 Mr 81 Viola Marie
  205 W E 205 243 275
MINGLE, John 158
MINISTERS, 281
MINOR, 257 Frank A 253 G A 167 R T
  253
MISH, Arnold F 164 Geo F 164
MITCHELL, Joseph 67 Thomas 142
MOCK, Bertha M 266 James M 155 Miss
  266 Reva 280
MOHLER, Adam 138
MOLER, Butler H 164

MONG, 95 Anna E 204 Mary 177
  Wendall 57 158 William 177
  William E 204 William H 204
  276 William M 279 Wm H 110
MONGAN, Melvin J 164
MONROE, James 65
MONTGOMERY, Gen 137
MOON, 57 Jacob 306 335 James 95
MOONEY, J B 157
MOORE, Albertj 159 Andrew M
  157 Cato 65 136 273 J 157 John
  281 Richad G 150
MOPIE, William 150
MORALS, 37-38
MORAN, Ernest W 164 Mary 300
MORE, John 229
MOREDOCK, William 142
MORGAN, 95 227 270 Alva Rea
  164 B S 193 Catharine 193
  Daniel 52 62 71-72 75-76 89
  146-147 193 199 223-224 235
  281 David 138 Enoch 155
  Ephraim B 193 Floyd H 164
  Gen 223 H V 164 J B 315
  James B 316 331 Morgan 18
  131 193 276 302 333 Morgan I
  193 Morgan II 193 Morgan VI
  193 Morgan VII 193 Old
  Wagoner 89 Raleigh 135-136
  Richard 19 William 61-63 136
  275 William C 189 273 Wm C
  280 Zackwell 193
MORGON, William 107
MORREL, A H 305
MORRIS, Wm G 164
MORRISON, 95 Annabel P 160
  Chas W 164 Daniel B 276
  Garnett P 164 Geo L 164
  William 275
MORROW, Charles 135 Harry C
  164 Jeremiah 281 John 135 170
  276 R W 277 Thomas 135
MORSE, Samuel F B 185 290
MORTON, William 24
MOSEBEY, L W 167 W M 167
MOSELEY, Alexander 235
MOSSER, 238
MOUNTSFIELD, Thomas 142
MOWERY, Wm H 164
MUHLENBURG, Charles 156
MULLEN, Lille D 300
MULLIGAN, Patrick 157

MULLIN, G D 300
MULLIS, Mrs G W F 319 Van C 160
MURPHY, Alonzo E 164 D D 111 Dennis
  154 279 Edward A 164 George 92 112
  George H 157 273 James B 158
  James R 164 James W 155 John W
  155 Patrick 141 Richard 158 William
  164
MURRAY, Charles 140 Henry 158 John
  58 Patrick 157
MURRY, James H 164 Lt 289
MUSSELMAN, Plant 322
MUSSER, Norman 164
MUSSETER, J P 276
MYER, William 155
MYERS, 95 187 A 123 Archibald 121 276
  Chas B 164 Clifford 237 Cromwell
  157 David E 164 Edward Wm 164
  Enos 155 Floyd 167 G W 114 158
  Harry 167 Harry M 164 Howard F
  164 Hunter John 58 223 J H 167 300
  Jacob 155 276 279 Jacob H 165 John
  58 223 John H 160 Ludwig 136 Mr
  223 237 Mrs Bernard 318 Philip
  Clyde 161 R S 160 S N 261 Samuel
  155 W H 158 William Albright 165
  William C 155 Willie H 165
MYRE, Casper 142
NADENBOUSCH, A C 280 Adrian C 201
  274-275 Frederick 201 J B A 111 276
  J L 192 J Q A 113 155 181 200 317 J
  Roy 201 288 John B A 110 John Q A
  151 199 249 317 John T 201 M C 113
  Mary Ella 181-182 199 Moses C 151
  273 277 Moses T 201 Philip 65 230
  273 275
NAPOLEON III, King Of France 173
NATIONAL, Road 88
NEAL, John 137 Richard 140-141
NEAVILLE, John 61 275
NEEDY, Mary 298 300 Rachael 299
NEELEY, M M 280
NEELY, 238
NEER, A W 280
NEILSON, James 140
NELSON, 218 Dorothy M 299 Thomas
  140
NESSEL, 334
NEVILLE, Carter N 165 John 107
  Samuel 160
NEW, Constitution W Va 125-130
NEWBRAUGH, A F 299 Rumsey 245

INDEX 359

NEWCE, William 8
NEWCOMB, Dayton 165
NEWCOMER, Alex 111 Alexander 110 209 276
NEWKIRK, Geo H 165 George 279 Henry 62 James 85 147 170 James M 279 James W 276 Virginia 300
NEWMAN, J D 157
NEWPORT, Christopher 7
NEWSPAPERS, 314
NICELEY, Collins L 274
NICELY, Chas E 165 Geo Howard 165 Thomas S 165
NICHOLSON, Thomas 156
NICKLES, E D 160
NICODEMUS, Chas M 165
NIHION, Katharine 298
NIPE, Geo 121
NIXON, John 141
NOBLE, Anthony 67 276 Mary 243
NOEL, 190
NOLAND, William 157
NOLL, 95 Albert M 165 Allen B 190-191 246 273 296 307 313 Chas R 165 Fannie 178 G Oliver 298 Gottleib 190 Henry V 165 James Mcs 165 James W 333 Mr 191 307 Mrs Frank 246 Mrs William T 246 Raymond 165 Robert M 165 William T 158 190 246 Willis 178
NOLLE, 190
NOLLVILLE, 333
NORLAND, Lt 289
NORRIS, John E 110 273
NORTH, George 65 276 Gorge 273 Mountain 16 18 88 95 291 Valley Orchard Co 322 W D 276
NORTHCRAFT, Harry 165
NORTHERN, Neck Of Virginia 28-29
NORTON, William 9
NOURBORNE, Parish 72
NOURSE, Catherine Burton 64 James 61-64 107 275 279 323
NOVINGTON, John W 155
O'BRIEN, George N 300
O'CONNOR, Charles 165 Michael 157
O'NEAL, John R 157 Nelson B 165 213

O'ROKE, Eber C 165 Ward B 165
O'ROURKE, Paul L 165
OATS, T K 322
ODEN, Alexander 276 Ann 66 Archibald 156 322 Charles 66 Elias 65-66 Mr 322
OFFICERS, County 63
OFFICIAL, Directory Schools 298
OFFUTT, Nellie 300
OGDEN, H C 315
OLD, Deeds 63 National Bank The 290 Pack-horse Ford 18 Pack-horse Road 61 89
OLDHAM, Conway 140 Samuel 62
OLIVER, Denton P 165 Grace M 300 John L 121
OMENS, Etc 39-40
ONDERDICK, Howard W 165
OPEQUON, 16 18 79 95 300
ORGAN, Chauncey B 165
ORME, Lt 52 Robert 50
ORNDORF, Nolan 165
ORNDORFF, Christian 135
ORR, Mary Ann 195 William F 165
ORRICK, Charles 273 276 Nicholas 85 108 147 171 273 William 65-66
ORT, Alice K 300
OSBORNE, J Nelson 165
OTT, John 88 John H 149
OTTERBEIN, Mr 304 William 304
OWENS, Holmes P 165 Horace E 165
OX, George 138
PAGE, C G 167 M W 167 Thomas S 276 Thos S 110-111 William H 149
PAINTER, George 55 Joseph 156
PAINTER'S, Fort 55
PALMER, Chas S 165 Harry P 165 John 64 Joseph 64 Kearney 157 Mary Ann 192 Ray R 165
PANNICCIA, Giovanni 165
PAOLO, Francisco 165
PARISH, 68
PARKE, James 124
PARKER, Richard 156 215 Richard E 274 Stacey C 165
PARKINSON, John W 165 L A 165 William R 276 Wm L 165
PARKS, Alexander 89 182 256 274 276-277 290 320 Alexander B 182 287-288 Alexander Sr 181-182 199 Capt 213 John M 165 John N 182 200 277 Mary Ella 181-182 199 Mr 182

PARSON, Charles E 165 Mr 36
PATRICK, Mason M 289
PATTERSON, 288 333 Frank 158
    G H 165 Gen 114-116 152
    James 167 William 67 70 276
    Wm A 165
PAULL, Mary C 177
PAYNE, Isabelle 300 J Tripp 158
    John D 168 Josiah 168 Martha
    Shepherd 168 Martin H 276
    Martin L 158 274 Martin
    Luther 168 Nathan D 111 O F
    158 Samuel S 165 Shields 77
PEACOCK, James 136
PEARCE, John 138
PEARE, James 149 John 149
PEARRELL, Allen E 165
PELHAM, J C 157 John 117 153
    205
PEMBROKE, Earl Of? 9
PENDLETON, Charles 147 171
    Chas 85 E Boyd 263 323
    Edmond 263 Edmund 279
    Elizabeth 215 232 Judge 171
    Nat 140 Nathaniel 72 141 215
    P C 157 Philip 62 87 215 221
    232 279 302 323 Philip C 221
    276 323 Sara Ann 221 William
    65 67
PENICK, W S 274 303
PENN, 101 William 20-21 24 28 48
PENNINGER, Christian 142
PENSIONS, 143-145
PENTONY, James 149
PEOPLES, Trust Co The 290 327
PERCY, Lee 165
PERKINS, C 154
PERREGORY, William 157
PERRY, E A 167 James S 155
    Marvin H 165
PERSHING, Gen 210 248
PETER, 105
PETERS, Chas M 165
PETRIS, Frank 165
PETTUS, 270
PHILLIPS, A C 165 Mrs A C 300
    William 156
PHOENIX, Garrett 161
PICKING, John T 275
PIERCE, Franklin 110 Mrs 263
    Mrs S P S 174 Pres 235
PIKE, Frank Jr 157

PIKESIDE, 57 333
PILE, William 140-141
PILES, Edgar C 155 Osborne H 155
PINE, George 333 Roland M 165
PIPER, John R 156 T H 160
PITCHER, Charles W 155 John W 155
    Mollie 205 Roger Williams 205 Viola
    Marie 205
PITSNOGLE, Daniel H 161 Percy M 165
PITZER, 95 Anna 245 Charles L 246 250
    276 288 Charles W 246 Chas L 251
    296 E Mong 187 Elias M 121-122 245
    276 296 Eliza 246 Ernest D 165 G W
    299 Geo D 187 George D 246 George
    V 76 246 George W 246 331 Gladys
    299 Glen M 246 Glenn M 165 250 276
    280 322 Harrison Taylor 246 Homer
    S 165 Ida 246 J Hensel 165 Jacob
    245-246 296 James S 15 121 John
    165 245 John W 245-246 273 296
    Lida 246 Martin 76 245 296 Michael
    K 246 Miss 246 Mr 245 Mrs Geo
    William 186 Ruth M 300 Stuart J 165
    T H 160 U S G 250 275 U S Grant
    246 273 296 W A 296 William A 246
PLEASANTS, James Jr 65 John
    Hampden 235
PLOTNER, Herman D 165 Howard E 165
    Lawrence 165 T H 160
PLUNKETT, Father 303
POE, Andrew 230
POFFINBERGER, J C 165
POINCE, Ada 175 Adah Dodd 265 John
    William 265
POISAL, Daniel 88 149 J W 165 Jacob 85
    147 171 John 126
POLAND, J R 300 327
POLK, 235 James K 149 269
POLLOCK, Robert 149 Thomas 141
POMPELL, Jerome E 154
POOLE, J W 159 X 322
POPULATION, 335
PORTER, Commodore 235 Robert P 129
PORTERFIELD, 95 152 A W 110
    Alexander 157 Archibald S 279
    Charles 237 George 237-238 273 275
    279 J Myers 161 John 279 322 M H
    165 Milton 157 William 273 276
    William Jr 63
POSITIONS, Of Trust W Va 281
POTOMAC, River 17 79 329-330
POTTER, Alfred 154 R 154

INDEX

POTTS, 51
POWELL, Alfred 323 Elmer T 165
  George 138 Samuel R 276
POWNALL, Minnie M 298
PRATHER, Lemuel 165 Socrates
  149
PREFACE, 4
PRESCIT, B F 154
PRESCOTT, 195
PRESTON, James P 65
PRETTYMAN, Joseph 299
PRICE, 95 250 Harry 165 Isaac 141
  Luther M 165 Mr 310 Raymond
  W 161 Reuben 273 Samuel 165
PRIME, Benjamin 140
PRIOR, Thomas 157
PROCTOR, Roy S 309 W F 165
PROGRESS, Of County 87-95
PROSECUTING, Attorneys 273
PROSSMAN, William 155
PRYOR, John 156
PUBLIC, Utilities 336
PUCKETT, John 275
PULASKI, 138
PULLIN, William 155
PULTZ, David 121 273
PUNCHEONS, 30
PUTNAM, Israel 239
PYLE, William 140
PYLES, Miflin 310 Mr 310
QUAGLIO, Lario 165
QUAKER, Letter 20-21
QUAKERS, 20-21 32 57 72
QUAY, Matt 270
QUENZEL, Quay 165
QUICK, Harry 165
QUIGLEY, Dr 177 Elsie 300 James
  63
QUINN, Martin 214 316-317
RACY, William 155
RADIO, 290
RAINER, George 158
RALEIGH, Walter 5-7
RAMER, 270 Fred R 300 Frederick
  Randolph 269 Juanita A 300
  Miss 319 Peyton H 322
RAMSBURG, 95 Elijah 155
  Frances 300 Geo W 165
RAMSEY, Charles 159 D C 256 O
  M 253 256 Oscar Mahone 256
  Otho M 257 Otho Moseby 256
  Vervenia 256

RANDALL, John 137 Sarah 204
RANDOLPH, Beverly 65 James L 185
  John 234 Mrs James L 185
RANEY, Reginald 165
RANSON, Matthew 279
RAWLINGS, Col 228 Geo R 165 Moses
  141-142
RAWLINS, John 215 Joseph C 110-111
  276
READ, Isaac 226
REAMY, John T 149
REARDON, John 157
REBERT, Ellen S 168
RECONSTRUCTION, 120-124
RED, House The 324 William C 165
REED, Abe 280 David A 165 Henry 165 J
  F 157 John 157 John C 149 Lena M
  300 Richard 165 Russell F 165
  Thomas Buchanan 209
REESE, Jeremiah R 149
REGAR, Burkett 136
REGER, Lemuel 136
REID, J Thomas 165
RENCH, Eliza 246
REVOLUTIONARY, War 71-74 133-134
REYNOLD, 95
REYNOLDS, C R 288-289 Elijah 155
  George 137
RHODES, C H 165 H M 165
RICE, R L 298
RICHARDS, John 165
RICHARDSON, George 112
RICKARD, William H 165
RICKEL, Charles W 165
RIDDLE, John 156 William 273 276
  William N 276 Wm 317
RIDENOUR, Charles 155 Elmer J 165
  James 155 Martin 157
RIDEOUT, Edward 167 Timothy 167
RIDER, Adam 140 142
RIDGEWAY, 334 Charles J 334 Ruth 300
  Sylvester 154
RIDINGS, Cleo E 165 Harry C 165 N B
  165 R H 165 William Paul 165
RIFE, Chas L 165
RIFFLE, Henry 165
RIGER, Burkett 136 Lemuel 136
RIGSBY, O S 328
RILEY, Jennie 243 John T 315 Lucinda
  168
RIND, Harry L 165
RINER, G P 129 274 276 Henry 122 124

RINER (cont.)
276 Jane 299 John 77 188 211
John H 266 274 Maggie 299
RINOR, John 149
RIORDON, Edgar M 165 Michael
W 243 Mr 243
RIPPLE, 253 William 122 276
RISER, Irine Lemaster 300
RITTENOUR, C A 165 Henry F 165
ROACH, Claud J 165
ROADS, 282
ROBB, Philip 136
ROBBIN, 95
ROBBINS, George T 149
ROBERTS, 223 Charles 231 E S
158 Geo D 158 James 140 142
Samuel R 165 William 158
ROBERTSON, Mr 79
ROBINSON, 95 H C 317 Israel 155
274 276 279 J H 167 James 297
James H 276 James W 273-274
315 326 John 103 John S 157
315 R K 111 279 Robert K 110
276 Ruby B 165 Thomas 61 107
275
ROBISON, Edgar 157
ROBY, Middleton 155
ROCKWELL, 255 F M 165 George
W 156 Wm M 165
RODERICK, J E 310
RODGERS, A L 298-299 Decatur H
262 James S 262 Mary 262
ROE, Owen R 165
ROGERS, A Kenneth 165 Decatur
H 165 274 280 L T 159 Peyton
167 Robert L 165
ROHERBAUGH, Perry A 273
ROMER, Edward L 165
RONEMOUS, Andrew 138 Conrad
138 Lewis 138
RONK, Alice 291 Benjamin 158
Mary 291
ROONEY, Lee G 165 Lewis 237
Michael 58 65 237 275 Mike
237 Mr 237 William B 299
ROOSEVELT, Col 256 Mr 326 Pres
183-184 207 331 Theodore 182
326
ROPP, 95 C H 277 Geo Wm 165
Jacob 121-122 276-277 298 326
Margaret 300
ROSE, A P 157

ROSS, Alfred 276 Gen 86 James O 154
ROUARK, Wm H 165
ROUSCH, Arlington 177 Carrie 177
Charles 76
ROUSE, John 132
ROUSH, Anna E 204 Arlington 76 129
204 Carrie 204 Carrie M 312 Charles
158 204 Conrad 204 George 204
George S 204 Margaret 204 Sarah
204
ROWLAND, David M 165
RUBLE, Charles 210 280 Charles W 210
Matthias 210
RUCKMAN, L A 300
RUDE, George W 155
RUMSEY, James 136 324 330 Mr 324
RUNKLES, Calvin F 165 Herbert H 165
RUSH, 95 Conrad 141 Dennis 141 Jacob
132 Jervice 132 William 65
RUSSELL, Nicholas 141 Thomas 144
RUSSLER, Harold S 165
RUST, William 156
RUTHERFORD, Andrew H 165 H H 322
328 Robert 63 71 76 132 224 278-279
323 Thomas 61 107 279 323 Thos 275
Van 276
RUTLEDGE, Edward 280
RYNEAL, Anny Lee Alonzo 218 E 155
George Jr 189 277 George Sr 189 O F
189 P 157
SADERFIELD, Ephraim 158
SADLER, John 154
SAILES, Richard 156
SAINTALBANS, Earl Of 24
SAINTCLAIR, 74 135-138 Arthur 145-
146 198 Gen 73 146 236 James P 155
SAINTCLAIR'S, Defeat 73 145-146
SANDERSON, William 6
SANDIS, George 8
SANTAANNA, Gen 149
SANTMAN, J M 160
SAVAGE, John 104
SAVILLE, Albert 156 Edgar 299 John E
165
SAYLES, William 158
SCHAFFER, 315 David 317 Jacob 317
SCHEIG, Adolphus 157 George 156
SCHEU, 327
SCHEW, Louis 317
SCHILL, Daisy May 242 George W 242
William H 257
SCHLEY, H E 167

INDEX 363

SCHMUCKER, Morgan 257 Rev 257 Roy C 257 305 S S 257
SCHNEIDER, Albert A 165 M G 328 Wm Geo 165
SCHOFFSTALL, Mary 192
SCHOOLS, 297-300
SCHOPPERT, (chopper) Ford-road 123 John L 165 Wm F 165
SCHRODER, John L 300
SCHULTZ, William 157
SCHURZ, Carl 202
SCOTT, Dred 109 112 Fred D 165 Geo 215 George 64 72 140 276 Harry 271 J E 167 James 271 John 274 Marion G 300 Perry 271 Perry Jr 271 Sydney 271 William 144
SEAFINI, Giasfetto 165
SEAMAN, Jonathan 132 R D 111 279 William 141
SEAMAN'S, Journal 50
SEATON, 235 James 61-63 275
SECKMAN, Rebecca 192 T 158
SECRIST, John B 122
SEFTON, Baker 308 Mr 311
SEIBER, Henry J 129
SEIBERT, 95 219 Abraham 158 Albert 178 Barnet C 177-178 C J 322 C M 275 277 Cleveland M 178-179 188 319 Cromwell 177 David H 165 Edna 298 Eli 158 Fannie 178 George 57 177 Harriet 178 Henry J 111 240 275 279 298 327 J B 158 Jacob 111 Jacob M 274 276 John B 158 Joseph 157 Leslie M 165 Louisa 177 Mabel E 296 Margaret A 177 Mary 177 Mrs Barnet 246 Otho 178 Otho W 177 Wade 76 Wendall 158 177-178 204 William 178 Wm C 165 Wm T 111
SEIGLER, William 150
SELLERS, Eugene 160
SENATORIAL, Districts 73
SENCINDIVER, 90 95 Jacob 110 John 111 Lydia 205 Roy W 165
SETON, James 107
SEVER, Peter 140
SEVERS, Ray 189 280
SEWARD, Secretary 174
SEYBERT, George 57

SHADE, Chester S 165 Geo A 165 M Eleanor 160 Mrs H S 318 Vernon 322 Zella I 300
SHADY, Ferris 165
SHAFFER, 95 203 Balser 155 D W 277 David 155 327 G H 327 J Guy 161 Jacob A 165 Jos H 165 Joseph H 327 Luther M 273 Peter 145 Philip 165
SHANHOLTZ, W B 165
SHANK, Jacob 149
SHARFF, Elias P 159 Nicholas 156 P L 327
SHARP, Gov 101
SHARPE, Capt 126 Gov 53 Horatio 52-53 75 Thomas E 126
SHAVER, George 137
SHAW, Edmond 273 William B 155
SHEA, John 157
SHEARER, Ann 66 Archibald 62 276 279 James 85 147 171 Mr 80 Thomas 279
SHEETS, Adam 140 David 165
SHELL, Nicholas 135
SHELLY, Harry D 165
SHELTON, E S 167 J W 167
SHEN, Val Bank And Tr Co 327
SHENANDOAH, Hotel 322 River 16
SHEPHARD, Thomas 18
SHEPHERD, Abraham 72 135 140-141 144 215 228 Abram 258 Alex 57 Alexander 57 287-288 Capt 228 David 63 269 273 Eleanor 258 Estelle 298 James 158 Lydia 269 M E 167 Moses 269 Thomas 19 198 324 William 140
SHEPHERDSTOWN, (new Mecklenburg) 18-19 132 135-140 323
SHEPPARD, Adam 276
SHERARD, 294 Paul E 300 Stewart 332
SHERIDAN, 217 234 Gen 209 242 249 256 Phil 208 239 Philip 242 247 255
SHERIFFS, 273
SHERMAN, Walter A 165
SHERRARD, William 88 149
SHERRER, George 156 Joseph 157
SHICKEL, D B 291
SHIELDS, John D 165
SHIFLETT, Edward 165
SHIMP, Jacob 188 John 188 Jonas 188 Nathan 188
SHIMPJOHN, 145
SHIMPJONAS, S 188
SHIPE, Carter D 165 James S 300

SHIPPER, 95 Geo D 165 Hester
    Virginia 243 James B 76 243
    James H 177 208 243 281
    Thomas 165
SHIRK, John 154
SHIRLEY, Ernest R 165 James 132
    John W 195 274 Walter 132
SHIRTZ, Adam 141
SHIVELY, John 256 Margaret 256
SHOAP, Calvin Lee 161
SHOBER, Charles 155 John 144
    259 Susan 144 William K 159
SHOEMAKER, William L 149
SHOPPERT, Jacob 302
SHORT, David 304
SHORTEL, Jacob 302
SHOVER, Alias 144
SHOWERS, Ezekiel 111 276
    George E 158 Josina T 300
    Margaret A 177 Philip 110-111
    177
SHRIVER, Boyd F 161 Harry R 165
    Jos W 165 Norman V 165 Wm
    E 165
SHRODER, Chas R 165
SHROUT, Andrew J 155
SHUART, W 122
SHUTT, A P 126 275 August P 317
SIBOLE, Eldridge 165
SIDLO, 176
SIGEL, Franz 202
SIGLER, Chas M 165
SILER, Charles E 248 Ernest O
    327 George 250 Isabelle 250
    John 156 Lee 248 250 300
    Philip 155 Wm G 298
SILVER, Francis 169 276 Francis
    3d 169 Francis III 168 Frank
    158 Gray 168-169 277 281 332
    Gray Jr 169 Henry 158 Kate
    169 Mary Ann 168-169 Mary
    Gray 169
SIMMONS, W 156
SIMPSON, C J 275
SINE, Thomas 300
SISCO, John 154 157 Joseph 154
    Peter 157
SISK, Charles E 165 Silas 165
SITES, E M 165 Edgar 287 Edgar
    M 288 320 Ethel 160 Jacob 273
    277 Mary Ethel 266
SKARTELIAS, Conlstantine 165

SLAUGHTER, Philip 141 Smith 276
SLAVE, Anthony 108 Betty 108 Bob 118
    153 Ede 108 Hannah 108 Jack 108
    Joe 27 108 Nell 108 Peg 108 Peggy
    108 Phil 108 Phill 108 Sam 108
    Sambo 108 Will 108
SLAVERY, 106-109
SLEEPY, Creek 79
SLOAN, J G 165
SLONAKER, Carl 299 331 Guy E 165
SMALL, 95 Adam 277 279 David 158
    Fred P 165 Harvey G 165 Homer 76
    Homer C 322 Jacob A 110 Jacob B
    111 John M 156 Palham Lee 165
    Reuben 156 Sam 332 W Ernest 165
    William 158
SMALLWOOD, Albert A 266 275 288
    Clara D 298 H T 165
SMALTZ, Andrew R 166
SMAPP, C M 166
SMELTZER, C W 156 Harlan 166 Harry
    166
SMITH, 250 256 294 A B 315 Albert K
    166 Almon W 251 274 276 280 288
    Arthur W 166 C G 166 327 Capt 54
    278 David 140 154 Duane D 300 E L
    185 E O 166 Edward 141 Elizabeth
    299 Emma 180 Frank 157 Geo A 166
    Gov 149-150 H L 321 H Lott 277
    Harry 185 Harry F 189 280 Helen M
    300 Henry Lott 180 Howard M 159 J
    W 327 James H 175 179 273 277 296
    321 Jeremiah 54 Jessie B 300 John 7
    155-156 278 John B D 235 John W
    129 180 248 Joseph D 185 Kirk 76
    Lott 180 Marshall 243 Mathias B 155
    Mr 180 Norman W 166 Stanley 166 T
    G 185 William 123 144 150 154 156
    179 277 William Dean 251 Wm F 166
SMOOTE, John 140
SMURR, Harry F 161
SNAIDERO, Renato 166
SNAPP, Fred D 213 G M 213 H L 213
    332 Joseph 213 Joseph W 213
    Katharine 214 Morris 299 Mr 213
    289 Raymond 213
SNIDEAL, Emily 242
SNODGRASS, 95 242 331 C S 166 Elisha
    Kelly 206 I B 179 John Fryatt 205
    229 Mary 205 Nancy 205 Philip 206
    Porterfield 156 Robert 237 Robert Sr
    330 Robert V 276 279

INDEX 365

SNODGRASS (cont.)
  Sarah Ann 194 Stephen R 276
  Stribling 281 William 205
  William I 205 William II 205
  William T 279
SNOOK, Lida 246
SNOWDEN, Charles 142
SNOWDON, E G 166 Mr 13
SNYDER, 89-90 Abraham 166
  Benjamin H 285 D W Jr 129
  Earl C 166 Isaac 166 Jacob 85
  147 171 James 274 James E
  166 John D 166 John W 161
  Luther 161 O L 166 300 Perry
  L 166 Peter 142 R N 166
  Raymond M 166 Robert S 166
  W B 129 W S Jr 166
SOILS, 44
SOLENBERGER, C M 299
SOMERS, H L 166
SOMERVILLE, William 144
SONNER, Edward R 166
SORBER, William 150
SORTWELL, Alonzo 229
SOUDERS, Christopher 65 Sally 65
SOUTH, Branch 16-17
SPAN-AMER, War 159-160
SPAULDING, Alva 166 Jas H 161
SPECK, B J 276 John 110 John C
  280 Thomas 330
SPEILMAN, George S Jr 245
SPENCER, Franklin 154
SPENDALOWE, Lt 194
SPENDELOW, Lt 50 55 267
SPEROW, 95 C R 181 281 Charles
  W 322 Chas H E 166 Cromwell
  R 128 Elizabeth 300 Elmer E
  166 Geo 110 George 156 200
  George O 200 H D 322 Harry
  166 Hunter D 77 Jacob 156
  John W 200 277 Luther 77 Mrs
  George R 246 Prof 200 Riner 77
  Virginia 299 William 276
  Wilson P 166 200
SPERRY, Elmer 289 Lawrence 289
SPIELMAN, Elena E 300
SPIKER, 294 Amos W 186 Arthur
  L 186 Edward 186 J W 76 186
  Miss 186 W R 159 William R
  186
SPILLMAN, 209 Frederick 317 H I
  166
SPILMAN, 250
SPONG, David 144
SPONSELLER, Mrs G J E 318
SPORTS, 34 40
SPOTTSWOOD, Gov 18
SPRECKER, C S 166
SPRING, Charles 160
STAFFORD, John 155
STAHL, Jonathan 155
STAKE, Mr 292 R W 291
STALEY, Susan 300
STANBURY, H B 155
STANDISH, Myles 33
STANLEY, Peter 137
STATE, Assembly Of Va 278 Road Com
  285 Senators 277
STATLER, Andrew J 155 Henry M 155
STATTER, Benj F 154
STAUB, John 260 John F 156 Julia 299
  R P H 156
STEANSBAUGH, Harry 154
STEDMAN, David 140
STEEL, 256
STEELMAN, Rev 310
STEER, Thomas 140
STEHLEY, Frank D 273 John E 277
STEIN, John R 166
STEPHEN, Adam 52 58-59 61-62 67-69
  71 73 107 132-133 198 225-226 262
  273 275 279 302 325 330 Gen 68-69
  73 226-227 254 Lt Col 226 Maj 226
  Mr 80 Robert 61-62 107 275 Sheriff
  226
STEPHENS, Adam 254 Alexander 85 147
  170 Gen 170 James 170 Peter 19
  Richard H 150 Robert 62-63
STEPHENSON, Capt 72 Col 142 215
  Hugh 71-72 139-142 193 215 224 228-
  229 236 James 74 236 273 276
STEVEN, Adam 281
STEVENS, Edna 300 Gabriel 142 John
  144 Peter 324
STEVENSON, Adlai E 264 James 279
STEWARD, T W 156
STEWART, 95 217 Amelia 191 Amelia L
  E 191 Barney 157 Charles 191
  Charles D 223 Col 115 David 110
  Elizabeth 191 F A 127 Gen 117-118 J
  B 268 J E B 52 112 114-117 205 J W
  321 James E 279 John 140 John P
  149 John W 191 326 334 M H 160 Mr
  191 Ralph W 166 Robert 64 276

STEWART (cont.)
   Robert H 158 191 Robert Jr
   110-111 S Allen 161 Sheridan G
   166 Spencer A 166 William S
   191 William T 191 225 327
STIGLER, William 276
STILWELL, Alex W 166
STISMITZ, A B 276
STOCKS, And Pillory 62
STOCKTON, Commodore 231
   Robert 19
STOGDON, George 62 Robert 61-
   63 107 275
STOKER, Thomas 155
STOLIPER, E R 166
STOTLER, Geo B 166
STOUT, Roy A 166
STOVER, Jacob 37
STOWE, Harriet Beecher 112
STRAIN, George 167
STRAINEY, Edward 157
STRAWSON, H W 155
STRAYER, A P 157 D J R 158
STREET, Lighting 122 127 William
   J 155
STREETT, Saint Clair 182 288
STREIT, Christian 301
STRIBLING, Adm 281 318 Mary C
   319 Mary Calvert 319
STRICKLER, James 160
STRINE, Elmer J 166 Jacob 276
   Jonathan 276
STRODE, Capt 258 Eleanor 258 J
   T 166 James 61-63 67 107 258
   275 Joseph 158 Mr 258 P H 158
   Phoebe 258 Rachael 258
STRONG, Ella 298-299 J W 332
STROOP, R B 166 William 19
STROTHER, David Hunter 184
   184-185 281 Elizabeth 215 John
   86 215 274 316 Miss 185
STROTHERS, John 316
STUABLEY, L H 166
STUART, 177 217 Charles 191 Gen
   153 J E B 153 205 331 Jeb 153
   John 230
STUCKEY, Anna 240 Arthur 299 C
   L 211 C Newton 280 Carlton B
   208 280 Charles 240 276
   Charles L 240 249 Charles W
   208 257 276 299 Chas Jr 110
   Chas L 166 277 296

STUCKEY (cont.)
   Daniel 240 296 David 274 David H
   240 296 Elizabeth 240 Harry J 166
   Hester Virginia 243 Jacob 58 208 240
   276 Jacob H 208 James D 76 John W
   157 Joseph 110 276 Lee F 166 Miss
   208 Newton 208 Samuel 208 Samuel
   A 156 Samuel K 88 Virginia 253 299
STUCKY, Charles 65
STULL, Holland Williams 229 231
STUM, Robet C 166
STUMP, Casper 110-111 276 J P 274
   John H 158 Mary E 183 Ralph R 166
SUCKEY, 95
SUDDITH, Joseph 156
SUITER, Charles 156
SULLIVAN, Edward 157 Gen 170 H E
   160 Paul 166
SULPHUR, Springs 81
SUMMERS, Minnie 216
SUTER, T C 157
SWAN, Pond 81 335
SWARTZ, Ella E 300 Fred F 166 Roy C
   166
SWEARINGEN, Joseph 72 135 140 144
   215 258 279 Josiah 140 273 Phoebe
   258 Thomas 19 107 Thomas Van 231
   281 Thos 275 Van 19 107 275 302 323
SWEENEY, Henty M 166
SWERENGAN, Thomas 62-63 Van 62
SWERINGAN, Thomas 61 Van 61-62
SWERINGEN, Joseph 276
SWIFT, Goodwin 70 276
SWIMLEY, 95
SWOPE, Elmer 160
TABB, 95 E W 158 Edward 78 George
   140 Robert 276 William 140
TABLER, 95 Adam Malachai 253 C C
   252 274 298-299 Carlton L 166
   Christopher C 298 Christopher
   Columbus 252 Duff H 166 E G 155 E
   H 188 239 273 E S 187 274 277
   Edward H 274 Elizabeth Green
   Claybourne 253 Ernest R 166 Esther
   V 298 H P 121 Harrison 276 Levi J
   277 Mark H 166 Martin 157 Maybury
   G 218 Mildred 298 Mr 218 252-253
   Peter 114 154
TABLER-GLETNER, Helen I 298
TABLERS, 334
TAFT, Mr 326 Pres 183-184 326 331
   William Howard 326

INDEX 367

TALBOTT, Holmes 245 Holmes S 166 Robert 245
TALMADGE, T Dewitt 325
TALMAGE, T Dewitt 264
TALTY, Andrew 303
TARLETON, 223
TATE, 89 95 A D 333 Magnus 233 273 279 281 Morganus 276 Robert 157
TAYLOR, Betty 268 Charles 166 Ephraim 155 Gen 171 George 141 James 155 John 19 John L 166 Monroe 269 Paul 144 Robt B 148 Samuel 19 121 276 Samuel H 155 W H 121 Zachary 233 268
TAYOR, George 140
TEACK, S 158
TEAL, Paul H 166 274
TEETS, Albert 154 Elisha 155 John 155
TELEGRAPH, 91-92
TELEPHONE, 290
THATCHER, 95 Charles W 260-261 266 274 276 Emma 180 Harlan 321-322 Harlan C 261 I B 260 J N 260-261 321 Jacob 158 James 260 Jonathan 180 260 Jonathan N 260 Jonathan Newton 260 321 Jonathan W 260 Leona 299 Mr 260 321 Mrs Stephen 260 Peter 260 Samuel 260 Stephen 260 306
THAYER, Annette 204
THIETH, James 62
THOBURN, Joseph 206
THOMAS, 89 95 A J 124 273 327 B 157 Douglas Graham 241 Emory F 322 Franklin 111 Gen 186 Jacob 158 Lt 228 Martha 240 Millicene R 241 Mr 241 P H 240 Richard J 276 Wilbur H 240-241 322 327
THOMPSON, Anna Lee Alonzo 218 Ben 219 Ben J 219 Charles 219 Charles E 219 Chas F 166 Chas H 166 Daniel 154 David 276 Downey 219 H S 219 Hobert T 166 J F 218 J Frank 218-219 J S H 166 James E 161 James F 129 218-219 John W 218 Joseph 218 Lewis H 327

THOMPSON (cont.)
Louis H 219 Mary 218 Mr 218 Robert 154 Robert S 219 Samuel 218 Samuel J 218-219 Virginia 219
THORN, H P 129 262 322 326 Mr 262
THORNBURG, Benjamin 306 C W 274 276 Collins W 121 David H 166 Thomas 137
THORNTON, C J 327
THORSWAY, Baron Of 24
THOUVENAL, M 173
THROCKMORTON, 57 89 95 212 Dr 256 J A 256 James E 65 Job 256 John 276 Robert 276 279
THRUSH, John M 156
THURSTON, Charles Mynn 323 Ray C 166 Sen 270
TICHNAL, Samuel 155
TIFFIN, Edward 281
TILLMAN, 270
TILLOTSON, Archbishop 205
TIMMONS, Bryan 142 John 303
TINKON, H G 266
TINSMAN, Harry D 166
TITLOW, R 156 Robert 157
TOBACCO, 46
TOBIN, Geo W 160
TOLL, Gates 287
TOMAHAWK, 335 Rights 36
TONKIN, Dr 249 308 312 H G 166 179 273 275 280 H Glenville 249
TOUP, H Clay 166 William 160
TOWNSEND, Clarence 296 Frank 296 Mabel Claire 196
TOWNSHIPS, 63
TRANSPORTATION, 282
TRAYER, Chas S 166
TREMBLE, George 61 227
TRENT, William 49
TRIGG, Harrison 116
TRIGGS, Chas B 166 Harrison 157
TRIPLETT, William 69
TROUT, Edgar C 166 Horace 308 Mollie E 300 Mr 308 311 Walter 307-308
TROXALL, E S 274
TROXELL, E S 327
TRUMP, Charles S 200 Charles S Jr 200 Chas S 166 Elizabeth 299 Frank M 166
TUCKER, Chancellor 171 Chemcellor 222 Harvey E 166 Henry St George 234 323

TULLIS, Aaron 140 Michael 140
TUNISON, Garret 140
TURNER, 95 Chas Mck 166
 Edward 167 Harriet 177 Henry
 323 J F 167 J W 160 John 273
 276 John A 158 Joseph 138 Mrs
 Anthony 246 Paul 296 Thomas
 136 Thomas M 296 Thomas W
 246 256 275 William 157
TUSCARORA, Creek 20 57 67 79
 95 Indians 14 67 Pike 286
TYLER, John 65 Pres 235
TYSON, Gilbert M 166 James E
 166 Robert G 166
U, S Fish Comm 281 S Senators
 281
UNGER, 95 257 John 154
UNSELD, Henry 137
UTENSILS, 31 94
VADEN, Paskil 150
VALLEY, Pike 19 60
VALUATION, 335
VANANSDAL, Jerry 155
VANBUREN, Martin 325 Pres 236
VANDERGRIFF, 126
VANDEVER, Jacob 63
VANDINE, Stephen 141
VANDOREN, 95 Jacob 273-274 279
VANDORN, 130 Gantt 275
VANHOHN, Daniel H 166
VANHORN, Daniel H 166 John C
 150
VANLIER, John 150
VANMATRE, 23 26 Machyken 208
 Abram 58 Isaac 19 25 208 Jan
 208 Jan Joosten 207-208 John
 17-19 25 58 208 282 Joost
 Janse 208 Thos J 111
VANMETER, 207 Smith M 129
VANMETEREN, Emanuel 207
VANMETRE, 48 95 207 288 Abishe
 296 Abraham 55 195 266 305
 Abram G 150 Allen 208
 Asahale 178 Bessie 254 E W
 208 Floyd 208 George W 189
 208 273 Haunce 254 I D 58 254
 I D Jr 254 Isaac 72 154 208
 Isaac D 195 Isabel 195 Jacob 19
 63 254 James 254 James Henry
 208 James Larue 254 James M
 186 195 254 276 John 20 72 81
 Joseph 144 Katherine 254

VANMETRE (cont.)
 Lafayette 166 Lillian M 300 Luther
 111 Margaret 195 Mr 189 254 Mrs
 George 76 Mrs Smith M 246 Polly 55
 179 194-195 266 Robert S 166
 Thomas H 166 Thos Earl 166
VANMETREN, 207
VANMETRES, 18
VARDEN, Stephen 140
VARLE, Charles 78
VATTAL, 100
VAUGHAM, Patrick 140
VAUGHN, Patrick 142
VEENEY, A I 167
VEST, 270
VICTORIA, Queen Of England 91-92
VILLA, 210
VIRGINIA, 5-11
VOGEL, John 157
VOLGAMOTT, Moses 155
VOORHEES, 270 George F 156 John 121
 John A 275
WACHTEL, M L 312
WADE, Alexander 155
WAGELEY, Arthur 166 Roy 161
WAGELY, Edmond 154
WAGGENER, Andrew 279 Andrew Jr
 279
WAGGONER, Andrew 86 148 221 232
 Andrew Jr 65 232 Mary 221 Philip
 140
WAGONER, Andrew 144 273 276
WAITE, Harrison 274 Obed 274
WALES, Prince Of 182
WALKER, 95 234 A Hunter 204 254 298
 Annette 204 Caranda 167 Col 203 E
 M 157 246 274 296 E W 167 Frank W
 166 G W 157 Henry S 290 J H 167
 James 167 James W 270 299 Joseph
 E 161 Mr 203 220 Mrs James 246
 Noah 166 Pernell 167 Stewart W 203
 Stuart W 31 129 220 277 Thomas 203
 William B 166 William Frances 270
 Wm W 110
WALKERS, 50
WALLACE, Edward F 166 James 140
 Lew 239
WALLER, William 140-141
WALLETT, George 112 P 157
WALLIS, Lew 188
WALTER, 95 Margaret 204
WALTERS, George 76 George B 260

WALTERS (cont.)
    Jacob 305 John P 110
WANDER, L A 166
WANDLING, Thomas 121 276
WANN, John 157
WAPATOMAKA, 16 18
WAR, Of 1812 58 85 147-148 With
    Mexico 148 150
WARD, 95 Joel 65 230 273 279
    William 63
WARE, Joel 275
WARM, Springs Road 61 286
WARREN, Adm 171 G K 252
    Thomas 141
WASHINGTON, 27 33 52 69 97 230
    258 Charles 324 Col 74 226 Gen
    19 70 105 139 170 199 223 253
    330 George 20 26 49 51 53 71
    131 198 203 222 254 301 323-
    324 330 Pres 74-75 146 Samuel
    61-62 70 107 273 275 323
    Warner 323
WASTPHALL, Charles 157
WATERS, Robert 166
WATKIN, Evan 51
WATKINS, 97
WATSON, Harry 166 Michael 160
WAUCH, Willilam H 165
WAYNE, 56 Anthony 74 145 Gen
    170 Mad Anthony 74 138
WAYS, Charles 92
WEAST, George L 150
WEAVER, Charles 156 158 D J 154
    George 156 158 John 156
WEBB, James E 166
WEBSTER, 269 Daniel 172 234 R A
    156
WEDDELL, George W 157 John H
    157 N Baker 160
WEDDING, The 34 94
WEDDLE, Albert W 159 John A
    159
WEIDMAN, Calvin 311
WEIGAND, Herman E 166
WEIGLE, Edward 166 John M 166
WEIL, David 218
WEISE, James E 160
WEIST, C W 166
WELLER, Charles 158 Earl C 327
    George 166 Harvey L 245 John
    317 Louis B 275
WELLING, Al C 160

WELLINGER, A G 166
WELLS, Edgar 167 George 158 R E 70
    Ross G 257
WELLSH, Eddie 166
WELSH, C W 155 Patrick P 155 Thomas
    S 155
WELSHANS, Levi J 154 Maud 300
WELTON, Kathleen 280
WELTY, H P 166 Joseph 166
WENTZ, Henry 157
WERT, H T 157
WEST, Garnet L 166 J I 166 Thomas 141
WESTENHAVER, 176 190 D C 177 191
    D O 273 David C 177 Harriet 177 J D
    166 John 331 Mary C 177
WESTERHAVER, David 177
WESTPHAL, W W 327 William W 327
WESTPHALL, 294 W W 277
WETZEL, Lewis 40 230
WEVER, 95 Anna Lee 257 C A 277
    Charles Albert 257 Geo L 166 George
    L 248 Jacob 273 275 John L 257 Nota
    K 268 318
WHARTON, H L 166
WHEELER, Matilda 214 Victor 214
WHETZEL, J C 166
WHIPPING, Post 62
WHIPPLE, Joseph 142
WHISKEY, Rebellion 146-147
WHITACRE, E K 166 H S 166 Nora 299
    S E 166
WHITE, Aexander 62 Alexander 62 76
    273 276 323 Alexander Jr 279
    Alxander 224 C C 166 Mr 224 Robert
    72 140 215 274
WHITEHOURST, James 157
WHITEMAN, Charles 150
WHITEMORE, G S 160
WHITING, Henry 276 Leota 300
    Matthew 108 R S 332
WHITLOCK, C A 166
WHITMORE, 242 Florence M 160 G F
    166 George F 210 John C 210 John L
    211 Joseph 211 Mr 211
WHITSON, George D 156
WHITTINGTON, C E 166 Francis 166 I
    L 166 R B 166 W B 160
WICKERSHAM, Jonathan 81
WIDMYER, R S 166 W H 166
WIDOW, Bedinger 3 51
WILAN, 241 William 121 276
WILBURN, J E 250 John 250

WILEN, 328 John 179 William 179 277 Wm 317
WILHELM, Henry 150
WILKENSON, 215
WILLARD, C E 166
WILLIAM, The Conqueror 192-193,
WILLIAM, The Third 170 193
WILLIAMS, A T 167 Allen P 161 Annie Laurie 194 C A 167 D T 166 E C 276 Edward Cleggett 194 Eleanor 300 H R 166 Howard E 129 248 J E 166 John R 150 Kathryn 300 Lee 166 Maj 228 Otho 242 274 Otho Holland 229 Sen 307 Thomas 142 Thos S 140 W J S 160
WILLIAMSON, 95 Ella 175 Ella Dodd 298 J E 166 S J 276
WILLIS, 95 L B 111 Lewis B 86 91 Mr 237 Nathan Parker 314 Nathaniel 237 314 Nathaniel Parker 237 Robert C 63 Robert Carter 61-62 67 107
WILLS, Lewis 142
WILSON, 95 Alexander 221 C L 166 C M 166 Capt 147 171 Claude 166 E A 166 F E 327 Howard 166 J L 158 James 64-65 144 273 276 John 142 John B 129 275 290 325 327 John S 323 Mr 315 325 Philip R 279 Postmaster-gen 176 Pres 176 203 219 261 281 290 R H 166 Robert 85 147-148 170 Stewart 167 Valerius 157 William 137 141 Wm L 176 Woodrow 326
WILSON'S, Berkeley Artillery 147
WILTSHIRE, Elizabeth 217 G B 188 217 275 G B Jr 217 Harrison 217 Lorena 217 Mrs G B 318-319
WINCHESTER, Pike 50 60 72
WINE, Jacob 141
WINN, Jacob 140
WINNING, Edward 276
WINSLIP, Winn 276
WINSLOW, Benjamin 104
WINTER, Richard 150
WISE, Gov 199 Henry A 65 113 173 196-197 200 214 Thomas 155
WISNER, J Nelson 273 290 315 Mr 315

WISTER, Benjamin K 155
WITHEROW, James 157
WOLF, Adam 154 Geo W 309 George W 310-311 J C 239 309 Jacob 239 Julia 220 Michael 142 239 Mr 311 R M 159
WOLFE, R M 160
WOLFENSBERGER, Dora E 300
WOLFES, L R 160
WOLFF, Bernard C 230 George 230 273 275
WOLFORD, A G 166 C F 166 E A 166 E B 166 Emory 248 Harry 248 J C 166 J R 166 John 248 R G 166 248 Reginald 166 Thomas 248
WOLLF, C A 156
WOOD, Cecil W 166 322 Howard 166 I W 273 277 J 65 James 65 Walter A 260
WOODS, Andrew H 181 Cecil W 299 David J 181 F M 181 303 Isabella 219 J M 181 203 250 262 273-274 307 319 Judge 251 Samuel 219
WOOLF, George 65
WOORE, A M 166
WORMLEY, Mr 20 Ralph 19 61 107 275
WORTHINGON, Thomas 230
WORTHINGTON, Robert 63 273 276 Thomas 281
WRIGHT, James 140 John 19 M H 166 R S 166 Thomas 167 W E 166 Wm 333
WYATT, Dudley 24 E V 166 Francis 8 Gov 8
WYNDHAM, George 166 J L 166
WYSONG, Fayette 136 Geo R 327 George R 276 326 Jacob 136 Mr 326
YANCEY, James 140
YEARDLY, George 8
YEARICK, 255
YEODER, N G 160
YOHO, Ezra 155
YOST, C C 166
YOUNG, Adam 85 147 171 Charles 144 Christy 138 John 157 Samuel 310
ZAMARELLY, Dominic 166
ZANE, Ebenezer 230 Elizabeth 269
ZEILOR, E N 274 Mildred 298 Mrs E N 186
ZEPP, Hattie L 266 James 166 W F 166 W J 167
ZILER, J W 167 W C 167 W J 167
ZIMMERMAN, E J 167 Martha 189
ZIRKLE, John H 322
ZOMBRO, G B 167 R B 167

www.ingramcontent.com/pod-product-compliance
Lightning Source LLC
Chambersburg PA
CBHW051627230426
43669CB00013B/2201